THE HUMAN STORY

An Introduction to Anthropology

THE
HUMAN
STORY

An Introduction to Anthropology

ALEXANDRA **BREWIS**

KELLY **KNUDSON**

CHRISTOPHER **STOJANOWSKI**

CINDI **STURTZSREETHARAN**

AMBER **WUTICH**

Arizona State University

W. W. NORTON & COMPANY

Independent Publishers Since 1923

W. W. Norton & Company has been independent since its founding in 1923, when William Warder Norton and Mary D. Herter Norton first published lectures delivered at the People's Institute, the adult education division of New York City's Cooper Union. The firm soon expanded its program beyond the Institute, publishing books by celebrated academics from America and abroad. By midcentury, the two major pillars of Norton's publishing program—trade books and college texts—were firmly established. In the 1950s, the Norton family transferred control of the company to its employees, and today—with a staff of five hundred and hundreds of trade, college, and professional titles published each year—W. W. Norton & Company stands as the largest and oldest publishing house owned wholly by its employees.

Editor: Andrew Blitzer
Project Editors: Carla Talmadge and Taylere Peterson
Assistant Editor: Elaina Sassine
Associate Director of Production, College: Stephen Sajdak
Managing Editors, College: Kim Yi and Carla Talmadge
Media Editor: Ariel Eaton
Associate Media Editor: Alex Park
Media Assistant Editor: Rachel S. Bass
Ebook Producer: Kate Barnes
Senior Marketing Research and Strategy Manager: Marlee Lisker
Associate Art Director, College: Anne-Michelle Gallero
Director of College Permissions: Megan Schindel
Photo Department Manager: Melinda Patelli
College Permissions Associate: Patricia Wong
Illustrations: Dragonfly Media Group
Composition: GW STL
Manufacturing: TC Transcontinental

Permission to use copyrighted material is included in the back matter.

Library of Congress Control Number: 2023947990

ISBN: 978-0-393-44118-5

W. W. Norton & Company, Inc., 500 Fifth Avenue, New York, NY 10110
wwnorton.com

W. W. Norton & Company Ltd., 15 Carlisle Street, London W1D 3BS

1 2 3 4 5 6 7 8 9 0

BRIEF CONTENTS

■ **1** Why Anthropology? 2

■ **2** Doing Anthropology 20

■ **3** Human Variation 50

■ **4** Primates: Our Closest Relatives 84

■ **5** Human Origins and the Earliest Hominins 120

■ **6** The Origins and Spread of Modern Humans 154

■ **7** Language and Our Worlds 194

■ **8** Human Settlement and Societies 220

■ **9** Food and Economic Systems 248

■ **10** War and Group Violence 284

■ **11** Gender 314

■ **12** Sex, Love, and Marriage 344

■ **13** Death, Dying, and the Dead 376

■ **14** Race and Racialized Societies 400

■ **15** Disease, Health, and Healing 430

■ **16** Anthropology, Environment, and Better Futures 462

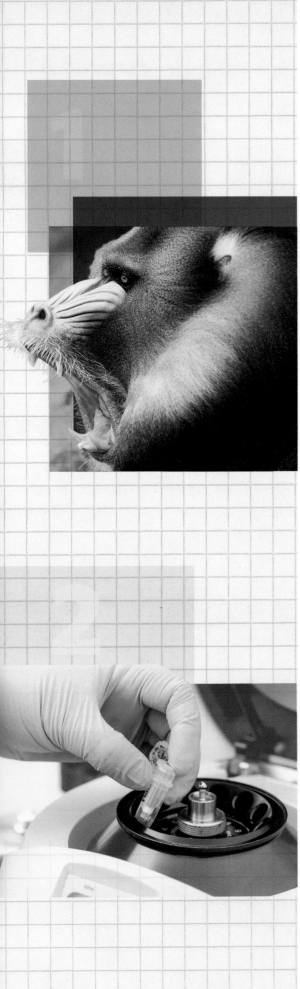

CONTENTS

1 Why Anthropology?   2

SECTION 1.1 / **THE SUBFIELDS OF ANTHROPOLOGY   4**

• Biological Anthropology
• Archaeology
• Cultural Anthropology
• Linguistic Anthropology
• Other Subfields
• Our Teeth: Views from the Four Subfields
• Integrating the Subfields

SECTION 1.2 / **WHAT MAKES ANTHROPOLOGY "ANTHROPOLOGICAL"?   10**

• Valuing Fieldwork
• Cross-Cultural and Cross-Species Comparison
• Embracing Diverse Scholarly Traditions
• Making Research Relevant
• Shared Ethical Standards

2 Doing Anthropology   20

SECTION 2.1 / **DOING CULTURAL ANTHROPOLOGY   23**

• Ethnography and the Study of Culture
• Quantitative and Qualitative Approaches to Culture
• Reflexivity and Positionality

SECTION 2.2 / **DOING LINGUISTIC ANTHROPOLOGY   30**

• Recording Language

SECTION 2.3 / **DOING ARCHAEOLOGY   33**

• Changing Questions and Concerns: Processual and Postprocessual Archaeology

SECTION 2.4 / **DOING BIOLOGICAL ANTHROPOLOGY   40**

• The Methods of Biological Anthropology

SECTION 2.5 / IMPROVING ANTHROPOLOGICAL PRACTICE 43

- *Coproduced and Shared Knowledge*
- *Ensuring Community Control of Research Materials*
- *Diversity within Anthropology*

3 Human Variation 50

SECTION 3.1 / BASICS OF HUMAN VARIATION: GENETICS 53

- *The Building Blocks: Cells, DNA, and Genes*
- *DNA Function: Protein Synthesis*
- *Reproduction and Inheritance: Meiosis*
- *Phenotypic Traits*

SECTION 3.2 / MECHANISMS OF MICROEVOLUTION 58

- *How New Variants Happen: Mutation*
- *Genetic Drift and Gene Flow*
- *Human Microevolution: The Larger Picture*

SECTION 3.3 / HUMAN VARIATION AND GENETIC ADAPTATION 66

- *Adaptation to Climate: Body Shape*
- *Adaptation to Ultraviolet Radiation: Skin Reflectance*
- *Adaptation to Disease: Antimalarial Phenotypes*

SECTION 3.4 / HUMAN CULTURE AND MICROEVOLUTION 69

- *Dairying, Niche Construction, and Coevolution*

SECTION 3.5 / DEVELOPMENT AND PLASTICITY 72

- *Developmental Plasticity: Secular Trends*
- *Plasticity: The Role of Social Stress*
- *Epigenetics: Inheritance and Environmental Stress*

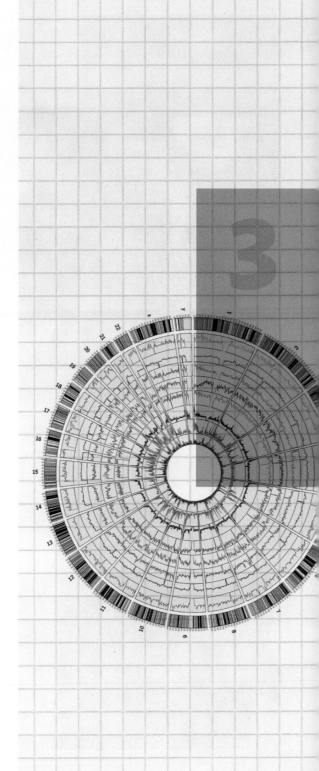

CONTENTS

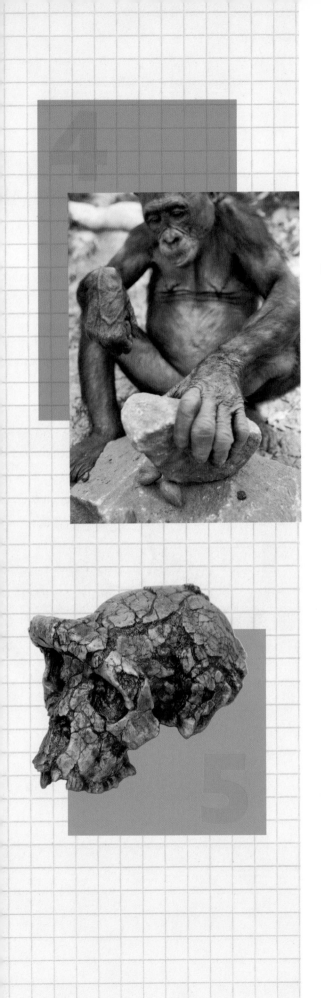

4 Primates: Our Closest Relatives   84

SECTION 4.1 / **WHAT IS A PRIMATE?**   87
- *Primate Anatomy*
- *Primate Behavior*

SECTION 4.2 / **DIVERSITY OF LIVING PRIMATES**   93
- *Strepsirrhines*
- *Haplorhines*

SECTION 4.3 / **FOSSIL EVIDENCE AND PRIMATE HISTORY**   103
- *Using the Primate Present to Interpret Our Primate Past*
- *Primate Pasts: The Fossil Evidence*

SECTION 4.4 / **PRIMATES IN PERIL**   112
- *Conservation and Human–Primate Interactions*

5 Human Origins and the Earliest Hominins   120

SECTION 5.1 / **THE PLIOCENE EPOCH AND THE CHALLENGES OF SCARCE DATA**   125
- *Fossil Evidence*
- *The Challenge of Dating*
- *The Challenge of Identifying Species*

SECTION 5.2 / **IDENTIFYING OUR EARLIEST ANCESTORS**   129
- *Identifying a Hominin*
- *Identifying Bipedalism*

SECTION 5.3 / **EARLY HOMININS**   136
- *The Earliest Hominins at the Miocene–Pliocene Boundary*
- *The Genus Australopithecus*
- *The Pliocene–Pleistocene Hominin Radiation*
- *The Genus Paranthropus*
- *The Genus Homo*

SECTION 5.4 / TOOL-MAKING PLIOCENE HOMININS 144

- *Early Tool Production*
- *Early Tool Producers*
- *Material Culture and Cultural Learning in Primates and Hominins*

SECTION 5.5 / TELLING THE EARLY HUMAN STORY 149

- *Paleoanthropology as a Narrative*
- *Diversity in Paleoanthropology*

6 The Origins and Spread of Modern Humans 154

SECTION 6.1 / HOMO ERECTUS 157

- *Stature*
- *Footprints*
- *Brain Size and Cranial Appearance*
- *Brain Size and Intelligence*
- *Tool Tradition and Behavior*

SECTION 6.2 / MIDDLE PLEISTOCENE HOMO 165

- *Anatomical and Behavioral Adaptations*
- *Tool Production*
- *Use of Fire*
- *Brain Development*
- *Fragmented Habitats and Regional Distinctiveness*

SECTION 6.3 / HOMO SAPIENS 173

- *Anatomically Modern*
- *Behaviorally Modern*

SECTION 6.4 / THE OTHER HUMANS AND US 184

- *The Neanderthals*
- *The Denisovans*
- *Other Recent Hominins*
- *Entwined Human Histories*
- *From Our Pasts to Our Futures*

CONTENTS

7   Language and Our Worlds   194

SECTION 7.1 / **THE STRUCTURES OF HUMAN LANGUAGE   197**
- *Phonological Rules*
- *Syntax Rules*
- *Language Variation*

SECTION 7.2 / **WHAT HUMAN LANGUAGE DOES   202**
- *Language and Meaning*
- *Language as Action*
- *Language as Identity Marker and Creator*
- *Language Is Social Organization*
- *Language Is Social Action*

SECTION 7.3 / **HOW LANGUAGE SHAPES HUMANS   212**

SECTION 7.4 / **HOW PEOPLE CREATE MEANING   215**
- *Linguistic Prejudice*
- *Discrimination as a Consequence of Linguistic Profiling*

8   Human Settlement and Societies   220

SECTION 8.1 / **THE ADVANTAGES OF COOPERATIVE COMMUNITIES   223**
- *Why Primates Live in Groups*
- *Cooperation in Hunter-Gatherer Societies*

SECTION 8.2 / **THE TRANSITION TO AGRICULTURE AND PERMANENT SETTLEMENTS   227**
- *A Changing Climate*
- *Cultivation of the Land*
- *The Domestication Process*
- *The Transition to Sedentary Agriculture*
- *Population Growth after the Transition to Agriculture*
- *Health Consequences of the Transition to Agriculture*
- *The Early Neolithic Site of Çatalhöyük, Turkey*
- *The Spread of Language in the Mesolithic and Neolithic Periods*

SECTION 8.3 / **THE RISE OF CITIES AND STATES** 235

- *The Emergence of Urbanization*
- *Social Stratification in Early Cities*
- *Why Human Societies Tend toward Complexity*
- *The Case of the Hawaiian Chiefdoms*

SECTION 8.4 / **GOVERNING COMPLEX SOCIETIES** 240

- *State Governance within Complex Societies*
- *Informality and Non-State Justice*
- *Informal Justice and Self-Governance*
- *Self-Governance, Inequality, and Modern Urban Life*

9   Food and Economic Systems   248

SECTION 9.1 / **RECIPROCITY: THE FOUNDATION OF HUMAN EXCHANGE** 250

- *Gift Giving*
- *Reciprocity as Social Insurance*
- *Beyond Reciprocity: Human Exchange Systems*

SECTION 9.2 / **MARKETS** 258

- *Markets and Money*
- *Transitions to Capitalism*
- *Socioeconomic Change: From Industrial to Neoliberal Capitalism*
- *Commodification of Language: Contemporary Capitalism in an International Call Center*
- *Postindustrial Capitalism*
- *Cultural Capital and the Commodification of the Body*
- *Beyond Simple Self-Interest: Expanding Conventional Economic Models*

SECTION 9.3 / **REDISTRIBUTION** 267

- *Redistributive Systems: Evidence from the Past*
- *Redistributive Economic Systems in the Postcolonial World*
- *Redistributive Systems Today*

SECTION 9.4 / **MIXED AND ALTERNATIVE ECONOMIES** 274

- *Moral Economies*
- *Building Better Economies*

CONTENTS

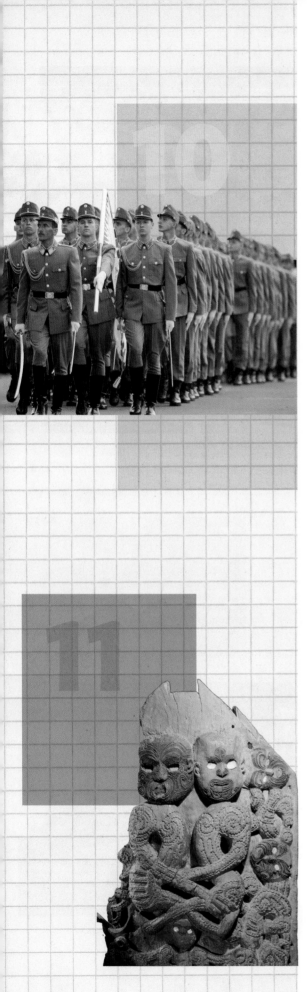

10 War and Group Violence 284

SECTION 10.1 / **WARFARE IN PRIMATES AND HUMANS** 287
- *Human Violence and Warfare in the Past*
- *Endemic Warfare*

SECTION 10.2 / **NORMS, RHETORIC, AND WILLINGNESS FOR WARFARE** 293
- *Group Identity and Willingness to Fight*
- *Rhetoric and Willingness to Fight*
- *Why Mostly Men?*

SECTION 10.3 / **STRUCTURAL VIOLENCE** 299
- *Root Sources of Structural Violence*
- *Structural Violence and Contemporary Suffering*
- *International Development Projects: Causing or Correcting Structural Violence?*
- *Redressing Coloniality in Anthropology*

SECTION 10.4 / **FIGHTING BACK: RESISTANCE, REFUSAL, REVOLUTION, RECONCILIATION** 308
- *Resistance*
- *Refusal*
- *Revolution*
- *Reconciliation*

11 Gender 314

SECTION 11.1 / **GENDER, SEX, AND GENDER*SEX** 317
- *Complicating Sex*

SECTION 11.2 / **BINARY GENDER AND BEYOND** 321
- *Signaling and Experiencing Gender*
- *Gender Roles and the Division of Labor*

SECTION 11.3 / **WHY DO WE HAVE (BINARY) GENDER?** 329

SECTION 11.4 / GENDER, INEQUALITY, AND POWER 333

- *Patriarchy and the Persistence of Men's Power*
- *Embodiment of Gender Valuation*
- *Gender Inequality around the Globe*
- *What Next for Gender*Sex?*

12   Sex, Love, and Marriage   344

SECTION 12.1 / HUMAN SEXUALITIES   346

- *Sexual Configurations*
- *Human Sexualities in the Archaeological Record*
- *Challenging Heteronormativity*
- *Resistance to the Oppression of Sexuality*

SECTION 12.2 / MARRIAGE AND MATING SYSTEMS   354

- *Marriage Systems*
- *Human and Primate Mating Systems*

SECTION 12.3 / WHY AND HOW HUMANS MARRY   362

- *Marriage and Economic Arrangements*
- *Marriage and Living Arrangements*
- *Women's Well-Being and Patrilineal Marriage*
- *Selecting a Spouse*
- *Romantic Love*
- *Alternatives to Marriage*

SECTION 12.4 / SEX WORK IN A GLOBALIZED WORLD   371

13   Death, Dying, and the Dead   376

SECTION 13.1 / DEATH AND ITS RITUALS   378

- *When Did Humans First Comprehend Death?*
- *Mortuary Practices in the Past and Present*
- *Mortuary Practices and Social Position*

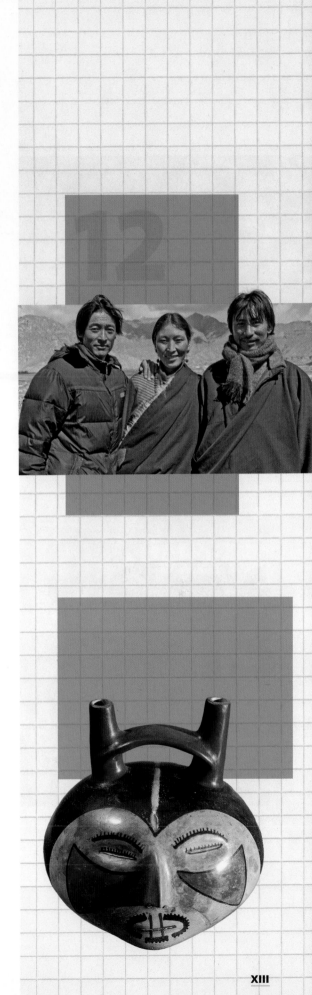

CONTENTS

SECTION 13.2 / **GRIEVING AND CELEBRATING THE DEAD** 386

- *Grieving Rituals*
- *Maintaining Connections with the Dead*
- *Between Life and Death*

SECTION 13.3 / **STUDYING THE DEAD** 392

- *Revealing Those Forgotten by History*
- *Seeking Justice for Victims*
- *Understanding Emerging Epidemics*

SECTION 13.4 / **ETHICS, ANTHROPOLOGY, AND HUMAN REMAINS** 395

14 Race and Racialized Societies 400

SECTION 14.1 / **SCIENCE AND THE ORIGINS OF RACIALIZED SYSTEMS** 403

- *What Is Typological Thinking?*
- *The Early Science of Race*
- *Social Darwinism and Eugenics*
- *Physical Anthropologists and the Support of Racial Typologies*
- *Early Anthropology Challenges Scientific Racism*

SECTION 14.2 / **STRUCTURAL RACISM** 412

- *Racism in the Hospital: Obstetric Care*
- *Racism and Embodied Stress*

SECTION 14.3 / **THE PERSISTENCE OF RACIALIZED SOCIETIES** 415

- *Colorism and Whiteness*
- *Racializing by the State: The Census*
- *Reinforcing White Supremacy through Institutions: Policing and Police Training*
- *Reinforcing White Supremacy through Institutions: Schooling*
- *Learning and Reading Race in Everyday Interactions*
- *New Ways to Self-Racialize: Genetic Ancestry Testing*

SECTION 14.4 / **ANTHROPOLOGY AND ANTI-RACISM NOW** 425

15 Disease, Health, and Healing 430

SECTION 15.1 / DISEASE AND HUMAN HISTORY 433
- *Evolutionary Medicine*

SECTION 15.2 / SOCIAL DIMENSIONS OF ILLNESS 439
- *Healing in the Human Lineage*
- *Recognizing Illness*
- *Experiencing Pain*
- *Illness as Communication*
- *Learning Stigma*

SECTION 15.3 / HEALING SYSTEMS 446
- *Personalistic Healing Systems*
- *Naturalistic Healing Systems*
- *Medical Pluralism*
- *Biomedicine as Ethnomedicine*

SECTION 15.4 / BIOMEDICINE AND POWER 453
- *Biomedicalization and the Commodification of Health*
- *Biopower and Bodies*
- *Power, Inequality, and Biomedical Training*

16 Anthropology, Environment, and Better Futures 462

SECTION 16.1 / THE ANTHROPOLOGY OF DISASTER 464
- *Disaster Anthropology Is Born*
- *Vulnerability and Resilience*
- *Adapting to Disasters: Archaeological Insights*
- *Disaster Capitalism: Profiteering and World-Building after Environmental Crises*

SECTION 16.2 / ENVIRONMENTAL INJUSTICE 473
- *Environmental Justice in the City*
- *Environmental Justice in Micronesia*
- *Indigenous Environmental Justice*

CONTENTS

SECTION 16.3 / ANTHROPOLOGY AND HUMAN ECOLOGY 478

- *From Materialism to Materiality*
- *Human Behavioral Ecology*
- *Human Ecologies as Systems*

SECTION 16.4 / BETTER WAYS FORWARD 483

- *Prioritizing Relationality*
- *Sustainability Transitions*
- *Pluriverse Transitions*
- *A Concluding Thought: Many Ways Forward*

Glossary   G-1

References   R-1

Credits   C-1

Index   I-1

PREFACE FOR INSTRUCTORS

Welcome, fellow instructors, to our first edition. We are excited to share our collective love for anthropology in a textbook that seeks to reflect an integrated, imaginative, and collaborative approach to *doing* anthropology with the following goals.

To Create an Integrated "Four-Field" Anthropology Text

Four-field texts are typically constructed by combining chapters from each of the four fields—such that each field artificially stands in isolation. Our goal was to write an introductory text that embraces the holistic ethos of anthropology, showcasing the complementarity of and interactions between all four fields. Among other things, this meant rethinking how an introductory text should be organized. Some topics, like the study of human violence or gender/sex, bring us close to the ideal; you simply cannot make sense of them without insights from anthropology's major subfields. Other topics, like those that cover the details of fossil evolution, lend themselves to a more conventional treatment, in part because there is less crossover research to draw on and less opportunity to diverge from covering a density of key evidence. With that said, our emphasis on synthesis suffuses the entire text so that students experience how all subfields interact today to shape our understanding of the world. The organization of the work done by anthropologists into four fields is of course an arbitrary imposition in itself, and notably most of the cases in the book highlight the exciting work happening at the interstices rather than the core of each subfield.

To develop a new textbook that was synthetically integrative of the field, we outlined and wrote all the chapters together as a five-person team. This collaborative process was complex; it involved long discussions about what anthropology is, what it should be, and how best to represent the discipline's diversity of methods and perspectives. Since there is no firm consensus on many of these big-picture questions, we had to make hard decisions about what to highlight, critique, and omit. We strove to provide students with a sense of how knowledge is produced in the discipline, explaining how and why reasonable anthropologists can disagree.

One very basic issue we had to grapple with together at the start of this project was defining exactly what anthropology is and what it is not. Many of the keystone methods from anthropology (like ethnography) are now widely deployed in other fields; many others used by anthropology are innovations adopted from other fields (like Indigenous studies, genetics, or chemistry). Also many people who define themselves as doing anthropology do not teach in anthropology departments. They may teach in medical schools or work for government agencies, nongovernmental organizations, or industry. Our decision was to define the scope of anthropology based on how people identified themselves: if those doing cutting-edge research were trained as anthropologists, referred to themselves as doing anthropology, or mainly spoke and wrote to anthropological audiences, then their work was considered in our schema as part of the wider anthropological project. By the same token, this also explains some of our decisions about what was not included.

To Bring Readers into the Text by Telling Stories

Our title, *The Human Story*, is purposeful. Humans love a good story, and stories are a well-established means for drawing people further into the experience of learning. We thus aimed to write in an accessible, narrative style to the greatest extent possible. We have placed anthropologists themselves at the center of our stage, more so than is perhaps typical, to bring real working people with their own backgrounds and orientations into the story.

To Illustrate Knowledge as Coproduction

Historically, public-facing anthropology has tended to elevate the notion of the lone ethnographer or highlight the "star" paleoanthropologist, suggesting that a single scholar (usually based at a U.S., European, or Australasian university) can make important discoveries or breakthroughs largely by themselves (often from evidence collected elsewhere). This is rarely, if ever, how research today works on the ground. Increasingly, the field is reorienting to identify that ethical and forward-looking anthropology always recognizes and embraces collaborations as key to knowledge production by partnering in meaningful ways and better recognizing the contributions made by those working in other scholarly fields or in the communities that are impacted by, care about, and support any research. One result of this orientation is that we tend to not just present findings from those doing anthropology but also explain them to students in the contexts of how they were produced, by naming people and specific methods as well as giving examples of how anthropologists' own lived histories were relevant to the research. We also tend to lean toward highlighting the work of less senior scholars; one reason is they are often clearer and more purposeful in their reporting of the research about such context and the coproduction processes.

To Adopt a Global Orientation

This text draws on case studies and examples of anthropologists-at-work from all regions across the globe. To explain this to students, we have attempted to identify and highlight a wide array of scholarly traditions and positions, including cutting-edge ideas and innovative practices emerging from active centers of scholarship in Latin America, Oceania, Africa, Asia, and elsewhere. But this text does include more cases based on the work and concerns of anthropologists who are based in North America. This is partly because the vision and practices of four-field anthropology emerged in and remain most directly engaged by North American institutions, both from universities and professional anthropological organizations (such as the American Anthropological Association). Also most students who take integrated Introduction to Anthropology courses will do so at North American universities. Although the North American focus of contemporary four-field anthropology has many problems attendant to it, not least of which is its historical ties to colonial and patriarchal worldviews and systems, we have tried to balance this as best we can in decisions about the most effective mix of regional examples and how they are presented.

To Welcome Diverse Students

We have all remained committed throughout our careers to teaching in public institutions that serve very large and diverse student bodies. We regularly teach required introductory courses to more than 500 students at a time, and those students come from a variety of backgrounds, countries, and experiences. To present anthropology as a field that values this diversity, we made a strategic decision to prioritize the work being done by a younger—and increasingly diverse—generation of scholars. Our hope is that this approach emphasizes to all our students that anthropology is a field that welcomes and values them and has valuable applications in their lives, even if they don't go on to become anthropology majors.

To Highlight Anthropology's Critical Role in a Complex World

We decided to highlight anthropological research that is geared toward understanding and addressing major challenges humans face now and will in the years ahead. Our wish is to communicate to students (and the broader public) that anthropology matters because it can advance such goals as sustainability, health, stability, and equity. Related to this, we also see no need to distinguish between anthropology that is applied and not: in our vision all cutting-edge anthropology should be relevant and applicable, and our role is to help highlight this for students in ways that will resonate with them.

To Enable Teaching in Varied Modalities

We have designed this book to be useful in classes that are large and small as well as taught in varied modalities of varying lengths. Many chapters, particularly in the second part of the text, are designed to stand alone so that they may be configured in nonlinear ways. For example, an instructor teaching an Applying Anthropology course can extract a subset of chapters, such as those on gender, health, death, sex/marriage, and violence, and focus on exploring each of those topics through a four-field perspective.

To Present an Optimistic, Future-Oriented Vision of the Field

Much of the most exciting work in the field has been produced very recently and reflects new methods (such as the amazing genetic revolution that is entirely changing how we see human evolutionary pasts) and new ways of understanding the roles of anthropologists in producing knowledge (such as efforts to redress the extractive nature of much past anthropological fieldwork). This recent flourishing of our field, rife with many (sometimes painful) reconsiderations of what we do and why, means we devote less space to direct discussions on the historical origins of anthropological ideas and practices. Rather, we weight more heavily the implications of ideas being produced by anthropologists now, many of which are explicitly about creating a better, more sustainable, more just, and healthier world.

The belief that anthropology is the best lens we have to better understand possible human futures is one that recurs throughout the text. Of course, the road into that future will be a bumpy one, perhaps most especially for our students. They are making decisions about their future professional lives while grappling with many seismic societal shifts. We wrote most of this first edition in a time of great social disruption—during the COVID-19 pandemic, climate disasters, contested elections, dramatic inflation, and the Black Lives Matter and #MeToo movements. A globalized, capitalist world system is one that will absolutely continue to be challenged by pandemics, profound inequalities, environmental disasters, and social and political instability. Anthropology, as we explore it here, lays bare much of the scale and suffering of such challenges. But this text is also, we hope, ultimately imbued with the optimism we together feel: that anthropology is a particularly powerful way to see humans at their best and imagine sustainable, just futures. And we hope this sense of the great things ahead for our field, even as it shifts and turns to redefine its purpose and obligations, is the lesson that will linger most for the reader.

Alexandra (Alex) Brewis
Kelly Knudson
Christopher (Chris) Stojanowski
Cindi SturtzSreetharan
Amber Wutich

Tools for Teaching and Learning

NORTON ILLUMINE EBOOK

The Human Story is also available as a Norton Illumine Ebook, which provides students and instructors with an enhanced reading experience at a fraction of the cost of a print textbook.

- **Check Your Understanding** questions allow students to review key terms and concepts from the section's content, receiving answer-specific feedback to explain why their choices are correct or incorrect. These questions can be assigned for completion grades that report directly into your learning management system (LMS).

  The Check Your Understanding questions were authored by Jimil Ataman at the University of Pennsylvania and have been reviewed by Seth Dornisch at the University of Massachusetts Amherst.

- **Anthropology in 3D models** allows students to interact with 3D bone and fossil specimens of primate species as they read to help them better understand human evolution and primate evolutionary traits.

- **Note-sharing capability** allows instructors to focus student reading by sharing notes with their classes, including their own embedded images and videos. Reports on student and class access and time on task allow instructors to monitor student reading and engagement.

ANTHROPOLOGY IN 3D MODELS

Anthropology in 3D models help students examine and interact with virtual primate bone and fossil specimens as if they were in a lab. The models include monkey, ape, hominin, and human examples, allowing students to compare and contrast different species' evolutionary traits.

These 3D models have been included in the Norton Illumine Ebook where relevant. They are also available to use in customized lectures, activities, and assignments in the Resources for your LMS cartridge and at digital.wwnorton .com/humanstory.

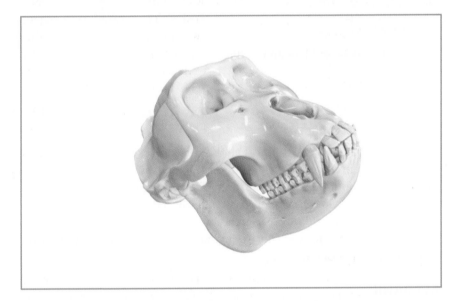

The specimens were largely provided by Sabrina Agarwal at the University of California, Berkeley. Some hominin specimens are hosted by Morpho-Source.

NORTON TEACHING TOOLS

The easy-to-navigate Norton Teaching Tools site makes designing or refreshing your syllabus easier than ever with our creative, equity-minded resources.

Every resource is aligned with chapter topics and organized by activity type, making them easy to find based on your course needs. The guide also features tips and best practices for assigning Norton's digital learning tools and addressing the most common course challenges. Example content includes the following:

- **Digging Deeper into Contemporary Anthropology assignments**, which spotlight the diversity of working anthropologists and their research

- **equity-minded and antiracist course design tips**, which give instructors ideas on how they can structure their courses differently to best help students navigate anthropology's key lessons, but also its complicated history

- **Modern Debate activities**, which have students reflect on current topics through an anthropological lens and form their own opinions on issues

- **conversion guides**, which will make transitioning easier for first-time adopters who have been using select competing titles

- sample syllabi

- lecture ideas

- class activities

- lists of suggested videos and media

- discussion questions

- chapter outlines

- lecture PowerPoints

Our textbook authors created almost all these resources based around their book's approach, interweaving their integrated, inclusive, and contemporary approach throughout these teaching tools. The Digging Deeper into Contemporary Anthropology assignments were authored by Jimil Ataman at the University of Pennsylvania. The original concept for these assignments was developed by Liz Soluri at Cabrillo College and Sabrina Agarwal at the University of California, Berkeley.

TEST BANK

Norton uses evidence-based assessment practices to deliver high-quality and pedagogically effective quizzes and testing materials. This test bank offers 35 questions per chapter, including 30 multiple-choice questions and 5 essay questions. Questions are classified by section and difficulty, making it easy to construct tests and quizzes that are meaningful and diagnostic. The framework to develop our test banks, quizzes, and support materials is the result of collaboration with leading academic researchers and advisers.

Norton Testmaker brings Norton's high-quality testing materials online. Assessments for a course may be created from anywhere with an internet connection, without downloading files or installing specialized software. Test bank questions can be searched and filtered by chapter, type, difficulty, learning objectives, and other criteria. Test bank questions can also be customized to fit a course. Then tests can easily export to Microsoft Word or Common Cartridge files for an LMS.

Our test bank questions were written by Jimil Ataman at the University of Pennsylvania and reviewed by Seth Dornisch at the University of Massachusetts Amherst.

LECTURE SLIDES

Available for each chapter covered in the text, these customizable PowerPoint slides feature images and bulleted chapter outlines for in-class presentation. The Lecture PowerPoint images include alt text, and the slides are designed to be accessible for all students, including students who use screen readers.

ART SLIDES AND JPEGS

All the art from the book, sized for classroom display, is available in Power-Point with alt text and in JPEG format.

RESOURCES FOR YOUR LMS

Easily add high-quality Norton digital resources to online, hybrid, or lecture courses through integrated links. All activities can be accessed right in an existing learning management system, and many components are customizable. Resources already integrated into the LMS include the following:

- **Norton Illumine Ebook** gives students an active reading experience. Along with answering Check Your Understanding questions, students can also take notes, bookmark, search, and highlight.

- **Biological anthropology animations** explain major scientific concepts in anthropology in more detail.

- **Anthropology in 3D** fossil and cast specimens allow students to interact with skulls, feet, and more, as well as analyze primate anatomy online as if they were in a lab.

- **Flashcards** help students review key terms in each chapter.

ACKNOWLEDGMENTS

James Alexander, Lake Michigan College
Janet Lynne Altamirano, Texas A&M—Kingsville
Alice Baldwin-Jones William, Paterson University
Anthony Balzano, Sussex County Community College
Melissa Beresford, San José State University
Brad M. Biglow, Florida State College at Jacksonville
Katie Binetti, Baylor University
Renee Bonzani, University of Kentucky
Matthew Boulanger, Southern Methodist University
Kelly M. Branam Macauley, St. Cloud State University
Ann L. Buckun, College of DuPage
Jennifer M. Cantú Trunzo, Augusta University
Choeeta Chakrabarti, Florida State University
Marie Elaine Danforth, University of Southern Mississippi
Anton Daughters, Truman State University
Paul Donato, University of Maryland, Baltimore County
Zachary DuBois, University of Oregon
Samuel Duwe, University of Oklahoma
Kelsey Ellis, Miami University
Amanda L. Ellwanger, Georgia State University
Georgia Ennis, Penn State University
Kristin Fitzgerald, Creighton University
Julianne Fontenoy, UNM Gallup
Catherine M. Fuentes, University of North Carolina at Charlotte
Celeste Marie Gagnon, Wagner College
Meskerem Glegziabher, Arizona State University
Marcus Hamilton, University of Texas at San Antonio
Christian Hammons, University of Colorado Boulder
Doug Henry, University of North Texas
Elizabeth W. Higgs, University of Houston
Bobbi Hornbeck, Stockton University
Rachel Horowitz, Washington State University
Jamie K. Johnson, University of North Texas
Lewis Jones, Gettysburg College
Eleana Kim, University of California, Irvine
Susan Kirkpatrick Smith, Kennesaw State University
Susan Krook, Normandale Community College
Aaron Leo, Savannah College of Art and Design
Daniel Loganbill, University of Kansas
Lily Malekfar, City Colleges of Chicago and Triton College
Aurelien Mauxion, Columbia College
Barbara J. Michael, University of North Carolina Wilmington
Aaron Michka, University of Notre Dame
Andrew Newman, Wayne State University

Osbjorn Pearson, University of New Mexico
Jarrett Phipps, Tallahassee Community College
Donna Rosh, Central New Mexico Community College
Michael Rutz, Brightpoint Community College
Margaret Sabom Bruchez, Blinn College
John D. Seebach, Colorado Mesa University
Nicola Sharratt, Georgia State University
Krystal Smalls, University of Illinois Urbana-Champaign
Marjorie M. Snipes, University of West Georgia
Robert Stokes, Eastern New Mexico University, Portales
Roger Sullivan, California State University, Sacramento
Yuki Tanaka-McFarlane, Saint Louis University
Aaron Thornburg, Eastern Oregon University
Matthew Tornow, St. Cloud State University
Janel Tortorice, Lone Star College—CyFair
Dr. Heather R. Triplett, College of DuPage
Rebecca L. Upton, DePauw University
Dr. Lisa Volle, Central Texas College
Jean Wynn, Manchester Community College
Shaozeng Zhang, Oregon State University
Molly Zuckerman, Mississippi State University

The authors wish to thank Jake Schindel, their colleagues at ASU, and their many other collaborators who have lent so many ideas and given such generous guidance over the many years of imagining and then writing *The Human Story*.

ABOUT THE AUTHORS

The coauthors are all professors in the School of Human Evolution and Social Change at Arizona State University (ASU), which has been repeatedly ranked as the leader for anthropology research impact and scale. They have more than a century of combined experience teaching four-field undergraduate anthropology, both in person and online, and have received numerous awards for their instruction and research. For information on the authors, their research, and anthropology programs at ASU, see **shesc.asu.edu**.

THE HUMAN STORY

An Introduction to Anthropology

Why Anthropology?

Viewed in the totality of life on our planet, our species is extremely young. We are but one of the many upright-walking primates or hominins that emerged in the grasslands and woodlands of what is now Africa. But we are the only one remaining today: *Homo sapiens*. Anthropology is the study of how we humans came to be, our present condition, and the possibilities for our future. Most simply, the scholarly field of anthropology is about understanding what it means to be human in the broadest possible sense.

This book explores what anthropologists have learned in the exciting and ongoing quest to understand our species, in all our dimensions, complexities, and contradictions. But studying anthropology is also a means to discover our own selves. It can spur you to reexamine every aspect of your life. Anthropology makes us more aware of how we identify ourselves socially, and how and why we relate and react to others as we do. Studying anthropology reveals that each personal understanding of the world is but one of many, and greater knowledge of this diversity of human experiences enriches the possibilities for our own lives.

LEARNING OBJECTIVES

1.1 The Subfields of Anthropology
Describe the diversity of work done by trained anthropologists across the four subfields.

1.2 What Makes Anthropology "Anthropological"?
Identify the defining features of anthropological research.

TEETH AND THE FOUR SUBFIELDS

Anthropology's subfields provide different, yet complementary, ways to look at the same issues or objects, such as our teeth. Comparison of human with living primate and fossil teeth helps us understand the evolution of human social organization and diet. Our teeth communicate information visually about our emotions and social identities, and create the sounds that underpin the remarkable human capacity for language. Dental health reflects the environmental and social conditions in which people live. Clockwise from top right: Smiling Hyolmo woman in Nepal; French dental students protesting reforms in state-funded dental services; fossil teeth from Gran Dolina, Spain; representing an extinct hominin species; a mandrill "grin" with their distinctively sharp incisors bared, used as a peaceful signal to others in their social group; the word "tooth" in British and American sign language.

hominin A human, extinct human ancestor, or closely related species that is more closely related to modern humans than chimpanzees.

Homo sapiens The only remaining species of humans.

anthropology The study of what it means to be human, in the broadest possible sense.

THE SUBFIELDS OF ANTHROPOLOGY

Anthropologists research an amazing range of topics, places, and problems. The work of anthropologists is often divided up into four traditional subfields, and explaining the characteristics of each is the focus of this section. The work of some anthropologists fits clearly within one subfield, but other anthropologists combine and integrate ideas and methods across two or more subfields (**Figure 1.1**). Ultimately, what ties anthropologists together as a scholarly community is a shared set of big-picture questions about what it means to be human and a core set of values about how we should proceed to answer those questions (explored further in Section 1.2).

BIOLOGICAL ANTHROPOLOGY

Biological anthropologists (sometimes called evolutionary anthropologists) recognize that humans today are a product of ongoing processes of evolution. Biological anthropology is the most explicitly scientific of the four subfields, and biological anthropologists often use assessments of past and present biological materials (like genetic markers in blood, skeletons, or fossil remains) to test hypotheses about the origins, patterns, and implications of past and present human biological diversity. They also study the anatomy and behavior of other primate species—our closest living relatives—to gain insights about the human past.

Biological anthropologist Sheela Athreya, for example, studies fossil evidence of early humans on the Indian subcontinent (**Figure 1.2**). Athreya looks for genetic similarities between living people today and fossilized human remains from rock shelters dating back 40,000 years, by comparing the shape of facial bones and other biological markers. Such data from regions that have been historically marginalized in the study of human evolution, like India, advance a more complete, global model of human pasts.

evolution The scientific theory that explains the appearance of new species as the accumulation of genetic changes across generations.

biological anthropology The study of human evolution and biological variation.

genetic Related to the basic biological materials of inheritance, which provide instructions for how organisms look and function.

fossil A remainder, trace, petrified form, or impression of a past organism that has been preserved in rock.

hypothesis A proposed explanation for a condition or phenomenon that guides scientific investigation.

biological diversity Variability in the biology of a population or species, in all its dimensions.

primate One of a group of related mammals that evolved as tree-dwellers with relatively large brains and forward-facing eyes; includes lemurs, monkeys, apes, and humans.

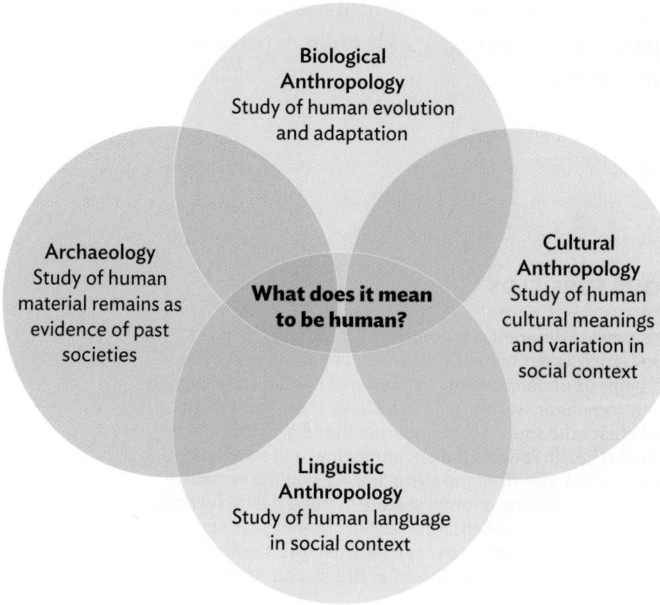

FIGURE 1.1

Although anthropology is usually described as having distinctive subfields, the work of many anthropologists integrates ideas and approaches from across them.

Biological Anthropology
Study of human evolution and adaptation

Archaeology
Study of human material remains as evidence of past societies

What does it mean to be human?

Cultural Anthropology
Study of human cultural meanings and variation in social context

Linguistic Anthropology
Study of human language in social context

FIGURE 1.2

Biological anthropologist Sheela
Athreya (left) and archaeologist Ravi
Korisettar collaborate on studies of
early human history at Bhimbetka
rock shelters in central India.

ARCHAEOLOGY

Archaeology is the study of the human past through the physical objects and artifacts that humans create and then leave behind in the archaeological record. Many archaeologists rely on excavation, the scientific technique of removing objects from the ground, to understand human societies that pre-date written records. Archaeologists also study human, plant, animal, or other organic remains to describe how past humans interacted with and within their local environments.

Archaeologist Li Liu's excavations in China span more than 10,000 years of human history (**Figure 1.3**). Liu's work explores what prompted people to move away from hunting and gathering wild foods and begin practicing agriculture. She is testing hypotheses regarding how cereals like rice and millet may have triggered the emergence of highly complex and hierarchical societies, like those of the earlier Chinese dynasties (successions of rulers descended from each other).

archaeology The study of material remains as evidence of past human behavior and societies.

artifact An object that people made or used in the past.

archaeological record The physical evidence of past human activity, including artifacts, built structures, and animal and plant remains.

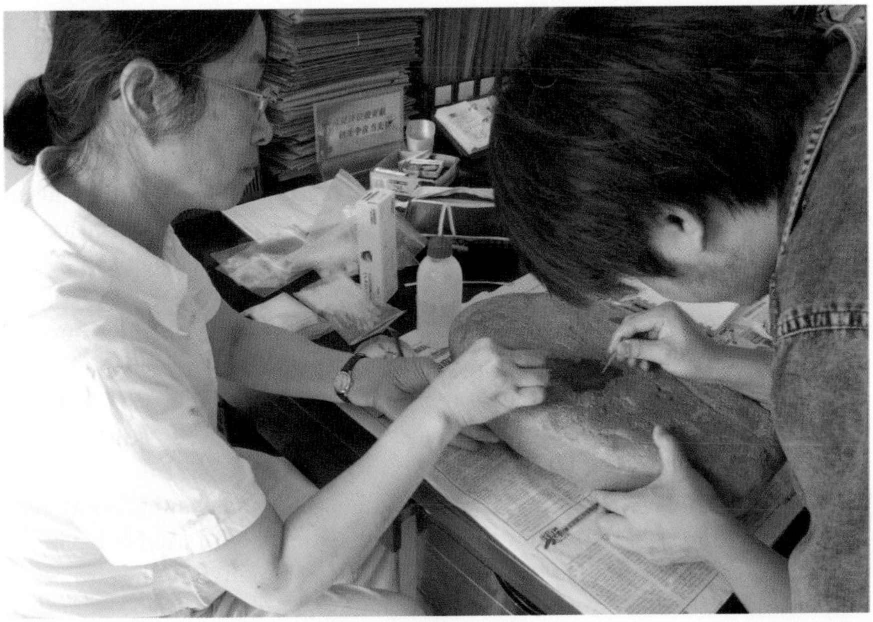

FIGURE 1.3

Archaeologists Li Liu (left) and Hao Zhao take residue from an ancient grinding slab in China; these samples show the stones were used to grind wild grass seeds, roots, and tubers to release starch and make them easier to digest.

FIGURE 1.4

Culture is based in symbols, with meanings applied to **(a)** objects (such as a headstone or flowers), **(b)** acts (such as prayer), or **(c)** images and sounds (such as written and spoken words).

(a)

(b)

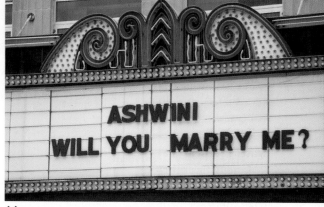

(c)

cultural anthropology The study of human cultural meanings and variation in social context.

norm A shared set of beliefs of what is ideal, acceptable, or to be avoided.

culture Shared meanings, norms, and practices that together shape how people collectively think and act.

society People in sustained communication, with rules and structures that organize them in relation to one another.

ethnography A research approach dedicated to describing cultures, based on understanding cultural insiders' own knowledge and worldviews.

participant observation An ethnographic research method that relies on cultural immersion; the researcher often lives alongside members of the culture under study, conducting careful observation and questioning to facilitate data collection and analysis.

symbol An image, sound, or action that we learn represents (but does not resemble) something else.

Indigenous, Aboriginal, and First Nation Terms that refer to original inhabitants of regions and their descendants, who often live with the legacy of being colonized by other groups.

descendant group People with direct and shared personal, spiritual, or ancestral connection to archaeological objects or human remains.

CULTURAL ANTHROPOLOGY

Cultural anthropology (sometimes called social or sociocultural anthropology) is the study of how people share, change, and dispute the meanings, practices, and norms that define culture and shape everyday lives. Cultural anthropologists are also invested in understanding how varied social arrangements within societies shape human experiences and the meanings applied to them. They study culture using ethnography, and seek an "insider perspective" through ethnographic techniques like participant observation.

Culture is based in symbols, in which specific meanings are given to objects, sounds, or acts (**Figure 1.4**). We are surrounded by symbols all the time, and we can only function in the world if we know how to decode them. For example, we might see a plain ring on a fourth finger of the left hand and recognize that means the person is married. The connection between such symbols and their meanings must be learned. We see "7" written on a page and know it refers to a number, but any other notation could potentially do the same job.

Paul Tapsell is a cultural anthropologist who was raised in the farmlands of New Zealand (**Figure 1.5**). His expertise in explaining the cultural meanings that people today place on archaeological objects from the past helps integrate Indigenous, Aboriginal, and First Nation community priorities and values into how museum objects are managed. He often consults on the return of Māori *taonga* (treasured objects) to descendant groups, many of which were taken for display in Europe in the 1700s and 1800s.

Even though cultural anthropologists are those who study culture most intently, all the subfields of anthropology are united by their interest in culture as a core concept for understanding humans, both past and present. Biological anthropologists consider the emergence of symbol-based behavior as a defining feature of our evolutionary past and fundamental to the success of hominin species thereafter. Archaeologists understand and treat the physical objects they excavate as material culture, meaning they reflect the specific cultural contexts in which they were produced, used, and even discarded.

LINGUISTIC ANTHROPOLOGY

Language is the most important symbol-based system learned and used by humans, and language is the core of how we relate to each other and interpret the world around us. Of all species, humans have evolved the most complex language and are the most dependent on it. Thousands of languages are used globally. Language use is the cornerstone of how culture is transmitted, and each society has its own language forms and conventions. Linguistic anthropology is the study of the ways that language diversity influences thought, as well as the ways that it contributes to maintaining or disrupting social reality and social relations. The study of languages in everyday use has long been a major focus of this subfield; more recent research also investigates the ideas that people hold about language.

Linguistic anthropologist Jonathan Rosa has conducted extensive studies of how urban U.S. schools attempt to change language use in immigrant youth to make them seem "more professional" (**Figure 1.6**). He showed how students navigated this socially complicated terrain by creating complex "school-kid" versus "community-kid" identities for themselves and switching between different language rules when in versus out of school. His research provides an explanation for why allowing for all different forms of language at school can improve educational outcomes.

OTHER SUBFIELDS

Although anthropology is traditionally said to have four subfields and is often taught in this way, sometimes other anthropological specializations are treated as their own subfields. Commonly encountered variants include

FIGURE 1.5

Cultural anthropologist Paul Tapsell (right) explains Māori worldviews to the president of Pakistan through examples of intricate carvings.

material culture The physical objects humans create, such as pottery or stone tools; once these objects become part of the archaeological record, they are known as artifacts.

language A systematic symbol-based signaling system that allows things to get done.

linguistic anthropology The study of human language variation in its social contexts.

FIGURE 1.6

Linguistic anthropologist Jonathan Rosa (middle) uses insights about language and culture to engage university and high school students in collaborative, community-based learning at Sequoia High School in California, United States.

medical anthropology and bioarchaeology. Medical anthropology uses tools and approaches from other anthropology subfields—including cultural, linguistic, and biological anthropology—to understand human experiences of health and disease. Bioarchaeology integrates approaches from archaeology and biological anthropology to study skeletonized human remains to understand human pasts.

OUR TEETH: VIEWS FROM THE FOUR SUBFIELDS

To understand how the four subfields are distinctive from and yet complementary to one another, we use the example of how each might differently confront the study of an object often given little consideration: our teeth (which anthropologists refer to as our dentition).

Our front teeth are highly visible to others. To a *cultural anthropologist,* the way our teeth look communicates social meanings that then shape social interactions and opportunities. Those who can't meet basic norms of hygiene, such as presenting obvious dental decay when they cannot access dental care, may find themselves systematically excluded from social invitations or excluded from paid employment.

Conversely, those who are able to modify their teeth into the most socially valued forms can gain social and economic benefits, such as a favorable marriage. The ideals of dental beauty vary greatly through time and across societies. Teeth may be filed to points, inset with jewels, blackened or whitened, or painfully straightened to create what is defined at that place and moment as desirable (**Figure 1.7**).

To *linguistic anthropologists,* tooth use can create sounds that in turn reinforce social distinctions. Sound, sign, and word differences can act as markers that identify who belongs within a group and who doesn't. For example, the "tooth suck" is a learned manipulation where the lips are pulled tight against the teeth and air is quickly sucked inward between clenched lips while the tongue rests on the soft palate. In some societies in western Africa and among African-descent populations in the Caribbean, the resulting hissing sound is used by women and girls to signal annoyance or anger.

For *archaeologists,* teeth (and other human remains) provide clues to the

(a)

(b)

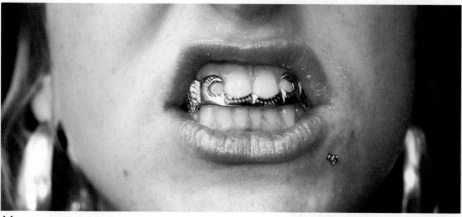
(c)

FIGURE 1.7

Examples of dental modifications are shown, each reflecting very specific local norms of beauty: **(a)** filed teeth in Ethiopia; **(b)** blackened teeth in Myanmar; and **(c)** a decorative teeth grill in the United States.

past social or environmental conditions in which that person lived. Teeth erupt in a set pattern and then wear down as we age, so the level of wear can indicate how long people were living into adulthood. Lines, ridges, pits, or retexturing in tooth enamel suggests hunger or acute illness while the tooth was developing. For example, one form of childhood enamel retexturing on the lip (labial) side of incisors was found in more than 90% of children living in one community in the Bolivian Amazon (**Figure 1.8**). Comparisons with dental studies of living humans allow archaeologists to use excavated human skeletal remains to draw conclusions about health and diet in past societies. For example, differences in the pattern of tooth wear of individuals from the same archaeological excavation area can suggest that they lived in a society characterized by marked social differentiation, such as men and women doing different types of labor.

For *biological anthropologists*, teeth are important for reconstructing an even deeper past of our ancestors and other primates. Teeth are preserved in the ground much better than most other organic remains, so they are some of the most important fossil finds for reconstructing human evolution. Tooth shape can reveal if the remains belong to a known human species or if the individual ate insects, fruits, or leaves. Comparing fossil teeth to the teeth of living primate species can give clues about social organization of past humans. For example, if the canine teeth of males are much the same size as those of females, it suggests the evolution of a socially monogamous species with stable, long-term living arrangements between one adult female and one adult male raising their young together (**Figure 1.9**). That is because biological anthropologists have observed that among living primates the most monogamous species tend to have males and females closer in size to each other.

INTEGRATING THE SUBFIELDS

While we have identified how the subfields can be viewed as complementary and distinct, many of the most useful and exciting applications of anthropological work come from their integration. In our example of front teeth, the case of refugee resettlement shows how examining a problem from the perspective of all four subfields at once can lead to important and practical insights.

The Second Sudanese Civil War (1983–2005) created a refugee crisis. Around 20,000 Dinka and Nuer peoples relocated from their homes in the south of the country to the United States in the 1990s. Some arrived with four to six teeth missing from their lower jaw. In interviews, these refugees explained to medical anthropologist Mary Willis that their permanent front teeth were removed as part of their coming-of-age rituals, marking the transition from childhood to adulthood. In their home communities in northern Africa, the gap had served as an important marker of their Dinka or Nuer social identity. While it was painful to have the removal performed, that gap and the distinctive sounds it produced while talking signaled beauty, maturity, and respect for tradition. In their natal communities, those without this modification could be teased or otherwise shamed by others.

Archaeological excavations have unearthed skulls that confirm that the tooth extraction practice (called ablation) has a long history in this region of northern Africa, dating back at least 15,000 years. Biological anthropologists, who understand tooth eruption and other skeletal patterns, have confirmed that the teeth removals happened around puberty, so they could have acted similarly as a marker of entering adulthood. However, only some groups in the region at the time practiced ablation. This suggests that the dental gap

FIGURE 1.8

Enamel changes, such as these "orange peel" marks and depressions documented for an adolescent in the Amazon study, can provide evidence of an individual's prior exposures to disease or malnutrition. Such studies also help interpret archaeological clues about the past conditions of people's lives.

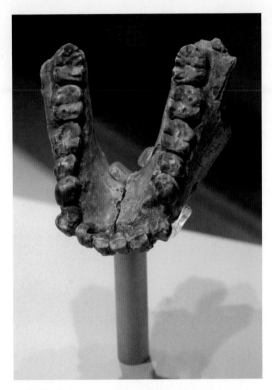

FIGURE 1.9

A cast of the fossil teeth of a proposed human ancestor, *Australopithecus anamensis*, shows relatively larger canines (eye teeth) compared to modern humans. Comparisons of dental form and wear patterns with modern humans and living primates give clues about this species' diet (lots of hard foods) and social structure (perhaps less monogamous than modern humans).

social differentiation The process of creating and reinforcing social hierarchies, aligned with differing roles within society.

social identity The self-recognized characteristics that make an individual or social group like or unlike others.

acted as a highly visible and important group social identity marker of some type.

But when members of these Sudanese groups arrived in the United States as refugees, they reported to Willis their observation that successful people in their new home all had straight white teeth. Within weeks, many asked for help to replace their missing front teeth. It wasn't just the aesthetics. They were also working to learn spoken English. The tooth gap made it difficult to speak in the ways expected in their new communities. The Dinka language, for example, does not rely on the sound "sh" (as in the word share). But American English does use this sound, which relies on both the upper and lower teeth being brought together to slightly inhibit the air. If the upper or lower teeth are missing, the air passes freely through the gap, modifying the sound quite a bit. Moreover, the diet in Sudan favors soft vegetables and grains that can be eaten without lower teeth. The harder and more chewy American foods prove much more difficult to eat. Inability to eat what everyone else is eating created a struggle to fit in at commonplace U.S. social events like group dinners.

Putting all this together, Willis used insights from across the four subfields to explain the importance of dental implants as refugee assistance. Working closely with dental experts, her team has shown that, after surgery, refugees were measurably happier because they were able to meet their goals to eat, speak, and look more like others in their new country.

SECTION 1.2

WHAT MAKES ANTHROPOLOGY "ANTHROPOLOGICAL"?

We've seen how dividing the discipline into subfields with particular focuses and methodologies helps anthropologists, as a community, better understand our species. We have also already identified that the concept of "culture" is central to all the subfields. In this section, we highlight some additional core values and practices that together define anthropology as a discipline. These include (1) conducting fieldwork, (2) comparison across societies and species, (3) embracing many different scholarly traditions, (4) prioritizing research that supports positive change in the world, and (5) sharing ethical standards. Together, these aspects greatly influence the topics anthropologists choose to study, who they do research with, and how they share the results of their work.

VALUING FIELDWORK

One thing that links the work of all the anthropologists we introduced earlier, and most other anthropologists, is the commitment to fieldwork as a means of scholarly discovery. The types of fieldwork anthropologists do are wide-ranging—archaeological excavations of abandoned cityscapes in Mexico, observing chimpanzee social behavior in Uganda, measuring children's growth in the suburbs of Canada, or interviewing people immersed in online gaming communities.

fieldwork The varied processes of collecting new data outside the laboratory, office, or classroom.

Why do anthropologists place such a high value on doing fieldwork? There are several reasons. First, the existing record of the full range of human diversity is extremely limited, spotty, and incomplete. Archaeological excavations done to date have uncovered only a very narrow window to past human lives. Many important phenomena within living human societies and the subcultures within them have never been documented. Fieldwork helps widen our evidence base, filling in more puzzle pieces.

Historically, anthropological fieldwork was done far away from home in distant locales. But increasingly, anthropologists also work close to home, including in the communities in which they live. Cultural anthropologist Laurence Ralph conducted fieldwork in the West Side of Chicago while living there (**Figure 1.10**). This allowed him to build detailed descriptions of life in segregated urban communities with high gang activity, where some residents face daily threats of physical injury. His research helps explain to unfamiliar audiences what solutions to urban violence could look like.

Second, societies constantly change, sometimes very rapidly. This means that data collected previously may no longer be relevant or usable. Studies by cultural anthropologists on gender norms in the early 2000s, for example, can be thoroughly out of date in many places today. Recent decades have seen significant changes in the social acceptance of more fluid gender roles and sexual identities.

Third, fieldwork requires anthropologists to go to physical places or engage socially in communities. This keeps anthropological research grounded, focused on understanding people in the contexts in which they live, work, and socialize now or in the past. This willingness to step away from their own lives to enter "the field" sometimes helps anthropologists question their own assumptions and consider how their biases shape what they look for and see. This effort to suspend personal moral values to better understand people as they are, and in their own terms, is sometimes referred to as cultural relativism.

FIGURE 1.10

Cultural anthropologist Laurence Ralph does detailed fieldwork in U.S. cities around urban violence, especially in Chicago, where he lived as an anthropology student.

cultural relativism The assessment of other cultures in the context of those cultures' own values.

CROSS-CULTURAL AND CROSS-SPECIES COMPARISON

Anthropology embraces comparative approaches to develop new insights about humans and their societies, past and present. Systematic comparisons across space and time provide information on the consistent features of human experiences, but also provide blueprints for the full range of possible variations in how successful societies can be arranged. For example, cross-cultural studies show that marriage is a characteristic feature of human societies, but monogamous marriage is not (Chapter 12). Comparing humans to other primate species is an important evidence base for understanding our deep past and how we evolved (Chapter 4). For example, comparison of dentition across past and present species highlights that primate bodies have evolved to accommodate very diverse (omnivorous) diets. The information gleaned from this approach can lead us to challenge the assumptions that underpin the ways we organize our own lives and societies and enable us to evaluate other possibilities.

Consider something all humans need to do every day: sleep. In large modern cities with electricity, many people expect to sleep in one long stretch, actively avoid ambient noise and light, and do it privately. Sleep deprivation and insomnia are cited as problems when long blocks of uninterrupted sleep become elusive. But anthropologists have consistently observed that people in communities living without artificial (electric) light typically sleep close to many

comparative approach Using data to compare features across societies or species, past or present, with the goal of identifying what is different and what is shared across them. In comparing contemporary human groups, this is sometimes termed cross-cultural research.

FIGURE 1.11

Celebes crested macaques (*Macaca nigra*) are one of many primate species that sleep together in groups, including for their afternoon naps.

FIGURE 1.12

Anthropologists have proposed that co-sleeping arrangements, done carefully, can reduce sleep disruption for parents and babies; such comparative research suggests new ways to look at what we define as healthy or risky.

science A systematic approach to creating new knowledge by testing falsifiable predictions about how the world works and came to be.

humanism An approach focusing on personal experiences, choices, expression, and meanings.

others, surrounded by noise and movement. Napping is common, and fixed bedtimes are viewed as odd or abnormal. Cross-species comparisons of humans with other living primates also suggest that both napping and sleeping in groups may be "normal" ways for humans to get rest (**Figure 1.11**).

Viewed by comparison both with other primates and across different societies, parents and babies have almost always slept together—an ideal human arrangement for ensuring babies benefit from nighttime feeding (**Figure 1.12**). But much medical advice in places like the United Kingdom and the United States tells parents that such co-sleeping is inherently dangerous. This then reduces breastfeeding of babies through the night, even while breastfeeding is promoted as good for them.

Beginning with an assumption that comparisons give us important clues about what is "normal" and safe for our species, biological anthropologist Helen Ball leads research on infant co-sleeping at the Durham Infancy and Sleep Centre in the United Kingdom. Her research on the safe ways for infants to co-sleep with their parents began with using infrared photography and physiological monitoring of families while they slept. Over the years, her team has also interviewed many mothers and tested the effects of different sleeping arrangements on both infants and parents. Ball's research challenges established medical advice and policies, and it includes recommendations that co-sleeping can be very safe (and the safest way to do so is by sleeping on a firm mattress and ensuring the child is positioned to avoid overheating).

The comparative approach helps anthropologists confront large and difficult questions: How should we raise our children? Is there a sustainable way to live on the planet? How do we create diverse yet stable societies? What is needed to prevent war and other deadly violence between human groups? How are new digital technologies, and the shrinking world they create, changing us? As you will find throughout this book, the comparative study of humanity provides many innovative blueprints for better options.

EMBRACING DIVERSE SCHOLARLY TRADITIONS

One of the main divisions in much current scholarly thinking outside anthropology is between science and humanism. Science is an approach that builds and organizes new knowledge based on testable, falsifiable predictions about how the world works. It values things that can be observed, measured, and tested. Humanism, meanwhile, emphasizes the uniqueness of people's own

FIGURE 1.13

Biological anthropologist Lisa Matisoo-Smith (red hat) collects genetic samples from rats in Papua New Guinea. Analysis of the animals that accompanied humans on their original migrations provides a proxy for tracing the history of human settlement across the Pacific region. Use of non-human DNA allows more communities to participate in comparative research projects, while recognizing and respecting differing local values around providing human biological specimens for scientific study.

experiences and the meanings people themselves apply to these. Anthropology fully embraces both science and humanism, often at the same time. This makes anthropology "the most scientific of the humanities, and the most humanistic of the sciences," as influential anthropologist Eric Wolf once said.

In practice, many anthropologists integrate both approaches in their research. For example, biological anthropologist Lisa Matisoo-Smith identifies the original migration histories of different groups within the Pacific region by comparing genetic similarities and differences today (**Figure 1.13**). While she does research on human biology in a scientific tradition, her research practices are shaped by ongoing conversations with humanists, addressing the ethics of data storage and ways to maximize benefits for descendant communities.

Anthropology recognizes there are many valid knowledge systems. Indigenous or other forms of local knowledge are created through long-term experience living in one place. This includes things like how to farm in a specific location or heal using local plants. A good example is the root crop cassava, which can be toxic if eaten raw but nutritious if prepared using learned techniques like sun drying, soaking and boiling, or fermenting. Some communities long ago figured out how to render cassava as safe, allowing it to become a dietary staple.

Anthropology is constantly evolving, bringing in new techniques and ideas from other scholarly fields but also learning from what participants and other community stakeholders think about the world. This openness makes anthropology special because it seeks to create knowledge *with* people, not just perform studies on or extract knowledge from them. Anthropologists are accordingly increasingly committed to knowledge coproduction, a process in which relevant research stakeholders, such as descendant groups, local communities, or policy-makers, are engaged as partners at all stages of a research project, from defining what is important to study to how research can be done ethically and how its usefulness and relevance can be maximized.

ethics A guiding framework to protect individuals and communities from harm while maximizing the benefits of research.

knowledge system An organized, systematic, and shared set of related ideas of how something works, based on careful observation, learning, and practice.

local knowledge A knowledge system that develops through long-term experience in one place.

knowledge coproduction A diverse set of research practices that seek to combine scientific integrity with creating knowledge to benefit communities through meaningful collaboration at all stages of a project.

research stakeholder A person with a direct interest or concern in a research project.

FIGURE 1.14

Bioarchaeologist Dawnie Wolfe Steadman (right) documents a donor grave site at the University of Tennessee's Forensic Anthropology Center.

applied anthropology The use of anthropological research and expertise in the solution of real-world challenges.

activist anthropology Collaborative research and action in partnership with communities, usually those with less power or otherwise marginalized, to challenge the political status quo.

FIGURE 1.15

Cultural anthropologist Maria Cruz-Torres's mother (left) shows her how to prepare arroz con pollo, a beloved staple of Puerto Rican cuisine.

MAKING RESEARCH RELEVANT

Almost all anthropological research is applied to some degree, in the sense that it is intended to be useful to the solution of human problems. Mary Willis's efforts to apply her dental research to improve government support for refugees is one example of a commitment to applied anthropology. Some anthropologists, especially those working in communities in which they have strong ties and long histories of connection, propose that varied forms of activist anthropology, with the overt goal of political change, are sometimes warranted or even necessary as part of ethical scholarship. Jonathan Rosa's media efforts promoting wider acceptance of alternative forms of English language use within the United States are one case in point. Rosa considers it a core professional responsibility to engage in contentious and difficult public debates using his expertise on language use in schools. For example, he has supported a campaign challenging widespread media use of the term "illegal" to label specific groups of immigrants in the United States. His own research shows the label is an outlier in the terms most people use in how they talk about immigrants and immigration, as well as being dehumanizing and demeaning. Rosa also argues this language choice leads to less effective political debate around immigration because the term is so polarizing. He has suggested the term "unauthorized" better allows productive public debate.

Bioarchaeologist Dawnie Wolfe Steadman's work is a very different example of applied anthropology, supporting law enforcement (**Figure 1.14**). Using donated cadavers, Steadman tests how different human bodies decay under varied environmental conditions at special university facilities. This provides important forensic information for police, legal, and other justice organizations that they can use to assess whether a death was due to murder or to establish evidence of war crimes. Her work on behalf of victims includes examining bodies related to possible crimes (including crimes against humanity) and testifying in court as an expert witness.

Increasingly, anthropologists are conducting and applying research in their own communities, bringing a rich insider perspective to their efforts. Cultural anthropologist Maria Cruz-Torres (**Figure 1.15**), who grew up on the island of Puerto Rico, now studies how people dependent on fishing understand and react to environmental destruction, whether from weather events or state-led economic development. Her work supports sustainable, mutually suitable, and meaningful solutions through large-scale government policy decisions concerning economic development in coastal zones in Puerto Rico and more widely in the Caribbean and Mexico. She's able to influence the shape of these policies because she can highlight both concerns and proposed solutions through an intimate understanding of affected local communities.

Anthropology projects are ideally suggested or spurred by local communities, encouraging anthropological research to develop in ways that can better support their applied or activist goals. Biological anthropologist Erin Kimmerle led a four-year excavation of the now-closed Arthur G. Dozier School for Boys, a juvenile reform school for boys. Located in Marianna, Florida, the school opened in 1900 and closed in 2011. There were many stories told by former students and families of missing boys over the years, especially of the Black students incarcerated in a segregated campus, and there was a growing call for action. Kimmerle used ground-penetrating radar to locate unmarked graves on the school grounds. These graves were excavated using archaeological techniques, and DNA samples of the children's remains were analyzed to establish their identities and link these boys to their living relatives. Her team's efforts located the remains of 51 boys previously recorded as "missing," and the forensic studies of their skeletons yielded heartbreaking evidence of the extreme physical abuse and starvation they suffered.

The research was initially difficult, as support from government leaders and other gatekeepers was uneven. Ultimately, the effort grew into a wider one, with the help of former students, community members, volunteers, law enforcement agencies, local government, and the state governor (**Figure 1.16**). Importantly, the findings were crucial to the Florida government passing resolutions acknowledging their role in past injustices and articulating a future commitment to "ensuring that children who have been placed in the State of Florida's care are protected from abuse and violations of fundamental human decency." In such projects, community reconciliation and healing can be seen as meaningful and important research results.

In Kimmerle's work, the school's survivors and relatives of the lost boys had a serious emotional stake in what research was conducted and how it was done. In this case, the desire of survivors and families for justice was satisfied, in part, by having an anthropologist help to recreate lost histories and buried truths. Such projects, which can be deeply meaningful for historically marginalized communities, are one way that outsiders to communities can—with appropriate care and attention—help produce impactful anthropological research.

Anthropologists also do applied research in very different types of settings, like industry. Elizabeth Briody worked for General Motors for 24 years as a cultural anthropologist. By using many ethnographic techniques, like working in the factory line and interviewing people in all parts of the company, she was able to trace complex but very consistent patterns of how people blamed others for low quality or slow factory output, and then recognize these as attached to how inventory was organized. This was crucial information for improving not only the quality of cars produced but also the experience of those who worked on the factory floor.

Some anthropologists had negative reactions to Briody working inside a large and powerful corporation like General Motors, making arguments such as "How can you work at a corporation that destroys the environment or exploits workers?" But for Briody and others who work in partnership with industry, these opportunities allow anthropologists to work outside the academy in ways that can make an immediate difference in the real world. Such challenging questions about the appropriate uses of anthropological expertise are central to scholarly conversations and are a good thing; the ways anthropology is done should never be static.

Even when anthropologists disagree about the value and implications of specific approaches to research, they share a commitment to questioning and correcting anthropology's practices. Anthropology as a field expands as research is conducted in new and experimental ways, building on but also challenging that which has come before. This is how anthropology as a field grows and improves (**Figure 1.17**).

FIGURE 1.16

Biological anthropologist Erin Kimmerle and Elmore Bryant, former mayor of Marianna (in hat), were key partners in the collaboration to reveal the full story of the "missing" boys from the Dozier School.

FIGURE 1.17

Anthropologists constantly debate how to define best practices for the field. Sometimes they use activist strategies to promote change within their own professional organizations, as this "die-in" protest within the 2014 American Anthropological Association (AAA) annual conference shows. Organized by the Association of Black Anthropologists, one goal was to push AAA leadership to address racialized policing directly (Chapter 14).

SHARED ETHICAL STANDARDS

Doing anthropological research raises particular ethical issues, and anthropologists share a basic set of professional requirements and expectations about how that work gets done. For anthropologists who are employed by universities or hospitals, oversight committees require all research processes that engage living humans to be deemed sufficiently safe through a formal legal approval process that often includes *informed consent*. The researcher must clearly and transparently explain to potential participants what they can expect from the research activities, including possible risks and benefits. Examples of possible harms include the physical risks of collecting blood or other physical samples, or social humiliation following failures to maintain confidentiality of personal and sensitive information shared by informants. Informed consent also ensures all participants make their own decisions to be part of any research project. For anthropologists working with primates or other animals, in the wild or in laboratories, separate ethical requirements focus on humane treatment.

There are also other shared expectations for ethical practice. Anthropologists are expected to prioritize the interests of individuals and communities who are the focus of their study or—if they are no longer living—their descendant communities and to carefully manage any power differences between the researcher and those they are researching. Plagiarizing, harassing colleagues or students, and failing to share research results are also considered serious ethical violations. **Table 1.1** lists the basic ethical principles established by one of the largest scholarly societies, the American Anthropological Association (AAA).

One way that anthropologists constantly reinvent and improve their field is through regular, careful ethical self-reflection. This entails consistently questioning assumptions, values, and practices, even when that leads to having to face and deal with uncomfortable aspects of anthropology's history. Early influential anthropologists like Bronisław Malinowski, Franz Boas, and Margaret Mead all emphasized the importance of fieldwork and considering both scientific and humanistic ways of understanding humans. These core values remain important to anthropologists. But some of the ways they did their research, often focused on locales they defined as "exotic" and doing research that had little benefit to the communities they analyzed, are unacceptable today.

These concerns about how past anthropologists have done research are not new, even as they have become more mainstream in recent years. In 1969, Vine Deloria Jr., a member of the Standing Rock Sioux Tribe, provided one of the first scholarly critiques of the standard North American practices of anthropology fieldwork (**Figure 1.18**). Deloria was himself not an anthropologist, but his aunt Ella Deloria was among the first generation of Indigenous North American anthropologists.

Deloria's 1969 book, *Custer Died for Your Sins*, questioned the purpose of the many anthropologists who came from the city each summer to study American Indian communities. He explained that the knowledge these anthropologists produced was totally disconnected from the local people's lived realities and did not provide any value to the communities being studied. This simple point has led to decades of intense debate among anthropologists about their own interactions with the people whom they study, how the knowledge they produce is or should be used, and even the very nature of what constitutes knowledge itself.

This process of critical reflection is an important and ongoing one. You will encounter examples of difficult debates in which anthropologists are currently engaged throughout this book. This includes how to acknowledge and confront anthropology's history of complicity with the systematic exploitation or

informed consent Permission granted with adequate knowledge of the possible consequences of participating in research.

FIGURE 1.18

Vine Deloria Jr. (1933–2005; right) talks with activist Vernon Bellecourt on the steps of the Federal District Court Building in Cedar Rapids, Iowa, on July 8, 1976.

mistreatment of one group over others—such as through support for colonialism (Chapter 2) and scientific forms of racism (Chapter 14). The aim of such reflection is to continue charting new ways forward for anthropology, such that it is performed in ever greater service of human well-being—the ultimate goal of this dizzying, dynamic field that tells the entire human story.

TABLE 1.1

Summary of the American Anthropological Association Principles of Professional Responsibility

Principle	Description	Examples of Ethical Violations
1. Do no harm	In designing and while conducting any research, anthropologists must carefully consider and address any possible ways that the research might cause harm, including loss of dignity.	• Research activities with living or past humans that violate people's dignity or bodily and material well-being • Failure to protect and steward the irreplaceable archaeological record
2. Be open and honest	Anthropologists must fully disclose the purpose, methods, findings, and sponsors of their work, including all interests they may have in the outcomes of research.	• Plagiarism • Falsifying evidence • Knowingly misrepresenting yourself or your study
3. Obtain informed consent and all necessary permissions	All participants must be fully informed about the nature and possible harms of research before they consent. Anthropologists must secure all required permissions or permits prior to the conduct of research.	• Failure to obtain informed consent • Failure to obtain required permits (such as to conduct research in other countries or to excavate an archaeological site)
4. Weigh competing ethical obligations	Obligations toward research participants are usually primary. However, anthropologists must weigh competing ethical obligations to their students, professional colleagues, employers, and funders.	• Failure to establish fair and appropriate guidelines with collaborators (such as guidelines around data access and credit in publication)
5. Make research results accessible	Anthropological research results should be made available to all and in a timely fashion.	• Doing proprietary or classified research without resolving any ethical issues it raises
6. Protect and preserve research records	Anthropologists must ensure the integrity and preservation of the evidence on which their findings are based, such as research data.	• Failure to document research adequately • Allowing collected materials to be used to harm participants • Failing to protect privacy of participants • Failure to appropriately safe-keep human remains or material artifacts
7. Maintain respectful and ethical professional relationships	In interacting with students, colleagues, clients, or staff, anthropologists must promote an equitable and supportive workplace. Anthropologists must communicate to their students the ethical responsibilities of anthropological work.	• Exploiting students, communities, animals, or cultural or biological materials for personal gain • Failure to report evidence of research misconduct to appropriate authorities • Permitting perpetuation of exclusionary practices (such as racism)

Why Anthropology?

Anthropology is a field that studies what it means to be human in all places and times.

KEY TERMS
> anthropology
> hominin
> *Homo sapiens*

1.1 | The Subfields of Anthropology

Describe the diversity of work done by trained anthropologists across the four subfields.

- Anthropology is often described by four different major subfields of study: cultural anthropology, linguistic anthropology, biological anthropology, and archaeology, each with its own set of core concerns and methods.

- In practice, these subfields are often integrated with each other, with other fields outside anthropology, and with other forms of knowledge, to encourage a holistic approach to understanding humans and their societies.

KEY TERMS
> archaeological record
> archaeology
> artifact
> biological anthropology
> biological diversity
> cultural anthropology
> culture
> descendant group
> ethnography
> evolution
> fossil
> genetic
> hypothesis
> Indigenous, Aboriginal, and First Nation
> language
> linguistic anthropology
> material culture
> norm
> participant observation
> primate
> social differentiation
> social identity
> society
> symbol

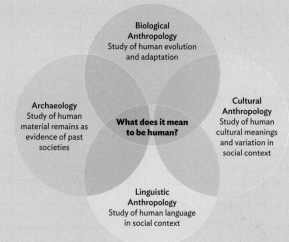

Biological Anthropology
Study of human evolution and adaptation

Archaeology
Study of human material remains as evidence of past societies

What does it mean to be human?

Cultural Anthropology
Study of human cultural meanings and variation in social context

Linguistic Anthropology
Study of human language in social context

1.2 | What Makes Anthropology "Anthropological"?

Identify the defining features of anthropological research.

- By employing comparisons that can encompass all human societies, now and in the past, anthropology has an unmatched capacity to identify the widest array of possible blueprints for successful human existence.

- Anthropology bridges scientific and humanistic forms of knowledge, putting the experiences of real people at the center.

- Anthropologists are expected to adhere to shared ethical standards.

- The growth of the field requires anthropologists to identify and address its weaknesses as well as its strengths, including past mistakes.

KEY TERMS
> activist anthropology
> applied anthropology
> comparative approach
> cultural relativism
> ethics
> fieldwork
> humanism
> informed consent
> knowledge coproduction
> knowledge system
> local knowledge
> research
> stakeholder
> science

Doing Anthropology

Katerina Teaiwa didn't grow up on Banaba, her father's home in the central Pacific. In 1945, along with everyone else on the tiny and remote island, he had been forcibly resettled in Fiji some 1,600 miles away. The British government was relocating people from Banaba's villages to make phosphate mining easier. Exporting the mineral to fertilize farms in British colonies, they also stripped the soil and polluted the water that had made Banaba habitable for some 2,000 years (**Figure 2.1**). Teaiwa spent a childhood in Fiji amidst stories and songs of a lost Banaba that her family loved and longed for but to which they could not return. She chose those memories as a starting point for studying the consequences of displacement for the Banabans, still living on the island of Rabi in Fiji today.

But doing ethnographic research around people's memories presented a serious challenge. She spent time in the archives documenting the history of Britain's colonial mining operations, visited Banaba, and interviewed former mine laborers and other displaced residents to detail their stories of life on the island and their forced resettlement. She further built the story of Banaban loss from old photos, shipping records, family videos, and recordings of Banaban songs and dances.

LEARNING HOW TO DO ANTHROPOLOGY

Training to be an anthropologist often means practicing hands-on techniques, such as sorting materials from archaeological excavations, participating in surveys to locate fossil remains, assisting with interviews or participant observation, taking biological measurements, or conducting genetic analyses. One means for learning many such skills is participating in field schools. Many universities offer opportunities for such fieldwork in nearby locations, working with local communities.

LEARNING OBJECTIVES

2.1 Doing Cultural Anthropology
Identify the core practices and challenges of ethnographic fieldwork.

2.2 Doing Linguistic Anthropology
Identify why and how anthropologists study human language.

2.3 Doing Archaeology
Explain key concepts that guide archaeological survey and excavation and the methods used to make sense of archaeological data.

2.4 Doing Biological Anthropology
Describe how biological anthropologists use scientific methods to study deep human history and explain contemporary human diversity.

2.5 Improving Anthropological Practices
Recognize recent changes in how anthropology is practiced that seek to address its historical harms.

FIGURE 2.1

Workers mine phosphate on Banaba, an island in the central Pacific Ocean, circa 1906.

colonialism A system of domination and exploitation, for settlement and other economic benefits, by exerting foreign rule over distant territories and the people in them.

While she developed her research into a scholarly book, Teaiwa shared the history she had reconstructed in other powerful ways as well. She designed a museum installation that lays bare for public audiences the ongoing impacts of **colonialism** on the Banaban people, using those images and sounds she had collected (**Figure 2.2**). These same materials are also being used to support activist Banaban struggles for adequate compensation and recognition of their rights for a restored island.

This chapter is about how anthropologists *do* their research. Teaiwa did her complex research piece by piece, using an array of ethnographic techniques and varied sources of data to identify how Banabans today understand their own history, navigating many practical, personal, and ethical wrinkles. Every different anthropological project deploys a different mix of methods to create new knowledge, drawn from one or more of the subfields. In this chapter, we outline each subfield's main forms of evidence, their methods to gather and assess that evidence, and how those methods are informed by the historical, practical, and ethical relationships each subfield has with the communities with which they engage.

FIGURE 2.2

Katerina Teaiwa is shown with her museum installation "Project Banaba" in 2017.

DOING CULTURAL ANTHROPOLOGY

For cultural anthropologists, understanding patterns of human culture is a particular focus. And there is one clear unifying method for studying it: ethnography. In this section, we describe the conventions and history of this set of methods in some detail, before we identify a number of current concerns and debates that are redefining the ways ethnography can or should be done.

ETHNOGRAPHY AND THE STUDY OF CULTURE

Ethnography is an intensive means of research that aims to identify and illustrate cultural patterns. It is done through learned methods for collecting cultural data, followed by a systematic interpretation of those data. What unites ethnographers is a commitment to describing and explaining the world from the perspective of insiders—that is, of those in the society being studied, through personal familiarity and physical proximity. Ethnographic practice has also long been guided by the idea of cultural relativism—that each social group should be evaluated in terms of its own histories and values, not by the standards of others.

The basic ethnographic approach to understanding human societies through fieldwork was first developed by early European anthropologists, beginning with Bronisław Malinowski (1884–1942). Stranded by World War I, he stayed in the Trobriand Islands of the western Pacific from 1914 to 1918 (**Figure 2.3**). His most iconic research concerned identifying a gift-giving system that he called the "Kula ring." This is a 1,300-km wide complex system of ceremonially

FIGURE 2.3

(a) Bronisław Malinowski (middle) conducts participant observation in the Trobriand Islands in 1918. **(b)** A sample of Malinowski's handwritten field notes is pictured.

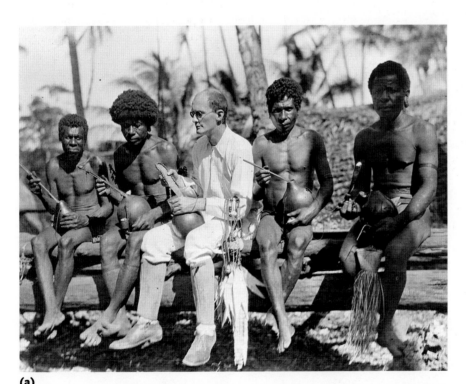

(a)

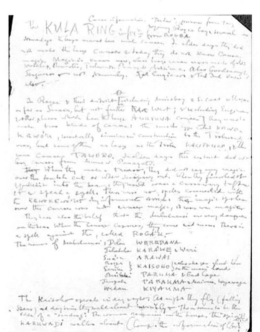

(b)

(a)

FIGURE 2.4

(a) A rendering of the map that Malinowski used to explain his ethnographic conclusions about the exchange patterns between islands that created the Kula gift exchange system. (b) A modern example of a highly prized Kula necklace received as a high-status gift.

(b)

exchanging red shell necklaces (clockwise) and white shell arm bands (counterclockwise) between communities, including Kiriwina Island where he based his research (**Figure 2.4**). Malinowski asked why people would sail across dangerous distances to exchange such small items. He concluded it was because of the powerful symbolic meanings people applied to the objects as a source of social prestige. Within Trobriand society, the givers accrued a higher status than those receiving the goods.

Malinowski's conclusions about the Kula exchange network as a distinct cultural pattern of gifting were based on evidence collected in a variety of ways, including interviewing, directly observing, participating in community events, mapping activities, and recording everything. Living in the community allowed him to participate and observe in great detail, providing the basis for his conclusions.

TABLE 2.1

Different Modes of Participant Observation

Types of Participant Observation	Examples
Nonparticipation	Observing without being present, such as collating and analyzing social media from the community being studied
Passive participation	Present in the community but acting as a bystander, such as observing children play
Active participation	Interacting with the community, such as developing relationships, actively asking questions, or attending events as a participant
Complete participation	Fully embedded as a member of the community, with defined social roles (in addition to being an anthropologist)

Each cultural anthropologist does participation and observation in different ways and to different degrees, depending on the community being studied and the nature of the research (**Table 2.1**). Often vital to doing effective participant observation are relationships with key informants, those in the community being studied who can provide particularly detailed or diverse insider explanations to the ethnographer of what is being observed.

As a key part of participant observation, cultural anthropologists typically keep detailed and careful field notes that form the raw data of their study (**Figure 2.5**), often accompanied by a more personal journal or diary. These notes become the basis for creating broader interpretations of patterns of culture within a society. Importantly, they are sufficiently detailed that later anthropologists can use them to expand on, reinterpret, or compare with the work of other ethnographers. The final stages in the ethnographic process are analysis and writing. Some anthropologists use techniques from literature to explore their data, while others use systematic techniques (including computer software) to identify cultural themes—shared, patterned, or repeated meanings.

Depending on the community being studied, ethnographic research might be located physically in one place (like Malinowski's work in the Trobriand Islands) or across multiple sites (like Teaiwa's study that spanned Banaba, Fiji, and historical documents housed in libraries further afield). Some ethnographic research sites today are not even physical places. Ethnographers can now join virtual communities as a means to do observation and participation, research some call "netnography." Cultural anthropologist Tom Boellstorff did his netnographic fieldwork in "Second Life," when it was a new virtual world, interacting with others through his avatar. He conducted a long-term study as the role-playing platform grew in popularity and expanded, using the same ethnographic techniques anthropologists have long applied: building relationships and interviewing key informants. But this was done by being a participating

key informant A cultural insider whose insights help the anthropologist understand the culture under study.

field notes Detailed notes made during or immediately after participant observation, a primary source of ethnographic evidence.

cultural theme A recurring symbol (word, image, or action) that defines a social group and reflects their worldview.

FIGURE 2.5

Cultural anthropologist Roy Rappaport writes daily field notes during research on how religious ritual could both balance and unbalance ecological systems (Tsembaga, Papua New Guinea, 1962–1963).

FIGURE 2.6

Tom Bukowski (shown here, on the left, in his "office"), the fieldwork avatar of cultural anthropologist Tom Boellstorff, interacts with other avatars on the Second Life online platform.

hunter-gatherer People who predominantly obtain their food through their knowledge of wild plants and animals, instead of reliance on domesticated plants and animals; sometimes called foragers.

BOLIVIA

South America

● Amazon rainforest

member of the online community, using his avatar instead of his physical self (**Figure 2.6**). His field notes included screenshots and chat logs.

Regardless of the community under study, participant observation requires the researcher to have sufficient knowledge to be able to interact effectively with people. This may include sufficient language capabilities (verbal, nonverbal, and/or sign) to talk to people directly, rather than relying fully on interpreters and translators. Quality of ethnographic interpretation improves through long-term and detailed familiarity with the context in which it is conducted. This increases opportunities to participate and observe but also builds the necessary rapport with community members. Achieving trust is central because participant observation is often heavily reliant on people revealing their worlds by sharing events, thoughts, and concerns that are often highly personal and meaningful to them. An insider view allows a researcher to better observe and understand rare but important events or comments, become privy to and discuss sensitive or private issues, and reevaluate constantly any initial interpretations or assumptions. Of course, even one to two years of fieldwork is not necessarily sufficient to gain full insider status, unless you grew up as part of the study community. And even if you grew up in the community, your status of being a trained anthropologist can complicate or change how others now view and react to you. So, part of doing ethnography is also awareness of what one doesn't know how to do or can't access and how this might shape the conclusions being drawn.

QUANTITATIVE AND QUALITATIVE APPROACHES TO CULTURE

Before the 1970s, ethnographic research was predominantly viewed as a scientific activity—one that provided objective reproducible research findings and assumed the anthropologist as a neutral observer. Many cultural anthropologists continue to build from this historical tradition of using hypothesis testing and quantitative research methods to assess theories about cultural difference, its meanings, and implications. Some enduring advantages of this approach are that it allows cultural anthropologists to work as peers in larger transdisciplinary teams with other scientists, and it enables them to contribute to incrementally building global scientific knowledge. This advances their capacities to address substantial and often global challenges and may allow them a more central role in policy discussions. For example, the Amazon rainforest and its many Indigenous communities are under constant threat of logging and other long-term environmental destruction. Cultural anthropologist Victoria Reyes-García does field research with Indigenous Tsimané [chee-mah-NAY] **hunter-gatherers** and farmers in the Amazonian region of Bolivia in South America, working in a scientific framework with a large international team of ecologists, economists, psychologists, agronomists, archaeologists, and computer scientists to understand and help craft some possible solutions (**Figure 2.7**).

Reyes-García tested hypotheses about Tsimané knowledge about the uses of forest plant species, comparing differences across generations. During semistructured interviews, Reyes-García asked individuals to sort pictures of 43 different plants into piles based on their main use as food, firewood, medicine, and canoe or house-building materials. She constructed a cluster diagram using specialized software. Reyes-García then used ethnographic interpretation

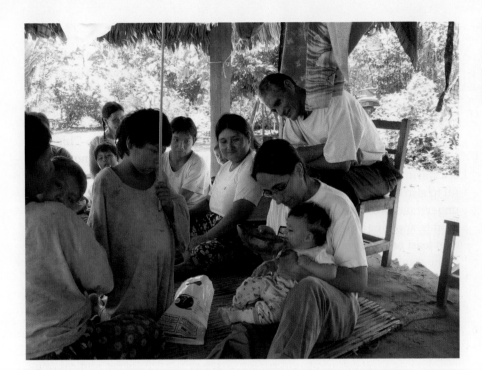

FIGURE 2.7

Shown here are cultural anthropologist Victoria Reyes-García (in glasses), her daughter, and longtime friends in the Tsimané community of Yaranda, where she tests hypotheses about local ecological knowledge and practices.

to organize the resulting pattern into different types of local knowledge (**Figure 2.8**). This analysis showed that Tsimané were passing on less of prior generations' accumulated knowledge about plants that could be used as food and medicine. Moreover, she also used statistical methods to show that recent changes in the economic activities people do (such as whether they work in the cash economy or farm full-time) have a crucial influence on the rate of loss of that community knowledge.

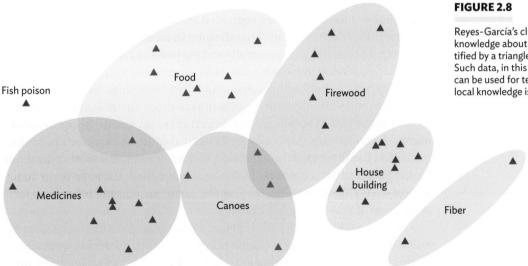

FIGURE 2.8

Reyes-García's cluster diagram shows how Tsimané knowledge about uses of different local plants (each identified by a triangle) is organized into different domains. Such data, in this case derived from systematic interviews, can be used for testing scientific predictions about how local knowledge is passed or lost between generations.

Starting in the late 1970s, however, another very different mode of ethnographic research emerged that provides an alternative or addition to these types of scientific approaches that pursue a single, knowable reality. Its proponents argue that if humans can have multiple viewpoints on the same objects, then we shouldn't assume that those objects can be reduced to single, definitive descriptions like those that scientific studies try to produce. This approach

ontology The study of multiple existing realities.

is sometimes termed ontology and is about being open to *any* possibility for understanding the human experience—not just those that align with a scientific worldview and practices.

Cultural anthropologist Martin Holbraad illustrated this point with a very different example of how to approach the study of human–environmental relations from his research on religious and spiritual healing in the Caribbean nation of Cuba. If a Cuban healer points to a tree and tells the ethnographer it is a spirit, is it correct to simply analyze that as a "belief"? Might it not be useful to also consider how the ethnographer could adjust their own worldview to understand that what looked to them like a tree might also be a "tree as spirit"? That is, applying an ontological perspective, there may be more than one truth, or at least no way to prove that a tree is not a spirit. This line of thinking suggests ethnographers can gain a full understanding of Cuban healing only by accepting trees or any other nonhuman objects—not as a singular or fixed phenomenon—but as something whose meaning can vary across time, space, and context. This approach to culture is an inherently exploratory and experimental form of ethnography, because it potentially allows for many simultaneous realities that the anthropologist can discover.

REFLEXIVITY AND POSITIONALITY

Cultural anthropologists are constantly experimenting with new forms of doing ethnography. However, many of the same data collection techniques first used by Malinowski and other early cultural anthropologists—such as long-term fieldwork, developing rapport, and detailed notes based on copious hours of participant observation—remain fundamental to ethnographic practice today. Ethnography is always a collaborative process, and the production of knowledge through fieldwork is based in stories told by, conversations with, and interviews of other people. That is why some ethnographers today refer to their research participants as interlocutors or collaborators, acknowledging that ethnographic insights are cocreated in those interpersonal interactions. Another thing that has changed significantly in recent years is how anthropologists place themselves more centrally and purposefully within their interpretations of their ethnographic texts and in relation to their interlocutors.

interlocutor A person who participates in conversation or interaction with the researcher.

Reflexivity refers to the purposeful effort to explore how the ethnographer's own self and interactions with others shape the research process and its interpretations. It entails careful reflection on any ties to the community or events being analyzed, as well as the historical contexts of power differentials embedded in the research process. Reflexivity purposefully inserts the ethnographer fully into the process of observation. It also tends to understand the subjects of study (like cultural insiders) as full participants and collaborators in the production of knowledge about them.

reflexivity Transparent self-reflection on the researcher's own social position, knowledges, and biases and how this shapes the course of research and its conclusions.

Cultural anthropologist Ruth Behar experimented with ethnography that included deep self-reflection (**Figure 2.9**). One of her scholarly books focused on the story of Esperanza Hernández (a pseudonym), a Mexican woman whom Behar met by chance in 1983. An Indigenous street peddler who sold fruit and vegetables from her garden, she had been accused of being a witch. Behar worked very closely with Esperanza to explore living as a woman in Mexico through the story of her life, seeing her as much more than a key informant and more as a "coparent" of the text they were creating and a close friend. And, inspired by Esperanza's story and courage, Behar's book also includes autobiographical reflections of her own personal history as a feminist and Cuban-American. For

(a)

(b)

FIGURE 2.9

(a) Cultural anthropologist Ruth Behar (left) and Esperanza Hernández (a pseudonym) are pictured with a copy of their 1993 book, *Translated Woman*. **(b)** Illustration by Behar's fellow Cuban-American, artist Rolando Estévez, shows the women developing an ethnography together, with Esperanza explaining the violence in her marriage.

Behar, her exploration of Esperanza's life experience is a "set of mirrors" that helps her understand better her own.

Behar's work also incorporated the idea of positionality—the recognition that anthropological knowledge is structured by the class, gender, ethnic, or other identities of the anthropologist. This recognition in turn requires also confronting questions of power in the relationship between researcher and those being researched.

Embracing notions of positionality, reflexivity, and knowledge coproduction (see Chapter 1) also widens the types of evidence that ethnographers can use as raw data. The ethnographer's own personal experiences—in such forms as memories, creative expression, and emotions—have also become accepted forms of evidence, alongside more traditional elements of participant observation. Reflecting on personal experiences can be enormously important in generating research insights in ethnography.

A good example of how being attuned to personal emotions can inform ethnographic insights comes from cultural anthropologist Timm Lau, who studied migrant Tibetan laborers in northern India. One afternoon, returning from a basketball game with a monk, Lau encountered a Tibetan and Indian man viciously swinging at each other with steel rods beside the bazaar. The Indian man was hit hard on the head and fell to the ground. Without thinking, Lau leapt forward to restrain the Tibetan man. The fight was quickly over. But when a highly respected local leader publicly scolded Lau for interfering, Lau felt confused, angered, and shamed. Over time, Lau realized that his own feelings of shame were a crucial part of Tibetan socialization: being shamed is an indicator that someone has acted "out of line" within the informal hierarchy of Tibetan society.

positionality The socioeconomic, political, and cultural positions of the researcher in relation to those of the research participants or communities.

DOING LINGUISTIC ANTHROPOLOGY

Of the four subfields, linguistic anthropology is the smallest in terms of number of trained professionals. It is also practiced mostly in the United States, where it first emerged as an academic field. In the late 19th and early 20th centuries, the U.S. government was concerned with the escalating losses of Indigenous languages and culture (often without acknowledging the broader context of their responsibility for that genocide). Accordingly, early linguistic anthropologists were funded to catalog Indigenous North American languages, which included describing and documenting the grammar of the languages as well as recording stories and songs (**Figure 2.10**).

Beyond the goal of language preservation, linguistic anthropologists of the first half of the 20th century used the detailed analyses of language to study human history, culture, and worldview. Many adopted scientific models of careful and rigorous data collection to test predictions about language relatedness. Languages change over time, so systematic comparisons of the forms of language between different places help identify historical connections, estimating how long ago groups migrated or otherwise separated into different societies. For example, by working closely with archaeologists, early linguistic anthropologists measured differences in Indigenous languages to provide corollary evidence for when and from where humans arrived in different parts of

FIGURE 2.10

This 1916 image shows early linguistic anthropologist Frances Densmore (1867–1957) interviewing Mountain Chief, a Blackfoot leader, as part of U.S. government-sponsored research cataloging "dying" Indigenous languages.

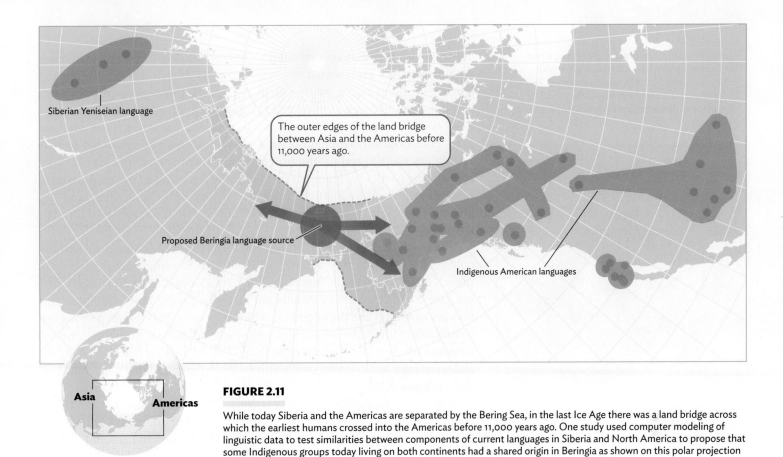

Siberian Yeniseian language

The outer edges of the land bridge between Asia and the Americas before 11,000 years ago.

Proposed Beringia language source

Indigenous American languages

Asia

Americas

FIGURE 2.11

While today Siberia and the Americas are separated by the Bering Sea, in the last Ice Age there was a land bridge across which the earliest humans crossed into the Americas before 11,000 years ago. One study used computer modeling of linguistic data to test similarities between components of current languages in Siberia and North America to propose that some Indigenous groups today living on both continents had a shared origin in Beringia as shown on this polar projection map. The current languages and their locations tested to build this model are shown in different colors.

the continents—a body of research that continues to be expanded and updated today (**Figure 2.11**).

Since the mid 20th century, linguistic anthropologists have increasingly explored how language shapes people's everyday lives. Many linguistic anthropologists today investigate not only how and why language changes but also the role of power in language—at individual, community, and societal levels.

RECORDING LANGUAGE

Linguistic anthropologists evaluate different forms of language to understand its role in culture and how it changes. As language is inherently social and cultural, linguistic anthropologists also consider ethnography one of their core tools, recognizing that language use, meanings, and implications can be understood only when they are interpreted in relation to the everyday contexts in which they occur. Thus, linguistic anthropologists use many of the same field techniques as cultural anthropologists to collect and manage their data, including participant observation, jottings on key observations or events, audio and video recording of interviews, and detailed field notes (**Figure 2.12**). Commitment to long-term participant observation within communities of language users has the advantage of allowing observation and recording of language with minimal disruption to its everyday use.

People use language constantly. This can create enormous amounts of spoken, signed, and written data for linguistic

FIGURE 2.12

Linguistic anthropologist Cecile Evers (right) interviews two French women. Her research with residents of Marseille's housing projects studies how young Muslims mix the French and Arabic languages to align themselves as both French and Muslim.

transcription The process of creating a text representing exactly what is said, often with relevant contextual information included. Transcripts are a primary form of evidence used by linguistic anthropologists to record language use.

LAOS

Asia

anthropologists to manage and analyze. For recorded spoken or sign language data, transcripts are created. Transcription is more than simply putting language content into a written form. A transcript may attempt to capture additional details such as overlapping utterances, interruptions, "backchannels" (such as uh-huh, yeah, or hmmm), gestures, pauses/silences, and eye gaze. Transcription is incredibly time-consuming, even as new voice-to-text technologies can speed up the process. Analysis of transcripts may include considering particular grammar forms people are using or not using, who is talking to whom (the audience), what they are saying (or not saying), and—by placing it back into its social and cultural context—what was achieved through language.

For example, in studying language and social life in Laos, linguistic anthropologist Nick Enfield uses audiovisual recordings to capture what people say to each other. Video recordings allow him to track eye contact and direction of eye gaze. So his transcripts include not just what people have said but whom they are looking at and the manner in which they say it. This research shows the complexity of interactional sequences through which the appropriate forms of language are used to get people to do things for one another (such as asking for and receiving a leaf to smoke) while also maintaining or building social relationships (**Figure 2.13**).

Linguistic anthropologists study language use in all its forms. Often this is based on speech or signs, whether recorded in formal interviews or captured as everyday conversation, as was the case in Enfield's work in Laos. But written language, as in official documents, newspapers, emails, or social media, can also be used as the basis for study. Urban cityscapes are especially littered with written forms of language, such as in billboards and other signage.

It is 9 o'clock in the morning. Women are chatting on a veranda. The woman to the right has just given the teenage girl by the doorway some tobacco to smoke. The teen calls to her "Aunty" (at back) to "pass some leaf" to roll a cigarette. There is no response, so she repeats her summons more insistently.

The woman to the left then turns and instructs the teen that there are leaves inside the storeroom. The teen then walks inside and quickly gets the materials she needs to make the cigarette.

FIGURE 2.13

Linguistic anthropologist Nick Enfield uses audiovisual recordings to capture what people say and with whom they are talking, and then tracks how this connects to subsequent social action. These stills, from a conversational sequence he recorded with Kri speakers in a village in eastern Laos, show how language is based in an assumption that others will cooperate to help us meet our unilateral goals.

FIGURE 2.14

Linguistic anthropologist Erin Moriarty (taking notes) conducts fieldwork to understand the emergence of new sign language communities in Cambodia.

Sign language also provides the material for linguistic anthropological analysis. Erin Moriarty, a linguistic anthropologist, has conducted research in both Cambodia and Indonesia on language use in deaf communities (**Figure 2.14**). Her field methods include recording and then transcribing sign language, using systems of notation that identify the shape, position, and movement of hands. Her position as a member of the global deaf community also helps her connect to her research participants and gives her a different way to understand their lives.

SECTION 2.3

DOING ARCHAEOLOGY

Archaeology is the study of human societies through physical traces left from past human activity. Archaeologists use the archaeological record (see Chapter 1), the preserved remnants of materials deposited in the past and their associated contexts, to better understand past human lives. Two important ways that archaeologists investigate the archaeological record are through survey and excavation.

Survey is often the first step in archaeological research and involves identifying archaeological sites over a large area. Some archaeological survey work is done remotely, using technologies such as images taken by satellites or ground-penetrating radar (**Figure 2.15**). These technologies can be used to survey and map relatively large areas and can visually strip away heavy forest vegetation so that archaeological sites are easier to identify. Archaeologists also rely heavily on traditional survey methods that involve systematically walking over the ground in the study region to identify and map visible artifacts, such as broken pieces of pottery on the ground, and archaeological features visible above ground, such as house walls or postholes.

FIGURE 2.15

Aerial light detection and ranging (LiDAR) uses lasers and Global Positioning System (GPS) receivers to measure the height of the ground surface to map the ground from above. This LiDAR map of the Maya archaeological site of Tikal in Guatemala reveals otherwise invisible archaeological features underneath the thick forest canopy.

archaeological survey Systematically mapping a study region and identifying archaeological sites and features, either from the ground or from the air.

archaeological feature A sign of past human activity that loses its form when moved, such as a posthole, hearth, or wall.

excavation Systematic and scientific process of uncovering and recording an archaeological site.

ecofact Material in the archaeological record that was not directly modified by humans, such as plant or animal remains.

stratigraphy The sequence of soil layers (strata) at a location that archaeologists can use to evaluate and date an archaeological site.

After surveying, archaeologists use scientific excavation to investigate parts of archaeological sites that are buried underground (**Figure 2.16**). It is a process of carefully and systematically exposing, recording, photographing, and collecting artifacts and ecofacts for future analyses and curation.

One challenge of collecting archaeological data through excavation is that it can never be investigated in the same way again. By excavating a site, archaeologists destroy the site as it was. This is why it is so incredibly important to excavate only when necessary, and to do so carefully, systematically, and with an eye toward recording information that might be relevant to future generations. While most excavations occur on land with trowels and wheelbarrows to move dirt, archaeological excavations can take place in other contexts, too. For example, archaeologists also put on wetsuits and scuba gear to map and excavate archaeological sites underwater (**Figure 2.17**).

Excavation is based on the principle of stratigraphy, which looks at the layers (or strata) in the earth and can be used to understand the ages of and relationships between sites and artifacts (**Figure 2.18**). Generally, strata are deposited sequentially, with the oldest layers underneath the youngest layers. So, as you dig downward in an archaeological site, you are moving from more recent to more ancient deposits. Clearly establishing the location of artifacts and ecofacts in archaeological sites, including noting in which depositional layers they appear, is essential for understanding what humans were doing at different points of the site's occupational history.

Different natural and human processes can complicate the stratigraphy. For example, digging a hole or plowing an agricultural field can move older materials above younger ones. The association of artifacts and ecofacts with surrounding soil and the use of direct dating techniques can help identify such displacements.

FIGURE 2.16

Archaeologist Ayana Flewellen (right) trains students in techniques in archaeology as part of the excavation of areas once occupied by enslaved Africans at a former sugar plantation in St. Croix in the U.S. Virgin Islands.

FIGURE 2.17

Archaeologists Justin Dunnavant (left) and Ayana Flewellen (right) also train students in underwater and maritime archaeology through the Diving with a Purpose organization, based at Biscayne National Park in Florida, United States. Their investigations of the park's 43 recorded shipwrecks are applied to better understand maritime history and the lives of enslaved Africans transported to the Americas.

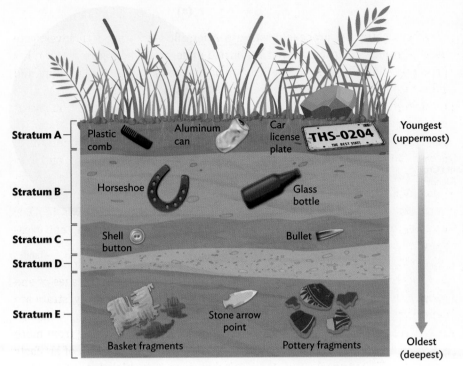

FIGURE 2.18

In this cross section, the oldest strata are the deepest, so that Stratum B was deposited before Stratum A, Stratum C was deposited before Stratum B, and so on.

The association of artifacts and ecofacts with one another and with the soil or area in which they were found provides the archaeological context. The importance of archaeological context in interpreting the past can't be overstated. For example, a piece of broken pottery found in a trash pit can be interpreted very differently compared to a piece of broken pottery found in a burial. One was a piece of trash that had been discarded after it was used, and the other could have been a valued heirloom that was important enough to be included in a loved one's grave. Both tell us different things about the people who made and used the pottery. This is also why looting of archaeological sites, which removes artifacts from their context, is so detrimental.

One challenge of interpreting the archaeological record and the contexts in which artifacts were found is site preservation, which varies widely because objects decay and can be easily destroyed by looting and construction activities. Densely occupied places such as cities can produce large archaeological sites. But if an ancient site has since been continuously occupied, the earliest levels may be underneath, and often damaged by, later occupation. Hunter-gatherers that moved around the landscape and did not build large, permanent sites are harder to see in the archaeological record.

Within the archaeological record, some materials are favored for preservation over others. Plant remains are often less common than animal bones, because they decay more quickly. Pottery and stone tools are hardier than artifacts made of wood or other plant materials, so pottery and stone tools are an important part of archaeological analyses (**Figure 2.19**). The presence of archaeological materials also reflects their differential treatment across sites and through time. In some communities, human remains were purposefully buried, so even though bone is an organic material that can easily decay, the bodies of the individuals who died are still preserved in the archaeological record. But when people cremated their dead as part of a mortuary ritual, archaeologists study their ashes, or cremains, instead.

archaeological context Placement and association of archaeological materials in the archaeological record.

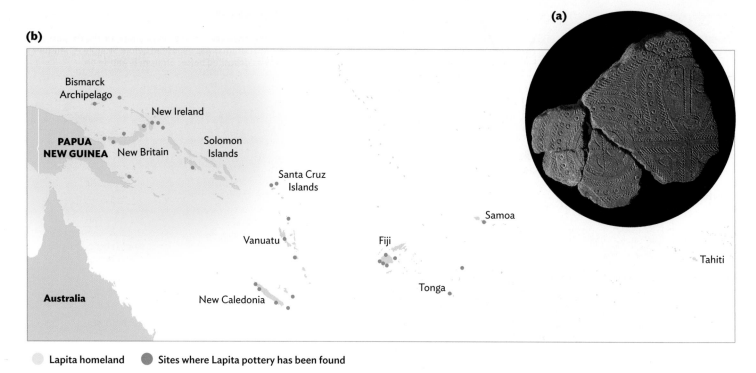

(b)

Bismarck Archipelago

New Ireland

PAPUA NEW GUINEA New Britain

Solomon Islands

Santa Cruz Islands

Samoa

Vanuatu

Fiji

Australia

New Caledonia

Tonga

Tahiti

(a)

○ Lapita homeland   ● Sites where Lapita pottery has been found

FIGURE 2.19

(a) Ceramic (pottery) remains of the Lapita maritime culture are pictured. **(b)** This map shows sites across the Pacific where Lapita sherds (broken pieces of ceramic vessels) have been identified, revealing past cultural connections through migration. The estimated dates for the earliest appearance of distinctive Lapita sherds on each island provides the timeline and direction of settlement, from the Lapita "homeland" in the west to later settlements to the east.

relative dating A method of determining whether one artifact or stratum is older or younger than another.

absolute dating A method of determining the age of an artifact or stratum in calendar years.

Such material evidence can be compared and constrasted across archaeological sites to document what was happening across whole regions. Archaeologists (working also with linguistic anthropologists) have used ceramic sherds to document the spread of the distinctive Lapita maritime culture of the western Pacific, with radiocarbon dating indicating the distinctively decorated pots were being produced from 3000 to 1500 BCE (Figure 2.19a). The ceramic sherds are the remains of large pots, probably used for cooking or storing food, with distinctive stamped geometric surface designs that can include faces and figures. The eastward spread of Lapita ceramics over time is used to trace the earliest colonization of Fiji from the Lapita homeland, and then further east into what is now Polynesia (Figure 2.19b).

Interpreting archaeological sites, and ultimately creating a wider view of human history, requires clear information on when the objects in them were in use. Archaeologists use both indirect and direct dating techniques, called relative dating and absolute dating, respectively. Relative dating allows archaeologists to use stratigraphy to determine whether a given layer—and thus the artifacts, ecofacts, and features in it—is older or younger than other layers at a site. Absolute dating gives the age of an artifact or archaeological site in calendar years. In this text, we give dates as BCE (before the common era) or CE (common era), which roughly correspond to BC (before Christ) and AD (*anno Domini*).

Absolute dating methods emerged through new technologies in the 1960s, and these methods revolutionized archaeologists' ability to ask and answer complex archaeological questions. Direct dating is now a hugely important and common part of archaeological investigations. For example, radiocarbon dating uses the radioactive decay of carbon isotopes in organic materials like plant remains or bone to determine when that plant or animal died. However, radiocarbon dating can't be used to date inorganic materials like stone, and it only works on organic materials that are less than about 40,000 years old. Different archaeological materials and different time periods require different dating techniques (see **Table 2.2**).

TABLE 2.2

Different Dating Methods Used in Archaeology to Establish Time Sequences

Archaeological Dating Technique	Materials Analyzed	Approximate Range of Dating Method	General Principles	Pros and Cons
Dendrochronology	Tree rings in preserved logs, especially long-lived species like pines	1–8,000 years	Annual growth rings in trees vary with rainfall, so trees with known histories can be used to create a detailed chronology of tree rings that can be matched with wooden artifacts or construction materials.	• Most accurate dating method • Provides a calendar date to the exact year the tree was cut down • Requires good organic preservation and detailed local tree ring records
Radiocarbon	Organic materials such as human or animal bone, plants, seeds, charcoal, or wood	500–40,000 years	The radioactive isotope of carbon (carbon-14) decays at a known rate, so the amount of carbon-14 in an object can be used to determine when the organic material died.	• Most commonly used direct dating technique • Only used for organic materials
Thermoluminescence (TL)	Ceramics, minerals (calcites), hearths, heated stones	100–50,000 years	Thermoluminescence is emitted when a mineral is heated, so archaeologists can heat the sample in a laboratory and measure the amount of light emitted, which can be used to calculate how much time has passed since the artifact was last heated.	• Useful for the period between radiocarbon and radiopotassium dating • Can be used to date ceramics and heated stone tools • Dates have large error bars associated with them
Radiopotassium (also called potassium–argon or K–Ar)	Volcanic rocks or minerals	500,000 years and older	Like radiocarbon, this technique is based on radioactive decay. As volcanic rock forms, potassium-40 decays into argon-40 gas, which is trapped in the rock and can be measured to determine when the volcanic rock formed.	• Important for dating early hominin sites • Requires volcanic rock, so not possible in some parts of the world
Electron spin resonance (ESR)	Crystalline stones and hydroxyapatite, which forms enamel and bone	30,000–2 million years	ESR measures the accumulation of unpaired electrons in crystals to determine how much time has elapsed since the crystalline material formed.	• Useful for dating very old hominin enamel samples • Few laboratories exist for this technique
Obsidian hydration	Stone tools made of the volcanic glass obsidian	200–15,000 years years	When volcanic glass is first worked, it begins to absorb water on the fresh edges; the longer the exposure, the greater the water penetration into the glass.	• Requires volcanic glass, so not possible in some parts of the world • Technique requires local calibration

After documenting the archaeological context and dating the age of a site or artifact, archaeologists undertake a number of specialized analyses. The range of methodological specialties in archaeology is large and growing as new scientific techniques are developed. These include using chemistry to understand where artifacts were produced or people lived or using botany and zoology to identify what people were eating in the past through study of their plant or animal remains.

CHANGING QUESTIONS AND CONCERNS: PROCESSUAL AND POSTPROCESSUAL ARCHAEOLOGY

Archaeology today embraces both scientific and humanistic approaches to interpreting human pasts through human material remains. Before the 1960s, archaeologists mostly focused on using the evidence from survey, excavation, and artifact analysis to characterize different human groups and to reconstruct the history of a region and its archaeological cultures (**Figure 2.20**).

In the 1960s, many archaeologists moved from simply describing changes through time in material culture to studying the culture change process itself. This new approach was called processual archaeology because of its focus on the *processes* that occurred in the past, not just the history of a place and its people.

Processual archaeology, which was also called the "new archaeology," reflected a shift toward more scientific approaches using a wider set of scientific tools. Lewis Binford (1931–2011), an early proponent of processual archaeology, employed a technique called ethnoarchaeology, whereby he used ethnographic observations to translate the production of archaeological materials

processual archaeology An archaeological approach that emerged in the 1960s, focusing on scientific study of the processes that created the evidence found at the site being studied.

ethnoarchaeology Using participant observation in contemporary groups to understand how archaeological sites could have been created.

FIGURE 2.20

At the time of this excavation directed by Princeton University's Howard Crosby Butler from 1910–1914, archaeological research was driven by search for "treasures." Many of the artifacts from his excavations of the site where the mythically rich Lydian King Croesus (died circa 546 BCE) once lived were purchased by the the Metropolitan Museum of Art in New York City. Basic methods, such as systematic survey and excavation, have long been central to the practice of archeology and will continue to be so. But the research motivations, ethical standards, and legal frameworks of archaeology have changed dramatically over the decades, making such extractive practices unacceptable and also often illegal.

into evidence of past human behavior (**Figure 2.21**). For example, using ethnographic methods of observation, Binford and his students recorded a yearly cycle of hunting and butchering techniques among the Nunamiut of Alaska in the early 1970s. They tracked the full experience of hunted caribou bodies and their parts, recording how carcasses were butchered and discarded by humans, how the discarded waste was treated by scavengers, and then how the animal materials were transformed into the archaeological record. By combining these data from living peoples with examinations of ancient artifacts, Binford and his team could deduce the human behaviors of the earlier populations, such as when and how they hunted and butchered animals.

Postprocessual archaeology emerged in the 1980s, challenging the idea that scientific methods alone were adequate to understand the archaeological record. Postprocessual archaeologists advocated for a purposefully *subjective* assessment of material evidence. Similar to perspectives found in cultural anthropology, postprocessual archaeology proposes that artifacts can also be viewed as social constructions and that archaeologists observe the past through the influences of their own positions in society. They can use awareness about their own biases and worldview and sensitivity to others' positionality to find new ways to read archaeological data.

Postprocessual approaches to archaeology have been long used to guide interpretations of archaeological evidence at the Turkish archaeological site of Çatalhöyük (sha-TAL-hoe-YOOK). Every excavator keeps a journal of their own personal thoughts and interpretations of what they have unearthed, and visitors share ideas too. These personal field notes are part of the public documentation of the project findings, intended to spur conversations among the crew and beyond and to trigger new ideas about ways to interpret the archaeological evidence of what was happening at the site 9,000 years ago (**Figure 2.22**).

FIGURE 2.21

Lewis Binford (1931–2011) demonstrates a sheep slaughter to students in an archaeology class at Southampton University in 1980.

postprocessual archaeology An archaeological approach focusing on multiple ways of knowing the past.

FIGURE 2.22

In the excavations at Çatalhöyük, each member of the crew keeps their own personal journal as part of the project's documentation.

(a)   **(b)**

FIGURE 2.23

(a) Archaeologist Verónica Pérez Rodríguez and her son are pictured, with the site of Cerro Jazmín in the background. **(b)** Pérez Rodríguez talks about the site with schoolchildren.

Current archaeological research often incorporates ideas and approaches from both processual and postprocessual perspectives. Archaeologist Verónica Pérez Rodríguez does research in the highland region of the Mixteca Alta in the southern Mexican state of Oaxaca (**Figure 2.23**). She uses an array of techniques to understand how and why the pre-Hispanic urban site of Cerro Jazmín was sustained for 600 years as a regional center, until it declined and was abandoned around 300 CE.

Pérez Rodríguez first used aerial mapping at Cerro Jazmín to identify the wider pattern of archaeological sites across the region. She conducted interviews with local community members to harness stories of their own history to develop new hypotheses. Then Pérez Rodríguez's team excavated a portion of the site and radiocarbon-dated some of the animal bones, plant remains, and other material collected. They also tested the chemical composition of human bones and teeth from the site through a method called stable isotope analysis. Through this combination of different forms of evidence, she concludes that Cerro Jazmín was able to support a growing urban population by growing maize (corn) as a staple but also by increasing reliance on the meat of corn-fed domesticated dogs. The exact reasons for the eventual abandonment of the city are not yet clear, but analysis of current data suggests it was not due to lack of food. Rather, changes in the city's layout suggest changes in how the city was being governed, which may have been one reason people moved elsewhere.

SECTION 2.4

DOING BIOLOGICAL ANTHROPOLOGY

Biological (sometimes called evolutionary) anthropologists look back furthest in time. They study human biology and behavior—past and present—in the context of evolution. They use dating, excavation, and survey tools as well as other specialized laboratory and field tools that allow them to ask questions about how humans are related to other primate species, contemporary human variation, and the ways human biology reflects both past and current adaptation to environmental stressors.

THE METHODS OF BIOLOGICAL ANTHROPOLOGY

Biological anthropology is the subfield that most directly and consistently uses quantitative, measurable forms of data as its means to characterize and classify human biology. Biological anthropologists use evidence of human biologies, from bone, blood, hair, or other biological samples—even ancient organic matter from fossils—to study the causes and consequences of human variation. This then expands the means to understand varied topics such as the divergence of human ancestors from other primates, to reconstruct past human migrations, or to identify how humans and their infectious diseases have evolved in relation to each other.

Most biological anthropologists get extensive training in one or more specialized scientific laboratory or field methods, as well as in statistics or other computer-based modeling approaches suited to large datasets. Technological advances mean that the suite of possible laboratory methods, especially around genetics, is constantly expanding. For example, new "big data" approaches—potentially analyzing genetic or other biological data from millions of people at once—are retelling the details of the histories of our species. Improving laboratory techniques for recovering and analyzing the tiniest amounts of ancient DNA allow us to observe directly the genetics of past humans, rather than just relying on the clues left by their living descendants.

But one of the most traditional methods in biological anthropology is using careful visual examination and measurement of fossilized skeletal remains to identify the lineage of extinct and extant hominin species. Hominin fossil evidence dating back millions of years is necessary to reconstruct deep human history, but this evidence is also extremely rare. To gather new fossil specimens and expand the range of data available, biological anthropologists learn how to conduct ground-based (often walking) surveys in the field in ways that will maximize the chances of finding them (**Figure 2.24**).

Identifying new species through fossil remains and placing them into our family tree also requires advanced training in comparative primate anatomy and how it relates to behavior and social organization (**Figure 2.25**). For biological anthropologists, comparisons of the behavior and biology of different species of primates, each of which is adapted to a slightly different environment, give clues for reconstructing how early hominins lived, what particular environmental challenges may have shaped the evolution of humans in the deep

ancient DNA Genetic material (often fragmentary) from humans who lived long ago, extracted from their skeletal or fossil remains.

FIGURE 2.24

Anthropology students at a field school in Hadar, Ethiopia, learn how to survey for fossils under the lead of biological anthropologist Kaye Reed (top right).

FIGURE 2.25

Anthropology students often learn primate observation techniques at local zoos (like this group in Memphis, Tennessee, observing gorillas), where they can record the behavior of captive animals.

(a) **(b)**

FIGURE 2.26

(a) Biological anthropologist Michelle Rodrigues, in Costa Rica, observes spider monkeys. **(b)** Rodrigues, in her laboratory, analyzes primate feces to determine stress levels.

stress The body's physical reactions to external challenges, both social and environmental.

past, and which aspects of human behavior today might be best explained by our particular evolutionary pathway.

Primate studies also help provide crucial information about how to help conserve our closest relatives, many at risk of extinction. Biological anthropologist Michelle Rodrigues has spent thousands of hours systematically recording the behavior of primates, such as spider monkeys in Costa Rica (**Figure 2.26**). Using lab techniques, she can also use primate feces to assess their stress levels by measuring the levels of stress-related hormones such as cortisol. Such detailed studies can show how primates are affected by increasing disruptions of their habitats and what changes in their habitats will make the greatest difference to their survival.

Biological anthropologists also work with communities of living humans, measuring and explaining biological and behavioral differences within and across populations. They might record growth rates, estimate dietary quality, collect blood pressures, or interview people using psychological scales to understand mental health. They then look to explain how these differences reflect the complex interaction of many different factors that must be considered, such as evolutionary histories and inherited genetics, age or life stage, dietary or work conditions, past or present social configurations of the community, or the status of the person being measured within it. This then provides blueprints to suggest different ways to create healthy and safe communities.

Biological anthropologist Pablo Nepomnaschy worked with Indigenous Mayan women in Guatemala, tracking how living with chronic stress from many sources (inadequate food supplies, infectious disease, or psychological trauma) interrupts reproductive hormones and makes it harder to become pregnant and increases the risk of miscarriage. Many biological anthropologists who do research with living groups employ this encompassing definition of stress as a basic means to understand the factors that worsen human health and what can be done about it.

FIGURE 2.27

Biological anthropologist Alyssa Crittenden (white shirt) observes how children are minded by Hadza women in Tanzania.

ethnographic analogy Using evidence from contemporary societies to inform reconstructions of past societies.

Biological anthropologist Alyssa Crittenden has done research in collaboration with Hadza communities in Tanzania (**Figure 2.27**). Through watching carefully how Hadza children interacted with adults over many months, she documented how many nonmothers provide them with high-quality child care. Her findings provide new models for considering how communities can effectively and safely manage child care while parents are working.

Studies of historical or contemporary hunter-gatherers are also sometimes used by biological anthropologists as ethnographic analogies for how now-extinct hominins may have cooperated to hunt, gather, share food, or otherwise cooperate. The assumption that modern hunter-gatherers like the Hadza are a direct analogy for early humans is, however, done with extreme care. First, hunter-gatherer populations today likely have access to different, and probably fewer, wild resources. Many now-extinct slow-moving herbivores were easier to catch, for example. Second, almost all contemporary groups are displaced from their historical ranges and into more marginal environments by miners, farmers, pastoralists, or growing towns and cities. The Hadza, for example, have lost as much as 90% of their land in the last 50 years, mostly cleared for cattle farming. Third, there is no human group today that is not connected to our global economies in some way, such as via tourism, trade, or schooling. Hadza regularly trade with nearby pastoralists, for example, and some have cell phones, some attend government schools, and some farm a little or work in tourism. Cultural anthropologists have even observed that paying visitors who go hunting with Hadza men or gathering with Hadza women may be one reason that some Hadza continue to hunt and gather as often as they do.

Biological anthropologists consider themselves scientists in how they approach the way they design their studies, collect data, and draw conclusions. But almost all such work by biological anthropologists with living peoples is done in the places people live and work in real-world contexts. So they often also use ethnographic methods—developed by cultural anthropologists—to help them both identify the most relevant and acceptable ways to design their studies from a community's perspective as well as allow for nuanced understandings of their scientific conclusions.

IMPROVING ANTHROPOLOGICAL PRACTICES

At the beginning of this chapter, we examined Katerina Teaiwa's work detailing the history of Banaba. Teaiwa, however, wasn't the first scholar to do anthropological research with Banabans. Decades earlier, anthropologist Arthur Grimble and his protégé Henry Maude had collected detailed ethnographic data while on the island, documenting rituals, recording people's songs and stories, and outlining systems of inheritance and land ownership (**Figure 2.28**). Both had studied social anthropology at Cambridge University in the United Kingdom. And both had arrived on Banaba as civil servants, managing Banaba and other nearby islands that were under British colonial rule. Maude was the administrator who designed the scheme to resettle all the Banabans in Fiji, work for which he was later honored with an Order of the British Empire.

Such entanglements between early anthropologists and colonial projects were not uncommon, and it is easy to trace how early anthropologists' basic practices were complicit in the harm done by colonizing powers, including the British Empire, to Indigenous groups around the globe. In fact, Grimble and Maude had both purposefully entered the colonial service after completing their training precisely because they wanted to get to the Pacific to do their own long-term anthropological fieldwork. Teaiwa's work is just one effort to recognize and challenge these historical practices.

FIGURE 2.28

Sir Arthur Grimble (middle) and Henry Maude (front, with his dog) were both British colonial administrators and anthropologists. Their administrative posts were based on Banaba, where they are shown posing with office staff (1932).

decolonizing methodology Designing and conducting research activities that recognize, challenge, and redress the historical and ongoing harms to colonized people, including by researchers.

decanonization Redefining a field's classic texts to include works previously excluded due to the scholar's nationality, race, and/or gender.

Many anthropologists, like Teaiwa, are grappling with how to move beyond some of the limiting practices of anthropology that stem from its intimate entanglements with its colonial past. This major effort, when applied to how research gets done, is sometimes termed decolonizing methodologies. This entails developing new ways of coproducing knowledge that identify and reject colonial practices (such as extracting knowledge for the benefit of outsiders or stereotyping societies) and instead build research relationships and design studies in ways that are empowering to communities. Key to this is centering their concerns, worldviews, and forms of knowledge.

Another related major effort has been around decanonization. The "canon" refers to the body of knowledge that people consider essential in a scholarly field. In anthropology, the historical canon centers the work of scholars such as Franz Boas (b. 1858 in Germany), Bronisław Malinowski (b. 1884 in Poland), and Claude Levi-Strauss (b. 1908 in Belgium). They were all cisgender, heterosexual White men born in Europe to relatively affluent families. The process of decanonization includes revisiting old texts that were unfairly ignored due to the author's nationality, ethnic identity, and/or gender and bringing them back into scientific debates. This process allows us to ask: What research questions and hypotheses did we fail to explore because we unduly ignored or discredited these works? Ultimately, decanonization and decolonizing methodologies are rapidly expanding the field of anthropology by adding new concepts, theories, and scholars. They are one important part of anthropologists' wider efforts to achieve justice, equity, diversity, and inclusion in and beyond the field.

In this final section we will highlight some of the specific ways that anthropologists have been active recently in rethinking and altering their practices across the subdisciplines in line with these goals. This effort impacts all the subfields of anthropology, with each updating their research practices in different ways.

COPRODUCED AND SHARED KNOWLEDGE

Most generally, anthropologists are increasingly centering their research to ask questions that matter fundamentally to communities collaborating in research and then answering them in ways that respect the histories, values, and right to self-determination of those communities. There are many examples of contemporary anthropology projects both inside and outside Indigenous communities that are successfully placing community concerns and values at the forefront of all research decisions, creating coproduced knowledge.

There is no one way to coproduce knowledge, and the practice is more about a commitment to acknowledge and redress past harms than any one way of going about that. Some examples in this and the previous chapter include Ruth Behar's recognition of Esperanza Hernández as a full partner in her scholarly work, Erin Kimmerle's collaboration with the families of the lost boys from the Arthur G. Dozier School for Boys in Florida to reveal better their abuses and help them seek justice, and the inclusive practices during the excavations at Çatalhöyük to bring in as many perspectives on the archaeological record as possible. Projects that partner fully with communities in the design, execution, and sharing of scholarly efforts can be referred to as community-based participatory research or CBPR. Basic principles of CBPR include a commitment to draw on all forms of knowledge and expertise held within communities, shared responsibility for and ownership of research materials, and using research results to take action that is defined by the goals of community members.

community-based participatory research (CBPR) A collaborative partnering with communities to ensure research is equitable, effective, and properly applied.

ENSURING COMMUNITY CONTROL OF RESEARCH MATERIALS

One way that archaeologists and biological anthropologists are beginning to redress past harms is by fully recognizing the rights of descendant communities to determine how their research materials should be collected, managed, displayed, or studied. An example of this is current concerns around who controls decisions around the use and preservation of archaeological artifacts from excavations. In the United States and many other countries, heritage laws have given professional archaeologists (who are often descendants of settler groups) this responsibility, rather than descendant communities.

Historically, archaeologists would often remove artifacts or human remains from the places they were produced and relocate them to distant museum displays or laboratory shelves, where descendant groups and other stakeholders no longer had access. This practice, which unfortunately sometimes continues today, reflects the ongoing power inequality between the descendants of the Indigenous and the colonizing communities. For example, in Australia, 43 years after the oldest known human remains on the continent were taken from Lake Mungo to the Australian National University for study, they were still stored there. The descendant groups were never consulted about the excavation and removal of their ancestors. The recognition that this violated Indigenous groups' rights to autonomy and self-determination in managing their own cultural heritage has been a first step in healing from the suffering caused. In 2017, some fossils were returned to the Mutthi Mutthi, Paakantyi/Barkindji, and Ngiyampaa peoples (the traditional owners of the Lake Mungo area); some of the returned materials were then reburied (**Figure 2.29**).

In recent years, handling of biological samples from living individuals has become another particular area of ethical concern. This includes invasive extractions of bone or blood, as well as less invasive procedures such as collecting hair, cheek cells, blood, saliva, or urine. Biological anthropologists who measure bodies can also take impressions of people, such as of their teeth or fingerprints. These materials do not exist in a scientific vacuum. Many Indigenous peoples and other descendant groups view biological samples as extensions of themselves and their communities. Blood, hair, or human remains can have powerful religious or cultural meanings, many of which are held *sacred* and not revealed to outsiders. So historical scientific practices in the treatment of biological samples can be highly distressing when they are misaligned with the community's own values. And such practices can do substantial psychological

sacred Things set apart from society, that are beyond the everyday and treated with care.

FIGURE 2.29

A hearse transports fossilized archaeological human remains to Lake Mungo descendant groups for reburial in a secret location. Indigenous Australian elders led ceremonies at stops along the way, like the one shown here.

FIGURE 2.30

In 2010, Havasupai representatives examine and ritually care for blood samples stored without their approval in university freezers. After a legal resolution, formal apologies were provided, compensations were made, and the materials weres returned to Havasupai, recognizing their rights to data sovereignty.

and spiritual harm to those people and communities from whom the samples were taken.

One such serious violation was by geneticists studying DNA collected from members of the Havasupai Tribe in northern Arizona. Originally, a cultural anthropologist worked with the tribe to recruit genetic researchers who could address the tribe's explicit concerns about rising rates of diabetes. But later, without consent of the tribe, the same samples were shared with other geneticists to study schizophrenia, something to which tribal members had never agreed. In discovering the violation, the Havasupai sued for damages and won, regaining control of the misused research materials (**Figure 2.30**).

In the wake of harms such as those done to Havasupai and other Indigenous peoples, their communities have increasingly sought to establish clear principles of data sovereignty over their biological materials. Such efforts aim to ensure that researchers are transparent about their intended uses of such material; that previously collected biological samples are not used for new studies without permission; that data are not used to write on topics that groups did not consent to have studied; and that all materials are returned immediately if and when requested by the community.

Improved legal frameworks that guarantee Indigenous and descendant-community stewardship rights over excavated materials are still needed in many places, and these efforts are making progress. For example, Canada enacted the Impact Assessment Act, which mandates that archaeology projects consider Indigenous knowledge and values alongside those of traditional science. Such legislation helps, but extensive local community consultation and involvement is necessary to fully integrate Indigenous peoples into the process of archaeological knowledge production. Furthermore, to be truly effective, anthropologists' treatment of material remains must also respect oral and ritual traditions as evidence in support of claims (**Figure 2.31**).

DIVERSITY WITHIN ANTHROPOLOGY

Historically, anthropology was a field where people came from the outside to study "others," guided by their own assumptions about what was important. This produced, directly or indirectly, some very harmful results. A more ethical, impactful, and relevant anthropology is advanced as its scholarly practitioners are more diverse, entering the field from many cultural backgrounds and different starting assumptions. Particularly, anthropologists who understand communities because they were raised in them are able to shape and guide innovative research practices, proposing better ways to design projects so they safely produce knowledge that can then be most effectively shared and applied (**Figure 2.32**).

FIGURE 2.31

Native American [Anishinaabe-Ojibwe] archaeologist Sonya Atalay uses comics as a means to communicate the issues of inadequate Indigenous and community voices in decisions around the disposition of archaeological materials, including human remains. (Comic cowritten with museum anthropologist Jen Shannon and illustrated by John Swogger.)

FIGURE 2.32

Chris Wilson, member of the Ngarrindjeri, Kaurna, and Latje Latje Nations, was the first Indigenous Australian to receive a doctorate in archaeology. Excavation on the River Murray's banks, informed by community elders, is connecting past with present knowledge about living in such environments. Such innovations in Indigenous archaeology are not only rethinking assumptions about the past but also suggest ways to manage precious resources (such as fresh water and fish stocks) for future generations.

For example, research in North America is improved significantly as more Indigenous people lead anthropological research projects. Indigenous archaeologists, like Kristen Barnett, are redefining best practices, centering communities in how research is defined and implemented. Barnett's research in southwest Alaska, her traditional homelands, initially prioritized helping the small community of Togiak with recovery of belongings and human remains that had been removed during archaeological fieldwork in the 1960s. Archaeologist Nicholas Laluk is a member of the White Mountain Apache Tribe in eastern Arizona. As Deputy Tribal Historic Preservation Officer for the White Mountain Apache, he has improved archaeological practice by incorporating Ndee (Apache) values and knowledge into the tribe's guidelines for how to best understand and manage their own cultural heritage. This improves both the conclusions drawn from archaeological research and the practices for handling of artifacts themselves.

Kānaka Maoli (Native Hawaiian) geneticist–activist Keolu Fox is proposing new solutions for bringing Indigenous knowledge into scientific practice that involves people collecting and then analyzing their own genetic data. He has also helped to build a genetics institute that is run by Indigenous people. Diné (Navajo) biological anthropologist Katrina Claw combines her scientific expertise with Diné ways of understanding the world and training in biology to advance Indigenous forms of genetic science that can improve the way the new field of personalized medicine is developing (**Figure 2.33**).

data sovereignty The right of a community to govern how data will be collected from their citizens, stored, protected, and used in research.

FIGURE 2.33

Anthropological geneticist Katrina Claw (left) and David Begay, a Diné traditional healer, perform a blessing ceremony in her new genetics laboratory.

2 Doing Anthropology

This chapter presents key points about how anthropological research is done across and within each of the four subfields. All aspects of practicing anthropology must balance complex ethical and practical challenges of how to create quality, reliable, and useful knowledge.

KEY TERM
> colonialism

2.1 | Doing Cultural Anthropology

Identify the core practices and challenges of ethnographic fieldwork.

- The core method of cultural anthropology is ethnography: identifying and illustrating cultural patterns. Ethnographers share a commitment to describing and explaining the world from the perspective of insiders, avoiding as many initial presumptions as possible.

- Early ethnographic research was viewed as a scientific activity that provided objective, reproducible research findings. Newer approaches also propose that humans can have multiple viewpoints and we shouldn't assume that there is a single, knowable reality. Both modes of ethnographic research yield important, but different, insights about humans and their societies.

- Recent changes in cultural anthropology emphasize the important roles of reflexivity and positionality in all forms of fieldwork.

KEY TERMS
> cultural theme
> field notes
> hunter-gatherer
> interlocutor
> key informant
> ontology
> positionality
> reflexivity

2.2 | Doing Linguistic Anthropology

Identify why and how anthropologists study human language.

- Early anthropologists recognized that the detailed and systematic study of diverse human languages provides crucial insights into human history, societies, and worldview.

- Linguistic anthropologists today study language as used in everyday context, gaining insights like how and why language changes and the role of power in language.

KEY TERM
> transcription

2.3 | Doing Archaeology

Explain key concepts that guide archaeological survey and excavation and the methods used to make sense of archaeological data.

- Archaeologists study the preserved remnants of materials deposited in the past and their associated contexts, through archaeological survey and excavation, to better understand past human lives.

- Dating is central to archaeological interpretations. Stratigraphy—the order of layers within archaeological sites—is a primary way to organize archaeological data in context. Techniques that can directly date objects, such as radiocarbon dating, allow archaeologists to refine further when and how the archaeological site was formed.

- Archaeological research continues to focus on the study of material evidence, from addressing changes through time to studying the culture change process itself. But increasingly subjective forms of evidence and community collaboration are considered integral to how research is designed and conclusions are drawn.

KEY TERMS
- absolute dating
- archaeological context
- archaeological feature
- archaeological survey
- ecofact
- ethnoarchaeology
- excavation
- postprocessual archaeology
- processual archaeology
- relative dating
- stratigraphy

2.4 | Doing Biological Anthropology

Describe how biological anthropologists use scientific methods to study deep human history and explain contemporary human diversity.

- Biological anthropologists study human biology in the context of our species' evolution and more recent adaptations to diverse environments.

- Comparing biological data within and across populations, such as that drawn from blood, hormones, or bone, is a primary method in biological anthropology. Often this involves combining field and laboratory research to understand evolutionary and adaptive processes.

- The systematic study of non-human primates provides an important evidence base for understanding the evolution of human biology in deep time.

- Technological innovations, especially in genetic analysis, are reshaping how biological anthropologists can study both human pasts and contemporary human diversity.

KEY TERMS
- ancient DNA
- ethnographic analogy
- stress

2.5 | Improving Anthropological Practices

Recognize recent changes in how anthropology is practiced that seek to address its historical harms.

- Anthropologists share a commitment to improving the practices of anthropology by admitting past mistakes, recognizing and valuing multiple ways of producing knowledge, and partnering meaningfully with communities: they are doing so in many different ways and to different degrees.

KEY TERMS
- community-based participatory research
- data sovereignty
- decanonization
- decolonizing methodology
- sacred

3

Human Variation

According to the archaeological record, people first arrived in warm and verdant Trinidad off the coast of South America some 8,000 years ago. But, according to later government records, these Indigenous communities all but disappeared after 1489 when Spanish colonization brought waves of deadly disease, widespread labor exploitation, and other decimating harms. To biological anthropologist Jada Benn Torres (**Figure 3.1**), this official account of Indigenous "extinction" seemed too simple. It also didn't match her own father's stories recounting their family history. And when she started genetic research in Trinidad and nearby St. Vincent in 2004, many others also talked of their own Indigenous ancestry.

Genetic laboratory techniques applied to samples from living people allowed Benn Torres to verify her working hypothesis: that Indigenous peoples were ancestors to many Caribbean people today, even while the islands had been more recently settled by enslaved Africans, laborers from Asia, and settler colonists from Britain. Her data collection began with a painless swab of the inside of the cheek to collect cells. Benn Torres then compared the genetic makeup of people in her biological samples to that of other Indigenous populations that had been sampled around the globe by many different research teams. She is one of many anthropologists who study the complexities of the biological basis of human variation today through an understanding of microevolution, meaning the ongoing processes of genetic change in human populations through time.

The genetic signatures collected by Benn Torres from people living in Trinidad and other nearby islands proved complicated, showing significant genetic overlaps with other groups living on the African and European continents today. But the genetic signals of Indigenous peoples from the American continent are

ADAPTABLE HUMANS

Humans can occupy a vast array of different environments, due to a combination of evolutionary (genetic) adaptations and technological innovations. Relatively recent evolutionary adaptations to new and localized environmental challenges have altered our visible phenotypes, explaining why humans from different regions can look so different from each other, even while we are so genetically similar. The circular map depicts a human genome.

LEARNING OBJECTIVES

3.1 Basics of Human Variation: Genetics
Identify basic mechanisms of human genetic inheritance.

3.2 Mechanisms of Microevolution
Distinguish the four forces of microevolution.

3.3 Human Variation and Genetic Adaptation
Explain why humans from different regions are similar genetically, despite looking different.

3.4 Human Culture and Microevolution
Identify how human cultural practices influence microevolution.

3.5 Development and Plasticity
Describe how a single genotype can result in highly varied phenotypes.

FIGURE 3.1

Biological anthropologist Jada Benn Torres (cloth mask, center) shares results of her genetic analyses of past Caribbean migrations with community members. Collaboration with cultural anthropologist Gabriel Torres Colón (right back), helps connect genetic research to how communities understand their ancestry, related identities, and sense of belonging.

ancestry A sense of one's biological heritage, often related to a particular group, place, or region.

population The set of organisms in the same region that can potentially mate and produce offspring. Human populations are rarely completely isolated from each other.

microevolution Any change in gene frequencies in a population between generations and through time.

genetic ancestry A shared biological history, as defined by genetic similarities.

genotype The genetic makeup of an organism.

phenotype The physical expression of a genetically influenced feature or trait, such as eye color or blood type.

unmistakably present, showing that ancestry has continued through the generations despite tremendous social and political upheaval. To Benn Torres, evidence of our genetic ancestry is important for providing a unique way to think about human connections through history. In this case, it can provide a marker of survival and resilience for communities in the region today, supporting their connection with their Indigenous ancestors (**Figure 3.2**).

Many people are personally interested in their genetic ancestry, as commercially available laboratory analysis of parts of their genotype can give clues about their deeper family history. Humans are also curious about visible phenotypes, why people appear physically similar to or different from each other, such as those from different parts of the world. But anthropologists place such genetic and phenotypic data into a much bigger picture, to document and explain not just our human history but also the implications of such human variation for our biology and societies today. This chapter explores why humans appear so phenotypically diverse, and how that relates to both our evolutionary histories and the varied environments in which our ancestors settled. Recent innovations in genetic technology are revolutionizing many aspects of how anthropologists study humans and will continue to do so in the decades ahead.

SAINT VINCENT

TRINIDAD

South America

FIGURE 3.2

First Peoples Communities in Trinidad supported Benn Torres's genetic research. They embrace the scientific evidence of their Indigenous ancestry provided by this collaboration as important to their shared social identities, as celebrated in this ceremonial walk in the capital of Port of Spain.

BASICS OF HUMAN VARIATION: GENETICS

Genetics and inheritance shed light on what defines us as a species and why we differ. In this section, we cover the essential background concepts.

THE BUILDING BLOCKS: CELLS, DNA, AND GENES

Each of us is a single organism composed of trillions of cells (**Figure 3.3**). Yet we all began life the same: as a single-celled zygote produced through the fusion of specialized sperm ("male") and ovum or egg ("female") cells called gametes. That single zygote is the source of all our somatic cells throughout our early physical development: these cells form all the organs in our bodies, including our hair, eyes, skin, heart, brain, testes, and ovaries. The zygote accordingly provides the genetic templates of the gametes that are passed on to the next generation through sexual reproduction.

Each human cell contains many tiny subcellular elements, including a nucleus that stores some of our DNA or deoxyribonucleic acid (more on DNA shortly). Each human cell also contains other internal structures called organelles. Ribosomes are organelles that are critical for making proteins, the building blocks of all the processes that happen in our body, including the hormones that cause hair growth at puberty and the enzymes that allow us to digest our food. The mitochondria are organelles that are responsible for supplying energy for cellular functions. Mitochondria also contain DNA that is only derived from the ovum (that is, inherited from the biological mother) and is an important source of information on human evolution.

cell The smallest basic structural unit of an organism, carrying out specialized functions.

zygote The first cell that replicates to create a new sexually reproducing organism, produced through fusion of ovum and sperm.

gamete A cell that carries genetic material intended for inheritance through reproduction (an ovum or sperm).

somatic cell Any cell in the body other than a gamete.

sexual reproduction The process that creates a new organism by combining genetic information from two different individuals.

nucleus The information and functional center of a somatic cell.

DNA Self-replicating material that transmits genetic information in all organisms, including humans.

organelle A structure that has a specialized function within a cell.

ribosome The organelle in which protein synthesis happens.

protein A large and complex molecule that performs one of many varied and critical functions in the body, such as growth, digestion, blood clotting, or immune response.

mitochondrion A plentiful organelle that produces chemical energy for the cell.

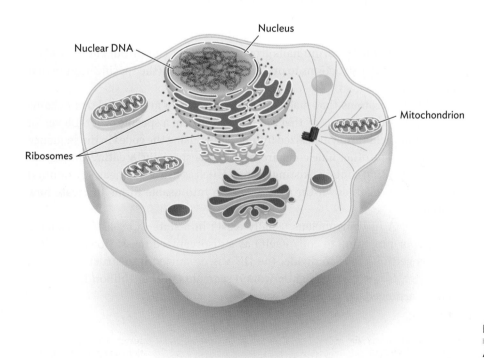

FIGURE 3.3

A depiction of the basic structure of a human cell, with some key organelles labeled, is shown here.

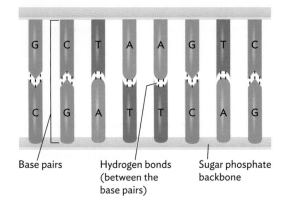

Base pairs   Hydrogen bonds   Sugar phosphate
             (between the   backbone
             base pairs)

Process of DNA replication

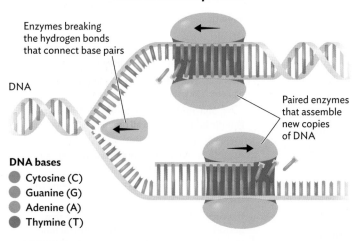

Enzymes breaking
the hydrogen bonds
that connect base pairs

DNA

Paired enzymes
that assemble
new copies
of DNA

DNA bases
- Cytosine (C)
- Guanine (G)
- Adenine (A)
- Thymine (T)

FIGURE 3.4

DNA bases pair in specific ways with each other to form rungs in the double-helix structure of the DNA molecule. DNA replication happens through splitting DNA strands, then rematching the bases to form copies.

molecule The smallest unit that has all the properties of a substance. Smaller molecules can combine to form larger molecules: for example, sugars, phosphates, and bases combine to make DNA, and amino acids join together to form proteins.

base A building block that pairs in a specific complementary way to form a double-stranded DNA molecule. Cytosine (C) always pairs with guanine (G), and adenine (A) always pairs with thymine (T).

protein synthesis The process by which cells produce protein molecules, using instructions encoded in DNA.

amino acid One of 20 compounds that, in different combinations, make up proteins.

chromosome The structure in the cell nucleus that carries and organizes genes.

The DNA in our nuclei has a double-helix structure, like a twisted ladder sharing a set of rungs (**Figure 3.4**). Sugar and phosphate molecules form the outside of the ladder. The rungs of the ladder, the sequence of which constitutes the genetic code, are composed of four molecular bases. Adenine (A) and thymine (T) are two bases that can bond together to form one rung, or step, in this ladder. Guanine (G) and cytosine (C) are the other two bases that bond to each other to form rungs. So, if one side of the ladder has the bases GCATAG, the other side has the sequence CGTATC. G always pairs with C, and A always pairs with T. These complementary bases are shaped to fit together and are held in place by hydrogen bonds. Human DNA contains about 3 billion base pairs that are partly (but as we will soon find, not entirely) responsible for our basic human biology.

So, what does our DNA actually do? It has two primary functions: to allow our bodies to function, grow, and repair through the synthesis of proteins, and to provide the basic genetic template for creating a new and unique human.

DNA FUNCTION: PROTEIN SYNTHESIS

The first function of DNA is protein synthesis. Animal bodies are formed from proteins that provide the structure. Muscle, for example, is made of protein, as are all other organs such as hair, skin, and nails. Collagen is the protein that forms the organic portion of our bones. There are also proteins that help regulate the body's functions, such as the enzymes, hormones, and antibodies that perform the bodily functions essential for our survival (such as breaking down food, fighting infections, releasing ova or making sperm, and acting as messengers to coordinate organ functions). The human organism is, at its simplest, proteins regulating functions within a body made of other proteins that provide structure and allow us to do things critical to our survival: locate and metabolize energy, find mates, and reproduce.

Protein synthesis is coded for in the DNA, and many different types of proteins made in our bodies are defined by different sections of DNA, each with a different function. When our nails grow, for example, cells in our cuticle are following chemical instructions to produce more keratin (the specific protein that forms nails).

All these proteins that make our bodies function are formed from chains of 20 different amino acids that are put together in a specific order. Eleven of these amino acids are synthesized by our bodies, using the codes in the sequence of our DNA. The other nine come from our diet, especially by eating animal and plant sources that contain existing protein (such as fish, eggs, meat, soy, or nuts) that can be broken down through digestion into usable forms to create new proteins.

The DNA in your nucleus usually exists in a state of stasis (not making proteins or preparing to copy itself) as a disorganized mass. However, when a cell is getting ready to divide, the DNA is organized into structures called chromosomes, which are tightly wound segments of the 3 billion DNA bases that are arranged in a systematic way.

The number of chromosomes differs from species to species. Humans typically have 46 chromosomes arranged in 23 pairs. The DNA for making a specific protein is located on the same chromosome pair in every human being. The section of each chromosome that has the DNA base-pair instructions (i.e., those long sequences of As, Gs, Cs, and Ts) for producing a protein is called a *gene*. Because both members of the chromosome pair have the same gene in the same place along their length, they are described as *homologous*, meaning they have the same purpose or function (**Figure 3.5**). Slight changes in the sequence of the relevant DNA bases situated along the chromosomes lead to the creation of slightly different proteins because the sequence of amino acids is altered. These gene variants are called *alleles*.

REPRODUCTION AND INHERITANCE: MEIOSIS

The second function of DNA is directing replication and cell division as a means for creating unique offspring. The complementary nature of the bases is what allows one cell to divide into two in a process called *mitosis* (**Figure 3.6**). The unique pairing of adenine with thymine and of guanine with cytosine is crucial because it provides instructions for *DNA replication* that result in two exact copies being made. The bond between each base pair breaks, and the two strands that make up the ladder uncouple. The bases on each strand pair with new complementary bases and so form two new ladders (Figure 3.4). And this capacity to split DNA strands down the middle is also how gametes can be produced. These strands can then be recombined (through sexual reproduction) with those from another person to create a genetically new person (i.e., a baby).

While all somatic cells are created through mitosis (simple cell division), gametes (sperm or ova) are created through a different process of cell division called *meiosis* that takes place in our reproductive organs (testicles or ovaries). During meiosis, chromosome pairs break apart before the cell divides, so that each resulting cell (sperm or ovum) contains only one chromosome from each of the 23 chromosome pairs. When a sperm and an egg combine to create a zygote, these combine to create the full complement of 46 chromosomes that makes a human a human.

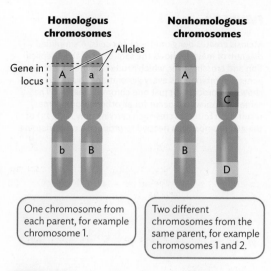

Homologous chromosomes   **Nonhomologous chromosomes**

Alleles

Gene in locus — A   a

A

C

b   B

B

D

One chromosome from each parent, for example chromosome 1.

Two different chromosomes from the same parent, for example chromosomes 1 and 2.

FIGURE 3.5

Homologous versus nonhomologous chromosome pairs are illustrated. In the homologous chromosome example, there are two copies of the chromosome, one inherited from each parent. Two genes, labeled A and B, are located at specific locations along the chromosome in each copy. The uppercase and lowercase letters indicate that different versions of the gene, or alleles, are present. The nonhomologous chromosomes do not code for the same genes.

gene The basic unit of genetic inheritance, identified as a sequence of DNA bases. Some genes provide the instructions to make the proteins needed for human growth, functioning, and reproduction.

homologous Having the same purpose or function. For example, homologous chromosomes, inherited from both biological parents, have the same genes that perform the same function in the same places on both halves of the chromosome pair.

allele An alternative form of a gene that codes for slightly different proteins that affect the development and expression of a trait (such as blood type or eye color).

mitosis Division of a single cell to create two identical cells, crucial to growth and maintenance of the body.

DNA replication The process of DNA making copies of itself.

meiosis The process in which a single cell divides twice to create four gametes (sperm or ova) with their own mix of half the genetic information of the original.

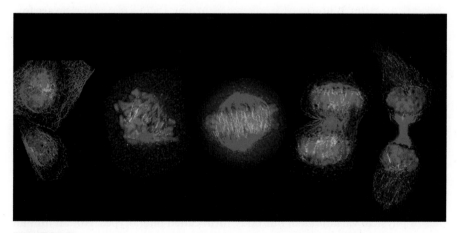

FIGURE 3.6

Human cancer cells are shown undergoing mitosis (division), creating full genetic copies of themselves as they grow. During replication, the chromosomes align in the center of the cell before copies are made. Then the two new full sets of chromosomes move away from each other and the cell splits to become two copies of the original.

FIGURE 3.7

Meiosis creates our gametes or sex cells. A simplified diagram of meiosis shows the sequence of DNA replication and crossing over, which produce gametes with new genetic combinations every generation. This diagram shows the process for just one chromosome pair. The same process would occur for all other chromosomes, resulting in four gametes each carrying only half (23) of the 46 chromosomes needed to produce a new offspring.

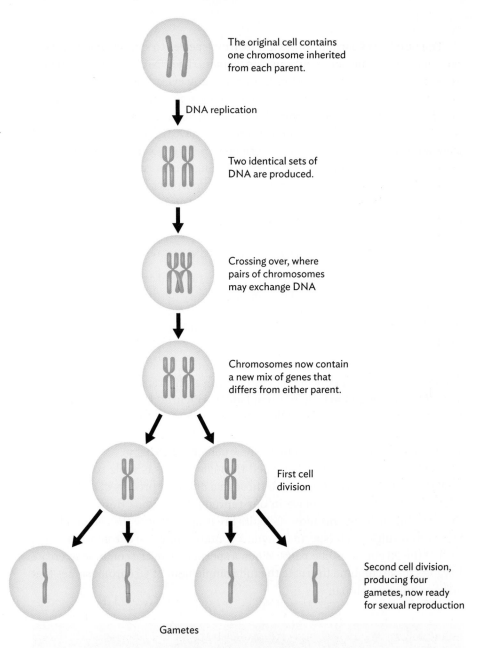

The original cell contains one chromosome inherited from each parent.

DNA replication

Two identical sets of DNA are produced.

Crossing over, where pairs of chromosomes may exchange DNA

Chromosomes now contain a new mix of genes that differs from either parent.

First cell division

Second cell division, producing four gametes, now ready for sexual reproduction

Gametes

crossing over Exchange of genes between homologous chromosomes during meiosis.

However, parts from one chromosome can be swapped with the corresponding part of its pair, a process called **crossing over** (**Figure 3.7**). This means that each gamete contains a combination of chromosomes inherited from a person's biological mother and father; neither contains an exact copy of a biological parent's chromosome. Every single gamete is unique. This chromosomal variation is critical for evolution to work, as we will discuss shortly.

PHENOTYPIC TRAITS

Our eye and skin color, our height, and even the hairiness of our toes are examples of physical variations in our body form called phenotypes. Not all human phenotypes are readily visible; incredible variation is also happening at a microscopic or molecular level. For example, some people have more T cells, allowing for stronger immune systems. Some have higher levels of testosterone or differently shaped red blood cells. Genetic (inherited) diseases (or the lack of them) are also examples of phenotypes. Behavioral traits with a clear genetic component (such as range of voice pitch) are also considered phenotypes.

Our phenotypes are the physical expressions of our genotypes. The genotype, our genetic makeup, is composed of our alleles, the alternative forms of a gene that code for the same trait. As noted, each person has two copies of each gene, inherited as one allele from each parent. If these match (that is, the alleles are the same in terms of the proteins they produce), they are homozygous. If the alleles from each parent produce proteins that would perform differently, they are said to be heterozygous. The specific homozygous or heterozygous combination is your genotype.

When the two alleles are heterozygous, they combine in different ways to determine the phenotype. For example, one allele may dominate the other so that it alone will determine what proteins are produced or regulated. Put another way, some alleles can mask the effects of others, which is called allele dominance. Recessive alleles are those that are suppressed if paired with a dominant allele.

The principles of dominance are easiest to observe in traits determined by a single gene. One example is cheek indentations, which have two phenotypic forms that result from different inherited genes: dimpled and nondimpled. The dimpled allele is dominant to the nondimpled allele. That means if a person has one dimpled allele and one nondimpled allele as their genotype, they will have dimples as a phenotype. Genotypes are often expressed in the form of two letters as a shorthand for the two alleles we each carry for a gene, with the dominant form of a gene represented by an uppercase letter (D = dimpled) and a nondominant ("recessive") form by the corresponding lowercase letter (d = nondimpled).

A Punnett square (**Figure 3.8**) can be used to predict what genotypes and phenotypes could be present in the offspring of two parents whose dimple genotypes are known. If you inherit two dominant D alleles from your biological parents, your genotype is DD and your phenotype will be dimpled. If you inherit two recessive alleles from your biological parents, your genotype is dd and your phenotype will be nondimpled. But if you inherit one D allele (dimpled) and one d allele (nondimpled), your genotype would be Dd and your phenotype will also be dimpled because the dimpled allele (D) masks the effect of the nondimpled allele (d).

However, many traits are determined by a much more complex process than a single gene with only two alleles. For example, each human inherits one of several different blood types, A, B, AB, and O, based on the combination of their biological parents' types. In this case, A and B are codominant and the O allele

homozygous **Describes alleles inherited from each parent that have the same genetic sequence.**

heterozygous **Describes alleles inherited from each parent that have different genetic sequences.**

recessive **Describes an allele that is expressed phenotypically only in the absence of a dominant gene.**

dominant **Describes an allele that is preferentially expressed in phenotypes.**

codominant **Describes alleles that equally influence phenotypic gene expression.**

FIGURE 3.8

Punnett squares illustrate examples of the basic pattern of inheritance of cheek dimples, which is a dominant trait over no dimples. While cheek dimples are a relatively "simple" trait that is mostly dominant, several different variants exist.

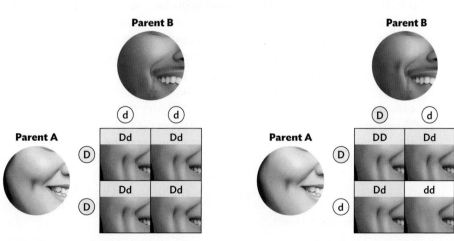

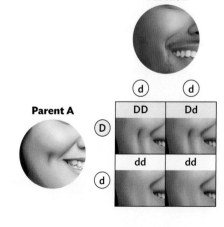

Ⓓ Dominant (dimples)

ⓓ recessive (no dimples)

is recessive, so the phenotype is determined by one gene with three different alleles that can result in four different outcomes. Alleles that are codominant result in a new phenotype that reflects the interaction of both alleles equally: in this case, the blood type AB.

Finally, most phenotypes are determined not by a single gene but by multiple potentially interacting genes, each with multiple alleles. Such traits, which include most of what we see in our bodies, are called polygenic. Even further, most polygenic traits are multifactorial, meaning many factors determine the phenotypic expression beyond just the genotype. We discuss some of these factors in Section 3.5.

polygenic Describes a phenotype whose expression or appearance is determined by multiple genes, each with multiple possible alleles.

multifactorial Describes a phenotype whose expression is determined by many factors, including the environment in which development happens.

MECHANISMS OF MICROEVOLUTION

Evolution is most simply defined as a change in allele frequencies in a biological population through time, often identified specifically by the term microevolution. So, if 5% of people in a population carry alleles for hairy toes in one generation and 6% in the next, then we are observing evolutionary change. Understanding what causes those changes in allele frequency over time, and how it underpins much of what we understand as human variation, is the focus of this section.

HOW NEW VARIANTS HAPPEN: MUTATION

One way changes in gene frequencies between generations happen is from the emergence of a new allele through genetic mutation. This process changes the DNA base-pair sequences that code for a protein, which we previously defined as an allele.

A gene that codes for blue eyes, for example, first appeared as a new mutation some 6,000–10,000 years ago. Originally, humans typically and likely almost always had brown eyes. But a single mutation in one gene (called OCA2) decreased the amount of melanin (the protein that causes skin and eyes to be colored brown) produced in the iris. This dilution of melanin results in blue eyes. Many blue-eyed people today share the same mutated gene in exactly the same locus (place) on their genome, suggesting a shared ancestry with just one initial blue-eyed individual.

Mutations happen when occasional random "mistakes" occur as base pairs are copied in the process of DNA replication (**Figure 3.9**). For example, GATTACA may get accidentally copied as GGTTACA or GATTACAA or -ATTACA at the same locus. Alternatively, the original sequence may get moved to another locus or get deleted entirely. Although these types of replication errors happen in all our cells, the mutations that most matter for evolution are the ones that we can pass along—that is, those that result in new alleles in gametes that

genetic mutation A permanent change in the DNA base-pair sequence of one or more genes, sometimes with consequences for how they code for the proteins that control body functions.

locus The position of a specific gene on a chromosome.

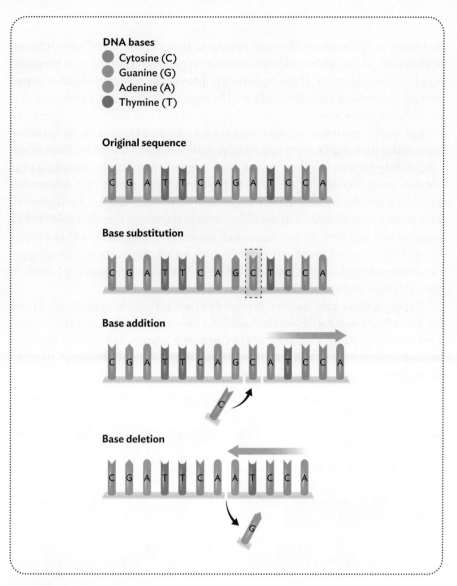

DNA bases
- Cytosine (C)
- Guanine (G)
- Adenine (A)
- Thymine (T)

Original sequence

C G A T T C A G A T C C A

Base substitution

C G A T T C A G C T C C A

Base addition

C G A T T C A G C A T C C A
C

Base deletion

C G A T T C A A T C C A
G

FIGURE 3.9

Genetic mutations can happen during DNA replication when new copies of each side of a DNA strand are made. Mutations can include substitution, addition, or deletion of bases in the sequence.

combine to create an offspring. The new allele can be transmitted to the offspring's own offspring, and in this way allele frequencies can change between generations. If one person is born with blue eyes in a population of previously all brown-eyed individuals, then evolution has occurred because gene frequencies changed across generations. But maintaining this new mutation and spreading it to other populations requires other forces to act on this genetic variant. Natural selection is one of the most important (more on this shortly).

Most mutations that happen during meiosis are in DNA that has no known function, so they are referred to as **neutral mutations**. What matters for evolution are mutations in those genes that produce proteins that

neutral mutation A change in DNA without any change in function.

deleterious mutation A change in DNA that impairs function of the encoded protein.

advantageous mutation A change in DNA that improves function of the encoded protein.

natural selection The theory that a comparatively better match between an individual's phenotype and their environment will favor inheritance of that underlying genotype to the next generation.

do things in the body, as they are able to change the ability of the organism to function. If the mutation impairs such an encoded protein, it is termed a **deleterious mutation**. If the mutation improves the function of the encoded protein, improving an individual's well being and chances of reproducing, it is an **advantageous mutation**.

But what constitutes a deleterious versus an advantageous mutation is not necessarily the same in every situation. A mutation's impact can be affected significantly by factors like the physical environments in which the resulting phenotypes exist. **Natural selection** is the evolutionary process that determines whether a genetic variant is advantageous or not within a given environment. This theory, first described in detail by naturalist Charles Darwin (1809–1882), explains one way that alleles change in frequency through time within a population. In developing the theory, Darwin drew on his observation of phenotypic variations among local finches (small birds) while sailing through the islands of the Galápagos archipelago off the coast of South America.

Darwin believed the finches he recorded were all originally descended from the same finch population on the mainland of South America. But the descendant finch populations on each of the dispersed islands had slightly different beak shapes and sizes, and the differences were pronounced enough to make them different species (**Figure 3.10**).

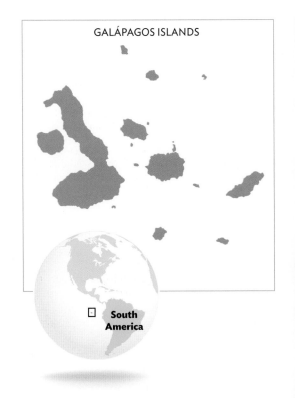

(a)   (b)

(c)   (d)

FIGURE 3.10

Four of Darwin's Galápagos finches are pictured, showing adaptations to the available food sources on different islands. **(a)** The large ground finch uses its beak to crack nuts. **(b)** The medium ground finch is able to eat larger and harder seeds as a food source during droughts. **(c)** The green warbler-finch and **(d)** the small tree finch both eat insects.

The different beak forms seemed to match differences in the foods available on each island. For example, the finches on an island where hard seeds were available tended to have shorter, stouter beaks able to crack the seed shell, whereas the finches on an island where fruit and pollen were available had longer, narrower beaks suited to accessing the food in this setting. Darwin proposed that beak forms that provided an advantage to individual finches (such as enabling them to eat less preferred hard seeds during droughts) were more likely to be inherited in future generations because those individual birds survived longer and had more offspring. Similarly, those birds with beak shapes that impaired their ability to get food would be less likely to pass their alleles to offspring, because they wouldn't survive long enough to breed or wouldn't be as able to compete for mates.

Such competition among individuals for access to food and mates is at the heart of natural selection. Phenotypic traits that allow an individual to outcompete others for such limited resources in ways that enhance its ability to pass genes to offspring are termed adaptations. Because individuals who have such advantageous adaptations are able to produce more offspring, they are said to have higher fitness. When future generations of that individual's descendants also benefit from that same trait, and themselves have more offspring, the advantageous alleles will become more common within the population over time.

There is an important point here. Selection, then, is the process by which populations of a species gradually become better adapted to specific environments over time, as better adapted (fitter) individuals produce proportionately more offspring in the next generation. Over many generations, if enough differences accrue though this ongoing process, a new species can form. This view of the evolutionary process that captures a much longer span of time and the accumulation of many microevolutionary changes is called macroevolution.

Modern genetic studies confirm this is exactly what happened on the Galápagos archipelago, where one initial species evolved, over many generations, into a number of different species, each adapted to be better able to survive in each of the varied island habitats.

In the 20th century, this central theory of natural selection developed by Darwin was explicitly connected to a clearer understanding of the principles of inheritance, such as meiosis and dominant and recessive alleles. This combined explanation for how evolutionary change happens came to be known as the "modern synthesis."

GENETIC DRIFT AND GENE FLOW

Although environmental factors are important in microevolution, allele frequencies can also change between generations (i.e., evolution can occur) entirely by chance, due to another mechanism called genetic drift. One way to understand genetic drift is to consider a coin flip where the sides of the coin represent different alleles of the same gene. If you were able to flip that coin a very large number of times, you'd expect the results to roughly even out to a 50/50 split between heads and tails. But if you flip the coin only a small number of times—say 10—it's much more likely your results would be more divergent from 50/50. You could get six heads and four tails, or three heads and seven tails, or even 10 heads and no tails. With fewer flips, chance plays a larger role in the resulting ratio of outcomes.

adaptation Any phenotypic variation that improves an organism's fit within a given environment.

fitness The success of an organism in passing its genes to offspring.

species A group of organisms sufficiently genetically similar to be able to breed with one another.

macroevolution The accumulation of evolutionary changes over long time frames, leading to the emergence of new species.

modern synthesis A consolidation of prior research that defined evolution as a change in gene frequencies across generations, potentially leading to new species (through mechanisms such as natural selection).

genetic drift Random changes in gene frequencies from one generation to the next.

This same effect applies to the sorting of alleles during meiosis. If in one generation you have a massive population in which half of all individuals are nondimpled with two recessive alleles (dd) and half are dimpled with heterozygous alleles (Dd), then you can say with some certainty that in the next generation roughly 50% of individuals will have no dimples (genotype dd) and 50% will have dimples (genotype DD or Dd) (see the right panel in Figure 3.8). But in a smaller population, that result is less certain because there will be random deviations from expected probabilities.

Sometimes larger populations split into new smaller ones, for example, when resources run out, as a result of group conflict, or simply from a desire to explore and settle elsewhere. Chances are that the genetic variation in the new smaller populations will not perfectly match that of the larger one it came from. In the human past, this could have happened when some individuals migrated away from the larger group to start a new colony (**Figure 3.11**). This effect on the frequencies of different alleles is called the *founder effect*. The small population of the remote Pitcairn Islands is descended from just six sailor mutineers who seized the English naval ship HMS *Bounty* in 1789 and six of the women who accompanied them from their last stop in Tahiti. Pitcairn descendants today have extremely low rates of myopia (nearsightedness). Their notably good eyesight is explained by a genetic founder effect, meaning the initial settlers were not carrying genes associated with inherited myopia.

Similarly, if a natural disaster randomly killed all of the dimpled people in a community, then this could operate as a related *genetic bottlenecking* that also reduces a group's collective genetic variability (i.e., removing the allele that causes dimpling). The smaller a group that undergoes a founder or bottleneck effect, the more significant such random changes in gene frequencies are likely to be, possibly even removing entire gene variants from a population.

The combined evolutionary effects of mutation, selection, and genetic drift work most quickly and lead to the formation of a new species when a smaller population remains fully isolated from others, like those Galápagos finches. The reverse scenario has the exact opposite effect. Increasing genetic interaction between once isolated populations is called *gene flow*, the fourth and final evolutionary mechanism. Gene flow can occur when people physically migrate, bringing their alleles into a different population. Gene flow can also result from changing social practices like marriage. If people switch from selecting their mates from within their own social group (called endogamy) to others from outside their group (called exogamy), gene flow increases and alleles are shared among formerly isolated populations. Gene flow introduces new genes from one population to another, meaning it can increase the genetic variation of a population. However, when populations share genes back and forth consistently, they become more genetically similar to each other as measured by the frequency of alleles in each population.

Through social and technological innovations (such as rapid global travel and online dating), humans have the ability to meet and mate with people from very different genetic backgrounds. Accordingly, gene flow is presently a particularly powerful homogenizing evolutionary force for the human species. Also, because gene flow makes the population (and thus the potential mating pool) larger, it actively works to counter the effects of genetic drift.

founder effect A change in gene frequency that occurs when a larger population divides into smaller separate groups, such as when settling new areas.

genetic bottlenecking A sharp reduction in population size (from events such as epidemics or natural disasters), resulting in a dramatic change in gene frequencies between one generation and the next.

gene flow Movement of genes between populations; it tends to make the populations more genetically similar to one another.

Genetic bottleneck

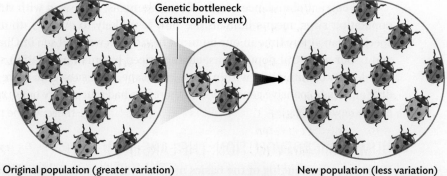

Genetic bottleneck
(catastrophic event)

Original population (greater variation)   New population (less variation)

The founder effect

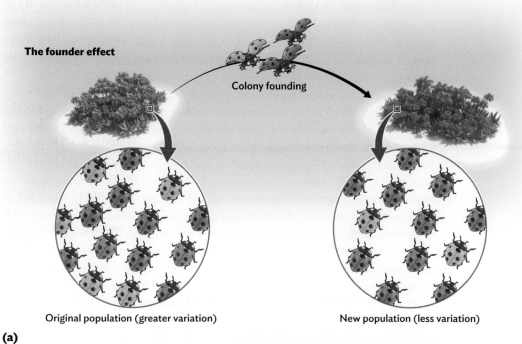

Colony founding

Original population (greater variation)   New population (less variation)

(a)

(b)

Pacific Ocean

PITCAIRN
ISLAND

FIGURE 3.11

(a) Genetic bottlenecking and founder effect, two forms of genetic drift, can rapidly change gene frequencies in small populations.
(b) The current inhabitants of Pitcairn Island in the eastern Pacific Ocean have unusually good eyesight, likely because they descended from a small set of founders without genetic variants that cause myopia.

The current abundance of gene flow in humans, combined with very large population sizes, means humans are now less likely to evolve into different species than at any time in our hominin history. As we shall see in Chapters 5 and 6, our ancestral populations, characterized by small population size and low-density communities within a vast landscape, were subject to more genetic drift and less expansive gene flow, and therefore had much more opportunity to evolve new species.

HUMAN MICROEVOLUTION: THE LARGER PICTURE

With an understanding of the basics of genes and the forces of evolution, biological anthropologists collect and compare genetic and phenotypic data from around the globe. This provides an important means of reverse-engineering the history of our species. The most basic conclusion is now well confirmed that the human species is exactly that—one species—and beyond that a species defined by a surprising lack of genetic diversity.

One reason for the significant genetic similarities observed across all human populations is because our species is so young, geologically speaking. Our current understanding is that anatomically modern humans (just like us) emerged as a single species in Africa around 250,000 years ago. All of us alive today are descended in some manner from these early humans, as the genetic ancestors of those groups that subsequently migrated out of Africa into the Middle East, Europe, Asia, the Americas, and beyond. These early human populations largely replaced (with limited gene flow) *other* closely related species of humans already living outside Africa, as we will explain in Chapter 6. However, the very complicated nature of genetic change, encompassing millions upon millions of cumulative microevolutionary changes through mutation, selection, gene flow, and drift, means this was a very gradual process. There is no exact place or definable time at which we suddenly became the species we are today.

FIGURE 3.12

Humans are curious and social, highly motivated to travel and connect, explaining why gene flow will remain a key influence on our species' ongoing evolution. Jemaa el-Fnaa square in the heart of Marrakesh, Morocco, has long been a market where people from many places have congregated and traded, and today it is a destination for tourists from all over the world.

Indeed, today genetic diversity is actually greatest within populations that live on the African continent, as opposed to other populations outside that region. This is because anatomically modern humans have been living in Africa longer than anywhere else, and so African populations have been accumulating new genetic variants (mutations) longer than humans living elsewhere. Furthermore, even if gene flow is greater now than in the past, significant gene flow has always been a key feature of human evolution. Being a highly social and curious species, early humans left Africa and settled new regions, and they continued to travel, trade, conquer, migrate, and intermingle with one another across generations in these new places just as they continued to in Africa (**Figure 3.12**).

The process of gene flow, introducing new genetic variants to make populations more diverse while also making populations more genetically similar to each other, has especially accelerated since the advent of farming and food production (Chapter 8), which led to increased population size and more migration, trade, and overall connectedness. This sharing of genetic material reduced the genetic differences between groups. Even in the isolated islands of the Pacific, the last region humans settled, human populations have never been fully isolated, fixed, or otherwise discrete for very long.

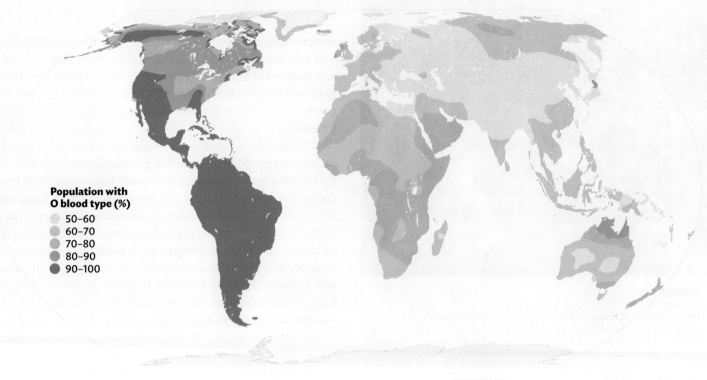

Population with O blood type (%)
- 50–60
- 60–70
- 70–80
- 80–90
- 90–100

FIGURE 3.13

Many initial scientific studies of human variation focused on blood types as an example of how genetic variation patterns through space, as seen in this early version of a clinal map estimating the percentages of people with ancestry in different world regions who have type O blood.

clinal variation A continuous, gradual shift in gene frequencies between one region and the next.

The global distribution of inherited blood types (and other genetic variants related to blood proteins) is a good way to illustrate this incredible global genetic overlap (**Figure 3.13**). Each person's blood type is based on a single gene, resulting in that person having an O, A, B, or AB blood type at the phenotypic level. About 63% of humans have blood type O. That means some 37% have rarer blood types: A, B, or AB. Frequencies of each type may be higher or lower in some regions than others, but the same types themselves appear in most regions. For example, type O is especially common in Indigenous peoples of the Americas, which reflects the reduction in A and B variants found in other world regions that were settled by humans earlier, likely through such microevolutionary processes as genetic drift. Ongoing processes of gene flow help explain how phenotypic traits like blood type map continuously along a spectrum and show gradual transitions across geography. Genetic variation that gradually transitions across geography is called clinal variation.

Recent studies using more sophisticated DNA-based analyses of the entire human genome (rather than just single genes) suggest that, on average, some 85% of genetic variation in modern humans is found within local biological populations rather than between peoples with ancestry in different world regions.

Ancient DNA (aDNA) extraction technologies allow anthropologists to directly sample the DNA of past humans, too, providing an incredible boost to the study of human genetic evolution (**Figure 3.14**). Currently, a DNA can be extracted from remains reaching back nearly half a million years. DNA extracts from people in past populations can also be compared to DNA from living humans. For example, the combination of studies of ancient and contemporary DNA suggests repeated genetic bottlenecking occurred as early humans left Africa and populated the globe. As populations kept splitting off through a sequence of migration events, the result was lower genetic variation within a given population with each event. Based on genetic data from modern and

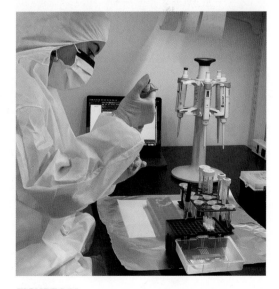

FIGURE 3.14

Biological anthropologist Maria Nieves-Colón collaborates with Jada Benn Torres to study the genetic connections between living and past populations in the Caribbean, by applying powerful newer laboratory tools that can extract and analyze ancient DNA from humans who were buried thousands of years ago.

FIGURE 3.15

Here Brahmin Indian women are attending a matchmaking event. Stricter community rules around who could marry emerged in India around 1,500 years ago, and these changing practices have created pockets of relative genetic isolation. In such cases, social practices that control who marries and mates with whom are leading to lower genetic diversity because they discourage gene flow and encourage genetic drift.

(a)

(b)

FIGURE 3.16

(a) Inuit people in Greenland tend to have more compact body shapes that function better in cold climates.
(b) Maasai people in warm and arid Kenya, in East Africa, benefit from long and lean body forms that better dissipate heat (note, though, that they also vary among themselves in height).

ancient humans, the evidence currently indicates that humans first migrated from Africa (higher genetic variation) to Arabia, and then to the Indian subcontinent, then to Europe and east Asia, and then to North America, and then into South America (lower genetic variation). We will discuss this in more detail in Chapter 6.

This isn't to say that these migrating human groups didn't themselves continue to diversify genetically through time. As they moved into new areas, they could become isolated from each other, so that both natural selection and drift could create greater genetic distances between them and other groups. Sometimes isolation can result from geographic barriers such as mountain ranges or oceans. Such isolation by distance is a common factor in the emergence of new species in plants and animals (such as Darwin's finches). However, humans have added complexity because sometimes populations will become more or less genetically isolated through social and cultural practices, such as marriage rules or language differences (**Figure 3.15**).

So, a key point from this background is that all humans are genetically very similar. Only 1 of every 1,000 DNA bases will differ between any two humans (i.e., we are 99.9% the same, genetically speaking). But if our relative youth as a species and our penchant for migration and intermingling make us so similar, it begs the question: Why can people from different regions appear to be so physically different?

HUMAN VARIATION AND GENETIC ADAPTATION

Most of the regional variations we see today in body shape, skin color, and other aspects of our phenotype emerged very recently in our species' history, after modern humans migrated beyond Africa. Rather than reflecting distinct biological categories into which we can group people, these regional variations exist along a continuum (or cline) and reflect the many ways humans have adapted to different environments—that is, how natural selection has helped human populations in different locations thrive in the face of new parasites, different potential foods, and unfamiliar climates. In this section, we discuss some examples of why and how natural selection has operated as it has, and how its impact is visible in our diverse modern human phenotypes. Many of these examples reflect relatively recent genetic adaptations to varied selective pressures encountered as earlier humans settled more widely in increasingly diverse new places.

ADAPTATION TO CLIMATE: BODY SHAPE

Generally speaking, human populations with ancestries tied to warmer versus colder climates tend to have different average body shapes (**Figure 3.16**). As a species that first emerged during a warm phase of African history, we initially had adapted a mammalian biology that dissipated heat efficiently. This included our relatively hairless bodies, ability to sweat, and relatively linear bodies with long limbs.

Two biological principles explain how different average body shapes differences emerge as adaptations to environmental stressors, even very quickly in evolutionary time. Bergmann's rule states that populations living nearer the poles should tend to evolve more compact shapes (greater body mass relative to height) allowing the body to conserve heat more efficiently. Similarly, Allen's rule states that limb proportions also reflect a similar adaptive process, whereby shorter-limbed bodies conserve heat better because they have less overall skin surface area from which heat can dissipate. This makes such bodies better suited to thrive in colder climates.

The adjustment to living in cold climates has come only relatively recently in our history, though, and the distinction between differently adapted body types doesn't break into just two categories. Rather, there's a spectrum of average body shapes seen among humans today that reflect many adaptations to specific regional climates.

ADAPTATION TO ULTRAVIOLET RADIATION: SKIN REFLECTANCE

Skin color is one of the most immediately visible and most variable phenotypic traits in humans, and its variation has become imbued with significant implications in contemporary life (Chapter 14). Based on measurements of skin reflectance taken in many different world regions, skin color is regionally patterned. The overall pattern is that individuals with the most reflective (light pigmented) skin tend to have ancestry in populations that historically lived nearer the poles where the sun and the ultraviolet radiation it emits is weaker (**Figure 3.17**).

This patterning reflects a complex biology of adaptation due to natural selection. The lightness or darkness of our skin is strongly influenced by genetic

isolation Physical or social barriers between groups of people that discourage gene flow and encourage genetic drift, meaning groups become less similar over time.

selective pressure An external factor that reduces or enhances the ability of organisms to survive or reproduce in a specific environment.

stressor A factor that disrupts normal or healthy physiological processes in an individual's body.

Bergmann's rule The tendency for populations living in warmer climates to have more linear, less compact bodies than those living in colder climates.

Allen's rule The tendency for populations living in warmer climates to have slimmer bodies with longer arms and legs than those living in colder climates.

FIGURE 3.17

This map shows one estimate of clinal variation in skin color, based on measurements of skin reflectance for people identified as indigenous to that region.

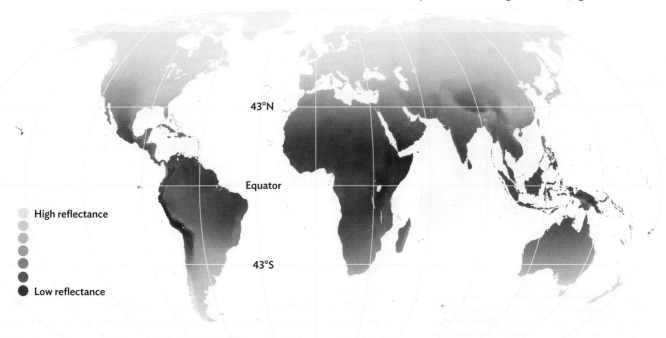

43°N

Equator

43°S

High reflectance

Low reflectance

FIGURE 3.18

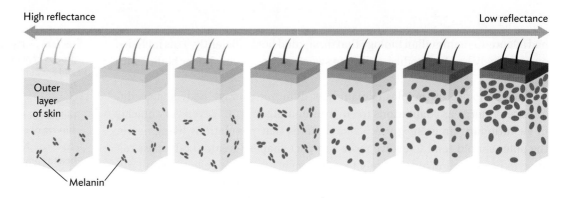

High reflectance   Low reflectance

Outer layer of skin

Melanin

There is a graduated relationship between melanin granules in the skin and skin reflectance. Low-reflectance skin is more protected from ultraviolet radiation damage but produces less vitamin D.

melanin A pigmented molecule that protects human skin from the harms of ultraviolet radiation.

traits that determine the density and distribution of melanin found in the outer layer of our skin (this pigment is also found in our hair and eyes) (**Figure 3.18**). Darker skinned individuals have more melanin granules in their skin and eyes, providing greater protection from burning, skin cancer, and other harms of sun exposure. For early humans in Africa, this was an important adaptation, especially because they were also relatively hairless.

Later, modern humans migrated out of Africa and moved toward regions—including northern Europe and northern India—where there are lower amounts of sunlight and diminished UV radiation. Here natural selection favored skin that could absorb more of the limited UV radiation to synthesize vitamin D, an important nutrient. A lack of vitamin D causes rickets, a serious and debilitating disease that weakens human bones. Lighter skin allows for greater vitamin D production in low-UV environments, which is the best explanation for why mutations for lighter skin variants were selected for in populations further from the equator, where the sun is furthest from the earth.

ADAPTATION TO DISEASE: ANTIMALARIAL PHENOTYPES

Diseases have been a major selective pressure in the human past, are in the present, and will continue to be in the future. When settling a new region or changing the landscapes in existing ones, humans can be newly exposed to deadly infectious diseases (Chapter 15). Existing genotypes that favor resistance to these can also emerge as adaptations. One of the deadliest diseases today is malaria. Caused by a parasitic microorganism transmitted through the bite of infected mosquitoes, the disease appears to have emerged prior to human migrations from Africa, probably initially transmitted to humans from apes. When humans began clearing and irrigating land for farming, this expanded the available ecosystem for the parasite's mosquito hosts, and they thrived in the expansion of standing water used to grow crops. The malaria parasite infects and destroys human red blood cells, causing terrible fevers and chills, and—most especially for children—can kill quickly if untreated (**Figure 3.19**).

Not everyone today, however, is equally susceptible to the effects of the malarial parasite. Some who are descended from populations in areas that have had malaria for millennia, such as the warmer and more humid parts of Africa, the western Pacific, and the Mediterranean, have inherited genetic variants that produce red blood cell phenotypes that are protective against malarial infection. In each region, different mutations emerged that provided survival advantages and then were inherited in higher frequencies by subsequent generations because of natural selection.

For example, one well-studied factor is a genetic variant of red blood cells in which some (but not all) cells are sickle-shaped rather than the more regular round shape (**Figure 3.20**). It results from a simple mutational switch from A to T in one gene, which changes a protein so that the hemoglobin (the main

FIGURE 3.19

Malaria remains a common disease in many tropical regions of the world, and efforts to eradicate it remain challenging. Here a temporary clinic in Malawi is testing for the signs of malarial infection, after severe flooding led to a rapid increase in the mosquito population that transmits the harmful parasite. This is one example of how extreme climate events matter for human biological evolution in the decades ahead.

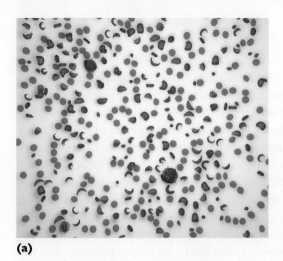

(a)

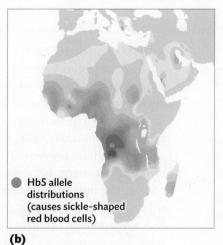

HbS allele distributions (causes sickle-shaped red blood cells)

(b)

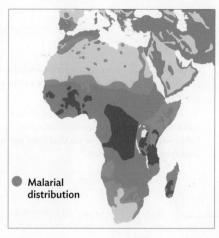

Malarial distribution

FIGURE 3.20

(a) Human red blood cells that are both sickle-shaped and fully round can be seen in this photo. Malarial parasites find it difficult to invade the sickle-shaped cells. Other blood components are stained purple. **(b)** The historic region of highest endemic (consistently present) malarial infection in Africa overlaps closely with high frequencies of sickle-cell genetic variants in populations living there.

part of blood cells) forms rigid clumps that change the cell shape. This mutation (called the HbS allele) was selected as an adaptation in malarial zones of Africa because it made it harder for the malaria parasite to attach.

The sickle-cell example also reminds us that crucial adaptations to extreme environmental stressors, such as malaria, often come with associated trade-offs. People who inherit two alleles for the sickle-cell gene (homozygous) have particularly strong protection from malaria, but they have difficulties with oxygenating the blood, resulting in a painful and debilitating illness called sickle-cell anemia. People who inherit just one sickle-cell allele (heterozygous) are protected both from malaria and from sickle-cell anemia. And people who inherit two alleles (homozygous) for the non-sickle-cell gene have no additional protection against malaria. So, selection continues to favor heterozygotes in areas where the mutation is present and malaria remains a deadly selection pressure. Once malaria is removed from a locality, so is the selective pressure that favors the ongoing maintenance of these sickle cell variants.

SECTION 3.4

HUMAN CULTURE AND MICROEVOLUTION

The evolved human capacity for cultural learning and accumulation of knowledge is itself a massive, species-defining biological adaptation that has allowed humans to adapt successfully in many different environments, and we explore this in detail in Chapters 5 and 6. In this section, we use the case of dairying to describe two concepts regarding how our genotypes, phenotypes, and culture interact to explain further the processes of human microevolution and how human biological variation is created: niche construction and coevolution. Along with the notion of developmental plasticity and of epigenetic inheritance described in Section 3.5, these concepts represent additional ways of thinking about evolution, collectively called the *extended evolutionary synthesis* (as they expand on the existing "modern synthesis" noted earlier). The relative importance of these processes in shaping human evolution is debated, but they provide frameworks to understand how culture and social arrangements might interact with microevolution to produce our varied human phenotypes.

extended evolutionary synthesis A revision and expansion of ideas about how evolution works to include mechanisms *beyond* natural selection, mutation, genetic drift, and gene flow.

coevolution A process in which two or more species mutually shape each other's evolutionary trajectories.

niche construction The process of an organism altering their adaptive environment, sometimes with consequences for that (and possibly other) species' evolution.

lactose tolerance or intolerance Ability or inability to digest milk sugar (lactose), related to the presence or absence of the enzyme lactase in the small intestine.

lactase persistence (LP) A genetic mutation that continues production of the enzyme lactase into adulthood, allowing digestion of lactose (milk sugar).

DAIRYING, NICHE CONSTRUCTION, AND COEVOLUTION

Coevolution refers to two species interacting in ways that shape the evolutionary trajectories of both. Niche construction refers to a species changing their own environment in ways that shift the pattern of selection they are subjected to. Niche construction can redirect or even reverse processes of natural selection and dramatically change the rates at which genes spread or disappear.

Humans have proven particularly masterful disruptors and creators of their own environments, because of their capacity to cooperate and deploy technology. The human invention and spread of farming as a subsistence strategy (Chapter 8) has been one of the most important niche adjustments for our species. Environment is meant in the broadest sense here: the climate, how we use the landscape to grow food or create cities, the technologies we create and use, and the institutions we rely on (like schools or hospitals). One example of niche construction and coevolution in humans relates to pastoralism, dairying, and using the milk of another species as a valuable adult food source. The growth of pastoralism transformed subsistence niches, and coevolution reinforced related genetic adaptations in both humans and cattle.

Babies and small children can digest lactose, the main sugar in mother's milk. However, for the majority of humans (like other mammal species), this ability is lost after weaning. Milk drinking in adulthood then leads to bloating, diarrhea, flatulence, and pain, a condition medically termed lactose intolerance. But some populations have high frequencies of lactase persistence (LP), a phenotype that includes an enzyme (lactase) that allows digestion of lactose (and so consumption of dairy products) with no discomfort as adults (**Figure 3.21**).

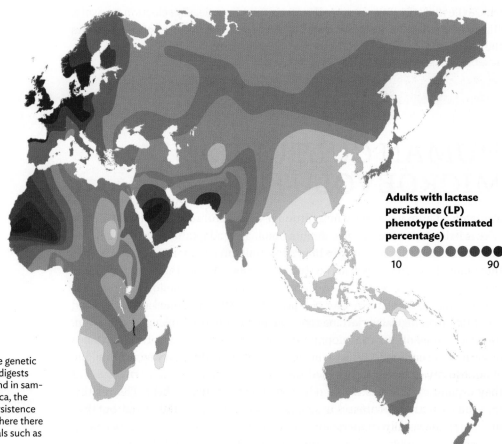

Adults with lactase persistence (LP) phenotype (estimated percentage)

10   90

FIGURE 3.21

Only about one-third of adult humans have the genetic variant that produces the lactase enzyme that digests milk, with the highest LP gene frequencies found in samples from Europe and some populations in Africa, the Middle East, and South Asia. These lactase persistence (LP) "hot spots" are mostly focused in areas where there have been long traditions of raising dairy animals such as cows, sheep, goats, or camels.

(a) **(b)**

FIGURE 3.22

(a) Polish people in eastern Europe and **(b)** Maasai people in eastern Africa both milk cows as part of their ongoing dairying traditions.

New LP mutations began to spread in both Europe and eastern Africa some 5,000 years ago, after humans were intensively domesticating cattle and other potentially milk-yielding animals such as camels. Ancient DNA analysis of excavated burials from a battlefield dated to 3,200 years ago in northeastern Germany suggests only a very small percentage of people—perhaps less than 10%—had the mutations for lactase persistence. Today, more than 80% of people living in that region have mutations that allow them to digest cow's milk as adults. This suggests the genetic variant was strongly and repeatedly selected for in recent millennia, likely because it was nutritionally advantageous.

Such traditions of dairying, learned and passed on over generations, show how learned human culture and innovations in technology are central to niche construction (**Figure 3.22**). Humans domesticated cattle initially for their meat. But over time they learned how to milk cows and increasingly adopted dairy products into their diets. Archaeological data from Europe, looking at the isotopes in ancient cattle teeth, suggests part of early dairying traditions included their weaning from the teat as very young cattle. This practice reduces available meat from those young cattle for human consumption but increases milk available from cows for other human uses. Interestingly, groups that adopted additional technologies for transforming the milk sugars to make them more digestible, such as fermenting milk to make cheese and yogurt, appear to have had less selective pressure for lactase persistence, such that their descendants have lower rates of the LP alleles today. But in other dairying groups, selection for LP alleles was created by consistent access to untreated dairy milk as a calorie- and protein-rich food source, and this is reflected in the higher level of LP gene variants seen today in places like Germany, Scandinavia, and Britain.

Cattle have coevolved with humans, as have many other domesticated animals and plants (Chapter 8). In northern Europe, genetic studies have shown that the local cattle populations in areas where human LP genes are most frequent are genetically more diverse (that is, more mutations related to variations in milk production have been retained). This indicates human-directed

FIGURE 3.23

This simplified chart shows an example of how human niche construction around dairying can dynamically drive human and cattle coevolution by selecting for certain alleles in both species.

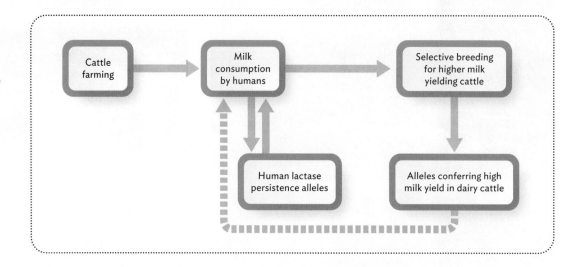

selection for alleles in cows produced more milk over time, in ways that affected selection for human LP genes, and so on (**Figure 3.23**).

Sometimes, humans have inadvertently created unwanted forces for coevolutionary selection through niche construction, such as the emergence of malaria in the wake of land clearing for tropical agriculture or infectious brucellosis from a more intimate relationship with domesticated cattle and their food products. Through urban development, deforestation, burning of fossil fuels, release of toxic industrial pollutants, and other activities that reconstruct our own evolutionary niches, we also continue to intentionally and inadvertently change the evolutionary trajectories of not just our own species but millions of others as well.

DEVELOPMENT AND PLASTICITY

So far, we have focused on how *genetic* variation underpins variation in our physical phenotypes (such as skin color or blood cell variants), and how that variation today reflects past adaptations to life in differing environments. But genetics do not account for all the phenotypic differences we see between people and across populations. Especially during childhood and adolescence, our genotypes interact with our environment to adjust our phenotypes. This can include exposures to varied climates, diseases, diets, and social conditions.

The same genotype can produce distinct phenotypes based on the conditions in which growth and development occur, through a process termed developmental plasticity. These often irreversible changes in the design of our individual bodies most commonly occur at critical points of growth: that is, in utero or when the skeleton is growing during childhood. These adjustments to the growth process allow human bodies to adapt to the specific challenges they will face within one's own lifetime—something that natural selection cannot do.

For example, around 85 million people live at high altitudes in the Tibetan and Ethiopian Plateaus and the Andes Mountains, where they face physiological challenges related to low oxygen (**Figure 3.24**). High altitude is usually

developmental plasticity The capacity of the same genotype to produce distinct phenotypes as a response to the environmental conditions under which development occurs.

FIGURE 3.24

People have lived in Phortse, a high-altitude (3,840 m) farming village on the Tibetan Plateau, Nepal, for millennia. Anthropologists have identified both inherited genetic and developmental adaptations that improve residents' ability to function in this and other similar low-oxygen environments.

defined as more than 2,500 meters above sea level. Humans started living in the high mountains in central Asia about 30,000 years ago, around 45,000 years ago in East Africa, and in the Andes in South America by 9,000 years ago. These populations today display genetic adaptations, such as proteins that allow oxygen to circulate better in the blood and protect against hypoxia or "mountain sickness" (in in the Tibetan Plateau) or that deliver more oxygen to growing babies during pregnancy (in the Andes).

But some important developmental adaptations that allow humans to function well at high altitudes happen during children's development, triggered by exposures to low-oxygen environments. In all three high-altitude regions, those who grow up there develop characteristic "barrel chests." These permanent alterations to the shape of the rib cage allow for greater lung size, in turn allowing deeper breathing and bringing more much-needed oxygen into the body. These developmental adaptations are not recent. Bio-archaeologists have found that skeletons of individuals buried at high altitudes in the Andes 1,000 years ago show the same larger and wider chest shapes as compared to skeletons of genetically related people who lived nearer to sea level.

Interestingly, there appears to be a trade-off associated with this process of developmental adaptation, as peoples in these higher-altitude environments tend to experience slower growth in early childhood, perhaps because more energy within the body is allocated to the development of the larger chest. But these processes also explain why peoples who are born and spend childhoods at very high altitudes are so much more effective physically in them. For example, the Tibetan Sherpas of Nepal, who have lived high in the Himalayas for thousands of years and spend their childhoods in lower oxygen environments, excel as elite mountaineers.

developmental adaptation A phenotype, resulting from developmental plasticity, that functions better under local environmental conditions.

GUATEMALA

North
America

DEVELOPMENTAL PLASTICITY: SECULAR TRENDS

Biological anthropologists sometimes refer to local biologies, meaning distinct phenotypes that reflect growing, reproducing, and aging in a very particular time and place with highly localized patterns of interacting stressors (like high altitude, dietary inadequacies, and disease exposures). When changes in environmental stressors—such as food availability—are widespread and sustained, these can be seen at scale over time as secular trends, or notable shifts in average biology through time within or across large groups of individuals.

Global changes in stature (height) over the last century are one of the best examples of a secular trend. Height is inherited to a large extent, and average differences in stature reflect histories of prior genetic adaptation to very different ecologies (such as cold or hot climates). But height, like other aspects of human growth and development, is also very plastic. With improving nutrition, better sanitation, and increasingly sedentary lifestyles, average height globally has been increasing.

A century ago, Mayan Guatemalan women had some of the lowest recorded average statures of any human group, and they still do today. But Guatemalan women born in 1996 are on average a dramatic 9 cm (4 in.) taller than those born a century before (**Figure 3.25**). The recent increase in average height among Maya and many other groups is mainly due to increased length of the long bones in the legs, related to diets providing better nutrition. Other secular trends are newly emerging in Maya (and almost all other groups globally), including higher body weights associated with changes from a diet high in fiber and vegetables to one with more salt, sugar, fat, processed foods, and sugar-sweetened drinks (including sodas and fruit juice). Anthropological studies of secular trends in

local biologies Phenotypic variation resulting from highly localized patterns of physical and social stress and their complex interactions.

secular trend A population-wide or group-wide shift in average growth patterns over time.

Maya Indigenous people who inhabit southeastern Mexico, Guatemala, Belize, El Salvador, and Honduras.

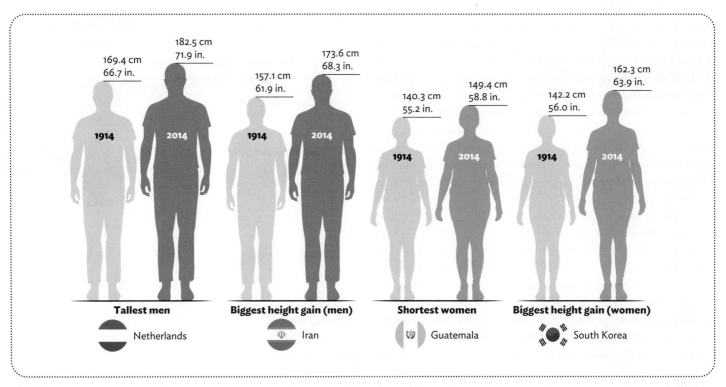

Tallest men — Netherlands
Biggest height gain (men) — Iran
Shortest women — Guatemala
Biggest height gain (women) — South Korea

FIGURE 3.25

Secular trends of increasing national average adult height for men and women have been observed in most countries over the last century, especially where nutrition is much better now than in the past. But genetic factors also continue to influence population differences in height, such as the differences between average heights shown here.

average bodies through time can thus reveal broad environmental, social, and cultural changes in societies.

Likewise, menarche (first menstruation) is a feature of biological maturation that is highly responsive to prolonged environmental exposures. In populations where the physical workload is heavy (such as farming communities) and nutrition is limited, bodies enter what is termed negative energy balance. Negative energy balance during middle childhood can delay the onset of menarche and the beginning of reproduction (**Figure 3.26**).

One of the highest median ages of menarche recorded by anthropologists was 18.2 years for a sample of Gainj women, part of a small community in the highlands of Papua New Guinea. This compares to median ages of menarche below 13 years that are now typical of people growing up in urban areas. At the time these estimates were made, Gainj practiced slash-and-burn agriculture on steep valley slopes; this hard physical work was performed by girls and women. They also provided most of the wood and water, collected wild foods and raw materials, and maintained house sites in addition to caring for children and the sick and dying.

Farming populations like the Gainj, with heavy workloads and more negative energy balances stressing the body, also tend to have lower levels of circulating reproductive hormones each month on average during adulthood, earlier menopause, and lower lifetime fertility (if not using contraception). But they also have lower rates of breast cancer and other cancers because of the reduced

menarche Onset of menstruation during adolescence.

energy balance The relationship between energy intake (through diet) and energy output (through workload or exercise).

FIGURE 3.26

Anthropologists have done many of their studies of the connections between energetic stress and human adaptation in places where agriculture is physically demanding and people must cope with chronic food shortages. But in urban settings today, young people subject to extreme physical demands in combination with food restriction, including competitive gymnasts and ballerinas, also have been observed to have delays in the onset of menstruation. This is an example of bodies going through the same developmental trade-offs in energy balance.

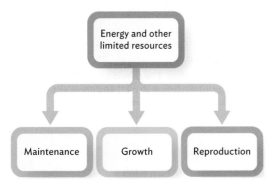

FIGURE 3.27

Life history is a means to explain how local human biologies result from trade-offs across the life span between different needs.

life history Patterns of growth and reproductive events across the life span.

reproductive hormone exposure. These are examples of how the outcomes of plasticity in reproductive biology during the development period have implications for our biology across our entire life span and for natural selection (in that it impacts the number of offspring we may produce). The study of these trade-offs across the life span, recognizing that the body can allocate limited resources (such as energy) in different ways with different costs at different life stages, is termed life history (**Figure 3.27**).

PLASTICITY: THE ROLE OF SOCIAL STRESS

Like physical environments, social environments impact phenotypes throughout development. Biocultural anthropologist Robin Nelson has been documenting and explaining the varied trajectory of gains in children's heights as they age (**Figure 3.28**). Mandeville, Jamaica, is a mountain town in a rural zone of bauxite mines and alumina processing. Many families struggle to get by. Nelson has measured and compared growth patterns of hundreds of children living with their families and those placed into three state-regulated homes after their families were unable to care for them.

Her measurements showed that 5–11-year-old children living in the residential homes grew more slowly and were relatively shorter when compared to those children of the same ages living with their families. Furthermore, when she compared the pattern of children's growth across the three residential homes, she found that the children in one home—called Guppy Pond—were growing as

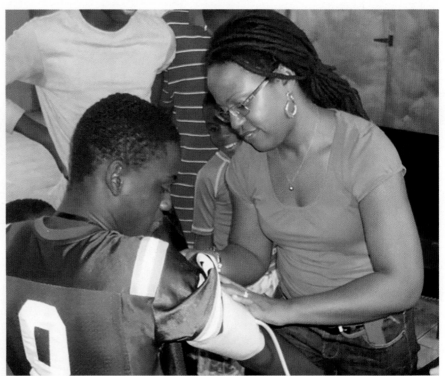

FIGURE 3.28

Biological anthropologist Robin Nelson (right) conducts fieldwork in Jamaica, testing theories of how social conditions like quality of childhood care affect human health, growth, and development.

well as the children living at home, while those in the other two homes were not. These discrepancies can't be explained by differences in genetics, physical environment, or health factors (such as access to food and nutrition), as the children of Guppy Pond and those in the other homes came from the same communities, and their overall amount of food and quality of diet were effectively the same.

After spending time observing at the homes, interviewing the children and the administrators at length, Nelson was able to develop a clearer picture of what the important differences shaping the children's growth trajectories might be. The director of Guppy Pond had created a local network of "parents" to support them emotionally and materially. Other policies also created more of a "home" feel for children, such as letting them eat if they wanted to outside set meal times. What was helping the children grow better was the feeling that they belonged and were valued.

Nelson observed that unrelenting exposure to stressors, such as the lack of adequate emotional care in childhood, can disrupt normal growth processes. While these sorts of systematic stress effects can impact anyone, they are especially deleterious (harmful) when they happen earlier in life, with lifelong consequences for health. The process by which such stress effects become our phenotypes, stemming from the way our societies are organized and our place within them, can be described as embodiment. That is, our physical bodies literally reflect and express the material, social, and political worlds in which we live.

EPIGENETICS: INHERITANCE AND ENVIRONMENTAL STRESS

Epigenetic mutation is a relatively new concept that blurs the boundaries between what we consider "genetic" and "nongenetic" determinants of human phenotypes. Exposure to environmental stressors can cause chemical modifications to our genomes that impact gene expression without changing the DNA sequence. These chemical alterations to DNA can also potentially be transmitted to offspring (**Figure 3.29**). A pregnant person's environmental exposures can trigger epigenetic changes not only in their own DNA but in that of their fetus. Offspring could also inherit epigenetic mutations from either biological parent if those alterations are maintained through meiosis and passed on via their gametes. If the reproductive cells of a fetus undergo epigenetic changes as well, it is also possible that these alterations could pass to a further generation. However, long human lifetimes and complex multifactorial phenotypes make it extremely difficult to demonstrate intergeneration epigenetic transmission in humans. But the possibilities open exciting new areas for anthropological research.

embodiment Incorporating and displaying in one's body the material and social worlds in which one lives.

epigenetic Refers to potentially heritable chemical modifications to genes that affect whether genes are switched on or off but do not alter the DNA sequence itself.

gene expression The process through which DNA codes for proteins that produce phenotypes.

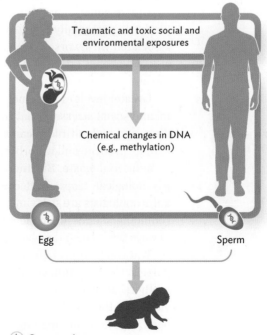

FIGURE 3.29

Many varied stressors, including social ones, can trigger methylation and other chemical alterations of DNA. The potential transmission of stress effects across generations is an emerging area of anthropological research on human variation.

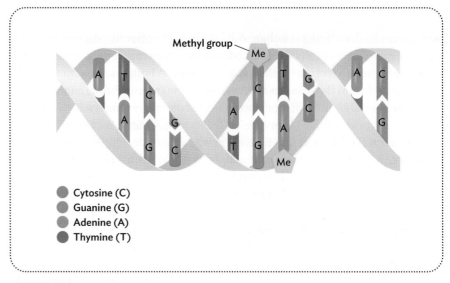

Methyl group — Me

Me

● Cytosine (C)
● Guanine (G)
● Adenine (A)
● Thymine (T)

FIGURE 3.30

Methylation of DNA strands involves the addition of "locking" methyl groups to either cytosine or adenine bases.

DNA methylation The chemical "locking" of sections of DNA, changing the way a gene codes proteins without changing the DNA itself.

trauma Profound, often ongoing, physical or emotional harms resulting from extremely stressful events or situations.

epigenome The full set of all epigenetic modifications to DNA as seen in a single cell.

DEMOCRATIC REPUBLIC OF THE CONGO (DRC)

Africa

One of the best-studied mechanisms of epigenetic change is DNA methylation (**Figure 3.30**). When methyl molecules attach to DNA base pairs, the genes associated with that locus can be locked into an "off" position. This gene suppression or silencing can then change fetal development and many other aspects of physiological function. These changed genotypes can be inherited for perhaps as many as three generations, but they do not seem to be passed down any further. DNA methylation can happen at any time in the life course. But the changes seem more likely and dramatic during embryonic development, which facilitates intergenerational transmission.

Unlike genetic mutations, methylation isn't random, and it rarely if ever produces potentially adaptive or positive benefits. Increased methylation is associated with worse health across the entire life span, including heightened risk of diabetes, asthma, some cancers, mental disorders, and even Alzheimer's disease.

Greater levels of DNA methylation are triggered by an array of environmental and social stressors that individuals experience. Famine, highly processed diets, and high altitudes can trigger epigenetic changes in DNA. So can exposure to airborne and waterborne toxins, such as cigarette smoke, air pollution, or industrial waste. But increased methylation also accompanies social and psychological trauma. Recognizing this has revolutionized how biological anthropologists are studying the relationship between genetics and social environment—such as how collective experiences of trauma can change epigenomes in ways that transmit negative biological effects across generations.

War can be especially traumatic, in many different ways. Biological anthropologist Connie Mulligan has been testing the relationship between Congolese mothers' adverse experiences while pregnant and the pattern of DNA methylation in their newborns. The Democratic Republic of the Congo (DRC) has been experiencing ongoing civil and international conflict since 1996. With brutal sexual assault used as a tool of war, many Congolese women both live with the fear of harm and must manage its aftereffects, which can include social ostracism. Half of the new mothers she tested had been refugees, and a quarter reported experiencing rape. Mulligan found that maternal trauma while pregnant was linked to specific gene deactivations in their children, through methylation, and these deactivations were associated with later-life health issues.

Other anthropological research has found similar effects of psychological trauma in other places. Anthropologist–physician Brandon Kohrt and his team worked with children conscripted into the 1996–2006 war in Nepal as soldiers. They have identified that early life adversity in children triggers epigenetic changes in regulatory genes relevant to reducing resistance to viral and other diseases, including cancer (**Figure 3.31**). But they have also observed some individual protective effects of psychological resilience, such as the belief in one's own abilities, against the genetic damage caused by childhood trauma as combatants. This suggests the complexity of epigenetic processes in shaping both local biologies and intergenerational health. Much is yet to be learned.

Cultural anthropologists are also starting to investigate how different groups interpret and apply the new types of evidence from epigenetic studies. For some Indigenous groups, this research is providing new means to speak out about health disparities as physical legacies of historical traumas resulting from oppression and cultural suppression. Indigenous Australians, for example, were traumatized through government policies of forced removals of their children from 1905 to 1967, referred to as the Stolen Generations. Researchers, communities, and policy-makers are working together to use epigenetic research to argue that addressing contemporary Indigenous health disparities is one means to provide reparation and healing from such historical traumas.

health disparity A difference in preventable disease, injury, or violence created through social disadvantage.

FIGURE 3.31

Brandon Kohrt (left) is shown here interviewing a former child soldier.

3 Human Variation

This chapter explains why humans—as regional populations and as individuals—are genetically similar, and yet have significant observable biological variation.

KEY TERMS
> ancestry
> genetic ancestry
> genotype
> microevolution
> phenotype
> population

3.1 | Basics of Human Variation: Genetics

Identify basic mechanisms of human genetic inheritance.

• Human cells contain DNA with two primary functions: to provide the genetic codes that allow our bodies to grow and repair, and to provide the basic template for genetic inheritance and unique reorganizations of DNA from two individuals through sexual reproduction.

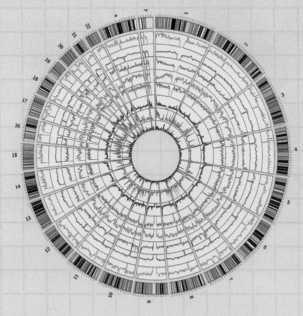

KEY TERMS
> allele
> amino acid
> base
> cell
> chromosome
> codominant
> crossing over
> DNA
> DNA replication
> dominant
> gamete
> gene
> heterozygous
> homologous
> homozygous
> meiosis
> mitochondrion
> mitosis
> molecule
> multifactorial
> nucleus
> organelle
> polygenic
> protein
> protein synthesis
> recessive
> ribosome
> sexual reproduction
> somatic cell
> zygote

3.2 | Mechanisms of Microevolution

Distinguish the four forces of microevolution.

* Human populations are continuously evolving, as allele frequencies change from one generation to the next via the processes of microevolution.

* Genetic mutation refers to changes in the DNA sequence, which results in a new allele and a modified protein being produced. The mutation may be advantageous, neutral, or deleterious depending on the environment.

* Natural selection is the process by which a population becomes better adapted to a specific environment over time, as better adapted (fitter) individuals produce proportionately more offspring in the next generation.

* Genetic drift refers to random changes in gene frequencies between one generation and the next and is most influential when populations are smaller or more isolated. It causes populations to become less genetically similar over time.

* Gene flow is when populations become connected or merge. It increases genetic diversity within a population and also makes interacting populations more similar over time.

KEY TERMS
> adaptation
> advantageous mutation
> clinal variation
> deleterious mutation
> fitness
> founder effect
> gene flow
> genetic bottlenecking
> genetic drift
> genetic mutation
> isolation
> locus
> macroevolution
> modern synthesis
> natural selection
> neutral mutation
> species

3.3 | Human Variation and Genetic Adaptation

Explain why humans from different regions are similar genetically, despite looking different.

- Humans from various world regions may look different, but humans overall are genetically similar (that is, our species has low genetic diversity). This is because we are a young species recently descended from a small population of African ancestors and because human populations today are rarely isolated.

- Genetic adaptations to localized stressors (such as climate) and genetic drift explain some observed differences in human phenotypes, such as skin color or body shape. These adaptations arose independently in different world regions at different times.

KEY TERMS
> Allen's rule
> Bergmann's rule
> melanin
> selective pressure
> stressor

3.4 | Human Culture and Microevolution

Identify how human cultural practices influence microevolution.

- Through their capacities for culture and technological innovation, humans constantly reshape the environments relevant to their own evolutionary trajectories; this is known as niche construction.

- Humans interact with other species in ways that shape the evolutionary trajectories of both, a process called coevolution.

KEY TERMS
> coevolution
> extended evolutionary synthesis
> lactase persistence (LP)
> lactose tolerance or intolerance
> niche construction

3.5 | Development and Plasticity

Describe how a single genotype can result in highly varied phenotypes.

- Human phenotypes reflect genotypes, but they also reflect the influence of varied environmental and social exposures during and beyond early childhood and adolescent development. Useful permanent changes in how the body functions in response to local stressors are referred to as developmental adaptations.

- Recent studies show that stress exposures in our lifetimes, including extreme psychological trauma, can reshape which genes are activated or not. These chemical attachments to our DNA sequences are referred to as the epigenome, are often harmful to health, and can potentially be passed to the next generation.

- Accelerating technologies and new knowledge about human genetic variation is expanding information on recent or more distant histories of groups, including revealing ongoing legacies of past harm. Anthropologists are well placed to support communities as they determine the best ways to share and apply the information.

KEY TERMS
› developmental adaptation
› developmental plasticity
› DNA methylation
› embodiment
› energy balance
› epigenetic
› epigenome
› gene expression
› health disparity
› life history
› local biology
› Maya
› menarche
› secular trend
› trauma

4

Primates: Our Closest Relatives

When biological anthropologist Stephanie Meredith first started observing the highly social ring-tailed lemur (*Lemur catta*) in southwestern Madagascar, an island off the eastern coast of Africa, she was fascinated by a highly unusual pattern of female behavior. Living in noisy troops of around 30 individuals, ring-tailed lemurs spend their days foraging for tamarind fruit, huddling for company, and sunbathing (**Figure 4.1**). Their vocalizations are some of the most complex among nonhuman primates, with purrs to communicate contentment, wails to signal predators approaching, and clicks to signal location to other members of their group. Yet, unlike humans, females hold much of the societal power.

Females are social and aggressive, approaching others often. Males spend more effort in marking their territories with scent glands. The species is unusual among primates (including humans) because the females in the group are often power-dominant over males, feeding on the best fruit first and biting, chasing, and hitting to maintain their positions.

Meredith credits her own childhood as a queer girl who didn't want to display expected "girly" behaviors as part of what attuned her to the question of why and how gendered behaviors develop and whether they're a uniquely human phenomenon (Chapter 11). She wanted to know how these dominant female behaviors developed in lemur society.

Meredith uses zoological animal observation techniques to identify and decode differences in young male and female lemur behavior and identify at what stage of reproductive maturity these differences emerge. Each lemur is identifiable by the colored dye she has squirted on its back; by the time it wears off, she knows them all so well that the dye is no longer needed. She follows each lemur in 30-minute rotations, recording everything they do and who they

LEARNING OBJECTIVES

4.1 What Is a Primate?
Identify the physical and behavioral traits that primates share.

4.2 Diversity of Living Primates
Classify primates into groups based on key physical and behavioral traits.

4.3 Fossil Evidence and Primate History
Explain how observations of primate traits today are used to interpret fossils and trace primate evolution.

4.4 Primates in Peril
Evaluate human impacts on, and responsibilities toward, other primates.

HUMANS AND PRIMATES

Anthropologists view other primates as important evidence of who we are as a species and where we come from because they are most like us. Many types of evidence explore this relationship, including observing living primate behavior and anatomy, genetic studies, and examining fossil evidence of primate pasts.

vocalization Sounds that transfer information to others.

REPUBLIC OF
MADAGASCAR

Beza Mahafaly
Special Reserve

Africa

Ring-tailed lemur
(*Lemur catta*)

FIGURE 4.1

Ring-tailed lemurs are often seen huddling together. This species is found in the wild only in southern and southwestern Madagascar. Meredith's research has focused on lemurs in the Beza Mahafaly Special Reserve where ongoing conservation efforts are providing some protection for threatened lemur species.

interact with. Over time, repeatedly following the same individuals over and over, she can build a detailed picture of the social behaviors of young lemurs within the group (**Figure 4.2a**).

Meredith also crawls under trees and trails behind younger members of the group, bagging their feces. Later, back in the lab, using methods from the medical field of endocrinology, she extracts measures of their reproductive hormones from their waste, giving her additional information about their physical maturity (**Figure 4.2b**). Combining data from observations with data on an individual's level of maturity allowed Meredith to make a key observation. She has found that young male and female lemurs living in the wild don't exhibit many differences in behavior before adulthood. Only after reaching adulthood does the female-dominant **hierarchy** develop in lemur society.

hierarchy A social arrangement among primates that is based in variations of power, with some individuals having dominance over others.

FIGURE 4.2

(a) Biological anthropologist Stephanie Meredith observes lemur behavior in Madagascar. **(b)** Feces collection allows Meredith to measure the reproductive maturity of individual lemurs, based on hormones excreted in the feces.

(a)

(b)

Meredith's research with ring-tailed lemurs is just one example of the broader reason that anthropologists study nonhuman primates: to understand more about what it means to be human. We focus on primates because they are our closest living relatives and we share relatively recent common ancestors. Understanding our common ancestry not only helps unravel the human evolutionary past but also helps us better understand—and question—humans' social patterning today (**Figure 4.3**).

In this chapter, we explore the remarkable diversity of primates, examining the classification of primates (including humans) according to their anatomy, biology, and behavior. We then examine what the available fossil evidence tells us about how and why they evolved into so many diverse species. Finally, we consider the conservation status of primates today. Increasingly, anthropologists who study living primates are recognizing that part of their ethical mandate is protecting the species they study.

FIGURE 4.3

When we observe primates, we are often seeing ourselves. Chimpanzee "tea parties" were a major attraction at New Zealand zoos into the 1970s, highlighting the way humans often anthropomorphize apes. Some letters to the editor of the local newspaper complained that the apes were "naked."

WHAT IS A PRIMATE?

Lemurs, along with apes, monkeys, and humans, belong to the taxonomic group called primates. Primates are primarily found in tropical and subtropical regions of the world, though in the past they had a wider geographical distribution (**Figure 4.4**). Estimates vary on the number of living primate species; the best guess is that there are 250–300 different species of primates alive today.

lemur A type of primate found only in Madagascar; mostly nocturnal and tree-dwelling species in which females are often socially dominant.

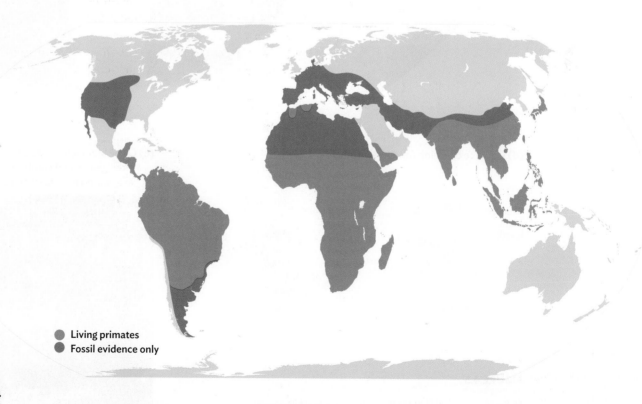

- Living primates
- Fossil evidence only

FIGURE 4.4

This map shows the distribution of living and extinct primate species.

derived trait An anatomical feature characteristic of the group in which it occurs that differentiates it from other, closely related groups.

diurnal Active during the day.
nocturnal Active during the night.

pair bond A social arrangement of residing and mating with only one other individual at a time.

Primates share biological and behavioral characteristics, known as *derived traits*, that were not present in the last common ancestor of primates and other groups of mammals but were presumably present in the ancestor to all primates. Examples of derived traits in primates include grasping hands, nails (instead of claws), large brains, and high levels of care given to infants within a highly social society (**Figure 4.5**).

But despite sharing derived traits, primates are tremendously variable. Body size ranges greatly, from the smallest pygmy mouse lemur weighing 30 grams (g) or about 1 ounce (oz) to the largest adult male gorilla weighing 160 kilograms (kg) or about 350 pounds (lb). Some primates are *diurnal*, while others are *nocturnal*. Some live in large social groups (chimpanzees and baboons), while others are mostly solitary (orangutans). Some live in female-dominant societies (ring-tailed lemurs), while in other species males dominate the social interactions (gorillas). Some form *pair bonds* where both parents raise their offspring (gibbons), while others live in one male/multiple female groups (gorillas) or multiple male/multiple female groups (baboons). Still others interact only for the purposes of mating (orangutans), with limited degrees of male contribution to raising offspring.

(a) Lack of anatomical specialization

(b) Prehensile hands and feet, usually with opposable thumbs and big toes

(c) Flattened nails, rather than claws, and sensitive fingertips

(d) Reliance on vision (and less on smell)

(e) Large brain relative to body size, high intelligence, and complex social lives with varied mating systems

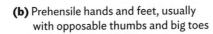

Reduced snout length

Elongated snout

versus

Monkey

Dog

FIGURE 4.5

Defining anatomical features shared by primates are illustrated.

Given this diversity, a key thing to note about primates as a group is that they are also defined by being relatively generalized; that is, there isn't a single feature we can point to that is shared by all primates and would also distinguish them from all other mammals. Rather, it is a combination of varied features that defines them.

PRIMATE ANATOMY

Primates today are found in a variety of habitats, including dense tropical forests, woodlands, swampy areas, grasslands, and even deserts. Some walk above the substrate (tree limbs or the ground), while others primarily leap from tree to tree, slowly climb throughout the forest canopy, or move by using their arms and suspend themselves underneath tree limbs and branches. Some primates are arboreal and live primarily or exclusively in the trees; others are terrestrial and only occasionally climb into the forest canopy; and still others, like the ring-tailed lemurs introduced earlier, range between both environments. How primates get about—their mode of locomotion—in these varied environments is reflected in anatomical differences that are shaped by generations of evolution selecting for energetically efficient bodies for a given environment.

For example, quadrupedal primates rely on all four limbs for locomotion. But even among quadrupedal primates there are subtle differences in anatomy reflecting natural selection. Arboreal quadrupeds have a greater risk of falling and thus need their center of gravity to be closer to the tree limbs they walk on, which is why their arms and legs are short in comparison to terrestrial quadrupeds. They also tend to have small bodies to avoid breaking the tree limbs. Terrestrial quadrupeds are not at risk of falling, so they are larger and have longer limbs that allow them to move further with each step they take. Knuckle-walking is a specialized form of quadrupedal terrestrial locomotion (seen in gorillas and chimpanzees) in which the palm of the hand doesn't touch the ground (as it does in most other terrestrial quadrupedal primates), and instead they support their upper body on one of the finger joints.

Quadrupedal leapers use all four limbs nearly equally to propel themselves from branch to branch and from tree to tree. They also tend to be small in size, and they have hands and feet adapted for gripping. Vertical clingers and leapers use their hind limbs to jump from one tree to another. These primates have a distinct body type with long, powerful hind limbs that generate their leaping force, long spines, and powerful grasping hands and feet.

Suspensory primates generally move slowly and deliberately underneath the branches using all four limbs and, in some species, a prehensile tail. Some suspensory primates get around by brachiation, or swinging from branch to branch using their arms (such as seen in gibbons). These brachiators have particularly long arms, a wide rib cage, and mobile shoulder, elbow, and wrist joints that help them swing.

Humans are the only living primates who are bipedal, meaning we habitually walk upright on two legs. A primate with relatively longer legs can move a greater distance on the ground with the same amount of energy; this is why bipeds tend to have long legs. In contrast, suspensory brachiators tend to have long arms, which allow them to swing farther with the same amount of effort.

Despite these differences in habitats and subsequent ways of moving about, all primates share *some* anatomical adaptations that reflect an arboreal

generalized Describes species that have not been shaped by evolution to perform one specific function very well but rather have anatomies that can do many things well.

arboreal Primarily living in the trees, which could include on the trunks of trees or on the branches.

terrestrial Primarily living on the ground.

locomotion How primates typically get around on the ground or in trees, reflected in their anatomy as shaped by evolution.

quadrupedal Reliant on all four limbs to move about.

suspensory Moving through trees by hanging from branches.

brachiation Swinging underneath from branch to branch.

bipedal Habitually walking on two legs.

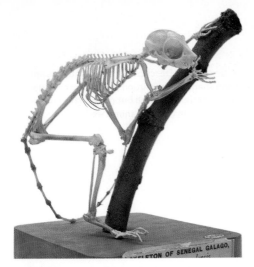

FIGURE 4.6

This skeleton of a galago shows the long, powerful hind limbs typical of quadrupedal primates.

Raccoon

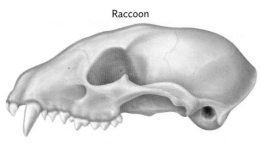

Lemur

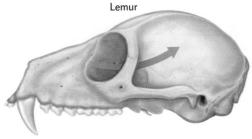

Gibbon

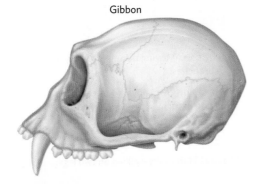

FIGURE 4.7

Three variations in the structure of bone surrounding the eye are depicted. In the raccoon (which is not a primate), the eye is exposed on the side of the skull. In the lemur, the eye is encircled by a ring of bone (postorbital bar). In the gibbon, the area around the eye is completely enclosed by bone (postorbital closure).

past, meaning primates originally evolved for life in the trees. There are three important locomotor features common to most primates that suggest that the first primates were arboreal.

First, primates have hind-limb dominated locomotion, which means the primate body has a center of gravity that is shifted backward, allowing for greater control of balance in the trees. The long hind limbs anchor powerful muscles that allow primates to propel themselves further and more efficiently by leaping. The legs are the primary means of locomotion. As such, there is a tendency toward a more upright posture. A typical primate is very different from a cow or horse whose limbs are much more even in length (**Figure 4.6**).

Second, primates have prehensile or grasping hands and thumbs, which are adapted to grasp tree branches and also to acquire food (see Figure 4.5b). Most primates (except humans) also have feet with opposable big toes. All primates also have a separate bone in the upper limb (the "collarbone" or clavicle) that acts as a strut to support greater mobility in the upper arm and shoulder joint, which allows primates to reach and swing with their upper body.

Third, most living primates have nails instead of claws on the backs of their fingertips, providing protection for the sensitive pads at the ends of their fingers (see Figure 4.5c). Some primates also have a precision grip, which helps them to grasp and handle even very small and delicate objects, such as insects or nuts.

Primates also have unusually good vision, as sight is the primary sense used to engage the world around them (in contrast, say, to dogs, who rely more heavily on smell). The reduced reliance on their sense of smell is reflected anatomically in the smaller snout of many (but not all) primates. Greater visual acuity, in contrast, is reflected in other characteristic anatomical features.

First, primate eyes are positioned toward the front of the skull with binocular stereoscopic vision, which helps them to accurately judge distances because the fields of vision of each eye overlap. This vision is also crucial to the safety of primate species that leap between branches, and it enables hunting for insects and lizards that some species feed on. Binocular vision helps humans to do tasks like cook a meal, park a car, walk up and down stairs, or conduct surgery. Second, many primates (including humans) have color vision, which is useful for detecting the ripeness of fruits or locating insects against a dense forest canopy. Third, all primates have a postorbital bar, a ring of bone that surrounds and protects the delicate eye from damage (**Figure 4.7**). In some primates, the area around the eye is completely enclosed by bone, as in humans, thus protecting the back of the eye from damage.

Primates also share a set of dental and digestive adaptations that allow them to process a wide variety of foods, such as fruits, leaves, tree gums/saps, and insects. One of these adaptations is their generalized dentition. Some animal species have teeth that can only process very specific types of foods, such as fruit or insects or meat. Shark teeth, for example, have been shaped by evolution to very effectively tear meat, but they cannot chew the meat (they just swallow it whole) and they cannot process plant material.

Primate teeth are much more versatile. Their dentition combines simple incisors, whose function is simply to bite off food pieces, and molars that can break down a variety of foods into smaller pieces that are easier to digest. Even in primates that have evolved to eat very specific types of foods, this generalized dentition is still evident (**Figure 4.8**). Many primates, including humans, have dentition especially suited to omnivores, meaning they can eat a diet of both plants and animals.

(a)

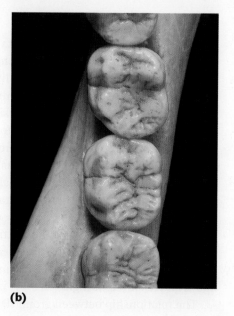
(b)

FIGURE 4.8

The generalized dentition of primates is reflected in their molars, which are not adapted for processing only a specific type of food. However, dietary adaptations are reflected within the general primate omnivore pattern: **(a)** shows molars with higher cusps and **(b)** shows molars with low, rounded cusps with more surface wrinkles.

hind-limb dominated locomotion A form of movement in which the body is propelled primarily through the power of the hind limbs.

prehensile Having the ability to grasp.

opposable The ability of the thumb or big toe to be placed against the other digits to grasp and hold objects.

precision grip The ability to touch the end of the thumb to the end of one or more fingers, allowing the handling of small objects.

binocular stereoscopic vision The result of two eyes working together to perceive depth and register an object as three-dimensional.

postorbital bar A strut of bone that encircles and protects primate eyes.

generalized dentition Having teeth that can process a diversity of foods, rather than being specialized for processing one type of food.

omnivore One whose diet is composed of both plant and animal food sources.

PRIMATE BEHAVIOR

Primates have relatively large brain sizes relative to body size compared with other mammals. This trait is associated with an enhanced level of cognitive ability (sometimes called "intelligence"). Primates also tend to live socially with others, though in highly varied social arrangements (**Figure 4.9**). This means that primate young are raised within a social context, interacting with others, and can develop strong and often enduring connections to those around them as they mature. Primate mothers have few offspring at a time and space them apart. Parents (particularly the mother, but sometimes also the father) or other

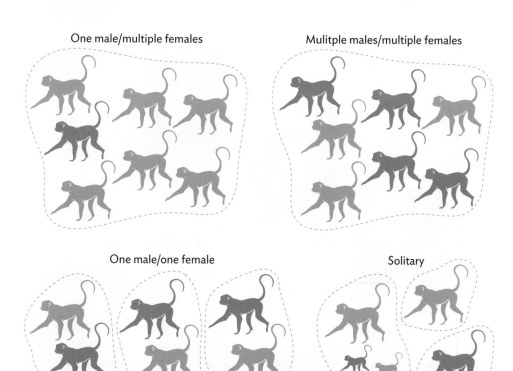

Female
Male

FIGURE 4.9

Some commonly observed primate social arrangements are illustrated.

alloparents Individuals, who are not the biological parents, that care for offspring.

group members acting as **alloparents** then invest considerable resources in provisioning, rearing, and protecting those offspring.

In solitary primates, the females live in groups with their dependent offspring and males live alone, only coming into contact with others for mating. The next smallest social grouping consists of pair bonds of one adult male, one adult female, and their offspring, as found in gibbons. Such groups are more common in small territories that one male can easily defend and monitor. One male/multiple female groups, such as gorillas and howler monkeys, consist of an adult male, multiple adult females, and their collective offspring, with groups of unaffiliated males vying to take over from the dominant male. Such groups are more commonly found in regions where food sources are widely dispersed. Finally, multiple male/multiple female groups, the largest grouping that includes baboons and macaques, consist of multiple adult males and adult females and all their immature offspring. In such groups, competition for both mates and resources is high.

The relationship between group size and habitat suggests a basic theory of why primate social arrangements vary so much: they reflect adaptations to the availability of food and mates for both males and females in a given location.

life history Patterns of growth and reproductive events across the life span.

Life history refers to the pattern of growth, reproduction, and aging throughout the course of an individual's or species' lives. The life histories of primates are extended overall, with larger primates such as apes and humans spending years as juveniles (**Figure 4.10**). Primate gestation times are typically

FIGURE 4.10

Primate life histories are compared across species.

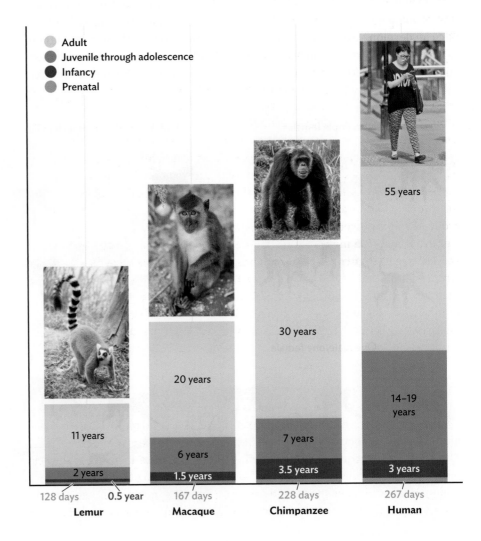

- Adult
- Juvenile through adolescence
- Infancy
- Prenatal

Lemur — 128 days, 0.5 year, 2 years, 11 years

Macaque — 167 days, 1.5 years, 6 years, 20 years

Chimpanzee — 228 days, 3.5 years, 7 years, 30 years

Human — 267 days, 3 years, 14–19 years, 55 years

longer than those of other animals, and they feed their young on mother's milk for longer as well. The extended gestation period allows greater in utero brain development. The extended period of infancy and childhood, and with it the relative delay of reproduction, allows primates to learn how to navigate their complex social worlds, rather than relying solely on instinctual behavior. The overall life span is also longer in primates than in most other animals of similar body size. Long life spans allow for more offspring to be born in a slow-growing species, supporting life-history strategies that emphasize having few young and investing in them heavily.

DIVERSITY OF LIVING PRIMATES

Thus far we have discussed the traits that distinguish primates from other mammals. In this section, we examine how primates are organized in relation to one another. Taxonomy is the science of classification, and it provides one means to understand how diverse life forms relate to each other. The actual evolutionary and historical relationships between different species are referred to as phylogeny, and a good taxonomy should reflect the true phylogeny of different species.

Formal scientific taxonomic classifications date back to the late 1700s, when the system of binomial nomenclature was first devised by Carolus Linnaeus to name and organize individual organisms. This system is still widely used today, as is the practice of developing taxonomies heavily based on anatomical (rather than behavioral) distinctions between groups of animals. But increasingly, genetic data are used to refine the overall arrangements of relationships among species. In other words, descriptions of similarities based on observed features are being replaced with assessments of genetic ancestry.

Anthropological researchers—combining studies of bodies, brains, behavior, and genes—worked for decades to identify key ways that primates can be grouped and arranged, particularly using features related to how distinct species are adapted to move around their environments, locate food, and eat. As you can see in **Figure 4.11**, all primates are organized into two major groups: strepsirrhines and haplorhines. Strepsirrhines are considered more primitive than haplorhines, by which we mean closer in anatomical form (and possibly in behavior) to the earliest primates. Understanding these groupings is very important to biological anthropologists, because it is the crucial framework for interpreting the fossil evidence of early human evolution (Chapter 5).

STREPSIRRHINES

Strepsirrhines include lemurs, galagos, and lorises. They exhibit a generalized mammal body pattern that doesn't seem to be clearly adapted to any specific niche. Many are nocturnal, and they have large eyes to be able to see at night. The word strepsirrhine itself refers to the shape of the nose and nostrils, reflecting a stronger emphasis on a sense of smell compared to other primates. As a group, they have longer snouts and a moist rhinarium (a hairless patch of skin connecting the nose to the mouth) with a split upper lip, as we see in many other

taxonomy A scientific system to define and organize species in relation to each other by grouping individuals into like types.

phylogeny The evolutionary history of a species and its relationship to other taxonomic groupings.

binomial nomenclature The "two name" system of naming and defining a species within a genus, for example, *Homo sapiens*.

strepsirrhine One of a group of wet-nosed, mainly arboreal primates with toothcombs; this group includes the lemurs, galagos, and lorises of Africa and Asia.

rhinarium A hairless patch of skin connecting the nose to the mouth.

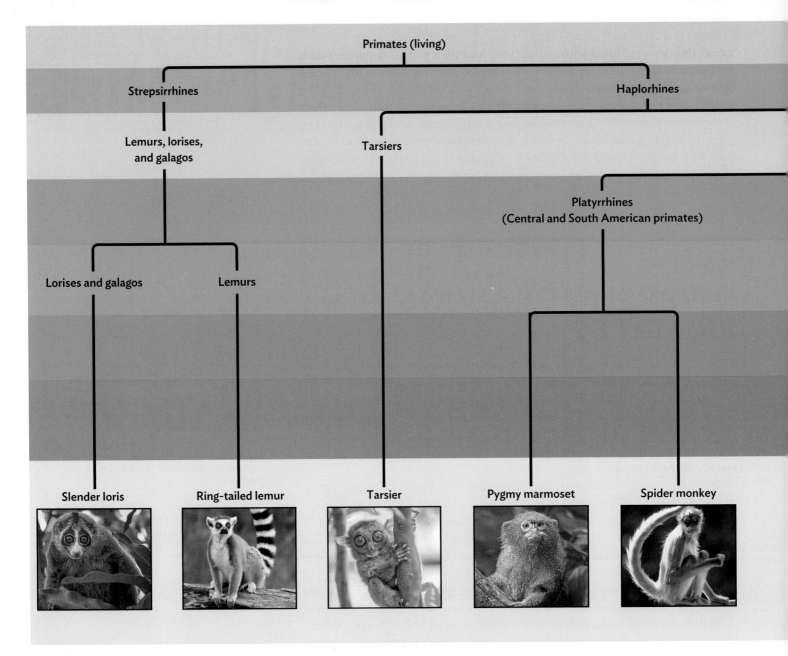

FIGURE 4.11

Simplified version of a standard taxonomy divides the primates into two main groups and multiple smaller groups. Primates (and people) are often described as being either from the "Old World" (Europe, Asia, and Africa) or the "New World" (the Americas). This terminology reflects historically incorrect European beliefs they "discovered" other continents, even though many peoples had long lived there. Increasingly, the term "Neotropical" is used to refer to the monkeys of North and South America. A similar term for the primates of Europe, Africa, and Asia is lacking, however.

mammals such as cats and dogs (**Figure 4.12**). Their brains are relatively small, and they live less complex social lives in comparison to haplorhine primates. Strepsirrhines give birth to larger litters than other primates; females have a two-horned uterus, multiple pairs of nipples, and a simpler form of placenta; and they are seasonal breeders, only mating at limited times during the year. These are all so-called **primitive traits** because they are present in other, nonprimate mammals and likely reflect an original, shared adaptation in an early ancestor of many mammal groups.

primitive trait An anatomical feature inherited from an ancestral species that may have given rise to many descendant species through time.

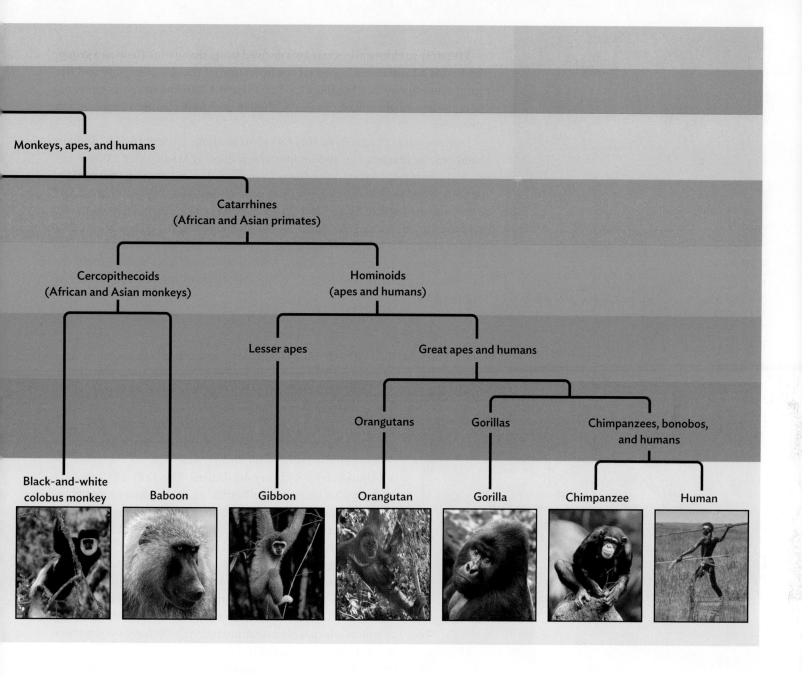

Monkeys, apes, and humans

Catarrhines
(African and Asian primates)

Cercopithecoids
(African and Asian monkeys)

Hominoids
(apes and humans)

Lesser apes

Great apes and humans

Orangutans

Gorillas

Chimpanzees, bonobos,
and humans

Black-and-white
colobus monkey

Baboon

Gibbon

Orangutan

Gorilla

Chimpanzee

Human

(a)

(b)

FIGURE 4.12

The two major groups of primates can be differentiated by their noses. **(a)** A typical "wet-nosed" strepsirrhine such as this ring-tailed lemur has a longer snout with an incomplete upper lip (although this may be difficult to see) and a moist rhinarium. **(b)** In a "dry-nosed" haplorhine such as this Hanuman langur, the snout is shorter, and the upper lip completely divides the nose from the mouth and is not moist.

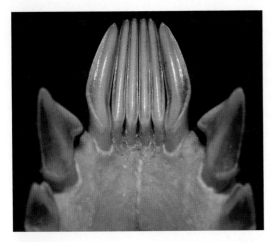

FIGURE 4.13

This toothcomb of a living ring-tailed lemur shows the lining up of four lower incisor teeth and two canine teeth in the mouth to form a comb.

The strepsirrhines also share two derived traits that define them as a group. The first is a toothcomb, a special configuration of the lower incisors and the canine teeth that is used to groom the fur (**Figure 4.13**). The second is a grooming claw instead of a nail on the second digit of each foot, also used for grooming purposes.

Lemurs range in size from tiny (30 g) to medium (10 kg or 25 lb) and are found only in Madagascar. Before humans arrived in Madagascar 2,000 years ago and accelerated extinctions, there were much larger lemur species, weighing perhaps 60 kg (150 lb). Galagos (also called bushbabies) live only in central Africa, subsist on insects and tree gums, have very large forward-facing eyes, and are agile leapers and climbers that live entirely in the trees. Lorises are also small-bodied arboreal insectivores, but they move slowly through trees by using all four limbs rather than by leaping. Lorises are found only in Asia. They are the only primate with a venomous bite, used in disputes with other slow lorises (**Figure 4.14**).

HAPLORHINES

Haplorhines include all the other primates: tarsiers, monkeys, apes, and humans. The word haplorhine means "dry-nosed," because members of this group lack the characteristic moist rhinarium or "wet nose" of the strepsirrhines. They also tend to be larger in size and larger-brained than strepsirrhines (tiny tarsiers are the exception), and they exhibit more complex social behaviors, have better vision, and rely less on a sense of smell for survival.

Almost all haplorhines are diurnal. This shift from a mostly nocturnal to increasingly diurnal existence was probably an important development during the primate adaptive radiation, as it expanded the range of environmental niches primates could explore and exploit.

There are several other derived traits shared by haplorhines. For example, the eye is completely surrounded by a cup of bone ("postorbital closure") rather than just a postorbital bar. Haplorhines are distinctive for having a single complete uterus; other mammals typically have two or more separate or only partially fused uterine organs. Combined with a more developed placenta, this means more nutrients can be exchanged between the mother and developing fetus. Pregnancies that are better nourished support infant brain development, underpinning the greater cognitive capabilities and more complex social lives of haplorhine primates. Furthermore, the upper lip is not attached to the nose by a rhinarium. This freeing of the upper lip allows for a greater degree of facial expressions facilitating nonverbal communication, which is important to larger-brained, more cognitively sophisticated primates.

FIGURE 4.14

The nocturnal omnivorous slow loris (shown here: *Nycticebus coucang*) found in Asia moves very slowly compared to other primates. It has foot and hand adaptations allowing it to hang at length from branches.

FIGURE 4.15

This tarsier is shown during the day, but its large eyes for nocturnal vision are evident. Note the vertical clinging posture and presence of nails on its hands and feet.

toothcomb An anatomical feature of strepsirrhine teeth in which the lower incisors and canine teeth are modified to form a comblike structure.

grooming claw An anatomical feature of a single claw instead of a nail on one foot digit.

haplorhine One of a group of "dry-nosed" primates, variously terrestrial and arboreal; this group includes tarsiers, monkeys, apes, and humans.

adaptive radiation A time period during which the number of species increases rapidly, resulting in much greater diversity.

prosimian A taxonomic classification that recognizes the more primitive appearance of tarsiers and all strepsirrhines but ignores the derived features linking tarsiers to other haplorhines.

platyrrhine A monkey of South or Central America (sometimes referred to as a Neotropical primate).

catarrhine A monkey or ape of Africa or Asia (and in the past throughout Europe as well).

There are three major divisions of haplorhines. The first includes the tarsiers, small-bodied primates that live only in the forests of Borneo, the Philippines, and Sulawesi in southeastern Asia. They are agile vertical clingers and leapers who live as nocturnal predators of insects and small vertebrates such as lizards, with extremely large eyes to support their night vision (**Figure 4.15**). Strepsirrhines (lemurs, lorises, and galagos) and tarsiers are sometimes together referred to collectively as **prosimians**. They share the features of a special claw for grooming, a two-chambered uterus, relatively poor color vision, and they are more similar to the earliest primates than other living species.

The two other major divisions of haplorhines are the platyrrhine primates and the catarrhine primates, a distinction based on the configuration of the nostrils (**Figure 4.16**) and number of premolar teeth. **Platyrrhines** have broad, flat noses with wide spacing between round nostrils that point to the side, as you can observe in howler monkeys, spider monkeys, and capuchin monkeys that you might encounter on a visit to a zoo. They all have three premolars in each quadrant of their dentition. **Catarrhines**, including humans, have closely set and narrow nostrils that point downward. They all have two premolars in each quadrant of their dentition.

Platyrrhines

Catarrhines

FIGURE 4.16

A primary anatomical distinction between platyrrhines and catarrhines is the shape and orientation of their nostrils.

FIGURE 4.17

The prehensile tail of the larger platyrrhines, such as this Geoffroy's spider monkey in Belize, enables them to grasp tree branches to move about more easily in the dense forest.

FIGURE 4.18

(a) A baboon yawns, revealing the four cusps on each molar. **(b)** Alignment of the cusps in clear rows is characteristic of African/Asian cercopithecoids.

FIGURE 4.19

A bonnet macaque uses expandable cheek pouches to store fruit; this adaptation is seen in many cercopithecoids.

Platyrrhines live only in South and Central America, hence the term Neotropical monkeys. Many platyrrhines are arboreal quadrupeds with mixed diets that include fruits and leaves. The larger of these monkeys have prehensile tails, which can be used as a fifth appendage for grasping branches and moving throughout the forest canopy (**Figure 4.17**). Some platyrrhines have prehensile tails, but this trait is not found in any other primate group.

Catarrhines are generally larger than platyrrhines, have larger brains, are more intelligent, are all diurnal, have more complex social groupings, and are found on the African and Asian continents. Catarrhines are further subdivided into cercopithecoids (African and Asian monkeys) and hominoids (apes and humans).

Cercopithecoids include both terrestrial (ground-dwelling) and arboreal (tree-dwelling) monkey species. Anatomically, they have characteristic bilophodont molars that set them apart from other primates, meaning the cusps (usually four) on their back teeth are aligned in clear rows (**Figure 4.18**).

(a)

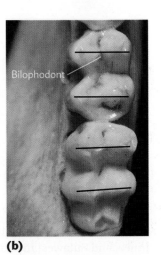

Bilophodont

(b)

Some are classified as cheek-pouch monkeys, so named because they can store food inside their cheeks in pouches. Examples include baboons (found in Africa) and macaques (found in Asia) (**Figure 4.19**). Other catarrhine monkeys, such as the colobus monkey in Africa and the langur in Asia, are leaf-eaters. They are arboreal and mainly active at night, and they rely on leaves as a dietary staple. As such, their molars have evolved sharper crests for shearing the tough plant material they eat. This grouping of monkeys has also evolved a multichambered stomach that allows them to better digest their tougher, leaf-heavy diets.

Formation of the two major groups of haplorhines (platyrrhines and catarrhines) resulted from a dramatic isolation event, creating an opportunity for a rapid adaptive radiation of platyrrhines in Central and South America. Current genetic, anatomical, and fossil evidence suggests all platyrrhines descended from a single monkeylike species from Africa that reached the coast of South America by chance. The best current hypothesis is that a small founding group floated across the Atlantic on eroded patches of forest about 30–40 million years ago. Africa and South America were closer together and sea levels were likely lower at the time, thus making this journey less harrowing.

This history of isolation between primate populations in the two hemispheres also explains why only monkeys (and not apes) are found in the

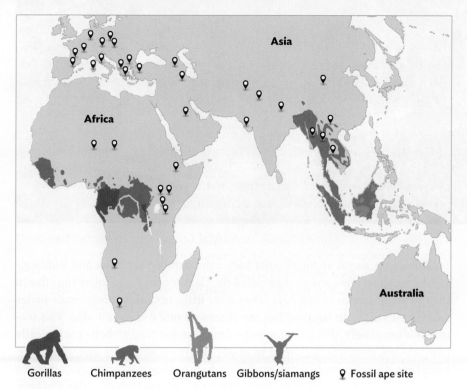

Gorillas Chimpanzees Orangutans Gibbons/siamangs ♀ Fossil ape site

FIGURE 4.20

The geographic distribution of living and extinct ape species is shown.

Americas: Apes evolved in Africa, Europe, and Asia only after monkey colonies became established in the Americas.

The founding group of monkeys that made it to South America must have been small, and accordingly they were unrepresentative of the population of monkeys living in Africa at the time. This created the opportunity for genetic drift, changing the range and frequency of alleles in the new population (Chapter 3). Additionally, differences in available food sources and predators in South America would have created new selective pressures, advantaging different traits in teeth, fur, or mating behavior. In other words, natural selection would have favored different adaptations on each continent. The isolation of the new colony prevented gene flow via mating between the two populations. Quickly, new species arose in the Americas, including some with the distinctive prehensile tails that greatly assist with getting fruit and other foods in dense tropical forests.

The taxonomic grouping hominoids includes the so-called lesser apes (gibbons and siamangs), the great apes (orangutans, chimpanzees, bonobos, and gorillas), and humans. Today apes are found only in sub-Saharan Africa and Asia, but in the past they had a much wider distribution, including in Europe (**Figure 4.20**).

Among living primates, hominoids are the largest in body and brain size and the most distinct from the original primates. All hominoids, including humans, are diurnal. They are also distinguished by a more vertical body posture with long arms relative to their legs, a broad chest and face, and lack of a tail.

Hominoids have a distinctive Y-5 cusp pattern on their lower molars, which is useful for chewing a variety of foods. This is a very important identifier for those who study the fossil record of primate evolution, because a single molar can easily differentiate a monkey from Africa or Asia, with its bilophodont molars, from a hominoid with its Y-5 molars (**Figure 4.21**).

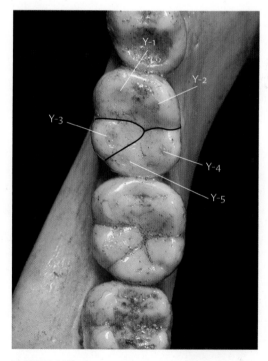

FIGURE 4.21

The Y-5 cusp dental pattern seen in some ancient primates is also seen in living apes today. It is called a Y-5 pattern because the grooves between the cusps on the lower molars (back teeth) are roughly in the shape of the letter Y and there are usually five cusps on the teeth. In contrast to apes, monkeys generally have four cusps aligned in rows.

FIGURE 4.22

FIGURE 4.22

Endangered Western hoolock gibbons (*Hoolock hoolock*, a lesser ape) seen here vocalizing. Males and females of this species are not sexually dimorphic but they are different colors.

sexual dimorphism The condition when males and females of a species are significantly different in size.

Hominoid social arrangements vary considerably. Gibbons and siamangs are the smallest apes, sometimes called the "lesser apes," and today they live in the forests of southeastern Asia. They have little sexual dimorphism—males and females differ in coloring but are otherwise much the same size. This feature is often observed in pair-bonded animals, and indeed gibbons are typically pair-bonded, meaning they tend to reside and mate with only one other individual at a time. Because of this, evolution does not favor larger male body sizes like it does in species with high competition over access to mates (like gorillas). The males in some of these species contribute significantly to raising their partner's offspring, such as helping with provisioning and guarding of a shared territory (**Figure 4.22**). Lesser apes are best known for their brachiation, which is among the most acrobatic form of locomotion in primates.

The great apes include orangutans, gorillas, chimpanzees, and bonobos. The orangutan (genus *Pongo*) is the only great ape found outside Africa today, living in the forests of Borneo and Sumatra in southeast Asia. Orangutans are slow, suspensory climbers (**Figure 4.23**) with significant sexual dimorphism (males may be up to twice the weight of females). They are the most solitary apes, meaning adult females and males each have their own territories. While

FIGURE 4.23

A very large male orangutan shows the cheek pads that develop as the orangutan matures.

males may defend females that they can mate with in overlapping territories, they otherwise have limited contact. Living much of their lives separately from females, males use a "long call" that can travel at distance through the forest canopy, advertising themselves to females or warning other males to stay away.

Gorillas (genus *Gorilla*) and chimpanzees and bonobos (both genus *Pan*) are all found in sub-Saharan Africa. All three spend considerable amounts of time on the ground and in the company of others. They move using knuckle-walking while on the ground. Gorilla social groups consist of females, their offspring, and typically one mature adult male (the silverback) that leads the group and reproduces with the females resident in that group.

Chimpanzee and bonobo societies consist of large multiple male/multiple female groups that often split apart into smaller parties, called a **fission–fusion society**. Chimpanzees, like gorillas, are sexually dimorphic, with the males noticeably larger than females. Chimpanzees mate more indiscriminately (that is, with more different partners) than other apes. Relatedly, while the bond between females and their offspring is strong, chimpanzee males do not particularly assist in caring for infants within their groups. Meanwhile, one interesting feature of bonobo society is the extent to which sexual activity is used to mediate social relationships and is not an act performed simply for reproductive purposes, much like with humans.

Genetic studies confirm that chimpanzees and bonobos are our closest living relatives (**Figure 4.24**), sharing some 99% of our DNA. Both chimpanzees and bonobos display learned social behaviors associated with high levels

fission–fusion society A form of primate social group with relatively unstable group membership in which different groups form and dissolve over time depending on circumstances such as food availability.

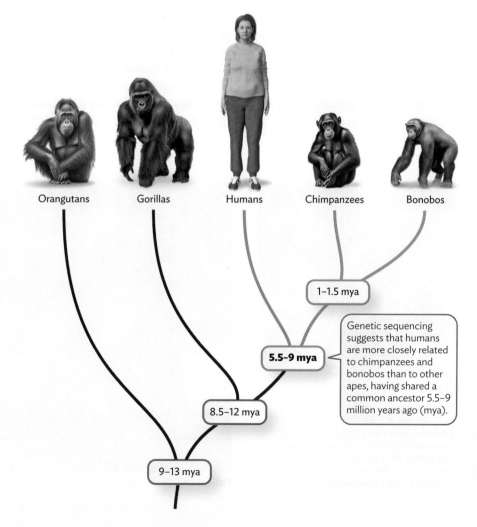

Orangutans   Gorillas   Humans   Chimpanzees   Bonobos

1–1.5 mya

5.5–9 mya

8.5–12 mya

9–13 mya

Genetic sequencing suggests that humans are more closely related to chimpanzees and bonobos than to other apes, having shared a common ancestor 5.5–9 million years ago (mya).

FIGURE 4.24

Relationships among great apes and humans are based on comparisons of their DNA sequences. The benefit of using genetic evidence to infer species relationships is the ability to estimate when those species diverged in the past, as shown here.

FIGURE 4.25

A chimpanzee uses leaves to collect water.

of cognitive ability. They can devise and use tools to do tasks such as "fishing" termites out of mounds with sticks, cracking open nuts with rocks, and soaking up drinking water with leaves (**Figure 4.25**). Gorillas have been observed using sticks to forage for food, a very basic form of tool use, but not to the same extent as chimpanzees and bonobos.

Biological anthropologist Jill Pruetz and her team have been observing chimpanzees at Fongoli in Senegal, in western Africa, since 2005. The Fongoli chimpanzee community of around 30 individuals lives in a mosaic of woodland, grassland, bamboo, and gallery forest habitats. Pruetz's team has recorded many instances of hunting behavior over the years, with chimpanzees using sharpened sticks to pierce smaller nocturnal primates such as bushbabies who are sleeping inside trees during daylight hours (**Figure 4.26**). At Fongoli, females are observed to hunt much more using tools than males.

Even though meat isn't central to their diets, chimpanzees at Fongoli and elsewhere will sometimes band together to hunt and then share the meat they obtain with other group members. Chimpanzee hunting can include coordinated barking sounds not heard in other activities. More barking spurs more chimpanzees to join and increases the likelihood and speed of capturing elusive prey (such as small monkeys).

(a)

FIGURE 4.26

(a) A sharpened stick (held by biological anthropologist Jill Pruetz) that was used by a female adult Fongoli chimpanzee to hunt for meat. **(b)** One of the most prolific recorded hunters is Nickel (left).

(b)

Food sharing, in general, is an interesting feature of chimpanzee behavior that also speaks to group cooperation. It occurs for a variety of reasons, such as helping feed relatives, building relationships with nonrelatives, or preemptively reducing harassment from members of other groups. These behaviors observed in chimps (hunting and food sharing) in many ways predict what we see in early human ancestors, for whom the importance of meat to brain development resulted in a feedback loop whereby greater intelligence and cooperation were required to survive.

Despite humans' close genetic and anatomical relationship with the living great apes, we are distinctive in being fully committed bipeds and fully reliant on language. Nonhuman primates typically use varied vocalizations, such as barks, to transmit warnings or other information. One important difference between this type of communication and human communication is that the latter includes recursion. Recursion refers to the idea that any communication can be made longer and more detailed by adding other units into it. For example, the "blue house" can become "the big blue house" and then "the big blue round house" and so on. All human languages include this property of recursion, but nonhuman primate communications appear not to include this feature. Although all primates use vocalizations to communicate, and some apes have been taught basic sign language, it remains true that recursive language is one of the defining uniqueness attributes of our species. In fact, language is so central to our being that it is defined as one of the four basic subfields of anthropology (see Chapter 7).

cooperation When members of a group work together for common or mutual benefit.

recursion Communication that can be made longer and more detailed by adding more language units to it.

SECTION 4.3

FOSSIL EVIDENCE AND PRIMATE HISTORY

Biological anthropologists rely on fossils to identify extinct species and use the evidence of preserved anatomy to understand these species' relationships with other extinct species as well as with living descendant species. They can also combine primate fossil evidence with that from other extinct animals to reconstruct the environments they lived in and what foods they ate. Combined with the information above about the comparative anatomy and behavior of living primates, fossils tell us the where and when of primate evolution and provide some information on why certain primates evolved the adaptations we see today, and ultimately the origins of us humans.

Fossilization is a process for preserving the shapes of bones and teeth that happens only under very specific environmental conditions (**Figure 4.27**). Upon death, an organism needs to be buried very quickly in an oxygen-free environment, such as when a flood layers sediments over a body before animals can scavenge it. Over time, the inorganic materials in bone or teeth are replaced by other minerals (such as silica and iron), forming what is essentially a stone replica. Because tooth enamel is more durable than bone, they are more often preserved. Accordingly, much of what we know about primate evolution is based on teeth, which happen to preserve rich information about a past organism's life. The organic component of a fossil can sometimes contain DNA, in which case the fossil can then also potentially serve as a source of genetic evidence in anthropology research. However, DNA preservation is rare in ancient fossils, in which usually little to no organic matter is left.

fossilization The formation of a stone copy of a bone or tooth by slow replacement of inorganic material by other minerals in the environment.

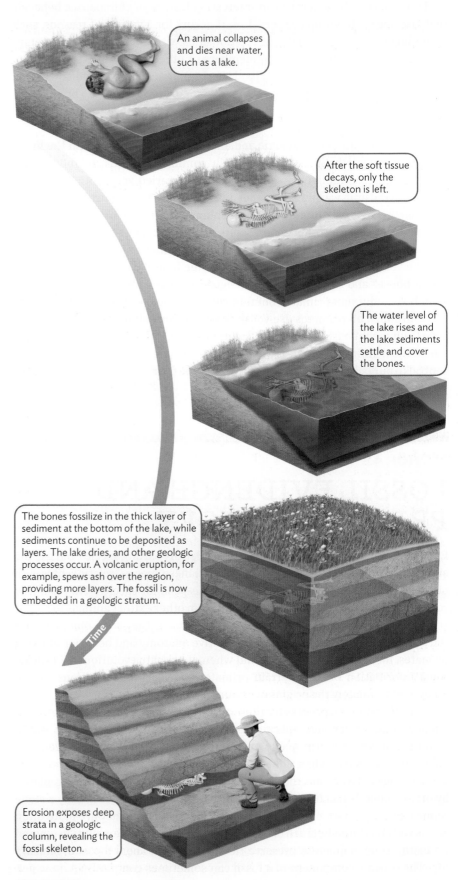

FIGURE 4.27

This depiction shows a common means of how fossils are created and discovered.

There are many challenges associated with generating conclusions from fossil evidence. Because fossilization occurs only under a rare set of circumstances, only certain places and time periods are documented in the fossil record, making our picture of the primate past very incomplete. Many species have come into being and gone extinct without leaving any fossil evidence at all. Finally, to construct primate histories from fossils, we also have to know where fossils are located in the geological timescale (**Figure 4.28**). Dating materials that are now inorganic generally requires relative rather than absolute dating methods (as discussed in Chapter 2), which means scientists can often place fossils only within very approximately dated time periods, based on geological changes in the landscapes in which the fossils are embedded.

USING THE PRIMATE PRESENT TO INTERPRET OUR PRIMATE PAST

Given these limitations of fossil evidence, how—on the basis of a very few specimens—do we know what long-extinct primate species were like when they were alive? How can we determine whether they lived in trees, if they were sexually dimorphic, if they walked upright, what they ate, how they mated, or if they had culture?

For this, anthropologists rely heavily on comparative studies of living species to develop theories about their function and their behavior. Specifically, the comparative method takes observations from living primates—some of which are observable in both extinct and living species (e.g., tooth shape), and some of which can only be observed in living species (e.g., what they eat, how they mate)—and uses these observations to generate predictions about ancient species we cannot observe.

For example, anthropologists might compare the molar tooth shapes of several living species with different diets (some that eat fruits, some that eat leaves, and others that eat insects) to draw conclusions about the relationship between diet and tooth shape. Those conclusions are then used to generate a prediction about the diet of an extinct species based on the appearance of their fossilized teeth. The same comparison can be done for just about anything we are interested in knowing about in the past, as long as the behavior is related to some aspect of hard tissue anatomy.

Let's run through a few of the ways anthropologists reconstruct details of past species using this approach.

Body Size and Dimorphism

Body size is relatively easy to reconstruct in extinct species, even on the basis of very limited fossil remains. We know from measuring contemporary species that the sizes of primate body parts are highly intercorrelated, which means that as one part of the body gets larger, so do most others. Taller, heavier primates tend to have longer bones, thicker vertebrae, bigger skulls, and larger teeth than smaller primates.

This relationship is robust enough that a species' body size can even be estimated from a single tooth. Knowing the overall body size of past species then tells us about such things as their metabolism or what they ate (for example, no primate over 500 g [1 lb] can subsist solely on insects). The larger the body, the more calories the species would need for growth and maintenance. Body size also provides clues about the life history of the species, such as gestation length, the period of lactation, and the length of adolescence. Larger primates tend to live longer lives and have more extended periods of development than smaller primates.

ERA	PERIOD	EPOCH
Cenozoic	Quaternary	Holocene
		Pleistocene
	Tertiary	Pliocene
		Miocene
		Oligocene
		Eocene
		Paleocene
Mesozoic	Cretaceous	Late
		Early
	Jurassic	Late
		Middle
		Early

FIGURE 4.28

The geological timescale is a nested set of time divisions. Eras are divided into periods and then periods are further divided into epochs. The story of primate evolution begins at the end of the Cretaceous period with the earliest primates likely evolving during the Paleocene epoch.

Another thing biological anthropologists want to establish about past primates is their degree of sexual dimorphism. On the basis of what we see in living primates, sexual dimorphism of body size, where males are much larger than females in body mass, suggests that males in that species are in competition with one another for reproductive access to females. Less sexually dimorphic species tend toward pair bonding, and in some such species the males invest more in their young.

Both sexual dimorphism and large canine teeth in modern primates are associated with greater male–male competition and behaviors like aggressive fighting over females, male rank hierarchies, mate guarding, more seasonal breeding, and less male investment in caring for young, as well as physiological features such as higher testosterone levels.

Locomotion

When we start to consider human evolution specifically, one key feature of our species is that we are terrestrial and walk upright on two legs, thus freeing our hands. The influence of this anatomical and behavioral trait on our lifestyles is enormous. So in interpreting fossil species, reconstructing their locomotor adaptation is especially valuable. Locomotion also tells us much about how members of a species find food, find mates, and avoid predation (being eaten by other species). We know from studies of living primates that larger primates, for example, are more terrestrial (living on the ground) because their weight cannot be supported as easily in the trees. But larger primates are also less vulnerable to predation, so living on the ground is less risky than it would be for smaller animals.

Diets

Studies of contemporary primates provide a rich understanding of the way primate dietary adaptations, such as relying on insects (insectivores), fruit (frugivores), or leaves (folivores), should be reflected in fossil species. Smaller primates today, like the tarsier, have lower overall energy requirements but must eat high-quality foods that they can digest quickly. Larger primates, like the gorilla, have higher overall energy requirements but can eat lower-quality foods that they can digest slowly. For this reason, larger primates tend to eat more leaves and smaller primates tend to eat more insects. The incisors of frugivores are larger than those of folivores because larger incisors allow them to bite off larger pieces of fruit. The incisors of gum-eaters (gummivores) and insectivores are large, thick, and forward-projecting, so that they can gouge trees that exude sap or find insects buried in tree branches and trunks. Relationships also exist for the chewing teeth, or molars. Insectivores have pointed molar cusps for piercing the tough exoskeletons of insects. Folivores have molars with cusps that form shearing crests when they chew to cut leaves into smaller pieces. Frugivores tend to have molars with low, rounded cusps to crush pulpy fruits into mush before swallowing. Ultimately, these adaptations increase the surface area of the food being eaten to ease digestion and the absorption of calories.

Primates with larger chewing muscles also have larger muscle attachment sites that are visible on the skull. Taken to the extreme, for example, an overly large temporalis muscle will result in a sagittal crest, a crest of bone that runs from the front to the back of the skull, most dramatically seen in gorillas (**Figure 4.29**). These large muscles are needed to chew tough and fibrous foods like wood stems, mature leaves, or underground plants like tubers. So, based on living primates, when a fossil shows evidence of a sagittal crest, we can generate predictions about the diet of that species even though it is now extinct.

insectivore One whose diet is composed mainly of insects, such as a tarsier.

frugivore One whose diet is composed mainly of fruits, such as an orangutan.

folivore One whose diet is composed mainly of hard-to-digest leaves; examples are mostly monkeys and apes of Africa and Asia.

gummivore One whose diet is composed mainly of tree sap and gums (usually also with insects); examples are some lemurs and marmosets.

sagittal crest A prominent ridge of bone projecting upward from the skull that supports extremely strong jaw muscles associated with powerful biting or chewing.

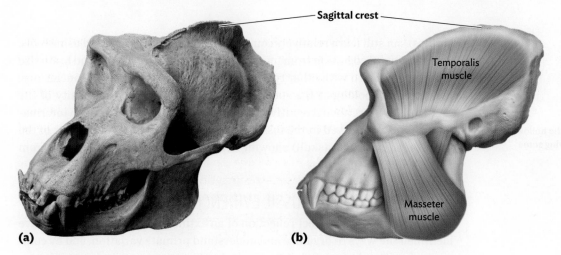

Sagittal crest

Temporalis muscle

Masseter muscle

(a)   (b)

FIGURE 4.29

(a) This side view of a gorilla skull shows a sagittal crest that extends along the top of the skull around the back. **(b)** This crest allows for the anchoring of the large temporalis muscle that together with the masseter muscle help with chewing tough and fibrous plant materials.

Social Behavior and Cognition

Cognitive abilities, such as are reflected in **tool use**, can also be very roughly estimated from fossils that indicate cranial capacity, and thus brain size. Here the "chimpanzee model" is important because it shows that—with an average cranial capacity of 400 cubic centimeters (cc), as compared to the human average of 1400 cc—bonobos and chimpanzees are able to devise and use rudimentary tools, communicate regularly with others in their group through gestures and vocalizations, and learn these behaviors from others. Thus, cranial capacity in fossils is often applied as a means to identify which fossil species may have been capable of more advanced cognitive tasks than others. The forms of tools that living apes produce are used to help identify what may have been very early rudimentary tools in the archaeological record. Bonobos (and other primates) use stones to crack palm nuts, leaving behind characteristic flake patterns referred to as "choppers" (**Figure 4.30**). Such documented behavior helps identify the differences between simple rocks and possible stone tools associated with fossil finds.

Notably, brain size of an individual, fossil or otherwise, does not directly equate to cognitive ability ("intelligence"). Humans with differently sized brains display no innate differences in capacity for tool use, language, or learning. Similarly, some species with smaller brains than humans (such as chimpanzees or

tool use Manipulation of objects to achieve a goal.

(a)

(b)

FIGURE 4.30

(a) Bonobos use stones to crack palm nuts. **(b)** Capuchins in Brazil have been observed smashing rocks but not using them as tools (suggesting that identifying the earliest tools from flaked stone needs to be done with extreme caution).

endocast A fossilized model of the hollow space inside a skull, often preserving some details of brain anatomy.

gorillas) can still learn relatively complex tasks, such as making and using tools. So, estimates of cognition from measures such as cranial capacity and brain size must be combined with other types of evidence to draw any such conclusions. For example, looking at the specific structure and surface complexity of the brain tells us more about cognitive abilities than brain size alone. Such information is rarely preserved in the fossil record, however, though endocasts of the inside of the cranium (skull) showing brain structures have been found from possible human ancestors.

PRIMATE PASTS: THE FOSSIL EVIDENCE

No living primate is a direct reflection of an extinct one. But now that we have identified the ways to organize and understand primate variation, and by comparing fossil evidence to what we know about contemporary primates, we can make some reasonable guesses about primate history. This then sets the stage for understanding our own early evolutionary history as tool-using, upright-walking primates. Current fossil evidence suggests species with characteristic primitive traits of primates first appear between 65 and 85 million years ago (mya), as depicted in **Figure 4.31**. This is a time period from which fossil

FIGURE 4.31

The best-known primate fossils, the species they are believed to reflect, and their placement in geological time are shown.

ERA	PERIOD	EPOCH	DATES	MAJOR EVENTS	EXAMPLE SPECIES
Cenozoic	Quaternary	Holocene	0.01 mya–present	Villages, domestication	Homo sapiens
		Pleistocene	1.8–0.01 mya	Genus Homo radiation	Homo erectus, Neanderthals, Homo sapiens
	Tertiary	Pliocene	5.3–1.8 mya	First definite hominins	Ardipithecus, Australopithecus, Paranthropus
		Miocene	23–5.3 mya	First apes	Proconsulids, Sivapithecus, Gigantopithecus
		Oligocene	33.9–23 mya	First haplorhines	Aegyptopithecus
		Eocene	56–33.9 mya	First definite primates	Adapids, omomyids
		Paleocene	66–56 mya	First likely primates	Plesiadapiforms

evidence is especially difficult to discover, and the earliest primates are not expected to look much different from other early mammals living at the same time. Therefore, identifying the earliest primate is very difficult. Still, some clues do exist.

The estimated date of 65–85 million years ago, derived from primate DNA research combined with the scant fossil evidence, places the first primates at the start of the Tertiary period (see Figure 4.31). But the story of primate evolution starts earlier in the preceding Cretaceous period when climate changes created the conditions that allowed primates to emerge. The end of the Cretaceous period was a time of massive global changes in plants and animals, most significantly the extinction of the dinosaurs (probably following a massive meteor event that upended Earth's climates), an expansion of flowering plants, and a resulting adaptive radiation of both mammals and insects into new niches. Flowering plants were central here because they provided two new food sources for small mammals: fruit and the insects who consumed the plants' nectar. There were also fewer predators of these early mammals after the dinosaurs disappeared.

The first primates evolved from a shrew-like mammal that had the capacity to eat different foods because of its generalized dentition. We cannot currently know for sure what the first primate mammals were, but possible candidates include the highly successful and diverse plesiadapiforms. They first appear about 66 million years ago in what is now the western United States, western Europe, Asia, and possibly Africa, during the Paleocene epoch (66–56 mya). These quadrupedal mammals had grasping hands and feet and some species had nails instead of claws, both primate traits (**Figure 4.32**). But they also had sideways-facing eyes, very specialized teeth (probably for eating fruit), a relatively small brain, and no postorbital bar around the eye, all traits that are not shared by primates today. No plesiadapiforms exist today. They survived for some 10 million years before going extinct, around the same time the planet got hotter and wetter and tropical forests expanded.

After this time, during the Eocene epoch (56–33.9 mya), we see fossils with traits that are from undisputed primates. The Eocene fossils suggest that an array of small species had evolved that share very primitive versions of features still seen in some living primates today, including forward-facing eyes and relatively large brains for their body size.

One proposed explanation for the development of forward-facing eyes, called the visual predation hypothesis, suggests that Eocene primates evolved as predators, hunting insects attracted to the flowers at the terminal ends of branches by using an improved sense of sight with forward-facing eyes. An alternative hypothesis, called the angiosperm radiation hypothesis, proposes that early primates focused more on fruits or a combination of fruits and insects, an idea supported by the observation that most primates today are not predatory hunters. According to this hypothesis, the rapid expansion of both flowering plants and primate species coincided, and the proliferation of fruits in trees was the primary factor driving early primate evolution.

Biological anthropologists group the roughly 200 identified Eocene primate species—found across modern-day Africa, Europe, Asia, and North America—into two main families: one that was larger and diurnal (the adapids), adapted for slow climbing and similar to modern-day lemurs, and one that was smaller and nocturnal (the omomyids), adapted for leaping and similar to modern-day galagos and tarsiers. However, whether these species are ancestral (directly related to) any living primates, including humans, is not currently known.

FIGURE 4.32

Carpolestes simpsoni was a plesiadapiform that lived around 56 million years ago. It had grasping hands and feet, nails on opposable digits, and teeth suggestive of a fruit-based diet, all indicating it as a possibility for a very early primate.

plesiadapiform One of an early group of mammals that lived during the Paleocene epoch and were very closely related to the first primate.

Paleocene epoch A division of the geological timescale that lasted from 66 to 56 million years ago and is associated with the adaptive radiation of early mammals closely related to primates.

Eocene epoch A division of the geological timescale that lasted from 56 to 33.9 million years ago and is associated with the adaptive radiation of early primates, in particular the adapids and omomyids.

visual predation hypothesis The theory of primate origins based on visual hunting of insects as the primary adaptation.

angiosperm radiation hypothesis The theory of primate origins based on visual collecting of fruits as the primary adaptation.

FIGURE 4.33

Biological anthropologists are shown excavating within the Fayum Depression in the Western Desert of Egypt. In the Oligocene epoch this was a swampy forest that preserved an abundance of early catarrhine primate fossils.

Oligocene epoch A division of the geological timescale that lasted from 33.9 to 23 million years ago and is associated with the adaptive radiation of early haplorhines.

Miocene epoch A division of the geological timescale that lasted from 23 to 5.3 million years ago and is associated with the adaptive radiation of early apes.

proconsulid One of a group of Miocene-epoch African primates that are candidates for early ape ancestors.

During the Oligocene epoch (33.9–23 mya), we finally detect what are almost certainly haplorhine primates related to those that still exist today. Much of what we know about primate diversity in this time period comes from an extraordinary fossil site in the Fayum region of Egypt containing evidence of many different types of primates alive at that time (**Figure 4.33**). The many diverse fossils of species found there lived in a swampy forest between 36 and 33 million years ago. The dry climate at the Fayum Depression today is very different. The wet conditions were excellent for forming fossils, and the dry desert today is excellent for being able to find and excavate them.

Because the fossil record at the Fayum Depression is so rich and well-preserved, it is possible to reconstruct more about the behaviors of species living there (**Figure 4.34**). One of the best-known fossils, dating to around 30 million years ago, was *Aegyptopithecus zeuxis*, a medium-sized (6 kg or 15 lb), diurnal, slow-moving, arboreal quadruped that has dentition suggesting a diet of leaves and fruits. With fossils found for both males and females of this species, we know they were sexually dimorphic (males larger than females), which suggests that males competed with each other for access to females, likely living in one male/multiple female social groups. *Aegyptopithecus* is also a leading candidate as an ancestor of all later catarrhines, including humans. This is why it is sometimes referred to as the "Dawn Ape."

With another dramatic spell of global warming at the start of the Miocene epoch (23–5.3 mya), primate habitats changed again. This is when apes first appear in the fossil record, in a much wider distribution than today. The best known are the proconsulids, which had the diagnostic Y-5 cusp pattern and lacked a tail. However, their bodies lack adaptations to knuckle-walking or suspensory locomotion otherwise seen in apes today. Like *Aegyptopithecus zeuxis*, proconsulids seem to have been sexually dimorphic, with the females being much smaller than the males. This suggests that social organization might have included male–male aggression, the guarding of more than one female for mating, and females doing most or all of the care for offspring.

After around 17 million years ago, during the middle part of the Miocene epoch, many ape species (mostly folivores) flourished across Africa, Asia, and Europe, displaying a variety of locomotor adaptations. Some species were clearly suspensory, such as the Asian ape *Sivapithecus* that had similar anatomy to modern orangutans.

Gigantopithecus, another Asian ape dating to around 8 million years ago, is the largest primate to have ever lived, weighing in at 300 kg, standing over 10 feet tall, and with molars measuring an inch across (**Figure 4.35**). The large teeth probably supported a diet of bamboo, much like pandas of today. This species survived long enough to live alongside human ancestors as recently as 300,000 years ago. Coexisting in the same habitats as humans in what is now southern China may have been part of the reason for their relatively recent extinction.

During the late Miocene epoch, after 8 million years, climates again became cooler and drier. Many apes did not survive the shrinking of forests and the spread of more open grasslands that followed. The African and Asian apes that survived were those located much as they are today, in the densest tropical

FIGURE 4.34

An artist's reconstruction depicts primates that inhabited the Fayum Depression during the Oligocene epoch. These primates were arboreal, using their hands and feet for climbing and feeding.

equatorial forests. European apes went extinct, although perhaps some successfully migrated back to Africa to fill the altered habitats the African apes abandoned. The ape fossil record from this time is very sparse, so it is hard to know exactly what became of the European ape species.

The global expansion of open grasslands, however, paved the way for the adaptive radiation of the monkeys. New monkey species proliferated across Africa and Asia, while the apes died out. Monkeys now represent the vast majority of primate species on the planet.

But some apes did survive. Sometime between 8 and 5 million years ago, probably because of an isolation event of some type, one of the species of ape that lived in Africa gave rise to two new branches in the primate family tree. One was the ancestor to humans, and we will pick up the story of what followed in the next chapter. The other was that of the bonobos and chimpanzees, which currently hover on the edge of extinction in the tropical forests of central Africa.

FIGURE 4.35

A reconstruction that shows what *Gigantopithecus* may have looked like is being assembled at the Museum of Us in San Diego, California, in 2006. Fossils provide no evidence for what color fur the ape had; it is just a guess based on modern orangutans, the only living Asian ape.

PRIMATES IN PERIL

Anthropologists study primates to understand our shared evolutionary pasts and to learn more about why humans are as they are today. But primate research is also critical to preserving primate species. The fossil record tells us that many now-extinct primates across wider geographic ranges lived in the past. Currently, more than half of all primate species are **threatened**, meaning they face possibilities of extinction in the near future. This includes 100% of living apes classified at the very highest risk of extinction (**Figure 4.36**).

Human encroachment plays the major role in this threat. Forest clearance fragments or destroys primate habitats, including wild food sources. For example, the small group of Fongoli chimps in Senegal, known for their female-led tool-based hunting, live in close proximity to a number of villages and to the regional capital of Kedougou. Wild weda fruit, a preferred and important food for the chimps, is harvested by humans to sell. Their habitat is also decreased

threatened Species that are critically endangered, endangered, or vulnerable to extinction due to small or declining numbers and habitat destruction.

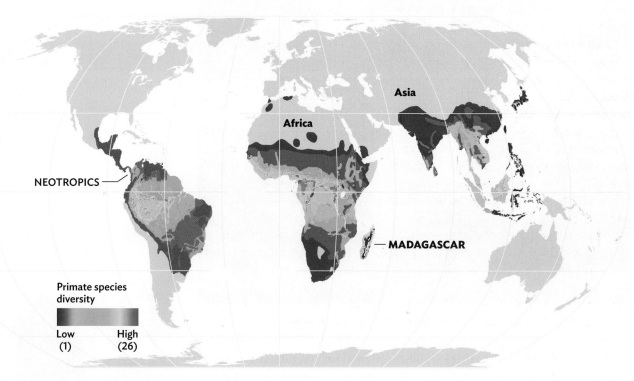

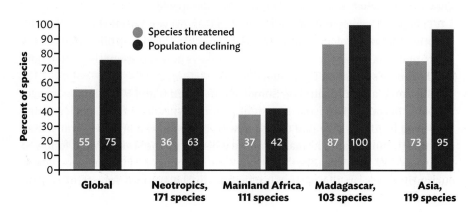

FIGURE 4.36

This figure shows a 2017 estimate of living primate species diversity and threats of extinction across world regions. The COVID-19 pandemic accelerated hunting threats to many species, as lockdowns reduced active wildlife policing. But land clearance for agriculture remains the single most important factor in driving declines.

and destroyed by local farming, ranching, and logging. Moreover, seepage from transient local gold mining camps introduces toxic mercury pollution into their habitat. Finally, in an area prone to long dry seasons with high temperatures, climate change is also placing them at additional risks of heat stress, hunger, and habitat loss.

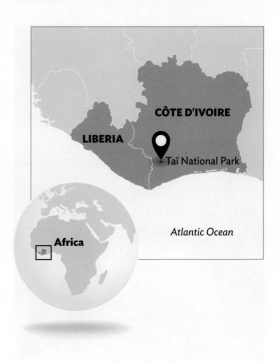

Ongoing hunting of primates has led to extinctions of species such as Miss Waldron's red colobus, last seen in western Africa in 1978. Humans have also long eaten primates as a meat source and continue to do so today. On the basis of fossil evidence, giant (now extinct) geladas from eastern Africa were being hunted 400,000 years ago. Today, wild primate meat represents a major source of both food and income for many communities in Africa and Asia that live in or near forests. New technologies, such as high-power night lights, make hunting easier. And species that are larger and slower, such as gorillas, are especially easy targets.

In some cases, hunting primates is for special ritual events that reflect cultural traditions, or primate meat is valued for its contribution to otherwise limited diets. Lemurs have long been hunted for food. Food insecurity is extremely common in Madagascar, meaning many families struggle to get enough food to eat. Studies suggest children in households that use primates as protein in their meals are healthier as a result.

In other cases, the meat is taken for sale in markets as a source of needed income. For example, in a survey of one riverside market on the border of Côte d'Ivoire and Liberia, West Africa, anthropologists traced all primates arriving on dugout canoes, recorded if the wild meat was smoked or raw, and estimated the approximate ages of the animals being killed. Based on repeated observations on market days, they calculated that more than 9,500 primates enter the market for sale as food each year, including many taken from the nearby protected World Heritage Site of Taï National Park. Wild meat that was being sold even sometimes included that of larger primates such as chimpanzees.

In Madagascar alone, one recent estimate suggests that 97 of 100 primate species are endangered, including the iconic ring-tailed lemur that opened our chapter. And for our closest living relatives—chimpanzees, orangutans, and gorillas—the outlook is particularly grim. These apes depend on relatively large territories to obtain the amount of wild fruit or leaves needed to provide energy for their larger bodies. As those territories shrink due to human activity, the impact on these populations is severe. Their large bodies also make them a target for hunting, and their rarity makes them a favored species in illegal pet trading.

The world's rarest primate is probably the Hainan gibbon of China (*Nomascus hainanus*), with fewer than 35 individuals remaining. Its territory was destroyed by the expansion of tropical plantations to produce rubber, a major Chinese export. Primates in China and elsewhere are also at risk because of the active global market for medicinal treatments based on primate bones and other body parts.

Another way humans can decimate primate populations is rooted in the human history of trade in wild-caught live primates. On the islands of Greece, murals from the Bronze Age (ca. 3500–1100 BCE) show varied monkeys that were not from the island, including baboons from northern Africa and langurs from central Asia, perhaps imported for menageries of wealthy residents (**Figure 4.37**). Archaeological evidence also suggests long-distance trade in primates who were found with other imported trade materials, such as tin sourced to modern-day Iran.

FIGURE 4.37

A close-up of a section of the "blue monkey" fresco on the island of Santorini, Greece. It was preserved in ash from a volcanic eruption around 1600 BCE, showing what appear to be langurs.

FIGURE 4.38

Pygmy marmosets are popular pets, including this one being kept by a Yagua teenager in the Peruvian Amazon, the area to which they are indigenous. They are also trafficked out of the region for illegal international sales as pets.

ethnoprimatology **The study of human and nonhuman primate interactions in a systemic way, focusing on how they coexist.**

habituation **The process of accustoming animals to be around humans.**

Trade of wild-caught primates continues today, often illegally. Some primate species are highly desirable as pets and accordingly are targeted by traffickers. Pygmy marmosets from Peru—the world's smallest monkeys—are one species that has become popular as imported pets through social media because they are so photogenic (**Figure 4.38**).

CONSERVATION AND HUMAN–PRIMATE INTERACTIONS

To address the threat that humans present, some biological anthropologists study not only nonhuman primates but also how humans and primates interact, a field of study termed ethnoprimatology. This research is increasingly important, as fewer and fewer primates live in zones that also don't contain people.

Most such interactions are beneficial to humans rather than primates. For example, primates can attract ecotourists, and with them tourist dollars, providing human economic benefits. But the corresponding impacts from increased ecotourism on local primate communities can be severe. Humans can transmit diseases to primates, especially respiratory illnesses. Being exposed to more diseases also results in a greater need for additional medical interventions by humans, which is itself very stressful for animals. Indeed, just being around humans increases stress levels in primates. Studies of gorillas at Dzanga-Sangha Special Reserve in the Central African Republic found that individuals being habituated to wildlife tourists had especially higher glucocorticoid hormone levels in their fecal samples, meaning being around humans correlated with higher degrees of physiological stress (suggesting psychological distress)(**Figure 4.39**).

FIGURE 4.39

In great ape tourism, accustoming apes to the presence of humans is a slow process. Here such gorilla habituation is underway at Dzanga-Sangha Special Reserve in the Central African Republic. Ethical great ape tourism must ensure the anticipated conservation benefits for the animals greatly outweigh the risks to their well-being from increased contact with humans.

The exchange of diseases between humans and primates that stems from close proximity is a threat to humans as well. As primates, we share generally similar biologies with nonhuman primates, particularly the apes, and hence have similar immune systems; this means infectious diseases are more easily spread between species. The viruses that evolved into human immunodeficiency virus (HIV) seem to have crossed originally from apes to humans around a century ago in the Congo Basin of central Africa. Macaque species thrive at many temples and other popular tourist sites around the world and have even become a tourist attraction in themselves. As monkeys climb over, scratch, and bite tourists wanting to hold and pose with them, they can potentially transmit an array of viral diseases not otherwise found in humans.

The Bukit Sari Temple and Sangeh Monkey Forest in central Bali, Indonesia, are such popular domestic and international tourist destinations (**Figure 4.40**) where visitors can interact with long-tailed macaques (*Macaca fascicularis*). Studies of human–macaque interactions at both sites have shown how these can transmit diseases not previously hosted by humans, such as simian foamy virus.

Not all interactions with humans devastate the local nonhuman primate communities, however. Studies tracking these interactions have revealed how some smaller monkeys do seem able to adapt to the many challenges of living in increasing proximity to humans. Working with local communities and park staff in Sulawesi, Indonesia, biological anthropologist Erin Riley combines

FIGURE 4.40

A tourist is pictured with an Asian macaque at the Sangeh Monkey Forest.

FIGURE 4.41

Biological anthropologist Erin Riley (left) with field team members Paisal and Amiruddin in Sulawesi, Indonesia, collecting data on human–macaque interactions.

methods from cultural and biological anthropology to observe and document the behavior of macaques on the sides of major roads that cut through national parks (**Figure 4.41**). People often throw food items and other trash from their cars. Riley and her team have recorded that this is changing where and how primates range in their territories. The macaques, in particular, spend much more time on the roads, where they can be hit by cars, but also closer to humans in ways that put them at greater risk of catching human diseases.

Riley's research also involves interviewing farmers and observing macaques raiding their fields for food. This work provides insights into how and why the two species come into conflict and what might be done to benefit both groups. This in turn supports macaque conservation efforts.

However, conservation efforts to protect threatened primates can come at some cost to local human communities. Protecting habitats—such as by turning them into national parks—means people may be cut off from obtaining food from forests they have relied on for generations. New protected areas can also bring more tourists, and without very careful planning, the benefits can flow to outsiders who are hired to manage parks and not those living in or near the park zones. Expanding primate populations can mean more foraging of farmers' crops, putting subsistence farmer livelihoods at risk. Environmental anthropologists are documenting the many ways that animal and human conservation can address the needs of both primates and the local community simultaneously.

The Madagascar ring-tailed lemurs that Stephanie Meredith observes have some protection in Bezà Mahafaly Special Reserve, one of the best places to see lemurs outside captivity. Collaborative conservation efforts were sparked by local community leaders in 1975, and subsequently developed in partnership with researchers from Madagascar and the United States and their universities. One focus has been on encouraging new ways for community members to get food or make money. Conservation efforts have included supporting the expansion and marketing of centuries-old artisanal salt production and teaching and providing the tools to expand fish farming, providing new streams of income to support both local families and park conservation initiatives (**Figure 4.42**).

FIGURE 4.42

In three rural villages closest to Bezà Mahafaly Special Reserve, conservation efforts have included expansion of artisanal salt production, as shown here. New and sustainable income streams for local communities are increasingly understood as fundamental to successful primate conservation.

But effective conservation programs are usually both complicated and expensive. They require legal protections and community buy-in and must consider economic trade-offs (such as the loss of ecotourism). They usually require expensive management operations as well as the costs of habitat protection and reconstruction.

As wild populations of primates dwindle, many zoos and research facilities are accelerating efforts to breed captive primates. This then provides the means to stock their own exhibits or share with other zoos, meaning primates need not be sourced from the wild. Potentially, captive breeding can help reintroduce captive-born primates into the wild to boost wild population numbers and genetic diversity. The captive primates can also act as "genetic reservoirs" for highly endangered species. However, efforts to reintroduce primates into habitats are often unsuccessful, and these primates tend to die at very high rates compared to those born outside captivity.

The Duke Lemur Center in North Carolina, United States, houses some 200 lemurs from 14 species in large outdoor enclosures, providing a facility for lemur observation studies. It also attracts many student anthropologists learning how to study primate behavior. The center has bred thousands of endangered lemurs (including ring-tailed lemurs), arguing that hopefully at some time in the future it will be possible to safely reintroduce them to build the lemur populations back up in the forests of Madagascar (**Figure 4.43**).

Given that so many primates are at risk of extinction, conservation is a complex endeavor, and captive breeding often fails, it isn't possible to conserve them all. So, how do we prioritize which species to work hardest to save? There are no easy answers, and different conservation efforts reflect different evaluations of such options. We are likely to lose many more of our closest primate relatives in the years ahead, even as we recognize their central importance to defining who we are as humans.

(a)   (b)

FIGURE 4.43

(a) This newborn lemur was bred at the Duke Lemur Center in North Carolina, United States. **(b)** Two ring-tailed lemurs (with tracking collars) are seen "sunbathing" in the center's large enclosures.

4

Primates: Our Closest Relatives

Humans are primates, and the study of the anatomy and behavior of other past and present primate species helps us understand what it means to be human. Anthropologists' engagement with living primates as our closest living relatives raises ethical challenges and responsibilities related to their well-being and conservation.

4.1 | What Is a Primate?

Identify the physical and behavioral traits that primates share.

• Primates are a diverse group of mammals that includes humans; they are collectively characterized by relatively large brains, a wide breadth of diets, and social living.

4.2 | Diversity of Living Primates

Classify primates into groups based on key physical and behavioral traits.

- The study of primates is central to anthropology, with comparisons across living and extinct species providing insights into human history, anatomy, cognition, behavior, and social organization. Living primates are organized into two main groups: strepsirrhines and haplorhines. Humans (and their ancestors) are haplorhines, which have larger brains and generally more complex social lives in comparison to strepsirrhine primates.

KEY TERMS
> adaptive radiation
> bilophodont molar
> binomial nomenclature
> catarrhine
> cercopithecoid
> cooperation
> cusp
> fission–fusion society
> grooming claw
> haplorhine
> hominoid
> isolation event
> phylogeny
> platyrrhine
> primitive trait
> prosimian
> recursion
> rhinarium
> sexual dimorphism
> strepsirrhine
> taxonomy
> toothcomb
> Y-5 cusp pattern

4.3 | Fossil Evidence and Primate History

Explain how observations of primate traits today are used to interpret fossils and trace primate evolution.

- From tiny amounts of fossil evidence—even just one tooth—comparisons with living primates allow anthropologists to describe long-extinct species, including how they moved, what they ate, and what their social behaviors were. This is important information for understanding the earliest stages of human evolution.

KEY TERMS
> angiosperm radiation hypothesis
> endocast
> Eocene epoch
> folivore
> fossilization
> frugivore
> gummivore
> insectivore
> Miocene epoch
> Oligocene epoch
> Paleocene epoch
> plesiadapiform
> proconsulid
> sagittal crest
> tool use
> visual predation hypothesis

4.4 | Primates in Peril

Evaluate human impacts on, and responsibilities toward, other primates.

- Most living primate species are at risk of extinction because of one of their own: humans. Anthropologists are deeply committed to identifying feasible, ethical means of primate conservation that consider multiple stakeholders in the decision-making process.

KEY TERMS
> ethnoprimatology
> habituation

Human Origins and the Earliest Hominins

5

Six paleoanthropologists crawled into the Dinaledi Chamber of South Africa's Rising Star cave system in late 2013. Hannah Morris, Marina Elliott, Becca Peixotto, Alia Gurtov, Lindsay Eaves, and Elen Feuerriegel had three things in common: they were small-framed, had prior caving experience, and had no problem with extremely enclosed spaces. To excavate the fossils deep in the cave system, they had to squeeze through a long vertical chute that narrowed to just 20 centimeters (about 8 inches) across, then work meticulously for hours in the dark (**Figure 5.1**).

On their first day, they carefully excavated a single, small mandible (jawbone) with oddly large teeth. On their second day, they realized the remains of more than one individual were present in the chamber. By the end of the first week, the team leader, paleoanthropologist Lee Berger, realized they were excavating the largest set of hominin remains ever discovered in South Africa—already a major center for fossil discoveries related to human origins. In three fast-paced weeks, they removed some 1,550 delicate pieces of fossilized bone that—pieced together through months of subsequent laboratory work—reflected some 15 separate individuals (**Figure 5.2**). The similarities of the leg and other bones of the individuals suggested they all belonged to the same species.

OUR EARLIEST ANCESTORS

Fossil, genetic, and archaeological studies, informed by comparative data from studies of living primates and humans, can tell us much about the earliest origins of the human species, despite the limitations of the fossil record. Together, these traces recreate a story of the evolution of many distinct species of human ancestor, leading up to the evolution of our genus, *Homo*, 2.8 million years ago.

LEARNING OBJECTIVES

5.1 The Pliocene Epoch and the Challenges of Scarce Data
Assess strategies and challenges in evaluating the scarce fossil evidence for early human evolution.

5.2 Identifying Our Earliest Ancestors
Distinguish early hominins from other primates.

5.3 Early Hominins
Outline the emergence of possible early human ancestors.

5.4 Tool-Making Pliocene Hominins
Relate tool use and production to the emergence of uniquely human behaviors.

5.5 Telling the Early Human Story
Identify how diversity in the study of early human origins supports improved interpretation and protection of the fossil evidence.

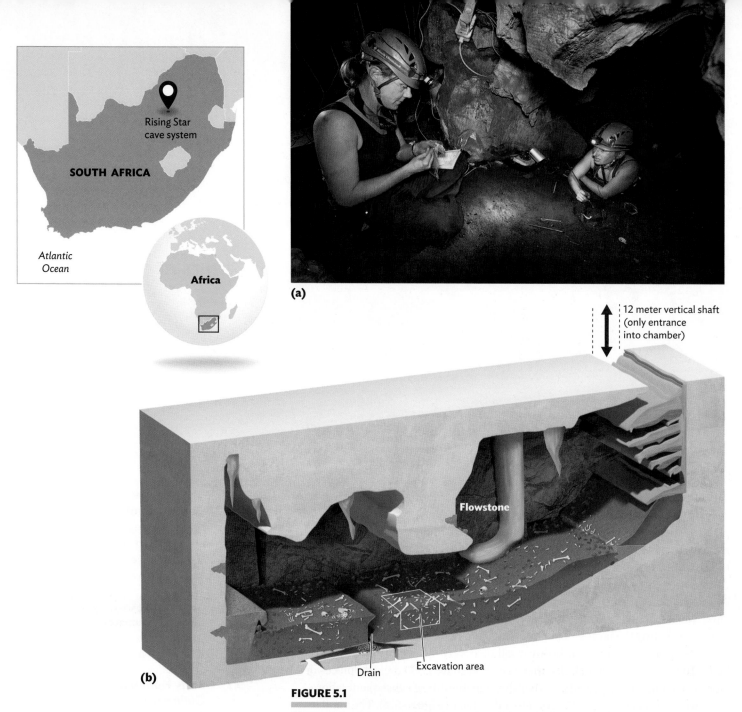

FIGURE 5.1

(a) Two of the six team members who conducted the original excavations in the Rising Star cave system were Marina Elliott (left) and Becca Peixotto. **(b)** This rendering of the chamber in the Rising Star cave system in which the *H. naledi* remains were discovered shows the tiny entrance to the Dinaledi Chamber at the top right.

paleoanthropologist An anthropologist who locates, examines, and interprets the early fossil and archaeological evidence for human evolution.

hominin A human, extinct human ancestor, or closely related species that is more closely related to modern humans than chimpanzees.

australopithecine A member of the successful genus of hominins *Australopithecus*, which first evolved around 4.2 million years ago during the Pliocene epoch (5.3–2.6 million years ago) in multiple locations throughout Africa, now extinct.

Homo The genus to which humans belong, which first evolved 2.8 million years ago, defined by having a smaller face and teeth and larger brain than other hominins living at the time.

But the remains also didn't look much like any other known fossil hominin species living in the region around the same time. Rather, the fossils had features that represented a mix of other species who existed millions of years apart. It had a tiny, orange-sized brain, and its apelike shoulders and torso suggested it was partially arboreal; these features are similar to the australopithecines from southern Africa that were dated to 3.3–2.1 million years ago. The anatomy of the hands, feet, teeth, and face, however, was closer to the genus *Homo*, which includes modern humans. Puzzlingly, too, no tools or cultural artifacts were found with them, despite their brain and hand anatomy suggesting they should have been able to produce them. It looked like a never-before-identified species. Perhaps, even, an early human ancestor.

(a)

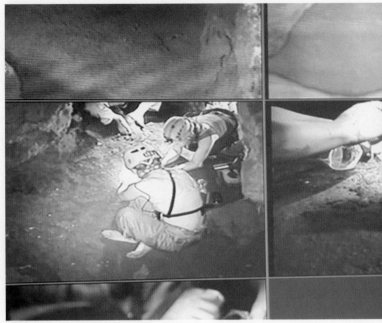

(b)

FIGURE 5.2

(a) The paleoanthropology field team views **(b)** the first images from the excavations taking place beneath them in the cave system.

But confirming this took time and effort. Additional lab-based studies needed to be conducted, including expert analysis of the inside of the braincase using three-dimensional modeling and a systematic comparison of the anatomy to all known species. In 2015, Lee Berger confirmed that they had, in fact, unearthed a new species: *Homo naledi*, a species that was right at the cusp of being human, perhaps bridging *Homo* to the australopithecines. A media frenzy ensued (**Figure 5.3**).

It wasn't until 2017, however, that scientists dated the fossil remains. This was no simple task. Varied geological techniques were needed to establish the relative age of the muddy sediments in which the skeletons were buried. Other more direct techniques such as radiocarbon dating were initially tried on some of the recovered teeth, before it was apparent that they were too ancient for the method to work. These methods together helped establish that *Homo naledi* entered the cave 230,000–340,000 years ago. In paleoanthropological terms, this is a very young (meaning recent) hominin species. Our own species, *Homo sapiens*, is about the same age and was living in southern Africa too. The exact placement of *Homo naledi* in relation to other fossil hominin species is yet to be resolved, but it isn't a modern human ancestor. Rather, it's another type of human contemporary with ourselves, if one noticeably physically different from us. This matters, because the dating placed it in a very different and later part of the human story—one that we return to in Chapter 6. And it shows how quickly the scientific narratives change, especially in the rather competitive quest to identify our "first" ancestors.

In earlier decades, many of the fossils we will encounter in this chapter were at different points proposed as paleoanthropological "stars": a possible direct *Homo* ancestor. As more fossils have been found that reflect more species—including more

FIGURE 5.3

Paleoanthropologist Lee Berger (right) and Deputy President of South Africa Cyril Ramaphosa are pictured in 2015, at the announcement of *Homo naledi* as a new fossil species.

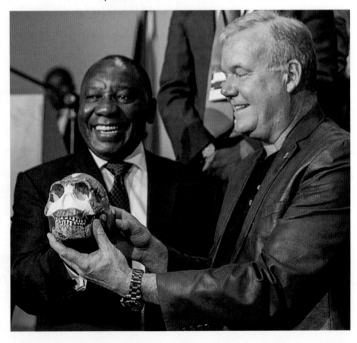

tool-using ones—and they become better situated chronologically in the human evolutionary timeline, the story has become more complicated (**Figure 5.4**). Currently, it isn't possible to pick one Pliocene species as a direct human ancestor; the more fossils that are located, the more possible narratives can be imagined.

Also, the way the science of human origins is often depicted, with humans at the top and center reflecting the ultimate outcome, is somewhat misleading.

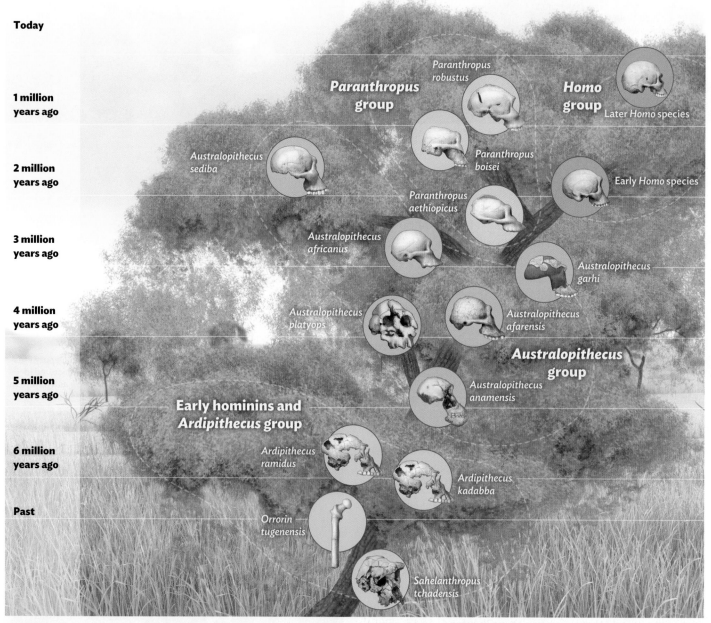

FIGURE 5.4

A simplified model and one possible arrangement of the human story shows a treelike configuration where the placement of each species is generally reflective of its earliest appearance in the fossil record. Of note here are the four major groupings, which represent distinct genera (plural of genus) within the hominin family: *Sahelanthropus, Orrorin, Ardipithecus, Australopithecus, Paranthropus,* and *Homo.* The proposed species and their relationships change with new fossil discoveries and better techniques for analyzing them.

There are other ways to organize and interpret our world that see us as primarily related to and connected with the other species around us (sometimes referred to as a relational perspective). Such approaches create different types of narratives that can better highlight the connections between all the many different and equally amazing tool-using Pliocene hominins, the challenges they also overcame, and the incredible journeys they made.

In this chapter, we explore the question of why and how human ancestors diverged from other apes. We examine the evolution of traits that distinguish early hominins from other primates, including the use of tools, and we consider how the scarcity of data has shaped the narrative about human origins.

THE PLIOCENE EPOCH AND THE CHALLENGES OF SCARCE DATA

A story needs a beginning. In choosing a starting point for the human story, many paleoanthropologists would place it at the time when the climate cooled and became drier at the end of the Miocene epoch, some 6–8 million years ago (mya). In Africa, tropical forests continued to fragment into smaller pockets, a process that may have began nearly 20 million years ago. Ape species living at that time either went extinct or adapted to the patchy forested environments. One population of apes was able to exploit the more open, less wooded environments of Africa particularly well, adapting to acquire and eat new foods and successfully avoid new predators (such as the giant grassland cats). Likely some degree of bipedalism (walking on two feet) helped them succeed.

By about 5 million years ago, these small-bodied bipedal apes had evolved to become more upright and better runners, and they and their immediate descendant species were called the australopithecines. One later australopithecine population was the likely ancestor of the first species in our own genus—*Homo*—that emerged around 2.8 million years ago.

There were at least two species of genus *Homo* living in sub-Saharan Africa by the end of the Pliocene epoch and the start of the Pleistocene epoch, between 2.8 and 2.4 million years ago. With significantly larger brains, smaller faces and teeth, and rounder skulls than the australopithecines, *Homo* was unambiguously a tool maker and user. Through the next 2 million years, new species of *Homo* emerged that ate more meat and had increasing capacities for tool use, language, and other cognitive improvements that helped their survival. But there were many other (mostly plant-eating) hominin species in Africa at the same time, sometimes living alongside one another, forming a complex mosaic of species on the landscape with distinct diets and behaviors. Modern humans like us didn't emerge until very recently, around 250,000 years ago.

While this broad outline of early human evolution is generally agreed upon by anthropologists, there remains much debate about how best to interpret the

Miocene epoch A division of the geological timescale that lasted from 23 to 5.3 million years ago and is associated with the adaptive radiation of early apes.

Pliocene epoch A division of the geological timescale that lasted from 5.3 until 2.6 million years ago and is associated with the evolution of fully bipedal hominins and the genus *Homo*.

Pleistocene epoch A division of the geological timescale that lasted from 2.6 million until 12,000 years ago and is associated with the beginning use of stone tools and the adaptive radiation of genus *Homo*.

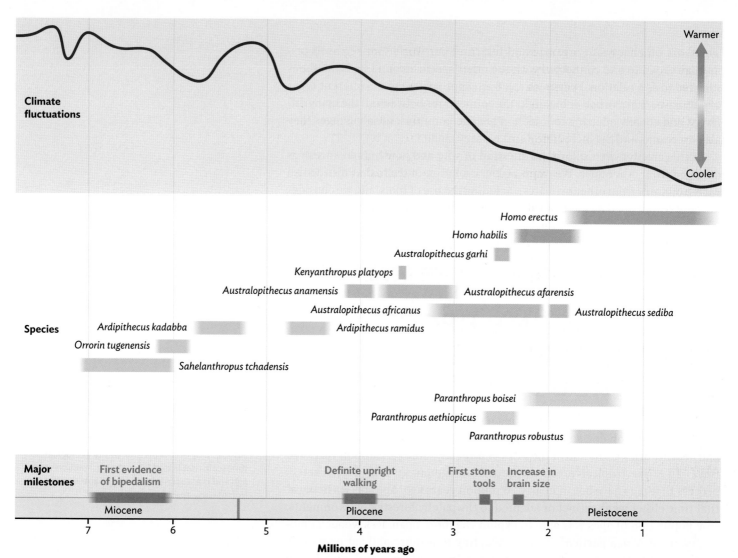

FIGURE 5.5

A more detailed view of a posited chronology of human origins shows distinct species names and approximate dates of their existence with major milestones of hominin evolution indicated on the time scale.

more specific details of the fossil record spanning the last 7 million or so years (**Figure 5.5**). The further we reach back in time, the more we find that physical evidence is very rare and incomplete, and it can be very difficult to sort into clear chronologies or distinctive species.

Paleoanthropology is an extremely exciting but also especially challenging endeavor that brings together experts in anatomy, geology, archaeology, and many other specialties to answer questions about the human past. It is important to consider these challenges in order to better understand how anthropologists derive knowledge about human evolution from fossils and what makes that knowledge so prone to revision.

FOSSIL EVIDENCE

One of the core challenges of paleoanthropology is its reliance on very rare material: ancient ape and hominin fossils and associated sediments that have survived intact for thousands or millions of years. The National Museum of Natural History, part of the Smithsonian Institution in Washington, DC, estimates so far there are remains from about 6,000 different early hominins worldwide. Many are represented by just a single tooth or a finger bone. Very few fossils are more complete sets of remains from a single individual, providing evidence of what different body parts were like, such as the size of the brain, the form of the legs, and so on, and how they vary within a single individual. This is one reason the Rising Star cave fossils were such a stunning discovery.

This scarcity of complete sets of remains is important because of human variation. A single family or village can contain both tall and short people, for example, for reasons both genetic and environmental (Chapter 3). Therefore, another challenge of dealing with the remains of so few individuals is that we can't necessarily know if they represent the average individual in the population from which they came.

Moreover, as scarce as the fossil evidence is, it is also not equally distributed geographically. Fossils form and survive under very specific conditions, and these conditions are more likely to be present in areas that were once lowlands, where swamps form, or where ash layers are deposited. The fossil record thus overrepresents species that lived in these types of regions and underrepresents species that may have lived in rainforests or other regions where conditions don't support the formation and survival of fossils.

This means that previously covered fossils that are later pushed to the surface are more likely to be found. This is why so many fossil finds have been located along the valleys of the East African Rift System, a tectonically active zone that exposes geological strata from the Pliocene and Pleistocene epochs (**Figure 5.6**). These ancient geological strata have been folded and uplifted and separated over millions of years and then rapidly eroded, exposing fossils. Although many of these sites are now in arid desert landscapes, millions of years ago they featured woodlands and grasslands, patches of forest, and many sources of water.

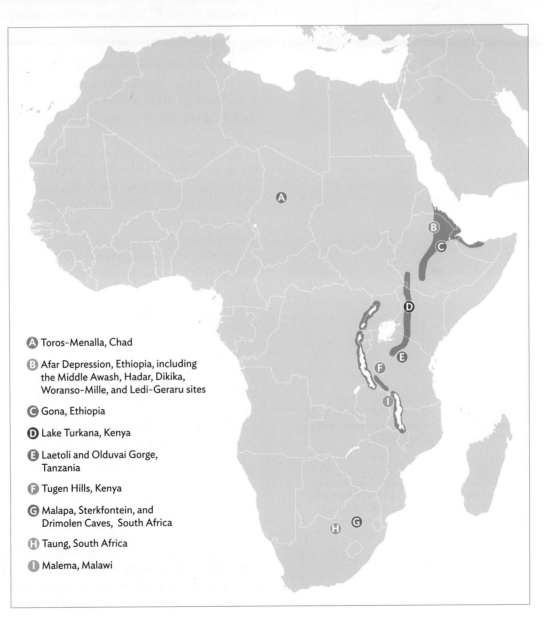

A Toros-Menalla, Chad

B Afar Depression, Ethiopia, including the Middle Awash, Hadar, Dikika, Woranso-Mille, and Ledi-Geraru sites

C Gona, Ethiopia

D Lake Turkana, Kenya

E Laetoli and Olduvai Gorge, Tanzania

F Tugen Hills, Kenya

G Malapa, Sterkfontein, and Drimolen Caves, South Africa

H Taung, South Africa

I Malema, Malawi

FIGURE 5.6

Key sites for the discovery of fossils of early hominin species are mostly found in the East African Rift System, shown in orange, or in cave systems in southern Africa.

The impact of this unequal distribution of fossil evidence is that we often cannot know if the absence of hominins in a place or time means that they didn't exist or just that their remains were not fossilized or remain too well covered to discover. And frustratingly, one of the periods most important to understanding human origins—the split between our hominin ancestors and other apes—is the one for which the fossil evidence is most lacking. This is because this ancestral species likely lived in a tropical forest environment, and generally, the further you go back in time, the harder it is to find fossil evidence.

THE CHALLENGE OF DATING

Even if we do discover fossils in a region, it is impossible to interpret them without knowing when the individuals they represent were alive. As we saw with the Rising Star cave remains, it was the combination of their unusual anatomy and their relatively young age that so surprised researchers. Unfortunately, fossils themselves are mostly far too old to use the well-known radiocarbon method that is integral to archaeological research (Chapter 2). Therefore, paleoanthropologists generally must use relative dating methods to determine the broad age of a fossil, but these methods may not be usable in all contexts where fossils are located.

For example, a common method for relative dating is to calculate the ages of the rock strata (layers) surrounding the fossil, by linking those strata to established geological events such as volcanic eruptions. This method has been used to date many fossils found in eastern Africa, which hosts numerous volcanic zones.

Conversely, it is much more difficult to date remains found in caves such as those in southern Africa. Rising Star was a typical case; the process of dating the fossils was an incredibly onerous one, requiring the combination of seven different methods and taking over two years to complete. This included dating nearby animal remains and dating flowstones and fossil teeth to cobble together a general time frame.

Finally, once a fossil has been dated, the work of interpreting it is just beginning. One of the most contentious, complex, and interesting questions paleoanthropologists tackle is whether two fossils with some common features—perhaps represented by only a few teeth—might be assigned to the same species or to different species.

THE CHALLENGE OF IDENTIFYING SPECIES

Understanding human evolution and when and how new species emerge through macroevolution is important for many reasons, including better understanding our place as humans in the world and charting our futures. New species also don't just "appear" one day. The transitions from one species to another are long and cannot be precisely defined.

A common way of thinking about species is the biological species concept. This defines a species as a set of organisms that can potentially mate with each other to produce offspring, which can then themselves reproduce at least as well as their parents. But how do we apply this in the fossil record? Modern genetic techniques do not work on most fossils, as they are too old and don't preserve DNA. Moreover, genetic evidence is unable in itself to define species' boundaries using this definition. So, the biological species concept is not very helpful when we attempt to define a species in the fossil record.

macroevolution The accumulation of evolutionary changes over long time frames, leading to the emergence of new species.

biological species concept A set of organisms that can potentially mate with each other to produce offspring, which can then themselves reproduce.

Rather, paleoanthropologists must make decisions about clumping or splitting species based on comparisons of anatomy alone (and usually very fragmentary anatomy at that) for very small numbers of individuals, with imprecise chronologies or timelines. This is a core issue in many debates between anthropologists and other scientists in the field. Clumping is based on the general principle that populations change slowly and rarely are fully separated, even by long periods of time. With splitting, smaller anatomical details matter more to distinguishing fossils, with many more supposed speciation events creating an evolutionary tree with more branches.

Overall, however, due to the lack of complete physical evidence, anthropologists frequently use words like "probably," "estimated," or "possible" when talking about the record of human evolution. One new single piece of evidence can change an array of assumptions. Dates, named species, their distribution, their characteristic anatomy, and so on are all best estimates and are likely to be tweaked and changed constantly in the years ahead. This is part and parcel of the scientific process, where revision of ideas is actually a sign of a healthy field where new ideas are accepted.

clumping The assumption that things are in the same biological category (such as one species) unless there is convincing evidence that they should be divided.

splitting The assumption that things are in different biological categories (such as multiple species) unless there is convincing evidence that they should be united.

IDENTIFYING OUR EARLIEST ANCESTORS

In Chapter 4, we outlined what is known about the shared origins of all primates, the taxonomic order to which humans belong. We know that chimpanzees and bonobos are our closest living relatives, based on numerous studies of our species' DNA dating back decades. In fact, chimpanzees are more genetically similar to humans than they are to gorillas, despite the similar appearances, habitats, and lifestyles of the living African great apes. What this means from an evolutionary perspective is that humans, chimpanzees, and bonobos share a more recent last common ancestor than they do with gorillas. That is, all three species are descended from a single species that was ancestral to this lineage. This as-yet-unknown species is colloquially referred to as "the missing link" but is more properly known as the human–chimp last common ancestor (HC-LCA), as shown in **Figure 5.7**.

lineage A group of species, both living and extinct, that are all descended from a common ancestor.

human–chimp last common ancestor (HC-LCA) The most recent ancestral species before humans diverged into a separate lineage from that of chimpanzees and bonobos.

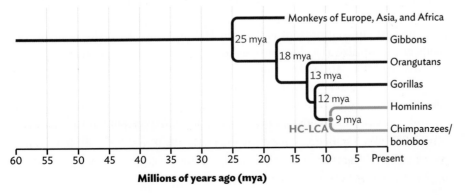

FIGURE 5.7

Estimated divergence times for several primate species are shown, based on genetic evidence. The estimated divergence times are based on accumulated independent mutations along each lineage, with the pace of those changes estimated by a molecular clock method. The human–chimp last common ancestor (HC-LCA) is noted here.

molecular clock method A method for estimating the possible date of past species' divergence, by comparing their later genetic differences and assuming a known rate of genetic change over time.

divergence The emergence of two or more species that shared one common ancestor.

We know that the HC-LCA probably lived in Africa, even if apes were more widely distributed in the past. Less certain is when the HC-LCA lived, exactly where it lived on the continent, or what its lifestyle and adaptations were (including whether it lived more in trees or on the ground).

Biological anthropologists have deployed numerous methods to estimate when the HC-LCA lived. One common approach is the molecular clock method, which aims to use the data from modern ape and human genetics to estimate when two species last shared a common ancestor (that is, to estimate the date right before divergence). Stated simply, the method aligns the DNA base-pair sequences of two species' genomes, focusing on those long "junk" sections that don't seem to code for much, and counts how many differences there are. Then, using an estimate of the rate of base-pair mutation over time (say, 1% mutation every 10,000 years), advanced computing techniques can estimate how long mutations have independently been accumulating in each lineage. For example, a 3% difference, at a rate of mutation of 1% per 10,000 years, would suggest the two species shared a common ancestor roughly 30,000 years ago. In reality, the calculation is more complex than that because different species have different rates of mutation. Much of the continued innovation around this form of molecular dating is related to more accurately determining the rate of mutation and trying to figure out how to account for the effects of gene flow as diverging species reconnect genetically before breaking away again.

Most current estimates place the HC-LCA in Africa somewhere between 6 million and 10 million years ago. When combined with fossil discoveries within this period, this window can be narrowed down to about 6–9 million years ago. Moreover, lineages do not usually diverge instantaneously; rather, the different populations of a species slowly accumulate genetic differences due to changing habitats, diets, or mating practices until they can no longer interbreed. This process can take millions of years as well.

Estimates of where precisely the HC-LCA lived and what its lifestyle was like can only be established from fossils and, as noted in the previous section, this is an especially sparse period in the African fossil record, which makes drawing conclusions very difficult. The last common ancestor of chimps and humans was certainly "apelike" in appearance, with an anatomy that allowed for moving about in trees. But it probably didn't look exactly like a chimpanzee, considering that chimpanzees have also been evolving away from the HC-LCA for millions of years just like humans have been. One fossil that provides a possible suggestion for what could have been the HC-LCA has so far been found in Greece and Turkey and dates to 9.6 million years ago: *Ouranopithecus macedoniensis* (**Figure 5.8**). This species is thought to have looked more like a gorilla than a chimpanzee, but it also shared some features (such as its smaller canines and thicker molar enamel) that were more like later hominins than the African apes.

The best guess at present is that our HC-LCA was about the same overall body and brain size as a chimpanzee—approximately 45 kilograms (kg), with a brain size of 300–400 cubic centimeters (cc)—and was covered in hair (early hominins were probably hairy, too). It was also probably a quadruped, which means it walked on all fours when spending time on the ground, and likely it was also able to grasp branches and move easily through trees, similar to a gibbon or an orangutan.

FIGURE 5.8

This illustration represents one guess what the last common ancestor of humans and chimpanzees (HC-LCA) could have looked like.

IDENTIFYING A HOMININ

If a paleoanthropologist finds a new fossil in Africa that dates to the right time period (6–9 mya), how do they decide if it belongs on our side of the chimp–human lineage and not on the chimpanzee's side? An important element is the presence of traits that correspond with differences between humans and apes today. For example, compared to apes, we walk upright all the time, we have bigger brains (allowing much more complex behavioral repertoires that include language and sophisticated tool use), and we have more diverse diets (including eating much more meat than the living apes). Thus, when examining early fossils, paleoanthropologists interpret evidence of a larger brain size (from the cranium or braincase), bipedalism (from the bones of the shoulders, arms, legs, hands, and feet), and a more varied diet (from teeth) to indicate that the specimen is a hominin rather than an ape.

However, these traits did not all emerge in our lineage at the same time. Language probably didn't evolve until the last 2 million years, hominin brain size only started to increase markedly around 2.8 million years ago, and manufactured technology in the form of stone tools developed only about 2.6 million years ago. The fossil evidence is clear that bipedalism evolved first, 7 million years ago, and set the stage for the evolution of many other traits (such as sophisticated language and tool use). Therefore, we look to the anatomical indicators of bipedalism to identify the earliest hominins.

IDENTIFYING BIPEDALISM

Understanding the anatomical changes associated with bipedalism is important for two reasons. First, reconstructing the functional anatomy of bipedalism provides insights into why this change in locomotion was so adaptively beneficial for early hominins. Second, understanding the body's anatomical changes caused by bipedal locomotion provides us with the skeletal indicators we need to identify bipedal hominins, including our direct ancestors, in the fossil record.

Fortunately for paleoanthropologists, the anatomical changes associated with bipedalism are dramatic. They are reflected in the reconfiguration of bones and muscles to shift the body's center of gravity directly over the hips (as opposed to in front of the hips, as in great apes). For example, one major change is in the gluteal (butt) muscles that reposition from the sides to the backs of the legs in bipeds in order to provide a more stable gait while walking. Associated head-to-toe changes include seven distinct markers of bipedalism that paleoanthropologists can detect in fossils (summarized in **Figure 5.9**):

foramen magnum The hole in the base of the skull that allows the spinal cord to attach to the brain.

1. **Foramen magnum position.** The foramen magnum (from the Latin meaning "great hole") is the hole in the base of the skull that allows the spinal cord to attach to the brain. In bipeds, the foramen magnum is located underneath the braincase in an anterior position. In quadrupeds, the foramen magnum is located posteriorly on the skull. This change positions the brain over the center of gravity of the body.

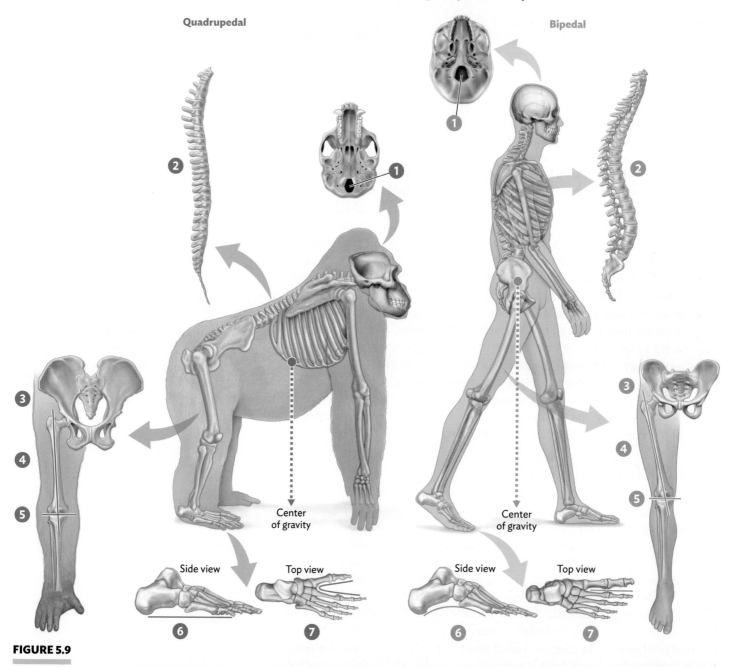

FIGURE 5.9

Seven markers of human bipedalism are compared to a quadrupedal gorilla. **(1)** The foramen magnum (the hole at the base of the skull) is moved forward and under the braincase. **(2)** There is an S-shaped curve in the spine. **(3)** The pelvis becomes shorter and wider. **(4)** The legs (especially the femurs or thighbones) are longer relative to the arms. **(5)** The bones of the knee angle inward. **(6)** The bones of the feet have arches that run from front to back and from side to side. **(7)** The big toe is in line with the rest of the toes, as opposed to diverging from the other toes.

2. **The spine.** In bipeds, the spine has an S-shaped appearance with two curves designed to keep the trunk over the center of gravity of the pelvis, which stabilizes the gait. Humans have a concave forward curve in the midback (thoracic) region and a convex forward curve in the lower back (lumbar) region. In quadrupeds, the spine is straight or C-shaped with only a single curve.

3. **The pelvis.** In bipeds, the pelvis is short and broad with the blades of the pelvis (called the ilia) turned inward, creating a bowl-shaped appearance. In quadrupeds, the pelvis is tall and narrow with the blades of the ilium turned anterior.

4. **Leg length.** In bipeds, the leg, and especially the femur or thighbone, is long relative to the length of the arms. Because our lower limbs are completely responsible for our efficient movement when we walk, natural selection favors increased leg length to move farther given the same amount of muscle effort. In quadrupeds, both the upper and lower limbs are used to move about the landscape, and the arms and legs are more equal in length. In some cases, such as suspensory climbers, the arms are longer than the legs.

5. **Leg angulation.** In bipeds, it is important to keep the mass of the body near the center or midline of the body. For this reason, our femora (thigh bones) are angled inward. This is reflected in the shapes of the joints that make up our knee; the femur and the tibia have joint surfaces that are angled, which is called a valgus knee. In quadrupeds, the knee is not angled inward and the joint surfaces are more symmetrical, meaning one side of the joint does not project lower than the other.

6. **Foot arches.** In bipeds, the foot forms an arch that runs from front to back (longitudinal arch). This allows the foot to flex as we push off with our big toe and then land heel first as we walk or run. This means our foot is designed for shock absorption. Our feet also have a transverse arch (side to side) that performs a similar cushioning function. In quadrupeds, the foot is flat and retains greater use in arboreal locomotion.

7. **Nonopposable big toe.** In bipeds, the big toe is brought in line with the other toes of the foot, forming a strut of support for the body. The big toe serves an important function in how we walk, as we push off with the ball of our foot located near the big toe. We have completely lost our grasping ability with our feet. In quadrupedal apes, the big toe is opposable like our thumbs, which is an adaptation for grasping tree limbs and climbing.

valgus knee Location of the knee toward the midline of the body caused by the angulation of the thigh bone.

longitudinal arch Curvature of the foot from front to back.

transverse arch Curvature of the foot from side to side.

opposable The ability of the thumb or big toe to be placed against the other digits to grasp and hold objects.

The emergence of bipedalism as part of the divergence between human ancestors and other apes must have provided a tremendous selective advantage, because it is followed by a flourish of bipedal hominin species. During the very late Miocene epoch, when hominins diverged from the chimpanzee lineage, the cooler, drier climate with more seasonal rainfall meant less tropical forest and more woodlands and grasslands. By being increasingly able to stand up and walk about, this made new food sources available, which then (through natural selection) favored changes in the jaws, teeth, and facial muscles suited to a more generalized diet that included both meat and more diverse plant foods.

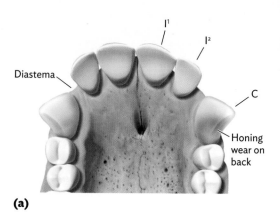

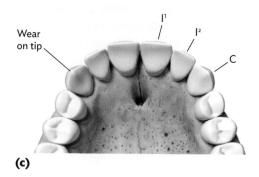

(a) (b) (c)

FIGURE 5.10

(a) This view of the teeth of a gorilla shows the large canines (labeled C) that are honed on their back edge. Diastema are present between the incisors (labeled I¹ and I²) and canines. **(b)** The diet of a gorilla involves chewing tough, fibrous plant materials. **(c)** In contrast, this view of the maxillary teeth of a human shows small, blunt canines and no diastema.

diastema A gap in the tooth row to accommodate large canines when the mouth is closed.

honing chewing A behavior seen in living apes but not humans, where the combination of a diastema and large canines creates a sharp edge on the canine that helps shred and cut tough plant food.

canine blunting The wearing of the canines on their tips, dulling the pointed cusp; characteristic of human dentition.

This diversifying diet is also reflected in dentition. Great apes, such as the gorillas and chimpanzees, have large, projecting canines that hold and shred plant foods when biting and are used in male–male competition for mates. The canines of living apes are so large that, in order for an ape to close its mouth, there must be a space between the canine and incisors in the lower jaw, which is called a diastema. Living apes also have very sharp wear surfaces on the back edge where the upper canine rubs against the first lower premolar, an action called honing chewing. This wear is probably an adaptation itself, creating a cutting motion that can cut, shred, and masticate (chew) tough leaves and fruits efficiently (**Figure 5.10**). African apes also have relatively thin layers of enamel on their molars, which is thought to reflect a dietary adaptation.

In contrast, humans have small canines and no diastema. Whereas in apes the canine wears along its back edge, in humans the canine wears on its tip, referred to as canine blunting. Humans also have relatively large molars compared to our other teeth and thickened enamel.

Bipedalism itself provided advantages to early hominins, which then allowed other changes in hominin anatomy and behavior with important evolutionary benefits (**Figure 5.11**). Perhaps the most important advantage is that it freed hominins' hands to do other things. They could gather more food, plucking fruits from lower tree branches or digging roots from the ground. They could better carry food and offspring, moving between daytime activities and a

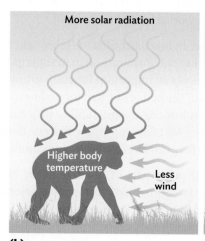

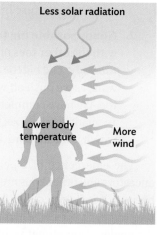

(a) (b)

FIGURE 5.11

The possible benefits of a bipedal gait to early hominins were numerous and included **(a)** the ability to collect and carry foods as well as **(b)** improved temperature regulation.

nighttime base. Having hands freed from locomotion also facilitates the use of and—when the cognitive capacity exists—the building of basic tools. All living apes, but especially chimpanzees and bonobos, can purposefully create objects to complete tasks (such as fishing termites from logs with a stick). This suggests the HC-LCA probably had this ability, too, but bipedalism set the stage for hominins to become even more adept.

Bipedalism was also probably a more energetically efficient way to navigate the landscape, meaning fewer calories were needed to exploit an increasingly patchy forest environment. An upright posture also reduced the surface area of a hominin's body that was directly exposed to the sun, perhaps making it easier to regulate body temperature in a climate that was getting hotter and drier.

Bipedalism also had some costs. Seeing better across the landscape also meant hominins could be better seen by predators. Walking upright and carrying loads also further strains the back, a cost seen in the common human ailments today of slipped disks, arthritis, and other forms of back pain. Such are the trade-offs common to many evolutionary adaptations.

But other anatomical adjustments, such as in the knees and feet, may also have minimized the impacts of upright walking. Studies of barefoot human endurance runners have shown that the way their foot hits the ground is very different than what we think of as a "typical" human pattern. When habitually running in sneakers, the back of the foot tends to hit the ground first. But for barefoot runners it is the front or midfoot. This toe-first pattern seems to protect the knee better from the shock of the foot repeatedly hitting the ground.

Biological anthropologist Daniel Lieberman and his team have established this through studies of the biomechanics of barefoot young Kenyan marathon runners and sandal-wearing Indigenous Rarámuri runners in northern Mexico (**Figure 5.12**). Systematic comparisons of such cases with runners using sports shoes give insights to early human bipedalism. This includes how to interpret fossilized footprint tracks and wear patterns on fossil foot bones. Lieberman has concluded that habitual barefoot running—as early hominins did—may do less harm to the body than running in sports shoes.

FIGURE 5.12

Rarámuri runners in northern Mexico excel at endurance running, typically done in hard and heavy leather sandals. By comparing the biomechanics of different running traditions—in sandals, shoes, and barefoot—biological anthropologists are better able to interpret fossil evidence of bipedalism, including the advantages and disadvantages it offered to early hominins.

EARLY HOMININS

Despite limited fossil evidence, paleoanthropologists have currently pieced together an evolutionary progression up until 1 million years ago (mya).

THE EARLIEST HOMININS AT THE MIOCENE–PLIOCENE BOUNDARY

There is no simple picture of the first hominins who evolved from the HC-LCA in Africa. What evidence exists is mostly scant. Anthropologists have identified fewer than a dozen fossil hominin individuals that have some of the expected skeletal characteristics and are found in Africa within the Miocene–Pliocene boundary time period (7–4.4 mya). At least four different hominin species have been identified based on the anatomical evidence that they were bipeds. All exhibit a mosaic of traits suggestive of both apes and later hominins. But the mix of those traits is a little different for each.

The oldest, *Sahelanthropus tchadensis*, dates to around 6–7 million years ago, right around the time of the HC-LCA. It was found at Toros-Menalla in modern-day Chad, far west and north of where most other fossils were found around the same time period in eastern Africa (see Figure 5.6). Its foramen magnum, the hole in the base of the cranium (skull), tells us *Sahelanthropus* was a biped, but its small brain and large brow ridges are much more like those of a gorilla, while evidence from postcranial bones suggest possible knuckle-walking adaptations (**Figure 5.13**).

Another early hominin is *Orrorin tugenensis* found near the Tugen Hills of Kenya (see Figure 5.6), which dates to around 6 million years ago. Its bipedal status was inferred from its leg bones, but otherwise little is known from the very fragmentary fossil evidence for this species. Slightly later in time, there were two species from the genus *Ardipithecus* discovered in the Middle Awash region of the Afar Depression in Ethiopia (see Figure 5.6). *Ardipithecus kadabba* dates between 5.8 and 5.2 million years ago, and *Ardipithecus ramidus* dates from around 4.8 to 4.4 million years ago. The hominin status of *Ardipithecus* is indicated by its nonhoning canines and multiple skeletal markers of bipedality, although still with many arboreal adaptations (**Figure 5.14**).

mosaic When a fossil species contains a mix of primitive traits and derived traits.

FIGURE 5.13

(a) The cranium of *Sahelanthropus tchadensis* is pictured. **(b)** An artist's reconstruction shows the many apelike features of this species, even though it was bipedal.

(a)

(b)

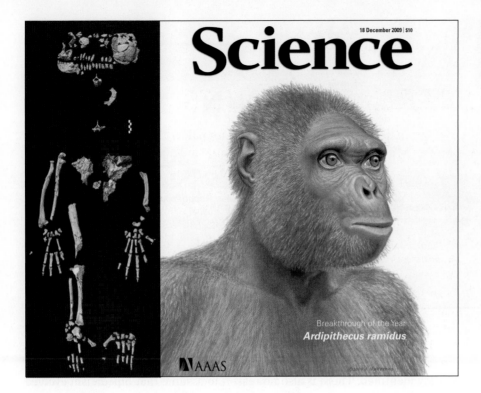

FIGURE 5.14

Ardipithecus skeletal remains from Ethiopia are shown, along with the reconstruction provided with the announcement of the discovery in *Science*.

One *Ardipithecus ramidus* specimen is especially important because its skeleton is more complete than the others. Nicknamed "Ardi," this specimen dates to 4.4 million years ago. Ardi's completeness allows us to see how the brain, teeth, and postcrania all fit together within a single individual.

Paleoanthropologists have been able to estimate that Ardi was biologically female from the pelvis shape, stood about 1.2 m (3.9 ft) tall from the leg bones, and weighed about 50 kg (110 lbs) through comparison of the bone sizes with other living primates. Ardi had a very small brain at 300–350 cubic centimeters (cc), similar to a chimpanzee's, but the small incisors and canines were not honed on their back edges, similar to human canines. Ardi's spine was located directly under the brain, indicating upright walking, and the shape of the pelvis was more similar to that of a modern human than a chimpanzee. But Ardi's body still retained arboreal adaptations for moving through trees, visible in the shape of the shoulder joint, the presence of an opposable toe, and curved fingers, suggesting considerable time in the trees. Ardi likely walked on tops of branches when in the trees, because the foot bones suggest that Ardi (like us) didn't have the mobility needed to swing below them without falling.

So what do we make of this earliest hominin fossil record, as scant as it is? First, the fossils of the four species that have been identified clearly show a mosaic of traits but without a clear linear trend of increasing "humanness" between apes and humans. Second, although all four species are considered to be bipedal, each also had significant arboreal adaptations, suggesting they spent considerable time in the trees. Third, and most importantly, the environments in which these species lived were not open savanna as was once predicted. Paleoenvironmental reconstructions using fossil animal evidence from the same time periods indicate they all lived in woodlands or mixed woodland/grassland environments, rather than in completely open grasslands (**Figure 5.15**).

Though these are the only species from this period we have yet uncovered, it is likely there were more species of bipedal hominins throughout Africa within this time frame—perhaps many more. Only one of these species can technically be our direct ancestor, and we do not yet know if it is one of the species we have

postcrania The bones of the skeleton below the cranium.

paleoenvironmental reconstruction The scientific determination of ancient environments in which fossil species once lived using methods from zoology, paleontology, and geology.

FIGURE 5.15

An artist's reconstruction depicts the appearance of *Ardipithecus* and the wooded environment they lived in.

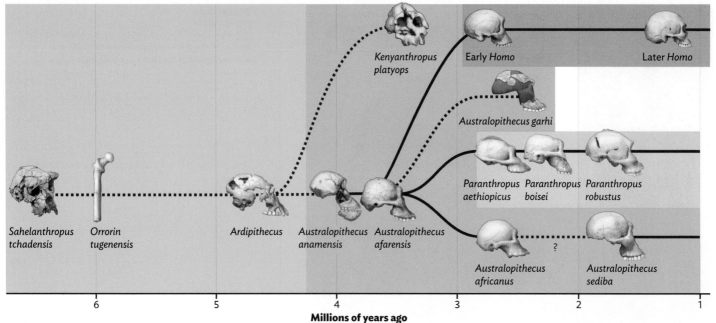

FIGURE 5.16

Age and evolutionary relationships between the earliest hominins, *Australopithecus*, and *Paranthropus* species discussed in this chapter are diagrammed. The evolutionary relationships among the different *Australopithecus* species are debated but suggest the appearance of two distinct lineages between 2.5 and 3.0 million years ago, one leading to *Paranthropus* and one leading to *Homo*. Dotted lines indicate putative relationships that lack scientific consensus due to limited fossil evidence.

already identified. There is also no reason to assume that bipedalism evolved only one time in one place. This part of the picture of the human story is, for now, unknown. But as more early hominin fossils emerge—and we develop new technologies to study them—we will learn more of the details and be better able to pinpoint the species that were our direct ancestors.

THE GENUS *AUSTRALOPITHECUS*

The fossil record becomes more detailed after 4.2 million years ago, in part because of the success of the newly emerged genus *Australopithecus* (**Figure 5.16**). While the earlier hominins such as Ardi have skeletons suggesting they spent at least part of their time in the trees, by the end of the Pliocene epoch, hominin fossils reveal fully bipedal, ground-based species with the remnants of some arboreal adaptations still present.

Overall, the australopithecines were intermediate in their anatomy between the apelike genus *Ardipithecus* and the bigger-brained but smaller-faced genus *Homo* to follow. But they were not just a link in the chain to humanness. The australopithecines had a number of unique features that were neither like apes nor like modern humans, reflecting evolution in action.

The australopithecines retained an apelike body size, ranging from 100 to 150 cm (40–60 in) in height and weighing from 25 to 45 kg (60–100 lbs). The range in size of the fossils suggests the species were probably sexually dimorphic, with male bodies much larger than female bodies, which in primates is associated with one male/multiple female or multiple male/multiple female mating arrangements. The postcranial skeleton, along with other fossil evidence such as the Laetoli footprints (which will be discussed soon), indicates the australopithecines were fully bipedal when on the ground.

The australopithecines had dentition that allowed them to eat tough plant foods that required a lot of chewing. Compared to earlier hominins, their lower face projects significantly forward, a trait called prognathism. This is combined with large jaw muscles, thick enamel, large molars and premolars, and little or no canine honing complex (**Figure 5.17**).

It is still debated whether australopithecines ate much animal protein, a distinguishing part of humans' general diet today. Certainly, they ate many

prognathism The projection of the face forward relative to the braincase, often associated with larger chewing muscles or large snouts in nonprimates.

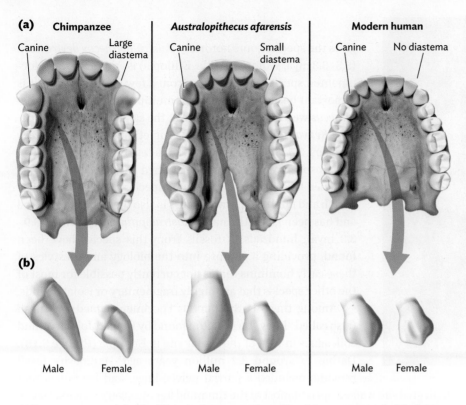

(a)

Chimpanzee	*Australopithecus afarensis*	Modern human
Canine — Large diastema	Canine — Small diastema	Canine — No diastema

(b)

| Male Female | Male Female | Male Female |

FIGURE 5.17

Dental features in chimpanzees, australopithecines, and modern humans are compared. **(a)** The maxillary dental arcade highlights the transitional nature of australopithecines with respect to diastema size and shape of the tooth row. **(b)** The transitional nature of canine size and shape for australopithecines—shorter and blunter than chimpanzees but not in comparison to modern humans—can be seen.

different types of foods, if only because they lived in more varied habitats. Whereas previous hominins were mostly based in woodlands, australopithecines were also found in more open or fragmented grasslands. As the Pliocene epoch progressed and the climate became drier and cooler, and thus fruit became less plentiful, their diet became tougher and centered around grasses, leaves, seeds, and roots. This diversity of environments and diets is what ultimately explains the variation we see in the fossil record, as different australopithecine species adapted to local ecologies.

Through the study of fossil crania (braincases), we also know that australopithecine species differed in brain size but averaged 450 cc. This is 30% larger than a chimpanzee's brain. Whether that means they had significantly greater cognitive abilities is not clear, because the structure of the brain, preserved in fossil endocasts, was similar to that of a chimpanzee. It lacked what we consider key human brain structures, especially in the front of the brain where higher cognition is centered. The increase in brain size could reflect initial steps toward more complex cognition, associated with early tool use, as we will discuss.

endocast A fossilized model of the hollow space inside a skull, often preserving some details of brain anatomy.

THE PLIOCENE–PLEISTOCENE HOMININ RADIATION

The australopithecines radiated widely from approximately 4.2 million to 2 million years ago, meaning they were especially well adapted to living in the African landscape. They were an extremely successful group of Pliocene primates, as at least six species have currently been identified in the fossil record.

Found in the Lake Turkana region of Kenya and the Middle Awash of Ethiopia (see Figure 5.6), *Australopithecus anamensis* (4.2–3.8 mya) is the oldest identified species from this genus. It may have been the ancestor to the subsequent radiation of other australopithecine species subsequently spread across much of Africa, including (but not necessarily limited to) Chad, Kenya, Ethiopia, Tanzania, and South Africa.

Between 3.5 and 2.5 million years ago, at least four distinct species of hominins lived in eastern Africa. *Australopithecus garhi* (2.5 mya, Afar Depression, Ethiopia) is poorly known but possibly the earliest maker of stone tools, which

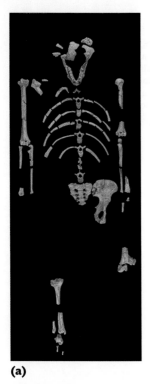
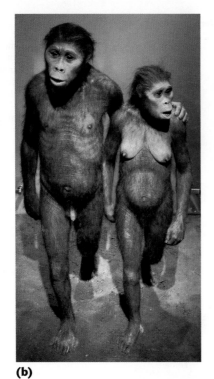

(a) **(b)**

FIGURE 5.18

(a) The fossil bones preserved in the 1974 find named Dinknesh or Lucy, the best preserved specimen of *A. afarensis*, are shown here. **(b)** This reconstruction shows an *A. afarensis* couple, including the female called Dinknesh.

gives the species some notoriety. *Australopithecus deyiremeda* (3.5–3.3 mya, Woranso-Mille, Ethiopia) is another poorly documented species, known only from a few fragments, but it is important because it shows that multiple species of *Australopithecus* were living in Ethiopia at the same time. A third species, *Kenyanthropus platyops* (or sometimes *Australopithecus platyops*; 3.5–3.2 mya, Lake Turkana region, Kenya), is known from a specimen with a badly crushed cranium that shows a flattened face very similar to some species of early *Homo*. The fourth and final species we discuss is also the best documented and has been given the name *Australopithecus afarensis* (3.9–3.3 mya); hundreds of fossils from this species have been found, providing a glimpse into the biology and lifestyles of these early hominins that is not currently possible for most of the other species that are highly fragmentary or isolated finds.

Among these is the famous specimen named Dinknesh (also called "Lucy"), a skeleton found by Donald Johanson and colleagues in 1974 at the Hadar site in Ethiopia (**Figure 5.18**). Dating to around 3.2 million years ago, Dinknesh's fossil remains included a partial pelvis, knee, and leg bones that indicated she walked upright most of the time, and her discovery provided some of the earliest evidence of clear bipedality in the hominin fossil record. Other notable finds include Selam or "the Dikika baby," discovered by Ethiopian paleoanthropologist Zeresenay Alemseged in the year 2000, which provides important information on the growth and development of *Australopithecus afarensis*. Also discovered near Hadar was a collection of 13 individuals of different ages, all thought to have died at the same time and referred to as "The First Family," which provides important information on group composition.

Several years after the discovery of Dinknesh's partial skeleton, archaeologist Mary Leakey, working in Laetoli in the Rift Valley in Tanzania, discovered the preserved footprints of three hominins who walked bipedally through volcanic ash 3.6 million years ago (**Figure 5.19**). The Laetoli footprints are one of the most world-recognized finds within paleoanthropology. Seeming to be from the same species as Dinknesh, the footprints were similar to those of a modern human in many ways. However, the footprints also exposed

FIGURE 5.19

(a) The footprint track at Laetoli, Tanzania, provides incontrovertible evidence of bipedal locomotion in early hominins. Here you can see the footprints as they were uncovered. **(b)** An artist's reconstruction imagines the landscape and the individuals who left their footprints in the volcanic ash.

(a) **(b)**

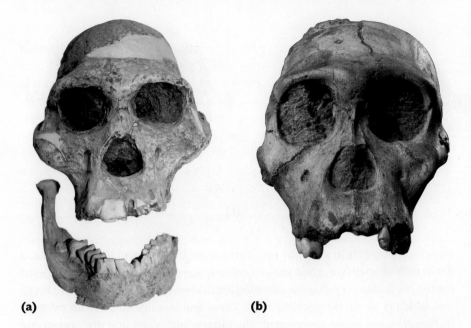

(a)   (b)

FIGURE 5.20

Two *Australopithecus* species lived in South Africa between 3.3 and 2 million years ago: **(a)** *A. africanus* (cranium and jaw of the "Mrs. Ples" fossil) and **(b)** *A. sediba* (cranium).

some key differences between *Australopithecus* and modern humans. The feet themselves were much smaller and suggested a slightly more divergent big toe and a less well-developed ball of the foot in comparison to humans. Their short legs and small overall height also suggest *A. afarensis* were less efficient walkers than modern humans and they may have still spent some time in the trees, perhaps when sleeping. The limb proportions with relatively long arms, the presence of slightly curved finger and toe bones, and the shapes of the fingertips suggest some arboreal adaptations remained in a species that was otherwise very human in its body form.

Hominins were not just restricted to eastern Africa during this time period, as was the case with the earlier australopithecines. At 2 million years ago, two species lived in southern Africa (**Figure 5.20**). *Australopithecus africanus* (3.3–2.0 mya), includes specimens such as "Mrs. Ples" (Figure 5.20a) discovered near Sterkfontein, South Africa, and the "Taung child" recovered near the town of the same name. *Australopithecus sediba* (~2.0 mya), a much more recently discovered species recovered from Malapa Cave, South Africa (see Figure 5.6), is among the last surviving species of the genus.

The success of the australopithecines provided the variation needed for natural selection to shape two distinct hominin pathways. One pathway led to the genus *Paranthropus*, while the other led to the genus *Homo*. There is a longstanding debate about which species of australopithecine was the ancestor to each of these lineages. Those debates will continue until better evidence emerges.

THE GENUS *PARANTHROPUS*

The genus *Paranthropus* (2.7–1 mya), sometimes informally referred to as the robust australopithecines, evolved initially in eastern Africa 2.7 million years ago from the older *A. afarensis* species that had been living there for over a million years. They were contemporaries of both several australopithecine species as well as early members of our own genus, *Homo*. Despite being a distinct genus, *Paranthropus* had a generally similar body type as *Australopithecus*. Body and brain size were slightly larger, but the genus was still a relatively small-bodied biped that was apelike in appearance. They are differentiated from the australopithecines by their adaptation to heavy chewing, reflected in their massive premolars and molars, massive mandibles, and hypertrophied jaw

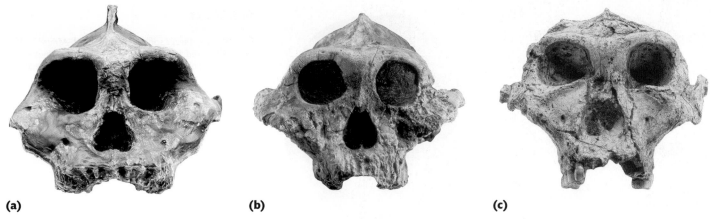

(a) **(b)** **(c)**

FIGURE 5.21

Crania from three species within the genus *Paranthropus* are pictured: **(a)** *P. aethiopicus*, **(b)** *P. boisei*, and **(c)** *P. robustus*. Note the distinct wide cheekbones and concave face of all three species as well as the presence of a sagittal crest on the top of the cranium.

muscles that result in a unique facial structure, including wide cheek bones, a flat or dish-shaped face, and a sagittal crest (**Figure 5.21**). The shape of the joint for the jaw is also very shallow, allowing for side-to-side movement of the lower jaw, which is useful for grinding food. These features are taken to an extreme in *Paranthropus boisei*, nicknamed "the nutcracker" when first discovered due to the massive size of its jaws. Species within the *Paranthropus* genus all had these teeth and jaws adaptations, resulting in very distinct cranial shapes and features (**Figure 5.22**).

Although the facial adaptations of *Paranthropus* are clearly related to heavy chewing, microscopic wear patterns and isotopic compositions of the teeth indicate the diets were also quite varied between the three species of *Paranthropus*. *Paranthropus robustus* found at numerous caves sites such as Drimolen, South Africa (see Figure 5.6), had a diet quite similar to *A. africanus*, which was heavily plant-based and included hard objects such as seeds and nuts. Both lived in southern Africa. *Paranthropus boisei*, found throughout eastern Africa as far south as Malema, Malawi (where the oldest specimens were discovered) (see Figure 5.6), appears to have eaten harder objects that scored and pitted the teeth but also subsisted primarily on grasses or leafy material. This again shows us how evolution can result in convergent (similar) physical anatomies such as dentition for different reasons. *Paranthropus aethiopicus*, found at sites such as Koobi Fora near Lake Turkana, Kenya (see Figure 5.6), is the third species within the genus, important for being the earliest member of the genus that was likely ancestral to both other species.

This hyperspecialization ended in extinction for *Paranthropus*, however. The paranthropines lived their entire 1.7-million-year existence alongside another more successful genus, *Homo*, whose diet was more flexible, an advantage in shifting ecologies such as at the Pliocene–Pleistocene boundary 2.6 million years ago, when the climate became much cooler. The genus *Paranthropus* disappears from the fossil record about 1 million years ago representing the end of a lineage that traded increased brain size for specialized chewing adaptations. Whether this demise came about due to the inability to adapt their diet as conditions changed or to encounters with other hominins remains debated.

THE GENUS *HOMO*

Working at the Rift Valley site of Olduvai Gorge, Tanzania, archaeologist Louis Leakey first excavated what appeared to be hominin stone tools in the 1930s. In 1960, his archaeologist wife Mary and son Jonathan discovered fossil remains in proximity to similar stone tools (**Figure 5.23**). These fossils appeared to have a larger braincase than other specimens they had discovered at Olduvai Gorge before. The Leakeys attributed the tools to a new species that they labeled

FIGURE 5.22

This image of *P. boisei* was reconstructed from skeletal evidence.

FIGURE 5.23

Archaeologists Mary (right) and Louis Leakey inspect the campsite of an early hominin at Tanzania's Olduvai Gorge.

Homo habilis or "handy human." This was the start of the enduring idea that genus *Homo* was the first consistent tool-producing hominin, and had greater potential as the ancestor to humans today.

These *Homo* specimens differed from australopithecines in other ways (**Figure 5.24**). Their heads were rounder and their brain size was larger, about 550–750 cc, suggesting they perhaps had greater cognitive capabilities. Their facial skeleton and teeth were smaller and less robust, suggesting changes that could accommodate the larger brain. From the head down, however, early *Homo* was much like other hominins, with a small body size and an apelike appearance, though certainly fully bipedal.

More fossils of *H. habilis* have since been located in many of the same places the australopithecines were living at the time, such as Tanzania, Kenya, Ethiopia, and South Africa (see Figure 5.6). The fossils uncovered have been

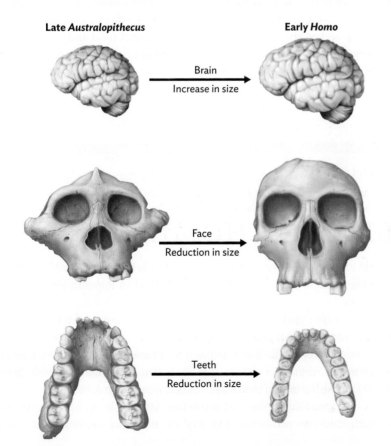

FIGURE 5.24

The major differences between the genus *Australopithecus* and the earliest members of genus *Homo* are listed here. These differences primarily manifest in the skull in the form of increased brain size and a reduction in the size of the teeth and the surrounding facial structure that supports the chewing muscles.

FIGURE 5.25

Paleoanthropologists have been doing research at Ledi-Geraru in the Afar region of Ethiopia since 2002. Chalachew Seyoum was the team member who found a crucial fossil mandible (jawbone) of very early *Homo* in 2020, here shown in his hand.

incredibly variable. Some adults were much larger, while others were smaller in size. Some early *Homo* fossils found in the Koobi Fora region of Lake Turkana in Kenya had much larger teeth, a taller, flatter facial structure, and a larger brain size (~750 cc). Some paleoanthropologists currently split these larger fossils into a separate species called *Homo rudolfensis*, though others continue to lump them as members of a highly variable single species, *H. habilis*.

Further adding to the complexity, in 2020 paleoanthropologist Kaye Reed and her team recovered a partial *Homo* mandible from the site of Ledi-Geraru, Ethiopia (**Figure 5.25**). The find is dated to 2.8 million years ago, and this extends the earliest appearance of *Homo* back further than previously known. The evidence base for this time period is so sparse, and there is still so much uncertainty regarding how these early *Homo* finds are related, that the team was not ready to name the species until more fossils can be found.

This very early *Homo* fossil in Ethiopia also raises new questions about the candidate *Australopithecus* species that could be ancestral to *Homo*. The species *A. afarensis*, *A. africanus*, and *A. garhi* are the best candidates because they were all present in eastern and southern Africa during the relevant time period. The problem is that none of these, nor any other australopithecine species, shows all of the features one would expect to see in the direct ancestor of genus *Homo* (such as a larger brain and smaller face and teeth). And our current estimate of when each of these species first evolved, and how long each species lasted, creates overlaps in their temporal ranges with early *Homo*, thus making a direct ancestor–descendant relationship difficult to determine. Hopefully, more and better-dated discoveries will help clarify this part of the story of our evolutionary origins.

To complicate matters even further, recent new discoveries of stone tools in association with other Pliocene hominin species have challenged the idea that early *Homo* alone invented tool production. Tools are what make humans so successful today, able to inhabit or at least extract food and resources from almost any habitat on the planet. But tool production may not be what makes *Homo* special after all, as we'll examine in the next section. We also evaluate the features paleoanthropologists look for in the earliest stone tools.

SECTION 5.4

TOOL-MAKING PLIOCENE HOMININS

Finding evidence of the use of stone tools in the early fossil record is a challenge because the earliest tools were likely very similar in appearance to naturally broken rocks.

Paleoanthropologists look for three types of evidence of tool production. First, hand anatomy can provide evidence of a precision grip and the manual dexterity needed for making and using tools. Preserved hand bones, then, provide evidence of whether a species was likely capable of making tools. Second, identifiable modification of stone into tools leaves evidence not only on the tool itself but also from the flakes that are removed to make a cutting edge. Being stone, such evidence preserves very well in the archaeological record and is the principal evidence sought of stone tool manufacture. And third, when tools are used to process dead animals, they can leave evidence of butchering on the animals' bones in the form of cuts, scrapes, and chop marks. This form of evidence is also relatively rare but provides direct evidence of meat processing/consumption by early hominins.

EARLY TOOL PRODUCTION

The tools found at Olduvai Gorge by the Leakeys were simple, round river cobbles that had been struck to create a very crude yet effective cutting edge. The production of these earliest hominin stone tools would have been very straightforward. A core would be held with one hand (or possibly placed on the ground or another rock) and struck by a hammerstone held in the other hand. Each strike removes a flake from the core (**Figure 5.26**). Tools could be fashioned from the core itself by removing several flakes to produce a large tool with a cutting or chopping edge. The flakes themselves could also be used as small tools, such as spear or arrow heads, though this didn't occur until much later in time. These basic stone tools could be produced from many different types of rock,

core A piece of stone from which flakes are removed to produce a cutting edge.

hammerstone A stone used to strike a core in order to remove flakes.

flake A piece of stone removed from a core by striking it with a hammerstone.

(a)

FIGURE 5.26

(a) Anthropology students learn how to create stone tools by watching and emulating. **(b)** An Oldowan-style tool is produced by removing flakes from one side of the core. This schematic demonstrates the simplest and most basic way to make a stone tool. **(c)** Flakes removed by striking during tool production leave "scars" with negative bulbs or concavities (arrow). This is one form of evidence to identify rocks with signs of tool manufacture versus normal wear.

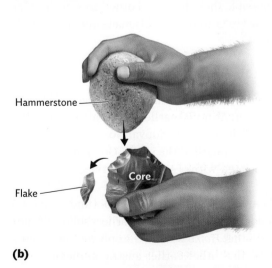

Hammerstone

Flake

Core

(b)

(c)

FIGURE 5.27

One reconstruction of how early tool use around 2.6 million years ago could have facilitated access to more meat, by making butchering more efficient. Some anthropologists suggest such collaborative activity may have been an important precursor to increasing reliance on language for communicating and organizing group activities.

knapping Making stone tools by hand.

Oldowan A style of very simple hand tools from after 2.6 million years ago, mostly produced by chipping a few flakes off a stone to reveal a single rough working edge.

but the best for knapping would be those that break in consistent ways when they are struck to form a sharp edge. Flint, obsidian, chert, quartz, and other rocks containing very small crystalline structures would have been best. To learn how to make these tools, younger individuals would likely have watched an experienced knapper and then practiced themselves until they got it right.

Since the first discovery of late Pliocene stone tools in association with *Homo habilis* fossils at Olduvai Gorge decades ago, many others have found evidence of similar toolmaking at many different locations in Africa. The exact uses Pliocene hominins had for these cores and flakes—sometimes collectively referred to as Oldowan tools—are also vigorously debated by those who study human origins. One hypothesis was that the tools were used to remove meat from scavenged animals. Core tools could also be used for scraping meat from the bones and also for breaking the bones to extract the precious high-fat, high-protein marrow (**Figure 5.27**). The flakes could also have been used for cutting meat from larger carcasses. It is also possible these tools had other uses, such as for processing plants, or even were used to craft other tools made out of materials (such as wood) that don't fossilize.

EARLY TOOL PRODUCERS

While Oldowan tools are undoubtedly purposefully made, the bigger mystery is which hominin species was the maker. As noted earlier, the Leakeys originally proposed *H. habilis* as the maker of the tools at Olduvai Gorge. In the 1990s, more examples of Oldowan tools were found at the site of Gona in the Awash region of Ethiopia, this time associated with a species identified as *A. garhi* (**Figure 5.28**).

These Gona tools were dated much earlier than previous tool finds, some 2.5 million years ago. Paleoanthropologists agree this is the earliest solid evidence of tool production and clearly shows that *Homo* was *not* the only tool-producing genus. It remains entirely feasible that other earlier australopithecines and

5 cm

FIGURE 5.28

This image shows the stone tools found at the site of Gona, Ethiopia, which were dated to 2.6 mya. These appear to have been made by members of the genus *Australopithecus*, not *Homo*. Prior to such finds, it was assumed only genus *Homo* produced tools.

later paranthropines were toolmakers as well. After all, there is really only one good basic method for producing choppers and other basic stone tools. This means many different groups of hominins could have potentially developed and used stone technologies completely independently of one another.

Regardless of the species making and using tools from 2.5 to 1 million years ago, they were a new—and more efficient—way that hominins were finding and processing their food in the fragmented woodlands/grasslands of Africa. Tool production also signals an increasing reliance on material culture and the social learning to transmit it. This is an early trend in human evolution that today distinguishes us from other living primates. Even if they were not necessarily direct human ancestors and are now extinct, these *Australopithecus*, *Paranthropus*, and early *Homo* tool users were extremely successful in evolutionary terms. They adapted to changing conditions, spread out across a vast continent, survived for millions of years, and developed the rudiments of culture.

MATERIAL CULTURE AND CULTURAL LEARNING IN PRIMATES AND HOMININS

The discovery of early tools at Olduvai Gorge and Gona was very exciting because it provided evidence that very early hominin behaviors (and not just hominin anatomy) were distinct from those of apes. Stone tools provide the earliest archaeological evidence we have of material culture—the objects we humans produce to help meet physical or social needs. As such, they also signal the existence of problem-solving and learning capabilities of those producing them. It is clear now that what we once thought were uniquely human traits, such as basic tool use and cultural learning, are widely observed in other animals, including many primates. Living apes and some monkeys manipulate objects occasionally to help with small tasks such as getting food.

FIGURE 5.29

In Uganda, chimpanzees use sticks to retrieve insects to eat from a termite mound.

cultural transmission The process by which cultural elements (behaviors, beliefs, and so on) are shared with and taught to and learned by others.

As our genetically closest living relative, it is no surprise that chimpanzees demonstrate numerous behaviors that are learned from other group members and passed down through generations, sometimes termed cultural transmission. These learned behaviors among chimpanzees mostly have to do with food procurement, such as hammering nuts with rocks, termite fishing with sticks, probing holes for food, or using spears to kill prey (**Figure 5.29**). However, other examples of learned behavior include grooming with leaf sponges, attention displays and greetings, and ways of devising greater personal comfort, such as fashioning sticks to shoo away flies.

These learned behavior patterns qualify as culture in part because they vary. That is, different behavioral patterns are being transmitted in different groups. To gather insects, chimpanzees will modify a stick and probe an ant or termite colony. The insects attack the stick, and the chimpanzees then withdraw it and eat the insects clinging to it. However, how the sticks are made and used differs across chimpanzee communities. In some, the sticks are made longer and the chimpanzee will use its hand to clean the stick of a large mass of insects to eat. In others, the sticks are made shorter and the chimpanzee eats the insects one at a time directly from the stick. The practice of using stones to crack open nuts is another excellent example of a regional pattern of chimpanzee culture because it only occurs in western African groups that are divided from those to the east by a river.

But some monkeys also display possible evidence of tool use and cultural transmission. One population of long-tailed macaques, worshipped at the long-used Buddhist shrine of Phra Prang Sam Yot in Thailand, interact often with visitors, including riding around on their heads. They have been observed pulling out human hair to floss their teeth, having learned to do this from each other (**Figure 5.30**).

Even while other animals exhibit cultural learning, human cultural learning is significantly different. Cultural expression in humans covers a much wider array of behaviors, not just those around food, communication, or grooming. The social learning that humans do to acquire this cultural knowledge is also far more complex. We imitate especially well. We learn quickly when being taught. Human children in particular are motivated and compulsive learners from a young age. They are seemingly programmed to trust what they are being told and can also quickly recognize the process and meaning behind a behavior rather than only imitating it. That is, human cultural learning is not only focused on an end result, which is a clear distinction from what we observe in other primates.

Most importantly, humans have cumulative culture. Cumulative culture refers to the fact that human behavior and technology have become increasingly complex with each new innovation and invention, building on an existing behavioral framework. That is, our entire species can potentially share the cumulative knowledge of past generations, whether passed one to one, such as parental instruction of a child, or shared with many others, such as through the internet or through formal schooling. This capacity is also linked to our abilities for massive and complex group cooperation, additional key features of our social behavior.

(a)

(b)

FIGURE 5.30

(a) In Thailand, these long-tailed macaques have learned to use rocks as stone tools to open shellfish. **(b)** At one temple location frequented by tourists, a single group of macaques have learned to floss with human hair.

SECTION 5.5

TELLING THE EARLY HUMAN STORY

In this chapter we have discussed how scarce fossil evidence is debated and interpreted to provide a basic scientific outline for the emergence of hominins, including our ancestors. When there is little evidence, as there is with early human evolution, there are gaps that need to be filled. And anthropology has other perspectives, drawn from a more humanistic rather than scientific tradition, to ensure an awareness of how that happens, and why that awareness matters.

PALEOANTHROPOLOGY AS A NARRATIVE

Dramatic fossil finds, such as those from the Rising Star cave system that opened this chapter, have an amazing ability to capture popular imagination. We want to know how these long-ago individuals relate to us, and what they tell us about who we are and where we come from. But to draw conclusions about millions of years of human history and fill in so many gaps in the scientific record, anthropologists must construct and continually revise a narrative to tie what we know together.

Anthropologist–writer Misia Landau has analyzed the ways that scientists have explained fossils and their relationship to us. Beginning with the early work of Charles Darwin and early paleoanthropologists such as Raymond Dart, Landau showed how their accounts of human evolution were often conveyed in the style of heroic journeys. They had key elements of folklore traditions: a hero, a primate ancestor often with a humble background that is somehow different than the others, who is in a relatively untroubled situation and then endures a series of challenges, like coming down from the trees, embarks on a dramatic and testing journey, like migration from Africa, and achieves the seemingly impossible, like becoming human. These same basic story elements are reproduced all around us in novels and movies.

Another way narratives of human evolution are conveyed is through artist interpretations. Science-based visualizations of key fossils are created by paleoartists who combine scientific knowledge and facial reconstruction techniques as guides to the final appearance. Reconstructions of hominins always rely heavily on best guesses about features, such as skin color or hairiness, that cannot be observed from the fossil record. Such choices become part of the way that these reconstructions then help create specific narrations of our past.

cumulative culture Traditions (such as tool use) that are built on and modified through time to expand and refine knowledge.

narrative Using language to create a coherent account of events or experiences.

folklore Traditional stories, crafts, rituals, festivals, and so on passed down as local knowledge and practice.

Artist John Gurche combines fossil evidence with techniques of facial reconstruction to create busts and bodies of extinct hominin species. His work was created from displays at the Smithsonian National Museum of Natural History. Each sculpture takes months and begins with a cast of an individual fossilized skull, which is then sculpted outward on the basis of forensic estimates of muscle, fat, and skin thickness. They are perhaps the best-researched renderings of their kind (**Figure 5.31**).

Piecing together narratives is required of other scientific fields. Developing a theory about how smoking tobacco causes cancer involved not only thousands of experimental studies but also assembling a "story" based on causal relationships. And, as Landau notes, explaining human evolution to nonscientists without imposing some type of narrative to pull the evidence together in a meaningful way is likely an impossible task. Yet unlike other human origin stories, such as Adam and Eve in the Garden of Eden, the narrative that paleoanthropologists advance is constantly changing as new evidence emerges and better ways of interpreting evidence are developed. This is again part and parcel of the scientific process of discovery.

FIGURE 5.31

These reconstructions of some hominins create one version of a visual narrative of the human story. Such reconstructions are shaped by scientific evidence, but because evidence is limited they also can reflect the world view of those creating them.

FIGURE 5.32

Kenyan paleoanthropologist Kamoya Kimeu receives an honorary Doctor of Science from Case Western Reserve University. Paleoanthropologist Richard Leakey, son of Mary and Louis, is at his left.

FIGURE 5.33

Ethiopian paleoanthropologist Yohannes Haile-Selassie (left), who trained in the United States in the 1990s, now leads the Institute for Human Origins at Arizona State University. On the right is another Ethiopian scientist, Berhane Asfaw, who became director of the National Museum of Ethiopia.

DIVERSITY IN PALEOANTHROPOLOGY

Paleoanthropologists, too, are sometimes portrayed as almost mythical heroes of science. Historically, the stories of the most famous fossil finds have highlighted the successes of White, non-African, and male researchers, in particular. Some examples are Raymond Dart's discovery of the first *Australopithecus* fossil uncovered by mining activity, the Leakey family's uncovering of very early *Homo* fossils at Lake Turkana in eastern Africa in 1960, and Donald Johanson's famous 1974 discovery of the australopithecine specimen that he named "Lucy" in Hadar, Ethiopia.

But African and non-male scholars have made important discoveries, too, in more recent decades. In 1984, Kenyan paleoanthropologist Kamoya Kimeu found an almost complete 1.5 million year old *Homo* skeleton, (**Figure 5.32**). Yohannes Haile-Selassie first discovered the 4.4 million-year-old skeleton of "Ardi" the *Ardipithecus* in 1994 (**Figure 5.33**). And Kaye Reed and her team unearthed a mandible (jaw) of what may be the earliest known *Homo* (2.8 million years ago) in Ethiopia in 2015 (see Figure 5.25).

One benefit of a more diverse scientific field is that the narratives that emerge highlight and notice different things, allowing scientists then to challenge each other in how they are interpreting evidence—ultimately building a fuller picture of what has happened in the past. To that end, many students of diverse backgrounds today are training as paleoanthropologists. This initiative is especially vital in eastern and southern Africa because it influences where fossil evidence gets housed and analyzed.

African nations are rightly concerned about possible misuse or removal of nationally important early hominin artifacts and other materials when projects are controlled by foreign interests, including universities and museums. Important early paleoanthropological artifacts have been removed from the African countries where they were unearthed, shipped out of the country, and displayed in hundreds of museums throughout the world This, then, becomes another form of wealth extraction, not gold or diamonds, but intellectual and cultural wealth. Many—but not yet all—of the most important fossil finds related to human origins have been returned and are now curated in the countries in which they were discovered (**Figure 5.34**).

FIGURE 5.34

The 300,000-year-old Kabwe or "Broken Hill" cranium was taken from a mine in what is now Zambia in 1921 and added to the collections of the Natural History Museum in London, England. Here it is on display as part of the museum's "Treasures" exhibition in 2013. The Zambian government has spent decades working toward repatriation of this remarkably complete fossil evidence of Middle Pleistocene *Homo*. As of 2023, they had not been successful.

5

Human Origins and the Earliest Hominins

In this chapter, we explore the questions of why and how human ancestors diverged from other apes, which ultimately led to the evolution of our species.

KEY TERMS
> australopithecine
> hominin
> *Homo*
> paleoanthropologist

5.1 | The Pliocene Epoch and the Challenges of Scarce Data

Assess strategies and challenges in evaluating the scarce fossil evidence for early human evolution.

- The fossil evidence for human evolution is scarce because it is so old and fragmentary. This means there can be significant debates around the scientific interpretation of limited evidence, and the need to constantly reassess our evolutionary story as new evidence is revealed.

KEY TERMS
> biological species concept
> clumping
> macroevolution
> Miocene epoch
> Pleistocene epoch
> Pliocene epoch
> splitting

5.2 | Identifying Our Earliest Ancestors

Distinguish early hominins from other primates.

- Early hominin fossils are found only in Africa and provide strong evidence that the first hominins (upright-walking primates) evolved on the continent after 7 million years ago.

- Some early hominin anatomical features, such as upright walking and the ability to digest an array of foods, proved advantageous to living in increasingly open and arid landscapes.

- By 2.5 million years ago, many hominin species were probably living alongside one another in eastern and southern Africa.

KEY TERMS
> canine blunting
> diastema
> divergence
> foramen magnum
> honing chewing
> human–chimp last common ancestor (HC-LCA)
> lineage
> longitudinal arch
> molecular clock method
> opposable
> transverse arch
> valgus knee

5.3 | Early Hominins

Outline the emergence of possible early human ancestors.

- There is no specific time and place that "humanness" emerges in the fossil record. Rather, skeletal features distinguishing humans from living apes, such as habitual upright walking (bipedalism) and generalized dentition, are shared by several different early hominin species and in varied (mosaic) combinations.

- We cannot easily identify the specific Pliocene species that was ancestral to humans because fossils provide only a limited view of ancestor–descendant relationships and mosaic evolution means no specific fossil can be claimed as our common ancestor.

KEY TERMS
- endocast
- mosaic
- paleoenvironmental reconstruction
- postcrania
- prognathism

5.4 | Tool-Making Pliocene Hominins

Relate tool use and production to the emergence of uniquely human behaviors.

- Hominin tool use appears around 2.6 million years ago and is significant as the first clear signal of humanlike behaviors that produce material culture. Members of other now-extinct hominin genera, not just our own genus *Homo*, produced tools.

KEY TERMS
- core
- cultural transmission
- cumulative culture
- flake
- hammerstone
- knapping
- Oldowan

5.5 | Telling the Early Human Story

Identify how diversity in the study of early human origins supports improved interpretation and protection of the fossil evidence.

- Diversity of scholars improves understanding of the fossil record of human evolution and management of the scarce evidence.

KEY TERMS
- folklore
- narrative

The Origins and Spread of Modern Humans

Archaeologists Jayne Wilkins and Ben Schoville have spent much of their careers excavating and analyzing stone tools—and the discarded rock fragments from tool production—at Pleistocene epoch sites in Africa. Their excavations at the Kathu Pan site in South Africa have yielded an array of triangular stone points, dating to 500,000 years ago (**Figure 6.1**). Wilkins and Schoville wondered who created these points and how they did so. Was it a very early *Homo sapiens*, or was it another Middle Pleistocene *Homo* species with similar technological capabilities?

The points look simple, but they are more refined than the crude Oldowan-style choppers found earlier in the same area that were associated with *Homo habilis*. It took some 10 to 15 sequential steps to create the geometric, balanced shape of the final tool. Many of these points also had additional working around the base that would allow a haft to be attached, suggesting use as spears.

To test this possibility, Wilkins and Schoville experimented using copies of points from Kathu Pan. They built a specialized backyard apparatus from a crossbow that could consistently simulate the thrust of a spear. They recreated sets of triangular stone points and hafted them to wooden dowels, using standard knapping techniques to create the same shapes from the same ironstone rocks found around the site (**Figure 6.2a**).

THE OTHER HUMANS

Major innovations in genetic technology are revolutionizing the ways anthropologists can study the other—now extinct—humans. But the longer-applied methods of closely examining dated fossils and experimentation remain important forms of evidence too.

LEARNING OBJECTIVES

6.1 *Homo erectus*
Explain what fossil and archaeological evidence suggests about *Homo erectus*.

6.2 Middle Pleistocene *Homo*
Identify the innovations and developments of Middle Pleistocene *Homo*.

6.3 *Homo sapiens*
Characterize the emergence of *Homo sapiens* and their anatomical, behavioral, and cultural traits.

6.4 The Other Humans and Us
Describe the groups that evolved from *Homo erectus* and their interaction through time.

Pleistocene epoch A division of the geological timescale that lasted from 2.6 million until 12,000 years ago and is associated with the beginning use of stone tools and the adaptive radiation of genus *Homo*.

stone point A shaped piece of rock typically used to create an arrow, spear, or other projectile.

haft To add a handle or strap to a tool, allowing more precision and force in how it can be used.

FIGURE 6.1

(a) Retouched points (~500,000 years old) from Kathu Pan in South Africa are pictured. The additional working at the base on some of the points suggests they were hafted onto wood to create spears. The *Homo* species that made the points is not absolutely known. Similar blades were invented elsewhere at around the same time, almost certainly independently. **(b)** Archaeologists Jayne Wilkins (left) and Benjamin Schoville examine points.

They then used the crossbow to repeatedly shoot the stone-tipped spear into an animal carcass, such as a springbok (**Figure 6.2b**). They compared the microscopic damage that resulted on the stone points to that on the excavated Kathu Pan points. While there is no absolute way to know how the points were used in the past, the wear and breakage patterns were similar to those created by spearing the springbok. This supports their hypothesis that the stone points

FIGURE 6.2

(a) These hafted stone spears were used in modern experiments to test their effectiveness. **(b)** This calibrated crossbow and springbok carcass (from a farm) experimental setup was used to test hypotheses that Kathu Pan stone points were used as hunting spears.

TABLE 6.1

Emergence of Different Tool Types[a]

~3.3 mya to ~300 kya	Handheld tools, initial stages represented by simple struck flakes, core and pebble tools (sometimes called "Oldowan"), followed by bifacially shaped handaxes, cleavers, and picks (sometimes called "Acheulean"). These simpler tool types are considered evidence of now-extinct hominins, including our ancestors.
~300 to ~40 kya	Retouched points, hafted tools, bone points, simple ornaments and jewelry; increasing variability in how tools are being produced through time. These more complex tool types are considered as evidence of early humans.

[a]mya = million years ago; kya = thousand years ago.
Note that tools made entirely from wood or other organic materials were certainly in use, but do not preserve as well in the archaeological record.

were used as spears for hunting—an important behavioral innovation that helped early humans adapt well to their environments by making it easier to safely extract meat as food.

In this chapter, we trace how anthropologists illuminate the complicated picture of our own species' emergence. We begin with what is known of the first member of our genus *Homo* to expand beyond Africa—*Homo erectus*, the longest surviving *Homo* species (thus far), thriving for around 1.5 million years. We then explore the many other species in our genus that followed—called Middle Pleistocene *Homo*, including those ancestral to modern humans. And we consider how our species arose and what makes us human—anatomically and behaviorally, how we interacted with other hominins, and why we are now the only hominin species remaining.

The fossil record of the Pleistocene is certainly complicated and sometimes hard to decipher. For the reader, this can mean juggling many potential species names, site names, and tool types. So to help navigate the pages ahead, several figures will provide summary maps that locate the major fossil discovery sites for *Homo erectus* (discussed in Section 6.1), Middle Pleistocene *Homo* (discussed in Section 6.2), *Homo sapiens* (discussed in Section 6.3) and close the chapter by discussing some contemporary, closely related species that lived alongside ours and with whom we occasionally reproduced, as reflected in our genes today (discussed in Section 6.4). When there is archaeological evidence of tool production that requires learning and skill, such as hafted spears, anthropologists often switch from referring to those that produced them as "hominins" and start talking instead about "early humans" (**Table 6.1**).

Homo erectus

Around 2 million years ago (mya), within an eastern and southern African landscape inhabited by *Australopithecus sediba* (the last surviving *Australopithecus* species), the large-toothed soon-to-be-extinct *Paranthropus robustus*, *Homo habilis*, and *Homo rudolfensis*, there arose a new kind of tool-using hominin with a larger brain. This was *Homo erectus*, our first established direct human ancestor. This new species did something remarkable that its other hominin contemporaries did not: it thrived in Africa but also expanded way beyond the continent. By 1.8 million years ago, *Homo erectus* had spread to areas as far away

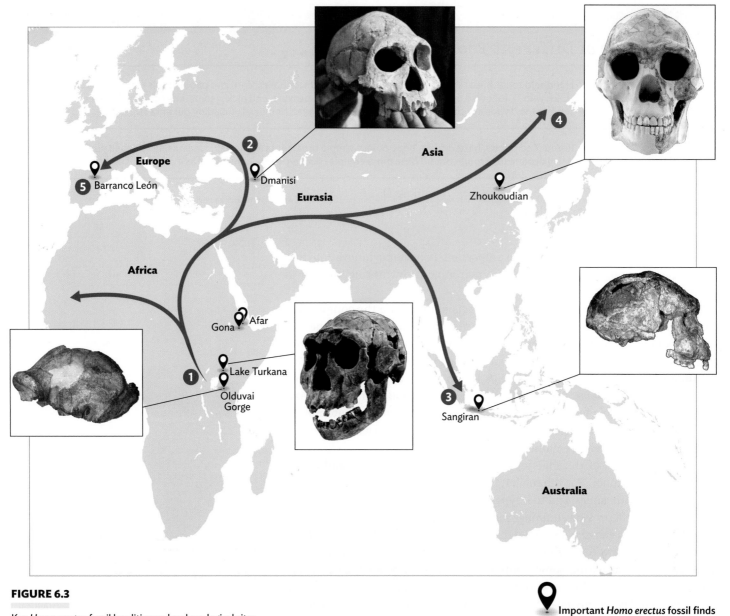

FIGURE 6.3

Key *Homo erectus* fossil localities and archaeological sites are shown. Suggested directions of expansions outside Africa by *Homo erectus* are also shown. The earliest *Homo erectus* fossils are found in eastern Africa 1.9 mya **(1)**, expand to Eurasia by 1.8 mya **(2)**, then rapidly expand into southeastern Asia **(3)** and eastern Asia **(4)** by 1.6–1.7 mya, and finally move into western Europe by 1.2–1.4 mya **(5)**.

Important *Homo erectus* fossil finds

as the Caucasus Mountains region of eastern Europe as well as throughout eastern and southeastern Asia (**Figure 6.3**). By 1.2–1.4 million years ago, *Homo erectus* populations were living in western Europe as well. From its first appearance at 1.9 million years ago, *Homo erectus* persisted in other parts of the world for an extraordinarily long time, with dates as recent as 140,000 years ago in southeastern Asia. But *Homo erectus* populations disappear from Africa around 800,000–900,000 years ago, seemingly replaced by new *Homo* species.

Homo erectus seems to have been better adapted to the cooler and drier late Pleistocene climate, as it survived while all the other contemporary hominins, confined to Africa, became extinct. *Homo erectus* successfully adapted to the more open grasslands and more seasonal environments of the early part of the Pleistocene epoch. *Homo erectus* was also able to survive in the northern latitudes of Europe and Asia, which were much colder than equatorial Africa where this species first evolved. As evidence of their success, in the span of only 200,000 years, *Homo erectus* occupied much of what is now Africa, Europe, and Asia.

Homo erectus not only flourished in many new and different environments but also did so for approximately 1.5 million years. As a result, *Homo erectus* fossils display much variability in brain and body size. In fact, they are so diverse that anthropologists debated whether *Homo erectus* should be considered a single, if widely spread, species or whether it might be two: *Homo ergaster* was earliest and found primarily in Africa while *Homo erectus* was later and found throughout Africa, Europe, and Asia. A major discovery in the 1990s at the 1.8-million-year-old site of Dmanisi, outside Tbilisi in the Republic of Georgia, provides some key evidence to this debate.

At Dmanisi, paleoanthropologists discovered fossil skulls and long bones from at least five individuals with the telltale cranial features of *Homo erectus*, alongside more than 1,000 stone tools of the types also typically associated with the species (**Figure 6.4**). The brain sizes of these fossils ranged from 550 to nearly 800 cubic centimeters (cc), reflecting the range of variation of all other

(a)

FIGURE 6.4

(a) In this overview of the Dmanisi site, medieval walls can be seen, as the site was later a medieval village. **(b)** This reconstruction is based on a *Homo erectus* specimen from Dmanisi. **(c)** Examples of flaked tools (labeled A–G; grouped and showing the same tool, not to scale, from different sides) were excavated at Dmanisi; they were most likely produced by *Homo erectus*.

(b)

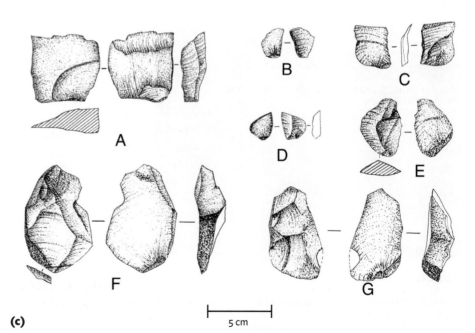

(c)

5 cm

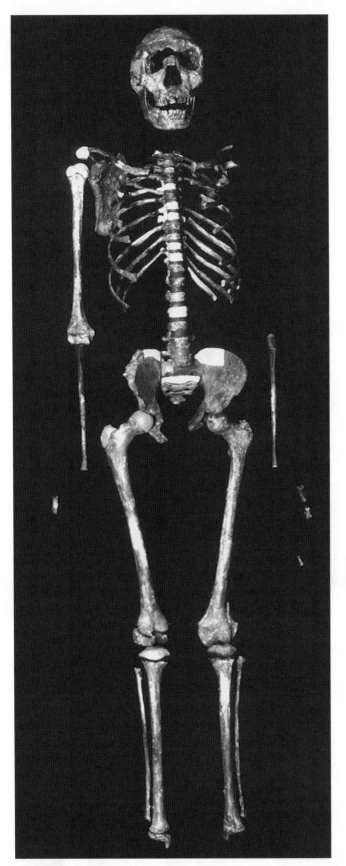

FIGURE 6.5

The so-called "Nariokotome Boy" was excavated in Lake Turkana, Kenya, in 1984 by paleoanthropologist Kamoya Kimeu and is dated to about 1.6 mya. It is an important *Homo erectus* fossil because it is so complete, which allows researchers to estimate height very accurately.

known hominin skulls from about 2 million years ago. On this basis, the Dmanisi collection provides evidence bridging the smaller crania of *Homo erectus* fossils found in Africa and the larger ones of eastern Asian fossils. It suggests a single, geographically diverse species united by extensive and ongoing gene flow. Some scholars still wonder if perhaps there were two different species living together at Dmanisi, a question that, it is hoped, more fossil finds will clarify further.

Despite their variation from one another, *Homo erectus* fossils collectively show a number of anatomical differences from other African hominins living at the same time. These distinctive body features—a taller stature, a fully bipedal gait, and modern limb proportions—may largely explain the comparative success of *Homo erectus*, by allowing for increased locomotor efficiency when traveling over long distances. That is, *Homo erectus* bodies could move well through varied landscapes to get food or other resources, using less energy to do so.

STATURE

Strong evidence of *Homo erectus* having a modern and taller stature was found near Lake Turkana in Kenya from a singularly spectacular find. Nicknamed the "Nariokotome Boy," this pre-adult fossil dates to about 1.6 million years ago and represents the most complete hominin fossil ever recovered. The skeleton is about 40% complete, providing significant information on such things as diet and growth patterns and walking ability (which was much the same as ours). Although we don't fully know whether *Homo erectus* children had a long period of adolescence like modern humans, the maturation of their teeth suggests they had a more delayed adolescence than earlier hominins, if not quite as delayed as modern humans. Therefore, we cannot identify precisely how old the Nariokotome fossil was when it died, but the suggested range is somewhere between 8 and 11 years (**Figure 6.5**).

The age is important because it helps estimate likely adult stature. Nariokotome Boy was about 160 centimeters tall, suggesting he would have achieved a height of close to 183 centimeters, or 6 feet, as an adult. This is the best direct evidence that some *Homo erectus* individuals were as tall as modern humans and taller than other contemporaneous hominins. Most notably, while all hominins show evidence that they walked upright, this skeleton shows an individual with none of the remaining skeletal adaptations to living even part of the time in trees. That is, like us, it had a narrow pelvis and shoulders, large joints, and short toes. This is one basic reason that *Homo erectus* is considered a likely ancestor of living humans.

FOOTPRINTS

Further evidence of a modern form of bipedality was discovered between 2006 and 2008, when paleoanthropologists uncovered 97 preserved footprints left by 15–20 individuals at Ileret, also near Lake Turkana in Kenya, dating to about 1.5 million years ago

(a)

(b)

FIGURE 6.6

(a) Excavations underway at Ileret, Kenya, near Lake Turkana, expose a track of footprints. **(b)** *Homo erectus* footprints preserved from this site are dated to around 1.5 mya.

(**Figure 6.6**). Using forensic techniques to reconstruct footprints (the same techniques used in crime-scene investigations today), paleoanthropologists showed that most footprints are indistinguishable from tracks made in the same fine sediments by humans living in the same location today who go habitually barefoot. That is, they have the same double arches, a big toe fully in line with the other toes, and a similar stride length and gait as us. This evidence leaves no doubt that *Homo erectus* was fully bipedal and walked just like us.

BRAIN SIZE AND CRANIAL APPEARANCE

Homo erectus had key cranial features that distinguished it from earlier *Homo* species. For example, even though the cranium was larger overall, the braincase was long and low with a receding forehead. The cranial vault bones were also quite thick. The brow ridges were much larger than in other hominins, and in some fossils, the brow ridge formed a shelf called a supraorbital torus. The back of the skull had a similar thickening of bone called an occipital torus. The top of the skull also had a thickening of bone down the center called a sagittal keel, which differed from a sagittal crest of *Paranthropus* in that it did not support muscle attachments for chewing (**Figure 6.7a**). It is likely these cranial features strengthened the skull, perhaps because of excessive stress caused by using the front teeth as a "third hand" for holding objects or biting and tearing foods. The face and teeth of *Homo erectus* were reduced in comparison to other hominins, especially the premolars and molars. The face was also less projecting (less prognathic), but there was no forward-projecting chin on the mandible, which we only see in our species, *Homo sapiens*.

cranial vault The rounded part of the skull that surrounds the brain.

supraorbital torus A thickened shelf of bone above the eye orbits, characteristic of *Homo erectus* fossils, especially those from Asia.

occipital torus A thickened shelf of bone near the back of the cranium, characteristic of *Homo erectus* fossils, especially those from Asia.

sagittal keel A thickened area of bone that runs from the top of the forehead to the back of the cranium, characteristic of *Homo erectus* fossils.

FIGURE 6.7

(a) *Homo erectus* crania exhibit a supraorbital torus, occipital torus, and sagittal keel. **(b)** *Homo erectus* had larger brain sizes than earlier hominins but also exhibited considerable variability in brain size through time. Relative brain size is estimated from endocranial volume, determined by internal measurements of the skull case (facilitated by computer scanning). Modern humans skulls average around 1500 cc. The graph shows the endocranial (skull interior) size in cubic centimeters (cc) of previously discovered fossil specimens compared to that of modern humans, as a means to estimate relative brain size.

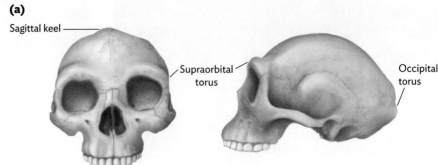

(a)

Sagittal keel

Supraorbital torus

Occipital torus

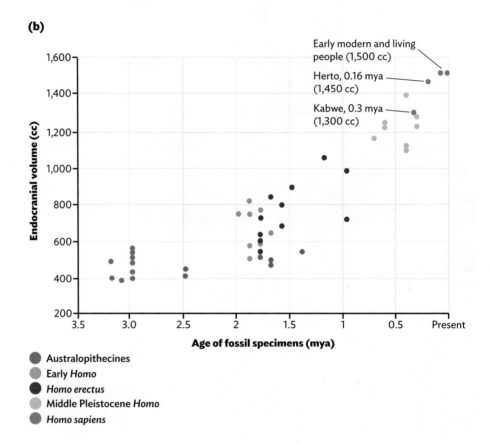

(b)

Early modern and living people (1,500 cc)

Herto, 0.16 mya (1,450 cc)

Kabwe, 0.3 mya (1,300 cc)

- Australopithecines
- Early *Homo*
- *Homo erectus*
- Middle Pleistocene *Homo*
- *Homo sapiens*

In addition to these skeletal differences, *Homo erectus* also had larger brain sizes than any of the other contemporary or preceding hominins (as well as living apes), averaging around 950 cubic centimeters (cc) when the species first evolved. A million years later, once the new species had spread out across Asia and Europe, its brain size was even larger, averaging around 1,200 cc—reaching the low end of modern human variation (**Figure 6.7b**).

BRAIN SIZE AND INTELLIGENCE

What can we surmise about the relationship between overall brain size, size of specific brain regions, and cognitive capabilities ("intelligence") of past hominins? Can estimates of brain size of different fossil species predict meaningful differences in ability? Adult human brains vary greatly in size without any appreciable difference in function (**Figure 6.8**). A human brain half the size of another can be just as socially and technologically capable, sometimes even more so.

But when we compare across species, differences in brain size and especially details of brain anatomy do seem to matter. Mammals with larger brains

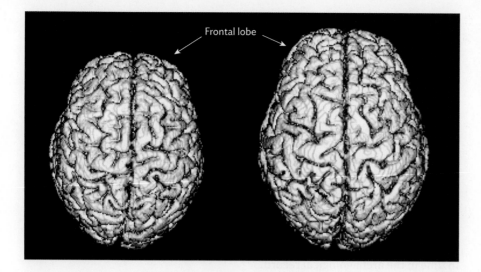

Frontal lobe

FIGURE 6.8

Three-dimensional reconstructions are shown of the smallest and largest brains of living individuals in a large dataset that was developed by biological anthropologists, through scanning, to test the relationships between modern human brain size and cognition. Despite the variation in size, note the similar degree of folding and complexity.

relative to body size are generally associated with both greater cognitive abilities and being more social as a species.

However, what seems to matter in distinguishing the human social and problem-solving capabilities from those of other living primates is not just brain size itself relative to the body but expansions in key brain regions such as the frontal lobe, which are associated with cognitive capabilities such as language, detailed memory storage, planning ahead, and awareness of both self and others.

Brains themselves do not fossilize. But sometimes, rarely, as the brain deteriorates it can be replaced by sediments, leaving an imprint of the outside contours of the brain called an endocast. These can help roughly extrapolate the capabilities of past hominin species.

On the basis of reconstructed endocasts, the brains of early *Homo erectus* from sites such as Dmanisi show an apelike organization of the frontal lobe. By comparison, *Homo erectus* specimens in Africa after 1.5 million years ago, and later in southeastern Asia, show brain forms closer to modern humans (**Figure 6.9**). This includes more prominence in regions associated with toolmaking and social cognition, indicating a brain that is "language-ready" even if not yet language-using.

A more reliable indicator of intelligence, however, can come from looking at other forms of archaeological evidence, such as the tools the species produced and used, to infer how these larger average brain sizes may have been linked to the types of social–behavioral capabilities that helped *Homo erectus* expand so successfully and last so long compared to most other hominins.

endocast A fossilized model of the hollow space inside a skull, often preserving some details of brain anatomy.

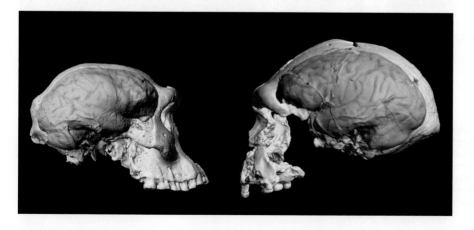

FIGURE 6.9

Endocast reconstructions of the brain topography of two *Homo* specimens are shown. The one on the left is from Dmanisi, Georgia (dated to 1.8 mya), and the one on the right is from Sangiran, Indonesia (dated to 1.3–1 mya). The brain shape on the left is much more like living apes, while the brain shape on the right is much more like modern humans, despite both specimens being associated with *Homo erectus*.

Homo erectus, over time, developed more sophisticated tool traditions than other species before it. In eastern Europe and most of Asia, *Homo erectus* continued to use the very basic Oldowan-style tools produced by *Homo habilis* that had only one flaked side. But in some sites, especially in Africa and western Europe, *Homo erectus* also developed so-called Acheulean-style tools (**Figure 6.10**). The handaxe is the most characteristic multifunctional tool form associated with *Homo erectus*, used for more than a million years. Handaxes are bifaces, meaning flakes were removed from both sides of a rock core, producing a more effective cutting edge useful for tasks such as cracking nuts or pounding open animal bones. A basic handaxe shape can also serve as the template for increasingly refined tools, such as spear and arrow points, found later in time in the archaeological record.

Over time, *Homo erectus* produced tools with even more refined shapes, with increasing symmetry and more uniform sizes, and using a wider array of rock materials. Crafting tools consistently from different kinds of stone is not done easily by simple imitation. It requires forethought and planning to learn a sequence of complex tasks, and probably the capability to teach and learn from others who are more experienced. *Homo erectus* was becoming more reliant on an array of specialized tools to get and process food more efficiently, perhaps from a shared home base that included some coordination of small-group activities.

Acheulean A style of tools, dating from around 1.8 million years ago, that includes two-sided handaxes and more functional diversity of tools, created from further working of removed flake edges to shape them.

handaxe A multipurpose bifacial stone tool, associated particularly with *Homo erectus*.

(a)

(b)

(c)

FIGURE 6.10

(a) Paleoanthropologists Michael Rogers (left) and Sileshi Semaw (right) at the site of Gona in the Afar region of Ethiopia, where findings show that *Homo erectus* individuals produced various styles of tools. Simpler choppers (Oldowan-style tools) are shown in the bottom rows of **(b)** and **(c)**, and more sophisticated retouched flakes, where the edges were later reworked to resharpen and refine them (Acheulean-style tools), are seen in the upper rows of **(b)** and **(c)**. These tools are dated with *Homo erectus* fossils from between 1.5 and 1.25 mya.

In short, the combination of improved efficiency in gait, for traveling across open landscapes, and larger brains, able to produce more sophisticated tools, allowed *Homo erectus* to better kill and process animals while making group activities (such as foraging parties) safer, faster, and more productive. The extent to which *Homo erectus* did such activities in cooperative groups is unclear, however. But the preserved footprints at Ileret, Lake Turkana, offer a tantalizing glimpse of one moment: It seems multiple (perhaps 15–20) males were walking together, perhaps even as a hunting party.

These early meat-eating efforts may have relied significantly on scavenging, such as from carcasses of prey taken down and left by giant cats and other large predators. Paleoanthropologist Briana Pobiner spent seven months measuring the remains of lion kills in a private reserve in Kenya, where lions (predators) are common but hyenas (scavengers) are rare (**Figure 6.11**). In their larger kills, such as zebras, she found that over half of all bones had significant amounts of meat left. Once eaten by a lion, a zebra carcass is left with, on average, around 15 kilograms (~30 pounds) of meat scraps, or some 60,000 calories. That could feed more than 30 *Homo erectus* for a day, if they were able to compete with other scavengers such as hyenas to get access to leftovers and use tools to crack open the bones.

The Middle Pleistocene *Homo* archaeological record is filled with examples of hunted and butchered large game, such as elephants and giant cats. Larger animal remains were transported back to home bases to process and share, and more tools were being produced to acquire and process both meat and plant foods. Access to slow-moving herbivores was facilitated by a cooling and drying climate, as herds of grazing antelopes or gazelles expanded with new grasslands.

Many questions about *Homo erectus* remain. We don't yet know if *Homo erectus* used speech-like symbolic communication. Better communication helps with coordinated group activities such as hunting or processing large animals, as well as with learning sequential skills such as tool production. It also isn't presently clear if *Homo erectus* used controlled fire to cook. Most paleoanthropologists think not. Regardless, the established set of features—tool use, bigger brain, and probably more coordination from a home base—were likely what helped *Homo erectus* spread so far and last for more than 1.5 million years.

FIGURE 6.11

Paleoanthropologist Briana Pobiner estimates meat-scavenging possibilities at Ol Pejeta Conservancy, Kenya, in 2011.

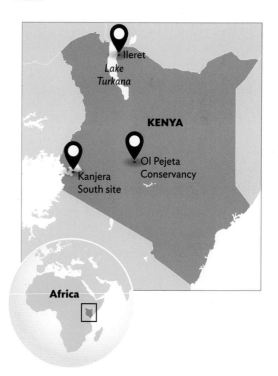

SECTION 6.2

MIDDLE PLEISTOCENE *Homo*

The Middle Pleistocene *Homo* fossils—spanning 800,000 to 300,000 years ago—are not anatomically *Homo erectus*, nor are they modern *Homo sapiens*. With brain sizes that approach those of modern humans, these fossils reflect a crucial evolutionary transition into the species that then evolves into *Homo sapiens* and a number of other species, as we see in Section 6.4. On the basis of inference from archaeological material about the behavior of these individuals, such as more refined toolmaking, use of fire, and cooperative hunting from home bases, some paleoanthropologists refer to these fossils as "archaic *Homo sapiens*." We

Middle Pleistocene *Homo* Describes a hominin that anatomically and behaviorally is neither *Homo erectus* nor *Homo sapiens*, who lived in the period between 800,000 and 300,000 years ago.

use the term "Middle Pleistocene *Homo,*" which is appropriate until there is better evidence to determine if these fossils really are best categorized as the earliest *Homo sapiens* or may reflect species that are not an immediate ancestor to us.

ANATOMICAL AND BEHAVIORAL ADAPTATIONS

These new Middle Pleistocene hominins had average brain sizes of 1,200–1,300 cc, larger than *Homo erectus* and even closer to the range of modern humans. Their head shape is clearly different as well: rounder and higher, with less forward projection of the face (though not as round and vertical as in modern humans). The teeth are also within the size range of modern humans but on the larger end of the scale, especially the front teeth (**Figure 6.12**).

(a) Modern *Homo sapiens* (~300 kya to present)

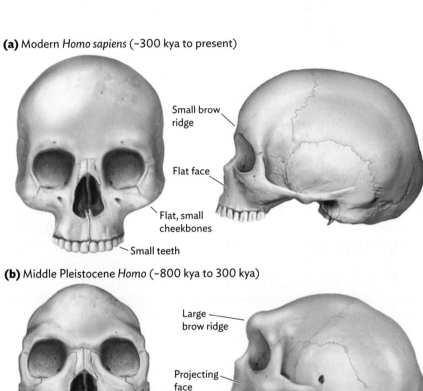

Small brow ridge

Flat face

Flat, small cheekbones

Small teeth

(b) Middle Pleistocene *Homo* (~800 kya to 300 kya)

Large brow ridge

Projecting face

Large, wide cheekbones

Large teeth

(c) *Homo erectus* (~1.8 mya to 140 kya)

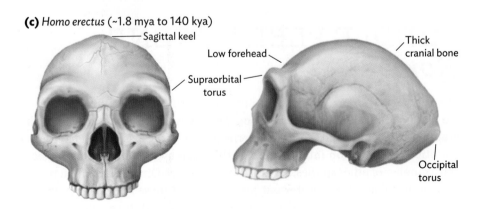

Sagittal keel

Thick cranial bone

Low forehead

Supraorbital torus

Occipital torus

FIGURE 6.12

Cranial features of **(a)** anatomically modern *Homo sapiens,* **(b)** Middle Pleistocene *Homo,* and **(c)** *Homo erectus* are compared.

The face overall was more prognathic (forward projecting) than ours and still lacked a chin. The long bones and crania were thicker than ours, with large muscle attachments. They were shorter than modern humans, though heavier, reflecting greater overall mass and muscularity. But they also show a lot of variation anatomically, with many different combinations of primitive and derived anatomical traits appearing at the same time, in the same region, and even within the same individuals.

The Middle Pleistocene was a period of overall cooling of the planet but also a time of more dramatic swings between colder and warmer periods. During cold periods, glaciers formed in northern latitudes. The rest of the planet was drier, as fresh water was locked up in the expanding ice sheets. This meant that it was also a period of increasingly fragmented forests and expanding grassland and deserts. *Homo* species thrived during this time period. They proliferated and spread, living in many habitats across Europe, Africa, and Asia: on varied coasts, lake edges and river margins, tropical and temperate forests, and savannas.

These new *Homo* species likely arose because their particular physical and behavioral repertoire was especially well adapted to obtaining food in these more varied landscapes. Populations on the coast ate fish, while those inland didn't, which highlights why there was no singular "paleolithic diet." Our ancestors ate varied combinations of lean proteins, roots, green vegetables, fruits, nuts, and honey; these unprocessed and varied diets are associated with better human health. Our bodies are not designed to be optimized to one specific mix of animals and plants, defining one "special" diet, despite various claims today. Innovations in technology, including hunting tools and fire, supported this crucial dietary flexibility.

TOOL PRODUCTION

Over time, Middle Pleistocene *Homo* produced increasingly refined tools, initially in Africa and then in Europe and Asia. For the first time, we see archaeological evidence that *Homo* was purposefully and repeatedly making smaller and specialized tools, including through use of a skilled technique called pressure flaking. These tools, used for hunting, butchering, and woodworking, include projectile points of various sizes, scrapers, knives, and picks.

One remarkable site near Schöningen, Germany, contained well-preserved wooden spears dating to more than 300,000 years ago (**Figure 6.13**). Experiments based on spears reconstructed with the same length and tapering suggests they were extremely effective long-distance projectiles, used to kill large animals without having to get dangerously close, unlike earlier thrusting spears.

Middle Pleistocene *Homo*'s more carefully crafted tools were finer and thinner, making it easier to do tasks such as butchering large animals. Their fossil remains and their tools are found near kill sites, where sometimes multiple species of large animals have been downed and—based on the cut marks on bones—expertly butchered. This doesn't mean that hominins with such weapons were not still gathering plants or scavenging meat when the opportunity arose. But it suggests that these populations were putting particular and focused effort into including more meat into their diets—a transition that occurred over time. And they clearly were hunting and not just scavenging, which requires more coordination, communication, and planning.

FIGURE 6.13

Wooden spears from Schöningen, Germany, were excavated in the 1990s. The spears have been attributed to a group of European Middle Pleistocene *Homo*.

pressure flaking Applying pressure (using a stick, bone, or antler) to chip away small stone flakes and create more refined shapes and sharper edges.

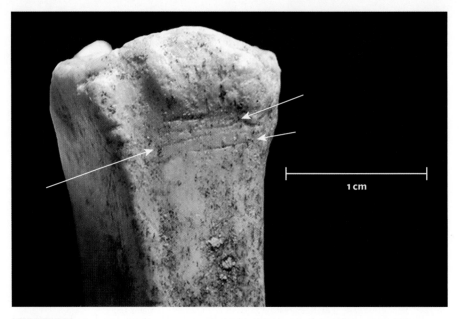

FIGURE 6.14

A small antelope leg bone with cut marks (arrows) was found at Kanjera South, Kenya, and was dated to ~2 mya. Stable isotope analysis of animal teeth at the same site suggests they were eating mostly grass, meaning the hominins were living in open grasslands.

Anthropologists use an array of evidence to understand the history of *Homo* diets, including the increasing importance of hunting, eating, and cooking meat. Meat-eating is first signaled by cut marks on bone, indicating animal butchery. The patterns of early butchery marks suggest hominins were extracting higher-fat organs, brains, or marrow from inside bones, an effort that was made much faster and easier by basic stone tools like choppers. One early site where *Homo* embraced meat-eating is Kanjera South in Kenya, which yielded 3,700 animal fossils and 2,900 stone tools dated to nearly 2 million years ago (**Figure 6.14**).

USE OF FIRE

Whereas evidence of the use of fire is at best equivocal for *Homo erectus*, Middle Pleistocene *Homo* certainly was fully able to control fire. Hearths have been identified at several sites dating to as early as 400,000 years ago. By 300,000 years ago, many of the Middle Pleistocene *Homo* have base camps that include hearths with burned bone (**Figure 6.15**), in a pattern of rapid diffusion across landscapes that suggests subgroups of hominins were sharing the innovation with one another.

Cooking was a remarkable innovation for gaining more energy from available foods, meaning less food needed to be hunted, gathered, or scavenged. Cooking (reflected archaeologically in burned bone) isn't apparent before 1 million years ago but becomes common after about 400,000 years ago. Cooking meat makes it easier to eat and digest, so that the body can extract more calories from a cooked portion than a raw portion. Burned mammal long bones also more easily yield the fatty marrow within. In addition, cooking allows plants to release more digestible starch (for example, a cooked potato yields twice the calories of a raw potato). Cooking also kills harmful bacteria.

(a)

Burned bone remains

(b)

FIGURE 6.15

Recognizing the archaeological evidence for cooking meat is assisted through experiments by archaeologists such as this one **(a)**, to see how meat purposefully roasted on fires enters the archaeological record as burned bone remains **(b)**.

Qesem Cave

ISRAEL

Asia

Beyond the benefits of fire for cooking, maintaining home fires was probably an important technological and behavioral adaptation for staying warm in a cooling climate, especially at higher latitudes. Controlled fire also enabled hominins to inhabit new environments, such as outside caves in areas with dangerous predators. It also can extend work and leisure hours into the night.

Excavations from Qesem Cave in Israel, for example, revealed a lakeside hunter-gatherer home base of Middle Pleistocene *Homo*, with fire hearths used for cooking meat (**Figure 6.16**). The layout of stone flakes and animal bones also suggests that the group allocated separate areas to different tasks, such as nut processing or fish preparation. Paleoanthropologists found plants in one space, tools in another, and animal remains in another. Additionally, these early humans produced tools from a greater variety of raw materials, which suggests that hominins had access to expanding social networks for trade.

Hearth

Hearth

FIGURE 6.16

Excavations at Qesem Cave, Israel, revealed a 300,000-year-old ash-filled hearth that was surrounded by tools for butchering animals, suggestive of a base camp arrangement organized around a fire.

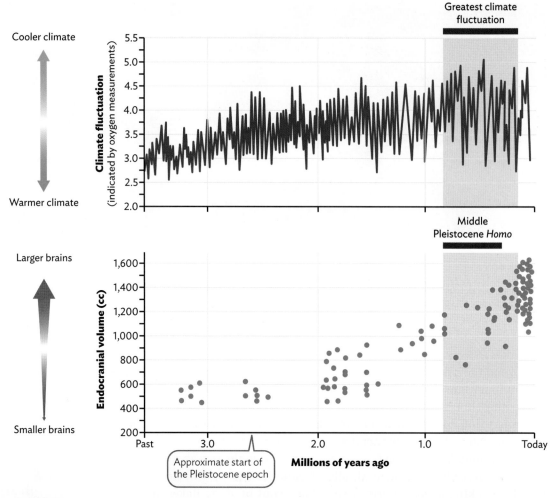

FIGURE 6.17

The relationship between hominin endocranial volume and climatic variability is plotted through time. Brain size shows the greatest increase during the period of greatest climate fluctuation. The orange dots reflect specific fossil finds or modern humans that are plotted on the far right side of the diagram.

BRAIN DEVELOPMENT

Throughout the Pleistocene epoch, from roughly 2.6 million years ago on, *Homo* brains steadily increased in size. An important observation from the fossil record is that the periods of greatest increase in average brain size were those in which climates were much more variable, suggesting natural selection for cognitive capabilities that could better manage unpredictable conditions (**Figure 6.17**). In other words, the enhanced cognitive abilities provided by brain size increase supported new means of tool production and more complex social behaviors.

Natural selection for larger brain size in the human lineage did not happen independently of other evolutionary anatomical and behavioral trends. Rather, all these changes related to and built on one another, including shifts in what hominins were eating across the Pliocene and Pleistocene epochs (**Figure 6.18**). That is, larger brains and increased cognitive abilities allowed *Homo* to make better tools and organize their foraging more effectively through communication and planning. Innovations such as cooking allowed even more calories to be obtained from their food during digestion even with a smaller gut, which in turn allowed brains to grow larger in a constant feedback loop of increasing cognitive capabilities, language, and social complexity.

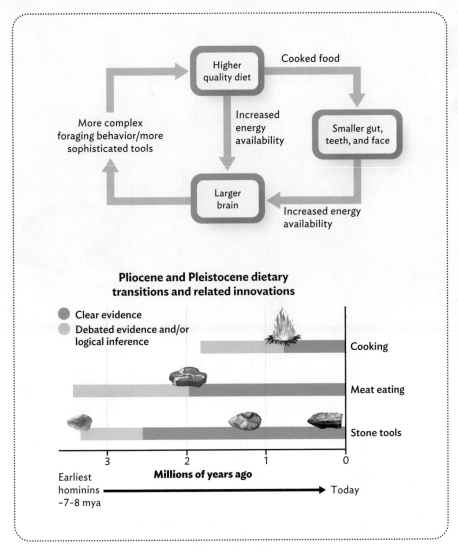

FIGURE 6.18

It is likely that some evolutionary synergies of trends in *Homo* diets, anatomy, and behavior developed throughout the Pleistocene epoch.

FRAGMENTED HABITATS AND REGIONAL DISTINCTIVENESS

Groups of Middle Pleistocene *Homo* became biologically isolated from one another as major climatic changes cut populations off from each other over longer distances, leading to genetic drift. Selection pressure for genetic adaptations to new habitats also likely encouraged biological differences to emerge in a short time span. This is the most likely explanation for why Middle Pleistocene *Homo* in Africa, Europe, and Asia display very clear anatomical differences (**Figure 6.19**). The relationship between this "regionalism" and the subsequent emergence of *Homo sapiens* (around 250,000 years ago) was one of the most hotly debated questions in paleoanthropology for several decades.

Specifically, fossils showing the larger brain and other anatomical features of Middle Pleistocene *Homo* appear earliest—800,000 years ago years ago—over much of the African continent. By 200,000 years ago, fossils are found in Africa that are nearly indistinguishable from modern humans. These populations are our most likely direct ancestors.

But the fossil record in Asia and Eurasia complicates the story. In Europe, numerous Middle Pleistocene *Homo* fossils have been discovered that show

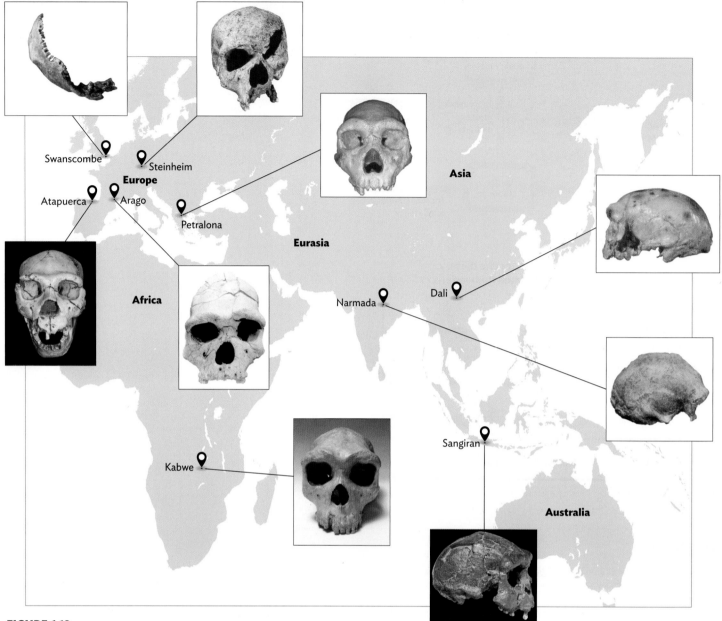

FIGURE 6.19

Middle Pleistocene *Homo* fossil remains from each continent demonstrate the degree of cranial variation in *Homo* individuals seen throughout the world, likely caused by fragmentation of *Homo* populations due to climate change.

considerable variability in cranial form. These fossil localities span the continent from England (Swanscombe) to Germany (Steinheim), Spain (Atapuerca), France (Arago), and Greece (Petralona). Asian sites such as Narmada in India suggest occupation sometime between 300,000 and 500,000 years ago, likely by *Homo erectus*. Fossils from sites further east in China (such as Dali) and Indonesia (such as Sangiran) also show a mosaic of *Homo erectus* and Middle Pleistocene *Homo* cranial features, leading to considerable confusion about which species of *Homo* were living in Asia during the late Middle Pleistocene epoch. Most likely, *Homo erectus* lived alongside a new arrival to eastern Asia sometime between 200,000 and 300,000 years ago. Asian lineages of *Homo* may have been evolving independently of those in Africa and Europe.

Based on such fossil evidence, the multiregional model (or regional continuity model) arose in anthropology, proposing that modern human anatomy emerged slowly and simultaneously within each region of the world. A single

multiregional model A theory of modern human emergence in which modern human anatomy is considered to have evolved within each continent slowly through time, where a single species was maintained across time by long-distance gene flow.

species maintained a shared gene pool across continents through long-distance gene flow, beginning with *Homo erectus*, the first to leave Africa. But more recently, advances in genetics have instead favored an assimilation model, which proposes that Middle Pleistocene *Homo* evolved into *Homo sapiens* first in Africa and then spread outward, ultimately replacing other *Homo* species in the Middle East, Europe, and Asia, but assimilating some of their gene pools through mating.

assimilation model A theory of modern human emergence in which modern human anatomy evolved in Africa and spread to other continents by migration of modern humans to other regions, largely replacing but also interbreeding with existing hominins living in Europe and Asia and assimilating their DNA into the modern human gene pool.

Homo sapiens

The Middle Pleistocene, and the proliferation of increasingly large-brained, meat-eating, tool-reliant, and cooperative species it yielded, represents a slow and uneven transition toward humanness. But around 250,000 years ago, we are able to identify what are more clearly anatomically and, later, behaviorally modern humans like ourselves. **Table 6.2** lists some features generally considered by paleoanthropologists to signal "humanness" in the fossil record. These features are not necessarily unique to modern humans, but they are especially well-developed in our species.

ANATOMICALLY MODERN

What does it mean to be "anatomically modern," like us? Or asked another way: How do you identify whether a fossil belongs to our species or is a Middle Pleistocene *Homo*? Paleoanthropologists identify *Homo sapiens* fossils from certain key features, including average adult brain size above 1,300 cc, a rounded skull

---

TABLE 6.2

Anatomical and Behavioral Traits Associated with Becoming Human

Anatomical "Humanness" in Fossil Remains	Behavioral "Humanness" in Archaeological Material
• Large brain relative to body size	• Group organization around productive tasks
• Enhanced brain structures relevant to memory, information processing, language use, social cooperation	• Hunting animals and eating meat, with an emphasis on sharing and cooperation
• Smaller teeth and face relative to body size with smaller chewing muscles	• Controlled use of fire, such as for cooking
• Body, legs, and arms suggestive of more efficiency in walking, such as thinner and lightly built bones and smaller muscle attachment sites	• Use of a home base, living in open areas
	• More sophisticated, consistent tool forms that suggest tool manufacturing traditions
• Facial features of reduction in bone mass, such as a forward-projecting chin	• Reliance on tools/technology to get and process food or solve other challenges
• Genome more similar to that of modern humans	• Group/personal identity, such as reflected in adornment
• Longer childhood/adolescence (seen in dental development)	• Larger social networks, such as trading materials or disseminating new technologies over longer distances
	• Ritual activity, such as purposeful burial
	• Symbolism and abstract thought, such as reflected in art
	• Manipulating ecologies as part of adapting to them

FIGURE 6.20

Cranial anatomical features of *Homo sapiens* are illustrated. These reflect a further reduction in the size of the face and teeth and further increases in brain size and overall skull height and skull roundness. Such features are critical for identifying new *Homo sapiens* fossils in the archaeological record.

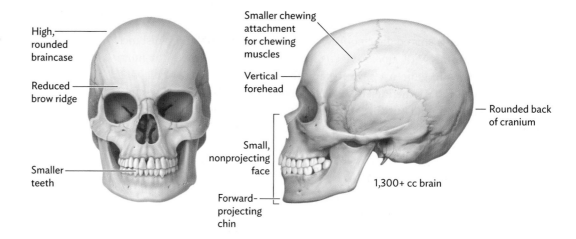

High, rounded braincase

Reduced brow ridge

Smaller teeth

Smaller chewing attachment for chewing muscles

Vertical forehead

Rounded back of cranium

Small, nonprojecting face

Forward-projecting chin

1,300+ cc brain

MOROCCO

Jebel Irhoud

Africa

with a non-projecting face but with a projecting chin, and smaller overall teeth (**Figure 6.20**). These differences are of course relative, as these features are all a continuation of trends we observe in the hominin fossil record dating back to over 1 million years ago. And there are examples of fossils that share features of both Middle Pleistocene *Homo* and *Homo sapiens* and cannot be easily placed as one or the other. This is one of the fundamental challenges of paleoanthropology: placing specific fossils into rigid species categories that reflect a much more dynamic evolutionary process.

For example, Jebel Irhoud Cave in Morocco yielded almost anatomically modern humans perhaps as early as about 300,000 years old, with the smaller face, rounded forehead, and jawbone with a chin that is most like those of modern humans but with much larger teeth than we see in our own species (**Figure 6.21**). These fossils seem to be transitional between Middle Pleistocene *Homo* and anatomically modern *Homo sapiens*, and they mark what is probably the very earliest time period for the anatomical changes that define our species.

(a)

(b)

FIGURE 6.21

The Jebel Irhoud site in Morocco contains 300,000-year-old fossils that preserve cranial features suggestive of a transition to anatomically modern humans. **(a)** This view shows the cave entrance where the remains were excavated. **(b)** Bone remains from Jebel Irhoud (yellow) are shown against a complete cranial reconstruction (blue), demonstrating how fragmentary the paleoanthropological record is and how computer modeling is used to estimate adjoining skeletal form from limited information.

The first definitive anatomically modern *Homo sapiens* fossils are found in sub-Saharan Africa at sites such as Omo Kibish and Herto (both in Ethiopia), from around 200,000 and 160,000 years ago, respectively. Other African sites associated with early anatomically modern *Homo sapiens* are slightly younger (100,000–150,000 years old) but are found across the continent at places such as Klasies River (South Africa) and Singa (Sudan), indicating our species rapidly expanded throughout the continent.

Anatomically modern human fossils are also found outside Africa from after 150,000 years ago (**Figure 6.22**). Early *Homo sapiens* fossils recovered from two cave sites in Israel (Qafzeh and Skhul) date to 110,000 years ago, meaning migrations out of Africa through the Arabian Peninsula must have happened before this time. The spread of anatomically modern *Homo sapiens* well beyond Africa subsequently accelerated, with the species reaching the continents of

FIGURE 6.22

This map shows some key early anatomically modern *Homo sapiens* fossil finds.

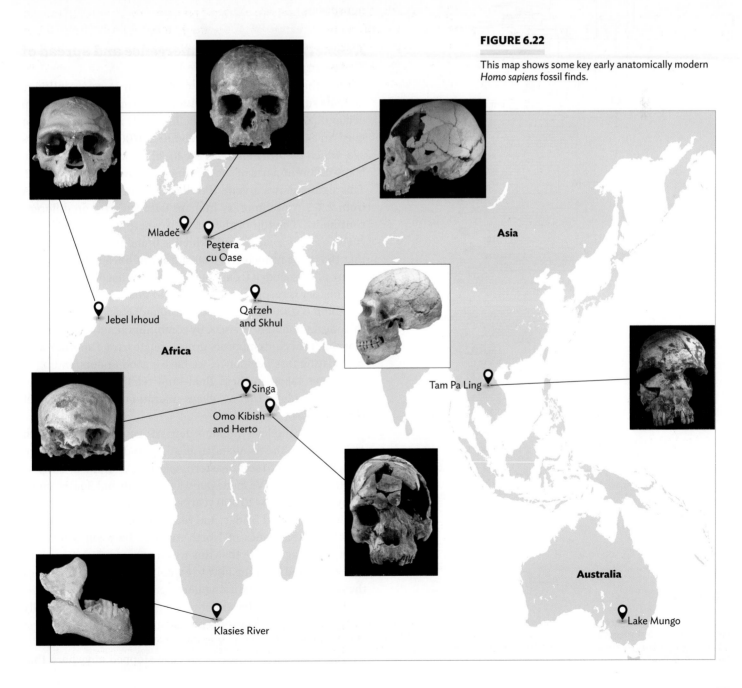

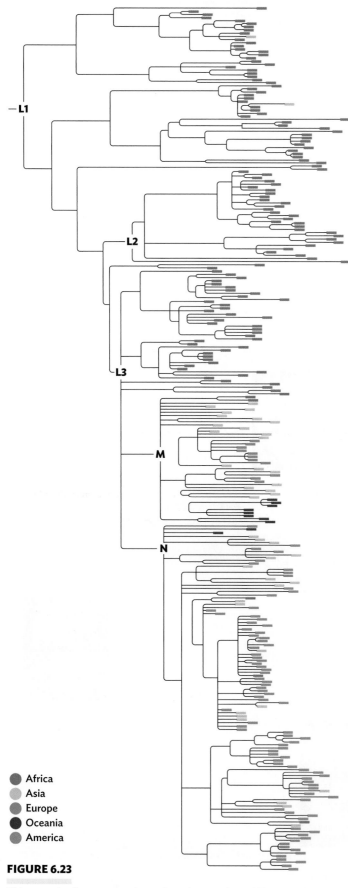

- L1
L2
L3
M
N

- Africa
- Asia
- Europe
- Oceania
- America

FIGURE 6.23

This example of a gene tree of 2,777 living humans from different world regions (shown by the colors) suggests that all are ultimately descended from a small group of early humans in Africa, represented by lineage L. Subsequent migrations out of Africa resulted in mutations represented here by lineages M and N.

Asia (at Tam Pa Ling) by 65,000 years ago and then Australia (at Lake Mungo) by 40,000–50,000 years ago. Europe seems to have been settled by anatomically modern humans later, with fossils clearly attributed to *Homo sapiens* dating to only 42,000 years ago at sites such as Peştera cu Oase (Romania) and Mladeč (Czech Republic) and sites without fossils attributed to our species as early as 48,000 years ago.

Despite these finds, the fossil record will always produce an incomplete picture of the emergence of our species. We never know if we have truly found the earliest fossil from a particular region, for example. Fortunately, the human story is also recorded in our genes, and major advances in gene sequencing and DNA extraction technologies over the last two decades have produced a wealth of new information on the origin of our species.

A Genetic View of the Emergence and Spread of *Homo sapiens*

Studies that measure the rate of mutation in genes in living humans suggest all living humans are descended from a group of about 30,000 anatomically modern early *Homo sapiens* that lived in sub-Saharan Africa about 200,000–250,000 years ago, which is consistent with the fossil record and recorded in many different parts of the genome, as shown in **Figure 6.23**. This figure shows a gene tree based on mitochondrial DNA from 2,777 contemporary humans with ancestry on different continents. The top of the figure is where it is rooted in the genetic lineage labeled L1, which is found in Africa. The fact that the other branches are all subsets of lineage L1 indicates we are all descended from populations that lived in Africa, and that history is recorded in our genes to this day.

About 65,000 years ago, populations of *Homo sapiens* began shifting to inhabit new areas. By combining genetic evidence of how different contemporary groups relate to one another with the existing fossil evidence, we have a good understanding of the routes taken in these final—and relatively rapid—major waves of modern *Homo sapiens* migration across the planet (**Figure 6.24**).

Initially, modern humans left Africa along a southern route through the Arabian Peninsula to India, then to eastern Asia, and finally to southeastern Asia and Australia as early as 60,000 years ago. We made our way to North and South America by about 15,000–20,000 years ago, crossing the then-above-water Bering Land Bridge, and reached the Caribbean and the extreme Arctic zones of North America between 8,000 and 4,000 years ago. Note that this was a process of shifting into new areas, and learning how to exploit new types of resources they offered, rather than singular migration events.

Reaching Australia and the Americas was an especially important watershed event for our species, as it was the first time *Homo sapiens* had expanded beyond the range of *Homo erectus*. *Homo erectus* seems to have stopped anywhere that

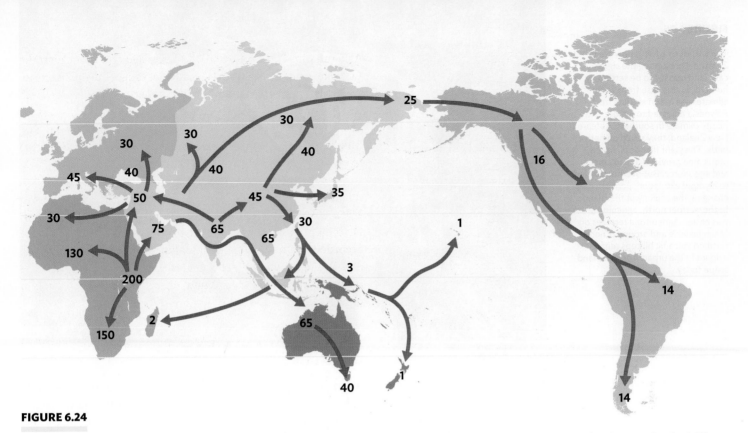

FIGURE 6.24

This is one reconstruction of the overall pattern of peopling of the world by early humans during the Pleistocene and Holocene epochs. The exact details of different reconstructions vary, based on the date estimates and data source being used, but the overall pattern is consistent. Numbers indicate the approximate dates of each major migration event (given as thousand years ago, or kya).

migration became more complicated, such as the edges of major land masses. So *Homo erectus* never crossed substantial bodies of water to settle places such as Crete, Madagascar, Australia, or Fiji.

The settlement of the final third of the planet's surface—the smaller islands of the Pacific—took longer because it required the development and refinement of extremely sophisticated sailing and navigation technologies. Modern humans began expanding into the more remote reaches of the Pacific Ocean around 3,500 years ago, finally settling the hardest-to-reach islands of Hawaii and New Zealand only about 1,000 years ago.

As smaller groups split off to settle new regions, they carried only a sample of the genetic variation from the original population. This resulted in a long series of founding events as modern humans expanded outward faster and farther, with each event reducing overall genetic variability in the descendant populations (Chapter 3). This is why African populations today have the most genetic variability and Pacific Island groups have less: overall diversity decreases with increasing distance from Africa (**Figure 6.25**).

Importantly, this spread of anatomically modern humans coincided with periods of considerable global climate change. The particular suite of features that allowed more symbolic communication, technological innovation, and group coordination meant our species was able to adapt effectively to varied and changing environments.

genetic lineage The pattern of mutations in genetic code that connect an ancestor's genome to that of its descendants.

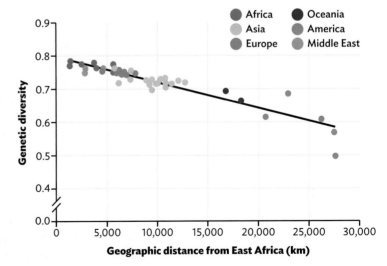

FIGURE 6.25

Genetic diversity in populations today is reduced the farther they are located from Africa, because populations were founded more recently and typically by smaller groups that carried only a subset of the diversity found in ancestral populations.

FIGURE 6.26

The islands of what is now New Zealand were among the significant land masses to be settled by humans, in this case from warmer climates. As Māori settlers from Polynesia adjusted to a more temperate climate in southern Aotearoa/ New Zealand, they relied on native birds. The giant flightless, herbivorous moa provided a ready meat and egg source. But overhunting led to its rapid extinction, permanently changing the ecology of the islands. In the warmer north, agriculture was easier. Agricultural terraces on Maungakiekie and around other fortified volcanic hilltops remain evident in the urban Auckland landscape today.

As humans began settling never-inhabited lands, they caused especially rapid and significant landscape changes, resulting from hunting new species and clearing land. Aotearoa (New Zealand) was the last major land mass settled by humans, by voyagers from Eastern Polynesia around 800 years ago. Māori settlers, coming from a tropical to a temperate climate, began a process of changing the landscape and species, which was accelerated further by the arrival of European settlers 500 years later (**Figure 6.26**).

The ability to organize and create new technologies provides the means to fundamentally change the ecosystems in which humans live, helping them live longer and in larger populations. This amazing capability for niche construction results from anatomical, but more importantly behavioral, adaptations of modern humans. Of course, the same amazing capacities to change ecosystems to meet our needs has been the primary driver of massive habitat destruction and declining global biodiversity (Chapter 16).

BEHAVIORALLY MODERN

What we consider "anatomically modern" humans, with bodies that function like ours, and "behaviorally modern" humans, with the ability to think and act as we do, did not emerge simultaneously. Anatomically modern humans emerged first, perhaps as much as 100,000 years earlier. Behavioral modernity refers to advanced cognitive capacities, which allow the learning of complex tasks, planning ahead, abstract thinking such as that needed to create art, symbolic communication, flexible social arrangements, social identities, norms and rules for behavior, and cooperation with non-kin. It also signals increasing reliance on culture to organize social groups and activities—the recognition of shared meanings and the capability to transmit those meanings.

Much like anatomical modernity, this shift to behavioral modernity occurred earliest in Africa and then spread to the rest of the world. It is visible in the archaeological record in Africa after about 150,000 years ago, and it becomes more definitely present archaeologically in Africa and elsewhere after 100,000 years ago. A remarkable combination of imagination, technological innovation, and accumulated knowledge gave rise to a new material culture reflecting complex cognition and sophisticated social worlds, much as we experience today.

FIGURE 6.27

Examples of early symbolic expression associated with modern humans include **(a)** colored engraved decorations, such as this engraved ochre from Blombos Cave, South Africa, **(b)** portable figurative art, such as this lion-man figure from Germany, and **(c)** cave paintings, such as this woolly rhinoceros scene from Chauvet Cave, France.

(a)

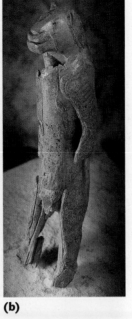

(b)

(c)

Art and Ritual

Modern humans are highly reliant on symbols (including language) to transmit accumulated cultural knowledge and traditions across generations. Art provides a clear indication of such symbolic communication in the past, and evidence of such art is used to estimate when human symbolic communication expanded.

For example, an early possible example of using colors to decorate is reflected in findings of scored red ochre at Blombos Cave in South Africa, dating to around 75,000 years ago (**Figure 6.27a**). Clearer examples of art are found after 45,000 years ago, including etchings on cave walls and portable figurines (**Figure 6.27b**). The spectacular cave paintings at famous sites such as Leang Bulu' Sipong (in Indonesia) and Lascaux and Chauvet (both in France) show particular artistic mastery of abstraction and meaning, all clear hallmarks of behavioral modernity (**Figure 6.27c**).

FIGURE 6.28

A cave wall from Grotte de Cussac, France, shows an engraving of horses.

ritual Describes a recognized social event that marks a life transition, such as death.

Another important marker of symbolic behavior that can be identified archaeologically is intentional ritual burial of the dead. For example, at the site of Qafzeh cave in Israel, dated to 110,000 years ago, the remains of an adolescent boy with severe cranial trauma were carefully laid in a pit. Two deer antlers were laid on the upper part of his chest near where the hands rested, which likely reflects an intentional inclusion with meaning. Burial decorations become increasingly elaborate through time, and especially in Europe, they were often entwined with art by 30,000 years ago. At Grotte de Cussac Cave in southwest France, early humans were buried using existing abandoned bear nests as the base, colored with red ochre pigment, and with some of the human bones organized into piles. The associated cave walls at Grotte de Cussac include beautiful etchings depicting animals and people created by torchlight (**Figure 6.28**).

Specialized Tool Production

Around 75,000 years ago, the archaeological record shows that *Homo sapiens* individuals were producing more specialized and standardized kinds of tools, including blades and microliths. Blades are stone tools that are long and thin, which allowed the longest possible cutting edge to be crafted from a stone flake. Microliths are very small tools that are hafted into wood and used to make lighter compound tools such as spears that are more effective for throwing long distances.

These new techniques for blade production were probably innovated multiple times by early African *Homo sapiens*, before arriving later in Asia and Europe after 45,000–50,000 years ago. Increasing effort put into the symmetry of tools over time also suggests the value placed on the aesthetics of the objects, not just their utility.

These new tools would have helped *Homo sapiens* to hunt and process food more efficiently than other *Homo* groups who were also hunting and gathering. For example, these new tools enabled fishing and the harvesting and processing of shellfish, which in turn provided an important additional (and very stable) source of protein for those on the coast or near large waterways. An atlatl was a later invention (after 18,000 years ago) that extended a throwing arm so a spear traveled faster and further; this helped especially in hunting larger and faster animals (**Figure 6.29**).

FIGURE 6.29

Effective hunting tools were likely invented over and over in many different parts of the globe. Here archaeologist Jason Nez shows visitors to Grand Canyon National Park how tools were used for hunting large animals by Indigenous people in the Americas. He is holding an atlatl in his right hand, which was a hooked stick used to throw projectiles further and with greater velocity.

FIGURE 6.30

This reconstruction shows the Upper Paleolithic mammoth bone huts excavated at the site of Mezhirich in Ukraine, which was used as a winter encampment.

Clothing and Shelter

Specialized tools also allowed for the production of material culture that expanded the means to adapt to even more extreme environments. Modern humans began wearing loose-fitting pelts as long as 200,000 years ago, at least according to genetic studies of the species of lice that are especially well adapted to live on our clothed bodies. New tools subsequently allowed humans to make tailored clothing to allow a tighter fit, which better maintained core body temperature.

The development of building traditions from locally available materials allowed people to erect safe freestanding structures for protection from the elements. At the site of Mezhirich, in what is now Ukraine (**Figure 6.30**), at least four huts were built from now-extinct mammoth bones around 25,000 years ago, and similar structures have been found across eastern Europe. The site of Kostenki in what is now Russia around the same time suggests a food storage facility made of the skulls of over 60 mammoths, evidence that these humans accumulated food to help bridge periods of food shortages (such as freezing winters).

Trade and Personal Adornment

One related feature of modern human behavior that is observable in the archaeological record is the emergence of wider social connections, via the development of trade and other networks across larger land areas. This can be seen archaeologically in the spread of raw materials and processed goods farther and farther from their points of origin, such as volcanic glass discovered far from any volcano (used to create sharp blades) or ivory transported far from where

it was collected. We can only see the materials humans traded archaeologically, but we can assume they also shared other things of value such as preserved food, mates, support in times of need, and new ideas for technological innovations.

We also only see evidence of personal adornment within the last 100,000 years. Early examples include 60,000-year-old carved ostrich eggshells from the Diepkloof Rock Shelter in South Africa (**Figure 6.31a**) and 82,000-year-old drilled shells recovered from the Taforalt Cave site in Morocco (**Figure 6.31b**).

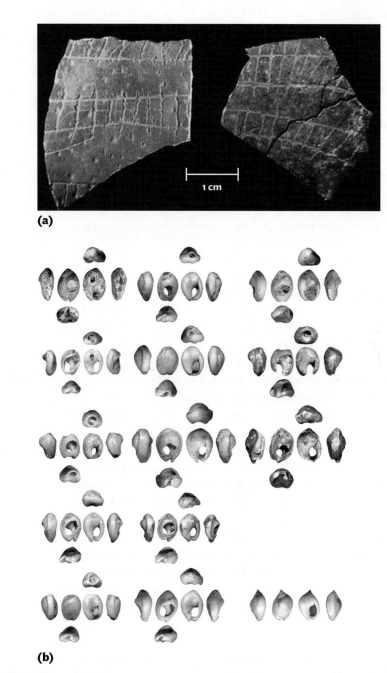

(a)

(b)

FIGURE 6.31

Beads were made from a variety of materials as early as 82,000 years ago, including **(a)** carved ostrich eggshells and **(b)** drilled shells. Such items were likely made into jewelry and reflect personal adornment, an important indicator of individual or group identity.

The emergence of personal adornments such as jewelry suggests another important aspect of human behavioral modernity: a sense of shared or distinctive social identities. Modern humans place very high value on signaling to others—through language, dress, diet, or the ways we move or modify our bodies—the groups we are (or want to be) part of. Gender, place of origin, religion, occupation, and sports teams are some examples. Wearing an engagement ring can signal that one is married or soon to be, but because it is worn usually by women it also helps others to classify gender, and an especially large stone can also suggest one is wealthy. Thus, proliferation of such adornments over time and in different sites suggests a clearer sense of identities was emerging, both within and between groups.

Language and Speech

Central to behavioral modernity is the ability to transmit knowledge in ways that allow it to be accumulated across generations, such as traditions regarding tool and food production or rituals around how the dead should be treated. This capability in using symbolic forms of communication probably improved very gradually. For humans, our language capabilities require both the physical means to control the sounds and body movement that create language and the capacity to understand novel vocalizations and signs. This is linked to direct neural connections between our brain's motor cortex and our larynx or vocal cords, something not seen in other living primates.

Signed or spoken words don't survive in the early human archaeological record. So how do we infer the language capabilities of past hominin species? Producing the sounds of contemporary human speech requires coordination of breathing, tongue, and mouth movements, while producing the signs of sign language requires coordination of the hands, torso, and facial movements. Anatomically, one important indicator of the potential to produce oral speech is the shape of the hyoid bone, which is suspended in the neck and anchors the tongue (**Figure 6.32**). The hyoid bones of living primates are shaped to support an air sac, not support speech; the same is true of the australopithecines. The fossils across genus *Homo*, by comparison, have a hyoid bone shaped much like ours. This suggests all *Homo* species had the anatomical capability to form words in a similar way to modern humans. But the fossil record cannot tell us whether or not they did so. Most paleoanthropologists conclude speech probably was not exclusively a modern human trait, but our species was certainly the most reliant on and effective in using it.

Genetic studies provide additional insights. One contemporary human gene, called FOXP2, suggests some past mutation enhanced our ancestors' speech ability compared to that of living apes. The FOXP2 is not a gene for speaking per se. Rather, it creates a protein that acts to control the expression of various other genes related to brain development, including functions such as vocal control and understanding words. These speech-related FOXP2 mutations (in just three base pairs) have been identified in genetic studies of early anatomically modern *Homo sapiens* but also in other Pleistocene hominins, especially the Neanderthals, who are discussed in Section 6.4.

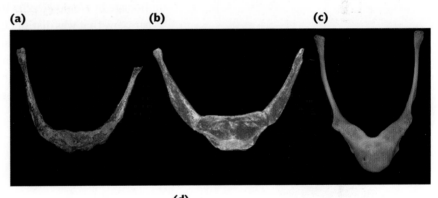

(a)   (b)   (c)

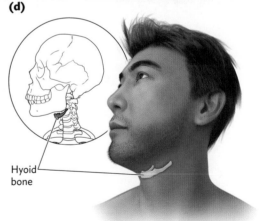

(d)

Hyoid bone

FIGURE 6.32

The hyoid bones of primates vary considerably, depending on their functions. Those of **(a)** modern humans and **(b)** Neanderthals differ from those of **(c)** chimpanzees and reflect the capacity for spoken language. **(d)** The position of the hyoid bone in modern humans is illustrated.

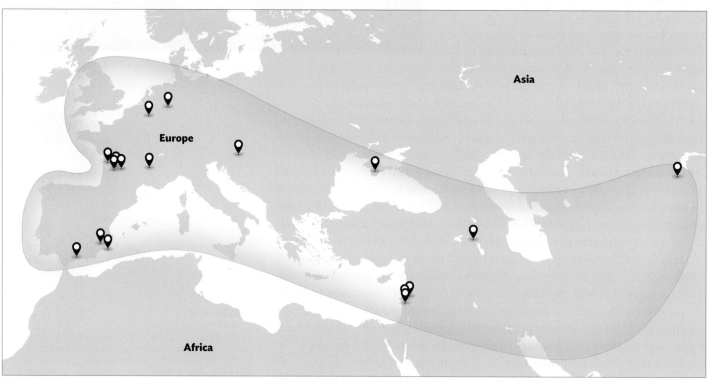

SPAIN

Sima de los Huesos

Europe

Neanderthal A now-extinct species of humans that lived primarily in Europe and parts of western Asia between about 430,000 to 35,000 years ago.

THE OTHER HUMANS AND US

At the same time that our behaviorally modern *Homo sapiens* ancestors emerged and spread, there were already other species of genus *Homo* living across Europe, Africa, and Asia. This raises an intriguing question: What happened during the later Pleistocene that transformed a diversity of thriving *Homo* species 200,000 years ago to just one single surviving species today? In this section, we consider these other species, how they are related to us, and what happened to them. By far the best studied of these species are the Neanderthals.

THE NEANDERTHALS

The Neanderthals lived across Europe, the Middle East, and western Asia from around 400,000 years ago to 35,000 years ago (**Figure 6.33**), including in areas that were extremely cold in the winter. They likely evolved directly from a lineage of *Homo erectus* that had been living in Europe for nearly a million years, one that was distinct from other *Homo erectus* populations in Africa. This is confirmed by DNA analysis from the 500,000-year-old remains of 28 Middle Pleistocene *Homo* individuals from Sima de los Huesos, Spain, as direct ancestors of the Neanderthals. It has clarified that Neanderthals and modern humans had been evolving along separate evolutionary lineages for at least half a million years.

Asia

Europe

Africa

Neanderthal site

Distribution of Neanderthal fossil sites

FIGURE 6.33

The geographic range of Neanderthals is depicted based on fossil and archaeological discoveries. Locations of key sites are plotted indicating a density of Neanderthal finds in western Europe.

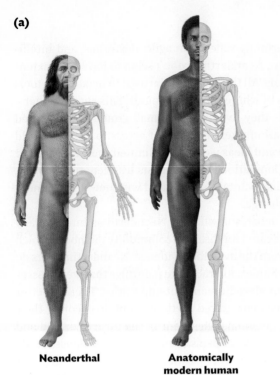

(a)

Neanderthal

Anatomically
modern human

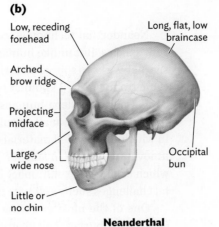

(b)

Low, receding
forehead

Arched
brow ridge

Projecting
midface

Large,
wide nose

Little or
no chin

Long, flat, low
braincase

Occipital
bun

Neanderthal

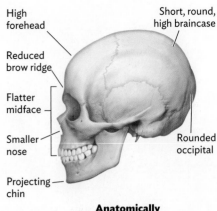

High
forehead

Reduced
brow ridge

Flatter
midface

Smaller
nose

Projecting
chin

Short, round,
high braincase

Rounded
occipital

**Anatomically
modern human**

(c)

FIGURE 6.34

(a) A comparison of Neanderthal versus modern human body proportions shows differences in stature and overall body mass, with Neanderthals being shorter and stockier than anatomically modern humans. **(b)** Cranial differences are reflected in several ways between Neanderthals and anatomically modern humans. The occipital bun of a Neanderthal is a broad expanded area of bone projection, not a shelf as was seen in *Homo erectus* but more prominent than the rounded occipital of modern humans. **(c)** An artistic representation of a living Neanderthal male shows the large nose and sloping forehead characteristic of this species.

Compared to modern humans, Neanderthals were short, strong, and stout, with big faces and even bigger noses, and *larger* brains. Otherwise they were anatomically much like us (**Figure 6.34**). Paleoanthropologists generally think their larger brain wasn't a continuation of the long-term hominin trend toward greater cognitive capacity, but rather the result of a scaling effect. That is, Neanderthals had greater body mass than modern humans and thus had larger brains as a result. Genetically, Neanderthals are closely related to modern humans, with perhaps one difference per 750 base pairs of DNA.

What do these biological differences really mean, though? Could they understand, talk, and act much like us? Because Neanderthals preferred living in protected caves, they have left significant archaeological clues in multiple sites spread across much of Europe. On the basis of this evidence, they can be defined as behaviorally modern humans because they sometimes did many of the things modern humans do, but not as consistently.

For example, Neanderthals almost certainly had controlled use of fire and used hearths for warmth and cooking. Neanderthals also developed their own distinctive tool style (sometimes called "Mousterian"). This style used a similar flake-based technology as *Homo sapiens* to make a range of different tool types (**Figure 6.35**). Some of these tools were spear points that were effective for hunting at close range, either as a thrusting spear or as a short-range projectile. Many Neanderthal sites are densely packed with both these stone tools and butchered animal bones such as those of red deer, bison, woolly rhinoceros, horse, and other medium to large herbivores. Stable isotopic analysis of Neanderthal bone remains suggests they were heavy consumers of meat, perhaps more so than modern humans. But there is no evidence they used fitted clothing, which may explain their reliance on dietary and skeletal adaptations for better managing cold rather than the tool-based solutions that typify modern humans living in cold climates.

Mousterian A sophisticated style of tools characterized by a technique of producing and refining sharpened flakes that are particularly suited to hunting.

FIGURE 6.35

Two examples of Neanderthal tools referred to as Mousterian are pictured. The image on the right shows a core that has been prepared to produce the specific desired shape of the spear point shown in place here (black arrow).

Neanderthal technology certainly reflects an agile, dexterous, and intelligent species. But unlike humans, Neanderthals don't seem to have used extensive networks to source materials. All the raw material used to make these tools came from within 5 kilometers of where they were found. This suggests that—compared to modern humans—they lived in very small groups, with limited mobility and very small population sizes. The lack of access to a wider world in which they traded materials and ideas would have limited their capacity for innovation. Living in smaller populations also suggests less genetic diversity, which can be an evolutionary disadvantage when faced with new environmental challenges such as climate change.

One of the most enduring debates is whether Neanderthals intentionally and ritually buried their dead or cared for disabled community members, which cannot be clearly established from the available evidence. Neanderthal sites do not show the development of complex abstract cave paintings that we see associated with their anatomically modern human contemporaries. There is better evidence that Neanderthals used ochre, a red earth pigment, to decorate their bodies and that they also used personal adornment in the form of drilled and painted shell pendants, beads made from parts of animals, and necklaces made from bird bones. Pierced seashells that were painted and likely strung together as a form of a necklace date to around 50,000 years ago in Spain, right before modern humans entered Europe.

What about language? Neanderthals have vocal anatomy that is similar to modern humans, with wide vertebral canals that are important for controlled breathing during speech and a hyoid bone that is identical to our own (as was shown in Figure 6.32). Recovery of ancient DNA from Neanderthal fossils shows they had the FOXP2 gene, which has some control over the development of our capacity for language. These findings are highly suggestive that Neanderthals could produce language, though not precisely the same way that modern humans do. But the overall evidence suggests that they seem to have some abstract and symbolic capability and sense of self.

THE DENISOVANS

We know much less about the Denisovans, who overlapped both with our species and with Neanderthals. The crucial fossil finds are from Denisova Cave in the Altai mountains of Siberia, where fragmented remains of Denisovans, Neanderthals, and *Homo sapiens* have all been located, dating between 20,000 and 50,000 years ago. The fossil and related archaeological evidence of Denisovans is so limited that we currently know very little about their anatomy or cognitive capabilities. Behavioral evidence of abstract thought, such as jewelry or art, is absent, though this may be because the populations were small enough that the chances of finding it are very low.

Denisovan fossils are very rare, but genetic analysis of DNA and proteins has identified them as distinct from both our own species and Neanderthals. **Figure 6.36** shows a fossil jawbone from Baishiya Karst Cave near Xiahe, China, which is located at high altitude on the Tibetan plateau, dating to 160,000 years ago.

In a remarkable study, researchers carefully removed 728 soil samples from Denisova Cave using a process of "genetic fishing" to search for tiny pieces of DNA shed from hair, saliva, skin flakes, feces, and dead bodies (**Figure 6.37**). In frozen soil like that in the bottom of a Siberian cave, traces of DNA can survive for millennia. This research showed that Denisovan genomes were highly divergent from modern humans, but they were also distinct from Neanderthals. The

Denisovan A now-extinct species of humans that lived primarily in Asia between about 200,000 and 50,000 years ago.

FIGURE 6.36

A fragment of a mandible (jaw bone) from Xiahe in Tibet, shown from the right side, has two molars still in place. Molecular analysis of preserved proteins indicates this mandible was from a Denisovan individual. Note the lack of a chin, a skeletal feature seen consistently in modern *Homo sapiens* fossils.

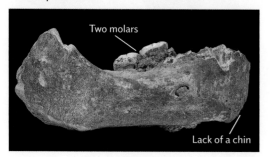

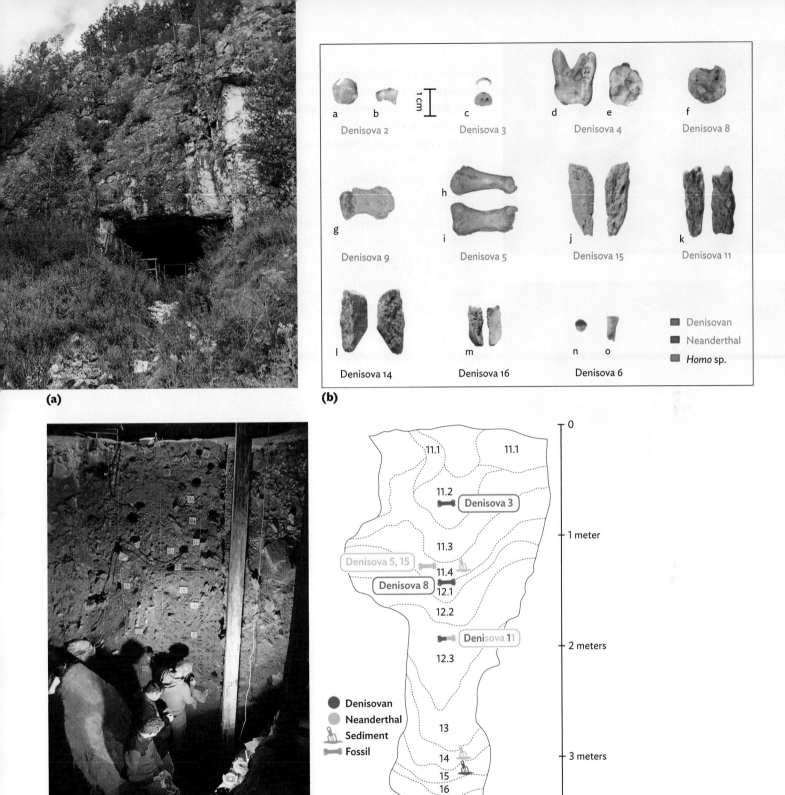

FIGURE 6.37

(a) The entrance to Denisova Cave is in the Altai Mountains, Siberia, Russia. **(b)** A summary of all fossils of Denisovans and Neanderthals, and hominin bones not assigned to either group, discovered at Denisova Cave is shown. Next to each fossil is the specimen number (for example, Denisova 2 in the top-left corner). Denisova 11 is a hybrid Neanderthal–Denisovan, which is why it is both colors. **(c)** Archaeologists Kieran O'Gorman, Zenobia Jacobs, and Bo Li collect sediment DNA samples from Denisova Cave's South Chamber, after carefully excavating the face of the layers and laying out a string grid. The coldness of the cave likely aided long-term preservation of trace DNA in the soil layers. **(d)** This diagram shows sediment layers and fossil skeletal remains that yielded Neanderthal (yellow) and Denisovan (green) mitochondrial DNA genomes. The different strata of sediment are labeled in the center of the diagram, showing the complex stratigraphy of the cave.

(a)

(b)

FIGURE 6.38

(a) Excavations at Liang Bua Cave uncovered the remains of *Homo floresiensis*. (b) This reconstruction shows *Homo floresiensis* hunting a stegodon on Flores, Indonesia.

Denisovan and Neanderthal genomes were more similar to each other than to those of living humans. Neanderthals and Denisovans may have shared a common ancestor 450,000 years ago, one that we did not share. The more distant common ancestor of Neanderthals, Denisovans, and modern humans is estimated to have lived between 700,000 and 500,000 years ago.

OTHER RECENT HOMININS

In Chapter 5, we introduced the Dinaledi chamber remains attributed to *Homo naledi* dating to between 230,000 and 340,000 years ago in South Africa. Their small size and recent date was a surprise to scientists at the time of their discovery but they are not the only surprise in the fossil record of Pleistocene humans.

Two sites on the island of Flores in the Indonesian archipelago provide evidence of an even more enigmatic lineage of genus *Homo*, dating to between 700,000 and 60,000 years ago. Excavations in Liang Bua Cave yielded remains of a dozen or so individuals who stood only 1 meter (3 feet) tall. The one complete skull suggests a brain size of only 400 cc. These hominins were found associated with Oldowan-style tools, although there is some debate about whether the tools were made by this species or by *Homo sapiens* who lived in the same area. Liang Bua Cave also contains cut and burned animal bones that suggest controlled use of fire for cooking, especially of stegodons (smaller relatives of modern elephants).

Subsequent excavation in the nearby Mata Menge Cave yielded the remains of three hominins that were even smaller than those at Liang Bua, dated to around 700,000 years ago. This reinforces the conclusion that the Flores Island hominins were a separate species, *Homo floresiensis*, perhaps found only on Flores (**Figure 6.38**). On the basis of a few teeth and finger bones from a single cave dated to about 50,000 years ago, some suggest another similarly small-bodied species on the island of Luzon in the Philippines, *Homo luzonensis*.

The best current explanation for these very recent and small-bodied species in islands off the coast of southeastern Asia is that they are descended from *Homo erectus*. Increasingly isolated when sea levels rose during warmer periods of the Pleistocene, these populations lived on well after *Homo erectus* populations had disappeared elsewhere. Biologically, their smaller bodies could be explained by natural selection. For example, "insular dwarfism" is a phenomenon whereby smaller bodies are selected for over time on islands or other constrained areas where food sources are scarce (**Figure 6.39**). It is also seen in some other extinct animals endemic to Flores, including the stegodons.

ENTWINED HUMAN HISTORIES

The current fossil and molecular evidence suggests that fully modern humans—our direct ancestors—arose in Africa around 250,000 years ago and then migrated into many new regions outside Africa, encountering many different hominin species. We now know that throughout Europe and Asia there was a remarkable diversity of extant hominins, all belonging to genus *Homo*, that our direct ancestors would have encountered.

We also now have increasingly compelling evidence, especially from studies of ancient DNA, that different human groups interbred toward the end of the Pleistocene but probably also across the last million years as well. Our species definitely mated with the Neanderthals, the Denisovans, and other Pleistocene human groups that we have not fully identified yet (**Figure 6.40**).

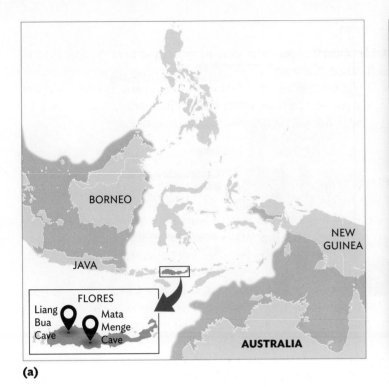

(a)

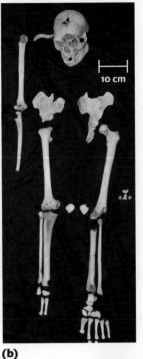

(b)

FIGURE 6.39

(a) *Homo floresiensis* evolved and was confined to the island of Flores in Indonesia, with a very small body size compared to hominins living on continents at the same time. This was likely because they were genetically isolated and evolved smaller bodies. The yellow areas were previously dry land, but Flores was always cut off from other land masses regardless of sea levels. **(b)** This skeleton of specimen LB1 shows a short stature of around 1 meter. **(c)** A left lateral view of the skull from specimen LB1 is shown.

Current estimates place the level of Neanderthal ancestry surviving in human populations at an average of around 2% for European and Asian populations. The much lower percentage of Neanderthal ancestry (~0.5%) in modern African populations is likely the result of subsequent gene flow and not direct mating between Neanderthals and *Homo sapiens* in Africa.

This level of genetic overlap suggests that mating was only occasional but occurred over a long period. The preponderance of mitochondrial (maternally inherited) DNA today associated with Neanderthal lineages suggests that there were many more surviving offspring between Neanderthal females and modern human males than the other way around.

Genetic analysis of the Siberian Denisovan remains shows that *Homo sapiens* also interbred with them after migrating into southern Asia. Indigenous people from Melanesia in the Western Pacific and nearby Australia (Oceania) have about 3.5% Denisovan ancestry, while Indigenous Asian and American populations have smaller but detectable contributions to their DNA.

These remaining archaic Neanderthal and Denisovan genes in modern human populations are mostly outside the coding portions of our genome. They are especially absent from the parts of our genome associated with language

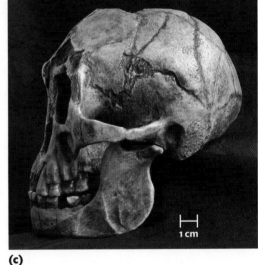

(c)

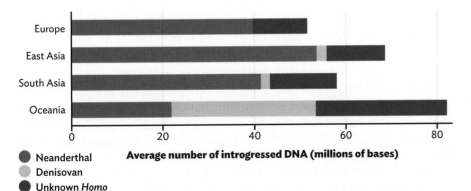

- Neanderthal
- Denisovan
- Unknown *Homo*

Average number of introgressed DNA (millions of bases)

FIGURE 6.40

This graph displays the amounts of introgressed (transferred) DNA from Neanderthal, Denisovan, and other, as-yet-unknown *Homo* genomes (represented in finds from Denisova Cave). It was created by comparing samples of living humans from different locations around the globe. The graph shows that the frequency of Neanderthal introgression is higher in populations in East Asia than in Europe overall. East Asian and South Asian samples show similar amounts of detected Denisovan ancestry, while Oceanic populations carry much more.

FIGURE 6.41

Organs and systems of living humans that include Neanderthal and Denisovan genes are illustrated.

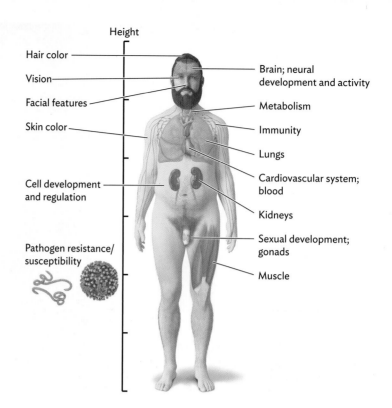

Height

Hair color

Vision

Facial features

Skin color

Cell development and regulation

Pathogen resistance/ susceptibility

Brain; neural development and activity

Metabolism

Immunity

Lungs

Cardiovascular system; blood

Kidneys

Sexual development; gonads

Muscle

and abstract thinking capabilities. Rather, most are found in the sections of so-called "junk DNA" that don't code for proteins.

Despite this, some inherited genes might have introduced variation into our gene pools that could pattern how we respond biologically to current and future threats. Some ancient genetic variants extracted from fossil Neanderthals that remain in human genomes today appear to make people more susceptible to infections of COVID-19. This variant is especially common in Asia. Other genetic variants appear to be at locations on the genome that influence aspects of human phenotypes such as hair color and body fat distribution (**Figure 6.41**).

This complicated genetic landscape highlights why a strict concept of species as reproductively isolated is especially problematic for organizing early humans. Some paleoanthropologists suggest that Neanderthals, Denisovans, and modern humans should be classified as separate species, while others suggest that they are all subgroups of *Homo sapiens*; still others consider a vagueness or indetermination to be appropriate for the current evidence. Some genetic studies also suggest that early humans had similar periodic interbreeding events with many other *Homo* species, including *Homo erectus*, further blurring the lines between species.

This periodic hybridization, or *introgression*, at some limited locales may be the best way to think of our shared genetic history as it relates to Neanderthals and Denisovans. The boundaries of species are created not only by an inability to mate and produce offspring but also by barriers due to location, behavioral practices, or just time. Speciation can accordingly be a fitful process. Populations can separate and differentiate, but they may also later reconnect. The current view of the last million years is one in which many hominin groups existed at once, disconnecting and reconnecting over time (**Figure 6.42**). Thus, modern humans are genetic mosaics, with a rambling history of dead ends,

introgression The transfer of genetic information (DNA) between diverged populations through limited successive mating, while the gene pools themselves do not merge.

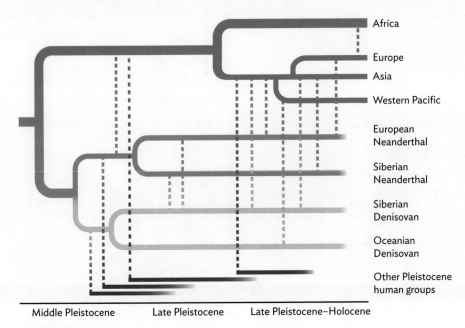

Africa
Europe
Asia
Western Pacific
European Neanderthal
Siberian Neanderthal
Siberian Denisovan
Oceanian Denisovan
Other Pleistocene human groups

Middle Pleistocene   Late Pleistocene   Late Pleistocene–Holocene

FIGURE 6.42

This reconstruction shows proposed introgressions between different human/hominin groups in the Middle Pleistocene, Late Pleistocene, and Late Pleistocene–Holocene epochs (time not to scale). Anatomically modern human populations are represented in blue. Horizontal dotted lines indicate suspected or known introgression events between populations.

dispersals, separations, and genetic reunions between human groups of all kinds in many places, not just ourselves.

Many aspects of the mating between modern humans and other human groups remain unknown. We do not know if these members of different groups connected emotionally, if they formed families, or even if the mating events were consensual. Ultimately, by about 35,000 years ago, it seems *Homo sapiens* was the last group of humans surviving, having displaced all the others. Perhaps other human groups, such as the Neanderthals, simply didn't have our capacity to adapt to changing environmental conditions, or their much smaller and less genetically varied populations proved a biological disadvantage. Perhaps modern humans were better hunters and outcompeted other groups for limited food supplies or were better at managing and processing emergency or famine foods.

FROM OUR PASTS TO OUR FUTURES

The behavioral features that made our species such adaptable, successful hominins have also contributed to the emergence of the greatest challenges we face today. Scaling of human technology-based innovations (such as factory farming, mass mining, industry, oil-based transportation, and commercial fisheries) are linked to increasing climate unpredictability, polluted landscapes, and increasing scarcity of basic resources. Continued reconstruction of our habitats is accelerating the extinction of other species and spurring the emergence of new diseases. The importance of group identities (religious, ethnic, or otherwise) in how we organize ourselves underpins ongoing conflicts around the globe.

The 21st century will be defined by continued upheaval, both ecological and social, based on the past evolutionary success of our species. But as we learn from our fossil ancestors, we are also a species with a long history of successful biological and behavioral adaptations to new and unpredictable circumstances.

Understanding where humans come from—and what got us here over the last million years—provides a unique window into what makes us "human" today, as well as where we are headed.

6.1 | *Homo erectus*

Explain what fossil and archaeological evidence suggests about *Homo erectus*.

- *Homo erectus*, the ancestor of later *Homo* species, initiated the migration of our genus out of Africa, surviving for more than a million years.

- The larger brain sizes of *Homo erectus* allowed them to thrive in more varied climates, both through the production of more sophisticated technologies for acquiring and processing foods rich in nutrients.

KEY TERMS
> Acheulean
> cranial vault
> endocast
> handaxe
> occipital torus
> sagittal keel
> supraorbital torus

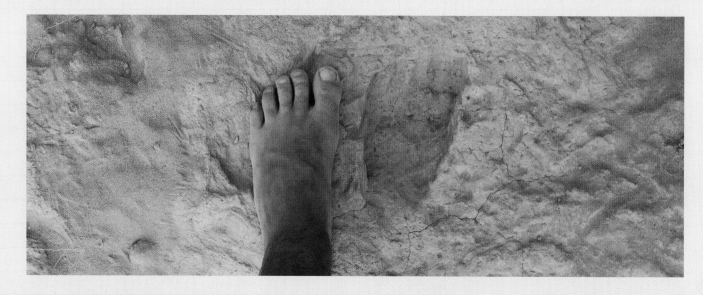

6.2 | Middle Pleistocene *Homo*

Identify the innovations and developments of Middle Pleistocene *Homo*.

- There used to be many *Homo* populations in and beyond Africa, including many other groups of humans very similar to us in their biology and behavior. All are now extinct, except for *Homo sapiens*.

- Key evolved and interrelated features of anatomy and behavior, including meat-eating, larger brains, increasingly sophisticated tool use, language, and social cooperation, allowed these early humans to inhabit an array of different environments.

KEY TERMS
> assimilation model
> Middle Pleistocene *Homo*
> multiregional model
> pressure flaking

6.3 | *Homo sapiens*

Characterize the emergence of *Homo sapiens* and their anatomical, behavioral, and cultural traits.

- Our direct human ancestry can be traced to a group in Africa that emerged around 250,000 years ago and began spreading across the globe about 65,000 years ago.

- *Homo sapiens* fossils are recognized by their large brain size, small faces and teeth, projecting chins, small brow ridges, and tall rounded skulls.

- With particularly sophisticated social, language, and technological capabilities, *Homo sapiens* was able to manage even dramatic environmental variations successfully.

- Anatomical modernity preceded behavioral modernity by about 100,000 years. Behavioral modernity is represented by archaeological evidence of symbolic thought and long-distance trade.

KEY TERMS
> genetic lineage
> ritual

6.4 | The Other Humans and Us

Describe the groups that evolved from *Homo erectus* and their interaction through time.

- Neanderthals, Denisovans, *Homo naledi*, and *Homo floresiensis* were contemporaries of early anatomically modern humans.

- Several scientific hypotheses as to why we are the only remining *Homo* species are debated, but genetic evidence is clear that we interbred with other human groups even as we also displaced them.

KEY TERMS
> Denisovan
> introgression
> Mousterian
> Neanderthal

Language and Our Worls

Language and Our Worlds

South Africans continue to face some of the highest rates of human immunodeficiency virus (HIV) infection in the world, resulting in acquired immunodeficiency syndrome (AIDS). Linguistic anthropologist and *ethnomusicologist* Steven Black began his research in South Africa in 2008, four years after the first retroviral drugs were rolled out, working with a Zulu-speaking gospel choir group. The activist-singers regularly performed in downtown Durban and even internationally, raising money for HIV/AIDS research and treatment (**Figure 7.1**).

The singers came from informal settlements around the city where, at the time of Black's research, infection rates were as high as 40%. Yet the stigma around the disease remained high. Those discovered to be infected were ostracized, thrown out of their homes, beaten, or even killed by neighbors or family. Not surprisingly, many South Africans went to great lengths to avoid any talk of the disease—including naming it directly.

The members of the choir lived in two geographically distinct realms: the informal settlements, where their HIV status was not safe to disclose, and the city, where they worked, visited medical staff, or met with support groups and where their HIV status was known. Even though all the performers were HIV-positive, Black discovered that they too avoided discussing the disease.

LEARNING OBJECTIVES

7.1 The Structures of Human Language
Explain the structures of human language.

7.2 What Human Language Does
Evaluate human language as a form of communication and social action.

7.3 How Language Shapes Humans
Assess how the structures of language impact human understanding.

7.4 How People Create Meaning
Analyze how language receivers encode and decode meaning.

THE MANY FORMS OF LANGUAGE

Linguistic anthropologists study all the forms that language can take, not just in spoken, signed, and written words but also emojis, body language, and other symbols that carry meaning.

ethnomusicology The study of music in its social and cultural contexts.

SOUTH AFRICA

Durban

Africa

FIGURE 7.1

Durban's Sinikithemba ("Give Us Hope") Choir performs on an international tour to raise money for HIV/AIDS programs in Africa.

Black hung out at choir practices to learn about Zulu choral music, becoming closer to group members over many months. Eventually they started to share more of themselves, including their HIV status. He was able to conduct interviews, videorecord performances, practices, and conversations and transcribe what people said and sang (**Figure 7.2**).

Partial transcript of *Into Enjani Lena* lyrics

Line	Lyrics
3	Abanye bahlekisa ngayo 'Some joke about it'
4	bayibiza ngeqhoks ((iqhoks = 'high heels')) 'They call it *iqhoks* ((some are teasing about it))'
5	Bayibiza ngamagama amathathu 'They call it "a three letter word" ((HIV))' [repeated 2x]
6	Abanye bayibiza nge-TB 'Some call it TB' [tuberculosis]

FIGURE 7.2

Linguistic anthropologist Steven Black uses lyrics to demonstrate how language can be used to challenge social stigma. This transcript shows the words to a choir song about HIV, titled *Into Enjani Lena*, which translates to "this thing that is like what." The words play on the ways people try to avoid naming the stigmatized disease when talking about it.

isiZulu One of the official languages of South Africa.

jargon Specialized words used by a group of people or a profession; often the terms are difficult for others to understand.

Black found that choir members deployed different language strategies to communicate about the disease and challenge its stigma. isiZulu is one of the official languages of South Africa. One strategy was the use of foreign medical jargon in English, instead of local isiZulu words, to describe the disease (such as referencing their ARVs [antiretroviral pills] or CD4 [cluster of differentiation 4] counts). This adoption of foreign medical terms extended the privacy of the clinic into choir conversations back in the neighborhoods. Within the city choir, members challenged stigma in the lyrics of their songs, while back in their own neighborhoods, these language choices helped connect them as a supportive community and avoid rejection and punishment by the broader communities in which they lived.

How we understand and use language matters because it shapes and defines every aspect of our lives, including how we relate to others. The use of at least rudimentary language—defined as use of symbolic forms of communication—is not unique to our species. Yet human language in all its forms—spoken, sign(ed), written, and tactile—is today very different from that of other animals because of what we *do* with it and what it *does* to us.

It is common for people to focus on words and the meanings of words when they think about language. But language is so much more than words. It is about all the other understandings embedded in the language moments as a whole. Language does so much more than "represent the world," "mean stuff," or convey information from one source to another (communicate). Rather, language is social action and actively builds reality; and, as such, it is a central aspect of the creation of societies.

The kinds of actions a person can perform with language are largely dependent on local language ideologies—the beliefs within a community about what language is and how it should be used. In the case of the South African activist-singers, the use of English medical terminology while speaking isiZulu wasn't just a matter of conveying the technical definitions of the medical terms. It was also a means to reduce threats of being rejected and excluded by others and to create a supportive community as they dealt with a highly stigmatized disease.

In this chapter, we examine human language and its complex systems of rules and grammar that inform the process of making meaning—encoding and decoding language. We investigate how language helps us arrange and manage our societies and how language acts to include and exclude people from various social groups. Finally, we explore how humans create meanings, too, through their perception of what is said, signed, or written.

language A systematic symbol-based signaling system that allows things to get done.

spoken Refers to language produced by using an oral method.

sign(ed) Refers to language produced by using a visual-manual or tactile-manual method.

language ideology Ideas and beliefs about language and language producers that vary across time, people, and place.

grammar The rules for how words, sentence parts, and sentences are organized to make meanings in a language.

THE STRUCTURES OF HUMAN LANGUAGE

In examining human evolution, we explored how the capacity to use and learn language was central to the emergence of behaviorally modern humans (Chapters 5 and 6). Yet great apes (bonobos, chimpanzees, orangutans, and gorillas) use vocalizations and gestures to communicate with one another in the wild and in captivity. Moreover, biological anthropologists studying primates have commonly observed that primates communicate with others like them. The interactions demonstrate taking turns like humans do as well as modifications based on changing contexts. So, why do anthropologists argue that our language abilities set us apart from primates—and even early humans?

Primate language is different from human language in significant ways. Researchers have taught great apes limited sign language. For example, the captive gorilla Koko mastered hundreds of signs based on American Sign Language for both nouns and adjectives (**Figure 7.3**). Notably, however, researchers have not observed great apes engage in novel production of human language. That is, they can mimic what they have been taught, but they cannot substitute a new item in for something else, a hallmark of human language. Consider the

FIGURE 7.3

A photo from 1972 shows Koko (1971–2018). The western lowland gorilla was born in the San Francisco Zoo in California and used signs, but did not create novel instances of language. For ethical reasons, such language training of apes for research is no longer done.

sentence: Throw me the ball. Humans could easily substitute the word "alien" or "dinosaur" in place of the object "ball" and we would still find the sentence acceptable. However, bonobo Kanzi has been credited with creating novel signs and being able to understand word order.

Many linguistic anthropologists are accordingly skeptical of claims that great apes *learn* languages. Almost all such training has been done in captivity, with humans trying to teach the apes language rather than observing apes using language to communicate directly with others in their own species. This has made it difficult to confirm exactly what language capacities apes have. It is possible that earlier researchers spent much time asking the wrong question; rather than figuring out if primates can learn human language, researchers perhaps should have been trying to learn the various primate communication systems.

Although vocalization is not a requirement of human language, apes do not have the vocal apparatus that allows humanlike speech. Due to a change in the shape of the hyoid bone during the evolution from *Australopithecus* to *Homo*, early humans gained the anatomical capability to develop a far more extensive vocal repertoire of sounds (Chapter 6). Humans used these sounds to develop language into a structured set of symbols that we use for various reasons, including communicating with one another. As a result, humans have an evolved capacity to acquire and use language in many, varied, and highly complex ways.

Language, moreover, is just one of the systems of symbols that humans use to mediate our everyday lives. The power of these collective symbols, termed semiotics, underpins every idea humans invent, have, and share.

Perhaps most significantly, humans speak and sign in many languages, and it is likely they always have. Today, around 7,000 languages are currently used throughout the world. Each language most likely has several varieties encompassed within it, including different sounds, signs, vocabularies, and structures (grammar). In addition, there are about 215 sign languages in the world.

Each language variety is based on the systematic organization of small units of sounds or signs into larger units of meaning. This complex system needs to be shared and learned, and so it also needs to be highly predictable. A fundamental feature of every language variety, then, is that its basic organization is rule-bound. All language varieties have rules about sounds or signs (phonological rules), how to make new words (morphological rules), how to organize words into longer units like phrases or sentences (syntax rules), and how to be polite, rude, or express emotions like love or anger (pragmatic rules).

PHONOLOGICAL RULES

Oral-auditory languages use various articulators, speech-producing anatomy such as tongue, teeth, and alveolar ridge, located in the physical structures of our mouth and voice box (larynx) (**Figure 7.4**). In most cases, air is drawn into the lungs and then expelled up through the voice box and out through the mouth and nose. Articulators affect the way that the air is modified, thus creating speech sounds. For example, the sound /b/ is created by pushing air out of the lungs through a closed glottis (a part of the larynx that includes the vocal cords and the space between them), causing the vocal folds to vibrate, and then into the mouth where the air is briefly but completely stopped by the lips before exiting the mouth.

semiotics **The study of the way that symbols, including words, make meaning.**

language variety **A form of a given language that is used regularly by speakers or signers within a society. The variety may be common to a group of age-related users or regional users or some other group within the society.**

articulator **Any one of several vocal apparatuses used to create and modify sounds.**

FIGURE 7.4

The human vocal apparatus is illustrated, with all articulators that are used in speech production labeled.

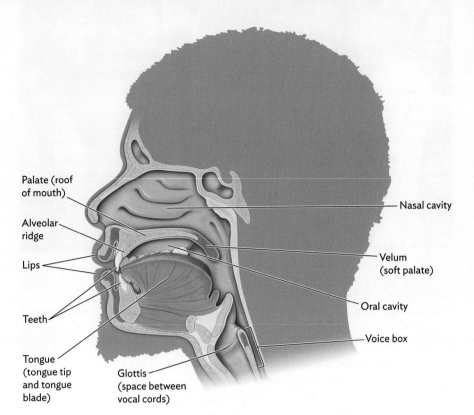

Visual-gestural language articulators include a signing space made up of the hands, upper part of the body, the head, and face; this three-dimensional signing space allows for morphological, syntactical, and pragmatical aspects of language to be realized. Sign languages are one obvious example of this.

The ways in which sounds (or signs) are combined and organized into meaningful units is guided by the *phonological rules* of a given language. In terms of rules about how we make sounds, consider the sound /t/ in the English words tip [tɪp] or stop [stɑp]. In using the rules of so-called "standard English," when the sound /t/ is at the beginning of a word, it is produced with a small puff of air called aspiration, represented by a superscripted h: [tʰɪp]. This production (in English) is predictable and rule-governed: in words such as tap or top or tapir, the initial /t/ is produced with aspiration. However, in words such as stop or stout, the /t/ is produced without any puff of air. It is the environment of the sound (e.g., what sounds come before or after the /t/) that determines the pronunciation used. Once this distinction is pointed out to English speakers, they can often perceive better the difference between these aspirated and unaspirated productions of /t/. But, without being made aware, these different instances of /t/ are perceived as identical. That is, what is actually produced and what is perceived are different. This is because we learn to ignore it.

Rules also govern sign languages. In American Sign Language (ASL), for example, the orientation of the hand (palm up or palm down) in phrases like MILK RUN OUT (meaning: ran out of milk) and TIME RUN OUT (meaning: ran out of time) demonstrates the same principle as we saw with the /t/ sound above: RUN OUT typically has a palm-up orientation, but when signing TIME RUN OUT, a palm-down orientation is used because the word TIME has a palm-down orientation. The palm orientation shifts due to the environment of the sign (e.g., what signs come near or before or after it).

phonological rule **One of a set of conventions, specific to each language, governing how sounds or signs are combined to make a specific language.**

FIGURE 7.5

Here Rotokas speakers without regular access to media get information about how COVID-19 spreads. As is common across all languages, new concepts are often introduced using foreign language terms. There are around 4,000 Rotokas speakers on Bougainville, where 19 Indigenous languages from three different language families are spoken on just one island.

constituent An individual piece of language that, in combination with others, makes up the grammar of the language. Subjects and verbs are constituents of every language.

rules (of a language) A systematized pattern of use that we learn when we acquire a language, mostly untaught and rarely obvious to speakers or signers.

Mainstream White American English (MWAE) Term used in place of "standard English" to make transparent how the assumption of "standard English" represents and legitimizes White, male, upper middle-class, and dominant ways of speaking English.

SYNTAX RULES

The rules are the grammar of the language, that is, the basic structuring of language constituents. All languages have constituents that serve as nouns (subjects and objects) and verbs (actions). Beyond nouns and verbs, language constituents may include determiners or articles (the, an, that), adverbs that describe verbs (gently, then), prepositions (at, against), postpositions (aside, ago), and adjectives that describe nouns (big, smooth).

All languages adopt or borrow words from other languages. Rotokas, one of many different languages spoken on Bougainville in the Solomon Islands archipelago of the Western Pacific, adopts words from English and Tok Pisin to accommodate new ideas and concepts (**Figure 7.5**).

No matter how many (or few) different types of constituents a language may have, all languages provide rules that outline a systematic way of organizing these pieces into meaningful segments of different-sized words, phrases, sentences, conversations, and so on. On the basis of the rules we learn for a given language, we combine different kinds of constituents into strings of meaning. Notably, these are not the rules taught in formal instruction but rather through using a language. When we use our languages, we are abiding by these mostly hidden, complex sets of learned rules, so that we have little or no awareness of them.

LANGUAGE VARIATION

These defining features of languages—rule-governed, systematic, and predictable—hold true for all language varieties. But within these rules, there is still a significant diversity in the morphology, syntax, and pragmatics used that vary by context (when, where, by whom, and to whom the language is being used). In discussing these types of language variations, linguistic anthropologists purposefully refer to language varieties instead of using terms such as "dialect" or "accent." This is to avoid the implication that there are default, typical, or normal forms of language that all speakers within a population agree on.

Notably, there are many different forms of English used by people. To be as clear as possible, when we are referring to the so-called "standard English" thought to be common in the United States, following linguistic anthropologist Samy Alim, we will refer to this form as "Mainstream White American English" (MWAE).

Because there is so much variation in language use, we tend to pay attention to only a fraction of it, and often we don't even notice most instances of language variation. What influences when we do become conscious of these variations? Some variation can become noticeable to us when it is unfamiliar, because it isn't one of the forms we are exposed to regularly. One example of this might be the use of "maths" by people who speak a British variety of English. Mainstream White American English varieties do not have this form; thus, a sentence like "My cousin is a maths teacher" may stand out to MWAE speakers and be noticed.

In other instances, variation is noticeable because we have been taught, explicitly or implicitly, to recognize it. It is common to associate some forms of language with being "more correct" or "better" than other forms. But the rules of the spoken language variety often referred to as "standard English" are not used by anyone. People often believe that they use "standard English," but that is an assertion about values, not about language rules. Standard language is an ideal that is not achieved by anyone, let alone a community of speakers. We think of it as a variety that exists only in people's minds. In particular, use of "standard English" tends to specifically represent (and also legitimize) White, male, upper middle-class, and historically dominant ways of speaking English.

One clear example of this is the **variable** forms of the verb "ask" used among English speakers and how the use of some variants can elicit very strong reactions. In the United States there are at least two very common pronunciations of the verb "to ask" (call for information, inquire): [ask] and [aks]. The pronunciation [aks] was the typical form used in English language literature and in central London until about 1600 (**Figure 7.6**), after which [ask] became the preferred written convention. Those unfamiliar with the history of [ask-aks] often assume that [aks] is only used by speakers of Black Englishes in the United States. But it is also commonly used in some White rural communities too, such as in Appalachia.

variable In sociolinguistics, a linguistic element that varies based on other linguistic elements but also based on social contexts including class, age, gender/sex, or situation.

- aks
- ash
- ask
- ax and ox

Europe

FIGURE 7.6

[Aks] and [ask] were both common pronunciations in England in the Middle Ages, as this map of late Middle English variants from the 15th century shows.

Black Languages English words with Africanized semantic, syntactic, morphological, phonological, and rhetorical patterns originating in the experiences of U.S. slave descendants.

indexicality A kind of meaning in language that relies on knowledge of the context in which the language occurred.

Many people who use [ask] react very negatively to those who use [aks]. Students who use [aks] in school classrooms in the United States are typically corrected by teachers. Adults who use it around others who don't may be belittled or otherwise encouraged to switch to the [ask] form. Why do many people who use [ask] react so negatively? It's because the specific usage has become stigmatized—that is, associated with a devalued social status. In other words, rather than being viewed as simply a variation of [ask], [aks] is perceived as incorrect and is assumed to be an indicator of poor language skills. In institutional contexts, [aks] signals for teachers or those in power a lack of education, lower class, and rurality. It can also today signal that the speaker is using a variety of Black Languages or Black Englishes. (We follow linguist April Baker-Bell in using this label for language varieties identified as being used by Black people in the United States.)

So, if [aks] is stigmatized in certain contexts, particularly those associated with more powerful sectors of U.S. society, why do people continue to use it (or many other stigmatized varieties of language)? This is a question that many linguistic anthropologists have pondered. In order to understand why stigmatized language forms like [aks] endure, we also have to consider what it means to belong to (and be cast out from) a community of speakers. That is, local language varieties have the ability to indicate that someone is an insider or an outsider to the community. Moreover, language that is deemed unacceptable or inappropriate in institutional settings may conversely create feelings of solidarity and belongingness in other noninstitutional settings (such as with family, friends, or in neighborhoods). This is achieved through indexicality; it also explains how language is able to signal inclusion or exclusion of people into or outside particular group memberships and is important for our next section on what language does.

WHAT HUMAN LANGUAGE DOES

Linguistic anthropologist Alessandro Duranti has defined language as a "nonneutral medium," meaning that language as a symbolic system isn't just something that humans shape and utilize; rather, language itself is a form of social action, shaping and impacting human experience just as profoundly as humans shape and impact it. In this section, we explore how language does this.

LANGUAGE AND MEANING

To begin, language is a system of signs. A sign is a basic unit of meaning. Semiotics, the study of signs as a means of meaning-making, proposes that these signs can take different forms, such as utterances and signs, gestures, and drawings and writing. The signifier, the form the sign takes, represents the signified, an object, concept, or relationship.

We come into contact with three kinds of signifiers on a daily basis: icon, index, and symbol. An icon is a signifier that resembles the object or concept being signified. For example, a road sign with an image of a deer running can signify that deer cross the road at the sign's location. An index is a sign that provides evidence of something that is being *represented* but is *not actually present* in the words or even the context (**Figure 7.7**). Consider seeing smoke billowing out of a chimney—the smoke is an index of the fire. The smoke implies the fire. A symbol, such as numbers and letters, bears no physical resemblance to what is being signified.

So how do we know what something means when another person signals it to us via signs? The answer to this question is not just a central element of the study of human language but is central to understanding how people operate effectively within the varied cultural contexts of their everyday lives. To create our meaning and signal it to others, we encode language. To take meaning from what others signal, we decode the signs it carries. We learn them through both implicit means, such as exposure and repetitive encounters, and explicit means, such as being overtly told how to interpret meaning (e.g., "That is *not* what I meant. I meant . . . ").

Symbols do not resemble what they signify in any way. This is called arbitrariness. The syllabic symbol す represents the sound su [sounds like "sue"] in Japanese. Written symbols (individual letters, syllables, logographs, and words) that represent the sounds of a language are acquired only through explicit study.

In contrast, humans learn how to interpret spoken or signed indexes naturally over time within their social or cultural context. People encounter and interpret arbitrary signifiers constantly throughout each day, and even while we dream. Interpreting signifiers requires us to apply both formal knowledge (things learned in school, found in dictionaries and encyclopedias, and so on) and informal knowledge (things learned through personal experiences or exposures to media, passed on to us by our friends, and so on). When we engage in decoding, we therefore do so without objectivity or neutrality.

Emojis are particularly clear and efficient visual representations of meanings. But even emojis are differently decoded depending on who is reading them, when, and why. The emoji 😤 is described on the Unicode website as "face with steam from nose." This literal description could be considered one meaning of the image, though it is not likely the first interpretation. But even the more common decoded meanings of it in English are notably varied; this emoji may communicate a range of negative emotions such as frustration, annoyance, or anger, and it can be directed at oneself (for doing something poorly, such as an exam), at other individuals (for letting us down), or at inanimate objects (such as a burnt pizza). Similarly, in a dating app versus a grocery app, receiving or sending an eggplant or peach emoji is decoded in very different ways. Additionally, a speaker and hearer, or a signer and viewer, might not fix on the same aspect of an emoji meaning. Those unfamiliar with emoji text conventions may only ever see a fruit or vegetable (**Figure 7.8**).

Some icons are also less straightforward than others in their approximations of what they represent. Consider the familiar logo that represents the powerful Apple Inc. brand: . When many people see this symbol, they don't

FIGURE 7.7

A sign exhibiting the index "today" refers to the particular point in time that the sign was placed. Without knowing what day the sign was installed, it is impossible to know when the yard sale will (or did) take place. An index relies on the context to recover the intended meaning.

icon A signifier that resembles the object or concept being signified.

index A sign that carries social meaning; it provides evidence of something being represented, but it is not physically present in the language used.

symbol An image, sound, or action that we learn represents (but does not resemble) something else.

encoding In language, the process of producing speech or signs that reflect what you are thinking about or desiring to express.

decoding In language, the process of producing meaning from someone else's language.

arbitrariness The absence of any connection between the sound or form of a word or sign and its referent.

FIGURE 7.8

Different audiences can read emojis very differently.

FIGURE 7.9

An ancient petroglyph from Puerco Pueblo, Arizona, is pictured.

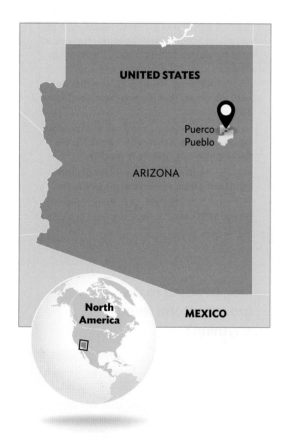

petroglyph An image carved on rock.

origin myth A shared, sacred story of where we come from and how and why we are, often including nonhumans (such as gods or animals).

oral tradition Knowledge passed down through generations using stories, song, signs, and other nonwritten means.

situated knowledge An understanding that reflects the contexts (including environmental and social) in which meanings are produced and applied.

necessarily or particularly see an apple, even though it depicts one. They have learned that it represents a multinational technology company.

How do people decode a sign with which they are unfamiliar? Consider one of the many petroglyphs created by Ancestral Puebloan farmers who lived at the Puerco Pueblo site in Arizona, United States, 600 years ago (**Figure 7.9**) We cannot know what the artist's meaning was when it was made, and viewers today interpret the symbols through their own origin myths and oral traditions. Most people who view the image recognize the large two-legged image as a bird. The meaning of the four-limbed creature at the end of the "bird" beak is decoded more variably: perhaps a frog or perhaps a human baby.

According to the inscription accompanying this petroglyph, some Indigenous Zuni people surmise that it is a form of "tagging," representing the signature of the artist. In this case, they suggest, perhaps the mother was from the Crane Clan and the father was from the Frog Clan. Meanwhile, some Indigenous Hopi people suggest that the image represents the story of a giant bird that eats bad children. Some non-Indigenous tourists visiting the park interpret it as a stork delivering a baby to parents.

Each of these interpretations—these means of decoding the language—relies on knowledge that is based on different myths, oral traditions, books, media, experiences, and common stories or ideas that circulate within each of these communities to explain and interpret the world. Put another way, the meanings of language symbols reflect situated knowledge as opposed to single, static interpretations.

Linguist James Gee, using the everyday example of "coffee," exhorts us to recognize how situated knowledge always informs our understandings, even in mundane announcements made in a grocery store.

> Announcement 1: Cleanup on Aisle 5, **coffee** spilled. Please bring a broom.
> Announcement 2: Cleanup on Aisle 5, **coffee** spilled. Please bring a mop.
> Announcement 3: Stop drinking Big Coffee! Fair Trade **coffee** is 50% off today.

The first announcement of the word coffee combined with the verb "spilled" could evoke a liquid. But the additional request for a broom cues us to reinterpret the word coffee as a dry substance. The second announcement to bring a mop reaffirms the original image of coffee as a liquid. The first sentence of the third announcement may seem nonsensical in itself. But the phrase immediately following contrasts "Big Coffee" with "Fair Trade coffee," and like "broom" and "mop," this allows us to understand the context implied. If we live in a culture in which the terms "Fair Trade" and "Big Oil" or "Big Pharma" are part of the lexicon, then we know to interpret the first sentence in the context of a critique of corporate labor practices in the coffee industry.

LANGUAGE AS ACTION

"Language as action" is an idea with a long history, often attributed to philosopher Ludwig Wittgenstein (1889–1951), who discussed language as a "game" with rules that must be learned. In the 1950s, philosopher J. L. Austin began to focus less on the ways that language represents information in general and more on the actions that language performs; this ultimately came to be called speech act theory. Consider a spoken claim: "I vow to clean my room." Speech act theory understands this utterance as being composed of three components:

speech act theory A set of ideas arguing that language does not just present information but also performs action.

(a) What was said: "I vow to clean my room."
(b) What was done: A solemn promise was made to perform the action of cleaning.
(c) What was (potentially) accomplished: The room was cleaned.

When it was first devised, speech act theory considered mostly the capacity of verbs that refer to or imply action (like "vow" in the example above). However, as language experts delved further into different types of language acts in the 1970s, they argued that language itself was also capable of social action even when the intended language act was not specified.

Consider the following sentence: "It is so warm in the kitchen." In this case, the implication of action is not encoded in the verb "is." However, if uttering this statement prompts someone to open the kitchen window or turn on a fan, the statement has resulted in direct action. In this way, language is action, both large and small.

Gossip is a feature of all human societies, and is one of the ways that humans create stories about those they know. Based often in negative innuendo and incomplete information, gossip is one way that social norms are communicated and enforced through language (**Figure 7.10**). It is so common for humans to gossip with one another that these rock formations have been named the "Three Gossips" as they resemble three people engaged in close conversation. Gossip is also inherently political and can shift power dynamics within a community by building or (more often) destroying people's social reputations.

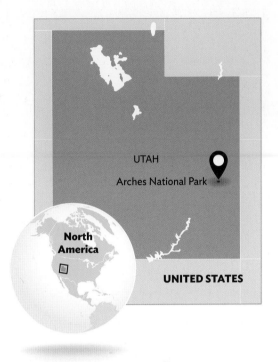

FIGURE 7.10

This formation at Arches National Park in Utah is called "Three Gossips."

LANGUAGE AS IDENTITY MARKER AND CREATOR

Language is one of the primary ways we constitute ourselves within our societies. By "constitute ourselves," we mean that we use language to show others who we are at a given moment in time and in a given space. Consider a snippet of a conversation that might happen between two university students.

PERSON A: "Hey! Are you goin' over to Juana's dorm later? They're gettin' pizza."

PERSON B: "Maybe. I have a test in anthro tomorrow, so I need to study."

The conversation here—the words chosen (dorm, test, anthro, study), the level of informality, the topics being discussed—reflects the two speakers each establishing their identity to one another. That is, language is central to how we present ourselves to others, in ways we often don't consciously consider or even notice. If this conversation were occurring in person or over video, it would usually combine with other visible symbols, such as clothing, hairstyle, or a backpack, along with the location of the interaction—on a campus or in a digital classroom—to create additional cues that shape the meaning and interpretations of what is being said.

We change our language—how we speak and sign and what we mean—based on both who we think we are or want to be (our presentation of self) and who we think the other person is. We take cues for how to understand who others are and how to speak and sign to them from how they talk to us. We use language in different ways when interacting with a religious leader than someone we are married to or dating.

register A cluster of language features (such as pronunciation, words, intonations, or other grammatical features) associated with a specific group of people or a specific context.

In many languages, *registers*, such as words, intonation, or grammatical features of a language, can produce or reflect the social status that exists between speakers and listeners. For example, Japanese has multiple forms of the verb "to eat" that are used when speaking in different contexts (**Table 7.1**). Knowing these different forms of the verb allows a speaker to demonstrate

---

TABLE 7.1

Japanese Variations on the Verbs Related to Eating

Verb "To Eat" in Japanese	When Expected to Be Used	Japanese Form	English Translation
Tabe-ru	In daily conversation among peers and family, or by a superior to a subordinate (boss talking to employee)	Ringo wo tabe-ru Apple object eat marker	[I] eat an apple
Meshi-aga-ru	By a subordinate to a superior (employee talking to boss)	Ringo wo meshi-aga-ru	[You] eat an apple
Ku-u	By men (but not usually women) when talking in peer groups or within the family	Ringo wo ku-u	[I] eat an apple
Itada-ku	Across many contexts to accept food provided by someone else; this form of the verb indicates deference by the person eating to the person providing the food	Ringo wo itada-ku	[I] eat an apple

their understandings of or produce hierarchy and power structures. These verb forms do not refer directly to social status. But over time, and in particular contexts, these status markers have informally come to be understood as part of the meaning encoded in the words.

Moreover, the appropriate use of these verb forms also signals the moral qualities of the people interacting: their politeness, and relatedly their upbringing; their willingness to adhere to cultural norms, including language ideologies; their ability to recognize social dynamics and rankings; and so on. In this sense, language contributes to the creation of social identity. How we use language, and how well we align our language use with a society's language ideologies, defines us as polite, rude, kind, arrogant, educated, funny, feminine, nonbinary, young, old, a business leader, etc.

LANGUAGE IS SOCIAL ORGANIZATION

Language not only marks social status but also maintains and creates our relationships to others. Labels like parent, family, best friend, co-worker, and stranger serve to indicate how we can and should interact with another person.

Language draws boundaries around people, placing them into identified groups. It defines some as "in" and some as "out." We distinguish family from others through labels like father and uncle. However, we can establish "fictive kin" by applying these labels to those who are not related to us, reminding us to relate to them as family. Fraternities, sororities, and other social groups, for example, may use terms like brother and sister to refer to other members, applying family terms to recall and reinforce the closeness and intimacy group members expect with each other (**Figure 7.11**).

Using nicknames for romantic partners is another example of how labels provide the guides for how we should interact. Use of English-language terms like bae, honey, or darling around others in public helps signal that an intimate relationship exists. It also denotes the person mentioned as taken: that is, it clearly assigns them to the category of romantically or sexually unavailable. Such use of language to signal categories that people belong to is often incredibly helpful to others. It helps them know what is appropriate to say and do, such as whether it's acceptable to flirt in this case. That is, the use of language sets up a frame of interaction that allows others to act in socially appropriate ways.

FIGURE 7.11

Members of the fraternity Phi Iota Alpha doing volunteer work. Fraternity members use kin terms such as "brother" to refer to one another. In the United States, such "Greek" fraternities are private, men-only social organizations for university undergraduates, and are seen as a potentially valuable source of lifetime social connections.

(a)

(b)

FIGURE 7.12

Elinor Ochs's research highlighted that language learning for children takes many forms, and it shapes how we learn to interact with others. **(a)** U.S. English speakers often use eye contact and speak directly to a baby. **(b)** Samoan speakers more typically orient a baby to listen to others.

Language can establish, maintain, or challenge social organization. Linguistic anthropologist Elinor Ochs has explained that the ways parents talk to their children are very different across societies. MWAE speakers in the United States tend to look their babies in the eyes and talk directly to them—the same way they talk to adults—while using a simplified and exaggerated "babyese" (**Figure 7.12a**). This can include combinations of verbal and nonverbal efforts, such as when a caregiver raises an infant's hand and waves it while encouraging the infant to "say bye-bye." But it also extends to asking or answering questions as though the baby were capable of holding a conversation, mimicking the forms of adult speech even though the baby is preverbal. Consider the following exchange while feeding carrots, which shows how a caregiver is interpreting the infant's behavior and narrating it aloud:

Caregiver feeding baby pureed carrots:

CAREGIVER:	"Is that good? Do you like it?"
INFANT:	Spits carrots out and wrinkles brow.
CAREGIVER:	"Oh, you don't like it? It's not yummy?"
INFANT:	Looks at caregiver.

This is very different than what Ochs observed of mothers interacting with their babies in Samoa (**Figure 7.12b**). Caregivers spoke directly to babies very little or not at all; instead they oriented the babies so they could observe typical language (not babyese) interactions happening around them. This is fitting in a society where those of lower social status (such as young children) are expected to listen rather than talk as a means of respecting those of higher status.

While the two ways of interacting with young children are very different, they result in children learning how to use language equally well and appropriately. These early childhood routines, repeated many times a day, are one way we learn to produce language sounds or signs and to interpret language in our environments. But we are also learning many related social cues and expectations, such as appropriate forms of eye contact and the importance of providing a response or silence in conversations. We learn not only how we are meant to talk but also how we are meant to think and feel through such interactions. These routines teach us how to be a competent member of any society.

Language practices can serve as a means of resisting change to social structures. Linguistic anthropologist Erin Moriarty has done research on language ideologies among deaf sign language users (signers) in schools in Bali, Indonesia. There are many different formalized sign languages across the globe, including several English variants such as American Sign Language (ASL) and Australian Sign Language (Auslan). As a result of colonialism and more recent developments, ASL dominates in Africa and throughout southeastern Asia, including Indonesia (**Figure 7.13**). ASL and other established sign languages often push out and replace existing signing systems in local languages.

In Indonesia, several sign languages are in use throughout the 17,508 islands that make up the nation. At the school for the deaf in Bali where Moriarty did her fieldwork, the students and teachers used Indonesian Sign Language (BISINDO) to communicate with each other but not with outsiders. Moriarty was specifically instructed not to talk (sign) directly with the students but rather to sign to the teacher in ASL, who would translate her signs into BISINDO. This

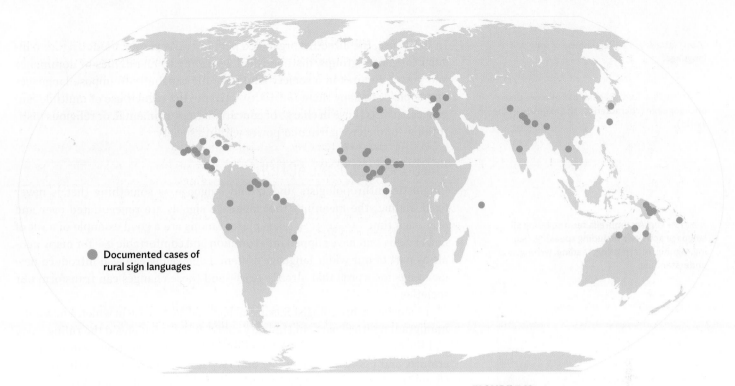

Documented cases of
rural sign languages

FIGURE 7.13

Rural sign languages are used by both deaf and hard of hearing individuals as well as by hearing individuals. These are unique sign language variants that have emerged in small villages ("rural") or other isolated locales where there is a high incidence of childhood deafness. Known cases are identified on the map, but—just like with spoken languages—there are many more undocumented cases.

was because the teacher was adamant that the students must not adopt any new non-BISINDO signs, even inadvertently (**Figure 7.14**).

Through this directive, the teacher was drawing clear boundaries between foreign and BISINDO language. It was linked to a language ideology that considered dominant sign languages such as ASL or International Sign Language to be powerful and destructive: able to easily topple "smaller" sign languages such as BISINDO, and therein contribute to the weakening of local group identities.

FIGURE 7.14

BISINDO or Indonesian Sign Language shares some, but not all, of the symbols for letters with other sign languages such as American or British Sign Language.

BALI

Asia

monolingualism Regular use of only one language.

multilingualism Regular use of more than one language (characterizes the majority of the world).

languaging An umbrella term covering all language activities including speaking, hearing, signing, interpreting, reading, writing, and understanding.

HUNGARY

Europe

In this sense, the directive organized people into separate, monolingual (singular language) groups, distinguished according to hierarchies of dominance and power. Figures in a society who have the capability to impose languages on people or to deny them multilingualism—the regular use of multiple languages, such as those in charge of educational, governmental, or religious institutions—often have particular power within a society.

LANGUAGE IS SOCIAL ACTION

Linguistic anthropologists understand language as something that is never fixed. Rather, the meanings that language signals are renegotiated over and over each time languaging takes place. Emojis are a good example of a set of newer signs that have slipped into common and comfortable use for many people as part of our wider language system. Languaging can also introduce new meanings for words that already exist—and these changes can transform our societies.

Lingustic anthropologist Susan Gal has analyzed a case in which a new anti-immigrant political party in Hungary called Jobbik challenged the ruling party and European Union immigration policies. In political writings, campaign literature, and public speeches, the Jobbik party began to refer to the Romani (Roma) community (a large, heavily discriminated against minority) as "Gypsy" (cigány), a known pejorative ethnonym (name for a group of people) in Hungarian. Jobbik also began to use the terms "gypsy-criminals" (cigánybűnöző) and "gypsy-crime" (cigánybűnözés). In this way, Jobbik's discourse about "gypsy-criminals" served effectively to turn them into criminals in the perceptions of many Hungarians and so bolstered public support for their own policies (**Figure 7.15**).

This demonstrates that language is social action: through simple phrases that sit comfortably within local language ideologies, it is possible to transform a group merely through language associating them with criminality.

FIGURE 7.15

Members of Hungarian far-right nationalist groups associated with the Jobbik political party protest against what they call a "gypsy-crime."

The ways that ideas get picked up and moved around through language is sometimes described as *circulating discourses*. Our contemporary global environment includes technologies that provide immediate access to many media platforms and their near-bottomless amounts of content, much of which reinforces the messaging we encounter in nondigital format (billboards, print media, and so on). In addition to all this media we now consume, we also have ready connections in person and online to friends and families. They, too, share value-laden information that impacts our lives. Through these various media outlets and personal networks, we become participants in circulating discourses that repeat and echo with similar content. These discourses nudge us to pick up some new language usages and interpretations while jettisoning others.

Exact meanings of words like "fat" are interpreted differently in different places, but the idea that thinner bodies are more acceptable and desirable is consistently messaged through language across multiple platforms and places (**Figure 7.16**). It is through circulating discourses that social action takes place.

circulating discourse An idea or belief that moves around communities (large and small) through language.

(a)

(b)

FIGURE 7.16

(a) A billboard advertising a weight loss product establishes and reinforces negative interpretations of non-slim bodies. (b) A response to a beach body ready campaign offers a different perspective. One note reads "Every body's beautiful!" and another "We're all beach ready."

HOW LANGUAGE SHAPES HUMANS

linguistic relativity The concept of language as a catalyst for a shift in perspective, such as how people perceive and interact with the worlds around them.

Yucatec Maya speakers

Kuuk Thaayorre speakers

Linguistic anthropologists have long been committed to understanding how language helps create people's worldviews, such as how we view and react to different bodies. This idea is sometimes called linguistic relativity—the idea that people and the worlds we live in are created through our everyday language practices. Or, in other words, words take hold of us, leading us in particular directions, and often urging us into patterns of perception and action.

Language mediates our experience of the world, broadly. Consider riding on a rollercoaster: Your body feels and experiences the ups, downs, and loop-de-loops, but when you tell someone about that feeling, the words are mediating the actual feelings. In this instance, "mediate" means that language intervenes between the feelings and the expression. And in this mediation, language can be a catalyst, a spark, that brings forth complex reactions and interactions.

As an example, let's consider linguistic anthropologist John Lucy's investigation of the role that grammatical categories have on our worldview in his experiment with Mainstream White American English (MWAE) speakers and Indigenous Yucatec Maya (YM) speakers in southeastern Mexico. Lucy was interested in comparing these two languages because of the treatment of the grammatical category of number by each language. In MWAE, marking number on objects is required: one tree or two trees; one rabbit or five rabbits. Some languages do not require grammatical number to be indicated. YM marks grammatical number in an optional but not required manner.

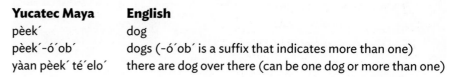

Yucatec Maya	English
pèek´	dog
pèek´-ó´ob´	dogs (-ó´ob´ is a suffix that indicates more than one)
yàan pèek´ té´elo´	there are dog over there (can be one dog or more than one)

Because marking number (plural) is required in MWAE and optional in YM, Lucy surmised that these two languages could reveal ways that this grammar difference mediated speakers' worldviews in terms of what they notice and attend to in their everyday lives. Lucy predicted that the YM speakers would give less attention to number than the MWAE speaker counterparts. Lucy had the two sets of speakers look at and sort various objects. Later, when asked about what they had seen, the two sets of speakers attended to and recalled the objects in ways that aligned with the linguistic relativity theory: MWAE speakers had attended to number more than the YM speakers.

Linguist Lera Boroditsky has conducted fieldwork in the small remote Indigenous community of Pormpuraaw in coastal northern Queensland, Australia, studying how humans using different languages also distinctly organize the realities of their worlds. Her work began with an observation that people in Pormpuraaw, who speak Kuuk Thaayorre as their primary language, don't use terms like left or right to denote direction. Instead, they use cardinal directions like north, south, east, and west. These terms are employed continuously in everyday interactions, such as, "Oh, there's an ant on my southwest leg," or "Move your cup to the north-northeast a little bit." Even a greeting in Kuuk Thaayorre takes the form of "Which way are you going?" Kuuk Thaayorre speakers in Pormpuraaw always use cardinal directions regardless of what they are locating in space. The terms used in Kuuk Thaayorre for east (kaw) and west (kuw) use the sun's trajectory for their definitions, but the terms north (ungkarr) and south (iparr) are defined by the local coastline. In comparison, English speakers use their body as a point of reference for locating objects, even if they use cardinal directions for travel or locations. In English, for example, people would say, "There's an ant on my left leg."

Boroditsky conducted a set of nonlinguistic experiments, asking English speakers to organize a sets of cards on the ground in relation to the passing of time. The cards depicted sets of various events, one set depicted a whole orange, a peeled orange, and a few slices of an orange. English speakers consider the future being "in front of them" and the past "behind them." When English speakers gesture, past events tend to be to the left and the progression of time moves to the right. Therefore, when English speakers are asked to arrange the cards in temporal order, they put the whole orange to the left, followed by the peeled orange, and finally the few slices of the orange, showing the progression of events (and time generally) from left to right.

But when Kuuk Thaayorre community members were asked to do this task, Boroditsky found that they arranged the cards from east to west (**Figure 7.17**). So, if the Kuuk Thaayorre person completing the task was sitting facing south, the cards would progress from east to west (left to right of their body); if the person was sitting facing north, the cards would progress from east to west (right to left of their body); and if the person was sitting facing east, the cards would progress from east to west (toward the body, with whole orange located further away from the body than the card with orange slices on it). In short, Pormpuraawans organize time sequences in a pattern of east to west, with the east representing more distant time and the west representing more recent time. This reflects thinking about time as connected to space in a way that American English speakers and other groups do not, in this case because other groups lack the necessary spatial knowledge acquired through their language.

Clearly, the way space is organized within a language is connected to how people perceive time and how they talk about time. The languages that we learn nudge us to pay more attention to some aspects of the world around us than others. This does not mean we can't learn other ways of attending to our world. It does suggest, however, that language impacts our thinking and the framing of our world.

Another example of how language guides our experiences of reality is provided through *evidentiality*—pieces of language that indicate how a speaker obtained the knowledge they're sharing. In MWAE, evidentiality is expressed through phrases like "I heard that," "I saw that," or "allegedly." But evidentiality is not obligatory in MWAE: this means that the grammar does not require evidentiality to be included in things we say. Consider:

A. Gary mopped the floor.

B. I saw Gary mop the floor.

C. Allegedly, Gary mopped the floor.

While each of these sentences describes knowledge of an action (mopping) Gary completed, examples B and C grammatically denote how the knowledge was acquired (B) or that the knowledge has not been proven (C). In using English, the speaker can use any of the forms and is not required by the rules of the language to specify whether they witnessed the mopping or not.

FIGURE 7.17

Lera Boroditsky conducts experiments with children in Pormpuraaw, an Indigenous community in Australia, asking them to lay out the temporal sequences of events like an apple falling from a tree.

evidentiality A piece of language that indicates how something is known.

FIGURE 7.18

There are few speakers of the oral Wintu language. The community has been working with linguist Stephan Liedtke to document the language, create a dictionary, and develop educational materials for classes, like the one shown here, so the language can be taught to the next generation. Given the entwined relationship between language and worldview, such efforts are important to cultural knowledge and discerning the world in usefully different ways, not just language preservation.

Winnemem Wintu tribe homelands

But other languages do have this requirement. Wintu, an Indigenous language of the Winnemem Wintu tribe whose homelands are in northern California, requires speakers to specify the source of knowledge (**Figure 7.18**). The following example, "Harry is chopping wood," is an illustration, showing the five different options speakers have for describing what Harry was doing with an axe. The underscored information approximates the text that appears to the left.

"Harry kupa<u>be</u>"	I see or have seen Harry chopping.
"Harry kupa<u>nte</u>"	I hear him, or a chip flies off and hits me.
"Harry kupa<u>re</u>"	I have gone to his cabin and find him absent and the axe is gone.
"Harry kupa<u>el</u>"	I know that Harry has a job chopping wood every day at this hour, that he is a dependable employee, and, perhaps, that he is not in his cabin.
"Harry kupa<u>ke</u>"	I know this by hearsay.

Consider this in the context of how quickly "fake news" can be spread among English speakers, whether in person or through social media. In English, one can say "There is a conspiracy" without having to specify exactly how this is known. In Wintu, passing along such information requires the speaker to identify how they know this—for example, if they witnessed the conspiracy directly themselves versus simply heard it as hearsay. In English, sharing information without attendant information about the veracity of the claim is, by comparison, much easier to do, which makes it easier for multiple (and sometimes directly conflicting) accounts of reality to coexist within the same society.

HOW PEOPLE CREATE MEANING

In many ways, encoding language seems much more straightforward than decoding it. As a speaker or signer, we have in mind what we intend to say or convey. But decoding language can be far trickier than we imagine, requiring quite a bit of guesswork.

In the prior sections we have explained how speakers bring many considerations, both conscious and not, to every interaction they have, including what and how things can be said or signed in given contexts. One of the newer areas of study in linguistic anthropology is how meaning is also produced by receivers of language. Much of the research to date has focused on how perceptions of speakers and signers produce particular social identities in the minds of the audience—and how these perceptions, in turn, can help create, maintain, and challenge social norms and structures.

We bring our beliefs about others to every interaction. In the 1970s, cognitive psychologists Harry McGurk and John MacDonald described a phenomenon that has come to be known as the McGurk effect. This effect occurs when an acoustic utterance (that is, a single sound or a syllable) is heard as a different utterance if paired with a visual image that people do not expect to match the sound. Experiencing a language variety that seems discordant with how a person looks is an example of this. The relationship between what we see and perceive affects our understanding of an event and impacts our subjective experience of it.

Linguist Ethan Kutlu did a series of what are called "matched guise" experiments in the United States. His studies examined how speakers judged two varieties of English— MWAE and Indian Englishes—when paired with faces that were perceived as concordant (matching) versus discordant (unmatching). Participants listened to a stream of speech from each English variety while looking at a photo of the face of a White woman or a South Asian woman. Participants rated each speaker's accent (**Figure 7.19**). Both the MWAE and Indian English speakers were judged to have less of an accent when participants were viewing the White face.

In a second study, Kutlu asked participants to transcribe (write down) what they heard when listening to American and Indian varieties of English in order to measure the intelligibility, or ability to be understood, of what is being said. The same voice was attributed to either a South Asian person or a White person, but the voice was routinely judged to be less intelligible when attributed to the South Asian person. This exemplifies how our beliefs about others shape the outcomes of human communication.

In ongoing work, Kutlu has suggested that people who live in multilingual societies with high language diversity, such as Montréal, Canada, report higher levels of comprehension of varieties of languages compared to those living in places of

McGurk effect The perception that results when we hear a sound or a stream of language while viewing an image we associate with a different sound or language.

– American English
– Indian English

– American English
– Indian English

FIGURE 7.19

Linguist Ethan Kutlu used faces like these in his listening tests, where the voice was the same but the accents were judged to be different.

FIGURE 7.20

Nelson Flores answers questions on a discussion panel. His research on language and race among dual-language students in a predominantly Latinx school in Philadelphia in the eastern United States, and his related policy work draw on his prior experiences as a teacher of English as a Second Language (ESL) and as a bilingual student in the same city.

raciolinguistics The study of how language ideologies produce racial difference and ideologies of racial difference produce linguistic differences.

Latinx A person of Latin American origin or descent. The -x ending indicates all genders.

racialize To categorize people into established racist typologies within a given cultural context.

linguistic prejudice Having biases or judgments about people based on their language, including the way they speak.

low language diversity, such as Florida, United States, in his study. Our brains tune our ears to listen differently, based on what we are regularly exposed to but also based on the contexts in which we are hearing language. In other words, if exposed to wide variation across diverse speakers and language varieties, we can learn to listen and achieve more consistent understanding.

Educational linguist Nelson Flores has written about a raciolinguistic perspective to describe the ways that listeners expect people who look a certain way (typically non-White or nonmajority) to speak. Flores, who is a member of the Latinx community, describes an event at an academic conference (**Figure 7.20**). He had 20 minutes to cover a lot of information and was trying to go as quickly as possible. The first question from the audience was a White student who asked why it was that Latinx people spoke so quickly. When Flores assured her that there was no research showing that Latinx people spoke more quickly than any other racial or ethnic group in the United States, her response was "Oh come on. You people speak way faster than we do."

A raciolinguistic perspective allows us to understand how such racialization impacts the audience's perception of the speaker. As language subjects, our beliefs about speakers and signers combine with our beliefs about language more broadly to impact how we decode specific utterances and interactions.

University campuses are increasingly internationalized, with both students and instructors migrating between regions and countries to learn and teach. Monolingual English speakers and multilingual English speakers are often in the classroom together. Studies on campuses have shown that students reflect many of the findings of the matched guise study discussed earlier. In one such study, a woman was audio-recorded reading the script of a classroom lecture using MWAE pronunciation. U.S. university students as research participants were divided into two groups. One listened to the audiotape while a picture of a White woman was projected in front of them. The other listened to the same audiotape but with an Asian woman projected as the speaker. Students were then quizzed on the content of the lecture material. Those who listened while looking at the Asian woman rated the speaker as having more of an accent and being difficult to understand, and they scored worse on the subsequent coursework than their classmates in the other group. Since the lecture was exactly the same for the two groups, this suggests that the reason students couldn't understand the instructor was not due substantively to the instructor's language proficiency itself but was due to a predisposal against some groups of multilingual English speakers.

The same study team also tested some possible "inoculations" that might improve students' comprehension and learning, such as informal contact (like doing puzzles together) with instructors. This did improve comprehension, like hearing less of an accent. This research highlights how university students benefit from an awareness of their language predispositions in dealing with teachers or classmates who look different from them.

LINGUISTIC PREJUDICE

While exposure can improve our decoding ability, situated knowledge and experience can develop into linguistic prejudice and inform how we interpret and react to language varieties. These prejudices can be acquired at a young age. Children's entertainment is one source through which ideas of race and gender are taught. Rosina Lippi-Green has written about the role of Disney animation in teaching viewers to connect language varieties with specific characters

FIGURE 7.21

Disney villains, such as these evil hyenas in the movie *The Lion King*, have historically been portrayed using varieties of English other than MWAE.

and the characteristics they display. Analyzing Disney films made between 1937 and 2009, she found the voices of most film heroes (such as Snow White) used MWAE, while villain voices used other English varieties. In *The Lion King,* for example, the villainous hyenas are voiced with Black English and Spanish accents (**Figure 7.21**). The hero Simba, on the other hand, is voiced in MWAE.

In such ways, Lippi-Green argues, children learn how to decode the kinds of language varieties they hear in the contexts of the characters' roles (hero, villain, sidekick) and associated traits, including their ethnicity, status, and power. In this way, we learn how to hear judgments about good and bad (or desirable and undesirable) qualities, teaching us how to be prejudiced. This reminds us that language is embedded in almost every aspect of our lives, in ways we are barely aware of but that are constantly nudging us toward understandings of how things are meant to be and what is valued in our society.

DISCRIMINATION AS A CONSEQUENCE OF LINGUISTIC PROFILING

From a young age, linguistic expert John Baugh code-switched between MWAE and Black English, and he noticed he was perceived and received in different ways when using each variety (**Figure 7.22**). These childhood experiences in urban Los Angeles would ultimately lead him to coin the term linguistic profiling. His research included language analysis of hundreds of phone calls made to real estate agents, loan officers, and potential employers. He found that such financial and housing gatekeepers made different judgments about a caller based on whether they spoke Black English, MWAE, or Mexican-style Spanish-English. Moreover, the quoted cost of the same apartment rental was higher for a Black English speaker and lower for a MWAE speaker. A job described as "already filled" to a Mexican-style Spanish-English speaker was still accepting applications from a MWAE speaker. Baugh's work documents discrimination based on language uses that can be used in courts of law to aid those targeted by such illegal actions.

code-switching Moving between two or more language varieties in the same stream of language.

linguistic profiling Deciding who someone is with regard to race/ethnicity, age, social class, or national origin based on the way that they speak or sign.

FIGURE 7.22

John Baugh participates as a language expert on a music industry panel in 2020, exploring the implications of the usage of words like "urban" in describing different music forms and the people who produce them.

7 | Language and Our Worlds

When we use language, we are not just hearing words or seeing signs. The complex symbolic system of language creates meaning and social action based not only on what is said, signed, or written, but also on how we perceive and interpret what we hear, see, or read.

7.1 | The Structures of Human Language

Explain the structures of human language.

- Understanding language requires not only knowing what words mean referentially but also understanding the ways that meanings not present in the words used in an interaction—along with context—create meaning.

- Interpreting language is not simply decoding the words and structures used. Social values and cultural norms underlie much of the meanings we produce from language.

7.2 | What Human Language Does

Evaluate human language as a form of communication and social action.

- Language produces social actions such as social organization, status, and experience.

- Language is a non-neutral medium that acts on humans at least as much as humans act on language.

KEY TERMS
> arbitrariness
> circulating
  discourse
> decoding
> encoding
> icon
> index
> languaging
> monolingualism
> multilingualism
> oral tradition
> origin myth
> petroglyph
> register
> situated
  knowledge
> speech act theory
> symbol

7.3 | How Language Shapes Humans

Assess how the structures of language impact human understanding.

- The grammatical structures and rules of a language influence how its speakers construct their worlds.

KEY TERMS
> evidentiality
> linguistic relativity

7.4 | How People Create Meaning

Analyze how language receivers encode and decode meaning.

- We learn to perceive others through specific lenses of understanding that often rely on ideas and values about the speakers. These ideas and values shape the way we create meaning, including what we are then prejudiced against.

KEY TERMS
> code-switching
> Latinx
> linguistic
  predjudice
> linguistic profiling
> McGurk effect
> racialization
> raciolinguistics

Human Settlement and Societies

Archaeologist Linda Manzanilla has spent more than four decades researching how the ancient metropolis of Teotihuacan was organized and ruled in the Valley of Mexico. First settled in 100 CE, Teotihuacan grew quickly into the first city in Mesoamerica, peaking with 100,000 residents and lasting six centuries. Teotihuacan was not just a city but also an early state, meaning it controlled a wide surrounding territory too. The inhabitants constructed massive, monumental buildings on an east–west axis, known as the Avenue of the Dead, that connects the so-called Pyramids of the Sun and Moon, which are still standing today (**Figure 8.1**).

Manzanilla excavated temples and houses at Teotihuacan (**Figure 8.2**). But early on, she wondered what this society was like and how it was governed. To answer these questions, she began collaborating with archaeologists with other specializations—in paleoethnobotany (study of ancient plants), zooarchaeology (analysis of ancient animals), archaeological chemistry, geoarchaeology, and mathematical modeling, as well as in political science and genetics.

Although they found no obvious signs of one ruler, such as a queen or king immortalized either in public artworks or in tombs, researchers believe that there must have been a centralized government that wielded significant control and power. The monumental buildings themselves indicate substantial control of a massive labor force and careful planning capabilities, including some form of hierarchical society. The Teotihuacan food system involved large-scale irrigation to grow crops such as maize (corn) and stable marketplaces for imported items such as cotton or salt; these also point to a strong, central government. Within Teotihuacan, Manzanilla excavated the Xalla sector, a palatial compound near the Pyramid of the Sun that included temples and contained jade

AN URBAN SPECIES

The city is a very new, human-created ecosystem. Living closely with others creates new opportunities and challenges, all of which are the focus on anthropologists' study.

LEARNING OBJECTIVES

8.1   The Advantages of Cooperative Communities
Illustrate how living in communities benefits primates, including modern humans.

8.2   The Transition to Agriculture and Permanent Settlements
Describe the drivers behind and the transitions to permanent settlements and agriculture.

8.3   The Rise of Cities and States
Connect urban settlement to increasing social complexity and inequality.

8.4   Governing Complex Societies
Assess mechanisms of state governance and the ways that people also self-govern from within larger-scale societies.

FIGURE 8.1

The Avenue of the Dead, at Teotihuacan in central Mexico, connects the Pyramid of the Sun (shown here) with the Pyramid of the Moon. The massive scale of the monumental architecture is shown by the visitors walking along the avenue.

state A large, hierarchical political unit with a centralized government that binds citizens by consensus or coercion and the power to decree and enforce laws.

hierarchical society A societal model in which people are ranked in grades, orders, or classes, with higher-ranked individuals gaining additional access to resources and power.

elite A person with significantly greater power and access to and control of resources than others.

ethnic group People who are identified by shared ancestry or heritage, language, and cultural traditions.

urban Describes the dense settlement of humans in defined areas.

FIGURE 8.2

Archaeologist Linda Manzanilla excavates at the Xalla sector within Teotihuacan.

and mica imported over vast distances. Xalla may have been one neighborhood from which elites co-ruled the city.

Studies incorporating stable isotope analysis and ancient DNA show that many people in the city were born elsewhere and had diverse backgrounds. Early residents may have first been driven toward living together in the Valley of Mexico by a series of volcanic eruptions. But many other communities migrated in subsequently. At least five different languages were commonly used.

This diverse city was, like many large cities today, organized into many distinct neighborhoods containing smaller temples, workshops for artisans, and market areas. Much like our cities today, each neighborhood also had a distinctive "feel," with people cooking and eating foods from their homelands, using pottery and other artifacts that were familiar to them, and burying their dead loved ones according to their unique traditions. The largest neighborhood was dominated by people drawn from Oaxaca to the southwest. Manzanilla excavated the smaller neighborhood of Teopancazco, where many artisans lived and the residents maintained strong ties to their originating communities on the coast of the Gulf of Mexico, eating imported marine fish and wearing cotton clothes with seashells sewn on them.

The evidence from neighborhoods excavated by Manzanilla and others, though, suggests that different ethnic groups in Teotihuacan enjoyed autonomy. Neighborhoods had easy access to a center, and housing was organized differently in each. The art and other creative expressions seen in material culture also suggest that a diversity of expression was valued, which is not generally associated with governance structures with centralized control. There were also surprisingly low levels of inequality across neighborhoods, at least in material wealth. This makes Teotihuacan quite different than most other urban centers, including those today.

FIGURE 8.3

A mural painting from the Tepantitla apartment compound at Teotihuacan depicts a number of people participating in a large-scale communal event.

However, the city needed some unity to survive for centuries and maintain institutions such as central markets. Shared religious rituals and a shared cosmology likely provided the shared purpose required for stable government not based in a single powerful leader (**Figure 8.3**). The huge, monumental temples, rising high above the city, would have reminded the residents that they lived in a sacred place.

By 550 CE, Teotihuacan was no longer a major center, but it remains a critical landmark in human history that provides insights into the process of agricultural settlement and urbanization. To those who study Teotihuacan's complex history, including Manzanilla, it isn't a story of societal collapse. Rather, it is an early and even hopeful example of a complex, multiethnic society that managed to thrive for centuries—longer than many of our major cities today have existed.

In this chapter, we will trace the path of human settlement from the earliest agricultural settlements to urban centers, investigating the how and why humans tend toward social complexity. We will analyze how governance occurs today to build a picture of how humans live together, even at incredible densities.

cosmology A theory of the universe (world) as an ordered whole, including beliefs, knowledge, and interpretations about its origins.

social complexity Describes a society with large numbers of people, large permanent settlements, and many varied social and economic roles.

SECTION 8.1

THE ADVANTAGES OF COOPERATIVE COMMUNITIES

For almost all of the last 200,000 years, modern humans lived in small groups, like most other primates, foraging for food. Kinship was the most important tie that people had to each other and was central to how communities and activities within them were defined and organized. By kinship, we mean patterns of very close relationships defined by the recognition of being related through birth (consanguineal kin) and those we then affiliate with in other ways, such as through adoption and marriage (affinal kin). Some primates do seem to recognize kin relationships in small ways, especially related to females with offspring. Primate cooperative activity tends to favor those with closer genetic

kinship Extremely close social relationships that have a density of expectations and obligations attached to them.

relationships. This is the case with humans also, but humans will also favor cooperation with genetically unrelated individuals who are socially defined as part of our kin groups (including adopted children).

Categories of kin vary from society to society. For example, the terms for cousins and siblings are the same in some Polynesian languages, meaning both should be considered as similarly close kin. In other languages such as Hindi-Urdu, the terms for cousins differ by gender and who you are related through and suggest a range of levels of closeness.

Regardless of how kin are defined, having kin helps meet complex social goals by defining both our level of obligations to help others and what we might then also expect in return. The support can be material, such as sharing food or maintaining a home. It can also define who we plan and spend holidays and celebrations with, who you can curse in front of, or who should provide physical and emotional care when we are young, sick, old, or sad. Kinship rules also provide important information that directs how societies are organized, such as who we should or shouldn't marry or who we should leave our property to when we die (**Figure 8.4**).

It is not clear exactly when humans started using kin categories to organize their relationships into different roles and expectations, but it was certainly tied to the emergence of early human capacities for shared language, culture, and identity. A willingness to share and cooperate intensely with others offered advantages for survival, even at times when no immediate reciprocity could be expected. It created the framework for being able to rely on others.

Today, the majority of humans live in cities, which are dense and complicated social settings. City dwellers cannot just cooperate with kin. They are also fully reliant on massive, globalized supply chains to get what they eat and otherwise need and on organized transportation systems to be able to get around. We interact with and rely on many different institutions that shape how we live, work, and relate to others, from local neighborhood associations and schools to corporations and city and national governments.

Viewed in the scale of human history, a reliance on kinship remains an important element of how we organize ourselves and share necessary resources, including how we pool or share our food and income and otherwise arrange households. But this change over the last 200,000 years—from living in highly dispersed kin groups to living in extremely dense societies with unrelated others—has been recent, rapid, and dramatic. Why would such a drastic change occur? We can find the beginnings of an answer by analyzing the advantages of cooperative communities that extend beyond just our own relatives or people we know well and can trust.

FIGURE 8.4

This historic wax recreation of the British royal family at Madame Tussauds in London reflects how birth and marriage together define categories of close kin in elite British society. It also shows how other types of dense, intimate relationships—even with other beings such as pets—can also be considered as kin or kinlike.

WHY PRIMATES LIVE IN GROUPS

Almost all primates live in groups. The only species that don't always live as group members are nocturnal strepsirrhines (such as lemurs) and orangutans—species whose food sources are very widely distributed and who consequently need to move about a lot to feed (Chapter 4). Yet living together has notable disadvantages. Living in close proximity spreads disease and means individuals often must share food that they find with others. So why do most primates, including humans, live in groups at all?

FIGURE 8.5

Chacma baboons cooperatively watch for predators in Kruger National Park, South Africa.

Anthropologists observing primates with varied social arrangements suggest that one major benefit is that larger groups are better able to defend a territory against others of the same species. This might include protecting patches of food that may only be available seasonally, such as ripening fruit.

Another benefit for primates living in groups is reducing their chance of being hunted by predators. Lions and leopards are primary culprits in Africa, but snakes and predatory birds also pose a risk to many primate species, especially the young. Living in large groups provides more sets of eyes and ears to be alert to potential predators. Social primate species use calls to warn each other, including specific calls for specific types of threats on the ground versus from the air. Smaller primates hide, while larger primates use mobbing behavior to deter a predator that enters their territory.

Baboons live in particularly large groups, up to 250 individuals, and males have large bodies and sharp fangs used to fight other males to maintain their place in the group's hierarchy (social ranking) and their access to estrus females. This also allows them the capacity to group together to ward off predators. Chacma baboons (*Papio ursinus*), for example, will confront a python, hyena, or cheetah by surrounding them, barking and showing their large, pointed canines (**Figure 8.5**).

Also, living in groups means the risk of predation is shared among all members of the group, so the chance of becoming a meal is reduced for all. This is referred to as the "selfish herd" effect, and it is one explanation given for why these behaviors may be selected through evolution as a primate adaptation. Finally, another reason to belong to large social groups—one perhaps especially relevant to humans today—is that it provides access to and options for mates with relatively little effort involved in locating them.

But there are also limits on how large primate groups can become, determined in part by the resources available in the group's territory. A major challenge of living in increasingly larger groups is how to gain enough resources, and—when there isn't enough to go around—how to negotiate sharing that food with other members of the group and avoid aggression and conflict.

Early human societies benefitted from our evolved capacity for prosocial behavior, which refers to actions that help others, even at possible costs to ourselves. Other primates sometimes cooperate and share resources such as food in some limited ways. But humans have the capacity to share more widely and more consistently than any other primate, and we do so more often with those unrelated to us. This capacity is an important reason why humans have been able to live in larger groups than other primates.

prosocial behavior Voluntary actions that are intended to help other individuals or groups.

Hunter-gatherer societies, such as these Ju/'hoansi (!Kung San) hunters in the Kalahari Desert of Namibia, are typically small, mobile, and egalitarian.

egalitarian A societal model in which access to resources and power is not controlled by some individuals or sectors of society; rather, involvement in decision-making and access to resources is evenly distributed, and social distinctions are based on age, gender, and individual qualities.

hunter-gatherer People who predominantly obtain their food through their knowledge of wild plants and animals, instead of reliance on domesticated plants and animals; sometimes called foragers.

FIGURE 8.7

This Gravettian carved mammoth ivory figurine shows evidence of woven head coverings.

COOPERATION IN HUNTER-GATHERER SOCIETIES

Until around 12,000 years ago, humans lived in small, mobile groups that were mostly egalitarian in their social structure, meaning that people were considered generally equal, with similar power and access to resources. These hunter-gatherer societies outcompeted other *Homo* species and were able to settle and thrive in a much wider set of ecologies (Chapter 6). These groups illustrate the great advantages of cooperative living, although today they are few in number (**Figure 8.6**).

Cartoons and films have popularized a distorted view of past hunter-gatherer groups as living in small, isolated family groups, barely eking out a living, lacking language skills, and living in damp and dirty caves. Moreover, hunter-gatherer groups cooperated far more extensively than previously thought. During the twentieth century, many anthropologists believed that hunter-gatherer groups consisted of kinship bands of 25–50 individuals within an isolated territory. Three or more of these stable bands formed a larger kinship group of approximately 150, which in turn had more distant ties to discrete societies of about 1,000 individuals. Recent research on present-day hunter-gatherer societies challenges these ideas, showing instead that early human societies were likely larger, more varied, and more complex. Rather, these societies may have been based in large ethnolinguistic social networks in which fluid bands of individuals without close kinship ties could arise. These bands might, for example, consist of unrelated co-workers.

The Gravettian case is an example of an early hunter-gatherer community engaged in complex cooperation that must have included non-kin. Between 29,000 and 21,000 years ago, during the Upper Paleolithic period, hunter-gatherer Gravettian societies at many sites in Europe left evidence of rich artistic, cultural, and technological achievements in the archaeological record. Clay figurines wearing hats, skirts, and other apparel and tools found at these sites indicate that these societies had woven textiles, basketry, nets, and cords (**Figure 8.7**).

People living in Gravettian sites hunted mammoth, bison, and reindeer with sophisticated projectile technologies that include the javelin, spear thrower, and bow and arrow. Plants were also important for food, and Gravettian hunter-gatherers ground wild grains to bake bread. They lived in caves, highly organized campsites, and semisubterranean houses with roofs constructed of mammoth bones and furs. At one site, these houses were arranged in an oval around nine hearths that warmed a central area.

THE TRANSITION TO AGRICULTURE AND PERMANENT SETTLEMENTS

For tens of thousands of years, modern humans enjoyed great success as hunter-gatherers. Today, hunter-gatherers constitute less than 0.001% of our population (**Figure 8.8**). What happened? How and why did we change from being a species in which everyone was a hunter-gatherer to one in which most people live in settled communities and rely on domesticated plants and animals?

Archaeologists still debate exactly why the transition to agriculture occurred. Since it happened in many different world regions at about the same time, some archaeologists look to universal factors, such as increasing population density or climate change, since the early Holocene epoch brought a more stable climate worldwide. However, these "prime mover" models only fit the archaeological data on the transition to agriculture for some (but not all) regions. For example, in the Near East, the first domesticated plants and animals are seen in areas where there is no evidence for population pressure, and different groups reacted to changing climatic conditions in different ways in this region. As archaeologists learn more about the transition to agriculture in different world regions, it is clear that large-scale factors such as climate changes played a role but that each region had a distinct and varied transition to agriculture that also relied on the wild plants and animals that were available, local ecosystems, and individual choices about resources.

A CHANGING CLIMATE

Around 12,000 years ago, the last major glacial cooling of the planet ended, and climates became more stable. This set the stage for the transition to agriculture and widespread domestication of plants and animals starting in the early Holocene epoch, one of the crucial turning points in the history of our species.

From approximately 21,000 to 15,500 BCE, glaciers covered much of the Northern Hemisphere, locking up water so that the climate globally was both cold and arid. Worldwide, deserts expanded while tropical rainforests contracted. By the beginning of the Holocene epoch, the planet began to warm. Glaciers retreated, grasslands gave rise to forests, and some large mammals, such as mammoths, died out. Sea levels rose dramatically, giving rise to the present boundaries of continents and island nations. As temperatures rose and rainfall increased, vegetation and animal life spread into new regions, closely followed by hunter-gatherer communities.

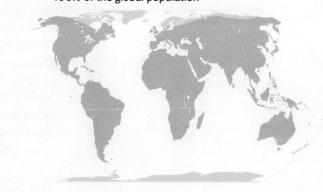

15,000 BCE: Hunter-gatherers made up 100% of the global population

1500 CE: Hunter-gatherers made up 1% of the global population

1960 CE: Hunter-gatherers made up 0.001% of the global population

FIGURE 8.8

These maps show hunter-gatherers as a percentage of the human population over time.

domestication **The process of adapting plants and animals to be dependent on humans for reproduction and to be used as sources of food, wool and clothing, transport, or milk.**

Holocene epoch **A division of the geological timescale that began about 12,000 years ago, after the last major glacial cooling of the planet, and has been associated (until very recently) with a relatively stable climate.**

CULTIVATION OF THE LAND

Tens of thousands of years prior to the appearance of the first agricultural villages, hunter-gatherers practiced the cultivation (active growing) of wild plants. For example, as Indigenous Australians maintain traditions of foraging for wild plants, they sometimes gather only a part of the plant—such as the side tubers of yams—leaving the main plant and its roots intact. They also cut up tubers to replant them elsewhere. Some hunter-gatherer societies burned vegetation, either to encourage the natural spread of a favored wild crop to that area or to plant seeds and cuttings there. They transplanted vegetation to new areas and even diverted streams to irrigate their wild crops.

THE DOMESTICATION PROCESS

The process of domestication occurred over many generations as humans slowly modified wild plants and animals so they would become more stable and predictable food supplies. They bred animals to make them easier to control and increase how much meat, milk, or wool they yielded. They bred plants so that they would grow faster and larger and be easier to harvest.

Archaeologically, animal domestication can be identified by rapid changes in the size and shape of animals' bodies or evidence of culling managed herds (such as animals of one sex or the same age being butchered). Plant domestication can be signaled by changes in the size and shape of seeds. Genetic studies of plant and animal remains can help confirm changes over time.

Widespread domestication happened independently in different parts of the world but around much the same time: between about 8000 and 5000 BCE. The same wild animal or plant was domesticated several times in different places (**Figure 8.9**). In the Near East, early domesticated species included wheat and

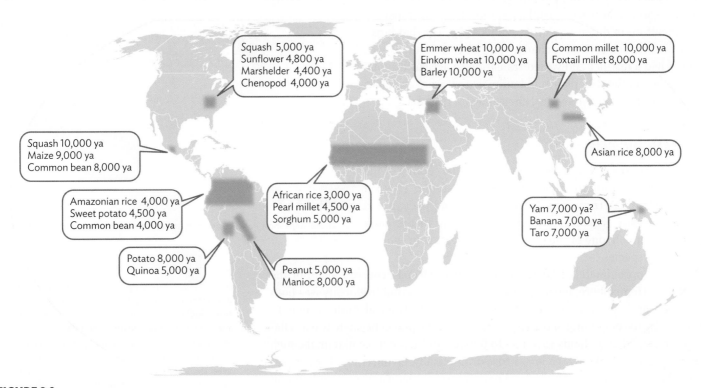

Squash 5,000 ya
Sunflower 4,800 ya
Marshelder 4,400 ya
Chenopod 4,000 ya

Emmer wheat 10,000 ya
Einkorn wheat 10,000 ya
Barley 10,000 ya

Common millet 10,000 ya
Foxtail millet 8,000 ya

Squash 10,000 ya
Maize 9,000 ya
Common bean 8,000 ya

Asian rice 8,000 ya

Amazonian rice 4,000 ya
Sweet potato 4,500 ya
Common bean 4,000 ya

African rice 3,000 ya
Pearl millet 4,500 ya
Sorghum 5,000 ya

Yam 7,000 ya?
Banana 7,000 ya
Taro 7,000 ya

Potato 8,000 ya
Quinoa 5,000 ya

Peanut 5,000 ya
Manioc 8,000 ya

FIGURE 8.9

This map shows the areas where plants and animals were independently domesticated with approximate dates in ya (years ago).

FIGURE 8.10

Rice has long been a staple food crop across Asia (including in Bali, Indonesia, as shown here) and comes in many varieties. Rice was also independently domesticated in West Africa and the Amazon. There is ongoing debate around how many different locations independently domesticated rice from wild grass.

sheep. In Mesoamerica it was maize (corn). In North America it was amaranth. In South America it was potatoes and guinea pigs. In sub-Saharan Africa it was sorghum and cattle, and in China it was rice and pigs (**Figure 8.10**).

Domestication often established a mutual relationship between other species and humans, in which each is dependent on the other to reproduce or otherwise thrive. Consider the domestication of maize in the Balsas River Valley in Mexico about 10,000 years ago. Domesticated maize looks very little like the wild teosinte grass from which it is descended (**Figure 8.11**). The early maize cobs had just two rows of kernels. It may not have been domesticated initially as a food but rather for the sugar in the stalk that can be chewed or converted into maize beer. Ancient DNA studies of cobs suggest that, by 5,000 years ago,

FIGURE 8.11

Modern maize (corn) was domesticated from wild teosinte grass.

genes were present in the cobs that made it easier to break off the corn ears and generate greater starch production. At about the same time, cobs with multiple rows appear (Figure 8.11). Following the emergence of these newer forms that were easier to cultivate and extract calories from, there is then evidence of accelerated clearing of forests in the region, presumably to create fields and plant more crops. Studies of pollen remains confirm that maize became much more common across the region. Analysis of human remains from Mesoamerican sites, using stable isotope analysis, confirms that maize was a prominent part of diets in some locations by about 3,000 years ago, with more maize being eaten by societal elites. This large time gap shows that many domesticated plants and animals were consumed alongside wild food sources for many years in some regions.

By Teotihuacan's peak, maize cultivation was the centerpiece of the food economy and necessary to its sustainability. The large flat areas around the city were suited well to the crop, in an area otherwise beset by inconsistent rainfall and winter frosts. Massive irrigation channels brought water to the floor of the valley. Corn also fed domesticated animals, such as rabbits. The production, storage, processing, and redistribution of corn were central activities of a city that needed 180 million calories each day to feed its population, equivalent to 50,000 kg or 100,000 lbs of corn. This is just one example of how plants and humans became mutually dependent through the long slow process of domestication.

Some of the plants and animals domesticated thousands of years ago are still key food sources for us today, such as wheat, rice, pigs, cattle, and chicken. Other early domesticated species aren't as common anymore. In the river valleys of eastern North America, marsh elder (related to sunflowers) was domesticated about 4,000 years ago for its oily seeds and was, for a time, an important food source. Today it is not cultivated, having been replaced once easier-to-grow corn crops were available.

Plants were generally domesticated first, followed later by animal domestication. For example, in the Levant, the earliest evidence we have for people living in settled villages is about 12,000 years ago. Fully domesticated cereal grains such as wheat and barley begin to make up a small part of the diet about 10,500 years ago. Domesticated animals such as goats are present a few hundred years later and begin to make up a larger part of the diet with domesticated plants. By about 8,000 years ago, we even see genetic evidence that farmers in the Levant were breeding animals for their color and other preferred traits.

THE TRANSITION TO SEDENTARY AGRICULTURE

The transition from a fully hunter-gatherer lifestyle to a fully agricultural lifestyle often took thousands of years, and is still ongoing in some societies. Many hunter-gatherer societies enjoyed a semisedentary lifestyle, in which they lived in one area for part of the year and then moved to another region once they had exhausted food supplies. These societies sometimes established agricultural villages but later abandoned them and returned to a more mobile lifestyle.

Archaeologists recently tracked the mobility of the Natufians, a group of hunter-gatherers in the Levant, through analysis of the molars of mice found at a handful of different sites. Approximately 200,000 years ago, all mice molar teeth belonged to a species of wild Macedonian mice. As the Natufians began to construct semipermanent structures, a new species of mice, called house mice, evolved that could better exploit food from human waste. By about 13,000 BCE, only house mice were present at the sites. Surprisingly, though,

Levant An archaeological term for the general region along the eastern Mediterranean shore where there was early emergence of domestication and complex societies.

FIGURE 8.12

The Natufian settlement of Jericho, shown here, was an early agricultural settlement that contained about 70 structures housing about 1,000 people by 9400 BCE.

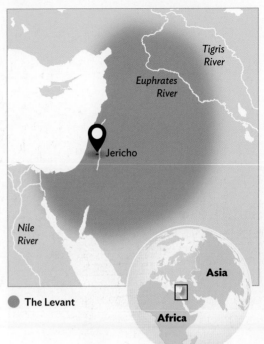

● The Levant

around 11,000 BCE, during the period in which the Natufians constructed smaller structures and made less use of the structures, the wild Macedonian mice enjoyed a resurgence. Only around 10,000 BCE did the house mice again outcompete the wild mice. At this point, people in the Levant had settled in villages near fields of wild grains. By 9400 BCE, approximately 1,000 people resided in 70 houses in the Natufian settlement of Jericho (**Figure 8.12**). They cultivated wild wheat and barley in fields that were easily irrigated from a stream that fed into the town. By about 6000 BCE, many villages had become fully dependent on domesticated agriculture for their survival.

This shift to sedentary farming defines the end of the Mesolithic period and the start of the Neolithic period of human history. It remains one of the key factors in how humans have completely and permanently recreated their ecological niches globally to better meet their need for stable, localized food supplies.

POPULATION GROWTH AFTER THE TRANSITION TO AGRICULTURE

Although archaeologists are still trying to understand why the transition to agriculture occurred in each region, it is clear that the shift to an agricultural economy transformed life in the societies in which it took place. Populations in these early farming villages grew much faster than they had in foraging societies. One genetic study indicated that population rates increased five-fold relative to the population growth rates among hunter-gatherers. It may be that societies became locked in to agricultural lifestyles once populations started to settle and then grow, because it was no longer feasible to support their populations from wild foods alone.

Several factors can explain this population growth. Access to easily digestible cereals as infant foods allowed earlier weaning. Exclusive breastfeeding tends to suppress women's ovulation after giving birth, which delayed new pregnancies. Correspondingly, faster weaning of infants from the breast allowed women to become pregnant more quickly and so have shorter intervals from one birth to the next and more children across their reproductive years. In addition, child labor is especially useful in agricultural societies for work such as tending animals or harvesting crops, so there could have been an incentive for families to be large.

Mesolithic period The part of human history during which humans were hunter-gatherers, generally dating to between 20,000 and 10,000 years ago.

Neolithic period The part of human history during which humans domesticated plants and animals, generally beginning about 10,000 years ago.

HEALTH CONSEQUENCES OF THE TRANSITION TO AGRICULTURE

Paradoxically, even as the transition to agriculture supported more stable food supplies for larger populations, it also introduced notable negative consequences for human health, and even led to rising death rates. Bioarchaeological evidence from excavated skeletons shows that early agriculturalists had reduced stature compared to previous generations, as people worked harder for a less nutritious diet and therefore didn't have the nutrients of earlier populations.

Similarly, analysis of human remains indicates more dental decay, probably because growing crops encourages higher carbohydrate diets that feed the bacteria that cause decay in our mouths. Moreover, reliance on a limited number of food sources places more people at risk of hunger if crops fail due to insects, plant diseases, droughts, or floods. For example, potatoes were domesticated in the Andean highlands of South America around 9,000 years ago (**Figure 8.13**). Potatoes were able to grow on otherwise marginal land and be stored for months, thus making them a highly useful plant. Once they were introduced to Europe, this high-carbohydrate root crop was associated with massive increases in population growth during the 17th and 18th centuries. With increasing reliance on potatoes, crop failures also led to many deaths in Europe, especially in Ireland where the "Great Famine" killed some one million people in less than a decade.

Clearing land to farm in tropical zones also led to the proliferation of diseases such as malaria where the mosquitos that spread the disease to humans thrived in stagnant pools of water used to irrigate crops. So even as farming provided much more consistent access to calories, dependency on it also sowed the seeds for intermittent larger-scale crises such as regional famine and new diseases.

FIGURE 8.13

Potatoes still play a major role in the Andean communities where they were first domesticated.

THE EARLY NEOLITHIC SITE OF ÇATALHÖYÜK, TURKEY

One well-studied example of early sedentary agriculturalists and the many substantial societal changes that the transition to agriculture brought comes from the archaeological site of Çatalhöyük (sha-TAL-hoe-YOOK), which is located in what is now south-central Turkey and dates to 9,000 years ago. At Çatalhöyük, thousands of people lived in densely packed mud brick houses during the Neolithic period. Because there were no streets between the houses, people entered via ladders through holes in the roofs and moved across the flat roofs from house to house (**Figure 8.14**).

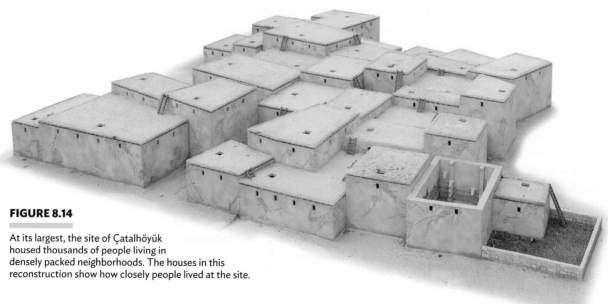

FIGURE 8.14

At its largest, the site of Çatalhöyük housed thousands of people living in densely packed neighborhoods. The houses in this reconstruction show how closely people lived at the site.

FIGURE 8.15

Archaeological excavations at the site of Çatalhöyük, located in what is now Turkey, have shown a large site where sedentary agriculturalists farmed wheat and barley and raised sheep and goats.

Inhabitants of Çatalhöyük farmed crops such as wheat and barley; raised domesticated animals such as sheep, goats, and cows; and also fished and hunted wild animals (**Figure 8.15**). The intricate and varied religious and ritual lives of people in the settlement are reflected in special rooms with large bull horns on altars and walls with elaborate murals.

Since the site was occupied for more than 1,000 years and has been extensively excavated by archaeologists, it provides unparalleled insights into the lives of early sedentary agriculturalists and the beginnings of human social stratification. One important finding is that relying on an agricultural economy and living in close quarters had significant negative health impacts for the people living there. Bioarchaeologist Clark Spencer Larsen's work on skeletons at the site bears this out. As increasing fertility caused Çatalhöyük to become more densely settled, its inhabitants were more likely to die with infections and dental caries. Bones in their arms and legs became thicker and denser, a sign of increased physical labor probably connected to agricultural work. They were also likelier to experience physical violence related to fighting, such as cranial trauma. Archaeologists interpret this as an indication of increased stress due to overcrowding.

Çatalhöyük is often described as an egalitarian society, mostly because there is no clear archaeological evidence of "royal" houses linked with elite activities or burials. Both men and women from different areas of the site ate the same kinds of foods. However, there are some signs of emerging social stratification. Most households used the same agricultural tools for farming, but larger grinding stones (for preparing grains) housed in some more elaborate buildings suggest craft specialization.

cranial trauma Injury to the head or skull.

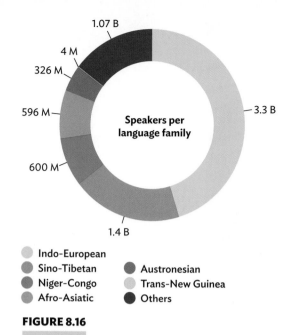

Speakers per language family

1.07 B
4 M
326 M
596 M
600 M
3.3 B
1.4 B

- Indo-European
- Sino-Tibetan
- Niger-Congo
- Afro-Asiatic
- Austronesian
- Trans-New Guinea
- Others

FIGURE 8.16

This graph depicts the number of speakers for different language families, in billions (B) or millions (M), as of 2022.

protolanguage A hypothetical undocumented ancestral language.

cognate One of two or more words that have a shared origin.

root (word) A word that does not have any affixes such as a prefix or suffix.

prefix A string of letters/sounds that go at the start of a root word.

Indo-European languages A language family that includes the overwhelming majority of Europe, the Iranian plateau, and the northern Indian subcontinent. English is an Indo-European language.

THE SPREAD OF LANGUAGE IN THE MESOLITHIC AND NEOLITHIC PERIODS

Anthropologists can also glean insights into the human experience during the Mesolithic and Neolithic periods through the study of language. Linguists can group languages into families that are traced back to a protolanguage from which these languages emerged. Today, people speaking languages in the Indo-European, Sino-Tibetan, Niger-Congo, Afro-Asiatic, and Austronesian language families make up the vast majority of the world population (**Figure 8.16**).

Reconstructing the history of languages proceeds much like reconstructing genetic evidence of human population history. Linguists compare language use now to identify cognates, words that share similar origins, common grammatical structures, and many other features such as the use of clicks or tones. For example, Afro-Asiatic languages tend to have words with two- to three-letter roots and use prefixes to shift a verb into past or future tenses. Changing the tone in Sino-Tibetan languages changes the meaning of the word.

Linguistic anthropology also gives us insights into our hunter-gatherer past. For example, genetic analysis suggests that the ancestors of Native Americans left Siberia to cross into North America about 25,000 years ago. However, the archaeological record only shows habitation in North America from 15,000 years on. Scientists began to hypothesize that these hunter-gatherers might have found a home in ancient Beringia, the land strip now covered by sea that once connected Asia and Alaska. A linguistic analysis of the Na-Dene language family, spoken in Alaska, and the Yeniseian language family, spoken in central Siberia, indicates that these two languages likely emerged from a protolanguage in Beringia (Figure 2.11). This then suggests that hunter-gatherer groups lived in Beringia and migrated both into North America and back to Asia.

Yet migration is not the only way language spreads. In reconstructing human experiences tied to the spread of Indo-European languages, some scholars have focused on the role of technological innovation. A group of words within the domain of vehicle or transport including "wheel," "axle," and "he transports it" share a cognate in eight Indo-European language branches. The shared

FIGURE 8.17

This map shows the present-day distribution of Indo-European languages and two proposed geographic sources for the initial speakers of a proto-Indo-European language (the Steppes and Anatolia). Both were regions of early agricultural settlements.

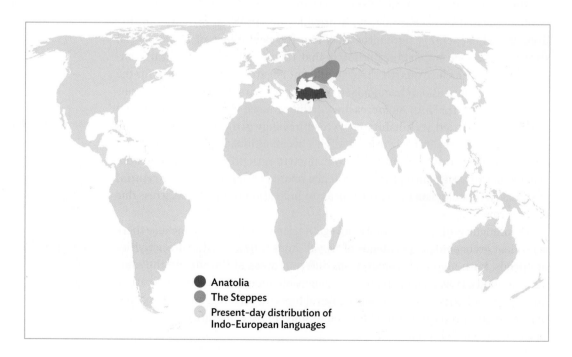

- Anatolia
- The Steppes
- Present-day distribution of Indo-European languages

cognate across such a wide set of languages suggests not only that new words were transmitted as groups connected in the past but also that the technology of horses and wheeled vehicles (valuable in farming and long-distance trade of goods) was an important part of those connections.

The original proto-Indo-European speakers were located in the steppes west of the Ural Mountains about 6,000 years ago (**Figure 8.17**), in a zone in which agricultural technologies included cattle and sheep herding, dairy foods, wool products, wagons, honey, and horses. Most scholars suggest that the replacement of original European languages was not based in conquest or even large-scale immigration. Rather, people adopted new language forms because they offered better opportunities. There were likely intermarriages and generations who were speakers of both Indo-European and non-Indo-European languages. But people who could speak Indo-European had greater social and economic security, such as through wagon-based technologies that allowed them to trade over long distances. Today, millions of people speak Indo-European languages, including English—and for much the same reasons of expanded opportunity.

SECTION 8.3

THE RISE OF CITIES AND STATES

The early sedentary agricultural villages, such as Çatalhöyük, paved the way for the growth of the first cities and states—though why and how is a topic that archaeologists are still investigating. One early theory argued that states emerged to manage the large, sophisticated irrigation systems that enabled agricultural production. Another early idea, the circumscription theory, describes a three-step process in which hunter-gatherers settled in areas with highly concentrated agricultural resources, the population grew, and wars erupted over access to these resources. In 1970, anthropologist Robert Carneiro noted that the first cities arose in regions that all had access to rivers or other freshwater sources for irrigating crops, but not all these cities developed into states. Looking at those that did, Carneiro noticed that they were surrounded by mountains, deserts, oceans, or other geographical features that limited access to—or circumscribed—the territory. States developed in the Nile, Tigris and Euphrates, and Indus Valleys as well as in the Valley of Mexico and the coastal valleys of Peru. Archaeologists have generally moved away from large, universal theories to explain state formation worldwide and toward more nuanced investigations of how urban centers arose and functioned around the world.

THE EMERGENCE OF URBANIZATION

The earliest origins of urbanization are seen in Mesopotamia—for example, the site of Uruk, which is located in what is now Iraq and dates to about 5,000 years ago (**Figure 8.18**)—and at the archaeological sites of Harappa and Mohenjo-Daro in the Indus Valley of Pakistan, which date to about 4,000 years ago.

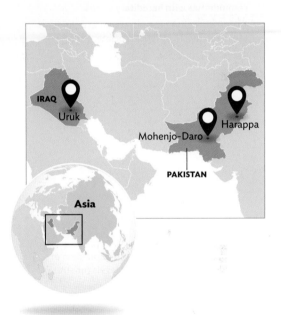

FIGURE 8.18

Uruk in modern Iraq was one of the earliest human cities, emerging after 5,000 years ago. The site was located on a channel of the Euphrates River that allowed productive farming and support of a large and hierarchical population; the river no longer flows near the site.

These early cities housed tens of thousands of people. The substantial changes in social organization that arose when small villages transformed into large, complex societies have led some archaeologists to call this period the "Urban Revolution."

What defined these new complex urban cities? Several important features include an economy based on large-scale agriculture, a dense population, hierarchical social organization, centralized government, specialized roles for individuals, and some form of recordkeeping, such as writing.

Notably, large complex societies in the form of cities and states are not the only type of group organization we see in the world today. Sometimes small-scale societies are described as bands of hunter-gatherers, while other small-scale societies that rely more on agriculture are considered tribes. In applying the terms bands and tribes, relationships are generally egalitarian. Chiefdoms, meanwhile, are then differentiated as agricultural societies with kin-based social status divisions that are inherited and passed down through families. Within a chiefdom, political authority is held by a chief, who along with close relatives possesses greater power and wealth than others in the society.

The relationship between these different forms of social and political organization isn't linear; that is, bands do not necessarily "evolve" into tribes, then chiefdoms, then states. Nor do these different categories neatly correspond to agriculturalist versus hunter-gatherer lines. In both the present and the past, some hunter-gatherers were organized into large chiefdoms, such as those of the Pacific Northwest of North America, while some agriculturalists lived in small, egalitarian, and quite mobile groups. There can also be varying levels of complexity within these different organizations. In this section, we now focus on why increasingly large and complex societies emerged in nearly every part of the world.

SOCIAL STRATIFICATION IN EARLY CITIES

The transition to agriculture also accelerated social stratification. At the root of this was the change in food production. Hunting and gathering would often provide just enough food to support small groups, and with sources varying seasonally, very little was able to be stored for the long term. Farming and herding created surpluses of crops such as grains, however, which can be stored for longer periods. These surpluses created varying levels of wealth within a society, tied to differences in access to stored food. This excess allowed people to begin specializing in tasks not directly related to food production, such as building tools for processing food, making textiles and pottery, or smelting and casting metals. Such craft specialization leads to wealth and power disparities based on how different specializations are valued.

It is important to note that food surpluses also markedly advanced the emergence of social stratification in some large groups of hunter-gatherers that were also able to generate the kinds of food surpluses accumulated in agricultural societies. Generally, these groups, including the large Haida, Tlingit, and Kwakwaka'wakw hunter-gatherer societies of the Pacific Northwest of North America, lived in rich environments where people could collect and store large amounts of food while staying largely in one place. Archaeologists have documented the complex social structures that existed in this area for at least 2,000 years. Within these societies, classes of elites controlled the labor of others, just as in agriculturally oriented societies. So, while on a global scale the transition to agriculture precipitated significant social stratification and later urbanism, it was not the foundational cause of stratification everywhere.

band A society of hunter-gatherers in which relationships are generally egalitarian.

tribe A small-scale society of agriculturalists where relationships are generally egalitarian.

chiefdom A hierarchical political unit with kin-based status divisions and composed of several communities with hereditary status.

social status A person's standing or importance relative to others in society.

social stratification The organization of human groups into different levels (or strata), such as elites and non-elites.

craft specialization The assignment of particular productive tasks to subsets of people in a community; these can include tasks that require skill, such as pottery production or weaving.

Signs of social stratification do appear in the archaeological record at sites all over the world following the rise of agriculture. Examples include materials associated with the presence of elites, such as houses with a greater diversity of everyday objects than others and more prestige goods (valuable items without practical functions that require skill and time to make). These societies also constructed buildings and areas that only elites could access (**Figure 8.19**). Burials provide particularly revealing evidence of stratification and inequality, such as separated burial locations or differences in the level of ornateness of burials (e.g., the presence or absence of valuable adornments associated with a burial).

Settlement architecture also provides archaeologists with evidence of stratification and with it the possible signs of increasing economic or social inequalities—some houses were more private and difficult to access, more heavily decorated, constructed from finer materials, or larger. Some featured uniquely large spaces dedicated to ritual activities (such as feasting, sports, or religious activities). Finally, larger variation in skeletal signs of nutrition within ancient agricultural societies versus hunter-gatherer societies is another line of evidence often used by bioarchaeologists as an indirect indicator of unequal distribution within societies in access to food or other resources.

Another way anthropologists assess the role of agriculture in driving stratification is by comparing societies whose transition to agriculture took different forms and extents. For example, when archaeologists looked at household size and distribution as a proxy for wealth and inequality in post-Neolithic sites from North and Central America, Africa, and Europe and Asia, they found that wealth disparities increased in all of these areas as sites became larger and more complex. However, the wealth disparities were not as large in the Central and North American sites, where the inhabitants had domesticated turkeys but not large draft animals such as cows and horses, as these animals were absent from these continents. In Europe, Africa, and Asia, the domestication of large draft animals allowed more intensive agricultural practices that eventually led to more wealth inequalities.

WHY HUMAN SOCIETIES TEND TOWARD COMPLEXITY

We've seen how the rise of agriculture allowed for increasingly complex, stratified societies. But given that this stratification is invariably tied to growing social inequalities that harm some members of society, it begs the question of why human societies nonetheless consistently (though not always) tend toward increasing complexity over time. Anthropologists have proposed many theories, and there isn't a clear consensus. We examine some of these theories here.

Evolutionary anthropologists (who combine methods from biological and cultural anthropology to evaluate contemporary human behaviors in the context of what advantaged survival in the past) suggest that humans may have always been concerned with social status. They note that even in small, noncomplex societies people sort themselves, at least to some extent, on the basis of prestige. In hunter-gatherer societies, for example, evidence suggests that hunting prowess may be one means by which people can accrue high social standing (**Figure 8.20**). According to this theory, a tendency toward stratification is inherent to our species, having enabled early humans to achieve greater productivity and effectiveness in obtaining food and other materials needed for

FIGURE 8.19

El Tajín in Veracruz, Mexico, an urban center that was at the height of its power from 800 to 1000 CE, included beautifully constructed and decorated ball courts (such as the one shown here) and buildings reserved for use by elites.

FIGURE 8.20

Among the Tsimané people of lowland Bolivia, and many other human groups, accomplishment in hunting elevates people's social status.

a population to thrive. Changes in the resource environment that made agriculture possible allowed this tendency to be realized on a larger scale in most subsequent human societies.

Another theory as to why human societies tend to grow more stratified and socially complex focuses on the distribution and availability of local resources. Some people will be in a better position to monopolize those resources than others. For example, upstream water users can dam or divert water, while downstream users are at their mercy. Such resource inequalities create new power dynamics in a society. Those with greater power generally work to develop political systems that benefit their own interests. These political systems may allow or encourage private control of resources, the accumulation of wealth, or the passing of wealth and power between allies and family (such as through inheritance).

Additional political elements then arise that control the relationships between those with more and fewer resources, locking in these inequalities over generations. Some of these institutions are based on ascribed leadership that is not earned, such as inherited positions (in contrast to a status that is achieved, for example, through an occupation). Other institutions may enable the emergence of professional administrators. Thus, the capacity to sequester resources that matter—water, food, marriage partners, or professional status—becomes the necessary foundation for the perpetuation of elites and for enduring social stratification.

Why might people who are not elites tolerate the persistent inequality that accompanies complex societies? Sometimes physical or social coercion is a reason, either through punishments or control of needed resources. Under such conditions, the acceptance of a subordinate position within a society may be the only way to access those resources. Patron–client relationships, such as those seen in feudal agricultural societies, exemplify this dynamic. Serfs in medieval Europe lived on and worked a parcel of land owned by an elite landowner, and in return they could expect protection and some of the food they produced (**Figure 8.21**).

Even without coercion, however, elites may be tolerated if the net benefit of going along with a stratified society outweighs that of resisting or leaving

ascribed Describes a status that is not earned but rather given, such as inherited wealth.

patron–client relationship An unequal political and economic arrangement in which a person of higher status protects and provides resources to a person of lower status while simultaneously extracting labor or other services from the person of lower status.

FIGURE 8.21

Serfs in medieval England are depicted harvesting wheat in this illuminated manuscript.

the society. Hierarchy, centralized decision-making, and craft specialization are required to organize complex human activities. Such complex activities include managing large-scale agriculture (including irrigation systems), building infrastructure, and engaging in warfare against competing societies (either to obtain their resources or protect yours from being taken). In such cases, whole groups might benefit by accepting such stratification even as it leads to inequality.

Many societies also develop core cultural values that encourage and support the idea that there is virtue or validity in embracing one's place within a hierarchy. Such values can be embedded within religious traditions, such as the role of Christianity in supporting the idea that feudalism in medieval Europe was morally acceptable. In short, there is no singular reason why human societies trend toward complexity, and many alternative explanations are related and interconnected. Past evolutionary influences on human psychology, the outcomes from uneven access to resources, and the need for centralized power to address large-scale collective action endeavors all likely play some role.

THE CASE OF THE HAWAIIAN CHIEFDOMS

The Hawaiian archipelago was settled by ocean voyagers from central-eastern Polynesia about 800 years ago. Archaeological data from Hawai'i is rich and, combined with historical accounts, provides a detailed record of how there can be a rapid shift to social complexity with a consolidation of elite power.

The first Hawaiian settlements were dispersed along the fertile coasts on the rainy side of the islands. People lived off the abundant local fish and other marine foods and the domesticated plants and animals they brought with them (including sweet potatoes, pigs, and chickens). As populations grew over the subsequent centuries, settlements gradually expanded inland toward the center of the islands. Taro (a starchy root) emerged as a primary crop, grown in systems of irrigated pond-fields that capture and control stream water. In this phase of Hawaiian history, with intensifying agriculture and denser settlements, the social organization based on kinship starts to shift to one based in ascribed chiefly power.

For the first six centuries or so, the Hawaiian economy experienced rapid growth, increasingly productive agriculture, and growing surpluses. A switch to dryland farming of sweet potatoes without irrigation made the agricultural economy even more productive but required much more labor. It thus became harder to produce a surplus. Interisland warfare and conquest escalated during this period as competition for resources became fiercer. By the time the first European explorers arrived at the island chain in the 18th century, chiefs controlled large territories organized into wedges called *ahupua'a* (traditional land subdivisions). Many ran from the top of mountains to the ocean following stream drainages, encompassing zones favorable to different crops for the communities within them. Control of military forces, religion, and agricultural production were all important to the emergence and maintenance of chiefly power.

While chiefs controlled the islands' food resources and warriors, different strategies and institutions emerged to organize power and social relationships within the society. These included alliances through marriage, ritual religious practice through cults, a tax system, communal labor, and restrictions on who could fish or gather certain plants. At the time of greatest stratification,

FIGURE 8.22

Puʻukoholā heiau has been restored and opened as a national historic site.

Hawaiian chiefdoms built very large ritual sites that required great sacrifices from commoners in labor, goods, and even lives. Puʻukoholā heiau was a sacrificial temple (*heiau*) in honor of the war god Kūkaʻilimoku completed in 1791 on the Big Island of Hawaiʻi (**Figure 8.22**). It was built by hand, with rock carried many miles, on the site of a smaller temple built some two centuries prior.

Such complex governance arrangements benefit members in giving them access to crops grown in a range of zones. They also provide recognized rules for how resources are distributed within society, and thus they may also reduce the need for overt warfare or other forms of costly conflict.

GOVERNING COMPLEX SOCIETIES

Within a few thousand years, once semisedentary human societies developed agricultural villages, cities, and states. Population size and population density increased in settled areas. Sedentary societies arose in resource-rich areas, pushing hunter-gatherers into lands unsuitable for farming. Agricultural innovations and technologies expanded the lands that could sustain sedentary communities. Hunter-gatherer societies raided or invaded cities or states, sometimes occupying those areas.

In China, for example, dynasties ruled by elites rose and fell, gradually occupying larger swaths of land (**Figure 8.23**). These dynasties built the Great Wall in the north to prevent invasion from more mobile groups. However, the Mongols, a nomadic society in the north, succeeded in invading all of China and extended their rule over a significantly larger area under their Yuan Dynasty. Yet the Yuan Dynasty was short-lived as the native Han people rebelled against Mongol rulers and founded the Ming Dynasty.

As the Han rebellion illustrates, elites are periodically overthrown from within. Living in larger groups demands governance, the rules, norms, power, and influence that organize and enforce decisions about how people within societies interact with each other. Rules are formal guidelines that are generally enforced through punishments such as fines, corporal punishment, imprisonment, or death penalties. In contrast, norms are informal understandings that are generally enforced through social mechanisms such as shame or loss of status.

governance The formal rules (such as laws) and informal social norms that manage and regulate how people interact within societies.

rule A formal guideline that dictates what can and cannot occur, especially regarding behaviors.

norm A shared set of beliefs of what is ideal, acceptable, or to be avoided.

Shang Dynasty (1600–1046 BCE)

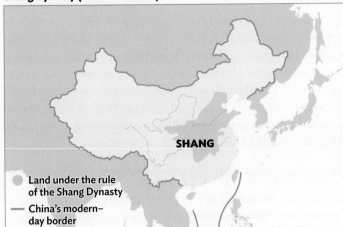

Western Han Dynasty (206 BCE–9 CE)

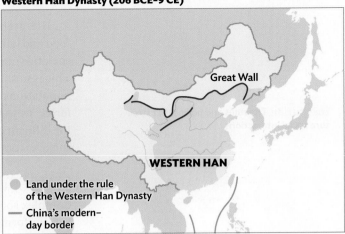

Eastern Han Dynasty (25–220 CE)

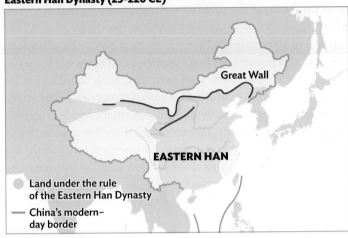

Mongol Dynasty (1206–1368 CE)

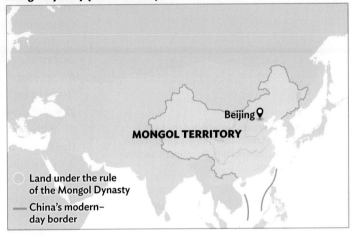

Ming Dynasty (1368–1644 CE)

People's Republic of China (2023)

FIGURE 8.23

The territorial expansion of selected Chinese dynasties.

institution The rules and norms that structure social interactions.

hegemony A process in which dominant groups consolidate consent to govern through shared norms, legitimating discourses, and historical narratives.

EL SALVADOR

North America

Hierarchical governance organizes how larger sets of resources such as food and labor were centralized and allocated. One consistent feature of urban societies (and the states that contain them) is social and economic inequality. This is nothing new; it represents a long-term part of the human condition as populations began to grow. The Hawai'i and Teotihuacan cases illustrate different ways that humans reorganize these institutions to deal with some of the difficult challenges—such as increased conflict over resources or increased social diversity—that are amplified by living in closer proximity.

STATE GOVERNANCE WITHIN COMPLEX SOCIETIES

Complex societies today are embedded in a range of democratic and nondemocratic forms of governance. In nondemocratic forms of governance, decision-making typically rests almost entirely within the elite. These elites may derive their elevated social status from birth (in monarchies and aristocracies), from religious status (in theocracies), or from technical training and expertise (in technocracies).

In democratic forms of governance, a broader range of people have a role in determining how society is organized, with the participation of people from different social statuses enabled by systems such as voting. Such societies are far from perfect, of course: they still have elites and experience ongoing power struggles and the monopolization of resources by some in ways that exclude others.

Elite power is often maintained by hegemony rather than violence. Although the threat of violence can be an effective means for one group to secure the cooperation of another, the other groups need only to acquire weapons and fighters in order to challenge and overthrow the elite. As a result, stable dominant groups consolidate consent to govern through shared norms, legitimating discourses, and historical narratives.

Consider the case of the El Salvadorean civil war. Cultural anthropologist Robin Maria DeLugan was involved in the reconstruction process in El Salvador, in Central America, in the wake of the devastating internal conflict (1980–1992). Her observations in her field seasons between 1993 and 2018 allowed her to consider the process of rebuilding governance with a focus on democracy, civil rights, and inclusion as core values. Unifying strategies included embracing those who had fled the country during the war as *hermanos lejanos* (faraway brothers/sisters) and remembering rather than hiding the memories of victims of the civil war massacres. The ways that nations erase or reconstruct traumatic memories are a very important part of how nation-building often proceeds through time.

To attempt to repair the fabric of society, the Salvadorean state was determined to recreate national identity and shared values and purpose. They changed school curricula to introduce new ideas of national identity, ones based in the idea of a blending of Indigenous and Spanish histories (*mestizaje*). They commissioned museums, including a new museum of anthropology, and promoted archaeological sites to present the idea of a shared Maya identity and history and the notion of a shared national culture (**Figure 8.24**).

Today, most humans live within a mosaic of states, both stable and unstable. States govern and maintain their authority through a sense of collective identity and purpose, based in ideas of shared culture, language, history, religion, and ideology. In addition, states maintain authority through coercion. States typically maintain a monopoly on violence that is perceived as legitimate, including policing, armed conflict, and executions. In unstable states, illegitimate actors regularly commit violence and uses of violence by the state may be considered illegitimate.

FIGURE 8.24

State museums are often central to governance and nation-building efforts. The Museo Nacional de Antropología Dr. David J. Guzmán was opened in El Salvador in 2001, specifically to promote a sense of national history and identity. This gallery focuses on the agricultural history of the nation.

justice A system designed to ensure each person or group gets their fair due.

informal justice Activity that is intended to ensure fair treatment but is not regulated or enforced through a formal legal system.

INFORMALITY AND NON-STATE JUSTICE

To maintain authority over citizens and noncitizens alike within their borders, stable states use formal laws and a range of punishments to enforce those laws. Formalized justice systems (such as courts of law) are a powerful force for hegemony, setting norms for what is "acceptable" and "expected" behavior and what is accordingly rewarded or punished. But many communities also have informal justice systems, which they build and enforce themselves. This can include justice systems implemented by subgroups within a community, such as those tied to religious practices that use shunning or shaming as a form of punishment.

Early anthropologists often studied the customary laws of colonized societies. Today, many communities have unique rules and norms for justice that pre-date and operate alongside (or outside) state legal systems. Morocco, for example, was colonized by the French. After decolonization, the legal system retained elements of the colonial French civil code, the dominant and preferred sharia (Islamic law), and an informal justice system for conflict resolution. A *qadi* (Islamic judge) in Morocco has the power to adjudicate issues such as divorce and property. In one case, for example, a wife insisted that her living situation near her husband's family was intolerable. After hearing the wife's and husband's views, the qadi ruled in favor of the wife—and the couple resettled in a new apartment farther from the in-laws. It is common for Muslims, Catholics, and members of many other religious communities to maintain elements of alternative legal structures that operate alongside state systems, determining who can marry and how, who may belong to the community, and so forth. Such hybrid legal systems—integrating the state and informal or non-state authorities—are found everywhere.

INFORMAL JUSTICE AND SELF-GOVERNANCE

Cities and states often do not implement justice systems uniformly across their territory. Elites are often able to secure physical protection. However, in many cases, non-elite communities are neglected by state justice systems, with no monitoring or enforcement of rules the wider society is expected to obey. Cultural anthropologist Daniel Goldstein studied how residents of the Zona Sur—informal settlements on the south side of the city of Cochabamba—were functionally abandoned by the Bolivian state. Largely Quechua and Aymara Indigenous migrants from Bolivia's rural countryside, these low-income and precariously employed residents had few practical legal rights. Often sold land

self-governance A system where people regulate their own conduct without intervention from an external authority such as a government.

that was zoned for agriculture rather than habitation, Zona Sur residents found their property rights unenforceable.

Ignored by the police, Zona Sur residents had little protection from crime. In response, communities built their own rules and norms for enforcing justice as a form of self-governance. They monitored their own informal settlements for crime, carefully observing outsiders' movements and behavior. And in hundreds of cases, Zona Sur residents self-organized vigilante lynching of accused thieves and criminals. In these lynchings, an angry mob attacked the accused criminal by, for example, tying them to a tree, stoning them, or setting them on fire with gasoline. Goldstein describes the vigilante lynchings as horrific spectacles designed to attract attention to the neglect and suffering of underserved communities.

Such neglected communities tend to be poor, rural, minoritized, or otherwise marginalized. In this case, Zona Sur residents hoped to be ultimately integrated into state justice systems and afforded the same security as others in the same city from more affluent neighborhoods.

SELF-GOVERNANCE, INEQUALITY, AND MODERN URBAN LIFE

People often move to and stay in cities today exactly because they are dense and diverse, filled with services and opportunity. This generates massive resource usage, creating the need for practical solutions to such problems as sanitation and waste. But one of the great challenges of modern cities is exactly what draws many people to them; social diversity and economic opportunity also tend to intersect with increasing inequality (**Figure 8.25**).

As we noted at the opening of this chapter, Teotihuacan was unusual among cities for its lack of extreme economic and social inequality. Today, most cities are defined by, and must grapple with, not just ethnic and cultural diversity but deep economic inequalities. Outside state efforts, humans rely on many creative

FIGURE 8.25

In Jakarta, the huge and densely populated capital city of Indonesia, high-income and very low-income neighborhoods exist in very close proximity.

FIGURE 8.26

Cultural anthropologist Teresa Caldeira has labeled arrangements like this one beside Favela Paraisópolis in Morumbi, São Paulo, as "fortified enclaves" that use physical barriers, surveillance, alarms, and guards to separate elites from non-elites within contemporary cities.

governance mechanisms to organize themselves within larger societies. Some of these self-governance mechanisms may create alternative justice systems to attempt to undo some aspects of inequality, such as mutual aid networks that redistribute food or provide shelter and material assistance to those who need it (see Chapter 9). Such networks may operate outside the formal economic system that governs the distribution of material goods using formal rules.

Other mechanisms of self-governance, conversely, reinforce inequality by protecting the status of elites. Cultural anthropologist Teresa Caldeira, in her ethnography *City of Walls*, examines how wealthy São Paulo residents constructed fortified condominiums and neighborhoods that completely separated them from public spaces and less wealthy neighbors (**Figure 8.26**). This was not just an attempt at crime prevention but also a response to democratization after the end of Brazil's military dictatorship in the 1980s. Although people's political rights expanded, the fortification of the city constrained people's movements and solidified social barriers between the rich and poor.

Fortified condominium arrangements such as those found in São Paulo are an example of an enclave established by a subset of people within a massive city, which serves as a smaller-scale community with its own formal and informal rules for governing members' behavior. In some ways these are continuations of what was happening in the neighborhood enclaves of the former Mexican city-state of Teotihuacan.

Contemporary forms of urban self-governance can be highly democratic, viewed from within, and are able to construct and maintain local cultures within a larger and more diverse society, as well as helping to defend group members from outside threats. These similarities illustrate an important conclusion from anthropological scholarship on the politics of living together: all forms of human governance involve some form of complex pattern of unequal power and wealth and political corruption. But they also encourage the emergence of creative means to ensure belonging, participation, collective decision-making, and intracommunity sharing.

Such cases also illustrate how the dominant state rules do not necessarily work well for everyone. Humans often leverage their skill in establishing culturally shared norms that allow people who have been disadvantaged by state arrangements and rules to thrive. This capacity for creating and maintaining informal justice systems is an important piece of how people manage to live together in the extreme densities of modern cities.

8

Human Settlement and Societies

This chapter considers how and why humans have become a predominantly urban-dwelling species and what that means for how societies are organized.

KEY TERMS
› cosmology
› elite
› ethnic group
› hierarchical society
› social complexity
› state
› urban

8.1 | The Advantages of Cooperative Communities

Illustrate how living in communities benefits primates, including modern humans.

- Most primates, including humans, live in groups, which provides many advantages.

- Around the world and for the vast majority of our history as a species, humans have lived in small, mobile, and largely egalitarian groups that emphasized kin relationships.

KEY TERMS
› egalitarian
› hunter-gatherer
› kinship
› prosocial behavior

8.2 | The Transition to Agriculture and Permanent Settlements

Describe the drivers behind and the transitions to permanent settlements and agriculture.

- Around the world, humans began to domesticate plants and animals between 10,000 and 5,000 years ago, marking the beginning of the Neolithic period.

- In many regions, the Neolithic period was also when people began to live in permanent settlements.

- While relying on agriculture provided many communities with a stable food source and their populations grew, there were also negative consequences for human health.

KEY TERMS
> cognate
> cranial trauma
> domestication
> Holocene epoch
> Indo-European languages
> Levant
> Mesolithic period
> Neolithic period
> prefix
> protolanguage
> root (word)

8.3 | The Rise of Cities and States

Connect urban settlement to increasing social complexity and inequality.

- Social complexity of human societies, including the emergence of urban centers, accelerated with and after the transition to agriculture during the Neolithic period.

- Increasing social complexity is associated with increasing inequalities.

- There is no simple or single theory to explain why inequality arises with complexity and why it persists, but the capability of some to control resources needed by others is a necessary precondition.

KEY TERMS
> ascribed
> band
> chiefdom
> craft specialization
> patron–client relationship
> social status
> social stratification
> tribe

8.4 | Governing Complex Societies

Assess mechanisms of state governance and the ways that people self-govern from within larger-scale societies.

- Humans are now a predominantly urban species, a very different context than that we experienced for most of our history. This brings new challenges that require complex systems to manage, most of which are unevenly experienced because they reflect the inequalities that characterize urban life.

- Large-scale societies (such as states) and the formal rules and laws they enact are inherently fragile, in part because of the remarkable human capacity to organize informally using norm-based institutions, even where they have limited or no legal status.

KEY TERMS
> governance
> hegemony
> informal justice
> institution
> justice
> norm
> rule
> self-governance

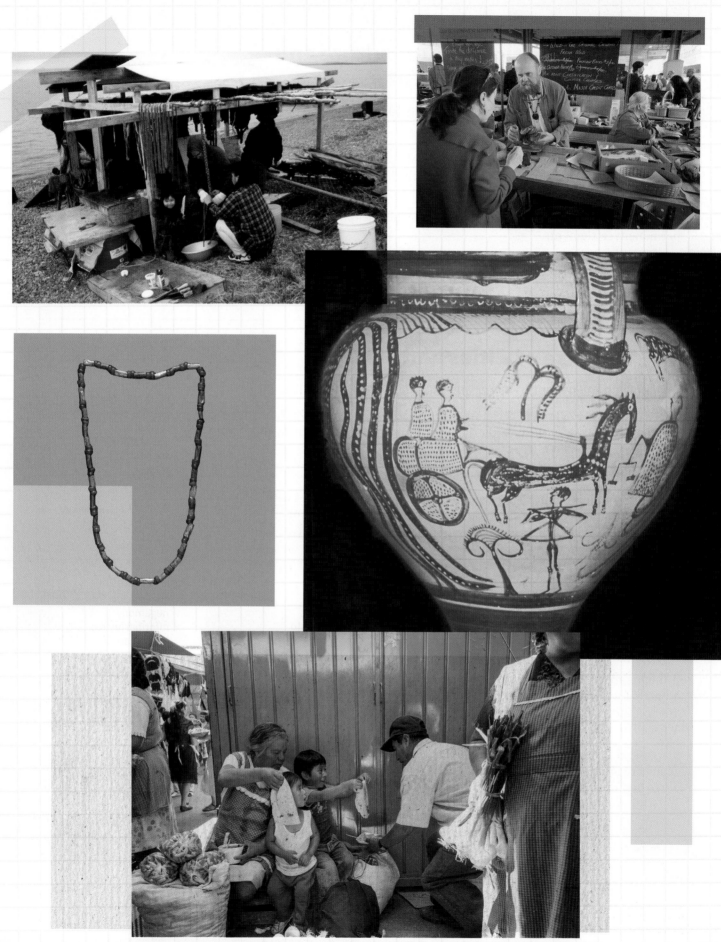

Food and Economic Systems

Cultural anthropologist Ashanté Reese grew up in rural eastern Texas, far from the nearest grocery store. Families in the small farming community often bartered to get what they needed. Reese remembers taking bunches of homegrown collard greens, running them down the street, and coming home with a bag of plums. Her uncle raised and slaughtered goats, pigs, and chickens for their meals, and she collected wild blackberries for desserts her mother would bake from scratch.

Rural towns, however, are not the only communities cut off from food markets. Reese's research focused on Deanwood, a mostly Black neighborhood in northeastern Washington, DC, United States, where residents struggled to get affordable, quality food. In the past, neighborhood grocers and other local businesses served the community's needs. There was a local milkman and other vendors who delivered fresh food directly to homes. But the neighborhood's 12 original grocery stores all eventually closed, reflecting a long-term trend in many lower-income sectors of cities and towns across the United States.

After these closures, residents either had to shop at small, expensive corner stores with little fresh or affordable food or travel outside the neighborhood to shop for fruit, vegetables, or fresh meat. The closest place was now a corporate-owned grocery store. People had to rely on neighbors to arrange rideshares to the store, traveling through neighborhoods where they felt unsafe. The corporate store itself felt dirty, people told Reese, lacking the care of owners with long-term relationships to everyone in the community. Shopping was no longer a social event, connecting people to others in the neighborhood. Rather, it was often described as an alienating and unpleasant experience.

Reese's interviews and observations—including attending planning events and shadowing gardeners—also revealed how residents found ways to push

LEARNING OBJECTIVES

9.1 Reciprocity: The Foundation of Human Exchange
Explain how reciprocity serves as a fundamental organizing construct in human economies.

9.2 Markets
Connect key turning points in the history of human societies to the emergence of different kinds of market economies.

9.3 Redistribution
Explain how redistributive economies have worked in the distant past, recent past, and present.

9.4 Mixed and Alternative Economies
Define mixed economies and efforts to build alternative economies to promote economic equity.

ECONOMIC SYSTEMS

Humans engage in many different types of economies, including gifts, barter, market exchanges, pooling labor and resources, and mixed economies. Anthropologists study them all.

FIGURE 9.1

Cultural anthropologist Ashanté Reese (right) and a Deanwood community garden volunteer check seedlings in 2014.

back against the loss of their trusted, valued community food stores. By working together on a community garden (with just three raised beds to begin), households were finding ways to connect to one another while also improving their food self-reliance (**Figure 9.1**). They were also symbolically demonstrating their determination to sustain their community and connect to each other.

Anthropologists have long studied human *economic* behavior: how people produce, exchange, share, and consume various resources. A *household*, made up of those people who daily share their food, water, and other vital resources, is the most basic human economic unit. Food and water are essential resources for human survival and well-being, and for that reason they have also often been a particular focus of anthropological research on human economies. But food, water, and other necessities also have profound meanings: They can act as the basis of our identities and create the means for us to connect and cooperate (or not) with others. They are fundamental to how societies are organized, including how inequalities are created and reinforced.

Throughout human prehistory and history, different sharing and exchange systems have developed to stabilize and improve our access to basic needs—and in some cases to also build wealth and power. These systems range from the smallest scale (households sharing items with a neighbor) to the large and complex (modern international food transportation systems or urban sanitation infrastructure). Some are imposed by the state, while others emerge—as seen in Deanwood—from grassroots efforts.

Anthropologists examine human economies across all these scales, but the field is especially adept at understanding the ways humans exchange and share resources outside conventional economic processes as in formal markets. We often assume our modern economies are based almost entirely on monetary transactions. But anthropology—which looks into humans in the past and present—allows us to see that there are many other important and effective economic arrangements. These may operate with, beyond, or in opposition to the predominant systems in our society, and examining them enables us to consider other possibilities when the predominant systems are not serving us adequately.

In this chapter, we organize our exploration of what anthropologists know about human economies of the past, present, and future. We begin with the three modes of exchange that anthropologists have long studied: reciprocity, markets, and redistribution. We then turn to two cutting-edge areas of research: mixed economies and alternative economies.

SECTION 9.1

RECIPROCITY: THE FOUNDATION OF HUMAN EXCHANGE

Reciprocity is the fundamental principle that underlies all human exchange systems. Reciprocity is about the exchange of objects, labor, or other things of value. Reciprocity is fully embedded in all human interactions, from the most personal and intimate to the most large-scale and public.

FIGURE 9.2

A bonobo shares fruit with other bonobos. Sharing is a relatively rare behavior in other primates compared to humans, who share food all the time.

economic Refers to human production, circulation, and consumption of resources.

household The small group of people who pool basic resources to meet fundamental daily needs (such as sharing meals and shelter); often members are also closely related kin.

reciprocity A form of transfer that has specific expectations of give-and-take, is infused with cultural meanings, and depends on the social relationship between people involved.

exchange system A set of rules and norms that governs how materials, services, symbols, and ideas are transferred between people or groups.

food sharing The form of reciprocity most fundamental to the history and survival of our species (and most studied by anthropologists), in which food is given, shared, or exchanged.

Nonhuman primate adults have been observed to share the food they procure, but this occurs relatively rarely (**Figure 9.2**). More often, primate males and females alike feed themselves. Humans, by contrast, tend to practice food sharing: We divide up tasks around hunting, collecting, and preparing food, often along gender lines, and then we share the resulting meals. There are no human societies in which getting food for oneself and eating alone is considered normal and expected.

A basic economic unit in human societies is the household, defined by the members (family or otherwise) living together and sharing food (**Figure 9.3**). Food sharing with our closest kin is fundamental to human social life all over the globe. But humans also share food (and other resources) generously and widely. This extends to giving away resources even to strangers and when we ourselves are in need.

Focused sharing of food and other resources marks an important behavioral shift in human evolution and one that then allowed the other forms of complex cooperation that define our species today. But why did humans begin to share food so intensely, consistently, and widely?

(a) (b) (c)

FIGURE 9.3

(a) A Uyghur family in Kashgar, China, shares a meal of laghman, combining noodles, mutton, and vegetables. (b) Don Cossacks share a family meal in their apartment in Novocherkassk, Russia. (c) A shared meal in the Gurage zone of Ethiopia includes vegetables grown on the family's plot of land.

labor Any work, including physical, social, emotional, and intellectual work.

Evolutionary anthropologists have proposed several explanations for why human food sharing (and, more widely, human cooperation) emerged as a key feature of human societies. One impetus to share more widely may have initially been based on the types of food that early humans evolved to eat, such as hunted meat, tubers, or nuts that require skill and time to both acquire and process before they can be consumed. The emergence of gendered divisions of labor enabled women and men to cooperate along gender lines to access and prepare different foods (Chapter 11). Once food-related and other everyday tasks were differentiated, consistent sharing within groups was of benefit to all. Other interrelated evolutionary features of humanness, such as increasingly sophisticated language and symbolism, memory, and group identity, would also allow for valuable social connections and alliances with outsiders as well, including as a form of insurance during tough times.

In studying the material evidence of early human food sharing, anthropologists have to rely on indirect signs. One proposed marker is archaeological evidence of "base camps" where human ancestors carried and shared food, slept, and socialized. Current archaeological evidence suggests that base camps can be observed after 450,000 years ago in Africa, Asia, Europe, and the Middle East. This may have been around the time humans started using fire to roast foods and employing a wider array of tools. Before that, humans appear to have been mostly living in open-air sites, where they were near water sources and butchered animals.

Cave dwelling meant living where food wasn't and bringing food back to a home base instead. Many anthropologists think increased cave dwelling and greater reliance on food sharing emerged together. However, some archaeologists, leaning more heavily on observational studies with contemporary hunter-gatherers, argue that the use of base camps is not in itself sufficient evidence of food-sharing practices. Rather, there should also be evidence of butchering practices that divide the meat into more equal sections or of the butchered pieces of animals being more evenly spread across sites (**Figure 9.4**).

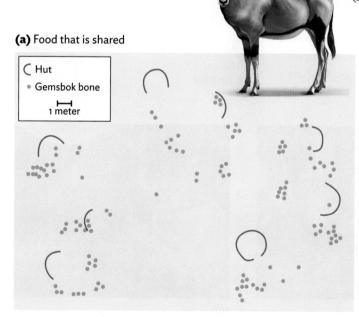

(a) Food that is shared

Hut
Gemsbok bone
1 meter

(b) Food that is not shared

Hut
Porcupine bone
1 meter

FIGURE 9.4

An archaeological study of how the remains of animals become distributed within a Ju/'hoansi (!Kung) base camp in southern Africa compares the pattern of **(a)** food that is shared (gemsbok kills) and **(b)** food that is not shared (a single porcupine kill). The unshared porcupine kill is mostly limited to one part of the site.

FIGURE 9.5

Excavations at Qesem Cave in Israel have yielded important archaeological evidence of early cooking and sharing of food.

By around 250,000 years ago, humans' home bases had become more confined and sophisticated, including more diversity of butchering and other tools. Especially important was the increasing use of hearth fires as the center of home bases. Such fires needed to be constantly tended, requiring basic forms of cooperative labor. By providing better means to cook and share food, these new fire-centered residential spaces also provided new places humans could plan and act together more effectively in other ways.

Qesem Cave in Israel, occupied from around 400,000 to 220,000 years ago, furnishes rich material evidence connecting home bases, hearths, and early food sharing (**Figure 9.5**). It contains fossil remnants of perhaps 10,000 animals that were hunted and brought to the cave, as well as evidence of possibly the oldest known use of human fire for cooking (dated to around 300,000 years ago). Qesem Cave inhabitants ate fallow deer, wild tortoises, horses, aurochs (a type of extinct wild ox), and goats. Early humans transported choice cuts of butchered animals (including heads) back to the cave, something not seen elsewhere at this time. Anthropologists have concluded that this is one of the earliest examples of a residential site with consistent food-sharing practices. The specific species of early humans that inhabited the cave at any given time has not been definitively determined, but the styles of butchering and the array of other tools found in the cave variously suggest *Homo erectus*, Neanderthals, and modern humans were all living in the region at various points (**Figure 9.6**).

GIFT GIVING

Marshall Sahlins was a prominent economic anthropologist and political activist who created "teach-in" protests in the 1960s. In his 1972 book *Stone Age Economics*, Sahlins conceptualized all human exchange as one of three forms of reciprocity: generalized, balanced, or negative.

In generalized reciprocity, people give to others without any expectation of direct payback. Gifts of food and birthday presents are good examples of generalized reciprocity. People receiving a gift might still later give something

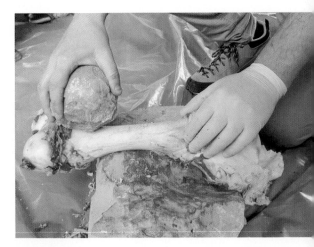

FIGURE 9.6

Archaeologists conduct experiments to identify which tools found in Qesem Cave would account for the butchering patterns and fat residues found on animal bones at the residential site. Bone marrow was an important source of high-quality fat, and stone balls seem to have been used to extract it.

generalized reciprocity **Giving without any expectation of direct payback.**

balanced reciprocity Giving with the expectation that payback has an equivalent value.

barter Direct exchange of goods or services, without the use of money.

negative reciprocity Giving where one party benefits more than the other.

back. It might not be a physical gift; it could be something else, such as respect or friendship. But with generalized reciprocity there is no immediate return.

In balanced reciprocity, people swap directly and expect a fair and balanced return. For example, when Greece was hard-hit by the economic recession of the late 2000s, people struggled to get enough money to buy needed goods. Small-town barter networks emerged to fill the gaps. Local fisherfolk, cheesemongers, butchers, gardeners, and seamstresses swapped goods and services.

In negative reciprocity, people attempt to get a thing for less than its value, or "something for nothing." Scams, such as selling fake plastic rice as food and price gouging during famine, are examples of negative reciprocity. While generalized reciprocity tends to happen between people who are socially close (such as kin), negative reciprocity is more likely when exchange partners are unrelated or, especially, strangers to each other (**Figure 9.7**).

The puzzle of payback—when, why, and how givers expect it (or not)—has long been considered by anthropologists. In his 1925 essay *The Gift*, French anthropologist Marcel Mauss put the question this way: How and why do humans feel so *obligated* to reciprocate gifts, even those with no expectation of return? Anthropologists find that gifts can increase the social status of the giver—at the cost of the receiver's social status. Reciprocating a gift resets the imbalance in power between the giver and the receiver, putting both back on even footing. From Mauss on, anthropologists have investigated how gifts tie people together in complex social networks of status and mutual obligation.

But what of supposedly unselfish charitable donations? Many people imagine charity as a gift that comes with no strings attached. Medical anthropologist Holly Ann Williams might differ in her thinking. Williams has spent much of her career at the U.S. Centers for Disease Control and Prevention, and she conducted a study with parents of children with cancer in the southeastern United States. Her work suggests that even charitable donations are perceived, by receivers, as coming with significant social and financial obligations that can be difficult to repay.

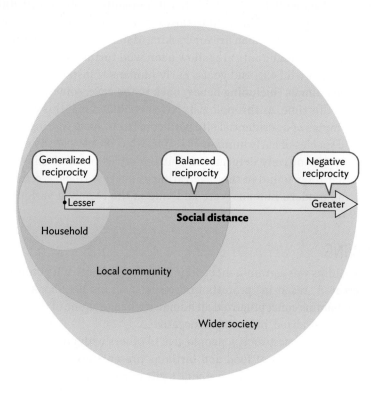

FIGURE 9.7

Marshall Sahlins's model of reciprocity suggests that greater social distance tends to encourage more self-interested forms of exchange.

In the United States, cancer treatment is extremely expensive. Williams found, at the time of her study, that many families lacked adequate medical insurance to cover the costs. The economic stresses parents faced forced them to juggle childcare, employment, and medical debt—often resulting in bankruptcy. Families bore the costs not just of medical care but also of meals and parking fees, even having to replace car tires after driving to numerous distant doctor visits.

These parents in crisis received gifts of money, food, labor, toys, and other goods from friends, family, co-workers, church groups, and community fundraisers (**Figure 9.8**). In interviewing parents, Williams found that receiving unreciprocated gifts—while kindly meant—created additional strain, regardless of their socioeconomic situation. It made parents feel uneasy, uncomfortable, and worried about how others saw them. They felt they were socially diminished unless they were able to return the gift later, which was often impossible for them to do. This experience is common for recipients of charity. Many gift-giving institutions and practices, including completely altruistic giving, can be laden with issues of inequality, power, status seeking, and burdensome obligations.

RECIPROCITY AS SOCIAL INSURANCE

Another way anthropologists think about sharing is as social insurance. That is, reciprocity can be a risk reduction system. Exchange partners can "store" people's obligations to reciprocate past gifts of food, water, labor, or household goods. This enables people to share risks across a community and to anticipate that others will come to assist them as needed, perhaps during difficult economic times or a pandemic.

Cultural anthropologist Polly Wiessner has conducted decades of field research in Ju/'hoansi (formerly called !Kung) communities of rural northwest Botswana and northeast Namibia (**Figure 9.9**). The Ju/'hoansi exchange institution of *hxaro* is an excellent example of this type of risk reduction through sharing. Ju/'hoansi families have *n!oresi*, inherited areas of land rights. Some contain large stands of nuts, others more permanent water sources, and some more game. Between hunting, gathering, and some domestic food production,

FIGURE 9.8

At a roadside donation stand, vegetables are offered as reciprocation for charitable donations given to fund children's cancer research.

social insurance An arrangement in which people can "store" obligations to reciprocate favors or gifts in long-standing relationships and then call on those relationship partners for help during times of scarcity or need.

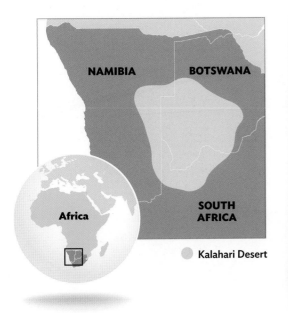

● Kalahari Desert

FIGURE 9.9

Ju/'hoansi people share fruit in the Kalahari Desert of Namibia.

Ju/'hoansi can often make a good living off their family's *n!oresi* with just 12–20 hours of work each week. But during drought, a family's land might not yield enough food.

In bad years, the *hxaro* relationship provides critically needed help, such as meat from a kill of larger game on someone else's land. A *hxaro* partnership is a lifelong Ju/'hoansi relationship that involves friendship, repeated small-scale gift-giving over time (of items such as beads, arrows, tools, and clothing), and—crucially—expected help in times of need. The Ju/'hoansi described the special lifelong relationships as "holding each other in their hearts" and being willing to offer various kinds of assistance when the other was in need. Many visits away from home were to communities where their or their spouse's *hxaro* partners lived. An important feature of *hxaro* relationships is they are formed between kin who live distantly from one another, in different geographic areas. This distance increases the likelihood that, at a given time, one partner will be faring better than the other and thus able to provide important insurance against hunger. Having several *hxaro* partners increases the insurance the system provides in times of need (**Figure 9.10**).

Reciprocal exchange systems are also observed in big cities where many people make a living through wage labor. Cultural anthropologist Larissa Lomnitz studied how people marginalized in such economies used reciprocal systems to help them manage. She studied an informal settlement in Mexico City, known as Cerrada del Cóndor, where around 200 households lived with no paved roads, drainage, garbage collection, or piped water. Renters lacked what many would think of as basic housing, steady jobs, or other securities. At the time of her research, unemployment was extremely high in Mexico. Almost everyone in the community who

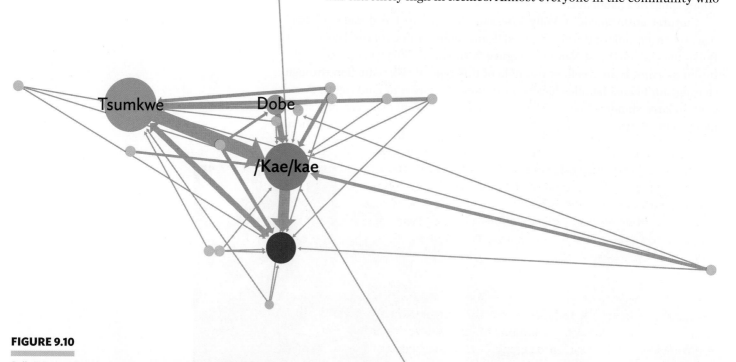

FIGURE 9.10

Polly Wiessner's painstakingly collected ethnographic data was visualized as a social network by Thomas Schweitzer. In this image, the nodes represent sites (camps or settlements), larger nodes and arrows represents more gifts (such as blankets or necklaces), and line length represents the real geographic distance between sites. In her response to Schweitzer's work, Wiessner praised the visualization for showing how individual gift giving can form a regional system, but noted a mixed-methods approach using the quantitative and qualitative (ethnographic) data she had collected would have given a richer representation of this reciprocal-exchange network.

FIGURE 9.11

Elders and children share food in a market in Mexico. Such reciprocal exchanges show how trusting relationships nurture human health, well-being, and survival across generations.

worked had jobs in the wealthier zones of Mexico City, such as food seller, construction worker, maid, or gardener.

Lomnitz found that people in Cerrada del Cóndor had active reciprocal exchanges that took many forms: information or gossip; assistance getting jobs; small loans of money, food, or tools; feeding and accommodating visitors; helping with construction projects; or friendship and emotional support. The networks between family members were especially stable and reliable. She found these reciprocal exchanges were embedded in ideas of *confianza* (trust) (**Figure 9.11**). Lomnitz argued that reciprocity endures over time, is embedded in meaningful social relationships (such as kinship and friendship), and is motivated by the maximization of security rather than profit.

While reciprocity can safeguard economic security, this does not mean reciprocity is utopian or even equitable. Lomnitz described many cases of conflict and status competition. One example was a woman whose marriage to a "worthless husband" meant she didn't have the necessary *confianza* for approaching her much wealthier sister to ask for help. Another example was a man who took a stable job and so he felt released from obligations to develop *confianza* with his neighbors. But Lomnitz's work showed, as have many subsequent anthropological studies, that even in a huge metropolis like Mexico City, reciprocal economies run on a very particular logic—a logic of mutual support and shared well-being.

BEYOND RECIPROCITY: HUMAN EXCHANGE SYSTEMS

Reciprocity is the oldest and most pervasive form of exchange in human societies, but as we stated at the beginning of this chapter, it's not the only form. Anthropologists have developed complex economic models to describe the full range of exchange systems.

Perhaps the most influential approach was developed by Karl Polanyi, an economic anthropologist and politician. He founded the Radical Citizens Party of Hungary and found employment in U.S. universities as a Jewish refugee intellectual during and after World War II. He opposed economic exploitation throughout his life.

FIGURE 9.12

Modes of exchange and production: Karl Polanyi's depiction of socioeconomic systems—reciprocity, markets, and redistribution—was published first in 1944. Eric Wolf later introduced an anthropological framework for understanding modes of production, which can be used in conjunction with the three modes of exchange.

Reciprocity
• Oldest form of human exchange
• Give-and-take that can be generalized, balanced, or negative depending on exchange partners' social distance
• Contemporary forms include gifts, sharing, and charity

Modes of production
• Kin-based (domestic)
• Tributary (ruler/subject)
• Capitalist
• All have exploitative features

Redistribution
• Centralizes goods and services
• Distributes goods and services out in new patterns
• Contemporary forms include food banks, social safety nets, and different forms of socialism

Markets
• Balanced to negative reciprocity
• Greater social distance between partners
• Privatization and commodification in capitalist markets

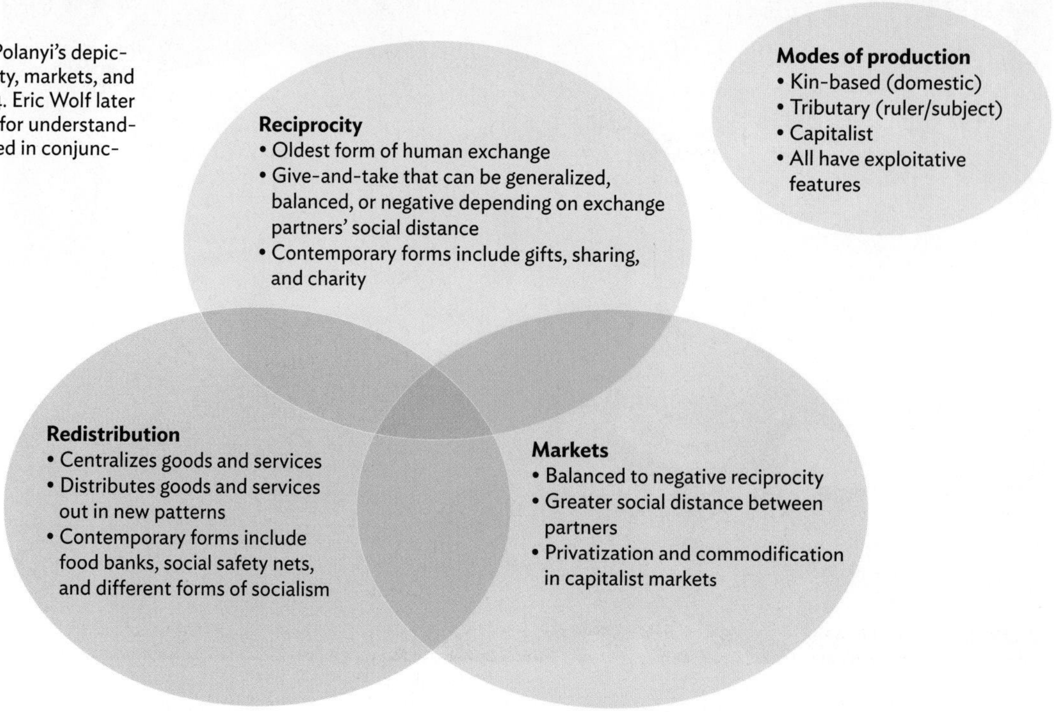

Polanyi described three forms of exchange that evolved over time: reciprocity, redistribution, and markets (**Figure 9.12**). All three modes of exchange integrate production and distribution involving cultural, political, religious, and familial organizations. Reciprocity, as we have seen in this section, is a form of exchange based on give-and-take; the amount of give versus take depends on exchange partners' social distance. Redistribution, which we will explore later in Section 9.3, is a form of economic exchange designed to centralize goods and services and then distribute them out in new patterns. We will examine market exchange in the next section.

SECTION 9.2

MARKETS

market A place (physical or virtual) where people meet to exchange goods, services, and money.

Today, markets account for an increasingly large portion of human economic activities. Market exchange is often said to be individualistic and based on rational maximization of profit. As we will discuss in this section, that's not always true. Many anthropologists see market exchange as a special case of reciprocity: The give-and-take is usually immediate, takes place between more socially distanced partners, and runs from balanced to negative reciprocity. Markets, like all economic exchanges, are deeply embedded in human systems of meaning. Markets connect people through culture, language, value, and symbols—and such connections are rarely truly individualistic.

MARKETS AND MONEY

Most humans across the globe today, including subsistence farmers and hunter-gatherers, engage to some degree with markets. But markets more generally have a long history. The earliest markets were based in barter forms of trading.

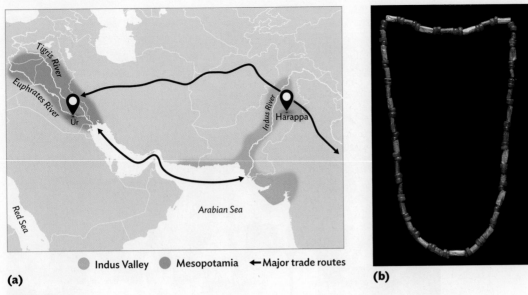

(a) Indus Valley ● Mesopotamia ● ← Major trade routes

(b)

FIGURE 9.13

(a) This map shows Harappa in the Indus Valley, where raw agate and carnelian were transformed into beads, and Ur in Mesopotamia, where Harappan carnelian beads were found. Identifying the movement of artifacts and raw materials across the landscape can inform our understanding of trade routes and relationships in the past. **(b)** These carnelian beads from the Indus Valley were found in the tombs of the Royal Cemetery of Ur, dating to around 2500 BCE.

Evidence of trade routes is thus one way that archaeologists can identify the existence of market economies of the past. By 4,000 years ago, during the Bronze Age, long-distance trade and exchange systems linked much of eastern and southern Asia with the Levant and Mediterranean region. People traveled along these routes by camels, donkeys, boats, and large caravan systems, and a market represented a nexus of these linkages. For example, beautiful reddish-orange carnelian stones were mined for Harappan workshops in the Indus Valley in what is now Pakistan. These stones were then transformed into long beads and traded to sites across ancient Mesopotamia and as far away as Egypt (**Figure 9.13**).

Because plants and, to a lesser extent, animal bone don't preserve as well as stone beads or pottery, evidence of the trade and exchange of food has been harder to identify in the archaeological record. However, archaeologists have started to look at plant microremains, such as phytoliths or "plant rocks," which are silica-based plant microfossils that can survive for thousands of years. Phytoliths in the dental calculus of people who died and were buried in Bronze Age sites in the southern Levant on the eastern edge of the Mediterranean Sea show that exotic imported foods such as bananas were traded at markets and then eaten along with local foods such as wheat and dates.

Evidence for markets and market exchange also comes from accounts in early Bronze Age written texts, which mention standardized weights and scales as well as money. Early money came in many forms: shells, strips or rings of copper, clay tokens, and eventually small metal coins. Some of the earliest metal coins appear to have been produced in China about 2,600 years ago and in Mesopotamia about 1,500 years ago. After that time, much more of what is definitely money is identifiable in the archaeological record.

Early complex societies—and then, especially, states and empires—had particularly dynamic economic systems with market exchange. These included dedicated and central city places filled with energetic trading in both goods and services, as well as systems of money. One of the best understood early market systems outside Europe was in the Aztec Empire, located in what is now Mexico. Written records, made by Spanish explorers when they first arrived in 1519,

money An object that serves as a medium of exchange and a unit of account in a market economy, such as a coin.

FIGURE 9.14

This painting by Mexican muralist Diego Rivera (1886–1957) shows his depiction of the Aztec capital of Tenochtitlán around 1500 in the background. In the foreground, people are buying and selling or bartering goods in the market of Tlateloco.

MEXICO

Tlatelolco

North America

Aztec Empire in 1519

describe the huge and bustling marketplace at Tlatelolco, where people could buy or trade foods such as corn, beans, or squash from farmers; salt, tropical bird feathers, or animal skins from professional traders called *pochteca*; or bronze tools, obsidian blades, or woven baskets from craftspeople (**Figure 9.14**).

Smaller towns and villages throughout the Aztec Empire also had regular markets. In these smaller towns, archaeologists have found evidence of people spinning cotton and weaving cotton textiles in their houses that then could be used as money in the markets, which were wide-open spaces in the centers of towns. Even in smaller towns, people traded for or purchased beautifully decorated pottery from other parts of the Aztec Empire to use as their "fancy china," alongside their "everyday dishes" that were made locally.

In Aztec society, both cacao beans and cotton textiles served as money. Purchases of food or other commodities could be completed using counts of cacao beans, but they were also (unlike modern cash) ground with vanilla beans and chile peppers to make hot chocolate. Cacao, along with vanilla beans, are tropical crops, and grow far from the Aztec capital in the lowland forests of Central America. Very large numbers of cacao beans were likely in circulation, leading also to evidence of fairly sophisticated counterfeit bean production. Archaeologists have found cacao beans that look real but are actually made of clay, and early Spanish accounts describe Aztec cacao sellers making counterfeit cacao with avocado pits or by filling empty cacao shells with mud.

TRANSITIONS TO CAPITALISM

While markets have been in existence for thousands of years, capitalism is a newer form of exchange that arose within the past 500 years. Capitalism brought big changes to how markets work, and over time it has expanded and globalized market systems. The basic tenet of capitalism is that people accumulate wealth by using privately owned resources to gain more money.

In capitalist economic systems, commodification makes it newly possible to own and sell things for money (for example, communally owned land or water), in ways that were not possible under the rules and norms of the preceding society. This is why the development and spread of economic, political, and legal systems that secure private property—and convert more and more

capitalism A market-based economy in which private ownership enables some people to profit from others' labor and consumption.

commodification The process by which something that was previously unable to be sold becomes saleable.

private property The bundle of rights that enable an individual or set of individuals to sell, access, manage, withdraw from, and exclude others from land, goods, and other resources.

resources to private ownership—are at the heart of capitalism. Over time, different forms and types of capitalism have created new ways to profit and accumulate wealth.

One early form of capitalism, termed merchant capitalism by some, focused on moving goods and people (such as by ship) in order to make a profit. The early expansion of capitalism was often violent and coercive. By around 1500, colonizers and early capitalists had begun to seize control of land, resources, and labor in other countries. Chattel slavery expanded in the 1600s to support the labor needs of this new global economic system. Plantation owners could own, sell, exploit, and control the reproduction and labor of humans for generations, and they could accumulate substantial wealth by doing so.

Many societies organize land, water, and other resources using common-pool resource institutions. Such systems lack private ownership, so members cannot individually own or trade common-pool resources. To facilitate privatization, then, communal lands were increasingly seized and enclosed in private property regimes as part of transitions to capitalism. When this happens, old farming, hunting, and migratory ways of life become impossible. When subsistence livelihoods are decimated by the privatization of common-pool resources, people must sell their labor to make a living.

By the 1800s, the rise of new technologies and newly displaced laborers fed another form of industrial capitalism. Industrial capitalism created new labor relations, such as those between the factory owner and wage laborers. This was facilitated by resource extraction, such as coal mining, and technological innovations, such as the steam engine. The increasing divide between those who provided low-value labor and those who could exploit it became a defining feature of industrial capitalism (**Figure 9.15**).

As new forms of social mobility emerged with each form of capitalism, old elite systems crumbled. Things that had been unattainable to non-elites—such as land or resources—could be obtained by anyone who could accumulate

merchant capitalism A market-based exchange system using long-distance trade for the acquisition, movement, and sale of raw materials to create profits.

chattel slavery A form of slavery in which a person is legally transformed into a commodity: The person and all their children become private property and can be owned and sold.

common-pool resource institution A governance arrangement in which a group of people communally owns clearly delineated resources (e.g., land, river water, forest) and collectively makes and enforces rules to protect and distribute these resources.

common-pool resource A natural resource that is finite but difficult to exclude people from using, such as a forest, fishery, grazing pasture, or fresh water.

private property regime A governance arrangement in which resources are individually owned, excludable (that is, open only to owners), and often tradable.

industrial capitalism A market-based exchange system using private ownership, wealth accumulation, mechanized production, and new wage-labor arrangements to create profits.

FIGURE 9.15

Boys are shown working evening shifts in a U.S. glass factory in 1908. In factory work, increasingly mechanized processes lowered the value of human labor.

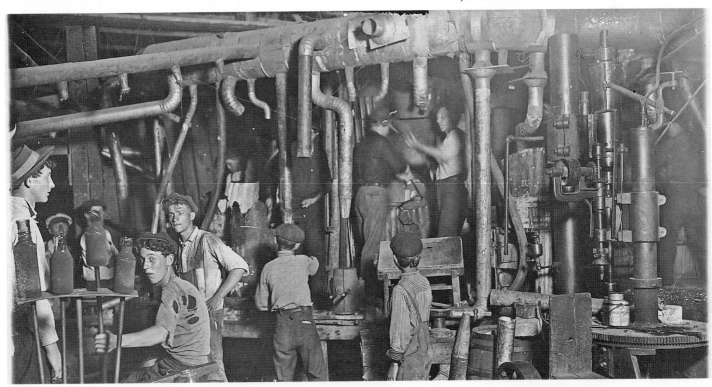

enough money. Social status became more directly aligned with these new forms of wealth. For some, the rise of capitalism and the dominance of market relations were profoundly freeing. This process continues today. As new forms of capitalism emerge, socioeconomic organization and related experiences of freedom and oppression are reshaped in novel ways.

SOCIOECONOMIC CHANGE: FROM INDUSTRIAL TO NEOLIBERAL CAPITALISM

Transitions to and within capitalism have transformed human ways of life globally. Karl Marx (1818–1883) famously argued that capitalism should be understood as a new mode of production, or a set of social relations that organized the economy. In industrial capitalism, for example, the capitalist class owns the means of production, buys the labor of workers, and keeps or reinvests the profits. As later forms of capitalism emerged, factory labor persisted but other kinds of labor arrangements drove major changes.

Anthropologist Eric Wolf (1923–1999; **Figure 9.16**), building on Marx's work, proposed three major modes of production: capitalist, domestic, and tributary. The capitalist mode of production has already been discussed. The domestic mode of production is kin-based. For example, hunter-gatherers or subsistence farmers might organize production by gender and age. The tributary mode of production is a social hierarchy based on, for example, kingship or religious rulers. Producers pay tribute, which is then controlled by the rulers. Like capitalism, domestic and tributary modes of production contain exploitative features. However, the forms of social organization and power differ widely in capitalist, domestic, and tributary modes of production.

Through ethnographic research, anthropologists have documented enormous cultural shifts, beginning in the 1980s, to a new phase of capitalism called neoliberalism or neoliberal capitalism. The functions of government were increasingly shifted into the market: Social services, such as healthcare and pensions, were privatized and replaced with market-based products. Anthropologists found that, in neoliberal settings, people learned to see themselves as consumers rather than citizens. People increasingly adopt ideas of personal responsibility for previously communal duties such as health, childcare, and education. Transnational businesses and their owners make up the capitalist class that has profited disproportionately from this large-scale privatization of government services. Meanwhile, many low-income workers and others at the economic margins have had to scramble to pay out-of-pocket for social services. As a result, income inequality has worsened globally.

Economic anthropologist David Graeber (1961–2020), who had been a student of Marshall Sahlins, became one of the foremost thinkers of the neoliberal era. A leader of the Occupy movement that promoted global democracy and economic equality, Graeber is credited with coining the slogan "We are the 99%" to draw attention to the disproportionate wealth and political power held by 1% of global elites (**Figure 9.17**).

One of Graeber's concerns was how current labor arrangements leave little time for people to imagine new and better economic futures. He argued that many of the well-paid jobs in contemporary capitalist economies—roles he called goons, flunkies, box-tickers, duct-tapers, and taskmasters—are far from efficient and generate very little value to society. Graeber described this as a kind of corporate feudalism, in which roles are assigned to perform status and maintain power, not generate wealth.

FIGURE 9.16

Anthropologist Eric Wolf developed influential ideas about human economic production through doing fieldwork in Europe, Mexico, and Puerto Rico.

FIGURE 9.17

Anthropologist and activist David Graeber leads a discussion about democracy and debt at the London School of Economics in 2016.

FIGURE 9.18

An international call center in Karachi, Pakistan, is pictured.

COMMODIFICATION OF LANGUAGE: CONTEMPORARY CAPITALISM IN AN INTERNATIONAL CALL CENTER

In 1983, the Oxford English Dictionary first recognized the phrase "call center" in its lexicon. The intended use of call centers is to sell products and provide services, most particularly to consumers in wealthier nations. But as demand for and competition around call centers have grown, the industry has increasingly moved to countries with lower labor costs, especially in south and southeastern Asia. Pakistan has emerged as one of the major centers for the burgeoning call center industry, in part because its colonial language was English, which continues to be taught widely in schools (**Figure 9.18**).

Linguistic scholar Tariq Rahman detailed staff and customer interactions in four large urban international call centers in Islamabad and Lehore, Pakistan, using participant observation (such as attending training sessions), interviews, and questionnaires. The call center preference was for staff dealing with English-speaking callers to use American or British varieties of English that resemble those of the customers. The physical environment of the workplace is reminiscent of high-tech industry environments, with avant-garde architecture, modern art, and posters that remind all workers that speaking Urdu (the national language of Pakistan) is not allowed (**Figure 9.19**).

In this example of a globalized capitalist workplace, Rahman describes how speaking the "correct" English variety is the product sold to the companies hiring call center services. Previously, the use of Urdu and Pakistani English was simply a result of language policies inherited from British rulers; while some people wanted Urdu to replace English in all contexts (government, education, etc.), others connected to the military and the urban middle class did not. Currently, abilities in both Urdu and English languages are important vehicles of upward mobility in Pakistan. English language abilities signal social mobility, urbanization, modernity, and formal education.

Under current globalized capitalist norms, however, being able to produce the "correct" telephone variety for eight hours a day is the source of profit, not pride. In this scenario, the globalized capitalist market pushes people to acquire a very particular language variety that is different from the Pakistani or Indian English learned in school and used in government spaces. Consequently, it denigrates the typical Pakistani English variety used by elites. Accordingly, the acquisition of the new variety opens some economic opportunities but closes

NO URDU POLICY

Do you Really want to improve your English?
If you do, then you need to stop speaking Urdu!
The only way to learn English (any language) is to force yourself to speak it *all the time*. Especially when you feel uncomfortable.

FIGURE 9.19

This message was displayed in one of the call centers that was the focus of Rahman's ethnographic study.

mode of production One of the varied ways that a society can organize human labor to produce what they need. Examples include kin-based (domestic) and tributary (ruler/subject) modes.

means of production The resources a society uses to produce goods and services.

neoliberalism A system of government that seeks to move service provision from public to market sectors and to move resource ownership and control from the public to the private sphere.

consumer A person who buys and uses goods and services.

citizen A person who has duties and is entitled to rights as a member of a political community.

off others. That is, by learning the call center variety of English, a person can be employed in the globalized capitalist economy but shunned from the elite spaces of Pakistani daily life.

POSTINDUSTRIAL CAPITALISM

In recent years, deindustrialization and the rise of postindustrial capitalism have driven another major transition. Due to the widespread mechanization of labor, wage labor and factory work are less important to profits. Postindustrial capitalism centers on profits made through services, technology, and knowledge. New forms of private ownership have again been created—such as, for example, cryptocurrencies and non-fungible tokens (NFTs), created in 2014. Some scholars have argued that wealth and power are now less about the accumulation of material goods and more about controlling the flow of information and services.

Economic anthropologist Karen Ho, in her book *Liquidated*, conducted an ethnographic study of financial labor, an important part of the postindustrial capitalist economy, on Wall Street in the 2000s (**Figure 9.20**). Working in the "middle office" of an investment bank as a business analyst in New York, Ho had access to the highly paid investment bankers working in the "front office." By interviewing Wall Street bankers, attending industry conferences and networking events, and following industry publications and reports, she was able to detail the investment banker work culture within companies such as Goldman Sachs, J.P. Morgan, and Merrill Lynch. She identified how these elite workers justify and legitimize capitalist market values while also embracing a grueling ethos of extreme overwork and accepting the need to shift jobs often.

Ho's Wall Street research found that these workers generally perceive themselves as belonging to an exclusive group, uniquely qualified to make quick decisions. Through their enormous impact on the national economy, this self-perception can have outsized consequences—including creating market conditions that result in the layoff of millions of workers. The combination of their sense of specialness and their own job insecurity meant their professional decisions were mostly designed to prioritize short-term payoffs, such as personal bonuses, over concerns about the potential failure of their decisions and the subsequent consequences for clients and other affected individuals. This cultural attitude motivated risky moves such as corporate takeovers, downsizing and restructuring, and credit default swaps, in pursuit of profit. Ho's work explaining why banking culture often encourages reckless levels of risk-taking helps contextualize and explain the Great Recession financial crisis of 2007–2009.

Economic anthropologists debate whether postindustrial capitalism will ultimately be better or worse, for the mass of people globally, than the forms of capitalism that preceded it. Perhaps this model will usher in universal basic income, sustainable economies, and shortened workweeks. Or it may lead to deepening wealth inequality, injustice, and economic exploitation. We return to this important and timely concern in Section 9.4, when we consider alternative economies in more detail.

FIGURE 9.20

Economic anthropologist Karen Ho's ethnographic research on Wall Street in New York, shown here, explains why changing the institutional culture of high-level finance and banking is central to global economic stability.

CULTURAL CAPITAL AND THE COMMODIFICATION OF THE BODY

In capitalist economies, many different aspects of human life, beyond just labor, are commodified, incluidng food, dress, and other consumer goods. High-value goods, then, signal social prestige. French scholar Pierre Bourdieu's

(1930–2002) work has been extremely influential to anthropologists' understandings of why people engage so enthusiastically in the processes of commodification. Commodified knowledge and goods convert into cultural capital. By communicating such messages as knowledge, taste, class, and power, they can help establish, elevate, or reinforce the heightened social position of the person displaying them (**Figure 9.21**).

Physical bodies provide a means to acquire cultural capital too. Slimness is increasingly valued as higher status, a trend that parallels the increasing average body size of populations in most parts of the world. Psychological anthropologist Anne Becker's studies of body image among young women in Viti Levu, Fiji, have shown how engaging in capitalist systems changes the ways people relate to and work on their bodies as individual projects, especially how they view and seek slimness. The idea of the individual here is key, because such body projects are based in cultural values of individual responsibility and self-care.

When Becker first began interviewing Indigenous Fijian women about their own body ideals in 1988, they had little interest in reflecting on their shape and size as a personal concern. But they were interested in talking about the bodies of others, such as how they were fed and if they were sick. Robust bodies signaled heath and elevated social status. Chiefs were stereotyped as big-bodied. This positivity toward largeness was linked to core cultural values where notions of the self were embedded in care for and relationships to others, and ideas about sharing food were part of the broader Fijian ethos of care. But, as television became widespread in Fiji, and then later social media, ideas about the need to attend to and work on their own bodies have become increasingly central to how young women see themselves and relate to others. Becker has been able to track not only the emergence of practices such as dieting but also the emergence of body image concerns and eating disorders.

This increased focus on individual body projects, such as maintaining slimness or gaining lean muscle, hasn't just been happening in Fiji (**Figure 9.22**). It is a cross-cultural phenomenon, expanding as communities become woven

FIGURE 9.21

As celebrity Kim Kardashian leaves her workout, she illustrates how bottled water, designer clothing, members-only gyms, and certain body shapes accrue cultural capital in ways that can reinforce social inequality.

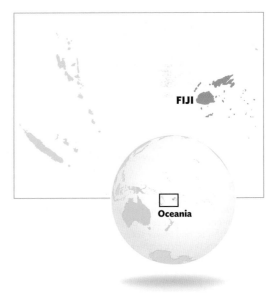

FIGURE 9.22

Bodybuilding competitions—such as this one held in Bhutan—reflect the individual social and economic capital created by body projects using extreme diet and exercise.

cultural capital A set of beliefs and behaviors that can be mobilized to help people enhance their social or economic status.

body projects Attempts to construct and maintain a desired social identity through attention to the form of the body, especially its surface.

into global networks of broadcast and social media, employment, migration, and social interaction embedded in capitalist economies. This trend is occurring alongside shifts in industrial farming, food production, and the rising cost of healthy foods—forcing people with lower incomes to eat diets heavy in cheap processed foods linked to weight gain. This is a good example of the complex effects of capitalist globalization.

BEYOND SIMPLE SELF-INTEREST: EXPANDING CONVENTIONAL ECONOMIC MODELS

Economic anthropologists, drawing from the entirety of human history, tend to study economics differently from other fields. One basic difference between theories from anthropology and economics is around self-interest. In economics, market exchange is conventionally viewed as individualistic and based on rational maximization of profit. The long search for a fundamental theory of motivation for human economic behavior led to a set of ideas called the rationality model or the canonical self-interest model. Some also call this *Homo economicus,* the economic human.

Proposer is given $50

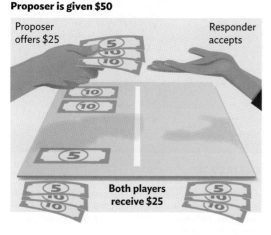

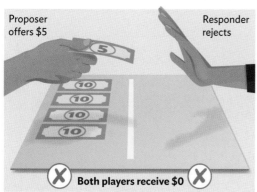

FIGURE 9.23

In the ultimatum game, the first player makes an offer to split money with a second player. Both players get the money if the second player accepts. But if the second player rejects the offer, neither player gets anything. Anthropologists use ultimatum games to study (1) social norms of fairness and (2) the cost people are willing to pay to punish unfair behavior.

bounded rationality **The idea that humans make economic choices that are rational given a specific social context, cultural values, and access to information.**

This model predicts that people will generally and consistently act to maximize utility or benefits, such as profits or monetary rewards. This model works reasonably well in explaining how people behave in capitalist market economies. The idea is that people will do what benefits them materially. So, for example, they will manufacture the product that will yield the greatest profit. But this self-interest model really only works well in predicting a narrow range of human behaviors—it cannot explain, for example, why we bring our neighbors meals or care for infirm elders.

And it performs particularly poorly for predicting people's economic behavior in the many human societies that aren't "WEIRD," an acronym for Western, Educated, Industrialized, Rich, and Democratic. Biological anthropologist Joe Henrich and colleagues have been collating experimental data from many different types of non-WEIRD societies. His team uses an "ultimatum" game-based bargaining experiment to identify the circumstances under which people choose to act generously toward others (**Figure 9.23**). One person is assigned an amount equivalent to one day's wages in their locale. They are then asked to choose the amount of that money they would like to offer the other player. If the other person accepts the amount, that is how the money is divided. If the other player rejects it, no one gets anything.

In their initial studies comparing experiments in 15 different societies, important patterns emerged (**Figure 9.24**). People typically act generously to others. On average across all the field sites, the offers tended to be in the 40–50% range, even if people in some societies were a little more generous than others. But, rationally, any offer should be accepted, however low it is, because it is certainly better than getting nothing. But the experiments also showed that people in all those studied societies were willing to pay a personal cost (giving up all money) to "teach a lesson" to others they considered to be acting selfishly by giving offers seen as too low (such as 10%).

Accordingly, anthropologists have worked alongside economists to explore how the idea of bounded rationality might better reflect human economic motivations and behavior. In bounded rationality, people make economic decisions in rational ways, but that rationality is always shaped by limited knowledge or attention. Anthropologists argue that factors such as social norms, culture, religion, and social status are also very important for understanding bounded

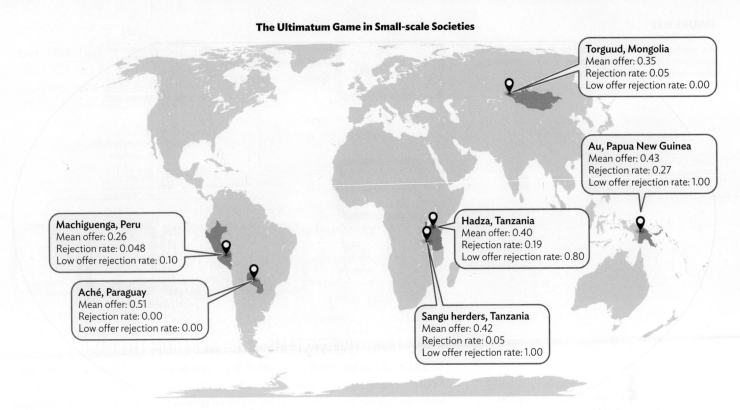

Torguud, Mongolia
Mean offer: 0.35
Rejection rate: 0.05
Low offer rejection rate: 0.00

Au, Papua New Guinea
Mean offer: 0.43
Rejection rate: 0.27
Low offer rejection rate: 1.00

Machiguenga, Peru
Mean offer: 0.26
Rejection rate: 0.048
Low offer rejection rate: 0.10

Hadza, Tanzania
Mean offer: 0.40
Rejection rate: 0.19
Low offer rejection rate: 0.80

Aché, Paraguay
Mean offer: 0.51
Rejection rate: 0.00
Low offer rejection rate: 0.00

Sangu herders, Tanzania
Mean offer: 0.42
Rejection rate: 0.05
Low offer rejection rate: 1.00

FIGURE 9.24

Acceptance and rejection rates of cash offers in some of the societies studied by Henrich's team are illustrated here. The rates are shown as proportions in the ultimatum game for each society; the low offer rejection rate refers to offers of 20 percent or less.

rationality and economic decision-making. And people do not necessarily want to maximize profit; their economic behavior is often motivated by the desire to maximize things such as family survival, solidarity, fairness, or even love. This perspective can help us understand economic behavior in a range of settings, including markets.

SECTION 9.3

REDISTRIBUTION

Capitalist economic systems tend to concentrate wealth and promote socioeconomic inequality. In this section, we explore the ways that people and societies establish systems for redistributing wealth and resources. There are many examples of redistribution across human history.

A redistributive economy generally requires a flow of resources to a pool controlled by a central administration, which can then reallocate those resources outward to others. A food bank is a very basic example of a small redistribution center. Food is donated from varied sources (such as churches or businesses) to a central place (the food bank) and then redistributed in portions (boxes of food) to other people. But the state itself can also act as a redistribution center, using taxation to fund public services. Sometimes redistribution systems are effective in accumulating resources centrally and sending them out to those who need them most. Sometimes they are not; redistributive economies, as we will see, can also be drivers of inequality and wealth accumulation.

redistribution A form of economic exchange designed to centralize goods and services and then distribute them out in new patterns.

FIGURE 9.25

A simplified redistribution model for Mycenaean Greece (1600–1100 BCE) shows how goods from local communities were redistributed to textile workshops.

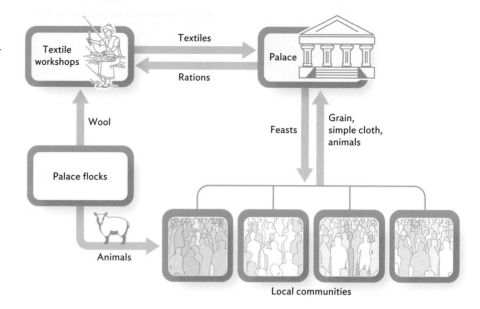

socialism A range of redistributive economies with the basic feature of partially or fully communal ownership and control of resources or production.

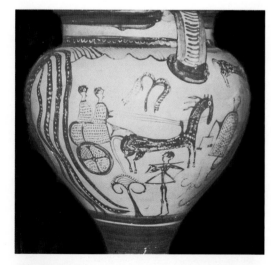

FIGURE 9.26

This Mycenaean ceramic vessel shows a chariot. Chariots were constructed in centralized workshops in the Mycenaean redistributive economy.

REDISTRIBUTIVE SYSTEMS: EVIDENCE FROM THE PAST

Redistribution has been a common form of exchange for thousands of years. Today, redistribution is often associated with socialism, but many other large- and small-scale systems also have redistributive elements. There are hundreds of contemporary forms of socialism, and they range widely in terms of their forms of governance and degree of market integration. Using the archaeological record, anthropologists have constructed examples of redistributive economies from a variety of time periods and places.

For example, in Mycenaean Greece (1600–1100 BCE) during the Bronze Age, the "palace economy" was based on a system of redistribution of multiple items, from food to textiles to tools (**Figure 9.25**). Mycenaean palace-based rulers didn't directly own much land. Rather, they received grain and other agricultural products, animals, and simple textiles from the local communities that produced them. These goods were then moved onward to workshops for treatment by skilled craftspeople. Palace leaders would provide food rations, such as grain and figs, to skilled workers such as spinners and weavers. The textiles were then likely distributed at feasts and to elite families. A similar decentralized Mycenaean redistributive system has also been documented for making chariots, which were constructed in workshops in the palace using wood and other raw materials that had been collected as taxes (**Figure 9.26**).

Not all redistributive economies in the past were associated with palaces. For example, a complex economic system with redistribution and a huge system of trade and exchange can be found in what is now northwestern New Mexico, in the United States, where a substantial population lived and farmed in Chaco Canyon between about 800 and 1350 CE. By about 1050 CE, as many as 5,500 people occupied these pueblos, sites with large multiroom complexes, which were connected by more than 350 miles (563 kilometers) of roads, many of which were the size of a two-lane highway. The largest site in Chaco Canyon, called Pueblo Bonito, was a huge D-shaped site that contained more than 800 rooms, many of which were five stories high (**Figure 9.27**). Archaeologists believe that the labor for these massive buildings and road systems was contributed in exchange for food and other goods that were redistributed at large feasts.

FIGURE 9.27

In this view of Pueblo Bonito in Chaco Canyon, located in northern New Mexico, round kivas, or ceremonial rooms, and multistory adobe buildings are visible.

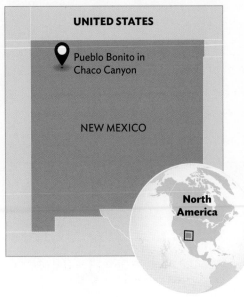

Archaeologists have shown that dietary staples such as deer, rabbits, and prairie dogs were imported from over 40 kilometers (km) away by looking at the isotopic values in the archaeological animal remains found in Chaco Canyon sites to determine where the animals lived. Similarly, archaeologists looked at the isotopic values in corn cobs found in trash pits in Chaco Canyon sites to determine that corn was grown and brought to the site from as far as 90 km away. Even the huge logs used for floors and ceilings in the multiple-story buildings were carried from spruce and fir forests in the surrounding mountains, up to 100 km away (**Figure 9.28**). Archaeologists have used *strontium isotope analysis* of the wooden beams to identify exactly where the timber came from in the Chuska and San Mateo Mountains more than 60 km away.

Some foods and objects found in the Chaco Canyon region came from even farther away, showing how redistribution systems can operate within much larger exchange systems. Copper bells and scarlet macaws from Mesoamerica show clear ties with people thousands of kilometers away. There are also

strontium isotope analysis An analytical method that compares the abundances of stable isotopes that vary in bedrock and geologic regions; often used by archaeologists to understand how past humans moved around landscapes.

FIGURE 9.28

Details of sandstone masonry and wooden supports for floors and ceilings at Chaco Canyon, New Mexico, are shown. Archaeological analysis has tracked the origins of construction materials as well as different artifacts found at the site to better understand the complex economic systems in the region.

FIGURE 9.29

Ceramic vessels like these are decorated in a black-and-white style, typical of other ceramics in the Chaco Canyon region, but they have a cylindrical shape commonly seen in Mesoamerican vessels used for a chocolate drink made with cacao beans.

ceramics decorated in typical Chaco Canyon styles but made in more typically Mesoamerican cylinder shapes found in Mexico and Central America (**Figure 9.29**). By analyzing the chemical residues inside these ceramic vessels, researchers were able to show that the ceramics were used for a chocolatelike drink containing the molecule theobromine, which is found in large quantities only in cacao beans; cacao is the main ingredient of chocolate and grows in the jungles of Central America, where it was also used as money, as previously noted. Clearly, bringing exotic plants, animals, and objects by foot over thousands of miles was important to people at Chaco Canyon, and some of these would have been redistributed at large ceremonial or feasting events.

Another archaeological example of a very large trade and exchange system in which redistribution was important comes from eastern North America. Around 1100 CE, much of this region was connected through a massive exchange system centered at Cahokia, an archaeological site outside what is now St. Louis, Missouri, United States. Cahokia was the largest site in North America and was located in the agriculturally fertile American Bottom, which is just south of the confluence of the Mississippi, Missouri, and Illinois Rivers. At its height between 1050 and 1250 CE, during what is called the Mississippian period, Cahokia probably housed about 30,000 people, some of whom moved to Cahokia from other regions. Huge earthen mounds covered an area of 6 square miles (16 square kilometers) (**Figure 9.30**), and the large urban center was surrounded by smaller towns and villages. Archaeologists have argued that Cahokia was the epicenter of a global Mississippian culture that spread from the Great Lakes in the north to the Gulf of Mexico in the south. Because of its location at the center of extensive trade routes, exotic materials such as copper and marine

FIGURE 9.30

Monks Mound, the largest earthen mound at the archaeological site of Cahokia, is the largest prehistoric mound in the United States and Canada.

shells came to Cahokia from thousands of miles away. Craft specialists and artists at Cahokia used the raw materials to create beads, carved shells, and pottery in distinctive styles that were then redistributed within and outside Cahokia by trading relationships throughout midwestern and southeastern North America (**Figure 9.31**).

However, much more than Mississippian-style artifacts was redistributed from Cahokia. The spread of artifacts was accompanied by changes in mound construction, mortuary behavior, and social and economic intensification. In this case, it is impossible to separate purely economic interactions from political and religious interactions. For example, at Mississippian sites such as Etowah, in what is now northwestern Georgia, Mississippian mounds are associated with archaeological evidence of social and economic stratification in mortuary behaviors as well as the use of artifacts that reflect their participation in the complex religious symbols and *cosmology* coming from Cahokia.

REDISTRIBUTIVE ECONOMIC SYSTEMS IN THE POSTCOLONIAL WORLD

Later examples of redistributive economies often come from the postcolonial world. After gaining independence, many former colonies experimented with socialist economies organized around principles of redistribution. Centuries of extractivism—in which colonizing countries extracted raw wealth (through mining, timber, slavery, and so on) to feed global capitalism—had undermined the preexisting health, education, political, and economic systems in these former colonies. Some people in these newly independent countries hoped socialist redistributive systems could help redress these problems.

Anthropologists have played many different roles, variously informing, promoting, and undermining these global experiments with socialist redistributive economies. One example is Kwame Nkrumah (1909–1972), born in the British colony in Africa known as the Gold Coast and now the Republic of Ghana (**Figure 9.32**). In 1945, he was admitted to the London School of Economics and Political Science (LSE) to study for his doctoral degree in social anthropology.

FIGURE 9.31

The sandstone Birdman Tablet were excavated from Monks Mound at Cahokia. It is an example of Cahokian-style artifacts that spread throughout North America during the Mississippian period.

cosmology **A theory of the universe (world) as an ordered whole, including beliefs, knowledge, and interpretations about its origins.**

FIGURE 9.32

Ghanaian President Kwame Nkrumah, once a doctoral student of social anthropology in England, dances with Queen Elizabeth II in 1961, during her state visit to Ghana after the country's independence.

GHANA

Africa

While in London, Nkrumah was involved in the 5th Pan-African Congress, laying plans to free African colonies from British rule. Nkrumah's academic mentors determined that his thesis was not the "right type" for the anthropology department, reflecting the ways academic departments policed the work of many non-White scholars. Returning home in 1947, Kwame Nkrumah went on to lead the successful independence fight and became Ghana's first prime minister in 1957 and first president in 1960. As a politician and scholar, Nkrumah critiqued then-contemporary anthropologists' vision of "African socialism" being promoted in places such as LSE and rejected their nostalgic tendency to idealize traditional precolonial African economies as classless, nonhierarchical, or idyllic. He argued, instead, that using contemporary redistributive economic systems was the best way to end the harms of exploitation in modern African societies.

Socialist governments of the 20th century sometimes came into being through class struggle—that is, people from lower classes struggling against people from upper classes to win control over a larger share of the economy. Anthropologists and others have done extensive research aiming to understand what conditions brought about the rebellions, revolts, and revolutions that sought to displace old economic systems with new forms of socialism. One proposal is that every unequal economic system—regardless of its form—has a breaking point at which the mass of people will no longer tolerate poverty, exploitation, or suffering. But this proposition does not seem well-supported by anthropological evidence. Throughout human history, there have been many societies with high degrees of inequality or exploitation; not all of these have had large-scale class struggle or revolts.

One perspective that anthropology offers on rebellions, revolts, and revolutions focuses not on the reality of material poverty or economic oppression but on how those subjected to it view it. That is, revolt against an economic system is brought about by a broken social contract. According to this hypothesis, people within a society have a shared set of cultural values and expectations about what their role in society affords them, especially regarding subsistence and survival. These values and expectations as to what people should be afforded can vary quite widely: There is a range of attitudes across societies toward how much hunger, poverty, inequality, or preventable death is tolerable.

But when enough people perceive that they are being denied the economic roles and the protections they *believe they should be afforded*, rebellions, revolts, and revolutions can result. This explains why such factors as ideology are so important to maintaining the exploitative features of economic systems. Neoliberal capitalism, for example, has been associated with a core belief that people's economic success directly reflects their talent and hard work, much more so than their life circumstances. If people are poor, the logic goes, this can be explained as a personal failure for which they should bear full responsibility. Such beliefs can permit and reinforce massive economic inequality, including promoting the idea also that there is no need to address its structural causes.

REDISTRIBUTIVE SYSTEMS TODAY

Anthropologists continue to study new efforts to experiment with redistributive systems, often in democracies and postcolonial settings. Socialist Cuba, with an active redistributive economy in place today, is a country that provides basic necessities, such as healthcare, to citizens. But Cuba is not without inequality. Based in Santiago de Cuba, the island nation's second-largest city, medical anthropologist Hanna Garth has been researching the changing eating patterns of post-Soviet era Cubans since 2008. Garth's work highlights the contradictions of contemporary Cuba, in which moral commitments to human well-being persist alongside booming market activity designed to fulfill desires for living "a good life."

In the wake of the socialist revolution of 1959, food and other goods and services were more equitably shared across society than they had been before. But after the fall of the Soviet Union in the early 1990s and the subsequent integration of more market-based economic institutions, Cubans found themselves increasingly responsible for managing the acquisition of food on their own. Garth's work reveals how, in a place where "nobody dies of hunger," the search for the right types of food nonetheless has become highly stressful. Everyday life in Cuba can now involve many hours of labor and stress related to accessing food that meets the standard of a "decent meal," an important component of a good life. This effort includes talking to contacts about where food can be found, undertaking long walks between different outlets to search for food, and waiting in shopping lines to get the items needed to prepare a complete meal (**Figure 9.33**). While people deploy many different tactics to get the foods they want, they rarely succeed. And because certain forms and combinations of food—such as tender seasonal corn or pork to accompany beans and rice—are so important to their cultural identity and social position, people feel forced to do things they resent, such as buying on the black market.

This is one of many reasons that anthropologists who study both economic and food systems often advocate for the importance of food sovereignty. While not eschewing markets and trade, advocates of food sovereignty envision mixed economies in which reciprocity and other nonmarket exchanges (especially of food) have a large role. The residents of Deanwood who opened our chapter, sharing the food from their community gardens, are one small but successful example of this. In Indigenous communities, in particular, this

food sovereignty The right of people to control how food is produced and to exercise this right to produce healthy and culturally valued foods.

mixed economy Economic activity in which multiple sets of rules and norms simultaneously operate to govern how materials, services, symbols, and ideas are transferred between people or groups.

FIGURE 9.33

A Cuban definition of a dignified and decent meal includes a specific balance of meat, vegetables, and starches, especially rice and beans (shown at top right).

means recognizing the right of people to govern their ancestral land, economic relations, and food production. Rather than seeing food as a mere commodity, Indigenous food systems can be understood as especially important to sustainable ways of life, because they prioritize living in a sustainable relationship with nature and upholding reciprocal responsibilities to care for the land.

MIXED AND ALTERNATIVE ECONOMIES

It is a mistake to view human economic development as a steady line of progression from reciprocal hunter-gatherers to redistributive agricultural societies to various forms of capitalism. Economic anthropologists see that perspective as mostly inaccurate because, while at each stage humans indeed added new forms of economic activity, the older systems never went away. Over time, human economies have become more and more mixed. Yet the illusion that there is only one economy that truly counts—capitalist markets measured by gross domestic product (GDP), stock prices, and economic growth—remains a major barrier for people to recognize the diversity within current economic systems and contemplate other possibilities.

Mixed economies—which interlace multiple modes of production—are present in almost every society today (**Figure 9.34**). Predominantly capitalist economies, such as those in the United States and England, nonetheless rely on kin-based gifts and exchanges of labor for childcare or household tasks. Social democracies, such as those in Sweden and Norway, have capitalist markets that are comprehensively integrated with redistribution strategies to reinforce

Kotzebue

ALASKA

UNITED STATES

North America

(a)

(b)

FIGURE 9.34

(a) Alaskan Native subsistence hunters braid seal gut for communal consumption in Kotzebue, Alaska. Anthropologists have found in Iñupiat communities that subsistence, reciprocity, and market exchange coexist in stable mixed economies. **(b)** A mushroom kiosk at the Wild Food Gatherers Guild in New York's New Amsterdam Market captures mixed economies—where gathering livelihoods interface with markets and alternative economies—in the context of contemporary capitalism.

equitable access to healthcare, education, and other social services. Contemporary socialist countries, such as China, are today deeply engaged with capitalist markets. Members of hunter-gatherer and subsistence societies, too, sell excess meat or crops at the market, engage in wage labor and labor migration, and pay cash for children's school fees. In American Indian, Alaskan Native, and First Nations communities in North America, for example, hunting and gathering are deeply intertwined with sharing economies, market exchanges, and government distribution of resources.

Mixed economies provide people with different ways to get food and other resources, from producing to bartering to purchasing. However, while mixed economies can help protect households from poverty, they are not foolproof. Sometimes mixed economies fail along multiple lines, producing food insecurity or famine.

MORAL ECONOMIES

One major contribution to our understanding of how people defend themselves against such failures has been anthropologists' work in revealing the moral economy. A moral economy has three elements: shared justice norms, economic practices that uphold the justice norms, and mechanisms of social pressure to enforce the justice norms. In Bolivia, for example, anthropologist Amber Wutich has detailed how people build moral economies—through the culturally shared belief that "water is life"—in water-scarce informal communities on the outskirts of the city of Cochabamba (**Figure 9.35**). Most water-insecure households are dependent on high-priced water sold by unregulated "pirate" water trucks. Yet in interviews with water vendors and clients, she found that unionized water vendors worked together to ensure that people could afford the water they needed. Using *yapas*—an Indigenous market practice of giving small gifts to customers—water vendors gave their clients extra gifts of water that lowered water costs. When households ran out of water, most could also depend on reciprocal relationships with their neighbors to provide a bucket or two of water. This mixed economy example illustrates how moral economies work.

subsistence society A society that produces the basic material necessities for survival, such as food, water, housing, and clothing, but without creating surpluses.

moral economy A system of economic beliefs and behaviors consisting of (1) shared justice norms that uphold a right to subsistence and survival; (2) economic practices, such as reciprocity, that uphold the justice norms; and (3) social pressure mechanisms such as gossip or protest to enforce justice norms.

FIGURE 9.35

Cochabamba, Bolivia, where many households do not have the water they need, has seen determined resistance to government efforts to privatize water (such as in 2000, shown here).

North America

MEXICO

Guadalajara

Living with poverty—having to worry continuously about how to meet basic needs—can fundamentally erode people's capacity to engage fully in a moral economy because they simply don't have enough to share. While doing research in Guadalajara, Mexico, before, during, and after the neoliberal economic reforms of the 1990s, cultural anthropologist Mercedes González de la Rocha found that people's time and money became increasingly scarce. Working extra jobs, or otherwise struggling to get by, meant people were too busy and stressed to even maintain the friendships and other social relationships in which reciprocal sharing is embedded. This highlights how social life is always entangled with economic life, including in complex mixed economies.

In any economic system, extreme scarcity can erode social connections, even where those relationships based in trust and reciprocity have historically been highly valued. When entire communities are impoverished, even the most active sharing economies can't protect people through risk-sharing and self-insurance. Anthropologists agree that some trends in neoliberal capitalism, such as low wages, loss of social safety nets, and focus on individual responsibility, have thus been an important component in eroding reciprocity-based social insurance systems. Moreover, many economic anthropologists find that the incursion of capitalist markets into social lives—such as through the commodification of many different aspects of family life and friendship—makes it harder for everyone, not just the poor, to draw on social support when times are tough.

Increasingly, anthropologists observe that people in many different parts of the globe are forced to rely on transfers of labor or goods secured through unstable, weak, and short-term reciprocal relationships. Examples include our reliance on "sharing apps," the gig economy, and the caregiving economy (such as childcare and eldercare). In such settings, relationships are formed quickly, used for support, and then abandoned. These sharing relationships are quite different from the rich and meaningful social ties that characterize Ju/'hoansi *hxaro*, Mexican *confianza*, and other systems based in lifetime relationships of reciprocity. Rather, these "throwaway" sharing relationships instead tend to violate the norms of moral economies or to adhere to them only during the brief duration of the relationship. These weakened reciprocal sharing networks may be linked to higher rates of emotional distress and social isolation.

BUILDING BETTER ECONOMIES

So, what are possible solutions that anthropological research suggests to the challenges posed by modern economic systems? Most anthropologists working in this area recognize and seek to amplify the sustainable, equitable, and solidarity-building economic activities that are already occurring all around us. Here we highlight four such practices: rotating credit associations, barter-based market systems, worker cooperatives, and community gardens.

Rotating Credit Associations

Tandas are a kind of trusted lending circle or rotating credit association found in Mexico and anywhere where people with cultural ties to Mexico live (**Figure 9.36**). Cultural anthropologist Carlos Vélez-Ibáñez tracked people's use of tandas in the western United States and northern Mexico. He found that tandas, usually containing 10–12 participants, are used by people in all walks of life: laborers, teachers, informal vendors, even upper-class elites. In Mexico, over 60% of people use tandas or other informal systems to raise credit. The group rotates payouts so that each person gets a turn. (For example, if 10 people

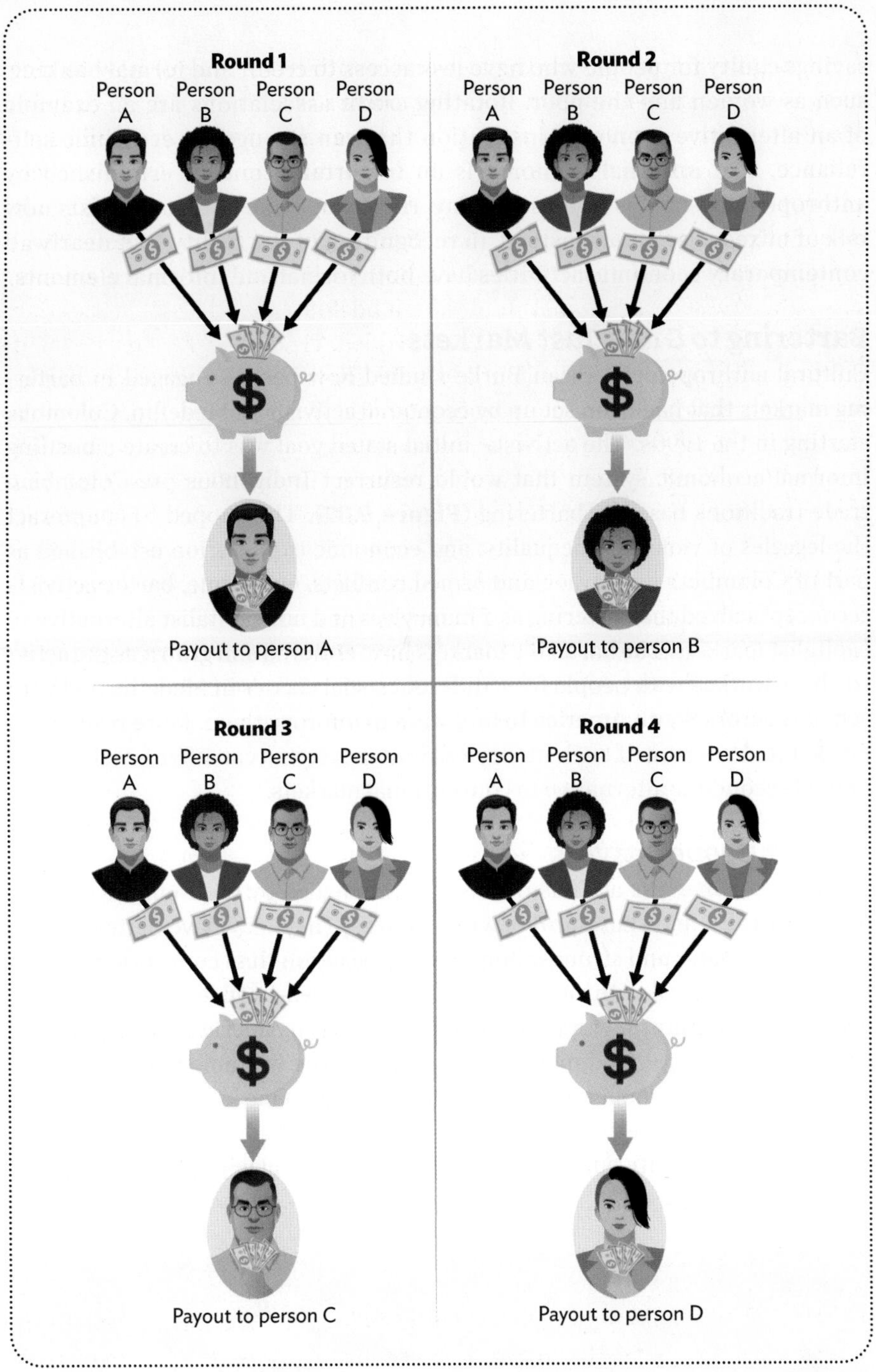

FIGURE 9.36

Every person pays in regularly for the duration of the tanda, no matter when they are scheduled to get a payout.

Round 1

Person A Person B Person C Person D

Payout to person A

Round 2

Person A Person B Person C Person D

Payout to person B

Round 3

Person A Person B Person C Person D

Payout to person C

Round 4

Person A Person B Person C Person D

Payout to person D

pay in $100 regularly, payouts to each person total $1,000.) Tandas are used for many reasons: to raise money for a business, to save money for a big vacation or gift, or even to pay for school. In U.S.–Mexican border communities, Vélez-Ibáñez found that tandas are one of the major sources of credit for low-income households and can help kick-start entrepreneurial ventures.

Rotating credit associations like tandas have been around for a long time and have emerged in many different places globally as a grassroots solution to economic problems. The detailed work of anthropologists has helped to demonstrate to those outside the systems that they work well and make a real difference in helping people get by. Rotating credit associations help people get established as entrepreneurs in the formal economy. They are especially important for those who are unbanked and working mainly in the informal economy, including undocumented immigrants. They improve

formal economy Legally regulated economic activity, estimated to characterize about 40% of the world's employed population.

unbanked Lacking access to formal banking institutions.

informal economy Economic activity that is not legally regulated or protected, estimated to characterize about 60% of the world's employed population (2 billion people). Examples include babysitting, cottage industries, unlicensed street vending, undocumented labor, criminalized sex work, and the black market.

COLOMBIA

Medellín

South America

worker cooperative A business that workers own and self-manage.

savings equity for people who have less access to credit and formal banking, such as women and the poor. Rotating credit associations are an example of an alternative economic institution that can strengthen economic self-reliance. The informal economy is an important concept established by anthropologists and is still used today. However, some anthropologists now talk of mixed economies instead, in recognition of the reality that nearly all contemporary economic activities have both formal and informal elements.

Bartering to Grow Just Markets

Cultural anthropologist Brian Burke studied how people engaged in bartering markets that had been set up by economic activists in Medellín, Colombia, starting in the 1990s. The activists' initial stated goal was to create a bustling informal economic system that would resurrect Indigenous pre-Columbian trade traditions based in bartering (**Figure 9.37**). They hoped to counteract the legacies of violence, inequality, and economic exploitation established as part of Colombia's drug trade and armed conflicts. Over time, barter activists reconceptualized the bartering as a moneyless and noncapitalist alternative to capitalist markets. The bartering markets have endured and grown as the activists have worked with people from different social classes in Medellín and with scholars across South America to find ways to improve them. More research is needed to determine if such moneyless barter systems can offer a viable, sustainable economic alternative to conventional markets.

Worker Cooperatives

Worker cooperatives are businesses that are owned by their employees, run democratically, and share profits with workers. They may have better worker productivity rates and stronger employee satisfaction than conventionally run businesses. Cultural anthropologist Marcela Vásquez-León led a major project examining agricultural worker cooperatives in Latin America as they struggle to compete in global food markets. In one study she was able to compare two small agricultural cooperatives in rural Paraguay. One cooperative exports organic sugar to Eastern Europe, and the other exports bananas to Argentina. The banana cooperative is more conventional, working with private for-profit

FIGURE 9.37

A Colombian barter market is shown.

FIGURE 9.38

A fair trade sugar cane cooperative in Arroyos y Esteros, Paraguay, is shown here.

companies and the government to sell their produce. Their efforts are relatively precarious financially, because they are directly competing with many very large international companies that produce and market bananas.

The sugar cooperative is organized around principles of social justice and is working with international development agencies (**Figure 9.38**). In doing so, the cooperative is able to market itself as "fair trade" to foreign buyers, and this has helped it gain an advantage over its market competition, as well as connecting it to larger global initiatives such as sustainable development. This work shows how even small worker cooperatives can promote positive social change by supporting grassroots development, reducing poverty, and addressing income inequality. Such innovative worker cooperatives, committed to and embedded in local communities, are a potentially important model for alternative forms of *solidarity economies*, worthy of further investment supporting their experimentation.

Community Gardens

Our final example brings us back to the opening of our chapter. Many communities are developing alternative community production efforts, with the hope of growing a solidarity economy to produce food and other goods. These efforts include community farms, handicraft collectives, and worker-led efforts to revitalize abandoned factories. Such initiatives aim to revitalize mixed and noncapitalist economies to support production and redistribution, often pushing back against social and economic inequalities. Like the Indigenous food sovereignty movement discussed earlier, many such alternative production efforts are ultimately focused on our most basic food needs: gardening, farming, and food sharing or trading. This is not only because food is a basic essential for life but also because food is culturally meaningful, historically shared, and intimately tied to exchange systems. The Deanwood residents, introduced at the start of the chapter, are building their collective food self-reliance through community gardening, bartering, and sharing. More than being a mere material food production effort, the community gardens are also an important symbolic way to highlight their collective care, concern, and resistance to external capitalist forces (such as the death of locally owned stores). Food sharing—dividing hunted, fished, or gardened items with others, giving gifts of cooked food, and eating meals together—has always been central to human social connections and likely always will be.

solidarity economy **An approach to economic development designed to put people over profit, such as fair trade, rotating credit associations, worker cooperatives, and community gardens.**

9

Food and Economic Systems

An anthropological perspective on economics examines all of human history to understand how diverse economic arrangements—including those defined by reciprocity, redistribution, and markets—have helped humans survive and thrive.

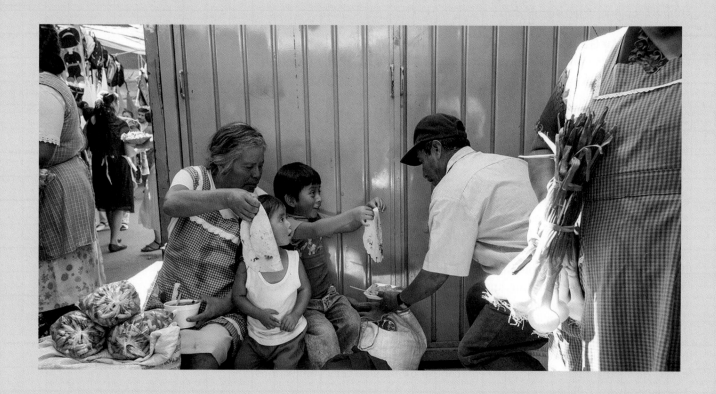

9.1 | Reciprocity: The Foundation of Human Exchange

Explain how reciprocity serves as a fundamental organizing construct in human economies.

- The earliest human economic systems were based on sharing and reciprocity, capacities that evolved as part of the human behavioral repertoire around 500,000 years ago.

- Reciprocity, or give-and-take, is the foundation of human economics. Reciprocity can be more or less self-interested, depending on the social distance of the exchange partners.

- Reciprocity can be used as a form of social insurance.

KEY TERMS
> balanced reciprocity
> barter
> exchange system
> food sharing
> generalized reciprocity
> labor
> negative reciprocity
> reciprocity
> social insurance

9.2 | Markets

Connect key turning points in the history of human societies to the emergence of different kinds of market economies.

- Markets and long-distance exchanges have been documented for more than 4,000 years.

- Markets are a special form of reciprocity, often with balanced or negative exchanges conducted between socially distanced partners.

- All economic systems can create inequalities in status and wealth, but the form this takes depends on the mode of production: kin-based, tributary, or capitalist.

- Starting around 500 years ago, new forms of capitalism (merchant, industrial, neoliberal, and postindustrial) emerged when different kinds of goods or services were privatized and commodified for profit. These radically changed human cultures.

- Anthropologists have contributed to understanding market economies by explaining how rational self-interest is bounded by people's knowledge, culture, and values.

KEY TERMS
> body projects
> bounded rationality
> capitalism
> chattel slavery
> citizen
> commodification
> common-pool resource
> common-pool resource institution
> consumer
> cultural capital
> deindustrialization
> industrial capitalism
> market
> means of production
> merchant capitalism
> mode of production
> money
> neoliberalism
> postindustrial capitalism
> private property
> private property regime

9.3 | Redistribution

Explain how redistributive economies have worked in the distant past, recent past, and present.

- Redistributive economies, which concentrate resources and services centrally and then distribute them out in new ways, have existed for thousands of years.

- Ideology has a role in causing or preventing revolts and revolutions that aim to change economic systems.

- Postcolonial states have experimented with many different kinds of socialist economies to address the harms of past extractive and unequal economic systems.

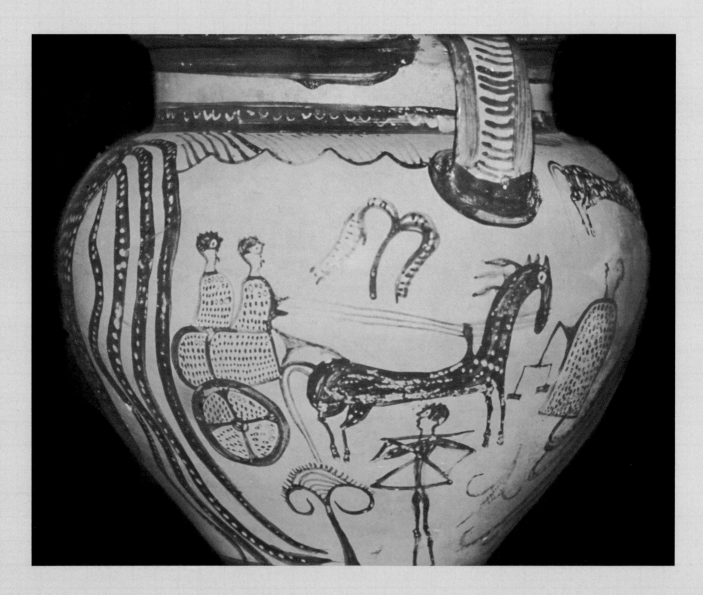

9.4 | Mixed and Alternative Economies

Define mixed economies and efforts to build alternative economies to promote economic equity.

- New forms of economic exchange keep emerging, but the older ones never go away. Today, anthropologists find that nearly all societies include elements of mixed (redistributive, market, and reciprocal) economies.

- Social insurance mechanisms, like generalized reciprocity, have been eroded by extreme poverty and inequality, a lack of time, and weakening social relationships.

- Moral economies help address this precarity. These exist where people (1) share a justice or survival norm that is (2) upheld by economic practices like sharing and (3) enforced through social pressure mechanisms like gossip or protest.

- Anthropological research is exploring how alternative economies (e.g., barter, rotating credit associations, worker cooperatives, community gardens) may support economic justice, social solidarity, and environmental sustainability.

KEY TERMS
> formal economy
> informal economy
> moral economy
> solidarity economy
> subsistence society
> unbanked
> worker cooperative

War and Group Violence

Forensic anthropologist Fredy Peccerelli arrived in New York as a political refugee in 1980, at the age of nine. His family had left Guatemala quickly in the midst of a 36-year civil conflict after his father received death threats by mail. The government, suppressing a leftist insurgency supported in part by Indigenous Maya, carried out *genocide*, in which an estimated 200,000 Guatemalan men, women, and children "disappeared" and were killed.

Over a decade later, Peccerelli returned to Guatemala as part of a team of forensic anthropologists to help search for the dead. The first few months of work digging in one village yielded 40 coffee sacks of teeth and bone fragments to take back to the lab. Several decades and some 10,000 bodies later, Peccerelli is still in Guatemala as the director of the Guatemalan Forensic Anthropology Foundation (FAFG), a nongovernmental organization he helped found. The foundation locates massacre sites and carefully cleans, exhumes, transports, and then examines the skeletons in their laboratory in Guatemala City. First, they establish the cause of death through evidence in the form of bullet holes and machete cuts on the skeleton. Then they try to determine who the individual was. They approach potential family members to request DNA samples to compare to the skeletons. The final part of the journey for each missing person is, hopefully, the return of their remains to their families (**Figure 10.1**).

A VIOLENT SPECIES

Humans are a highly cooperative species. One consequence of the human trait of identifying with and organizing around varied social identities—and with that the ability to form in-groups and out-groups—is that sometimes people come together to do harm to others. Sometimes this harm is physical, but the ability for one group to harm another is also built into the way societies are organized as structural violence. Anthropologists study all of these processes, past and present.

LEARNING OBJECTIVES

10.1 Warfare in Primates and Humans
Compare organized aggression in primate and human societies.

10.2 Norms, Rhetoric, and Willingness for Warfare
Identify conditions that encourage modern warfare.

10.3 Structural Violence
Assess the processes that underpin structural violence.

10.4 Fighting Back: Resistance, Refusal, Revolution, Reconciliation
Evaluate ways that groups fight back against violence, and identify potential supporting roles for anthropologists.

genocide Sustained and purposeful intent to destroy a group of people, in whole or in part, through killing and other acts of violent removal.

FIGURE 10.1

Forensic anthropologist Fredy Peccerelli (right) and survivor and human rights activist Rosalina Tuyuc Velásquez pay their respects at the gravesite of a Guatemalan genocide victim recovered and identified by Peccerelli's forensic anthropology team.

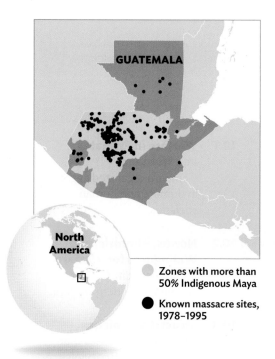

GUATEMALA

North America

● Zones with more than 50% Indigenous Maya

● Known massacre sites, 1978–1995

aggression **Behavior motivated by a desire to harm another.**

violence **Use of extreme aggression intended to hurt or inflict lethal or nonlethal damage.**

warfare **Organized violence between socially distinct or autonomous groups of people.**

Importantly, the foundation's forensic analysis of the skeletons has resulted in unassailable scientific evidence of massacres, which has been used to corroborate videotaped witness accounts. Together, these have led to convictions of military leaders for crimes against humanity, even decades later.

Cultural anthropologist Linda Green spent several years doing ethnographic fieldwork in Guatemala listening to the widows of men killed in that same state-sponsored violence in the 1970s and 1980s. Her research shows that even after the massacres stopped, the fear of violence continued to permeate everyday highland Maya lives. People didn't want to speak out because they were, as Green says, "socialized to fear." The fear of retribution by the government was so profound that it had become a collective societal experience, not just one felt by individuals. It created wedges of distrust within previously close communities, families, and friendships. The FAFG's work, in bringing those responsible to justice, is helping alleviate the fear and distrust.

Humans seem to be the only species to engage in organized aggression, violence, and warfare for solely ideological reasons. In Guatemala, this warfare took the form of removal and subjugation by the state of its own citizens who were deemed politically threatening (mostly Indigenous Maya), through genocide and related fear tactics. And it was the officials supposedly meant to protect those people (government leaders, their military, and the police) who organized, approved, or did most of the killing.

Why are humans not like other animals that only kill because of a physical need or a real threat? Why do humans sometimes band together to harm each other in such extreme ways? And can we stop it from happening? In this chapter, we explore what anthropological research has revealed about how and why humans wage war and engage in other, less overt—but equally devastating—forms of organized, institutionalized violence. Such knowledge can inform the recovery from the deep societal harms of organized violence (as demonstrated by the work of anthropologists such as Peccerelli and Green), as well as help us find ways to predict, avoid, and deter it.

We begin by examining the evidence for the history of human warfare using primate, archaeological, and cross-cultural ethnographic data. We analyze the factors that tend to encourage forms of group violence such as warfare. We then explore harder-to-see violence that stems from oppressive societal structures and inequalities. Finally, we identify how groups that are the target of all these forms of violence find ways to fight back and how anthropologists can help with that effort.

WARFARE IN PRIMATES AND HUMANS

Warfare and other forms of systematic violence committed against one group by another are based on people's identification as members of socially distinct groups. This capacity for constructing social identities based on group membership is a basic trait of our species. But many monkey and ape species are also able to form and re-form clearly defined groups, distinguishing between their own in-group from members of other groups. However, warfare also requires the capacity to engage in coalitionary aggression, meaning that two or more individuals join together in an effort to harm others of the same species.

Other than humans, chimpanzees are one of very few primate species that have been observed to use coalitionary aggression. This insight came from thousands of hours of careful observation of the chimpanzees (our closest living relatives) in the Gombe area in Tanzania (**Figure 10.2**). Jane Goodall and her team began observing the wild Gombe chimpanzees in the 1960s. Over time, they saw chimpanzee social groups form and split. In the 1970s, the researchers documented a rash of lethal raids between two chimpanzee alliances in the north and south of Gombe. The conflict began as a larger group split, after which

coalitionary aggression When at least two individuals jointly direct aggression at one or more individuals from the same species.

FIGURE 10.2

Jane Goodall has been observing chimpanzees at Gombe, Tanzania, since she established the Gombe Stream Research Center there in 1965. Here she follows a family group on a foraging expedition in 2014.

two alliances formed, following different dominant males. The two groups then engaged in a four-year conflict that resulted in the violent death of every male in the southern alliance. The northern group males took over their territory and mates.

But is this coalitionary violence exhibited by chimpanzees akin to human warfare? There are important differences in both motive and scale. The Gombe raids seemed to be motivated only by access to more food and mates, whereas humans will organize large groups to attack or otherwise dominate other groups for purely ideological reasons. For example, in all the decades of observing the primates at Gombe, never was a chimpanzee seen to attack another as revenge. The intensive killing in the four-year Gombe conflict was also an anomalous series of events, not repeated since. Human warfare, since the first establishment of agricultural villages and city-states, is far more common. Male chimpanzee raiding parties are careful to avoid confronting similarly sized or larger groups, preferring to attack and kill only when they have a clear numerical advantage. This means the chimpanzees who raid in groups face relatively little risk. Organized warfare among humans often carries substantial physical risks on both sides. Chimpanzee raiding parties are often composed of related males. Humans willingly fight together with others they are unrelated to, a key characteristic of many modern human armies but one that is a very recent part of our history as a species.

HUMAN VIOLENCE AND WARFARE IN THE PAST

Given these distinctions, modern humans appear to be meaningfully different than other animals in their willingness and capacity to engage in warfare for psychological (that is, nonmaterial) reasons. Does this behavior have a deep history in our species' lineage, or is it likely a product of more recent, complex human societies? One proposal is that early humans became fully capable of organized aggression alongside the developments in language, group identity, and social cooperation that allowed other complex, coordinated activities. This happened after 250,000 years ago. But humans' expanding symbolic capabilities would also have allowed for emerging moral frameworks for deciding when violence should and should not be used.

Certainly, early *Homo* species were capable of physical aggression against their own. Isolated incidents of violence have been identified at the cave site of Gran Dolina in Spain, dating to around 800,000 years ago. Excavations revealed the preserved remains of several individuals who seem to have been butchered and cannibalized (**Figure 10.3a**). Other sites across Europe, Africa, and Asia that date to 500,000 years ago have also yielded fossil bones that indicate interpersonal violence among Middle Pleistocene *Homo*, such as cut marks and healed fractures in locations on the long bones of the skeleton indicative of hand-to-hand fighting (**Figure 10.3b**).

On the basis of the available fossil evidence, though, such cases appear to be rare. It seems that humans and our hominin ancestors perhaps sometimes attacked and even killed others but that, for most of our evolutionary history, our ancestors lived in small, cooperative groups with little evidence for systematic and organized intergroup violence.

The first archaeological evidence of organized warfare does not appear until about 13,000 years ago. Prior to that time, human societies were mostly composed of mobile hunters and gatherers. Such groups left little trace of their

(a)

FIGURE 10.3

(a) Excavations at the site of Gran Dolina in Spain have recovered early evidence for violent trauma and cannibalism in the genus *Homo*. **(b)** Sites with fossil evidence of possible human violence in the Pleistocene epoch are depicted on this map.

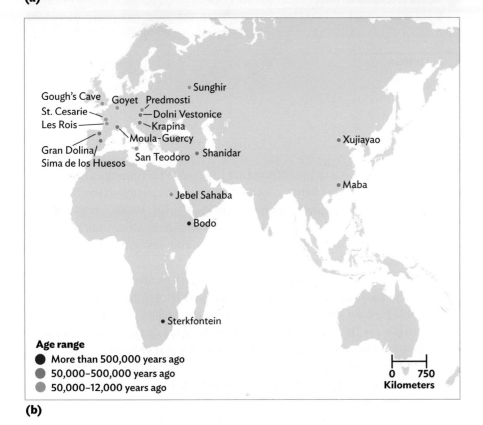

(b)

settlements or their activities in the archaeological record. This makes it hard to say for sure whether or not organized warfare (as opposed to smaller-scale physical fighting) predates the development of sedentary societies.

But starting about 13,000 years ago, when cemetery use became more common, we see the first clear evidence for mass fatalities probably attributable to organized tribal or ethnic warfare. The clustering of multiple skeletons with similar markers of trauma on the bones is one key way bioarchaeologists can recognize this.

tribal or ethnic warfare Conflict between social groups centered on, or legitimated by, distinctions in their ancestry, traditions, languages, cultures, or ideologies.

FIGURE 10.4

Burials with signs of violence were found at the archae-ological site of Jebel Sahaba in the Nile Valley of Sudan, dated to approximately 13,000 years ago. Many of those buried at Jebel Sabaha showed evidence of violent deaths, making it one of the earliest likely examples of warfare in the archaeological record.

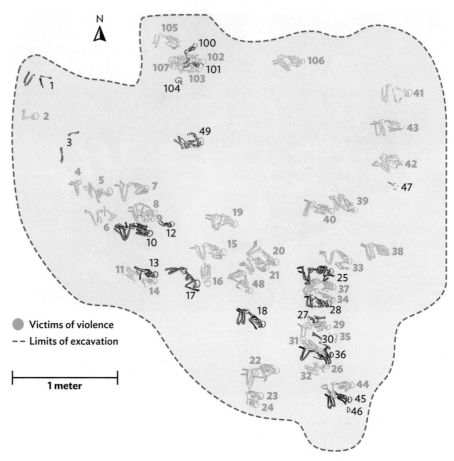

One of the earliest examples from that time period is from the archaeologi-cal cemetery site of Jebel Sahaba, located on the eastern bank of the Nile River in Sudan and used by hunter-gatherer groups. In the 1960s, archaeologists recovered the skeletal remains of 61 adults and children. More than half of the burials showed signs of death by violence, including several with stone arrow points embedded in their skeletons (**Figure 10.4**).

Around 7,000 years ago, when there were more permanent human settle-ments and population densities had increased, skeletal signs of violent trauma became much more obvious and common in the archaeological record. This is especially so as the earliest city-states emerged (as discussed in Chapter 8). Excavations at Hamoukar in Mesopotamia in what is now northern Syria have yielded signs of heavy bombardment using sling bullets on the former city walls about 5,500 years ago. These walls appear to have been destroyed in a single event, resulting in the city being sacked.

So, based only on archaeological data, warfare (as an institutionalized form of coalitionary aggression) was less commonly practiced prior to the start of such city-states. Our human ancestors evolved to be cooperative, highly social animals, and the highly organized violence that warfare represents is a very recent aspect of our shared history. What changed? One hypothesis is that competition intensified as populations increased in settlements located on and around land, water, and other resources that supported agriculture. For exam-ple, we saw in Chapter 8 that Robert Carneiro proposed in 1970 that agricul-tural settlements emerged into states wherever a concentration of resources, increased populations, and warfare existed in a circumscribed territory.

Yet, could this be the only reason? To try to answer this question, anthropol-ogists study present-day endemic warfare.

ENDEMIC WARFARE

In addition to the archaeological evidence that preurbanized humans had at least the capacity for warfare, studies of smaller-scale societies show that warfare can be endemic. That is, warring can be maintained as part of societal activities over a long period of time.

In seminomadic Turkana communities in Kenya, in eastern Africa, combat has been common for two centuries. Biological anthropologist Sarah Mathew began participant observation with Turkana warriors in Kenya in 2014 (**Figure 10.5**). Turkana are cattle-keeping pastoralists with relatively egalitarian communities. But Mathew's work has shown how Turkana sometimes quickly form war parties, composed of up to 300 men. Groups coalesce informally. Any warrior or local leader can propose and send messages out to other settlements to recruit friends and peers. Blessed and celebrated in their communities as they leave, and armed these days with assault rifles, the groups travel to villages outside Turkana territory with the ostensible goal of raiding for more cattle. Turkana homesteads depend on their cattle and other herding animals for food and long-term economic security. For example, men cannot marry until they have a sufficient numbers of cattle to give to their wife's family as a bride-price payment. After successful raids, won cattle are split among participants.

But Turkana warfare is not just about seizing cattle. Some of the attacks are in revenge for previous raids on their own communities. Social norms that emphasize the need to display bravery through raiding also seem to trigger men's willingness to join war parties and assume a social role as a warrior. Turkana men who refuse to fight or who desert a fight can be punished by their peers. The consequences can be severe, such as being tied to a tree and whipped and being required to sacrifice an animal from their herd.

endemic warfare Chronic state of low-intensity warfare between groups with little or no death and where the primary aim is not to control or destroy the enemy.

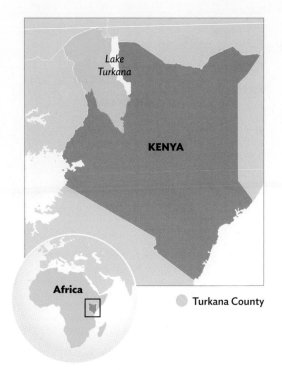

Turkana County

FIGURE 10.5

Biological anthropologist Sarah Mathew (far right) and team in community meetings in Turkana County, Kenya. Her research seeks to understand the cultural and psychological bases of endemic warfare.

Men who fight suffer different consequences, including injury and even death. The work of Mathew and her team has also highlighted that Turkana men who have seen more combat, especially those who have killed others or witnessed morally unsettling events such as civilian deaths, exhibit some symptoms associated with post-traumatic stress disorder (PTSD). PTSD is a psychologically debilitating condition affecting soldiers and others who have experienced violence. However, because being a warrior is so highly valued within Turkana society, there are postbattle rituals that help soldiers know they are supported by their communities. One purification ceremony held after a warrior kills an enemy for the first time involves being stripped of clothing and smeared with the blood of a slaughtered goat; the value of the goat and the donations of replacement clothing signal community support. Such communal rituals are held to help warriors manage combat-induced traumas.

Anthropologists have documented other small-scale societies engaging in endemic warfare. The 1963 documentary *Dead Birds*, a classic of anthropological documentary cinema, shows sequences of ritual battles among neighboring Grand Valley Dani (Ndani) groups in the central highlands of the island of New Guinea (**Figure 10.6**). Bouts of long-spear and bow-and-arrow fighting erupted as revenge for a death or stealing a pig. The warfare is described as ritual because it is often conducted with the goal of symbolic victory, rather than an overt effort to kill others. Fighting would pause for rain or cease if someone died. Communities celebrated capturing weapons in dances of victory. These patterns of Dani coalitionary aggression suggest the fighting was about more than competition for resources. It was also about valuable enhancements to social status, especially for men. It could serve as a means for men to build a reputation for courage or masculinity, or it could provide the mechanisms to

FIGURE 10.6

Dani boys practicing to become warriors, recorded as part of an anthropological study in 1961. At that time, the Dani were still engaged in endemic warfare. The "dead birds" in the ethnographic film released in 1963 refers to the spears or other items taken by warriors as battle trophies.

restore and reinforce group (not just family) honor after being the victims of recent raids or battle defeats.

Sarah Mathew and her colleagues have proposed, on the basis of Turkana, Dani, and other case studies of endemic war, that natural selection has favored the continued inheritance of cognitive traits in humans that allow a propensity toward coalitionary aggression under certain conditions. Mathew suggests that when warriors in one village band together to create a war party and raid another group, they aren't reflecting an evolved "war psychology" in humans. Rather, warring is one result of the evolution of a basic human psychology to want to follow group cultural norms and institutions. That is, while willingness to join in violence might enhance human survival in some limited cases, it can be better explained as a byproduct of the otherwise extremely adaptive psychological mechanisms that encourage us to want to live in groups and be willing to defend them.

NORMS, RHETORIC, AND WILLINGNESS FOR WARFARE

As we have seen throughout this text, humans are intensely cooperative and have evolved to live in highly complex social groups. We didn't evolve to be warlike and violent but rather to be cooperative, with clear and strong ties to the groups to which we belong. As a result, humans want to follow group norms and customs and to live harmoniously in groups. But this sometimes also leads to warfare.

GROUP IDENTITY AND WILLINGNESS TO FIGHT

Human group affiliations can lead to strong sentiments of "us versus them." A range of studies has shown that humans are much more willing to help those they identify with most closely (their in-group). For example, we generally are more likely to support spending on humanitarian assistance if it is for people from the same social groups to which we ourselves belong. Similarly, humans are more tolerant of harm happening to those beyond their in-group (their out-group). When direct conflicts arise between groups, many humans are willing to provide enormous resources, and even sometimes their lives, to support their in-group.

Group affiliations were likely common in our ancestral past, but they are hard to identify in the fossil record. However, we know that our close primate relatives establish group affiliations, suggesting it is part of our species' evolutionary history. For example, chimpanzees, like humans, yawn when they see another chimpanzee yawn. However, contagious yawning is more common when a member of their in-group is yawning, rather than a member of the out-group. And as we saw in the first section of this chapter, coalitionary aggression is also seen in chimpanzees, revealing some kind of group or community membership.

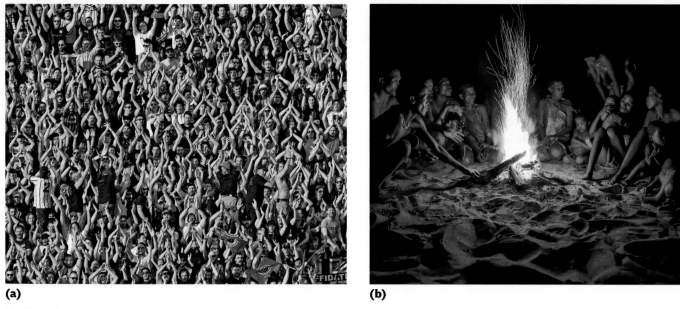

(a)
(b)

FIGURE 10.7

The strong alliances that help people band together to fight others can form in many different contexts, including **(a)** between strangers today around sports teams (as shown by Atalanta soccer fans in Bergamo, Italy) or **(b)** in sharing stories around a fire (as in a Ju/'hoansi community from Namibia).

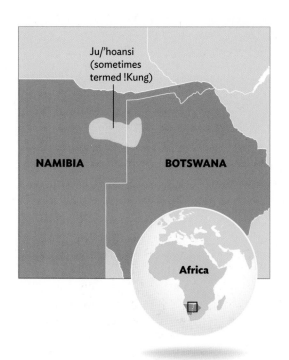

Today, we identify our in-group communities based on factors such as ethnicity, religion, nationality, gender, age, geography, language variety, or even sports fandom (**Figure 10.7**). Some group identities are remarkably durable, while others are quite flexible, forming rapidly and dissolving or morphing as situations change. Allies can split to become competitors, and competitors can join together to fight what is seen as a greater threat. This is often seen in large legal or political groupings, for example, where new conflicting groups can emerge around events such as elections, law changes, or key policy decisions. These new groups often dissolve quickly afterward.

Anthropological studies with hunter-gatherer societies show that communication and language (including gossip and arguments) are crucial to impacting how small groups strengthen their alliances. For example, cultural anthropologist Polly Wiessner has documented not just *what* the Ju/'hoansi hunter-gatherers living in the Kalahari desert around the Botswana-Namibia border talk about but *when* they talk about it. She has shown that gossip is used throughout the day as one means to sanction and correct social behaviors within the group. The evening talks around the fire focus on communicating larger cultural ideals and bonding the group through storytelling.

The strength of our in-group ties depends on how similar we believe we are to those in our group, how much we interact, the ways in which we are dependent on one another, and how much group membership is tied to our own social identities. Narratives regarding a group's past, sometimes informed by interpretations (accurate or not) of the archaeological record, can also drive group identity in ways that propel group violence. For example, in the lead-up to World War II, German leaders in the Nazi party sponsored excavations to "prove" Germanic groups had long lived outside the contemporary boundaries of Germany. These distortions of the archaeological evidence were then used to justify the Nazi invasion and genocide of other groups.

Similarly, colonists and, later, the U.S. government deployed archaeological rationales to justify genocide committed against Indigenous people in North America. Early excavations of elaborate mounds and earthworks were used to

FIGURE 10.8

The site of Cahokia has the remains of a complex of structures on elevated earth mounds built and occupied on the Mississippi River by Indigenous North Americans over 1,000 years ago. With 30,000 people living there at its peak, it was an important trading and ceremonial center. At that time, Cahokia may have been larger than the emerging center of London in medieval Europe.

advance a myth that Native Americans of the colonial period would not have been able to build the impressive structures and so must have killed the "Mound Builders" (**Figure 10.8**). Following this rationale, settler-colonists justified displacing and killing Indigenous people because they were not credited as the original occupants of North America.

Humans have evolved psychological mechanisms that make us desire and value group membership, and these mechanisms can motivate acts of violence that reinforce and protect our membership alongside unrelated others. But does this mean that the violence of war or genocide is inevitable? Definitely not. Anthropologists have identified some cultures that socialize members strongly against violence. Through comparisons of cross-cultural case studies, anthropologists have been able to identify the social mechanisms that characterize social groups that are less prone to engaging in both within-group violence and intergroup conflict. These include having an equitable social structure, marrying and exchanging with people in outside groups, having child socialization practices and decision-making procedures that prioritize nonviolence, and socially reinforcing nonviolent values and norms such as severely shaming, excluding, or otherwise punishing people who use violence to solve conflicts in their everyday lives.

For example, the Semai people of the central Malay Peninsula are semisedentary subsistence farmers who clear forests to grow rice and root crops. They view themselves as nonviolent people, and aggression is seen as immoral. Within villages, conflicts are settled and justice is restored by talking things through in long formal meetings. People who show aggression toward others are shamed, and displays of anger in daily life are discouraged by gossip and social rejection. More generally, when anthropologists looked at the records of lethal aggression in ethnographies from 21 contemporary hunter-gatherer groups, most of the lethally violent events were what we could characterize as homicides. Only a minority of the violent events would be classified as warfare.

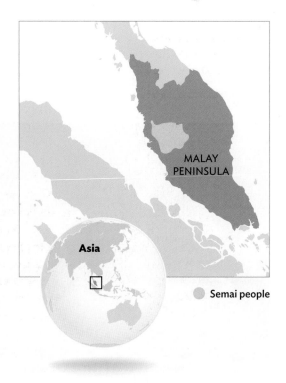

Semai people

Ancestral lands
of the Waorani

FIGURE 10.9

Waorani people, from the Amazon region of Ecuador, march in 2021 to demand justice around the government bidding of an oil project in their territory.

rhetoric Persuasive use of written, spoken, and visual language to organize and maintain social groups, construct meanings and identities, and consolidate power.

dehumanization The act or process of removing human qualities, traits, or dignity from a person or group of people.

metaphor theory The idea that metaphors impact how we think about an idea or object.

FIGURE 10.10

U.S. print media used the rat metaphor to describe terrorist attacks on New York's Twin Towers in 2001.

"WHY DOES EVERYONE JUST ASSUME MY GUILT?... "

Norms around violence can also change within groups over time, shifting from more violent to more peaceful and back again. The Waorani people in Ecuador are former hunter-gatherers who are now mostly settled in the Amazon rainforest. They value individuality, self-reliance, and independence, and they understand violence as a way to assert and reflect these values. They have historically had some of the highest homicide rates ever recorded, because many disputes are settled through physical altercation using spears and other hunting tools. However, attitudes toward violence as a means to resolve conflict are changing in this group. Waorani have become increasingly savvy at instead deploying peaceful political protest, for example, as a means to fight back against outsider incursions on their rights, such as from those seeking to extract resources from rainforests (**Figure 10.9**).

RHETORIC AND WILLINGNESS TO FIGHT

Rhetoric—in the form of speeches, radio broadcasts, or memes and other social media—is an important factor in driving group willingness to engage in conflict. Linguist Adam Hodges has analyzed the speeches given by U.S. President George W. Bush following the Twin Towers terrorist attack in New York in 2001, which killed almost 3,000 people. Hodges identified an array of metaphors used in the speeches to remove all sympathy for the terrorists.

Consider this quote from President Bush, who was also head of the U.S. Armed Forces: "We will find who did it, we'll smoke them out of their holes" (September 15, 2001). In this quote, language is used to convey burrowing animals or those that live underground, such as rodents. When language likens people to animals, it is a form of dehumanization. Authority figures often dehumanize people that are viewed as enemies, undesirable, or threatening (**Figure 10.10**). It is easier to motivate a nation to join in hunting down and killing nonhumans. This example demonstrates the metaphor theory in anthropology, which posits that metaphors impact not only the way we discuss ideas but also how we think about and experience them.

Leveraging a sense of group identity—and generating a sense of threat to that identity—can be a powerful means to promote the worst forms of organized aggression, including genocide. Cultural anthropologist and lawyer Darryl Li uses ethnography to understand the way these beliefs are created and spread in international conflicts. One of his techniques is to interview former fighters after a war is over. This reveals how the people who instigate conflicts understand and justify them. One of Li's first ethnographic studies was in Rwanda, Africa, where government forces and the Hutu ethnic majority killed members of the Tutsi ethnic minority. In 100 days in 1993–1994, over half a million Tutsi people died. Six years later, Li interviewed prison inmates who had pled guilty to participation in what became known as the Rwandan genocide. Li also interviewed farmers living in the conflict zones, activists, and government officials.

One of his most notable observations was the influence of radio broadcasts in shaping people's understanding of the conflict as it was occurring. Access to printed materials was limited for many people living rurally in Rwanda at that time. Radios, which were cheap and widely available, were the main way that rural Rwandans connected to the wider world. Li described how radio propaganda encouraged genocide across the countryside, using an accessible "street style" of discussion alongside popular music. Authoritative-sounding radio disc jockeys used a range of rhetorical devices to build hate toward Tutsi people. For example, radio broadcasters persuasively lamented the loss of the cultural identities of the Hutu-dominant majority. The broadcasts also included information on where Tutsi were located—and encouraged Hutu farmers in rural areas to hunt Tutsi people out and massacre them. Some referred to the station as "Radio Machete," implying that killers had a machete in one hand and a radio in the other (**Figure 10.11**).

FIGURE 10.11

Radio Machete was broadcast from this office building in Kigali, Rwanda, during the Hutu genocide against the Tutsi.

Li's work was about radios, now a waning technology. But his findings about the role of rhetoric to spread tolerance for hate crimes is useful for understanding the potential implications of newer and farther-reaching media, such as Twitter (X), Facebook, TikTok, and other social media platforms. Some sites, for example, have in recent years become hubs for the dissemination of White-supremacist sentiments and propaganda (Chapter 14), which in turn have led to real-life violence against minority groups.

WHY MOSTLY MEN?

One of our important social identities within human societies is tied to gender (Chapter 11). Notably, across most human and nonhuman primate communities—from the Gombe chimpanzees to the Turkana and Dani groups to urban street gangs—it is overwhelmingly males who (often willingly) engage in violence. And warriors in all standing armies around the globe are predominantly young adult men working in male-dominated systems.

Studies of chimpanzees suggest that male-initiated violence against other males and females is directly or indirectly related to gaining better access to mates and reproduction. This may mean that chimpanzee males are inherently more aggressive than females. There is currently no clear evidence one way or the other that human males have evolved to be more innately aggressive beyond dealing with material threats. However, anthropologists have gathered significant data to show how critical social context is to learning and enacting aggression, most especially for males (**Figure 10.12**).

One reason that men, more so than women, engage willingly in modern warfare is that it appears to provide benefits by signaling and enhancing masculine identities and maintaining their social status. Ideas around war as masculine and masculinizing dominate contemporary military operations, and they affect how soldiers understand their roles and goals within conflict settings. In 1999–2000, cultural anthropologist Liora Sion conducted an ethnographic study of the "Grizzly" artillery battery and the "Bulldog" infantry company, two Dutch peacekeeping units of the North Atlantic Treaty

FIGURE 10.12

The world's standing armies are highly skewed toward men and masculine values; here army soldiers are on parade in Budapest, Hungary.

Organization (NATO). Sion lived and participated with the peacekeeper unit members from the first stages of their training in Germany through periods of deployment in Kosovo and Bosnia and Herzegovina, joining them on patrols, while they manned checkpoints and guarded missions, and during off-duty time. She found that the peacekeepers from the Netherlands identified strongly with masculine self-images, talking about how the military was composed of "real men." In depicting masculinity in relation to their military service, combat was at the center of that imagery.

Yet, as the name suggests, peacekeeping operations often use military-trained forces to do the opposite of waging warfare, such as orchestrating humanitarian missions. This created a disconnect between what the male peacekeepers wanted and expected to do (fight and win) with what their role as peacekeepers required them to do (avoid conflict and help). The warrior attitude and the belief that humanitarian work was "feminine" and fighting was "masculine" meant that the peacekeepers sometimes viewed the locals as enemies rather than people to help. The military leaders had to deal with peacekeepers who wanted more conflict, even though this was the opposite of their mission. And the Dutch military often talked about the mission in the traditional military language of fighting and war. This masculinized rhetoric around fighting was one of the reasons, Sion explained, the soldiers were so frustrated about their roles as "peacemakers."

STRUCTURAL VIOLENCE

So far, we have been discussing overt physical aggression between and within societies, as reflected in warfare and genocide. But harmful violence need not be carried out directly. It can be built into the structures of society in ways that indirectly create systematic violence by one group (those with power) toward another (with much less power). Anthropologists use the term structural violence to describe harms done by social structures that result in highly inequitable patterns of human suffering. Slavery is one of the clearest examples of a structurally violent institution, enforced by powerful strata in a society through their collective beliefs of how things should be. We will encounter many examples of the forms and effects of structural violence in the chapters ahead, such as through patriarchy (Chapter 11) and racialization (Chapter 14).

Suffering here, as anthropologists use the term, includes not only pain but also other disabling losses, circumstances that prevent people from meeting their most basic physical and emotional needs. By expanding the idea of the harm of structural violence to include all types of extreme harm—from illness to hunger to psychological trauma—anthropologists then have a way to recognize root causes and so better alleviate many forms of human suffering.

structural violence When social, economic, and political systems prevent some groups from meeting their basic needs, creating and reinforcing inequities in ways that benefit other groups with more power.

suffering Pain, distress, loss, or deprivation that results from the enactment of unequal power structures within society.

ROOT SOURCES OF STRUCTURAL VIOLENCE

Throughout human history, more powerful groups have dominated weaker groups to gain access to resources, and they have used social, cultural, regional, and political differences as the justification. Imperialism occurs when a country uses military, economic, or political power to take control over another

imperialism The efforts of a government to control another country or peoples using military, economic, or political power.

settler colonialism A system of domination and violence in which people are removed from their land through displacement or genocide; often involves the annihilation of the prior inhabitants' language, culture, livelihoods, and ways of life.

Wari Empire

country or group of people. Imperialism harms humans in many ways: It undermines political freedom, removes wealth and health, destroys language and cultural systems, and demotes social status. This is particularly evident in the patterns of physical, psychological, and social damage that anthropologists have recorded in postimperialist nations. Colonialism is a form of imperialism in which governments or settlers take over territory with the goal of exploiting its people and material resources. In settler colonialism, the goal of exploitation is linked with the goal of replacing the original inhabitants through depopulating the area, enslaving or forcibly removing people, and/or forcing assimilation. Colonialism has been an especially profound force in reshaping human societies and cultures, and it appears to reach back to the emergence of complex societies.

Imperialism, too, is not a recent human practice. The Wari empire emerged around 1,500 years ago near the modern city of Ayacucho in Peru, pre-dating the Inca empire that came later. By tracking the spread of archaeological sites with known dates that contain particularly distinctive Wari items (such as their ceramics), archaeologists have determined that the Wari quickly spread to dominate a large area that engulfed many other cultural groups. New Wari sites were often located in agriculturally productive areas, and thus their acquisition of the land of other culture groups likely benefited people from the Wari heartland by expanding access to food crops.

The land seems to have been captured through military-style might and conquest as the Wari empire grew. Rates of violent trauma in skeletons excavated from burials also went up markedly at the same time Wari artifacts start appearing at those locations, and Wari-style ceramics depict Wari warriors engaged in battle (**Figure 10.13**). Between 600 and 1000 CE, these distinctive ceramics spread throughout Peru, providing a means to track Wari colonization of new agricultural areas as their empire expanded. But violent conquest may also have been accommodated by other strategies common to imperial expansion, such as religious conversion. Studies of isotopes in people's bone and teeth, which indicate where people spent their childhoods, suggest people may have been purposefully brought from other parts of the Wari empire as ritual sacrifices.

Often imperialists use war or other threats of violence to assert dominance over other groups and their resources, as appears to be the case with the Wari. Other forms of imperialism use economic coercion or enticement to advance the best interests of the dominant states. For example, when Europeans migrated in large numbers to the Americas after 1492, they engaged in settler colonialism, in which they remade the American territories entirely, decimating cultural institutions including foodways and gender relations. In addition, the European colonists and settlers also killed millions of Indigenous people by introducing new diseases—such as measles, smallpox, and typhoid—to populations that had not yet acquired immunity.

Some physical signals of suffering associated with the earliest Indigenous residential contact with Europeans are especially evident in what are now the U.S. states of Georgia and Florida. This zone of Spanish missions is especially well-

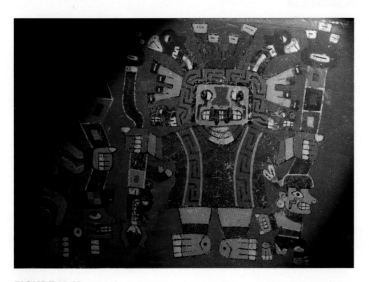

FIGURE 10.13

This Wari-style ceramic shows a staff god from Conchopata, Peru, a secondary center of the Wari empire. The spread of Wari items like this allows archaeologists to track the expansion of the empire through time and across space.

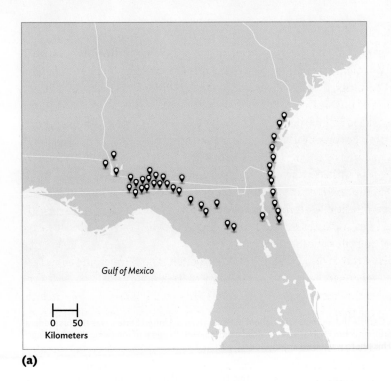

(a)

Gulf of Mexico

0 50
Kilometers

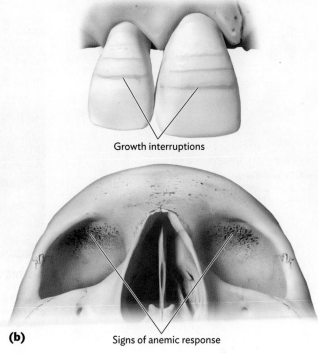

Growth interruptions

(b)

Signs of anemic response

FIGURE 10.14

(a) This map shows Spanish missions in what are now Florida and Georgia circa 1670. **(b)** Archaeological human remains show more signs of anemic response in the bones of the eye sockets and growth interruptions on teeth, both associated with worsening nutrition, compared to before the establishment of Spanish missions.

documented through historical documents, archaeological excavations, and bioarchaeological examination of the remains of people buried there (**Figure 10.14**). As local Indigenous groups were integrated into Spanish colonial priorities, such as producing maize (corn) for the European markets and engaging in Catholic religious practices, the health of bodies measurably degraded. In the periods after the establishment of Spanish missions, bones show increased evidence of childhood illnesses such as anemia or parasitic infections, due to poor sanitation. The teeth also recorded more signs of malnutrition and stress during childhood, shown as lines of slowed growth appearing across their surface. These signals of new physical harms seem to be associated with a less diverse diet consisting mostly of maize (identifiable in the stable isotope analysis of bone) and a likely more sedentary lifestyle that exacerbated the additional harmful effects of newly introduced infectious diseases.

Structural violence embedded in European colonialism and imperialism certainly harmed the health of Indigenous peoples. But there are many other related ways these types of structural violence can decimate—or even eradicate—whole cultural groups. Because culture is so embedded in language, the imposition of new languages can rapidly undermine the identity, autonomy, and culture of colonized people. Language death, when there are no remaining speakers of a language, is closely associated with the loss of land and cultural knowledge. Because they are so central to people's identities, these multiple losses can also be profound sources of long-term grief and trauma.

European settler colonialism in the Americas also profoundly devastated surviving local cultures through social institutions, such as schooling policies. For example, in the late 1800s, the federal governments in the United States and Canada sent agents to forcibly remove Indigenous children from their families, land, and culture. This was part of a broader effort to assimilate, subjugate, and eliminate Indigenous peoples. In these compulsory schools, children were banned from speaking their own languages or practicing their own cultural

language death When a language is no longer used and has no living speakers; also called extinction.

FIGURE 10.15

Opened in 1879, Carlisle Indian Industrial School in Pennsylvania, United States, was the first federal government boarding school for Native American children, with the goal of removing their language and traditions. This photo was taken around 1900.

traditions, and they were often subjected to physical and sexual violence as well as malnutrition (**Figure 10.15**).

Although the boarding schools have now closed, the harm they inflicted continues to be felt today. Studies by biological anthropologist Zaneta Thayer, in collaboration with public health experts, have revealed that individuals with parents from Northern Plains tribes that were forced into residential schools continue to have higher rates of suicide. And individuals who had both parents and grandparents attending the schools have even worse mental and physical health today, suggesting how the harms of structural violence can continue to accumulate across generations.

The latest studies of residential schools and similar culturally devastating policies are incorporating epigenetic data to track harm across generations. Thayer leads studies of how people's experiences of social discrimination and oppression in New Zealand later manifest as greater physical and mental risk in their children or grandchildren (**Figure 10.16**). Epigenetic studies suggest that trauma exposures due to institutional violence can impact DNA expression—and with it, negative health effects—up to two generations later (Chapter 3). On the basis of cases like this, public health officials increasingly recognize historical trauma as a potentially significant determinant of health disparities today.

STRUCTURAL VIOLENCE AND CONTEMPORARY SUFFERING

These studies of health effects consider the transmission of past trauma across generations. But many new and updated forms of structural violence are evident today, continuing to harm whole groups. Imperialism and colonialism created many of the notable features of our current global political and economic system, one today characterized by global health inequalities and the dominance of European languages and practices in areas such as politics, trade, and education.

As a result of centuries of such structural violence, some countries (collectively referred to as "the Global North") are enriched and empowered, while other countries ("the Global South") are relatively impoverished and

FIGURE 10.16

Biological anthropologist Zaneta Thayer (right) conducts research on intergenerational effects of social stress in New Zealand.

historical trauma Cumulative, multigenerational trauma resulting from extreme physical or psychological violence (including oppression) targeting specific communities, including social decimation and cultural erasures.

disempowered. Countries that are seen today as "underdeveloped" largely became so as a result of historical colonial-imperial processes that destroyed their local economies, resources, governments, languages, and cultures. Anthropologists use the term coloniality to describe the social structures that were put in place during European colonialism, persisted after its end, and are still with us today. And these continue to develop into many different forms of violence.

Physical health is an arena where impacts of coloniality are often most apparent. Physician–anthropologist Paul Farmer (**Figure 10.17**) worked in Haiti for decades, and much of his influential work focused on explaining very high rates of human immunodeficiency virus (HIV) infection, resulting in acquired immunodeficiency syndrome (AIDS), as well as other infectious diseases. He explained the very high rates in Haiti today are a result of historical processes of coloniality, a manifestation of these indirect structural forms of violence against people. A long history of colonial abuse, political instability, corruption, infringement of human rights, and outright poverty are associated with low levels of education, poor healthcare, and hunger. These factors act in complex interrelationships to produce vicious cycles that lock in poverty and suffering across generations.

Farmer explained the way unfair social forces differentially impact people through the story of Acephie Joseph. When Haiti's large Péligre dam was built to provide electrical energy, Acephie's home valley was flooded. The dam provided money and power to the Haitian military. The only way to support herself and her family was to sleep with a general who had a family of his own. But soon after, he died. So Acephie moved to the capital to do domestic work as a maid. She met a new man, became pregnant, was diagnosed with AIDS, and died. If Acephie had not been poor, female, and displaced, she probably wouldn't have been exposed to HIV. The decisions to flood her valley were far removed from her, and they benefited others at the cost of her own life. Women and ethnic or

coloniality Exploitative and ethnocentric social structures that were established during colonialism and are still in place today.

FIGURE 10.17

Paul Farmer (1959–2022, far right) was a physician–anthropologist who cofounded Partners in Health, a nongovernmental organization that provides direct medical care to people in Haiti and other countries with severely underfunded health systems and high rates of HIV and other infectious diseases. He suggested the provision of basic healthcare is one means to reduce the suffering associated with structural violence.

globalization The increased economic, social, and political linkages between nations and peoples due to the rapid movement of people and exchange of ideas both within and across national boundaries.

North America

—•— Triqui migrant route

racial minorities, because of their lower power within many societies, tend to be more severely impacted by structural violence—suffering more and dying sooner.

The legacy of coloniality allows for much of the structural violence in the world today, including Acephie Joseph's experience in Haiti. But new forms of structural violence are also being invented and propagated through globalization. One example is a system of governance known as neoliberalism, in which markets are less regulated, government services are shifted to the private sector, and citizens are treated as consumers (Chapter 9). Opponents of neoliberalism argue that it turns people's basic rights (such as health and education) into commodities only available to those who can afford them. As such, neoliberalism can be a powerful driver of structural violence.

Another cultural anthropologist who is also a physician, Seth Holmes, spent five years working with migrant Triqui Indigenous farmworkers from Oaxaca, Mexico (**Figure 10.18**). Traveling alongside the farmworkers, on a harvest route that runs from the Arizona border to California to Washington and back home to the highlands of Oaxaca, Holmes documented profound structural violence within their strawberry-picking work. He shows how farmwork keeps people in poverty while destroying their bodies with grueling work, inadequate housing and healthcare, and dispiriting discrimination that can impact mental health. Holmes explains how neoliberal systems—including the laws, policies, and agreements that regulate markets and immigration—provide cheap labor for competitive global agribusinesses.

In this context, migrants provide cheap labor to employers that can be easily and maximally exploited, since their immigration status makes them unable to pursue rights to fair pay, workers' compensation, sick days, healthcare, or other labor rights. The net result is a form of structural violence that keeps low-paid workers at the bottom of the economic ladder and reinforces the wealth and power of those at the top—and further benefits, if in a smaller way, anyone who buys a cheap container of fresh red strawberries or iceberg lettuce at a North American supermarket. Holmes's work also shows how such practices become so routine as to be unquestioned. He documents how managers and social workers who could help improve farmworkers' conditions think of Triqui bodies as innately better for the hard, damaging tasks at the bottom of the social ladder, a determination justified in part because the Triqui are "closer to the ground."

FIGURE 10.18

Triqui migrants from Mexico pick strawberries on Washington state farms, where cultural anthropologist and physician Seth Holmes studied how exploitative labor practices and lack of healthcare access for immigrants act as harmful forms of structural violence that literally "break" their bodies while they work to provide food for society.

FIGURE 10.19

South Asian "guest workers" are pictured in the fields of Barbar, a village in the Kingdom of Bahrain.

Cultural anthropologist Andrew Gardner similarly tracked the ways in which the labor system in the Kingdom of Bahrain created structural violence against immigrant "guest workers" (**Figure 10.19**). Gardner explains that in Bahrain and the other wealthy countries of the Persian Gulf, the *kafala* system allows citizens to import migrant workers from India and elsewhere in southern Asia. Citizen employers control immigrant workers' free movement, labor, and legal status. These employers sometimes abuse this power by using the threat of deportation to force the workers to accept low wages, physical abuse, and other forms of violence. Gardner documented abuses against guest workers, including murder, rape, stabbing, illegal imprisonment, workplace injuries, suspicious suicides, and many kinds of scams. This structural violence, Gardner argues, is primarily shaped by the kafala system of labor migration but is also informed by inequities born of gender, class, and religion. This is another powerful example of how social structures can be leveraged to enact violence against some groups for the benefit of others, by marginalizing members of some groups to the point they cannot meet their most basic physical and emotional needs. It was no surprise, then, that migrant workers in places such as the United States and Bahrain—living with substandard housing, little healthcare access, and low wages—were at heightened risk of death from COVID-19.

INTERNATIONAL DEVELOPMENT PROJECTS: CAUSING OR CORRECTING STRUCTURAL VIOLENCE?

At any moment, there are thousands of large international development projects being implemented in lower-income countries in Latin America, Africa, Asia, and the Pacific. The nations and agencies that initiate these projects, such as the United Nations Development Programme, the World Bank, the U.S. Agency for International Development (USAID), or the China International Development Cooperation Agency, are funded by high-income or otherwise powerful nations.

Development projects intend to improve human well-being predominantly through economic means, such as building a tourism infrastructure to provide new forms of employment, designing programs that keep young people in school to reduce unemployment, reducing corruption within legal systems, or improving water systems to increase small-scale agricultural productivity. In these ways, economic development draws people and countries more tightly into the global network of laws, banks, businesses, and values that were established (and are largely run) by wealthy countries. Development itself is also a large and lucrative transnational industry, comprised of myriad large and small agencies funneling vast amounts of money.

Deepening and unretractable poverty is one consistent outcome of structural violence. Some development projects have been shown to not alleviate poverty so much as to make inequalities worse and further marginalize the very people the projects were meant to serve. Development projects can also impose and reinforce norms and values that align with those of capitalist donor nations, such as consumerism and individualism. The ways people become integrated through projects into global markets and media consumption can affect what foods people want to eat or clothes they wear. For example, people may begin to desire, save for, and purchase expensive sneakers produced by multinational corporations. These sneakers become important for people because they signal wealth and taste, and they can improve people's social status. But the sneakers are produced through the growing cheap labor pools in lower-income countries. Who benefits? The large multinational corporations and their shareholders in the wealthier nations.

Moreover, the donor agencies often provide development assistance to poorer nations even as large foreign-owned companies from the same countries accelerate ownership and extraction of a nation's most precious mineral or other natural resources—often for vast profit.

Some cultural anthropologists, informed by observing how these processes impact people on the ground, propose that international development is sometimes merely colonialism in a newer form. That is, development is a means for more powerful and wealthier countries to continue to maintain indirect control over, and extract benefits from, the resources of poorer countries (including labor). If colonialism is a form of violent domination, and development is a modern-day form of colonialism, then some anthropologists argue that we should be highly suspicious of the motivations behind development projects and concerned about the costs they will accrue to the countries accepting the aid.

Yet other anthropologists propose development projects provide an overall net benefit to the local communities. Some anthropologists work in international development, whether as their primary employment or serving as consultants. They help to design, deliver, or monitor projects. Anthropologists have unique and important skills that can improve the way projects work. Particularly, they have insights that can better predict some of the potentially harmful, often unintended, negative consequences of projects that fail to take local conditions, priorities, and needs into account. Development agencies recognize that community-based projects tend to become more effective and sustainable (and less likely to derail) when anthropologists are involved. Cultural anthropologists with long-term familiarity with the communities targeted in development projects can provide an important role, helping projects avoid creating new social divisions or further harming the most vulnerable.

For example, in Lesotho in southern Africa, a development project put up fences to privatize pasture as part of an effort to improve livestock management among local cattle farmers during drought (**Figure 10.20**). But the land had long been held by Basotho farmers as a "commons," a collectively owned resource.

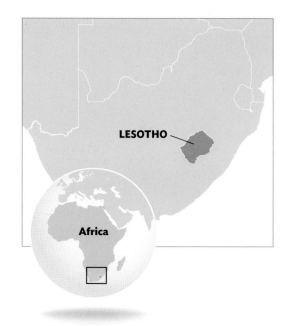

LESOTHO

Africa

FIGURE 10.20

Basotho people in Lesotho use cattle to plow agricultural fields.

So, the fences were pulled down. Any cultural anthropologist or archaeologist who knew about land use in the community could have predicted the fencing efforts would fail and been able to explain why. It could have saved time, money, and annoyance.

Looking at the big picture, though, the overall effort to change livestock management had many more problematic elements. The project was seeking to reallocate land to a few, making them wealthier and driving others into poverty, with the argument this was necessary to make the commercial management of livestock "sustainable." The wider effort also helped reinforce a repressive government in a rural area that had been resisting its power. The state's interests were being served more than the interests of local people.

In wider regional terms, cutting people off from farming livelihoods (by enclosing their lands and denying them access) also helped create a cheap migrant male labor pool for neighboring South Africa. These types of tensions, deciding what does good versus what does harm, are part of the reason that few topics in anthropology are as controversial as the ethics of engaging in international development efforts.

REDRESSING COLONIALITY IN ANTHROPOLOGY

Anthropologists have played an important role in showing how the legacy of colonialism continues to do structural violence. Decolonizing scholars are finding new ways to undo the influences of this legacy on anthropologists' own research practices and avoid additional harm done by applying traditional anthropological modes of investigation influenced by colonial projects.

Carolina Alonso Bejarano led a team of anthropologists and activist–researcher collaborators in a decolonizing study of undocumented migrant workers in New Jersey. By integrating less conventional research techniques with conventional ethnographic data such as interviews and field notes, the authors showed that the tools of ethnography can be used for social change. For example, the collaborators wrote and performed a one-act play as a way to communicate the findings of their research on work accidents. The researchers also

decolonization The act of challenging and removing enduring power structures created through colonization.

used their ethnography as a platform to inform undocumented workers about their rights under state and federal law. Focusing on workplace accidents and wage theft, the researchers urged immigrants to engage in direct action as a form of activism and to defend their rights as workers in the U.S. legal system.

As another example, the decision of Alonso Bejarano's coauthors, researcher–activists Lucia López Juárez and Mirian Mijangos García, to publish an academic monograph on immigrant rights in the United States under their own full names, given the risks associated with their unauthorized status, may inspire social change through fighting back. Furthermore, by doing research collaboratively with community members, the team was making efforts to displace the usual dynamics of coloniality, in which settler society researchers lead the study of people from colonized societies and marginalized groups. These kinds of experimentations with research practices are more common in linguistic and cultural anthropology but are increasingly being adopted across anthropology's other fields as a means to find ways to ensure anthropology itself is not complicit in any indirect form of violence.

FIGHTING BACK: RESISTANCE, REFUSAL, REVOLUTION, RECONCILIATION

resistance Pushing back against oppression and other forms of structural violence.

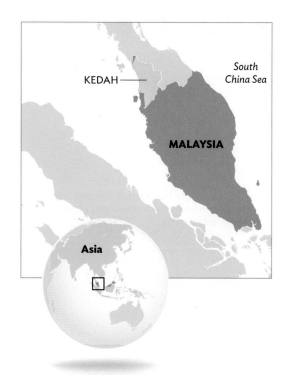

If dominance of one group over another is enacted through overt aggression, threats of violence, and more indirect structural violence such as that associated with the privileged systems set in place by colonialism, how do groups with less power fight back? Anthropologists' research is helping reveal how groups dominated by the threats of physical violence or subject to structural violence variously resist it, refuse it, revolt against it, and reconcile with it. We cover each of these tactics in turn in this section.

RESISTANCE

Resistance is the act of pushing back, publicly and privately, against oppression and other forms of structural violence. Cultural anthropologist James Scott proposed a theory of resistance in his books *Weapons of the Weak* and *Domination and the Art of Resistance*. Drawing on archival research and two years of ethnography in a Malaysian village in Kedah state, Scott explained how peasants and other marginalized groups resist material, status, and ideological domination. For example, people resist material domination in public ways by making petitions, boycotting, and striking. But they resist in hidden ways, too, with work slowdowns, by abandoning jobs and places, or by illegally occupying or poaching from restricted lands.

People can also resist status or ideological domination in other hidden ways, such as spreading rumors and gossip, telling stories and myths, and engaging in symbolic violence (e.g., burning a politician in effigy). After writing *Weapons*

FIGURE 10.21

Ngoni people perform in Songea, Tanzania, the site of a mass grave for more than 100 of their ancestors, as part of a commemoration of those killed in the Majimaji war.

of the Weak—but before publishing it—Scott went back to the same Malaysian village to ask people what they thought of the book. Scott recounts, "they corrected me in so many ways that I was faced with the possibility of writing a rather stupid book" and so, in keeping with decolonizing anthropological practices, he rewrote it. Resistance, it turns out, works for pushing back against anthropologists, too.

Sometimes resistance is very public and visible. For example, after years of forced labor following the occupation and colonization of Tanzania, multiple ethnic groups in Tanzania joined together in actively resisting German rule. This became known as the Majimaji war, taking place between 1905 and 1907, and it is estimated to have led to the deaths of well over 100,000 Tanzanians. South African archaeologist Nancy Rushohora is investigating the battlefields of the Majimaji war, first through archaeological survey and then through excavations at two battlefield sites (**Figure 10.21**). Although the Majimaji war was well-documented at the time, the written sources are almost always from the perspective of the German colonizers, not the leaders of the resistance or the lives of the Tanzanian fighters. Rushohora sees this work as important in documenting the resistance of people throughout Tanzania to German invasion and as resisting the dominant narratives of German colonization and conquest.

Language revitalization is another important way that colonized groups resist colonial violence, reclaiming some forms of power. Even when languages no longer have living speakers, they can still be reclaimed. If a language is documented, it is not extinct and can be awakened if and when people decide to study, practice, and learn to speak it. Daryl Baldwin (Kinwalaniihsia), an Indigenous linguist and citizen of the Miami Tribe of Oklahoma, and his collaborators revived the Indigenous language of the Myaamiaki people.

By 1846, most of the Myaamiaki, also called Mihtoheseeniaki, had been removed from their homelands in what are now the U.S. states of Indiana, Michigan, and Ohio and forcibly resettled to "Indian Territory" in what is now

language revitalization Process by which a formerly dead or "sleeping" language begins to be used and taught again.

Myaamiaki territory,
1650–1850

Oklahoma, United States. The dislocation and decimation of the Myaamiaki in the late 1700s was motivated in large part by the demand for beaver fur by White settlers. Many Myaamiaki were killed in warfare incited by White traders and settlers, but many also were killed due to infectious diseases for which they had no immunity. The era of federal boarding schools—in which English was compulsory and enforced with punishments—also exacted a high price on the everyday use of the Myaamia language. Through death, land decimation, and displacement, the Myaamia language was threatened and eventually the number of speakers decreased to none in 1960.

Typically, when language awakening (also called revitalization) is undertaken, the people revitalizing the language have access to written documentation, audio recordings, and elderly speakers of the language or "rememberers" (people who don't speak the language but had exposure when they were younger and thus have some knowledge of the language). In the case of Myaamia, there were no elderly speakers or even older members who could help with the language awakening. There were, however, documents by French missionaries in the late 17th to mid-18th centuries, followed by more documents developed by linguistics from the 19th and 20th centuries. Using this documentation, Baldwin and colleagues substantially awakened the language; there are now hundreds of people with some Myaamia language knowledge and a dozen or so people who are conversationally fluent. Today perhaps 500 people in Oklahoma speak the language regularly. The story of Daryl Baldwin's work and the revitalization of the Myaamia language is a hopeful one. It shows how acts of resistance can push back powerfully against attempts at linguistic and cultural erasure (**Figure 10.22**).

REFUSAL

Refusal describes acts that reject dominance in ways that go far beyond resistance. It is about refusing to acknowledge or engage with a dominant power and living in alternative ways, with or without the permission of the powerful. Examples of refusal include rejecting the sovereignty claims of a colonial power, declining an offer of citizenship or ethnic identity, or refusing to adhere to laws or norms that are unjust.

FIGURE 10.22

Like Myaamiaki members working to reawaken their Indigenous language of Myaamia, Elisabeth Mesa Calfunao is a rural primary school teacher. She grew up in Santiago, Chile. At the age of 25, she opted to fully embrace her Mapuche roots and migrated to what remains of her ancestral lands in Araucania. As an adult she learned to speak Mapuzungun, the Mapuche language, and now teaches it in rural classrooms.

refusal Acts that reject dominance, such as disobeying unjust laws.

Kahnawà:ke Mohawk anthropologist Audra Simpson introduced the concept of refusal as it relates to Indigenous sovereignty. Mohawk territory straddles the border between the United States and Canada, two colonial powers that refused to respect Mohawk rights to land, self-government, and self-determination. Simpson shows how Kahnawà:ke people incorporate refusal into their own political responses to such domination. For example, one strategy is to refuse to travel on a Canadian passport—traveling only on a passport that represents the Iroquois nations (including the Kahnawà:ke Mohawk). In this case, the act of refusal is also a demand for recognition of Iroquois sovereignty.

Importantly, Simpson critiques past anthropologists' representations of Mohawk culture. Using historical and ethnographic analysis, she explains how their accounts came to be incomplete, biased, and politically naïve. Simpson commits to refusal as part of her own research practice. In doing so, she refuses to reveal protected knowledge or facts that could compromise the fight for Kahnawà:ke sovereignty.

REVOLUTION

Revolutions are challenges to the state that seek to overturn its authority and establish a new government. They can be peaceful or violent, and peaceful protests can become violent in the face of state repression. Revolutions are aimed at overturning political orders that are seen as unjust or illegitimate.

Cultural anthropologist Carwil Bjork-James started his career in the United States as an activist, working in social movements to build solidarity among unions, environmentalists, and opponents of corporate globalization. His experiences sparked his passion to become an "ethnographer of revolution" while doing fieldwork in Bolivia (**Figure 10.23**). In the early 2000s, Bolivians protested against the privatization of water and exploitation of their national natural gas reserves. During the "Water War" and "Gas War," as the protests came to be known, Bolivians coordinated successful, large-scale labor strikes and blockades. By 2005, these protests—and the backlash against violent government repression—forced the resignation of two Bolivian presidents. Leading a majority coalition of Indigenous Bolivians aligned with unions and rural workers, Evo Morales rose to power as Bolivia's first Indigenous president.

Bjork-James's work details how Indigenous-led social movements created political reform that remade Bolivian society. Using oral histories collected from protesters, he explains how grassroots space-claiming actions, such as blockades and sit-ins, were essential to winning political power.

After 13 years in power, however, Indigenous President Evo Morales was forced to resign from the presidency in what many have called a coup. As a public anthropologist, Bjork-James led on-the-ground coverage of the resignation and its violent aftermath, as anti-Indigenous right-wing opponents sought to undo the plurinational society established by Morales and his political coalition.

RECONCILIATION

Reconciliation is a process designed to expose the truth about state repression and violence, establish responsibility for acts of genocide and terror, and enable a society to move forward in peace. We opened our chapter by discussing the work of Fredy Peccerelli and the Guatemalan Forensic Anthropology Foundation (FAFG).

Such processes of reconciliation, aided by anthropological forms of evidence, need not be on a national scale. Small local efforts matter, too. The collaborative community-based efforts in Florida related to the lost boys of the Arthur G. Dozier School for Boys (Chapter 2) were crucial to the Florida government passing resolutions acknowledging their role in past injustices and articulating a future commitment to "ensuring that children who have been placed in the State of Florida's care are protected from abuse and violations of fundamental human decency." In such projects, community reconciliation and healing can be seen as meaningful and important research results.

More broadly, anthropologists understand one of the ethical responsibilities of the field is to ensure that research clarifies how structural and all other forms of violence are caused, linking the symbolic, structural, political, and environmental conditions that reinforce domination and inequality and that undo people's capacity to resist it.

FIGURE 10.23

Cultural anthropologist Carwil Bjork-James has collected oral histories in the cities of Cochabamba, Sucre, and La Paz to explain how Indigenous grassroots actions led to winning political power and creating political reform in Bolivia.

revolution Challenges to the state with the goal of establishing a new government.

reconciliation A process designed to expose the truth about state repression and violence, establish responsibility for acts of genocide and terror, and enable a society to move forward in peace.

10

War and Group Violence

This chapter provides anthropological perspectives on violence and warfare in the past and present, including how and why people enact violence toward others.

KEY TERMS
> aggression
> genocide
> violence
> warfare

10.1 | Warfare in Primates and Humans

Compare organized aggression in primate and human societies.

- Human war and other forms of organized, coalitionary aggression differ from those of other species in greater scale, frequency, and motivations based in ideology.

KEY TERMS
> coalitionary aggression
> endemic warfare
> tribal or ethnic warfare

10.2 | Norms, Rhetoric, and Willingness for Warfare

Identify conditions that encourage modern warfare.

- Human social groups of unrelated people can form rapidly and use group identities to distinguish "us" and "them," providing the means for organized aggression at scale.

- While the human capacity for violence and warfare likely has a long history, war and other intergroup violence are not inevitable. Human societies can be configured to dissuade aggression and violence.

KEY TERMS
> dehumanization
> metaphor theory
> rhetoric

10.3 | Structural Violence

Assess the processes that underpin structural violence.

- Power is created and maintained through structural forms of violence that can exploit other groups and extract their resources. Anthropology provides tools to reveal and redress structural violence, such as the ongoing legacies of settler colonialism.

KEY TERMS
> coloniality
> decolonization
> globalization
> historical trauma
> imperialism
> language death
> settler colonialism
> structural violence
> suffering

10.4 | Fighting Back: Resistance, Refusal, Revolution, Reconciliation

Evaluate ways that groups fight back against violence, and identify potential supporting roles for anthropologists.

- People fight back against different forms of violent dominance and control through resistance, refusal, revolution, and reconciliation.

KEY TERMS
> language revitalization
> reconciliation
> refusal
> resistance
> revolution

Gender

Ethnographer C. J. Pascoe spent 18 months observing student behavior and language at school and during ritual events, such as dances and rallies, at River High, a school in California. "Damn, I was going to hit on you," said one 16-year-old boy, on discovering she was a researcher and not a fellow student. Such utterances are objectifying rituals, exemplifying the ways school social interactions are spaces of gender dynamics that help create notions of masculinity. Her analysis showed that one of the main ways that strict notions of masculinity were enacted at River High was through boys acting in hypersexual ways toward girls.

Students demonstrated little tolerance of male classmates for speech, dress, and acts deemed feminine, and they policed social behaviors by insulting one another with slurs such as "fag." Pascoe found, too, that while girls were expected to follow feminine gender schemas, their behavior was less trenchantly policed. This was partly because masculinity was so highly valued that cliques of girls engaging in more masculinized activities (such as basketball) actually got a status boost.

The strict (and sexualized) notions of acceptable masculinity that pervaded the school weren't just enacted by the ways students conversed. They were embedded in the entire way the school was organized, including the jokes teachers made in class, school dress codes, elective classes offered, sports participation, and school dances (**Figure 11.1**). Together, these examples built a hegemonic (dominant) form of masculinity, one in which men are situated socially above women. Masculinity isn't so much what males do but a social category based on what men are *expected* to do and constantly reminded about if they do not.

LEARNING OBJECTIVES

11.1 Gender, Sex, and Gender*Sex
Explain how gender is a fundamental organizing construct in human society, and describe why the combined term "gender*sex" captures both biological and social realities.

11.2 Binary Gender and Beyond
Explain how gender is constructed and performed.

11.3 Why Do We Have (Binary) Gender?
Assess the role gender may have played in human evolution.

11.4 Gender, Inequality, and Power
Assess how and why gender inequalities persist.

EXPRESSING GENDER IN APPEARANCE AND ACTION

Binary world views of gender shape our *habitus*, the ways we learn to perceive and thus move through the world. Habitus includes our body size and modification, the ways we dress, notions of beauty, and physical action.

gender Social, cultural, and/or learned phenomena relating to femininity, masculinity, and gender diversity.

masculinity Along with *femininity*, the collection of social roles and behaviors that are understood to be expressions of gender within a particular society or community.

femininity Along with *masculinity*, the collection of social roles and behaviors that are understood to be expressions of gender within a particular society or community.

schema A set of related social norms and rules that establishes how things should be within society.

FIGURE 11.1

Schools and other childhood institutions are organized in ways that can impose dominant views of masculinity and femininity. Historically in the United States, high school sports such as cheerleading and football exemplify this. However, increasingly young adults—including those in U.S. high schools—are actively challenging societal norms that require strict binary gender identities and that punish or reject those who do not conform.

binary Divided into two oppositional groups.

gender performance Repetition of socially sanctioned and recognized acts that create and cement gender identities for both self and others.

gender script Culturally shared gendered expectations, values, and practices within a society.

Societies have myriad ways to enforce how we think and act based on gender. School is one environment where such gender policing can be significant, with lifelong effects. But the processes of gendering start when we are born, or even earlier. As we will discuss shortly, sex assignment happens for most people at the moment of birth and is most commonly done along a binary male/female categorization. In this act of sex assignment, the new baby is immediately linked to complex social expectations of their distant adult self—including how they will look, who they will marry, and what jobs they will take.

It's important to note that having these gender expectations imposed on us is not the same as having a particular sexual-reproductive biology at birth. As influential gender scholar Judith Butler made clear in their research, we aren't born gendered but rather become gendered by interaction with others through repeated gender performance in front of others (in talk, dress, and so on). These interactions can include insulting or demeaning those who don't follow the expected gender script. So for many scholars like Butler who study gender, prior to acting like a man or woman (according to our society's norms regarding those categories), a person is without gender and must constantly create gender in every interaction. This can be described as "doing gender"—a set of actions that has to be redone every moment to maintain the identification.

Gender influences almost every aspect of human life. Right from the first moment that others assign us a binary gender (usually assigned at birth on the basis of having a penis or not), we are treated in a certain way because of it. Classifications of each of us as female, male, both, or something else are core to our social identities and constrain our opportunities. The binary gender system of River High was less rigid than some we will encounter in this chapter and more rigid than others. But the fundamental organizing principles it follows—of a social world composed of people categorized as boys and men versus girls and women—is recognizable anywhere across the globe. Anthropology helps us to recognize and understand how such binary gender schemas shape almost every aspect of our lives, to consider why they persist, and to imagine other possibilities. Challenging inequalities, both small (such as the dress code at River High) and large (such as pervasive male economic advantage), is a necessary aspect to consider in the analysis of gender in societies, because—as we will show—they are so pervasive and almost universal. Anthropology contributes to our understanding of why this is so in many ways.

In this chapter, we outline how the term "gender" both overlaps with and differs from that of "sex," and we observe the amazing spectrum of both sex and gender expressions. We then investigate how gender is constructed and performed. Looking at the specific experiences of people who don't belong to binary male/female categories further highlights the complexity of the interaction between gender and sex.

We explore the many ways that living with these binary gender schemas shapes our social identities, behaviors, experiences, and life trajectories. We take a deeper dive into one aspect of gender organization within societies that has been a particular focus of anthropological research for decades: the division of household labor by gender.

This discussion provides the background for considering two important puzzles related to gender. We investigate why we have gender at all and whether it can be understood as a function of our evolutionary past. Finally, we explore how and why it is that cisgender men consistently control most social institutions and maintain power over those of other genders. As we see, this pattern of inequality has direct implications for health and human rights on the basis of gender*sex, gender identity, and gender expression.

GENDER, SEX, AND GENDER*SEX

Defining gender is complicated by its intimate but often awkward relationship to sex. Ostensibly, sex is a concept based in our sexual-reproductive biology. Prior to the 1970s, anthropologists exclusively used the term "sex" to refer to both social and physical differences between men and women.

The term "gender" first appeared widely in academic use in the early 1970s as a means of challenging mainstream ideas about how these biological differences determined the kinds of things (e.g., jobs, sports) that men and women should or shouldn't do. The concept of gender as distinct from sex allowed women's social power to be discussed in new ways, challenging the assumption that their lower status in many areas was just a product of the natural order—assumed to be just the way things always were and should always be.

Over time, the two terms have often come to be used interchangeably in everyday English usage. An example is medical or governmental forms that ask you to check the box for either your sex or your gender.

But in recent years it has become clear that a distinction between sex and gender remains useful, especially for understanding the ways that people's sexual-reproductive biology and their social identities can diverge. For cisgender people, sex assignment at birth aligns with their later gender identities. But this is not always the case for transgender and nonbinary people.

cisgender Having one's internal sense of gender identity align with one's assigned sex at birth.

transgender Having one's internal sense of gender identity not align with one's assigned sex at birth.

nonbinary Not identifying as either man or woman.

FIGURE 11.2

A U.S. Marine punts a football sent by his wife, containing a gender reveal. The specific format of this ritual reflects cultural associations of footballs with boys and masculinity and the color pink with girls and femininity.

COMPLICATING SEX

Sex is often perceived as a stable and easily identifiable binary category—either male or female. But sex is more complex than that. At birth, babies are generally assigned a sex based on their external sexual-reproductive anatomy. This is recorded in their birth certificate, for example, as their legal sex. But this crude process of infant sex assignment often fails to recognize that a person's sexual-reproductive biology is a combination of many features that then become simplified to be defined in medical terms as male or female. This complexity includes primary characteristics such as the genetic makeup of one's sex chromosomes and the internal and external reproductive organs present at birth, as well as secondary sex characteristics that emerge at puberty, such as hormonal profiles, body hair, and amount of muscle mass or breast tissue.

Celebrations termed "gender reveals" have grown increasingly popular in a range of countries over the past two decades, aided by medical technologies. Symbols consist of pink colors for girls and blue for boys; these form a shorthand for biological sex (since sex organs themselves are rarely on public display), fusing gender and sex together in highly concrete ways (**Figure 11.2**).

But the presence or absence of a penislike sex organ does not tell us anything about other aspects of sexual development differentiation, and sometimes human bodies develop in ways that straddle male versus female, being both or neither. For example, in one small community in the southern Dominican Republic, a cluster of children sex-assigned at birth as girls suddenly started to develop male sex organs as they went through puberty. These children, who were raised as girls, subsequently chose male gender identities. Genetic tests helped to explain what was happening biologically. The children were born chromosomally male (XY). But they also shared a genetic mutation that delayed the development of the male external sex organs until they went through puberty.

In typical cases of fetal development in a designated male, it is around eight weeks after conception that a regular Y "male" chromosome becomes activated, and designated male sexual differentiation begins by transforming the undifferentiated gonads (sex organs) into testicles. Without this activation, a clitoris develops. In the Dominican case, the activation occurred once more hormones were present at the beginning of puberty. These children are medically termed as intersex, because they don't fit clearly into predefined male or female categories. Intersex individuals are but one example of the complexity and spectrum of characteristics that can influence our sex assignments.

● Chromosomal
● Gonadal
● Genitalia
● Physical manifestations

Female	Subtle variations	Moderate variations	46,XX testicular differences of sex development	Ovotesticular differences of sex development
● XX	● XX	● XX	● XX	● XX, XY, or mix of both
● Ovaries	● Ovaries	● Ovaries	● Small testes	● Both ovarian and testicular tissue
● Female internal and external genitals	● Female internal and external genitals	● Female internal and external genitals	● Male external genitals	● Ambiguous genitals
● Female secondary sexual characteristics (e.g., breasts)	● Subtle differences such as increased amount of male sex hormones or polycistic ovaries.	● Variations in sex development such as premature shutdown of ovaries. Some caused by variation in sex-development genes.	● Presence of male sex-determining gene *SRY*.	● Rare reports of predominantly XY people conceiving and bearing a healthy child.

Figure 11.3 provides examples of phenotypic variation within the sex spectrum. Human zygotes usually form with one of two chromosomal combinations, XX or XY, where XX is most often designated female and XY is designated male. Some XX and XY people are born without uteruses or testicles. But there are also people with differences in sexual development, including those who are XX chromosomally but have testes and functional sperm, those who are XY or XXY chromosomally but also have ovaries and give birth, and those who have one testis and one ovary.

Even with three possibilities for assigning sex at birth—female, male, or intersex—these descriptions don't fully encompass the wide variation in the array of sexual-reproductive traits actually present at any one time in any one person. In other words, the labels "female sex," "male sex," and even "intersex" are best thought of as social categories, not fully confirmed biological realities. These terms cannot capture the full complexity of human reproductive biologies, but rather they serve to approximate our socially agreed-upon ideas of "female sex" or "male sex." They reflect constructed social categories based on a "best guess" of an implied biology, not on a truly complete set of biological information or on our own self-identification. And as the Dominican case shows, assigned sex may be changed later in a person's life due to new information.

Because of the inherent limitations of sex assignments, and because the assumption that sex and gender identity are always exactly the same often socially devalues people for whom this is not the case, some scholars (Anne Fausto-Sterling and Sari van Anders, among others) propose joining the two terms together as *gender*sex*. This is meant to capture the idea that sex biologies and gender identities are potentially diverse and have a complex relationship in all individuals. The term "gender*sex" also recognizes the ways that our physical appearances are perceived by others as simultaneous expressions of both sex and gender categories. It should be noted that even this combined term may not be preferred in all cases; for some gender-nonbinary people, integrating the concept of sex with gender can lead to erasure of some identities and experiences. But because gender*sex reflects notable scholarship being conducted today and best acknowledges the nuanced connections between sex and gender, it's the term we'll use through the remainder of this chapter.

Table 11.1 helps organize the terms we've introduced thus far (and will use throughout this chapter), indicating which are associated with sex, which with gender, and which reflect the integration of the two concepts.

sex chromosomes A pair of chromosomes (designated XX, XY, or combinations thereof) that is partially responsible for biological differences in sexual and reproductive anatomy and physiology. Those assigned male at birth are assumed to have XY chromosomes while those assigned female at birth are assumed to have XX chromosomes, though exceptions exist.

hormone A chemical created in the body that controls and regulates the activities of certain cells or organs. Estrogen (produced in ovaries) and testosterone (produced in testes) are two important hormones that play key roles in reproduction and contribute to differences in secondary sex characteristics that emerge as people mature biologically.

gender*sex Whole people and identities; aspects of women, men, and gender/sex-diverse people that involve both gender *and* sex.

46,XY differences of sex development	Moderate variations	Subtle variations	Male
• XY	• XY	• XY	• XY
• Testes	• Testes	• Testes	• Testes
• Often ambiguous genitals	• Male external genitals	• Male internal and external genitals	• Male internal and external genitals
• Hormonal variation called "persistent Müllerian duct syndrome" results in male external genitals and testes, and also a womb and fallopian tubes.	• Anatomical variations such as urethral opening on underside of penis.	• Subtle differences such as low sperm production. Some caused by variation in sex-development genes.	• Male secondary sexual characteristics (e.g., facial hair)

FIGURE 11.3

People born with XX and XY chromosomes can manifest a range of primary and secondary sex characteristics for an array of different reasons. In every one of these cases, the individual could potentially identify as male, female, both, or neither.

TABLE 11.1

Sex and Gender Terms Used in This Chapter

Sex Terms	Gender Terms	Inclusive and Integrative Terms
Assigned sex (or sex) refers to an individual's classification as female, male, or intersex, based on observable patterns of primary and/or secondary sexual-reproductive biological characteristics. Sex is considered a multidimensional social construct based on a cluster of anatomical and physical traits usually assigned as male or female. Sex can change based on new information, such as gender identity or development of secondary sex characteristics.	**Gender** is a social construct regarding what it means to live within society as a man, woman, both, or something else. It is a multidimensional construct referring to cultural, social, and psychological factors that shape experience and how people operate within society. These involve gender-based norms, gender identities, and gender expressions.	**Gender*sex** is an academic term used to integrate the reality of gender (social) and sex (physical) as entangled and influencing one another in complex ways. One's gender*sex identity acknowledges biology, individual behaviors, and preferences.
Terms of reference: female, male, intersex		
Primary sex characteristics are sexual-reproductive biological features present at birth. For assigned sex classification, external reproductive organs are typically used (e.g., the presence of a penis or vagina). There can be variation in the features present in any one individual.	**Binary gender** is a basic organizing principle of human societies, whereby people are generally expected to look and act as either men (masculine) or women (feminine), usually in alignment with their assigned sex.	**Cisgender** means having one's internal sense of gender identity align with one's assigned sex.
	Terms of reference: woman, man, girl, boy	*Terms of reference: woman, man*
Secondary sexual characteristics are sexual-reproductive biological features that emerge through puberty, such as body hair, breast development, and voice pitch. There is variation in when, if, and how these features emerge in any one individual.	**Third gender** is a label for a third gender that is neither man nor woman, recognized by some societies (see Section 11.2).	**Nonbinary** means not identifying as either a man or a woman. There is a wide range of experience encompassed in this term, including people who feel their gender is between man and woman and those who experience their gender as something else entirely. This term is not used interchangeably with transgender.
	Terms of reference: Use the specific cultural label for the third gender. Avoid "third gender" as a term of reference for transgender individuals, as it suggests disallowance of normative gender identities of men and women even if they use these.	*Terms of reference: Highly variable; ask what the person uses and pay attention to the answer. Pronouns may include them/they or any of set of neopronouns (i.e., xe, ze, fae, ey).*
Sex spectrum encompasses the recognition that people's sexual-reproductive biology can reflect a mix of features that are typically classified as both male and female (see Figure 11.3).	**Gender schema** refers to a set of related social norms and rules within a society that establish gender-based characteristics and associations.	**Transgender** is an umbrella term referring to people whose internal sense of gender identity does not align with their assigned sex. Transgender identity is not dependent on sexual development characteristics or on past medical procedures or therapies.
		Terms of reference: transgender woman, transgender man, woman, man. Transgender is used as an adjective to modify a noun, so avoid usages such as transwoman, transman, a transgender, transgenders, or transgendered.

TABLE 11.1

Sex and Gender Terms Used in This Chapter (*continued*)

Sex Terms	Gender Terms	Inclusive and Integrative Terms
Sexual dimorphism refers to distinct differences in average body measures between individuals classified by sex. In humans, males are on average larger than females in many measures (such as height).	**Gender norms** are patterns of gendered social behaviors and ways of thinking about gender differences that are accepted and expected within a society. People who do not adhere to gender norms may be stigmatized or otherwise mistreated to encourage conformity.	
Intersex is a general term for patterns of sexual-reproductive anatomy that do not fit the typical definitions of female or male. There are over 30 officially recognized differences in sexual development that are characterized with this term.	**Gender identity** refers to a person's internal sense of their gender (not necessarily visible or obvious to others). This may not match their assigned sex or fit neatly into binary or third gender categories.	
	Gender expression refers to external displays of gender identity and/or norms that can include personal names, pronouns, voice, behaviors, body characteristics, clothing, and haircut. These signals or cues are labeled "masculine" and "feminine." These cues change over time and vary across space (see Section 11.2).	
	Gender role is a gendered social position occupied in everyday contexts. Typically, gender roles are determined by a person's assigned sex at birth.	

BINARY GENDER AND BEYOND

Despite numerous societies recognizing additional or third gender categories (as we'll explore in this section), binary distinctions between male/men and female/women continue to play a dominant role in shaping broader gender schemas in societies worldwide. The prevalence and persistence of these binary schemas at the societal level have much to do with historical and present systems of power within societies, as we will see. In this section, we begin to explore how those schemas of binary gender can be arranged and how these arrangements then define our social identities and roles.

Throughout our lives, we are repeatedly assigned into gender and sex categories by others, on the basis of a constellation of "markers" that reflect femininity and masculinity: the shape of our face and body; our height; our hairiness; and our manner of standing, walking, or sitting. We apply these same assignations to others. Identifying a person's gender gives us a clear, prescribed, learned, and comfortable gender script we can follow as we interact with that person.

FIGURE 11.4

Men and women wear distinctive clothing that identifies gender as they await guests in the Andean village of Misminay, near Cusco, Peru.

Dress is often an extremely obvious scripted gender marker. Societies often have very clear scripts about what is appropriate dress for women and men. In Japan, women often wear *kimono* or Japanese attire to formal events, while men wear suits. In many Indigenous Andean communities in South America, women wear brightly colored skirts, shawls, and hats, while men uniformly wear more soberly colored pants (**Figure 11.4**). In formal international business settings, a globally shared corporate culture suggests men's appropriate dress is constrained to specific items that include neutral-colored suiting, ties, collared shirts, and closed-toe shoes. Women are conventionally permitted a more elaborate dress code that includes bright colors, large necklaces or scarves, heels, skirts, and even bare legs and sleeveless tops in appropriate climates.

Language can be another marker of stereotypical gender. "You talk like a boy," friends told American linguistic anthropologist Cindi SturtzSreetharan when she was a high schooler studying abroad in Japan. She was just learning the language, and it took her some time to figure out what they meant. In Japanese, men often use *na* at the end of their utterances to invite a response from their listener. Japanese women are thought to use *ne*. SturtzSreetharan was saying *na*. By telling her that her language use wasn't quite right, her friends were teaching her something about how to be a girl in Japanese society (**Figure 11.5**). The lesson also helped inspire SturtzSreetharan to become an anthropologist, who decades later studies how language reflects and shapes ideas about masculinity and femininity in Japanese society.

This isn't to say that Japanese society doesn't also accommodate gender expressions outside the binary schema or that the schema itself hasn't changed (and continues to evolve) over time. For example, compared to 70 years ago, more Japanese women work outside the home, including in full-time career paths and at large companies that were once the exclusive domain of men. Moreover, Japanese society now accommodates gender expressions outside the binary schema. Popular Japanese fashion model Satsuki Nakayama identifies as genderless. Designated male at birth, Nakayama says, "The androgynous look has been great for my career, but what's more important than that is the fact that I feel comfortable." And some Japanese people define their own gender identities by explicitly rejecting the binary schema (**Figure 11.6**). But linking gender to particular ways of using language endures.

FIGURE 11.5

Linguistic anthropologist Cindi SturtzSreetharan (left) has been studying how language reflects and shapes ideas about masculinity and femininity in Osaka, Japan, for two decades. Here she is doing participant observation of "women's work" in the kitchen with Sachi, a Japanese housewife, long-term study participant, and friend.

FIGURE 11.6

Japanese actor Ryosuke Miura, famous for his role in the film, Kamen Rider. While identifying along the binary as male, many fans note that Miura often presents himself androgynously.

In some languages, including English, pronouns indicate the gender*sex of another person, as in he/she or her/him. In these cases, being able to easily identify someone as a woman or man provides the rules for how to interact with that person. It also reminds the listener about their gender*sex assignment. In other languages, the same pronouns are used to refer to anyone regardless of gender*sex, reducing misgendering. For example, in spoken Mandarin Chinese, the third-person pronoun *ta* is not marked for gender*sex and can be used as he, she, or a nonbinary singular pronoun. However, in written form, *ta* does exhibit gender*sex: 她 is used for she/her and 他 is used for he/him. Recently there have been some suggestions for adding a third written option, either *ta* written in roman letters or x也 to denote a nonbinary third-person pronoun.

But even in these cases, language is used to make assumptions about a speaker's gender*sex identity via the way the person speaks. The pitch of a person's voice influences a hearer's perception and designation of a speaker as male, female, or ambiguous. There are other ways that how we talk plays a role in gender expression and perception. Creaky voice (also known as "vocal fry") is produced when the vocal folds around our larynx vibrate at a very slow rate. It results in a low, shaky voice. Sociocultural linguist Lal Zimman has shown that some gay cisgender and transgender American men use statistically higher frequencies of creaky voice when speaking, compared to straight cisgender men. Furthermore, listeners asked to rate recordings of speakers identified creaky voice as more "gay sounding."

pronoun A word that takes the place of a noun or noun phrase such as a personal name.

SIGNALING AND EXPERIENCING GENDER

Yet another scripted gender marker is the way that individuals "take up" space. In the United States, United Kingdom, and many other countries, "manspreading"—public sitting with legs spread wide—is more often done by men. Women's sitting postures, on the other hand, are more likely to be with legs crossed or knees close together (**Figure 11.7**). This reflects the ways that individuals learn to move and hold their bodies so as to be considered culturally appropriate based on their gender. Learning these normative ways to move and hold one's gender*sex body begins as early as three months of age.

FIGURE 11.7

A woman and a man sitting on a public park bench in London show gendered differences in their public sitting positions.

ARGENTINA

Arroyo Seco

South America

Cultural scripts for gender make social performance and interactions easier in many ways, by providing road maps for our own behavior and for engaging with others. But they can also create oppressive and even dangerous boundaries around how one can identify and express themselves. For example, cisgender men who do not adhere closely enough to a masculine cultural script—such as by wearing "women's" clothing—are at higher risk for verbal and physical violence, not just at school (as the example of River High showed) but in almost every other public context of their lives.

Despite being learned, the actions that create gender*sex identities are often unrecognized by those doing them. Even social scientists perform gender in these subtle ways. Archaeologist Joan Gero (1944–2016) studied women and men conducting archaeological fieldwork at the Pleistocene site of Arroyo Seco in Argentina in the early 1990s. All the students and archaeological technicians were trained in the same excavation methods. This included how to construct pedestals while excavating, so that discovered artifacts are left in the exact place they are found. In this method, rather than disturbing the find, the excavator removes the soil around the artifact, which creates a column or pedestal of soil upon which the object rests, remaining easily visible and undisturbed while the dig proceeds. Gero found that men produced larger and more visible pedestals than women (**Figure 11.8**). While this may seem like a minor detail, it had significant implications. Artifacts displayed on smaller pedestals were treated as less important by the larger archaeological team, and consequently they were given less weight in drawing scientific conclusions.

Because of the importance of such performances in daily life, most people expect to feel confident in their ability to accurately assess other people's gender*sex. For some, a sense of not "knowing" someone's assigned sex can make social interaction potentially very uncomfortable. This may be because clearly understanding and following a cultural script means we don't have to think hard about how we are meant to interact with others.

Biological anthropologist Zachary DuBois, himself a transgender man, designed *The Transition Experience Study* to explore the way that gender is experienced in the United States. He interviewed 65 transgender men in the northeastern United States who were using testosterone hormonal therapy about their transition experience and also collected multiple biomarkers of stress (including salivary cortisol, ambulatory blood pressure, and blood-spot tests of inflammation levels). His study participants explained why social gatherings such as weddings or birthdays proved especially stressful. These

FIGURE 11.8

Joan Gero's study of the field practices of archaeologists at Arroyo Seco, Argentina, found differences in gender performance. **(a)** Women typically excavated smaller, more modest pedestals, just large enough to support the objects they discovered. **(b)** In contrast, men on the project typically excavated much larger pedestals.

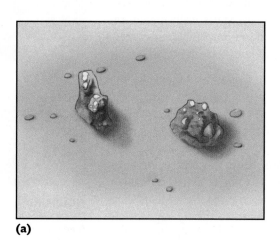

(a)

(b)

occasions brought together family members long practiced in interacting with the individuals as women and newer friends who were practiced in interacting with them as men. Having to navigate both cultural scripts simultaneously was very challenging.

With the expanded awareness of nonbinary identities and experiences through new media, there is a constant broadening and shifting of terminology. The important note here is that all people, whether they identify as women, men, transgender, nonbinary, or even agender, are nonetheless successfully creating core social identities around the basic idea of gender*sex itself. This includes personal identities defined in terms of opposition to the social prescriptions for what constitutes being female/woman or male/man.

In many cases, people who are nonbinary have to work to create their own sense of self, not defined by binary male/man and female/woman categories. In the United States, there is recently some evidence that we may be making greater room for gender categories that do not adhere strictly to a binary model. One example is U.S. fashion influencer féi hernandez (b. 1993), who was raised in California and is a trans nonbinary visual artist, writer, and healer. They are active in reshaping norms and culture that make room for nonbinary gender and allow for their equal treatment within society.

Other places in the world have accommodated alternative gender categories for nonbinary individuals for much longer. Two examples are the *fa`afafine* in Samoa and *hijra* in India—both cases where people sex-assigned as males at birth have made the choice to assume existing culturally recognized gender identities and roles that are neither women nor men.

In the small independent nation of Samoa in the central Pacific, the third gender is termed *"fa`afafine"* (FAH-ah-fa-FEE-ney), meaning "in the manner of a woman." *Fa`afafine* are sex-assigned as male at birth but often choose to do women's work, and they dress, walk, and talk in ways suggestive of Samoan ideas of femininity, such as growing their hair longer. Traditional Samoan society places service to family and community above individual needs or desires. This means that value is placed on identities that are closely linked to an ability to contribute to the extended family. Many *fa`afafine* talk of how they eschewed boyhood tasks such as learning how to farm or fish. Instead, they took on roles designated for girls/women within their rural households, such as cooking and laundry. *Fa`afafine* are mostly accepted within families and by other Samoans as just different expressions of gender—perhaps sometimes less than ideal in a society where getting married and having children are viewed as central to being adult, but explicable and loved just the same. They are, people locally say, probably just "born that way."

As more Samoans have opportunities to work in the modern cash economy, there are more gender-neutral ways to labor in support of the family. Many of the estimated 5,000 *fa`afafine* are employed in the capital city of Apia in the same jobs women would be more likely to occupy, including as seamstresses, in retail, and in social services (**Figure 11.9**). This shift into urban areas and away from village life is changing *fa`afafine* identities. Most influential is the increasing interaction with global gay and drag culture, which is changing how *fa`afafine* are seen; outside of Samoa, *fa`afafine* are often described using terms such as "drag queen." But this fails to capture the place of *fa`afafine* within Samoan society. They are not people who identify as men or who are dressing and acting as women through drag. They are something else, a third category defined as different and distinct from both men and women.

FIGURE 11.9

Fa`afafine* represent a gender category within Samoan society that is recognized as neither woman nor man but rather additional to those. Here a *fa`afafine is selling fruit in the market in Apia, the Samoan capital.

FIGURE 11.10

A group of *hijra* is pictured in Rajasthan, India, at the shrine of Sufi Saint Khwaja Moinuddin Chishti.

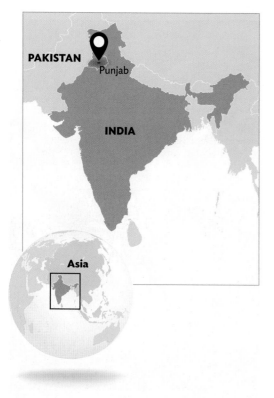

Another well-known example of a neither-man-nor-woman gender category has been detailed by anthropologist Serena Nanda, based on her ethnographic fieldwork in Punjab, India. In parts of southern Asia, *hijra* (HEEJ-ra) may include intersex people and transgender women, along with people assigned male at birth who may or may not undergo castration and/or other body modifications such as breast enhancement. It is noted that those who do undergo castration accrue higher respect than those who do not. Transgender women and *hijra* have different identities. *Hijra* must go through an initiation process that includes adoption into a chosen family based on *hijra* customs. *Hijra* typically wear saris, grow their hair long, take feminine names, and move their bodies in ways that reflect Indian ideals of womanhood (**Figure 11.10**). *Hijra* live together in what can be described as a "guru-disciple system" that functions as a socially stratified complex kinship system. It requires the patronage of a *hijra* guru (a powerful holy figure) who offers protection, a place to live, and a social network/community in exchange for domestic labor. There is even a distinct language that they learn and share, known as *Hijra Farsi*.

In India, Pakistan, and Bangladesh, *hijra* were granted formal legal status as a third gender*sex in 2014. And in 2018, India decriminalized "homosexual sex," a law that had been put into place by the British 160 years prior. But even though the gender category and the special spiritual status of *hijra* are recognized in Indian society, this doesn't mean that the people who are labeled with it are always respected. *Hijra* report being rejected by families and assaulted on the street.

GENDER ROLES AND THE DIVISION OF LABOR

One area in which the influence of gender norms is particularly obvious is in how household productive and reproductive tasks are allocated. Differences in what each gender is expected to contribute is sometimes referred to as the *gendered division of labor*.

gendered division of labor A system in which gender norms influence the formal or informal work roles assigned to people, such as in household chores or paid employment.

FIGURE 11.11

Margaret Mead's three fieldwork locations in Papua New Guinea.

Gender norms regarding division of labor can vary greatly. Indeed, one of the most influential early works in anthropology, Margaret Mead's *Sex and Temperament in Three Primitive Societies*, used the comparison of three small-society cases to demonstrate the flexibility of men's and women's roles (**Figure 11.11**).

Beginning in late 1931, Mead visited the western Pacific region to study the differences between women and men and to test the idea that gender (which she at that time termed "sex") could be culturally organized in an array of ways. She chose the Sepik River region in the north of Papua New Guinea for a very particular reason: It was (and remains) one of the most culturally and linguistically diverse areas in the world. Over the next 15 months, Mead did fieldwork in three very different, very small *polygynous* Sepik communities, all within 100 miles of each other, taking copious daily notes about the lives of men and women in each society.

Among the mountain-living Arapesh, as Mead described them, men and women often cooperated in both farming and childcare. Men were expected to be gentle and caring, like their wives. Mundugumor men (now Biwat), living on the muddy banks above a swift-flowing river, had more wives than the Arapesh, and the relations between men and women were much less sedate. Men and women were similarly less engaged in childcare, and both were expected to be sexually aggressive and quick to fight. For the lakeside-dwelling Tchambuli (now Chambri), Mead described a society in which gender was differently configured yet again, with men expected to be vain, concerned with making art, and emotionally dependent on their wives. Women, by contrast, were independent, unconcerned with frivolity, and did all the necessary fishing and weaving work.

Mead used these cases to highlight how different the societies were, not just from one another but also from prevailing ideas about gender*sex in the United States at that time. Arapesh men and women both acted consistently with U.S. norms for women (calm and responsive to children). The Mundugumor men and women alike had temperaments consistent with those expected for U.S. men at the time (assertive and fearless). The Tchambuli suggested a reversal of gender roles, as norms in U.S. society established the men as the independent providers (**Figure 11.12**).

polygyny A marriage system in which men are permitted or expected to have more than one wife at the same time.

FIGURE 11.12

In addition to conducting fieldwork in several different world regions, Margaret Mead (1901–1978) was also a social activist, challenging conventions around gender and many other issues of her day. She also was a recognized public figure, as seen here with actor Robert Redford.

South America

PERU

Chiribaya Alta

In the decades since Mead's research, anthropologists have documented how gender*sex is organized and experienced in a vast array of societies. What is perhaps most surprising about what we have discovered is that, counter to the intended point of Mead's book, and despite there being notable variation in gender norms and roles among different societies, there are nonetheless some very consistent overlaps between societies when it comes to gender roles. Specifically, whereas men participate in childcare to varying extents in different societies, women overwhelmingly have or share the primary role in childcare and many other core domestic tasks. Likewise, whereas women participate in nondomestic or public sphere–related tasks to varying extents in different societies, men overwhelmingly have or share the primary role in these areas. As we will see later in the chapter, the prevalence of this gendered division of labor across societies has roots in, and important implications for, global issues of power and inequality.

Is this dynamic regarding labor a relatively modern phenomenon? It would appear not. Archaeologists have been able to confirm gendered divisions of labor in past societies. This is done by comparing skeletons designated as male or female with the items buried with them. People living at pre-Inca Chiribaya sites, in what is now southern Peru between about 1100 and 1400 CE, were buried in bundles of intricate woven textiles. Graves also held the tools people used, presumably so they could continue to use their skills in the afterlife. At the archaeological site of Chiribaya Alta, the differences between the grave goods of skeletons designated as male versus those designated as female were dramatic. Both were wrapped in the same cloth, but skeletons designated female were buried with wide, heavily decorated woven belts, alongside skeins of raw and dyed llama and alpaca wools, spindles for spinning wool into thread, weaving looms, and additional intricately finished textiles. Male-assigned skeletons had hats and tools for farming, fishing, or hunting, including fishhooks and bows and arrows. This suggests that weaving highly valued and complex textiles, such as ponchos, hats, and bags, was women's work (**Figure 11.13**). Men's labor contributions were instead dominated by farming, fishing, or hunting.

Despite the persistence of a gendered division of labor, there are societies that provide examples of other, more equitable possibilities. The Aka live in hunter-gatherer communities in the forests of the Congo Basin of central Africa, and everyday tasks are flexibly arranged between men and women. Aka men hold many of the community leadership positions, but women hunt game with spears and fish with nets, even when well into their pregnancies and with newborns strapped on their backs. Still, more of the hunting overall is done by men. Likewise, while Aka men join women in gathering edible plants, tubers, and nuts, the majority of this work is done by women. Perhaps most notably, though, Aka men contribute very significantly to childcare (**Figure 11.14**).

Cultural anthropologist Barry Hewlett carefully observed Aka fathers to see exactly how they interacted with children. He estimated that they did 47% of infant holding. They would even sometimes let their babies suckle at their breasts to comfort them if the mother wasn't there. Generally, hunter-gatherer societies like the Aka do seem to be more egalitarian regarding the domestic division of labor and other social roles than are farming or other forms of subsistence communities. Nevertheless, Aka women undertake the majority of childcare.

In the new millennium, historical norms based on highly gendered division of labor are softening in many societies. Global economic and societal shifts, such as women's rising educational and employment opportunities, are encouraging

FIGURE 11.13

Goods buried with skeletons sexed as female suggest that women in Chiribaya Alta, Peru (1100–1400 CE), were acquiring expertise as weavers and producing highly valued textiles like the Chiribaya-style textile redrawn here.

egalitarian A societal model in which access to resources and power is not controlled by some individuals or sectors of society; rather, involvement in decision-making and access to resources is evenly distributed, and social distinctions are based on age, gender, and individual qualities.

FIGURE 11.14

Aka fathers spend much time in childcare, as seen here.

married men to explore new family roles, such as taking primary responsibility for domestic tasks and childcare. Yet notably, even in the wealthiest nations with the highest levels of women's education, such roles can be stigmatized and women remain, on average, paid less than men for the same jobs. Furthermore, women still bear the brunt of responsibility for childcare, as highly evidenced in the long-term closing of schools in the United States due to the coronavirus pandemic. The lack of in-person schooling led to many instances of women—rather than men—being the ones to reduce or stop working as a family's means for coping with the challenges.

WHY DO WE HAVE (BINARY) GENDER?

What accounts for the near-universal reliance on binary gender as a fundamental organizing principle in human societies? And why do we find certain consistencies in gender roles across cultures? Evolutionary perspectives on the possible advantages of binary gender systems to the early history of our species provide one possible answer to this question.

Primates show patterned differences in behavior related to their biological sex characteristics. But gender isn't just patterned behavior. It requires socially determined roles to overlap with sexual-reproductive characteristics that are incorporated into personal identities. It is more difficult to establish whether primates have what can be considered gender by this definition—that is, whether chimpanzees or other great apes have a sense of maleness, femaleness, or nonbinariness or whether they treat their infants differently depending on their infant's sexual characteristics. There is some evidence that grooming, play, and food-collecting strategies are learned behaviors and differ by sex characteristics in some nonhuman primate species. For example, female primates tend to spend more time holding, grooming, and feeding infants. But there is no evidence suggesting that nonhuman primates socialize male and female offspring differently.

So, humans are probably unique among primates (and other animals) for organizing societies around gender*sex, not just sex. This suggests gender likely emerged sometime in the hominin lineage. This process may have started around a million years ago, well before the emergence of anatomically modern humans. The chemical analysis of fossilized teeth from southern African hominins such as *Australopithecus africanus* and *Paranthropus robustus* (see Chapter 5) is one of the few early clues we have. It seems that males and females had different ranges for collecting food, which could indicate some sort of basic division of labor. The differences between the teeth on the presumed male (larger) and female (smaller) specimens also suggest females moved outside the region in which they were born more often than did the males (a behavior pattern seen today in both chimpanzees and bonobos).

By the time of the Neanderthals, around 50,000 years ago, the archaeological evidence is more substantial yet still hard to interpret. For example, based on signs of physical trauma (such as breakages) on skeletons, it seems both sex-assigned male and female Neanderthals equally engaged in dangerous hunts. However, differences in wear (damage) on male versus female teeth suggest they were using their teeth to do different types of work. Tooth damage is common in tool-using hominins and in modern human hunter-gatherers who use their teeth as a "third hand" for holding objects. In comparison to sex-assigned males, sex-assigned female Neanderthals had longer striations (patterns of ridges or other marks) on their teeth caused by sharp objects being dragged across the front surfaces. This means females were doing something different with their mouths than males, perhaps processing the hides from the animals that men hunted. Female Neanderthals also chipped the surfaces on their lower teeth due to some kind of currently unknown task they performed. Males had the same types of damage but on their upper teeth.

There is also evidence of *sexual dimorphism* in early hominin species—that is, differences in size between males and females (**Figure 11.15**). These differences persist in modern humans today. Once they reach full adulthood, sex-assigned males are on average larger than sex-assigned females in almost every measure imaginable. This includes features such as head circumference, amount and distribution of body hair, and pattern of body fat deposition. For example, the global average height of males (69 inches or 175 centimeters) is significantly greater than that of females (64 inches or 162.5 centimeters). Additionally, almost all adult females (99.9%) have muscle mass measures that are below the male average.

But whereas sexual dimorphism and the other physical differences observed above appear in our hominin ancestors, we can't say if these differences are themselves evidence of gender. As with the living apes, identifying

sexual dimorphism The condition when males and females of a species are significantly different in size.

FIGURE 11.15

These trace fossil footprints were made by *Australopithecus afarensis* in volcanic ash at Laetoli in eastern Africa some 3.6 million years ago. The significant differences in size between different sets of Laetoli prints are often interpreted as a sign of sexual dimorphism in the early hominin species.

archaeological signals in the fossil record of the emergence of hominin gender identities—as opposed to simply sex-differentiated behaviors—is tricky.

One compelling hypothesis suggests that patterns of division of labor based on sexual biologies could have provided an important survival advantage for a hunter-gatherer species increasingly reliant on raising highly dependent, large-brained offspring. One way to think about this is that people with female-characterized sexual-reproductive biologies (including the capacity to breast-feed) would have a relative advantage over males in assuming the roles of caring for children. If these females cooperated to accomplish most of the childcare and if this aligned with gender identities that recognized this as fitting into and contributing to the community, then males who were motivated to develop complex, cooperative skills at hunting or fishing could do so.

Ancient humans were distinct among the large primates in their dietary preference for big game and other hard-to-get foods. Studies of modern societies that engage in hunting for larger animals reveal that it requires significant range, time, and physical effort. For example, for the Tsimané people in the Bolivian Amazon, hunting and fishing form an important part of their diet (along with subsistence farming). Men contribute around 8% of their time to childcare, mostly playing. Much more of their time is spent hunting. An average man's hunting expedition includes ranging for 17 kilometers, lasts 8.6 hours, and has only a 61% chance of success. Perhaps the comparatively high levels of testosterone production and larger muscle masses of male human bodies that characterize human sexual dimorphism allowed hominin males to range further and obtain the varied, calorically dense foods needed to support their big-brained babies (**Figure 11.16**). If so, the broader socialization of sex-assigned males and females into gendered social systems could then have provided an additional advantage for our ancestors over competing hominin species that didn't arrange themselves into such gendered systems.

FIGURE 11.16

A Bolivian Tsimané father and son fishing. Tsimané men spend much of their productive time hunting and fishing, while women provide almost all of the child care.

FIGURE 11.17

A goanna lizard being prepared for a meal by a Martu community member in the Australian desert.

Desert

WESTERN
AUSTRALIA

Oceania

cooperative parenting A system in which children receive care from group members other than their biological parents (such as grandparents or siblings; also called *alloparents*), enhancing the children's well-being and survival.

Ecological anthropologist Rebecca Bliege Bird studied how and why Martu Indigenous women hunt in the deserts of Western Australia. In this arid zone, men's and women's gender roles around food acquisition are often cooperative and flexible. Women spend more time foraging for fruits or insects, but they also lead cooperative hunting expeditions for smaller animals such as goanna lizards (**Figure 11.17**). They actually bring home as much meat as men, but only men hunt the large, fast kangaroos. A Martu woman's capacity to hunt is completely dependent on supportive reciprocal arrangements with sisters, daughters, and co-wives, also called alloparents, who help with childcare; this arrangement is sometimes referred to as cooperative parenting. The emergence of gender-based cooperative childcare may even have assisted women to hunt more effectively, to the nutritional benefit of our species.

If there is consistent evidence of women big-game hunters in the past, this suggests early human societies were not arranged around clearly differentiated economic roles for men versus women. Certainly, humans have long had technologies to support women as efficient hunters. The atlatl, a tool that propels a spear farther and with greater velocity—used by hunters since perhaps 30,000 years ago—allows even those with relatively limited upper body strength to down a large animal.

One means that archaeologists use to clarify whether women hunted are the objects accompanying their burials. The assumption is that these objects tend to reflect who they were within their society. One such example is a skeleton of a 17–19 year old sexed as female based on DNA analysis of dental enamel and excavated from a burial in the high Peruvian Andes in South America, dated to around 9,000 years ago. She was buried with a projectile point toolkit used in big-game hunting (**Figure 11.18**), alongside nearby mammal bones. Isotopic analysis of her bones also indicated that she had substantial meat in her diet.

Such interpretations of prior archaeological discoveries are also changing perceptions of women's societal roles in the nearer past. In 1878, a presumed Viking male was excavated from an elaborate grave in Birka, Sweden. The presumption was based on the warrior being buried with the remains of two horses, one of which was bridled for riding, and multiple weapons, including two shields,

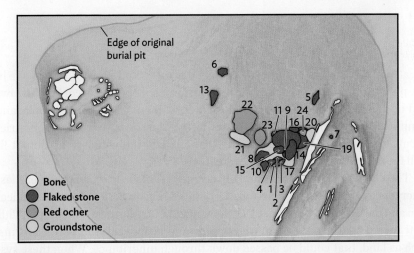

FIGURE 11.18

A female whose skeleton was excavated at Wilamaya Patjxa in southern Peru was buried 9,000 years ago with accompanying tools (shown) as part of the grave goods. The kit was likely buried together in a bag and includes projectile points used with short hunting spears (numbers 1–7), flakes suited to cutting (8–13), a possible knife (14), flaked scrapers and groundstone choppers associated with butchering and scraping hides (15–21), and red ocher used as a pigment (22–24).

a sword, an axe, a fighting knife, two lances, and 25 arrows. A full gaming board with gaming pieces was placed next to the body, which specialists interpreted as evidence that this warrior had a strategic leadership role because full gaming sets are most common in burials of Viking military leaders. However, more recently, archaeologist Charlotte Hedenstierna-Jonson and her team reanalyzed the skeleton and the grave goods. Genetic analysis confirmed this individual had two X chromosomes. It can't be known how this person self-identified, but there are examples of Viking "shield-maidens" in the historical record, so this may have been a biologically female warrior who was gendered as a woman rather than a man.

SECTION 11.4

GENDER, INEQUALITY, AND POWER

As we've seen, the current evidence suggests early humans occupied different and complementary roles, reinforced by gender*sex, that served the human species well at very specific points of evolutionary history. But that doesn't explain why these patterns have continued to define how most humans live, now that we are not competing with other hominin species for survival. It also doesn't explain why cisgender men tend to dominate so consistently across human societies and in so many aspects of human life. The reason may lie in the patriarchal social systems that predominate in most of the world's societies.

PATRIARCHY AND THE PERSISTENCE OF MEN'S POWER

A patriarchy is a system in which cisgender men hold most of the power in the public, and often private, spheres. Patriarchies operate according to laws and norms for gender behavior that exclude women, transgender people, and nonbinary people from positions of authority. Moreover, patriarchy sets strict norms of masculinity and femininity that alienate individuals who do not fit well into the rigid gender schema it creates.

The deeper origins of patriarchal societies seem closely tied to the earliest emergence of complex human societies—that is, tied to agricultural intensification and increasingly permanent settlements 12,000 years ago (Chapter 8). This shift meant that people could now accrue and keep wealth in various forms, such as land, that could be passed down through inheritance. When these systems favor cisgender men or preclude women, they tend to support patriarchal structures. For example, the widespread practice of patrilocality requires newly married couples to live near or with the husband's family. This practice is particularly useful for reinforcing patriarchal systems because it serves to isolate women, diminishing their capacity to gain support from their own kin. This arrangement is by far the most common one across the full range of human societies, including among hunter-gatherers (Chapter 12).

European nations have long histories of highly patriarchal societies. European colonialism exported these systems to many other parts of the world, along with the gender-based inequalities these systems produced. Prior to British settlement of Aotearoa/New Zealand in the 17th and 18th centuries, for example, Indigenous Māori men's and women's respective importance within society (and within Māori mythology) was seen as distinct but complementary and balanced (**Figure 11.19**). Living in extended family groups (*whānau*) meant multigenerational care for children, giving women options in how to spend their time. Gender roles were more fluid, too, with men sometimes caring for children.

But this situation fundamentally shifted as British immigrants introduced new norms that restricted political and economic power according to rigidly defined masculine and feminine roles. Now men alone had to financially support the nuclear family, and women's contributions were restricted to homebound duties supporting the men. British common law identified women and children as legally under the control of their husbands and fathers, with far fewer rights. For Māori women, the imposition of these sexist and more binding notions of femininity and domestication severely limited the behaviors considered normal or acceptable for them, and it meant new forms of personal isolation and a smaller zone of social and political influence.

The legacy of patriarchal systems can persist long after they have been reformed to prevent the legal exclusion of non-cisgender men. In the United States, for example, over 70% of women change their last name to that of their husband when marrying, but the converse is extremely rare. Almost all the leaders of Fortune 500 companies, the most economically powerful businesses, are cisgender men.

Cultural anthropologist Alexander Edmonds conducted a study of women and cosmetic surgery in the early 2000s in the beach city of Rio de Janeiro, Brazil. The Brazilian economy was booming at that time, and women had unprecedented access to low-cost, even government-supported, surgical procedures, such as rhinoplasty, liposuction, or abdominoplasty ("tummy tuck"). Edmonds conducted ethnographic fieldwork with women struggling at the margins of the market economy and found that many of these women viewed

NEW ZEALAND

Oceania

FIGURE 11.19

An 18th-century Māori carving shows the cosmological connection of Rangi the sky father (left) and Papa the earth mother as an entwined couple, who emerged together from the dark at the point of creation, forming the two connected, complementary halves of the world.

the surgeries as a means to ascend social class. In practical terms, it could help in getting a slightly better job, such as shifting from housecleaning to office work. Thus, by using one unfair system to push back on other unfair systems, those in society with less power had one way to slightly improve their own situations. Female genital cutting/mutilation is another example of a painful and potentially harmful cultural practice that women may endure to meet stringent norms of femininity but that can also allow them to gain some additional benefits from their society as a result, such as social or economic elevation through better marriage.

It's not women/men alone that support and maintain patriarchal arrangements within society, though. Cisgender women also can sometimes act in ways that confirm the gendered expectations and performances that maintain such systems. Moreover, patriarchal systems are also not always to the benefit of men themselves. In many cash economies, the dominant expectation is that men will financially support the family. This can be a source of considerable stress, trapping men into singular earner roles within the family. During the Great Recession in the United States from 2007 to 2009, when men's employment became more precarious, their depression and rates of suicide went up substantially compared to women's. This same pattern was also true in the earlier major economic recession in Japan in the late 1990s.

This leads us to the question: Are there any societies in which the dominant social structures channel more power to women and better meet women's needs than those of men? That is, are there **matriarchies**? The evidence is generally slim. One society that may fit this description is the Islamic Minangkabau of West Sumatra in southeastern Asia (**Figure 11.20**). Land, houses, and other assets are inherited by and mostly owned by women. While women marry, they manage their own households day to day, often with their brothers living with them. This means they are economically independent and can make decisions about what happens to them and their children. Husbands visit but are expected to return to their own sisters' homes or men's longhouses to sleep. Men, however, still control many of the elected political leadership positions within villages.

patriarchy A society that is organized such that cisgender men have dominant authority and advantages over women and transgender and nonbinary people.

power The capacity to do and get what you want, including the ability to access resources and influence the decision-making of others.

patrilocality A system in which married couples live near or with the husband's family.

sexism Ideas and practices suggesting the inferiority of one sex compared to others; usually directed toward women.

matriarchy A society organized such that women have dominant authority over men.

FIGURE 11.20

A Minangkabau bride and groom are pictured.

diarchy A society organized such that women and men generally share power.

embodiment Incorporating and displaying in one's body the material and social worlds in which one lives.

health disparity A difference in preventable disease, injury, or violence created through social disadvantage.

growth faltering When the normal growth of children slows or stops because of undernutrition, disease, or mistreatment.

FIGURE 11.21

A mother breastfeeds her son in Totonicapán.

Another way to understand a case such as the Minangkabau is as a **diarchy**, where men and women generally share power. They may lead in different spheres of social, political, and economic influence, or the control of key institutions might oscillate or shift between the genders as circumstances change over time. Whereas patriarchy is a remarkably persistent form of social structure, cases such as the Minangkabau remind us that societal forms of gender power sharing are possible and workable.

And even entrenched patriarchy can be substantially undone, although it often takes massive societal shocks for this to happen. In the 1900s, women in Rwandan society did not own much property and were mostly excluded from the professional workforce. But in the wake of the genocide in 1994, in which as many as 1 million Tutsis, Twa, and moderate Hutus were killed, the remaining population was skewed to about 70% women. By 2016, women held 64% of seats in the Parliament of Rwanda. Universal paid maternity leave for women in the workforce was then introduced, allowing women more opportunity for financial independence and upward mobility. Recent global movements empowering people whose gender identities or gender expression challenge or reject binary categories altogether suggest that if the traditional binary sex/gender system can be destabilized, so too can the historical persistence of the patriarchy.

There is no evidence of any kind that the emergence of gender*sex divisions of labor meant that women's social status needed to be lower or less than that of men. Yet through much of our species' written history, men have had access to much greater power than women, and this access to power has had particular kinds of consequences. We explore the implications of gender inequality and the relatively greater access to power and resources by men, considering why it is consistently observed in human societies. We first discuss how the different treatment of people on the basis of gender*sex translates into our biology—in particular, how it sickens and otherwise damages our bodies. Patterns of contemporary gender inequality across the globe are explored in light of efforts to improve human rights by addressing gender inequality. Finally, we tackle a deeply significant question: Why is gender inequality so widespread and persistent in human societies today?

EMBODIMENT OF GENDER VALUATION

The cultural gendering of social and productive roles can have profound effects on our physical and emotional selves, both when we're young and as adults. Our gender norms—how we should be and what we should do, and how we feel about these rules—can become literally **embodied**, or expressed through our bodies. The experience of being treated differently or being exposed to elevated risk because of our gender can show up in physiological measures, such as rates of growth, blood pressure, or depression, and so can produce significant **health disparities** between genders.

Consider how boys and girls are often treated differently as babies, because they are differently valued and cared for using gendered cultural scripts. In Indigenous Maya K'iche' villages in the rural highlands of Guatemala, food can be scarce. K'iche' mothers believe their boy children are fussier, hungrier, and need more to eat. They feed them differently throughout their childhood because of this belief (**Figure 11.21**).

The pattern of young children's **growth faltering** (growing at a below-appropriate rate) observed by anthropologists in one K'iche' community is the literal embodiment of these cultural ideas about gender (**Figure 11.22**). Boys—understood by mothers as needing and demanding more food—are viewed as being less satisfied at the breast. This means they are given supplemental food sooner than girls, such as a thin gruel of ground corn dough mixed with water and sugar. But this poses a new set of problems that are solved through further reliance on cultural ideas about gender.

Consider that, in early childhood, breast milk is not only more nutritious but also considered safer, as introducing supplemental food early exposes a child to more infections. Such early-life infections use up body stores of energy and undermine growth. As a result, the boys' growth begins to deteriorate in the first 6 months of their infancy as they are weaned sooner. Girls' growth continues on a healthier track, as they continue to be fed mother's milk. But once the girls are shifted to weaning foods, their growth then falters compared to boys. Girls are then fed less than the boys. By 3 years of age, girls display more physical evidence of malnutrition, including shorter heights, compared to boys of the same age.

During adulthood, another way gender differences can become embodied is through trauma related to the gender norms surrounding household tasks. For example, about one-quarter of households globally are without ready access to water. This means it has to be hauled from rivers, springs, wells, or community taps. Women are most often responsible for this task (**Figure 11.23**). They are also more often expected to do other household tasks that depend on this fetched water, such as cooking and laundry. Water is very heavy (~8 pounds or 3.8 kilograms per gallon) and often needs to be carried over long distances, multiple times a

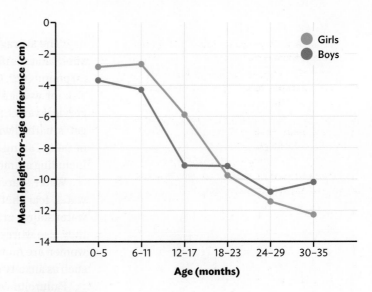

FIGURE 11.22

These curves were generated by plotting mean height-for-age differences (in centimeters) of 119 girls and boys in Totonicapán, Guatemala, at 6-month age intervals. The study began with an ethnographic observation that mothers were feeding young boy and girl children differently based on gendered ideas about children's needs for food. The effects of earlier introduction of solid foods for boys was confirmed through longitudinal study of growth. Initially girls were advantaged compared to boys because they were weaned later, but by the age of 2 years the boys were taller, reflecting their better nutrition.

FIGURE 11.23

In eastern Ethiopia, these women visit this community well several times daily, hauling multiple heavy jerry cans of water back to their homes.

day. The average time it takes to collect water in water-scarce communities in sub-Saharan Africa, for example, is 30 minutes per trip, with weights often over 50 pounds (22.7 kilograms). Doing this work every day results in a much greater risk for women of skeletal damage and pain from chronic compression in the cervical vertebrae of the neck. Paths to water can often be steep or wet, with gates, barbed wire fences, and large rocks, meaning women face enhanced risks of falls. Taking trips at night can increase the risk of other physical traumas, including animal attacks and sexual assault.

Water scarcity is also emotionally stressful, as people worry about getting water, fear that water will run out, and worry about an unsafe journey to the water source at night. Since women are those more often responsible for water, they also worry more about it. Consequently, in water-insecure communities, women are much more likely than men to experience mental health conditions such as anxiety and depression.

Failure to complete water-requiring tasks that women are expected to do, such as preparing dinner, can also trigger *gender-based violence*, such as beating, hitting, or verbal abuse by husbands or other family members with more power. This is yet another way that women's roles within societies place them at different risks of emotional and physical harm compared to men.

We can detect gendered embodiment in the archaeological record of past societies, using skeletal evidence of trauma (Chapter 10). For example, bioarchaeologist Christina Torres examined skeletons dated to about 400–900 CE, from the site of El Torín, located in what is now northern Chile. She found that some excavated individuals who were sexed as males had been buried with labrets (pronounced la-BRETTS; **Figure 11.24**). Sometimes called lip plugs, labrets are worn through a slit in the lower lip. These skeletons had damage on the lower jawbone that suggested chronic rubbing by the labret (that is, they wore them long-term). Those skeletally assigned males buried with labrets had much more skeletal trauma, suggesting violent injury. It seems likely that some form of masculine gender identity was indicated by use of labrets. And those who performed this particular form of masculinity were more involved in potentially violent activities such as warfare. That is, the social performance of maleness resulted in patterns of increased skeletal traumas.

This case also reminds us that not all gender-based violence must be against women, even if most victims are cisgender and transgender women and girls. Gender role expectations can also place men at increased risk of violent trauma and death, such as during warfare (see Chapter 10).

gender-based violence Serious physical, sexual, verbal, or emotional mistreatment directed at an individual because of gender norms and inequalities. This includes violence in response to perceived violations of the norms associated with assigned sex, gender presentation, or identity.

FIGURE 11.24

These labrets made of quartz were excavated in the Andes in northern Chile and dated prior to 600 CE. They are found associated with skeletons assigned as male.

GENDER INEQUALITY AROUND THE GLOBE

Identifying embodiments of gender-different treatment is one way that anthropologists can identify a pattern of disadvantage related to gender within communities. At the national level, gender equality within societies is assessed by factors including the following:

- women's economic participation and opportunities, including any wage gap between men's and women's earnings

- women's autonomy or capacity to make decisions about their daily life, including where they go, how they spend their money, and how they dress

- literacy and educational attainment

- women's control of their own bodies and reproduction (such as access to family planning contraceptives and decision-making)

- recognition and rights for LGBTQIA+ (lesbian, gay, bisexual, transgender, queer, questioning, intersex, and asexual) people

- equity in health and survival of women (women tend to live longer than men)

- women's relative political empowerment through representation in leadership positions

Based on this framework, there are currently no gender-equitable nations (**Figure 11.25**). But the goal of equitable gender status by such markers is considered both a moral necessity and a practical goal by human rights groups and other international agencies.

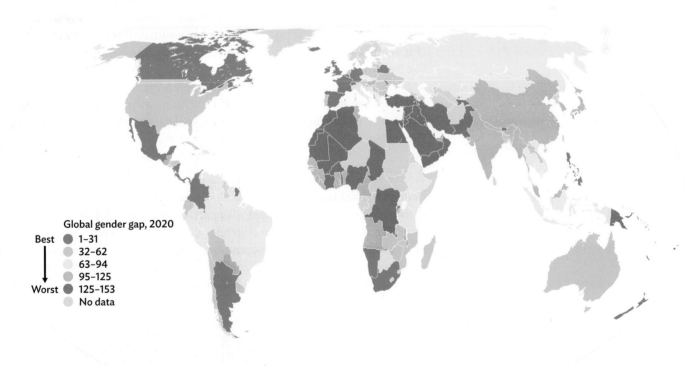

FIGURE 11.25

Gender equality differences across nations are illustrated. Higher numbers reflect greater gender inequity.

FIGURE 11.26

Cultural anthropologist Madawi Al-Rasheed has openly shared her insights on Saudi politics, religion, and gender through media appearances. The Saudi government removed her citizenship in response.

At the very bottom of national gender equality rankings are some African nations, such as the Republic of Congo and Mali, and Muslim-majority countries, some of which are wealthy nations in the Middle East such as Saudi Arabia. These include societies where women's and men's strict gender roles are not just socially expected but also legally mandated. Saudi women have little autonomy from men, and they cannot make decisions or move freely without men's permission; this includes legal permission to get a passport, have cosmetic surgery, or get married. In public, women are required to cover their entire body with a *hijab* (head scarf), *niqab* (face veil), and *abaya* (cloak), excepting the eyes and hands. Much of this is embedded in a guardianship (*wali*) system, where all women are under the protection/control of their husbands or other male relatives. It is also tied to deeply held ideas about the need to control, preserve, and protect women's sexuality.

Saudi anthropologist Madawi Al-Rasheed has used ethnographic interviews combined with studies of media and state documents to show how the control of women and the policing of gender presentation is nonetheless based in and enforced through strict and nationalist interpretations of Islamic law. More broadly, she explains that women's marginalization (which she refers to as a "hostage" dynamic) within Saudi society remains in place because it is embedded in the use of religion to maintain state political power (**Figure 11.26**).

Cultural anthropologist Lila Abu-Lughod has been doing ethnographic research with Muslim women in the Middle East for several decades, mostly in Egypt. She provides a different perspective on gender inequality, considering how people outside the Muslim world perceive practices such as veiling. She explains that many outsiders see veils as symbols of women's oppression. But Muslim women may also view them as "portable seclusion," allowing women the freedom of leaving home while still meeting strict Islamic requirements that women must be separated from men in public spaces. Moreover, viewing all Muslim women as similarly oppressed erases the vast diversity of this group of women who live in an array of different ways with different levels of autonomy (**Figure 11.27**). Abu-Lughod also points out that North American women, just like Saudi or Egyptian ones, dress to reflect their local cultures. And focusing on a "moral crusade" to "save" all Muslim women in the Middle East from men's authority, she says, deflects from self-reflection about the state of oppressions within other more familiar and privileged societies, including places such as the United States, Canada, and the United Kingdom.

WHAT NEXT FOR GENDER*SEX?

Gender and sex exist on a spectrum. Societal adherence to binary gender systems persists in close alignment with patriarchal power, because it acts to disempower anyone who is not a cisgender man (that is, women and transgender or nonbinary people). Men, too, can be negatively affected by patriarchal systems, because they require conformity to rigid definitions of masculinity.

Gender*sex in many societies is currently in flux, broadening how its social categories are imagined and acted on. Women globally have been gaining more

FIGURE 11.27

Women are veiled to differing degrees in Cairo, Egypt.

rights, including economic and political power. Changing medical practices and innovations, such as hormone prescriptions and surgeries, permit physical transitions between male, female, and intersex assignments. The social and legal recognition of nonbinary gender identities is growing. Twenty-first-century forms of communication and media provide an extraordinary and unprecedented arena in which to question and redefine what gender is and how it matters. The increasing practice of naming one's own pronouns (he/she/they/ze/xe) in email signatures and social media profiles, for example, creates an opening for broader conversations about gender identity and helps us all to recognize the unconscious way we make assumptions about gender identities and expressions. Representations of gender diversity in television shows and other entertainment can normalize transgender and nonbinary people, showing them acting and living in ways presented as positive and accepted. Social media, too, allows communities to grow and support members even at a physical distance and can help normalize a diversity of gender expressions. LGBTQIA+ communities are emerging in ways that provide the support and space for physically separated individuals to be able to perform and define gender identities in ways that challenge binary classifications. While there will never be any universal definitions of what constitutes either masculinity or femininity, this disrupts and broadens mainstream, culturally dominant ideas about what it means to live in our societies as a man, a woman, neither, both, or something in between.

11

Gender

Gender identities, in particular societal notions of masculinity and femininity, are enormously influential in how we see ourselves and interact with others.

KEY TERMS
> binary
> femininity
> gender
> gender performance
> gender script
> masculinity
> schema

11.1 | Gender, Sex, and Gender*Sex

Explain how gender is a fundamental organizing construct in human society, and describe why the combined term "gender*sex" captures both biological and social realities.

- Gender is deeply entwined with biological sex. This is why it is sometimes useful to talk of gender*sex as a combined concept.

KEY TERMS
> cisgender
> gender*sex
> hormone
> nonbinary
> sex chromosomes
> transgender

11.2 | Binary Gender and Beyond

Explain how gender is constructed and performed.

- Gender expectations are culturally defined and systemized through institutions, rituals, and our own performances of them. In this way they become core to our social identities. But these identities need not be solely based on binary sex options (female/woman versus male/man). Societies can accommodate and accept other gender expressions and categories.

KEY TERMS
> androgyny
> egalitarian
> gendered division of labor
> polygyny
> pronoun

11.3 | Why Do We Have (Binary) Gender?

Assess the role gender may have played in human evolution.

- There is evidence to suggest the notion of gender has evolutionary roots in our species, though the circumstances in which it would have proven useful to our ancestors aren't present today.

KEY TERMS
> cooperative parenting
> sexual dimorphism

11.4 | Gender, Inequality, and Power

Assess how and why gender inequalities persist.

- Gender beliefs and dynamics consistently favor and support men's power, although the degrees of inequality differ markedly across societies.

KEY TERMS
> diarchy
> embodiment
> gender-based violence
> growth faltering
> health disparity
> matriarchy
> patriarchy
> patrilocality
> power
> sexism

12

Sex, Love, and Marriage

C ultural anthropologist Dinah Hannaford was conducting research with Senegalese migrants working in western Europe. Most were in difficult and low-paid jobs in industries like construction or agriculture, including seasonal grape-picking. She noticed an interesting pattern. Almost all were men, and almost all were living apart from their wives and families. This was the seed of what grew to be a *multisited ethnographic* project on love, intimacy, and transnational marriage that spanned three countries and two continents. She attended weddings and interviewed men in the places they were working in France and Italy, and she interviewed their wives back in their homeland of Senegal (**Figure 12.1**).

As her research progressed, Hannaford estimated that perhaps a quarter of Senegalese marriages might be defined as transnational, with either a husband moving away for work or a woman marrying a Senegalese man who was already living overseas. Sometimes the absences are just a few months, but in many cases they are for years. Why would people be willing to marry or stay married to a partner living in a distant country, one they would rarely see and be unable to create a physical home with?

Men's migration away for work overseas, such as to France or Italy, was often motivated explicitly by the hope of building sufficient wealth to marry initially or to marry again. Muslim Senegalese men marry within a polygynous marriage system that allows them up to four wives. For women, however, only one husband is permitted. Some women were willing, however, to marry men already

LEARNING OBJECTIVES

12.1 Human Sexualities
Summarize the diversity of human sexualities.

12.2 Marriage and Mating Systems
Identify defining elements of human marriage and how these relate to primate mating systems.

12.3 Why and How Humans Marry
Assess the range of reasons humans marry and how and why these are changing.

12.4 Sex Work in a Globalized World
Explain how ethnographic findings expand how we view sex work.

MANY FORMS OF MARRIAGE

Archaeological and primate studies help us understand the very wide array of possible forms of intimate relationships among humans. Human marriage is found globally, and formalizes intimate relationships to create new kin support and obligations. The idea of monogamous, love-based marriages has grown in many places in the last century, but arranged or polygamous marriages remain the preference in others.

multisited ethnography **Research that purposefully collapses the distinction between local field sites and the global systems in which they are embedded.**

FIGURE 12.1

In this photo taken by cultural anthropologist Dinah Han-naford at a Senegalese wedding, the bride arrives at her wedding reception, accompanied by her uncle.

marriage A socially (and often legally) recognized intimate union, creating obligations to each other and other kin.

sexual orientation The kinds of people, roles, or experiences a person is sexually attracted to or oriented toward.

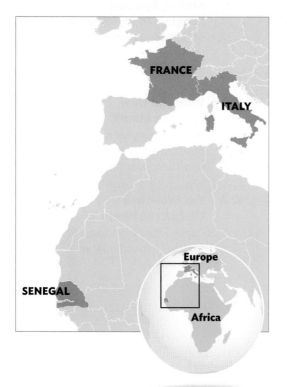

FRANCE

ITALY

Europe

SENEGAL

Africa

living overseas, entering marriage with clear expectations: it would provide them with adult status, social respectability, representation, and economic stability facilitated by easy smartphone transfers of cash from Europe to Senegal.

Many transnational couples had little or no physical element to their marriage and yet described their relationships as caring and intimate, meeting their expectations for what marriage and their roles within it should be. Still, the distance was hard on couples. Wives were unable to engage in the sort of day-to-day activities—cooking for and feeding their husbands, sex, and showing their beauty—that normally allowed them some influence with their partners. And the husbands expressed concerns about having their wives join them abroad, as living with them away from the obligations and expectations of Senegal could lead to wives gaining too much independence and challenging their authority. Lack of physical intimacy also fed husbands' worries about their wives' fidelity. Yet, for many, the economic, nurturing, and status benefits far outweighed the costs.

In Senegal, love, sex, and marriage have changed dramatically in recent years, aided by new technologies and influenced by complex global labor markets, migration, and changing laws. But this is a global story, too, as these practices and institutions are shifting almost everywhere.

In this chapter, we examine how anthropologists make sense of these complex and fluid dynamics of contemporary human sexuality and intimacy, and we examine the range of practices across societies. We then identify the different forms of human mating and marriage systems and explore how they underpin wider social organization. Finally, we consider why humans marry at all, how practices are changing, and some ways anthropological research challenges our assumptions about marriage, intimacy, and sexuality, including the now-globalized industry of sex work.

HUMAN SEXUALITIES

In Chapter 11, we explored what it means to live in society as sex-assigned and the implications and nuances of gender—the performance or other expressions of an internal feeling of being masculine, feminine, nonbinary, and so on. We also explored how gender identities should be understood as separated from those related to sexuality, such as sexual orientation. We now turn to the types of research anthropologists have done on human sexuality, how it expands our understanding and recognition of the myriad possibilities for how humans can express themselves sexually, and how shifts in what is researched are related to broader societal trends and concerns.

Since the beginning of ethnographic fieldwork, anthropologists have documented wide variations in sexual practices across human societies. Earliest efforts reveal far more about the observers than the objects of their study. English physician, colonial administrator, and early anthropologist Walter

Roth published *Ethnological Studies among the North-West-Central Queensland Aborigines in 1897* (**Figure 12.2**). The chapter that documented sexual practices was noted as "not suitable for perusal by the general lay reader," emphasizing his effort to present objectified and dehumanized accounts of non-European sexual practices as scientific knowledge for European audiences. Anthropologists now use such archival materials to understand Victorian sexual anxieties and desires, tracing how such merging of science and spectacle shaped colonial views of "native" peoples and their bodies. Such treatments are now recognized as racialized images that are highly sexualized in ways that grabbed the colonial imagination, creating and reinforcing harmful stereotypes.

The work of subsequent anthropologists such as Bronisław Malinowski and Margaret Mead explicitly described sexual practices that were distinct from what was considered acceptable or normal in mainstream, affluent European society of the early-to-mid-20th century. For example, in his fieldwork in the Trobriand Islands in the western Pacific, Malinowski made detailed notes about sexual practices, such as the biting of eyelashes as a signal of passion. Moreover, premarital sex was both frequent and expected. *The Sexual Life of Savages in North-Western Melanesia* was salacious to his English and European-language readers at the time, and its title reinforced the racism common in European perceptions of the peoples in other regions. But nevertheless, Malinowski's book—and other such ethnographic studies from that time—advanced the important argument that what is defined as normal and desirable in human sexual expression is highly variable across time and societies.

This point was made especially clear in the 1951 book *Patterns of Sexual Behavior*, by anthropologists Clennan Ford and Frank Beach. The book drew together all the existing anthropological research on sexual behavior available at that time. Ford and Beach used a statistical approach to compare patterns based on the observations of anthropologists who had recorded practices in 191 different societies. This included evidence on preferred sexual positions and common types of foreplay. Their book concluded that the only extremely consistent observation about sexual behavior across societies was an incest taboo. That is, all societies they surveyed had cultural rules and often serious sanctions against sexual relations between specified close kin. The exact kin defined as taboo varied, but it always included parents and children.

Otherwise, there was a remarkable amount of diversity among societies regarding what constituted "normal" sexual behaviors, as well as what was deemed erotically, romantically, or aesthetically attractive. Early anthropologists, for example, identified many societies in which male-with-male sexual activity was accepted or even normalized. This notion, that sexuality can be configured within societies in many different ways, remains central to how anthropologists study intimate relations today.

SEXUAL CONFIGURATIONS

Sexuality categories (gay, straight, asexual, and so on) are helpful in many ways but are also limiting in that they do not capture the full spectrum of what people actually desire and do. For example, the notion of sexual orientation makes no distinction between cisgender men who are romantically interested in or sexually intimate with other cisgender men versus cisgender men who are interested in transgender men or transgender women. All of these varied possibilities are observed across human societies. Yet many of these possibilities have been left unacknowledged, unnamed, and/or unspoken, reducing the human experience of intimacy mainly to binaries.

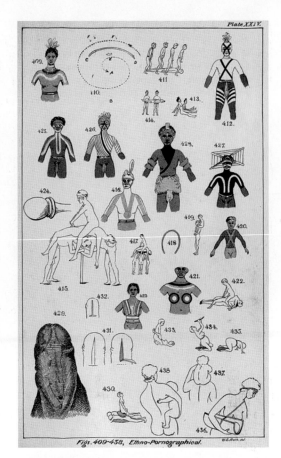

FIGURE 12.2

This panel of sexualized images from Walter Roth's 1897 monograph was intended to be viewed by scientists rather than the general public. Today it tells us more about European sexuality at that time than that of the people being studied.

incest taboo A cultural rule (usually strictly enforced) that prohibits sexual intimacy between kin defined as too closely related.

sexual configurations An approach to describing sexuality that seeks to incorporate as many varied lived experiences as possible, avoiding frameworks that categorize or constrain possibilities.

The concept of sexual configurations, as developed by Sari van Anders, provides an inclusive framework that recognizes both the fluidity of human sexualities and the dynamic relationships between gender*sex, sexual orientations, and sexual practices (**Table 12.1** and **Figure 12.3**). Sexual configurations considers all possible variations and combinations of these identities, preferences, and practices as encountered in the lived experiences of real people, not just those that are most common or considered to represent an "average." This model for understanding sexuality allows for our sexualities to change as we age. It also more easily accommodates new—even unexpected—sexualities that emerge as society changes.

The sexual configuration model also offers a clear distinction between two different aspects of human sexuality: eroticism and nurturance (as shown in Table 12.1). This is a distinction between what people do that is sexually or physically pleasing (eroticism) and how they seek and express emotional intimacy or love (nurturance). It is a useful distinction because people commonly assume these elements must go together in a social institution such as marriage. But, by looking across various case examples, such as the Senegal example that opened our chapter, we can see that pulling these ideas apart can be helpful to our understanding.

van Anders's map of sexual configurations allows sexual majority and minority persons alike to identify nuanced sexualities based on changeable variations in self-identified gender, sex, and gender*sex; desired gender, sex,

---

TABLE 12.1

Aspects of Sexuality as Distinguished from Gender*sex and Each Other by Sexual Configurations Theory

Term	Definition	Examples of Phenomena	Examples of Social Labels
Gender*sex (see Chapter 11)	Whole people and identities; aspects of people that involve both gender *and* sex	Internal sense of self, others' recognitions of self, whole impression, social groups, etc.	Nonbinary, woman, man, trans woman, trans man, cis woman, cis man, intersex, etc.
Sexual status	What people are doing, will do, have done; behaviors, actions, existences, etc.	Penetrative sex, flirting, cuddling, kissing, commitment, etc.	Partnered, married, single-by-choice, multipartnered, not sexually active, women who have sex with women, men who have sex with men, etc.
Sexual orientation	What people are drawn to, feels right, and/or resonates, etc.	Interests, attractions, desires, responses, fantasies, arousals, intimacies, loves, etc.	Heterosexual, bisexual, homosexual, monosexual, asexual, male-oriented, female-oriented, etc.
Sexual identity	Terms and labels people and others use to name themselves, groups, and communities; communities people are accepted in; etc.	Label, identification, politics, community, positioning, etc.	Asexual, polyamorous, heterosexual, queer, bisexual, kink-oriented, lesbian, gay, slut, etc.
Eroticism	Phenomena that are sexually tantalizing, arousing, pleasureful, etc.	Orgasm, genital pleasure, sexual arousal, fantasies, having sex, phone sex, sexting, sexual chemistry, etc.	
Nurturance	Phenomena that are tied to warm, loving feelings and closeness	Support, affection, cuddling, emotional connection, hugs, etc.	

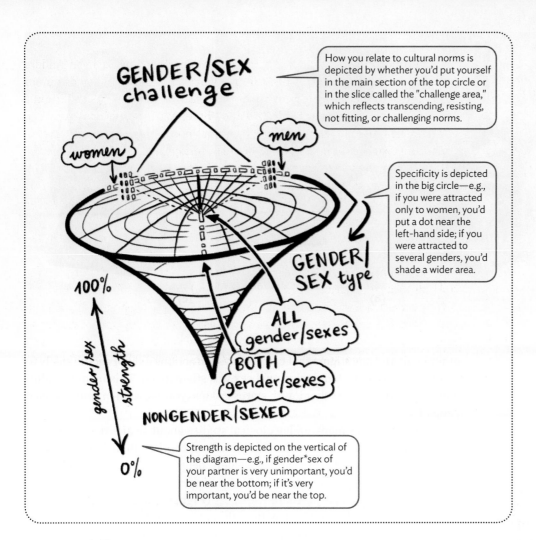

FIGURE 12.3

van Anders's map of sexual configuration is pictured.

and gender*sex of erotic partner; desired gender, sex, and gender*sex of nurturance partner; and number of partners. The ends of each ring indicate the norm boundary (binary gender*sexes: men or women), and the space between the ends of the incomplete ring represent norm challenges (multiple partners, nonbinary, transgender, and so on).

HUMAN SEXUALITIES IN THE ARCHAEOLOGICAL RECORD

Can we confirm such varied sexual configurations in our human pasts? Some archaeologists have focused on erotic sexualities, sexual identity, and sexual orientation. However, the nature of the archaeological record can make drawing conclusions about past sexualities difficult. For example, archaeologists may uncover depictions of various artifacts of men having sex with men. But without a substantial written record, they may not be able to determine what these acts meant to the people involved.

For example, nonanthropological researchers have focused on sexualities, particularly same-sex sexual desire, in ancient Greece and Rome, where a variety of sex acts, including those between men, are depicted on ceramic vessels and in paintings and murals. Classical scholars, who study the history of Mediterranean societies, initially argued that these depictions were evidence of same-sex practices in the past. However, more recent analyses of extensive written records have helped to contextualize the images and suggest that same-gender*sex attraction as we understand it today didn't exist in the classical Greek and Roman worlds. Rather, many men participated in sexual acts with

FIGURE 12.4

Moche ceramic vessels depict what is interpreted as **(a)** an individual portrait, **(b)** performing oral sex, and **(c)** a masturbating skeleton.

(a)

(b)

(c)

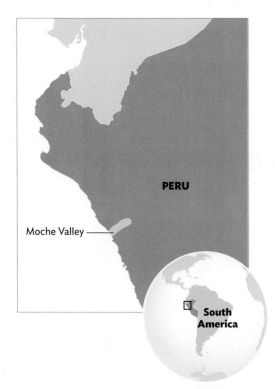

PERU

Moche Valley

South America

other men. And any stigma that came from such actions did not accrue solely to men: anyone penetrated during anal sex was stigmatized. This included adult men but also people in other lower-status groups (youths, women, and enslaved people).

There are not as many archaeological studies about sexualities in the past in areas without written records. One notable exception, though, comes from northern Peru about 1,500 years ago, where people living in the Moche Valley and the neighboring region created stunning ceramic vessels with graphic depictions of single and partnered sex acts (**Figure 12.4**). Oral sex, masturbation, and anal and vaginal sex with both same-sex and different-sex couples are all depicted in very detailed three-dimensional pots. Moche pots contained nonsexual images as well, and were used to store liquids and interred (buried) with human burials.

Sometimes people call these examples of ancient pornography or evidence of "homosexuality" in the past. But what did these acts mean to the Moche people? For that, we need to look to the archaeological context rather than imposing our contemporary ideas regarding sexualities, where the concept of non-heterosexuality as a sexual orientation may not have existed as it does now. Most Moche "sex pots" have been found in high-status tombs, where they were mortuary offerings. Cultural anthropologist Mary Weismantel has argued that, when they were placed in elite tombs, the pots may have symbolized the transfer of reproductive fluids such as semen from the ancestors to the living. When contextualized this way, Moche artisans' ceramic work cannot simply be labeled as evidence of gay identities, pornography, or other sexual orientations as we understand them today. We simply don't know enough to be able to interpret their meanings in Moche terms.

Relatedly, anthropological analyses can illuminate our biases with regard to how we interpret the archaeological record. For example, two people were buried hand-in-hand in Italy, interred about 1,600 years ago. They were initially and romantically referred to as the "Lovers of Modena," assumed to be a man and woman in a loving embrace. With other bones poorly preserved, bioarchaeologists recently used a new technique that looks at different proteins in tooth enamel. Through tooth protein analysis, they discovered that these so-called "Lovers of Modena" were both most likely biologically male.

Archaeologists are able to identify some economic aspects of sex in the past from material remains. For example, excavations at brothels in Los Angeles, California, and St. Paul, Minnesota, in the United States have shown that the front of the house, where sex workers would have been entertaining male clients, have remains of high-status foods, such as bones from expensive cuts of meat, and a wider variety of foods served on expensive dishes compared to neighboring houses. However, the rear yard areas, which were private and would have been used by the women who worked at the brothels when they weren't with clients, had remains of inexpensive foods served on plain dishes. Archaeological excavations at brothel sites have also uncovered personal items such as bottles of medicine used to prevent or treat sexually transmitted infections, as well as evidence of infants and children living at the brothels, such as baby bottles and children's toys. Although the women and children living at brothel sites in the United States during the 1800s can't tell us about their lives directly or how they experienced sex work as a profession, excavations can give important information about how some aspects of their lives were arranged.

CHALLENGING HETERONORMATIVITY

Anthropological research has been important for challenging assumptions of universal heteronormativity. New understandings of how people understand their own sexualities combined with understandings of how people behave can provide new information to considerations of law, medicine, and other aspects of social life. Yet even as an increasing number of societies come to recognize the lived reality of nonheteronormative sexual statuses, acknowledging the fluidity and further diversity of sexualities has represented an ongoing challenge.

heteronormativity The assumption that heterosexual orientation and sexual activity are "normal," meaning other sexual configurations are considered abnormal or not considered at all.

For example, beginning in the late 1980s, much anthropological research on sexuality focused on the human immunodeficiency virus (HIV)/acquired immunodeficiency syndrome (AIDS) crisis. Public health researchers did not fully understand nonheterosexual statuses, and so they were unable to accurately trace the sexual transmission of the infectious disease. Health officials assumed that all men who had sex with men had a singular and fully overlapping sexual status, orientation, and identity, all defined by being gay. Research by cultural anthropologists showed that, to the contrary, men who had sex with men sometimes avoided terms like gay. Rather, some said they described themselves as "normal" because they also had wives and children. This failure to understand the complexities and fluidities of sexual identity left a large set of men who have sex with men out of HIV/AIDS prevention efforts. Ethnographic research conducted at that time in the urban United States helped public health efforts by explaining how plural forms of sexual status operated and why this mattered.

Linguistic anthropologist David Valentine's ethnographic work in New York City in the late 1990s reiterated this point with reference to the then-emerging recognition of transgender status. Again, it was a case of a singular category being imposed on much more complicated ideas of gender, sex, and sexuality. Valentine conducted his fieldwork while working as a safe-sex activist, riding his bicycle across the city late at night, visiting organized social events, bars, support groups, and clinics. Valentine intended to study transgender communities (specifically transgender women), but he discovered many people he encountered were unfamiliar with or avoided using the term. They simply didn't use the term transgender; rather, they defined themselves in terms of sexuality such as gay.

FIGURE 12.5

Gay sexualities remain marginalized and unacceptable in many places, including much of Indonesia. The most extreme Indonesian sanctions are found, where provincial government laws allow for public caning (shown here) for men identified as having sex with men.

FIGURE 12.6

Once a slur, the term "queer" now is used by some historically marginalized communities to recast their sexual identities in positive terms. This was observed during a 2019 pride parade in Helsinki, Finland.

Despite their limitations and the importance of keeping these in mind when considering the spectrum of human sexuality, singular categoric terms can nonetheless become helpful in other ways. Labels that represent inner feelings of selfhood, such as transgender, gay, lesbian, and others, can provide the basis for the emergence of real, supportive, and meaningful communities. Such communities, defined by shared, nonnormative sexual identities, may develop their own dress codes or language, inscribing individuals' membership in—and reinforcing their sense of belonging to—a particular group. In addition, having access to such language contributes to defining their differences from others.

In Indonesia, those who identify as gay men and those who identify as *waria* (a combination of the words *wanita*, "woman," and *pria*, "man") sometimes use a style of speech termed "Bahasa gay." This language register (a cluster of pronunciation, words, intonation, or other grammatical features) uses the systematic substitution of standard Indonesian (Bahasa) first syllables to create unique word forms individuals use to speak to one another within the community, helping to create a sense of belonging. For example, *semangka* (watermelon) is used in place of the word *semak* (to like); in this case, the first two syllables (sema[ng]-) of the words match. Or, the brand name *bodrex* (a cough syrup) replaces *bodoh* (stupid). Even as openly gay sexual expression remains variously marginalized, discriminated against, and illegal across the archipelago (**Figure 12.5**), Bahasa gay has also been adopted by other people who do not identify as gay and appropriated in various forms of popular culture such as Indonesian television talk shows. These identities, signaled through language and other expressive cultural symbols, serve to gather people into collectivities of inclusion and belonging.

Newly recognized shared identities that get labeled can help to enact social change through the communities that are created around those identities (**Figure 12.6**). In 2014–2015, Syrian anthropologist Fadi Saleh studied nonbinary gender identities, including transgender, in refugee camps in Istanbul,

Turkey. When living in Syria, the idea of identifying as transgender was unthinkable (and possibly life-threatening, due to discrimination). But with the United Nations' recognition that minoritized sexualities and genders are at greater risk for discrimination, violence, and even death, refugees were empowered to assert their identities in order to seek political asylum. Saleh's work shows that the spotlighting of these identities allowed minority gender identities and sexual orientations to become more visible within wider Syrian society.

RESISTANCE TO THE OPPRESSION OF SEXUALITY

Anthropological research, such as the study of Syrian refugees just described, shows how gender identities and sexuality labels can be used as a means of actively challenging gender and orientation-based (and other forms of) oppression. So can sexual statuses, including how people choose to be physically intimate with others.

Ethnographic studies conducted in Tehran in 2000 found that in the decade after the death of the leader of the Iranian Revolution and the end of the Iran–Iraq War, many Iranian exiles returned and young people yearned for sexual and social change. Iran had one of the youngest populations in the world, with youthful concentrations who lived in the city and were well educated, living under the rule of an Islamist regime that emphasized traditional, highly conservative social values (**Figure 12.7**). Premarital or extramarital sex was subject to extremely harsh punishment, including public execution. Confidential interviews, sexual history surveys, and participant observation at parties, shopping malls, and the university by cultural anthropologist Pardis Mahdavi described how the defiant clandestine acts of dating and sexual connection were a means for young Tehranis to express their political dissent. Even as sexual activity is constrained by social conventions and laws, sometimes to extremes, its privacy means it is also a way that people can nonetheless exercise agency.

agency The capacity for individual power, such as acting independently and making free choices.

FIGURE 12.7

Sex outside marriage is illegal in Iran, punishable even by death. For young Iranians, embracing desire and pursuing sexual intimacies in private can be understood as a form of rebellion and resistance to living under a politically and socially oppressive regime. Here are some young people in Tehran hanging out in a bowling alley.

FIGURE 12.8

Cultural anthropologist Kim TallBear emcees an evening of sexy storytelling, performances, and audience participation in "Tipi Confessions." The show purposefully embraces the widest array of sexual configurations and doubles as a "research-creation laboratory" at the University of Alberta, Canada.

FIGURE 12.9

In this boundary stone from the archaeological site of Sippar, in what is now Iraq, the cuneiform script describes a conflict between two families who argue about the land that passed from one family to the other through marriage. The image at the top of the boundary stone shows the Babylonian ruler Nabu-mukin-appli, who ruled from approximately 978–943 BCE.

Studies of sexuality can themselves be a form of personal and professional activism, aimed at expanding recognition of minority sexualities. Cultural anthropologist Kim TallBear has been exploring autoethnographic approaches to challenging the dominance of monogamy as the only ethical sexual status within the United States and Canada (**Figure 12.8**). Her work—drawing on her perspective as an Indigenous Dakota woman—is both personal and political. She practices and studies what she terms "ethical nonmonogamy" or polyamory as a means to challenge and destabilize assumptions of what intimate relationships can and should be. Her activist scholarship shows that what is considered "normal" in mainstream North American society today reflects a relatively recent and particularly stringent set of settler society ideas. Her work further reveals that her own Dakota ancestors practiced alternate sexualities such as polyamory in the past. However, colonial efforts were successfully able to dictate that acceptable sexualities must entail different-sex attraction and monogamy and that families must consist of one man, one woman, and their children living together on one piece of land.

SECTION 12.2

MARRIAGE AND MATING SYSTEMS

In this section, we further explore human intimacy by considering the range of possibilities of human marriage practices and the wider context of human mating systems. Marriage as a legally codified institution probably extends back no further than about 5,500 years ago (**Figure 12.9**). But marriage is defined more broadly as a socially recognized and sanctioned pair bond that creates new family ties, and this can be traced back much further into the human past.

Marriages today are sometimes legally codified and marked by a religious ceremony or confirmed by a judge. However, some marriages are marked by neither. As a topic of anthropological research, marriage is generally considered to be the effort of a couple joining together with the intention to create new, socially recognized families—connecting love, sex, and reproduction through institutionalized pairing as spouses.

Marriage—as formal social recognition—is an institution that is social, economic, and cultural all at once. It creates extremely important human social relationships that extend well beyond a bonded pair and have profound implications for if and how we reproduce. Marriage also has significant implications for how humans care for and invest in children. It encourages others in the extended family to provide care and legitimizes economic and personal aspects such as inheritance.

Perhaps most notably, marriage creates new affinal kin (or nonbiological kin). Kinship is an extremely dense, reciprocal (two-way) relationship that entails specific roles with expectations, rights, and obligations. We are born with consanguineal kin or affinal kin, related to us by birth or adoption, such as siblings, parents, and grandparents. Our kin are typically those we feel particularly emotionally connected to; we rely on them for support in our daily lives and call on them for additional assistance in times of crisis.

Studies by evolutionary anthropologists in small-scale societies suggest that people can feel as emotionally close to affinal kin, and act as enthusiastically to protect and avenge them, as they do to consanguineal kin. This makes sense, as in-laws share genetic interests in the next generation—that is, all are equally vested in children that result from marriage.

Kinship rules differ from society to society, and they provide a map for navigating social relationships. For example, among the Mukogodo, a Maa-speaking cattle-herding group in north-central Kenya, widows do not typically remarry. But they can continue to have children with new partners and remain living in their husbands' settlements, raising the children as their recognized and legal offspring.

These newly formed kin relations created through marriage institutions are both created by and reflected in the ways that we talk to one another. As new obligations and rights arise as the result of marriage, the language also shifts. Consider, for example, the shift we may experience in American English from "my significant other" to "my spouse/partner" upon marriage. While the speaker may feel like the person being referred to is "the same," others may interpret this shift as monumental. It has been observed and reported across many languages that when a couple starts a family, they begin to refer to and address one another with parent-kin terms, adopting the term that a child would use toward a parent (e.g., papa or mama).

Many Indigenous Australians explain that their worlds are divided into relatively discrete categories of kin and nonkin, friends, neighbors, and strangers. Language forms, including forms to be avoided, create and signal these relationships among people. Using this language register creates the relationship of the speaker to the listener. Across Indigenous Australia, a man is to avoid his mother-in-law or, if it was necessary to interact, to do so with extreme care and deference. Men use "mother-in-law language" in several Indigenous Australian communities. Mother-in-law language is a form of avoidance speech used most commonly by a man toward his wife's mother, but it is also used when speaking to one's wife's mother's brother, when referring to a mother-in-law (even if she is not present), and in the presence or within earshot of a mother-in-law (even if she is not the addressee). It requires particular words to be changed or avoided due to taboos around those words (**Table 12.2**).

KENYA

Mukogodo Hills

Africa

autoethnography Ethnographic research that fully centers on personal experience and reflection as a means to investigate and understand societies.

monogamy The practice of being with one intimate partner at a time.

polyamory The practice of being with multiple intimate partners at a time, with the consent of all involved.

pair bond A social arrangement of residing and mating with only one other individual at a time.

affinal kin Family relationships created through marriage, such as in-laws, or by adoption.

kinship Extremely close social relationships that have a density of expectations and obligations attached to them.

consanguineal kin Family relationships created through shared blood relationships.

language register Different ways of using language according to the audience.

avoidance speech A particular, restricted speech form in some languages that must be used in the presence of, in reference to, or in conversation with certain relatives.

TABLE 12.2

Examples of Mother-in-Law Language in Gooniyandi, an Australian Indigenous Language

Mother-in-Law Term	Everyday Word	English Equivalent
balija	yoowooloo	man
mayamarlami	goornboo	woman
gilwili	barndi	arm
goombarloorloo/goomboo	yilaa	urine

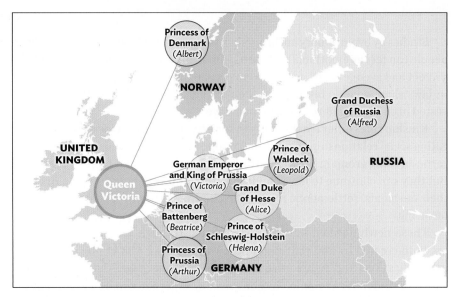

FIGURE 12.10

Queen Victoria of England carefully orchestrated marriage matches for her children. Of her nine children, eight married into other European royal households (shown). Ultimately, her grandchildren ruled seven countries (Germany, Russia, Norway, Spain, Greece, and the United Kingdom).

Likewise, when one recognizes someone as equal to a mother-in-law, this style of language is used to signal that relationship. That is, a person may not consider someone to be their daughter/son-in-law, but when that individual uses mother-in-law language toward them, the daughter/son-in-law is creating that relationship (and the obligations that come with it) with that person. This is an example of a way that language is social action.

Common categories of words that have specific mother-in-law terms include body parts (e.g., shoulder, arm, ear, head), objects made by humans (e.g., spear, boomerang), and things related to food (e.g., water, fire, meat). It seems that mother-in-law language has terms for things that are personal and significant to humans.

Marriage can also be a means to secure political and other alliances between tribes, clans, or even nations. This was the case in many marriages between European royal families until very recently. Queen Victoria, monarch of the United Kingdom of Great Britain and Ireland from 1837 to 1901, arranged the marriages of eight out of her nine children into other European royal families (**Figure 12.10**). Seven of the resulting grandchildren went on to ascend thrones. This soft but tightly binding form of political alliance helped to keep Europe relatively stable and Britain globally dominant for decades.

This brings us to a further point: In many societies, the choice of mate can't be left to individuals alone. There's simply too much at stake.

MARRIAGE SYSTEMS

Marriage takes place within the context of social and legal rules about who can unite legally, socially, and economically with whom. No matter what kinds of marriage systems a society recognizes, political or religious institutions establish clear rules for the system.

The majority of societies globally allow polygyny, a marriage system in which one man has a socially sanctioned relationship with more than one wife,

polygyny A marriage system in which men are permitted or expected to have more than one wife at the same time.

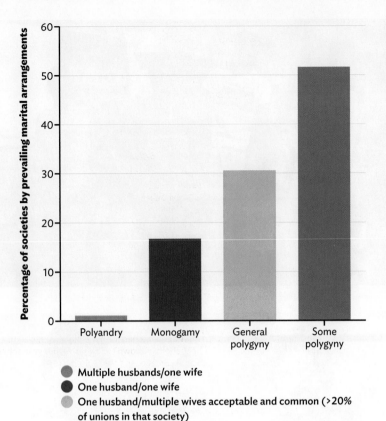

FIGURE 12.11

Within what is termed the "Standard Cross-Cultural Sample" of 186 human societies documented by anthropologists before 1961, polygynous marriage (one man/multiple women) was allowed in the majority. Polyandry (one woman/multiple men) was identified in only two.

Percentage of societies by prevailing marital arrangements

- Multiple husbands/one wife
- One husband/one wife
- One husband/multiple wives acceptable and common (>20% of unions in that society)
- One husband/multiple wives acceptable but uncommon (<20% of unions in that society)

supporting the women and their children (**Figure 12.11**). In groups that practice polygyny, there are typically rules and hierarchies that dictate the status of wives in relation to their shared husband as well as the other wives.

A less typical example of polygyny centers on allowing both the husband and wife to have sex with people other than their main spouse. Some Herero groups in rural Namibia engage in practices that can be viewed as informal polyamory woven into formal systems of polygamous marriages (**Figure 12.12a**). The first marriage is considered a serious obligation and is arranged between different lineages. It includes living patrilocally (with the husband's family). This relationship may or may not involve sex. Rather, marriage is about forming important symbolic, political, and economic alliances. The social standing of not just the couple but their families as well is based in a successful marriage. Beyond the marriage, both spouses may form additional, long-term different-sex sexual relationships, with a partner chosen from among their cross-cousins (the children of a mother's brother or a father's sister), a preferred marriage partner in many African societies. These relationships are understood as being for enjoyment rather than as part of an obligation, and they can include gift exchanges.

Polyandrous marriage and mating, in which a woman has more than one sanctioned husband or long-term male partner, is exceptionally rare. In societies that permit polyandry (generally alongside polygynous and monogamous marriage forms as well), there is often a principal or senior husband (often the oldest), who may be considered the father of all children even if the wife has sex with other men. But in some cases, co-husbands may share rights as father to any children.

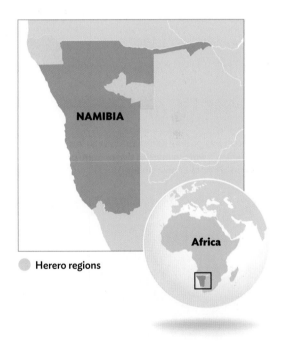

Herero regions

polygamy A marriage system in which a person can have more than one wife or husband at the same time.

lineage A group of people who trace their descent from one common ancestor.

polyandry A marriage system in which women are permitted or expected to have more than one husband at the same time.

FIGURE 12.12

(a) Herero families, like this one captured at their homestead in Namibia, are configured within a flexible polygynous system of formal marriage and additional sanctioned relationships. Herero lifeways have historically been based around cattle pastoralism. **(b)** A Tibetan woman from the high-altitude agricultural zone of Humla, Nepal is pictured with her two husbands.

(a)

(b)

fraternal polyandrous marriage A system in which a woman marries two or more brothers (who are not her own siblings).

Importantly, in sustained *fraternal polyandrous marriage* systems, the co-husbands are also brothers. In these cases, husbands don't just share a wife; they often also share land or other highly valued resources, and this co-ownership is what allows the marriages to remain stable.

Anthropologists have documented as many as 28 societies in the Himalayan zone in Asia—including India, Nepal, Bhutan, and Tibet—that sanction polyandry, in many cases fraternal polyandrous marriages. One of the most detailed studies was conducted in 1982–1983 by cultural anthropologist Nancy Levine, in the small ethnically Tibetan villages of the Humla district in northeastern Nepal. Levine was conducting a study to understand how different family and reproductive arrangements were linked to how people managed the very limited amount of agricultural land in the high-altitude valleys between the mountains. The most common marriage pattern she identified was sons who grew up together, married the same woman, and continued living together as adults. This provided the means to keep limited family land holdings together, shared by one household instead of being split into smaller plots (**Figure 12.12b**). This also helps explain why, as more men globally work for cash wages, polyandrous marriage systems seem to be growing even rarer.

Today, however, monogamous marriage between just two partners is the most common form of marriage worldwide despite the fact that polygyny is legal in the majority of societies. Some societies that legally allow only monogamous marriage may nonetheless tolerate informal forms of polygynous

FIGURE 12.13

Monogamy is the only legal marriage form in France, but how people arrange their intimate relationships is more complex. At the state funeral of President François Mitterrand (head of state from 1981 to 1995), his mistress and their daughter (far right) were present and acknowledged alongside his legal wife (far left).

arrangements, in which one man may support more than one partner and family (**Figure 12.13**). Most also allow for serial monogamy following divorce or death of a spouse. Notably, even in polygyny-preferring societies, such as the Senegal case that opened our chapter, only a minority of men end up marrying more than one wife because it takes wealth to do so. So even if men prefer to be married to more than one woman at the same time, they often end up living monogamously anyway.

Biological anthropologists have been able to test some assumptions about whether polygynous marriages serve the interests of men at a cost to wives and children. In a study of 1,764 ethnically diverse households in northern Tanzania that were variously monogamous and polygynous and included wives of varying ranks, household wealth, child growth, and food security were measured. According to these basic dimensions of well-being, polygynous households were not harmful to wives and children because those households were wealthier to begin with and so could support the children.

In general, human marriage systems tend to pattern in some very basic ways according to how communities have historically made their living. In places where resources such as food are highly dispersed, as in some hunter-gatherer societies, monogamy seems more common. When resources are concentrated or clustered and can be controlled more by some men while others are excluded, such as in subsistence farming societies (with regard to livestock herds), polygyny is more common. The main exception is societies in which monogamy is legally enforced. For example, there are major differences in wealth and access to the resources that drive wealth in the United States, but the wealthiest men are still limited to one legal spouse at a time. Furthermore, where divorce is easier to obtain, monogamy tends to be the only legal form of marriage.

serial monogamy The practice of engaging in more than one monogamous relationship over one's life span.

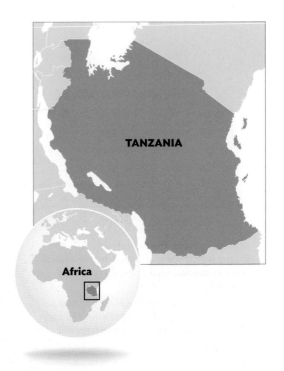

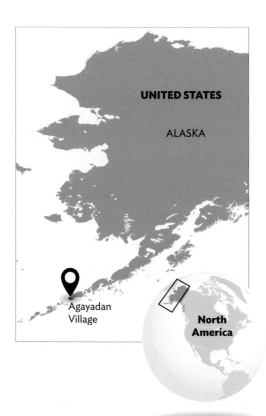

Agayadan
Village

North
America

Archaeologically, marriage systems, just like past sexualities, can be hard to document in regions without written records. For example, written records indicate that polygyny was common in Viking-age Scandinavia in northern Europe, but these groups would have been described as monogamous based on excavation data alone because of the cemeteries where one man and one woman, presumably husband and wife, were buried together.

Nonetheless, in areas without written records, archaeologists can use excavation data to look at how households were organized in the past. For example, household archaeology focuses on small-scale individual residences to learn about people's daily lives. Detailed excavations of large communal houses at Agayadan Village in Alaska showed how multiple family groups lived together in one larger house, with separate sleeping areas and storage pits for each family group, plus centrally located hearths for the larger household group to prepare food together. This would have allowed them to conserve and most efficiently use driftwood, which was valuable but rare in the Aleutian Islands, for cooking, heating, and lighting the whole house. However, without written records, it is hard to know if these households were composed of one husband and multiple wives with their children, one husband and one wife and their adult children and grandchildren, or some other configuration of social relationships.

HUMAN AND PRIMATE MATING SYSTEMS

Evolutionary anthropologists tend to study sexual and reproductive behavior at the level of the species as mating systems. Primatologists have identified four basic systems that characterize the range of mating strategies of living primate species (**Table 12.3**). Humans are unusual among primates because they variously apply all of the different mating systems, from short-term mating to enduring relationships known as pair bonds, suggesting our species is exceptionally flexible in this regard. One male/one female (monogamous) mating systems are more common in primates than in other mammals and are the typical arrangement in one-third of primate species. Monogamy between just two partners is the most numerically common, socially recognized pair bond arrangement in humans, as already noted, despite the fact that polygyny is acceptable or even preferred in the majority of societies.

In monogamous primate species, both males and females seem to exhibit a high level of selectivity regarding with whom they mate. They also tend to have a lower degree of sexual dimorphism; that is, males are not much larger physically than females. Polygynous species, by contrast, tend to have significant sexual dimorphism, where males are much larger than females; this seems in part linked to being able to defend from encroachment by other males of the same species, not just protection from predators.

Biological anthropologists have considered the evolutionary benefits of a longer term, even lifelong, pair bonds as a mating strategy using a variety of possible hypotheses. One suggests that when males and females work together, they can better defend limited resources, such as food. Another is that pair bonding is an evolved response to males' inability to defend multiple females at once. An additional idea is that pair bonding benefits females, as it assists in their caring for or protecting their young, improving chances of survival for all. Monogamous mating systems tend to also have higher paternity certainty, meaning that males invested in caring for a pair-bonded mate's offspring have a better chance of contributing to their own (rather than another male's) infant's survival.

mating system The typical pattern of sexual and reproductive arrangements of a social group or species, such as number of mates acquired.

paternity certainty The likelihood that a male caring for the offspring of a bonded partner is likely to be caring for his own genetic offspring.

TABLE 12.3

Primate Mating Systems

System	Description	Examples		
One male/ one female (monogamy)	One female mates exclusively or almost exclusively with one male. Females and males tend to be closer in body size, and males tend to contribute more parental care for their offspring than the males in other mating systems. Females tend not to seek out additional mating partners.	Found in Central and South American owl monkeys and titi monkeys and in Southeast Asian siamangs and gibbons		Dusky titi monkeys of South America bond deeply as a pair—often for life—and males invest heavily in caring for their offspring. Pairs become highly distressed when separated.
Multiple males/ one female (polyandry)	One female mates with multiple males to the exclusion of other females. Polyandry is rare in primates and only occurs in a few species; it is relatively unstable compared to the other systems.	Observed sometimes in the smallest monkeys in Central and South America		Geoffroy's tamarin is found in Panama and Colombia. Females often choose to mate with several males, and males will provide some care for all infants in the wider social group regardless of paternity.
One male/ multiple females (polygyny)	One male mates with multiple females to the exclusion of other males, with significant competition among males. Species tend to have significant sexual dimorphism, with males much larger than females; this may be linked to being able to defend from encroachment by other males of the same species, not just protection from predators.	Seen in galagos, lorises, some lemurs, some tarsiers, some baboons, and gorillas		Gorilla family groups are composed of a dominant male, their females, and their young, as seen here in Mgahinga National Park, Uganda.
Multiple males/multiple females (polygynandry)	Both males and females have more than one mate. Often associated with male-dominant hierarchies within groups that allow some males preferential access to more (or more fertile) females.	The most common mating system in primates, observed in many species of lemurs and monkeys including macaques, most baboons, squirrel monkeys, and capuchins		Ring-tailed lemurs of Madagascar live in multiple male/multiple female groups.

Just as with humans, primate mating systems in practice are often more complicated than they seem on the surface. Asian gibbons are often cited as among the most monogamous of primates, living much of their lives in groups consisting of one male, one female, and their offspring. Yet primatologists have observed gibbons engaged in extrapair mating, and gibbons can also decide to transfer to new partners after staying with another for years. This is one reason that primatologists are increasingly questioning whether "monogamy" is

extrapair mating When members of a monogamous species mate outside of their bonded pair.

FIGURE 12.14

A female bonobo with estrus swelling is shown here.

estrus Notable changes in female sexual attractivity (swellings, olfactory, and color changes that attract males), proceptivity (female initiation), and receptivity (willingness to mate) around the time most likely to result in conception.

bridewealth Payment to a woman's family to confirm a marriage (also called bride-price) and often to compensate for the loss of a daughter.

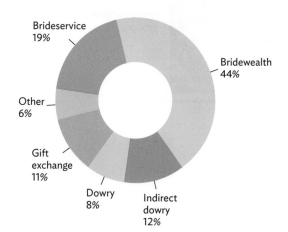

FIGURE 12.15

This chart depicts types of economic marriage transactions across the 186 societies recorded in the "Standard Cross-Cultural Sample" prior to 1961.

really the correct term to use to describe when one male and one female live as a bonded primate pair.

Moreover, some primate sexual activity—such as that of humans—is not only about reproduction. While primates are most sexually active during estrus, bonobos (one of our closest living primate relatives) also often engage in sexual interactions in everyday life at all ages and when not in estrus (**Figure 12.14**). Genital rubbing, touching, and mounting are common forms, and help contribute to reconciliation after conflicts around food, comfort others in distress, or otherwise alleviate social stresses and "keep the peace."

But, compared with all living primates, human sexual behavior is much further disentangled from reproduction because there is no discernible estrus. Humans are sexually receptive when pregnant, post-menopausal, engaged in same-sex intimacy, and otherwise unable to conceive. Several explanations have been proposed for this apparent "loss" of estrus in hominin evolution. Perhaps, released from the chaotic distractions of estrus, males could better invest in raising their own children while females could also then harness stable emotional and physical support. Currently, we can only guess, but our non-estrus human sexuality crucially defines how we can and do relate to each other today, and makes the human universal stable social arrangement of marriage possible.

SECTION 12.3

WHY AND HOW HUMANS MARRY

Marriage is one of the main social means for creating close new relationships. Kinship is a social mechanism that tells who we are compelled to care for (and who is compelled to care for us). Kinship is created through birth, adoption, or marriage, with varied lifelong material and emotional obligations such as gift-giving, moneylending, inheritance, or care when young or old. Consequently, families typically care greatly who marries whom, because marriages create new affinal relationships and, with those, new obligations and opportunities. Marriage may move people in and out of households, taking their labor or income with them, and may have other implications for family wealth and inheritance. Parents and other family members can exert substantial sway regarding who marries whom, in part because it involves religious and social values that help maintain their communities and inform their personal identities.

MARRIAGE AND ECONOMIC ARRANGEMENTS

Marriage itself often entails significant exchanges of usable resources, labor, or other valued things between the new kin. This can shape whom potential spouses and families consider acceptable and desirable partners. For parents in China, the education level of the potential spouses is an important consideration. Sometimes part of the negotiation over a marriage involves considering how it will include transfers of wealth or goods from one family to the other (**Figure 12.15**).

In some societies where women's labor is considered central to family wealth, it is tradition for a groom's family to pay bridewealth. This may be understood by those involved as a negotiated compensation for the loss of a valuable daughter by her natal family, especially if she is moving to the husband's village or city. The agropastoralist Kipsigis people in southwestern Kenya make a single bridewealth payment as a lump sum of cash and an agreed-upon number of livestock at marriage. The choice of a husband by a woman and her family will take into account the amount of land he owns and the amount of bridewealth being offered.

Brideservice is another way a bride's family might be compensated for their loss, consisting of an intended groom living with and working for the bride's family for some time before she moves away. Among the Ju/'hoansi (!Kung) of the Kalahari Desert, a new or prospective husband could join the bride's family for several years. By hunting for and feeding them, his future wife and family can ensure he measures up as a suitable spouse before she moves away. Brideservice as a gift of labor to a wife and her family has become less common in many places as more men can work in the cash economy. The ability to earn facilitates direct payments of bridewealth instead.

Dowry moves wealth in the opposite direction and is an agreed-upon payment—often cash, goods such as jewelry, or household items such as those for cooking—from the family of the bride. The goods come with her at the time of marriage. These payments can either be given to the bride and stay with her, sometimes acting as insurance in case of divorce or widowhood, or they can be given to the groom's family directly. This form is more common in societies where women are blocked from earning or accruing their own wealth and their labor in the house is devalued. The dowry is then viewed as compensation for the family taking on the "burden" of supporting the wife.

One of the most famous dowry systems was the one practiced legally across India until the mid-20th century. Large lavish weddings were common, with huge amounts of cash, clothing, and other goods handed to the groom's extended family. The amount given was taken to reflect the status of the bride's family, and social pressures toward generosity meant debt was often incurred. There was a significant gray area, however, regarding whether the dowry was coerced versus freely given. Humiliation and physical abuse suffered by some brides when the dowry was viewed as insufficient led to the legal prohibition of dowry in India in 1961. However, extravagant weddings continue today, and an informal dowry system is also still in effect in many places in India (**Figure 12.16**).

brideservice Work provided by a prospective or new husband to a bride's family, prior to or early in marriage, cementing his relationship with them.

dowry Transfers of wealth from a bride's to a groom's family to confirm a marriage (and often to compensate for the cost of supporting their daughter).

FIGURE 12.16

The wedding of English actress Elizabeth Hurley and Indian businessman Arun Nayar was particularly lavish. It included ceremonies at a castle in England and a palace in India, with pop legend Elton John performing.

MARRIAGE AND LIVING ARRANGEMENTS

Marriage often involves changes to living arrangements, whether moving to a new residence down the street, in the next village, or across the world. The Senegal couples who opened this chapter and were separated across countries didn't necessarily live together once legally married, but in many cases, the wife moved to the home of her new in-laws. Most societies have some basic norms about where new couples settle. These can vary greatly even in the same region (**Figure 12.17**).

Patrilocality, which is the most common rule on postmarital residence in human societies, refers to the expectation that brides move with or near their husband's family, even if it is a long way from their natal family location. **Matrilocality**, in which the man moves near or in with the woman's family after marriage, is less common. **Ambilocality** means either living arrangement is acceptable and both are practiced within a society. **Neolocality**, in which the new couple establishes their own new household that is away from both sets of parents, is now especially common in urban areas where people are working in cash economies and housing is affordable. It also usually occurs with less expectation of marriage compensation.

Biological anthropologists and archaeologists have been able to reconstruct marriage practices in the past by comparing the ancient DNA or other aspects of the phenotypes (see Chapter 3) of buried individuals from the same communities. This can identify if women or men relocated into communities, by

patrilocality A system in which married couples live near or with the husband's family.

matrilocality A system in which married couples live near or with the wife's family.

ambilocality A system in which married couples can live near or with either the wife's or the husband's family.

neolocality A system in which married couples move to a new household that is away from both sets of parents.

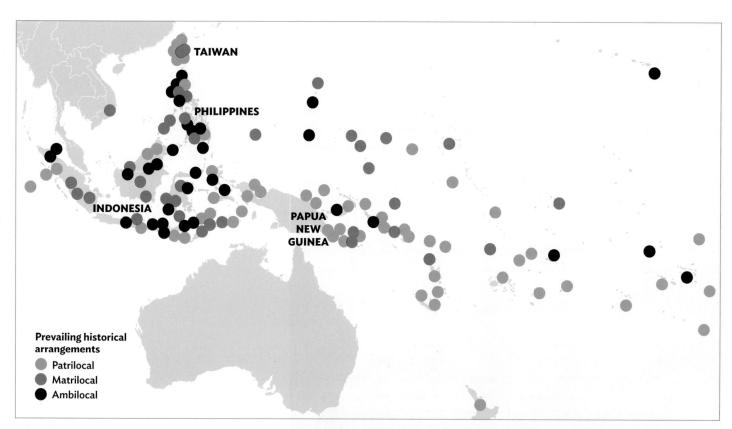

FIGURE 12.17

Societies can be differentiated on the basis of where they typically expect newlyweds to live. In the Pacific region, anthropologists identified a dizzying mix of historical practices between norms of living with or near a husband's family, a wife's family, or either. Neolocal arrangements have increased dramatically with urbanization and working in the cash economy.

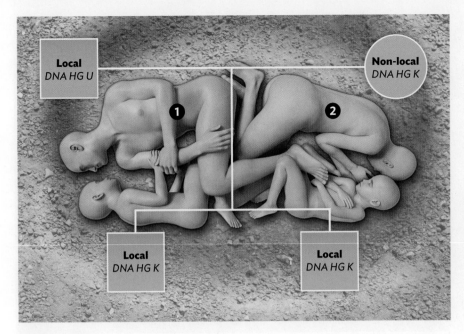

FIGURE 12.18

Grave 99 excavated in Eulau contained a man **(1)**, woman **(2)**, and their two sons. The ancient DNA shows that the male (upper square) and female (upper circle) were parents of the two other males (lower squares) buried with them. Analysis of each individual's teeth showed that the woman spent her childhood elsewhere, while the children and man grew up in Eulau. This is what would be expected if women move patrilocally to their husband's community when they marry.

identifying whether there is more relatedness in females or males within a site. Isotopic analyses of teeth or bone remains can also help identify whether individuals moved to the location as children or adults, because strontium isotopes from food and water that are preserved in the teeth or bones during childhood growth reflect the soil and bedrock in the area.

At Eulau, an archaeological site in Germany, excavated burials dated to 4,600 years ago included 13 adults and children placed carefully together—some with hands interlinked—alongside burial goods such as stone axes and animal tooth pendants. Arrows and skull fractures suggest they met a violent end, as might be expected after a raid. One burial with a male, female, and two children was confirmed as a family group by DNA analysis. The strontium isotope analyses then revealed that the women at the site had lived in a different geologic zone originally, whereas the men and children likely grew up near Eulau. This, in turn, suggests that the community was based on exogamous (out-group) marriage and patrilocal residence rules (**Figure 12.18**).

WOMEN'S WELL-BEING AND PATRILINEAL MARRIAGE

There are certainly marriage systems in which the exploitation of women is apparent, especially when marriages occur at younger ages or are arranged without the consent of the bride. Patrilineal, patrilocal systems, especially ones in which women move far away from their families at marriage, often at young ages, tend to be ones in which women's risk of abuse within marriage is amplified because they are so isolated from their natal support systems and do not have control of their own resources that would allow them to pursue other options. Matrilineal societies, in which women inherit and are more likely to stay close to their consanguineal kin after marriage, tend to be ones in which women have more social and economic power.

patrilineal A societal form in which ancestry, inheritance, and identity are related to men's familial lines.

matrilineal A societal form in which ancestry, inheritance, and identity are related to women's familial lines.

FIGURE 12.19

Sukuma wedding celebration in Tanzania is shown here.

TANZANIA

Africa

● Sukuma region

exogamy A practice that encourages marriage to people outside your own group (also called outmarriage).

endogamy A practice that encourages marriage to people inside your own group (also called inmarriage).

assortative mating Nonrandom selection of reproductive partners based on similarity (e.g., speaking the same language or having the same color hair).

In southern Asia and sub-Saharan Africa, in particular, women marry for the first time at relatively young ages, with perhaps half being under 18 years of age, and many of these are arranged marriages. The energetic international efforts to end early or "child" marriage are based on the idea that young women—especially those under 18—are exploited and physically and emotionally harmed by arranged marriages where they do not have enough power or experience to give meaningful consent. The large and powerful Nike, Ford, and Gates Foundations all have committed to this goal of "saving" these women, who are perceived as extremely vulnerable due to their young age at marriage.

But anthropological research is highlighting that we cannot assume that all arranged marriages of young women within patriarchal societies are inherently exploitative, dangerous, or damaging. Particularly, young age in itself may not necessarily be the problem. In Sukuma societies of northwestern Tanzania, about a third of women marry between the ages of 15 and 18. Farming and cattle-keeping are central in this patrilineal and patrilocal society. Evolutionary anthropologist Susan Schaffnit's interviews and focus groups revealed that these young women see themselves as being the ones to decide when and whom they marry, even as parents might assist and guide their decisions (**Figure 12.19**). She has observed that age in itself is mostly irrelevant. Rather, what matters is whether the woman believes she is ready for marriage. Early marriage can be an attractive proposition for a woman, as it accelerates her status as an adult in the community: someone who is now able to earn her own money outside the home, gain a partner, and have legitimate children.

SELECTING A SPOUSE

Social or religious rules or norms about who is an acceptable or desirable marriage partner can greatly influence choices, in both arranged marriages and "love matches." Tibetan fraternal (brother) polyandry is one example of the way local marriage rules can dictate who people can or should marry. In that case, only a set of brothers, and no one else, can marry the same woman at the same time.

More generally, in some societies and situations, the expectation or preference is to encourage marriage outside the group (known as *exogamy* or outmarriage), even while others expect or encourage marriage within the group (known as endogamy or inmarriage). Cousin marriage is one of the most common marriage endogamic rules anthropologists have recorded, wherein the ideal marriage partner is the child of your mother's brother or father's sister (cross-cousin marriage) or mother's sister or father's brother (parallel cousin marriage) or either.

The Yanomamö people of the tropical forests of the northern Amazon region (between Brazil and Venezuela) practice prescriptive cross-cousin marriage. That means men marry their father's sister's children and women marry their mother's brother's children (**Figure 12.20**). This practice is sufficiently central to Yanomamö culture that the words for cross-cousin and spouse are the same (**Figure 12.21**). Marriages are normally arranged by parents or other closely related male relatives in each lineage.

Problems arise when a suitable cousin is not available to marry, as then the person is expected to find and marry someone unrelated in the same generation—not always easy in a smaller-scale society. Sometimes, a father may recast his niece as a "sister" so that their children can marry each other. Yanomamö men can potentially marry more than one wife, following the same marriage rules. Some very small Yanomamö groups instead prefer marriage with people from outside villages, as a means to gain military support.

Even in societies where people are expected to find and choose their own spouse, marriage itself isn't random. Individuals left to make their own choices tend to end up with mates with similar family backgrounds, and similar heights and looks who share religious views or practices, who speak the same language, and who live close by. This is an example of positive assortative mating, wherein we tend to reproduce with those more like us. Sometimes this is by choice, and sometimes it is due to lack of choice. Religious affiliation is one area where families or laws may strongly encourage or even demand marriage only to others within the group.

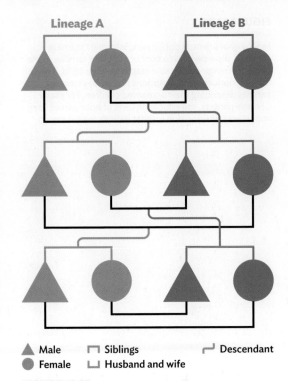

▲ Male   ⊓ Siblings   ⌐ Descendant
● Female   ⊔ Husband and wife

FIGURE 12.20

The ideal of Yanomamö marriage is cross-cousin marriages on both male and female sides of the family in each generation, as this kinship diagram shows. This means the persistence of very close alliances between related families.

FIGURE 12.21

A Yanomamö husband and wife are pictured in Irotatheri community, Amazonia, Venezuela, in 2012.

Yanomamö region

FIGURE 12.22

In Shanghai's central public park, informal "marriage corners" allow parents to connect to other families in the hope of arranging a suitable match for their child. The hanging notices are descriptions placed by attending parents describing their unmarried children. For many Chinese parents, the education level of both parties is an important consideration in what defines a good match.

romantic love An ideal of courtship and marriage characterized by feelings of desire, emotional intimacy, companionship, and mutual choice.

Since the late 20th century, some urban parks in China have transformed into informal "marriage corners" where parents matchmake on behalf of their unmarried—often professional—children (**Figure 12.22**). Although formalized matchmaking is not allowed, parents may bring photos and listings of their children's income, education, temperament, and body size. The efforts link to concerns that their children have spent time advancing their salaries and careers but are getting to an age where they also need to settle down and produce grandchildren. The aim of the events is to find another family with a child that will be compatible with their own. In the wake of China's strict former one-child policy, most older Chinese citizens are single children, as are many of their children. This raises the stakes for finding the right marriage match, as it represents their one hope of becoming grandparents and continuing the family line. If the families are compatible, they arrange a meeting and hope that love will happen between the children. By participating in these weekly marriage corners, parents are reminding their children that marriage is not optional nor solely their own decision. They are working to ensure their children marry someone as like them as possible and living in the same area, keeping the family and family traditions together.

ROMANTIC LOVE

Until recently, cultural anthropologists viewed marriage in many cultures as a mostly pragmatic affair related to establishing kinship, legitimizing inheritance, or gaining resources. This contrasted with the idealization of romantic love that has become a growing expectation for choosing a partner in much of the world today (**Figure 12.23**). Yet once anthropologists started questioning this assumption that romance, love, and arranged marriage could not coexist, they uncovered many different variants of romantic love across societies, some bound and others unbound to pragmatic considerations such as political alliance, economic need, or social opportunity.

Although arranged marriages remain common, there is an overall global trend toward more couples choosing their own partners, living neolocally (forming their own household), and placing primacy on emotional closeness and emotional compatibility in selection of partners. This trend has led to the

FIGURE 12.23

The notion of romantic love as the basis for marriage is more common today, but it appears historically too. Arguably the most romantic piece of architecture in the world, the Taj Mahal in Agra, India, was a mausoleum commissioned by emperor Shah Jahan as a resting place for his most beloved wife, Mumtaz Mahal.

primacy of the nuclear family—living and economic arrangements that focus on the married partners and their children.

The widely shared ideal of romantic "true" love, devoid of any economic considerations, emerged particularly clearly in early Medieval literature of western Europe. This ideal for deciding who to marry, based in Christian worldviews, often entwines love with the ideals of humility and self-sacrifice. These settler-colonial ideals were spread widely through European missionary efforts, and they continue to inform the character of romantic-love models of marriage around the world, though today other large-scale global trends are driving this model's spread—notably new technologies, education, and capitalism.

Linguistic anthropologist Laura Ahearn used written love letters to detail how women's access to writing changed how people found their marriage partners. Ahearn initially came to a small Magar town in western Nepal to teach as a Peace Corps volunteer. When she first arrived, some men could write, having been taught while serving in British or Indian army units. Women couldn't write, because they had no such opportunity to learn. Marriages were mostly arranged between families. Disillusioned with the development work she had gone there to do, Ahearn left, but she returned to the same village a decade later as an anthropology student. Things had changed. In the interim, "love marriages" had started to appear, with more young people quietly courting and then marrying those they chose themselves.

Formal education was an important factor in this transition. The establishment of a new village school meant that both women and men had learned to write. Love letters could thus now be written back and forth without parents knowing of a courtship. Trusted friends shared with Ahearn the new means of their clandestine courtships, which she was able to take to the city to photocopy and then return. Over the following years, she gathered more than 200 letters to identify how the act of writing was connected to major social changes: the emergence of romantic love as a desired ideal and the changing roles of younger people in society, such that they now had more autonomy from their families (**Figure 12.24**).

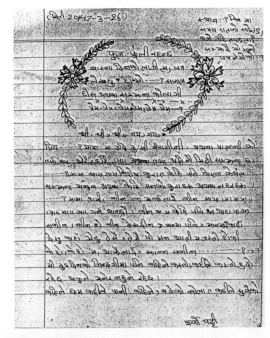

FIGURE 12.24

This love letter written by a Magar woman was shared with Laura Ahearn during her study of how the expansion of literacy transformed courtship rituals and marriage systems in western Nepal.

FIGURE 12.25

In Ho Chi Minh City in Vietnam, young people are pursuing romance and love as the basis for marriage while working to also please their parents with their matches. Motorbikes, affordable to the growing middle class, allow young people new forms of public intimacy for courtships based on emotional connection.

Trends away from arranged marriage have accelerated further with smartphones and other technologies that allow direct communication and the ability to establish emotional relationships away from the view of family, making it much easier for matches based on romantic love to happen (**Figure 12.25**). But the forms that intimacy takes in relation to courtship and marriage remain very dependent on local economic and social circumstances. In some societies, the economic circumstances make companionate (romantic love)-based legal marriage the easiest or most obvious option. This is increasingly the case for couples who can choose to live and work apart from their natal families. Both modern romantic notions of love and neoliberal capitalism are based on the shared idea that the self is prioritized above family and community needs and desires, and that the individual is then also expected to make their own decisions and take care of themselves. The economic circumstances in other societies, such as those in which young couples must co-reside and contribute to a parent's household, can make fully independent marriage decisions impractical.

ALTERNATIVES TO MARRIAGE

Increasingly, marriages accommodate or embrace the notion of emotional compatibility and romantic love as central to partner choice, same-sex marriage has been legalized in many countries, and the age at first marriage has generally been ticking upward. This last trend is creating new patterns of delayed entry into what is considered full adult status in many societies, a phenomenon termed "waithood." In some cases, waithood is related to expanding alternate opportunities, such as increasing access to higher education and employment. In others, waithood is based on constraints or barriers, such as lack of independent housing, lack of prospective partners, or inability to pay bridewealth or finance a wedding.

Cultural anthropologist Julia Pauli has been conducting ethnographic and survey research in northwestern Namibia in southwestern Africa since 2003, much of it in the company of her anthropologist husband and their daughter. In the small communities in which she has worked, wealth is based in livestock, and wealth inequality is severe. Marriages are "love matches" but require extended and expensive rituals that the couple must mostly pay for themselves. These include ritual gifts of cattle and jewelry to solidify the engagement, transporting and accommodating relatives, slaughtering and cooking animals, wedding pictures, facility rental for the reception, and so on. Having a small or civil wedding is embarrassing, suggesting "you do not have a family."

FIGURE 12.26

A Namibian marriage reception, attended by cultural anthropologist Julia Pauli, is pictured here.

As a result, most couples simply don't marry, despite it being considered socially desirable. In this way, marriage ceremonies in themselves become vehicles by which wealth and social status in the society are communicated (**Figure 12.26**). Moreover, because of the prohibitive cost of weddings, the vast majority of births in the community Pauli studied now occur outside legally sanctioned marriages.

In societies where marriage is important to adult social status, becoming divorced, widowed, or otherwise staying unmarried can lower a person's social and economic standing—most especially that of women. Educated women in urban areas are increasingly able to compete within the workplace to support themselves fully, making more viable the choice of singlehood. For example, in Japan in 1975 about 5% of women between the ages of 35 and 39 had never been married, whereas today it is around 25%.

Ethnographic studies globally suggest that both purposeful and unintended singlehood comes with advantages and disadvantages. Singlehood may release individuals from some adult responsibilities and give women, in particular, more independence and autonomy in their daily lives. Prolonged singlehood can provide time to explore potential love matches or build a career. But in most societies, to differing degrees, marriage is still an expected social norm. In these cases, singlehood often opens people up to varied forms of pressure and criticism from their family and friends, as well as discrimination and loneliness. Singles of all ages find other ways to create social support and emotional belonging with other single peers. These connections are increasingly possible to arrange and maintain thanks to social media.

singlehood Remaining unmarried or without an intimate partner, including by choice.

SEX WORK IN A GLOBALIZED WORLD

Marriage legitimizes sexual intimacy and cements social status in many societies. It is one of many dimensions of human sexuality that are defined by and recreate power structures within society. It is embedded in complex, dynamic ways in our political, economic, and legal frameworks. Ethnographic research by anthropologists provides a means to expand how we think about these connections, providing perspectives on human sexuality that can challenge mainstream ideas. Sex work is one of the best examples of this, and such research is helping to rethink complicated issues such as identifying and preventing sexual exploitation.

Sex work (also sometimes termed "survival sex") emerges from structural factors, such as poverty or discrimination, that limit economic or social opportunities or otherwise disempower people. Sex work now is also highly globalized, often being most intense as an economic activity where tourists and migrant workers overlap with easily exploitable sexual labor (**Figure 12.27**).

sex work Labor that employs the body in exchange for money, services, or goods.

FIGURE 12.27

Sex work in Germany is legal, relatively safe, and controlled by the state. Yet stigma around the profession persists, and many of those in sex work are minority nonnationals who came to Germany because they were discriminated against or unable to support themselves in their home countries. Accordingly, sex workers remain marginalized and at risk of exploitation and harm.

The Super Bowl sporting event in the United States is a significant site of human sex trafficking, and other global hot spots include many cities or tourist towns in southeastern Asia and the Caribbean islands.

Sex work is often dangerous, placing those providing services at physical harm from disease or assault. It can also be socially damaging, given the profound stigma that accompanies it. When coerced, such as through trafficking, participation in the sex industry results in unarguable harm as a contemporary form of slavery. In many countries, transgender women, gay men, refugees, and undocumented migrants are particularly vulnerable to being forced economically into sex work due to lack of other viable options. But ethnographic studies of both workers and clients are showing how difficult it is to define exactly what does and does not constitute exploitation, adding significant nuance to how we can advance human rights protections for those living with poverty or on the margins of society.

One set of insights from ethnographic studies comes from efforts to understand sex work from the perspective of clients. Ethnographer Megan Rivers-Moore did research in the Gringo Gulch neighborhood of San José, Costa Rica, an area where tourists (mainly U.S. men) travel explicitly to seek sexual services. Her interviews with U.S. clients revealed part of the value they received in the transactions of sex was more than simply physical. Sex with young and beautiful women changed their sense of self, enhancing and redefining their own masculinity. Many of the male tourists were "non-elites" at home, working in low-status jobs and considered less desirable as boyfriends or husbands. Transactional sex was a way to manage their own low status, and the exchange of emotions as well as money showed how this sex work was clearly operating as a relational economy, where clients value interpersonal closeness or loyalty (Chapter 9).

Notably, not all transnational sex clients are male. Economically disadvantaged Caribbean nations, for example, have also attracted numbers of female sexual tourists, and some "host clubs" in Japan cater to women seeking the focused attention of men. The economic and social inequality between tourists and locals is part of the motivation, whether consciously recognized or not, and local bodies are eroticized for the novelties of their skin color or shape. Ethnographic research on women's sex tourism reveals that being able to control men sexually while still meeting their own cultural ideas of femininity is a significant draw (**Figure 12.28**).

Ethnographic research focused on sex workers also suggests that they do not necessarily view themselves as exploited. Medical anthropologist Mark Padilla conducted fieldwork with sex workers in the beach town of Sosúa in the Dominican Republic in the mid-1990s, a country almost entirely dependent on tourism. The male and female sex workers alike in Padilla's study viewed their client relationships as building global connections and the means to advance themselves and their families socially and economically. This desire to connect meant there was then a need to "perform love." The capacity to convince clients of their genuine affection for them was at the heart of how they could be economically successful and open the possibility of their ongoing support in months and years ahead.

FIGURE 12.28

Specific resorts in the Caribbean are well-known destinations for middle-aged middle-class women tourists seeking the attention of local men.

Sex workers may also not necessarily view themselves as lacking in agency or choice. Activist–anthropologist Heidi Hoefinger spent over a decade interviewing, living with, and forming close friendships with the women who work in "hostess bars" in Phnom Penh, Cambodia, as part of the tourist-focused sex and entertainment industry (**Figure 12.29**). For foreign male tourists, companionship in Cambodia is extremely cheap, which is a main reason they arrive in such numbers. The women who work from the bars did not consider themselves victims and consequently didn't participate in the efforts of advocacy projects by nongovernmental organizations to provide them with avenues to leave sex work. Rather, they identified as respectable, hardworking, and liberated. None of these women, Hoefinger notes, have real power as such. And yet they still exercised it anyway through their entrepreneurism and efforts to create and follow opportunities.

For many young women in Cambodia, bar work is a stigmatized option often weighed against other terrible opportunities such as underpaid garment factory work, street hawking, or working rice fields. Describing what happens between bar girls and their foreign "boyfriends" entails much more than fits neatly into descriptions such as "sex worker" or "client." Sometimes they would engage in sex-for-fun, blurring the lines between paid companionship and love. Some felt free to experiment sexually. They built communities, pooling money to live and even raise children together in the absence of their natal kin.

But Hoefinger also warns against tendencies to romanticize the bar girls' lives. Even as bar work provides some economic freedom and the ability to elevate themselves and their families back home with money and goods earned through their work, they still deal with the consequences of having very low economic power relative to those who pay them. These consequences include having to endure unwanted sexual advances, verbal harassment, and racism.

Research such as Hoefinger's highlights the complexities surrounding the commodification and transnational movement of physical and emotional intimacies. Specifically, it reveals how difficult it is to define the boundaries between paid forms of sexual intimacy and those assumed to be given freely, or to define when workers are or are not exploited victims of the sex trade.

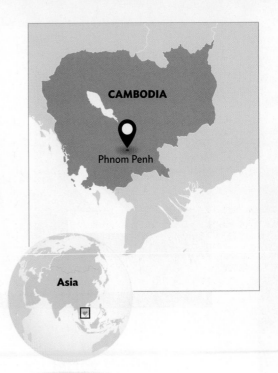

FIGURE 12.29

A "hostess bar" in the central nightlife district of Phnom Penh, Cambodia, in 2019 is pictured.

12

Sex, Love, and Marriage

Examining a variety of practices challenges our assumptions about marriage, intimacy, and sexuality and helps reveal insights into why people make the choices they do.

KEY TERMS
> marriage
> multisited
  ethnography

12.1 | Human Sexualities

Summarize the diversity of human sexualities.

- Anthropologists have documented the many ways human sexual configurations are highly flexible.

KEY TERMS
> agency
> autoethnography
> heteronormativity
> incest taboo
> monogamy
> polyamory
> sexual
  configurations
> sexual orientation

12.2 | Marriage and Mating Systems

Identify defining elements of human marriage and how these relate to primate mating systems.

- Humans are a "mostly monogamous" species in practice, even if more societies historically allowed or idealized polygyny. Among primates, humans have the most flexible mating systems, allowing many ways to configure how humans create families.

KEY TERMS
> affinal kin
> avoidance speech
> consanguineal kin
> estrus
> extrapair mating
> fraternal
  polyandrous
  marriage
> kinship
> language register
> lineage
> mating system
> pair bond
> paternity certainty
> polyandry
> polygamy
> polygyny
> serial monogamy

12.3 | Why and How Humans Marry

Assess the range of reasons humans marry and how and why these are changing.

- Human marriage is a universally important—if highly variable—institution that creates new kin alongside varied expectations of sexual intimacy and economic and reproductive cooperation.

- The globally spreading idea of romantic love, in which people expect to choose their own spouses, coexists with neoliberal capitalism and is enhanced by technologies that provide privacy.

KEY TERMS
> ambilocality
> assortative mating
> brideservice
> bridewealth
> dowry
> endogamy
> exogamy
> matrilineal
> matrilocality
> neolocality
> patrilineal
> patrilocality
> romantic love
> singlehood

12.4 | Sex Work in a Globalized World

Explain how ethnographic findings expand how we view sex work.

- Ethnographic studies show how difficult it can be to define when sex work is exploitative or not.

KEY TERM
> sex work

Death, Dying, and the Dead

Archaeologist Jason De León had initially set out to study blades made of obsidian (volcanic glass) in Mexico. But conversations with local people excavating with him inspired him to apply his archaeological expertise to a more urgent topic: the lives of Latin American migrants who died making dangerous, unauthorized journeys north. For the many who die each year crossing the Mexico–U.S. border in the company of smugglers, their bodies remain unburied, abandoned to the elements.

Combining methods from archaeology with cultural anthropology and *forensic anthropology*, De León devised what he called a "desert *taphonomy*," studying the human remains and personal effects left behind on the migrant trails (**Figure 13.1**). One of his experiments included dressing dead pigs in clothing to understand how scavengers disturb human bodies left in the desert sun. He also interviewed hundreds of migrants.

This research documents the dreadful scale of the uncounted deaths of border crossers, creating evidence important for border policy debates. De León was also able to give names and stories to some of the border dead, such as Maricela from Ecuador, who died of dehydration in the Sonoran Desert. In interviewing families of those he could identify, De León analyzed the grieving process, which carried on interminably, because there was no body, no *funeral*, and no closure.

LEARNING OBJECTIVES

13.1 Death and Its Rituals
Trace the development of death rituals in humans.

13.2 Grieving and Celebrating the Dead
Describe how the dead continue to interact with and impact the living in different societies.

13.3 Studying the Dead
Assess how scientific research of the remains of the dead can contribute useful knowledge.

13.4 Ethics, Anthropology, and Human Remains
Consider ethical complexities involved in anthropological studies using human remains.

A GOOD DEATH

The ways humans define a good death varies across cultures and religious traditions. Death rituals help humans come to terms with one painful result of our cognitive sophistication: the knowledge that we will die.

forensic anthropology A subdiscipline of anthropology focused on the examination of human skeletal remains to assist in the detection of crimes and the identification of victims.

taphonomy Study of the processes that affect human, animal, and plant remains as they decay and become part of the record anthropologists study.

funeral A ceremony honoring a deceased person, usually involving the disposal of their remains.

FIGURE 13.1

Jason De León and his team map the location of each artifact left behind by migrants as they stop to rest on their journey across the Mexico–U.S. border.

De León's research on migrant death captures several of this chapter's main points. First, anthropologists can gain important information for the living by studying the physical bodies of the dead, but one that also often raises complex ethical issues. Second, death is a symbolic event for human beings. More than any other animal, humans are aware that death is inevitable. We grieve the loss of those close to us, and greatly benefit from rituals to ease the painful transitions that death brings. And third, the way we are treated in death tends to reflect who we were in life. In this chapter, we explore these and related insights that anthropology provides through its studies of death and the dead.

ritual Describes a recognized social event that marks a life transition, such as death.

DEATH AND ITS RITUALS

Humans place great meaning on the way our remains are treated. In this section, we consider the array of *rituals* surrounding death humans use and how these reflect religious and cultural traditions and social positions. To begin, we consider when such ritual treatments of dead human bodies first arose, signaling the emergence of the acute human awareness of death itself.

WHEN DID HUMANS FIRST COMPREHEND DEATH?

Human beings are fully aware of death; we know that every human being, including ourselves, will eventually die. We devote considerable effort to avoiding, explaining, preparing for, and coming to terms with death. Is this a uniquely human quality, defining our species? Or do other animals also understand what death is? We know that many animals, such as elephants, attend to the dead bodies of group members (**Figure 13.2**), sometimes removing the dead from the living area. A few animals appear to display something akin to grief. For example, chimpanzee mothers in the wild have been observed grooming and carrying the remains of their infants for weeks after they die.

But among all animals, only humans purposefully and consistently treat their dead in patterned ways, using ritual acts such as burial. Indeed, our

FIGURE 13.2

Humans are not the only animals who seem to understand the concept of death. Here, elephants in Serengeti National Park in Tanzania gather around a dead member of their herd.

burial The intentional action of placing the body of a dead individual in a grave or pit.

universal understanding of the inevitability of death, and our concerns about managing it, are hallmarks of our species.

At some point in their evolutionary history, humans emerged as unique among animals for their intellectual capacity to fully comprehend death as an end to existence. When might this have occurred? One way to answer this question is to identify when humans began to practice rituals that marked the line between being alive and being dead.

One key sign is archaeological evidence of intentional burial. If we define "burial" as a patterned way of treating dead bodies, then most paleoanthropologists agree that Neanderthals were the first hominins to routinely bury their dead. They purposefully dug pits, placed bodies in set positions within the graves, and covered them up. Some of the earliest such Neanderthal sites with burials date to around 60,000–40,000 years ago and include La Chapelle-aux-Saints, France; Kebara and Amud Caves, Israel; La Ferrassie, France; and Shanidar, Iraq (**Figure 13.3**). Whether these intentional burials demonstrate that

FIGURE 13.3

Shanidar Cave, located in what is now Iraq, contains intentional burial of Neanderthals around 50,000 years ago. These are some of the earliest examples of intentional burial and suggest an important cultural transition for humans.

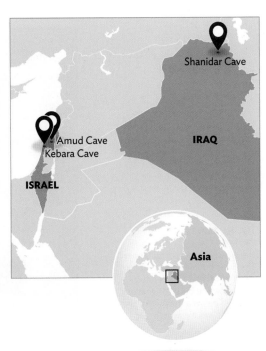

grave goods Objects, often valuable, buried with deceased individuals.

Neanderthals had a full comprehension of death, or even ideas about an afterlife, is heavily debated by anthropologists. This is because Neanderthal graves often lack the types of grave goods that would suggest complex rituals taking place during those burials.

The debate surrounding the Neanderthal fossils discovered at Shanidar Cave in northern Iraq is a good example of how difficult it can be to sort out what is a purposeful burial and to determine whether rituals surrounding death were involved. So far, 10 individuals have been excavated from the enormous, vaulted cave that was home to groups of Neanderthals from around 60,000 years ago. Most of those found buried seem to have either been covered in accidental rock falls or perhaps interred for practical reasons such as keeping predators off a decaying body. There was, however, an exception. One burial excavated, a male around 40 years of age, seems to have been buried more purposefully and with related mortuary rituals. In his grave, he was arranged in a flexed position on his left side, facing the cave's mouth. Soil samples from the immediate vicinity contained pollen from brightly colored flowers, perhaps indicating decoration on the grave. But this interpretation isn't certain. Paleoanthropologists returned to Shanidar in 2014 to apply techniques unavailable during the original excavations, such as better dating of the stratigraphic layers in the cave. Their data suggested that the flower pollen was simply tracked into the grave by burrowing rodents.

MORTUARY PRACTICES IN THE PAST AND PRESENT

It wasn't until about 30,000 years ago that we have clear signs of burial rituals being practiced by anatomically modern humans. The first such graves are found in open-air sites, often close to recognizable settlements. Well-known examples include the archaeological sites of Arene Candide, Italy; Dolní Věstonice, Czech Republic; and Sunghir, Russia (**Figure 13.4**). And unlike Neanderthal burials, those associated with anatomically modern humans were clearly intentionally buried with grave goods that include shells, shell and antler jewelry, ivory beads

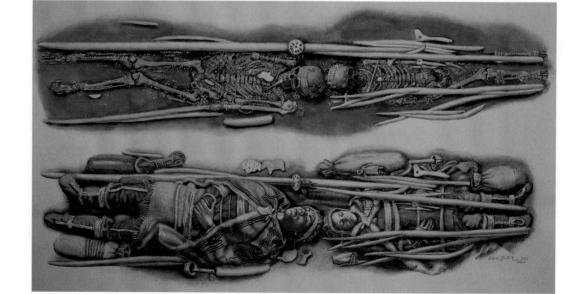

FIGURE 13.4

This reconstruction of an Upper Paleolithic burial from Sunghir, Russia, shows an artist's depiction of how the burial originally appeared below a drawing of the burial as it was excavated.

and drilled animal teeth, and animal bones. The bodies in several burials were stained red, indicating the use of red ochre in mortuary practices.

This association of personal objects buried with bodies suggests that the humans burying them had the cognitive capacity to comprehend death. While other apes may share with humans the capacity to mourn the loss of those they love, humans now understood that, sooner or later and regardless of anything they could do, they themselves would die. This is likely the same time that human beliefs about an afterlife—about how one can ultimately transcend death into a different life—began to emerge. Such beliefs would have made death something other than an ultimate demise and eased the fear that comes with that.

More recently in the human past, we see mortuary rituals becoming complexly organized and institutionalized, suggesting a further significant shift in how the living relate to the dead. The earliest known cemeteries, defined as planned areas set aside specifically for multiple burials, appear around 15,000 years ago in locations as varied as Italy, Morocco, and Jordan. Kow Swamp in southern Australia is the largest Late Pleistocene cemetery yet found, with burials starting around 20,000 BCE. It contained the crania (brain cases) of more than 40 individuals, ranging from small babies to adults. In 1991, the archaeological human remains from Kow Swamp were repatriated to Indigenous peoples and then reinterred, following the ethical concerns of the descendant groups whose ancestors were buried there.

For fully modern humans, all societies have meaningful and often complex mortuary rituals. The forms these rituals take typically connect to beliefs about life after death, and so they are shaped by and affirm religious and spiritual beliefs about the afterlife.

The cremation ceremonies that happen around the clock every day in Varanasi, India, illustrate how mortuary practices are embedded in religious and cosmological views. For centuries, Hindu individuals have been burned after death on wooden pyres on the steep steps alongside the sacred Ganges River (**Figure 13.5**). For those who believe in reincarnation, there are long cycles of rebirth and death. However, being cremated on the banks of the Ganges River

mortuary practice A rite or activity surrounding death.

cemetery A planned area set aside specifically for the in-ground burial of multiple individuals.

religious Describes a set of beliefs and formalized rituals regarding ideology, the supernatural, morals, and values in society.

spiritual Describes beliefs relating to unseen realms of existence.

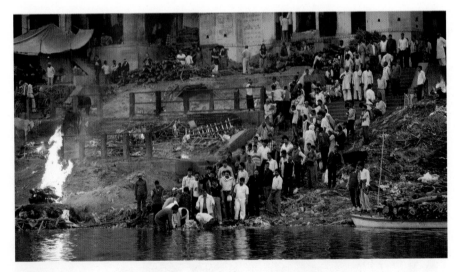

FIGURE 13.5

A body is bathed in the sacred Ganges River as part of a Hindu cremation in Varanasi, India.

FIGURE 13.6

Cultural anthropologist Beth Conklin (white shirt) is pictured with Wari' in the Brazilian Amazon while doing fieldwork in the 1980s. She is being painted in preparation for a festival.

BRAZIL

South America

Amazon rainforest

can provide a release from the cycles of death and rebirth. When a person's ashes are released into the river, their reincarnation cycles can end, and finally the person can reach nirvana (a state of release and happiness).

Mortuary rituals take an amazing array of forms. The Wari' (wah-EE), an Indigenous population from the rainforests of western Brazil, historically practiced what cultural anthropologist Beth Conklin has termed "compassionate cannibalism" as part of their mortuary rituals. At the time of first visits by Brazilian government agencies in the 1950s, the Wari' lived in villages of around 30 people in several family households. By the time Conklin was living with the Wari' in the 1980s, compassionate cannibalism had disappeared (**Figure 13.6**).

But she collected the accounts of older Wari' people who participated in or watched other Wari' in rituals in which the body would be dismembered and eaten (**Figure 13.7**). A wooden beam taken from the roof of each house in the village was used to construct the cooking fire. The meat was consumed by distant relatives and nonkin; close kin were considered to share the same body substance as the deceased and so didn't partake.

Wari' stories told to Conklin suggested that consuming a corpse was a difficult and emotional but ultimately healing experience. Consuming the dead aided the family in breaking their ties with the dead individual, removing the distress around the loved one in the state of death. The destruction of the corpse through dismemberment, roasting, and consumption also signified the dead individual's transformation from a mortal human to an immortal animal. The consumed would also remember their living kin, sending them peccaries (wild pigs) and fish from the spirit world to the land of the living to eat in exchange.

Small details in the way mortuary rituals are practiced can have profound meanings regarding identity and membership in cultural groups. In San Francisco's Chinatown, for example, Chinese American funerals are serviced by locally owned funeral homes and include viewing the body, transportation by hearse, and earth burial, as is common across the United States. But offerings of food and paper models of a home and money are often displayed near the casket. These are later burned graveside for use by the deceased in the spirit world, following Chinese traditions of ancestor veneration. The casket is

FIGURE 13.7

A funerary roasting rack used in past Wari' funerals is depicted, including bundles with internal organs. The image was drawn for Beth Conklin by by Wem Quirio Oro Nao, a Wari' elder.

FIGURE 13.8

Funerals in San Francisco's Chinatown ideally include a procession with a band, such as the one pictured here.

typically transported to the cemetery in a procession that includes a hearse, as well as a band and a likeness of the deceased displayed in a "picture car" (**Figure 13.8**).

Many Haitian families, meanwhile, including some Haitian Americans, use Vodou (Voodoo) mortuary practices, even as they also identify as Catholic or Protestant Christians. In Vodou, the spirit can leave the body at death, but it hovers nearby for the next week or so. This is a hazardous time for the newly dead, because others can take their revenge for insults and offenses incurred while the person was alive by using Vodou rituals to malevolently block the soul from finding peace. On the ninth night following death, the family gathers to eat, drink, pray, and chant, and the *hougan*, or Vodou practitioner, performs the *demier priye*, a prayer ritual. This ritual moves the soul farther into the afterlife. For the next year, the soul is held in the island's water, trees, caves, mountains, or wind. One year and one day after death, the family can perform a commemorative celebration honoring the dead. At this time, the soul can fully pass into spirit world and can live with other ancestors.

These mortuary rituals and the associated coffin and church burials can be very expensive, pushing many families into debt. But without treating the dead with the necessary care and respect, the deceased family member cannot find peace and the wider social order can become unbalanced. The heightened importance of death in human life explains why mortuary rituals often combine elements of different religious beliefs, as in the use of Vodou practices alongside Catholic or Protestant ones in Haitian funerals.

MORTUARY PRACTICES AND SOCIAL POSITION

Mortuary rituals can reflect a dead person's social status during their life. Married couples may be interred together. Sometimes children are buried separately from adults. The bodies of elites might be disposed of very differently than those of non-elites, in spectacular tombs instead of mass graves. These differences reflect the relative power of the individuals during their lives, with elites using wealth and power to forge a better chance for continued prosperity in the afterlife.

FIGURE 13.9

This map depicts the tomb and mortuary complex of Qin Shi Huang, located outside the city of Xi'an, China, much of which has not been excavated.

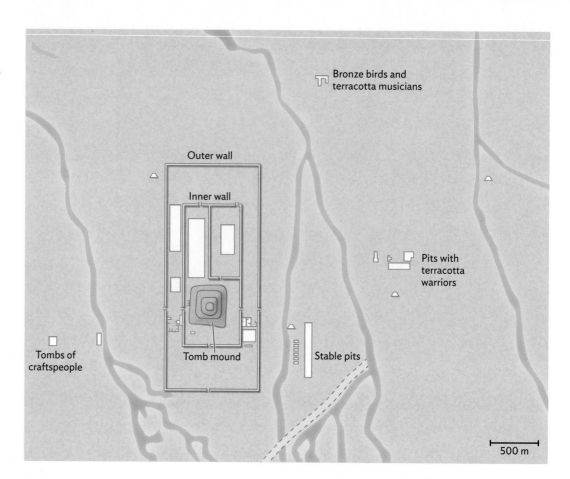

One of the most dramatic examples of an elite tomb was constructed at Xi'an for Qin Shi Huang (秦始皇, CHIN shuh-hwang), the first emperor of China. Qin Shi Huang ruled in the Qin dynasty from 246 BCE after taking the throne at the age of 13. After several unsuccessful assassination attempts, he began constructing a massive underground palace that would serve as his tomb (**Figure 13.9**). Chinese historical records indicate that it took 700,000 workers at least 36 years to complete construction. The palace was more than 10 stories deep and was designed to mimic the ordered layers of the cosmos. The major waterways of China were recreated in shimmering liquid mercury, and key constellations were painted on the ceilings with pearls indicating the stars. The coffin itself was hammered from copper, and the body was surrounded with fine pottery, precious stones, and a protective system of mechanized crossbows.

Above the tomb was a 46-meter-tall earthen mound, called Mount Li, shaped into a city with temples and a giant wall. The total area was about 55 square kilometers, roughly the size of Manhattan Island in New York. While the tomb itself remains unexcavated, archaeologists have opened a 3-acre (1.2-hectare) chamber. It contains more than 8,000 life-sized terracotta warriors that guarded the east gate of the tomb complex (**Figure 13.10**). Dressed in uniforms and carrying real weapons, no two statues are alike. For Qin, obsessed with living forever, the tomb allowed him to transport his massive domain with him into the afterlife.

In contrast with powerful, high-status individuals such as Qin Shi Huang, the bodies of people devalued by sickness, poverty, imprisonment, or enslavement may be disposed of in ways that speak to their marginal position within societies. Those who are unnamed or without rights may end up in mass graves, as medical specimens, or in other contexts that individuals of higher social status rarely experience after death.

FIGURE 13.10

The tomb of Qin Shi Huang was guarded by thousands of terracotta warriors. The ceramic sculptures were originally painted in bright colors, and their detailed and personalized expressions imply that they were individual portraits of warriors in the emperor's guard.

In the widely traveled "Body Worlds" and "BODIES" exhibits, the water and fat in cadavers of unnamed people are replaced by plastics. In this postdeath transformation, the muscles, nerves, and bones are exposed, while intact eyes, ears, and lips give the impression of the living human. Some bodies are shown riding bicycles or playing sports. In one display, a male and female body are posed as during intercourse; the dissected genitals are easily viewed, but a tender gaze is shared between them.

To many viewers who recognize that the bodies are those of real people who lived and died in the relatively recent past, the displays can be shocking as well as fascinating, posing ethical questions about what is an acceptably respectful way to display the dead. The company that runs the Body Worlds exhibits says it uses voluntarily donated bodies from many sources, but the BODIES exhibit uses bodies from unclaimed individuals from medical schools in China; in both exhibits, instances have arisen of bodies from unconsenting individuals being transformed into long-term displays. A plastinated gorilla named Artis, exhibited with Body Worlds and treated similarly to unnamed, anonymous human cadavers in the same show, had died in a German zoo (**Figure 13.11**). Animal rights activists have protested inclusion of the gorilla in the human display, on the basis that it is a protected species.

Such socially stratified treatment of the dead is not universal. Indeed, some places with dramatic inequalities in wealth have a surprising lack of variation in contemporary burial practices. For example, funeral practices in the United States are very uniform overall, with bodies being either buried or cremated using licensed for-profit commercial funeral homes.

For those being buried, embalming (treating the body with preservative) is common in the United States. Furthermore, for cremations and burials alike, the corpse is often groomed, dressed, and placed in a coffin to be viewed by mourners during religious rites. This is followed by transport via a specialized vehicle (hearse) to a cemetery and burial in a standard-sized rectangular earth plot with some form of floral display.

Challenging the standard practices are "green burials," without any preservation of the body, and the "home death" movement, which purposefully avoids use of funeral homes. Both are done, ultimately, to give desired forms of dignity to the deceased.

FIGURE 13.11

A plastinated gorilla named Artis was exhibited with Body Worlds in 2003.

GRIEVING AND CELEBRATING THE DEAD

rite of passage A ritual, ceremony, or event marking an important life stage, such as birth, puberty, marriage, or death.

grief Emotional pain caused by losing someone you care about.

lament A type of language and performance used to express grief, usually with weeping and a songlike quality.

● Karelian language

In Section 13.1, we gave examples of funerals as rites of passage with many ritual elements, outlining how the body is prepared and how people attending should act. Now, we explore the ritual ways that humans cope with emotional and social aspects of death, including what anthropologists have described of the varied ways we express grief and stay connected to the dead.

GRIEVING RITUALS

Humans openly grieve the loss of those they love. Death rituals bring people together; they can be highly comforting and provide meaning to people in a time of profound loss. Without funerals marking the transition from life to death, for example, managing loss is even more challenging, as the example of the migrant borderland deaths that opened our chapter showed.

While sharing our grief is a human universal, the ways we grieve are culturally and religiously prescribed. For people in many parts of the world, laments, which combine song, story, and weeping, are a crucial element of grieving rituals. Anthropologists have been studying laments and particularly women's crying songs for decades. One example studied by linguistic anthropologists is the lamenting practiced by elderly rural Karelian (kah-RELL-ee-an) women in the region located between Finland and Russia. In funeral ceremonies, their lyrical, musical laments help guide the souls of the deceased to Tuonela, the Karelian land of the dead. The lament isn't addressed to the dead person but to ancestors and divine powers located in the afterlife. The laments accompany all the preparations for the burial, from making the coffin to dressing the deceased. They are sung again at later memorial feasts. Through their emotion-laden songs, the lamenters offer themselves as bridges between the world of the living and the otherworld of the dead.

All Karelian laments are performed by women, who are said to "cry with words," whereas men "cry with the eyes." The language used in laments diverges significantly from everyday speech because the laments are meant for those in another world, which means that most living audiences cannot understand the laments being performed. Anthropologists studying these lamenters and their living audiences note that this lack of understanding is not a hindrance to the effectiveness of the laments as a comfort to those left behind. They ensure that connections between the living and the dead will endure, as the supernatural audience understands what is being communicated.

Lamenting is not the only ritual by which humans show grief and connect those alive to these who are leaving. One of the better described funeral rituals, also performed only by women, comes from the western highlands of New Guinea. Women of the Dani (dan-EE) tribe would remove the end of a finger after the death of a beloved family member. They would tie a finger with string to numb it, and then they would remove the top of the finger with an axe, transforming emotional suffering into physical pain. Among the Dani, fingers are symbolically important and are seen as working together to represent unity and harmony, like a family. The terrible loss of family then can be translated into loss of a finger, signaling emotional grief and physical pain, while honoring the dead

FIGURE 13.12

Among the Dani of Western (Papua) New Guinea in Indonesia, women used to remove the top of one finger after the death of a child or close family member. While this practice is now legally banned, some older community members still carry these lifelong markers of grief and mourning.

and helping their spirit rest. This practice is now legally banned but many older Dani women still carry these lifelong markers of their grief (**Figure 13.12**).

The ways we understand and react to death reflect our moral worlds—our socially reinforced ideas of right and wrong. These shape how we view what is a good or bad death and who and how we should grieve.

Catholic mothers in informal settlements in northeastern Brazil have long lived with the very real risks of losing their babies to contaminated water, lack of food, and inadequate access to healthcare. Funerals were usually quick and relatively subdued events. Coffins of infants could be carried to burial by neighborhood children. There may have been a few flowers scattered, but burial itself was sometimes unmarked, in a plot that might soon be reused. The mothers in northeastern Brazil typically contained and controlled their grief, limiting how much they wailed or even complained over the death, according to the cultural belief that they should only cry on the inside. Crying slows the child's transition into heaven, weighing down their wings so they cannot fly upward. These mothers recognized that there are better and worse deaths: A bad death happens before the child is baptized and means the child suffered while dying.

Cultural anthropologists who have done ethnographic research in northeastern Brazil with such mothers, including Nancy Scheper-Hughes, who based her research in Recife, have debated how to interpret this relatively low level of exhibited grief. Some suggest this moral worldview allows mothers to detach in a place where infant death is so very common, emptying themselves of emotion as a means to guard against grief itself. Others suggest rather that the grief is profound but muted in ways that help impoverished mothers with few options to save their children navigate otherwise overwhelming feelings of guilt and blame over the death of their small children.

MAINTAINING CONNECTIONS WITH THE DEAD

Living humans remain connected with the dead in many different ways, incorporating the dead into daily life for years, even generations, after death. In many Buddhist homes, a physical piece of furniture (of varying size) serves as a space

FIGURE 13.13

Buddhist annual O-bon ceremonies remember ancestors and welcome them back into the home. Daily feeding of the *butsudan*, or family altar, may also be a part of family life in Japan.

to house the family ancestors, who are represented with names on small tablets. In Japan, for example, this *butsudan*, or family altar, will usually include photos of the most recently deceased family members (parents and grandparents) along with an incense burning pot, flowers, and space for food offerings (**Figure 13.13**). Typically, the butsudan is located in the eldest offspring's home. Children are often taught to greet their ancestors with daily cheerful choruses of "Good morning!" Food may be given to the ancestors in small dishes that are miniature replicas of everyday dishes used by the living. Everyday foods given to ancestors include rice, vegetables, and soup. When the family receives a gift of food—sweets or fruit—these food items may be placed on the butsudan for a day or so as a way of sharing the gift with the ancestors and thanking them for their protection, support, and help. Then the food items will be removed and consumed by the people in the house.

The festival of QingMing—"Clear and Bright Festival" or "Grave Sweeping Day"—is a Chinese tradition that takes place annually to honor ancestors. This holiday blends Confucian ideals with Buddhist and Taoist traditions. QingMing signifies the day when the gates between the earthly world and the afterlife are opened so that people can more easily communicate with their ancestors.

The festivities of QingMing include preparation of the gravesite and symbolic consumption rituals (**Figure 13.14**). Gravesite preparation includes clearing grass around the graves, bringing fresh potted flowers to the graves, and burning sticks of incense. Food and drink offerings, such as roast duck, pastries, fruits, tea, and wine, are also brought to the graves. The dead symbolically consume the gifts. The burning of "ghost money" (or joss paper, printed to look like money) at the gravesite is one way that venerators ensure that their ancestors have wealth and comfort in the afterlife. Following a series of prayer rituals, the family may celebrate and consume the offerings themselves as well.

In China, this ancestor worship was forbidden after the Cultural Revolution of the 1960s. But it resurged after official government opposition to the practice was dropped. In Taiwan, this ancestor worship has been an unbroken cultural practice going back thousands of years.

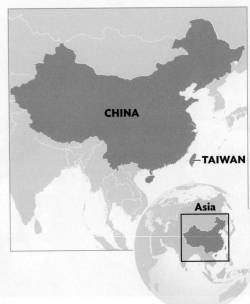

FIGURE 13.14

During the annual QingMing Festival, family members clean and prepare the tomb site and leave offerings for their ancestors.

Día de los Muertos ("Day of the Dead") is a holiday that was historically celebrated across Latin America. Its origins can be traced to the pre-Hispanic period, and the purpose is to communicate with and honor one's deceased familial ancestors. Commonly, family members go to the burial places of loved ones, decorating or cleaning the gravesite, preparing their favorite foods, sharing a picnic as a family in the burial place, and leaving an offering, such as a sugar skull, for the deceased loved one (**Figure 13.15**). The event also involves a brief

FIGURE 13.15

Offerings of favorite foods and sugar skulls can play a part of Día de los Muertos remembrances in Mexico and the United States.

FIGURE 13.16

During the Malagasy *famadihana* ritual in Madagascar, family members remove the remains of family members wrapped in burial shrouds. The shrouds are replaced before the remains are reburied.

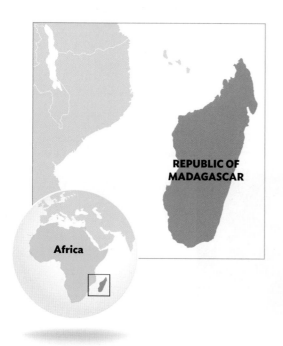

visit from the spirit of the deceased relative, street celebrations, and parades with costumed participants.

Among the Malagasy people of Madagascar, rituals called *famadihana* (fa-ma-dee-an) momentarily physically reconnect the living and dead. In Madagascar every five to seven years, the skeletons of the dead, wrapped in their shrouds, are removed from their tombs and carried around in celebration by the living (**Figure 13.16**). With singing and dancing, the community members replace burial shrouds, construct new tombs, and renovate old tombs. The famadihana rituals strengthen family relationships through honoring and remembering the deceased. Dozens to hundreds of family members and friends are invited to the celebration. Stories of the lives of the deceased loved ones are told to children. For the Malagasy people who participate in this mortuary ritual, famadihana is a celebration of shared heritage and family members, both living and dead.

While we can't directly observe important rituals such as the QingMing or the famadihana in the past, studying the archaeological record can reveal how the dead were incorporated into the lives of the living. One example comes from Andean South America, where people who lived in the Nazca Valley of southern Peru between 300 and 800 CE transformed the skulls of some people who had died into trophy heads, which were thought to impact the health of the agricultural fields and the living community even after their deaths.

Archaeologists have found both actual trophy heads and pottery that shows the heads and how they were used. Nasca artisans created stunning multicolored pottery vessels. Some depicted warriors with trophy heads—mummified human heads with cactus spines holding the lips and eyes closed—held in their hands or attached to their belts (**Figure 13.17**). Archaeologists have also found actual trophy heads at Nasca archaeological sites, sometimes in burials and sometimes in caches of many trophy heads. Like the heads painted on the pots, the decapitated heads had a hole drilled into the forehead for a carrying cord, and the eyes and lips had been closed with cactus spines.

But who were the people transformed into trophy heads? For a long time, they were presumed to be conquered enemies from outside the Nazca Valley. But more recently, bioarchaeologist Kelly Knudson and her team studied the trophy heads and extracted tiny pieces of bone and tooth enamel from the mummified heads, using isotope analysis to test various hypotheses about the trophy heads. Geologically unique strontium isotopes in bedrock are absorbed by plants and the animals, including humans, that eat them. Similarly, oxygen isotopes in the water humans drink can give information about the specific environment in which someone lived. Knudson's team compared the strontium and oxygen isotopes in the mummified heads with those of other individuals buried at Nasca sites. The isotopic data suggests that the individuals transformed into trophy heads weren't taken in battle after all but rather came from within the local Nasca population.

On the basis of this evidence, a better explanation would be that many trophy heads were beloved ancestors, carried as a form of veneration, helping with success in battle or ensuring fertile agricultural fields. While we can't directly observe the ways that Nasca trophy heads were incorporated into the lives of the living, we can use archaeology to see the ways that the dead were incorporated into life in the past, for many years after the person had died.

BETWEEN LIFE AND DEATH

These examples of mortuary traditions and ways of grieving suggest communities often do not see a clear line between life and death, with the living helping the dead in the afterlife and vice versa. Mortuary rituals such as those in Haiti recognize that a complete physical death precedes a complete social death, because they create a key social role for loved ones no longer physically alive. The examples from Asia and Latin America also show how the dead can long stay with the living, such as through festivals.

Medical technologies blur the lines between life and death, although exactly how differs across societies. Organ transplants mean that one person's death can give another person life. Ventilators and other medical measures keep people alive even after their bodies alone are unable to do so. Accordingly, many countries have developed complex legal codes to define when life ends, which is crucial to the legal and economic status of the rest of the family. Mostly, these are based on medical criteria, such as "irreversible cessation of circulatory and respiratory functions" (also called "brain stem death") or "irreversible cessation of all functions of the entire brain" (also called "whole-brain death").

However, the idea of "brain death" is not embraced in all societies. In Japan, for example, there is not widespread acceptance of the idea that doctors can declare someone dead and that their organs can be given away while their heart is still beating. Similarly, cutting into dead bodies is considered cruel and disrespectful, and many Japanese people consider organ transplantation between unrelated individuals unnatural and repulsive. Very few organ transplants are performed in Japan. Those that are performed are frequently surrounded by controversy and charges of murder.

Ultimately, the time and meaning of the moment of death in a given society is determined by the social relations that are disrupted by it and the social meanings that mark it. This raises an important moral and legal question: If the moment of death is defined by cultural ideas and varies from group to group, how do you decide when death is allowed to happen?

Medical aid in dying, which allows terminally ill and suffering individuals to take medication to bring about a peaceful death, is the subject of great debate around the world. Euthanasia involves the direct administration of a lethal medication to a terminally ill patient at the patient's request. Proponents of legalizing medical aid in dying argue that these practices enable dying persons

FIGURE 13.17

Pottery found at Nasca sites in Peru (100–600 CE) can depict the taking of trophies. Here, the pottery depicts a trophy head, and the red lines near the mouth represent the cactus spines used to close the lips.

to maintain autonomy and reduce needless pain and suffering. Opponents of legalizing medical aid in dying argue that it would undermine the integrity of the medical profession, cause psychological stress to survivors, and could be used coercively and against the will of the patient or without full informed consent. While the laws are changing, at the time of writing, medical aid in dying is legal in a small number of states within the United States, and is also legal in Belgium, Canada, Colombia, Luxembourg, the Netherlands, New Zealand, and Switzerland.

SECTION 13.3

STUDYING THE DEAD

As the previous sections make clear, death has great meaning within all human societies. But dead bodies themselves are also an important source of scientific information. In this section, we explore examples of the many ways anthropologists gain important knowledge through the study of human remains, using laboratory methods from fields such as forensics, chemistry, and genetics.

REVEALING THOSE FORGOTTEN BY HISTORY

The study of human remains by anthropologists can reveal the past lives and deaths of people whose stories are otherwise left out of written history. Records are often biased toward the people writing them, which historically has more often been those who were more educated, male, and of higher social status. And for societies whose histories have been suppressed or erased, these groups became "people without history." Archaeological analysis of human remains can help the living learn their stories.

During the Great Famine in Ireland (1845–1852), potato blight destroyed the rural population's most crucial food crop. At least a million people emigrated to countries such as the United States to escape starvation. More than a million people stayed in Ireland and died. They were the poorest and the least powerful.

Although many eyewitness accounts and other written records exist from the time of the Great Famine in Ireland, very few are from the people most affected. To tell their story, bioarchaeologist Jonny Geber analyzed the skeletal remains of almost 1,000 individuals who lived and worked at the Kilkenny Union Workhouse, in an area where the entire potato crop had been wiped out. For those who remained in Ireland and were starving, workhouses could give some relief, as workers provided their labor in exchange for food and shelter. Workhouse systems were designed to be as unpleasant as possible, so that people would only use them as a last resort (**Figure 13.18**). Families were separated, and conditions were reported to be miserable.

Geber's team examined the bones for an array of indicators of their overall health. This included skeletal indicators of vitamin C deficiency, indicating a diet without any fresh fruits and vegetables. They also looked at the bones for signs of trauma or heavy work, such as fractures and osteoarthritis. While historical documents show that people went to the workhouse to escape starvation in rural villages, the bones show that infectious diseases were common in the workhouses, likely because of overcrowded conditions. The risk of dying was high overall but highest for infants under two years of age. Yet there is also evidence of people receiving basic medical care. Four individuals had limbs

IRELAND

Kilkenny Union Workhouse

Europe

FIGURE 13.18

During the Great Famine in Ireland (1845–1852), institutions such as the Kilkenny Union Workhouse in southeastern Ireland housed people trying to escape starvation in the Irish countryside.

amputated. Two probably survived the amputation only to die of something else. Two did not survive the procedure, and their amputated legs were buried with the rest of the body. Such examinations of people omitted from written history help us understand a more detailed and complete picture of the past, most especially of the lives of those most at risk and with the least power during such major social and economic upheavals.

SEEKING JUSTICE FOR VICTIMS

The same techniques used to study long-dead skeletal remains—physical examination, isotopic analyses, and genetic testing—have applications in modern forensic work as well. A key component of a forensic anthropologist's work is establishing the biological profile of a *decedent*, when the remains are mummified or skeletonized, as a step to uncovering their identity and ultimately returning the deceased body to their loved ones. Initially this involves determining the sex, age, height, and (most controversially) ancestry based on the appearance of their skeleton that can then be matched against missing persons databases.

decedent Term used by forensic anthropologists to refer to a deceased, or dead, individual.

Forensic anthropologists can also analyze bodies for evidence of violent trauma and produce findings about the type of weapon used in a crime, based on bone signatures that leave diagnostic evidence of different weapon types. Forensic anthropologists can also assist with estimating time since death, as they study processes of taphonomy, or how dead bodies decay over time. Some of this research is done at university facilities, sometimes controversially called "body farms," where donated bodies are exposed to varied environmental factors such as sun, heat, cold, insects, and rain to identify how quickly they decompose. These methods allow forensic anthropologists to help law enforcement and legal investigators solve crimes by identifying the victim of a crime, estimating how long ago the crime happened, and determining what weapons were used to commit the crime.

UNDERSTANDING EMERGING EPIDEMICS

Another important reason to study past human remains is to document the long-term genetic history of diseases. Understanding how diseases evolve is vital to both predicting and reacting to new disease outbreaks. Cross-species transfers of genetic material in particular are very worrisome from a public health perspective, because they can more easily provide new genetic materials that can

zoonosis (plural, zoonoses) A disease that can be transferred between animals and humans.

tuberculosis (TB) An infection, caused by the tube-shaped *Mycobacterium tuberculosis* bacterium, that initially affects the lungs.

bacterium (plural, bacteria) A one-celled microorganism, with cell walls but without a nucleus, that can cause disease.

trigger mutations into more infectious and deadly strains. Recent examples of virus outbreaks include severe acute respiratory virus (SARS) in 2002–2004 and the Ebola virus in 2014–2016. The study of ancient human and animal remains reveals a very long human history of such dangerous zoonotic transfers.

Anthropologists use human remains to study tuberculosis (TB), which is transferred from animals to humans and is currently the leading cause of death by a single infectious disease. Infection by the tube-shaped *Mycobacterium tuberculosis* bacterium is focused in the lungs and is mostly spread through aerosol droplets (**Figure 13.19**). TB bacteria are harbored by both wild and domesticated animals. Previously, tuberculosis was almost eradicated with the introduction of modern antibiotics. But in the 1980s, new strains of tuberculosis began evolving that were resistant to drug treatment. Different strains of tuberculosis are found in a range of other mammal species and can potentially pass between them as zoonoses.

To a trained eye, the signs of chronic tuberculosis infections can be detected in archaeological skeletal material. Advanced infections eat into bone, eroding and eventually collapsing the spine, hips, and knees. Since the bacterium that causes tuberculosis can be preserved in bone long after death, it is possible to compare the current genetic profile of the disease to that from excavated skeletons. On the basis of these two types of evidence, the bacterium that causes tuberculosis originated in Africa in humans, who also gave tuberculosis to cows.

Interestingly, ancient DNA analysis also suggests that other early strains of tuberculosis were passed from animals to humans in more than one way and in more than one region. In the Americas, DNA from three individuals living in the Osmore River Valley of Peru around 900 CE had tuberculosis strains closely related to those found in sea lions that live on rugged ocean coasts. The work of a team lead by biological anthropologist Anne Stone has established that people living in the Osmore River Valley were likely first exposed to the disease while hunting and butchering marine mammal meat. Tuberculosis was likely passed from humans to marine mammals in Africa, and over time the marine mammals then passed tuberculosis to humans in South America well in advance of the first Africans or Europeans arriving in the Americas (**Figure 13.20**).

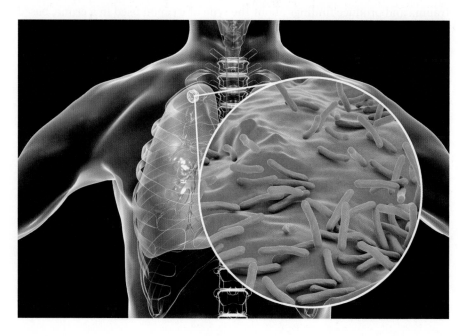

FIGURE 13.19

Mycobacterium tuberculosis bacteria (shown in blue in the inset) thrives in human lungs, but also in those of other mammals. Human contact with both domestic and wild animals (including sea lions and cattle) has allowed for repeated transfers of infection between species across many centuries, and allowed tuberculosis to reemerge in new places.

FIGURE 13.20

This tree shows proposed evolutionary relationships based on genetic comparisons of 261 different genomes of *Mycobacterium tuberculosis*, the bacterium that causes tuberculosis infections, taken from different mammal species, including humans. The dates are given as years before present and show the estimates of when the bacterial strains diverged from each other. In this figure, the colored lines each represent a human sample from different parts of the world. MRCA in the center of the diagram is the Most Recent Common Ancestor of all strains. Such genetic analyses are very important to understanding how novel strains of infectious disease emerge and spread through time and space, and hence both predicting and responding to epidemics and pandemics.

By the 18th century, when the age of European maritime exploration and colonial expansion was fully underway, many different strains of tuberculosis were circulating the globe. Analysis of the remains of 26 high-status parishioners interred between 1731 and 1838 in the crypt of a Catholic church in Vác, Hungary, showed signs of advanced tuberculosis on their bones. The subsequent DNA analysis then revealed exposure to multiple strains of tuberculosis, suggesting that at that time many people were being exposed to multiple genetic versions of the disease as the world was rapidly globalizing. This increasingly detailed genetic record of how and why different infectious strains have spread and died out through millennia is a crucial tool kit for dealing with new emerging strains of the deadly disease, including COVID-19 and those yet to evolve.

ETHICS, ANTHROPOLOGY, AND HUMAN REMAINS

Although the scientific study of human remains offers important evidence that cannot be gained in other ways, such remains have important symbolic meanings in human societies. This is why using the remains of the dead for anthropological science is ethically complex.

For those who died recently, the process of informed consent can provide clear ethical and legal guidelines, because such a process confirms if people or their closest relatives agree for their bodies to be used for scientific or medical

Native American Graves Protection and Repatriation Act (NAGPRA) Legislation passed by the U.S. federal government to protect and return archaeological human remains and culturally significant artifacts to affiliated Native Americans.

purposes after their death. Examples of how bodies could be used include organ donation, for medical training, or forensic decomposition studies; all of these require informed consent.

But for the remains of those longer dead, often the focus of anthropological research, deciding what is appropriate and respectful treatment can be a trickier issue. There are no consistent rules, and what is defined as appropriate is often linked to cultural ideas that vary across groups and societies. For example, some descendant groups are very interested in learning more about their ancestors by having their remains excavated and studied, often via genetic testing. They feel it is a new and exciting way to become more connected to them. But others see these same actions as violating religious practices and disrespecting the dead.

Generally, anthropologists agree that those most closely related to the remains should make decisions about whether and how they are used for scientific study and what should happen to them subsequently. But sometimes identifying who is most closely related can be challenging in itself, creating additional ethical considerations. "Kennewick Man" was the name initially given to an 8,000–9,000-year-old skeleton discovered in 1996 on the bank of the Columbia River in the state of Washington, United States. Local tribes, including the Umatilla, demanded return of the remains for reburial. They did not want them used for scientific study, and under the United States' **Native American Graves Protection and Repatriation Act (NAGPRA)**, they can make this determination for the remains of ancestors. But because the remains were so old and direct relationships to a tribe couldn't be confirmed, initially these claims were denied and scientific study of the skeleton began at the Smithsonian Institution, despite tribal protests. But subsequent DNA testing showed that The Ancient One, as he is now known, had genetic ties to several contemporary tribes, including the Colville, one of the tribes that initially claimed a relationship. In 2016, legislation returned the remains for reburial to a coalition that includes the Confederated Tribes of the Colville Reservation. Study of The Ancient One ceased.

Regardless of legal issues, each anthropological project needs to find the ethical balance between the scientific value of studying human remains and their symbolic value to relevant communities. The African Burial Ground project on the island of Manhattan in the United States provides an example of how the two can work well together. For about a hundred years, between the 1690s and 1794, free and enslaved Africans were buried outside the city walls of New Amsterdam, now New York City. Barred from burial in most churchyards at the time, they were buried in what was referred to in a map made in 1755 as the "Negros Buriel Ground" [sic]. It was rediscovered in lower Manhattan in 1991 during the construction of the Ted Weiss Federal Building. The remains of 419 men, women, and children of African descent were excavated. The human remains were taken to Howard University, a historically Black university, for study by bioarchaeologist Michael Blakey.

Working with descendant groups in New York City, Blakey's team focused their scientific study on learning all they could about the origins and daily lives of those 419 people. They found some had strong ties with Africa, reflected in grave goods transported from Africa or the genetic material extracted from their skeletons. For example, one adult female was buried with waist beads around her hips, and she also had incisors that had been filed into an hourglass shape and into a point. This suggested she was born in western Africa, forcibly enslaved, and taken to New York City.

Wooden coffins were used to transport the remains of enslaved Africans for reburial at the African Burial Ground. The archaeological human remains were transported from Howard University, where they had been studied, to the African Burial Ground in New York City as part of a ceremony called the Rites of Ancestral Return.

After a decade of analysis, further consultation determined how the remains should be returned. They were reburied in 2003. The ceremony, called the Rites of Ancestral Return, included reburial in wooden coffins that were made to replicate the coffins that may have been originally used at the site (**Figure 13.21**). In 2006, the African Burial Ground was named a national monument and was opened to the public. It has become a place for annual celebrations relevant to descendant communities, such as Kwanzaa, Juneteenth, and Black History Month, linking present and past.

Jason De León, whose work on the U.S.–Mexico border opened this chapter, is similarly connecting the study of the dead to the world of the living through anthropology, in ways accessible to both affected communities and the public more widely. He launched the Undocumented Migration Project to raise public awareness about the scale and violence of death on the U.S.–Mexico border and how border policies impact people. This collaborative effort includes applying tools from visual anthropology, such as photography and museum installation, to reflect and share evidence of the violence of migrant deaths (**Figure 13.22**). Yet ethical questions about what to display regarding deaths arise, even when human remains are not shown. Such issues include whether it is appropriate to display images related to those who died terrible deaths—abandoned, in pain, and otherwise marginalized.

The study of the dead remains central to anthropological study, but it will also continue to raise complex ethical concerns about how it should be done. How we treat the dead is profoundly important within all human societies; it speaks to who we are and what we value. This is the case within science as well.

FIGURE 13.22

This installation of the Undocumented Migration Project indicates the locations of deaths at the Arizona section of the U.S.–Mexico border (black line). The orange toe tags represent the locations of bodies that remain unidentified, while the beige tags represent people now identified.

CHAPTER REVIEW

13

Death, Dying, and the Dead

This chapter examines anthropological research on death, dying, and the dead from the first examples of hominins intentionally burying their dead to contemporary mortuary practices and grieving rituals from around the world.

KEY TERMS
› forensic anthropology
› funeral
› taphonomy

13.1 | Death and Its Rituals

Trace the development of death rituals in humans.

- Humans, as the only species that fully comprehends the inevitability of physical death, have found ways to look beyond it—to connect the living and the dead together spiritually through rituals and practices.

KEY TERMS
› burial
› cemetery
› grave goods
› mortuary practice
› religious
› ritual
› spiritual

13.2 | Grieving and Celebrating the Dead

Describe how the dead continue to interact with and impact the living in different societies.

- While grief at the loss of loved ones is a universal human emotion, how people react to these feelings varies widely in line with cultural and religious beliefs and practices. Reactions to grief can include elaborate funerals and laments, body modification, or efforts to control and minimize emotional repsonses.

- Many such practices act to connect the living to the dead.

KEY TERMS
› grief
› lament
› rite of passage

13.3 | Studying the Dead

Assess how scientific research of the remains of the dead can contribute useful knowledge.

- The study of the remains of dead bodies, such as skeletons, has been an important source of basic information for anthropologists, who are able to spread new knowledge on the history of our species and our vulnerabilities to disease, and to seek justice for those who can't speak for themselves.

KEY TERMS
> bacterium
> decedent
> tuberculosis (TB)
> zoonosis

13.4 | Ethics, Anthropology, and Human Remains

Consider ethical complexities involved in anthropological studies using human remains.

- Because the dead do not fully disappear from society, studies of their remains need to consider and resolve complex ethical questions.

KEY TERMS
> Native American Graves Protection and Repatriation Act (NAGPRA)

14

Race and Racialized Societies

For most people, a simple handbuilt brick drain in a soggy yard behind a modest two-story house is not worth noticing, let alone studying in detail (**Figure 14.1**). But to archaeologist Anna Agbe-Davies, such apparently mundane features can provide nuanced, otherwise overlooked insights to recent human history. We can learn a lot about life in the United States in the 20th century by examining written documents such as personal letters, newspapers, government documents, and other media. But the archaeological record can tell us about facets of life that were left out of the written record. Agbe-Davies uses excavation and artifact analysis to provide a different perspective on historical events, particularly the U.S. Civil Rights Movement, and to better understand both how people were treated differently on the basis of race and how people resisted the nation's legacy of racism.

Agbe-Davies excavated that seemingly unremarkable waterlogged drain at the childhood home of Pauli Murray (1910–1985) in Durham, North Carolina. Murray was a pioneering Black and genderqueer civil rights leader as well as a lawyer, author, university professor, and the first Black female-presenting Episcopal priest in the country. Agbe-Davies searched for clues about what could have inspired Murray's important work on civil rights and anti-racism.

The Murray home was built downhill from a segregated White cemetery that housed slaveholders, Confederate soldiers, and other prominent White residents in Durham, who did not live near the cemetery. Disamenities such as cemeteries are often found in minoritized communities even today, either because state or local governments placed them in neighborhoods where

LEARNING OBJECTIVES

14.1 Science and the Origins of Racialized Systems
Explain how race is a social construct.

14.2 Structural Racism
Connect the history of scientific racism to the development and persistence of racialized worldviews.

14.3 The Persistence of Racialized Societies
Appraise how racism operates today, including how it creates inequalities and destabilizes societies.

14.4 Anthropology and Anti-Racism Now
Evaluate anthropological approaches for accomplishing anti-racist goals.

REVEALING RACIALIZATION'S HARMS

In racialized societies, the organization around social constructs of race does many types of harm. Some are readily observable and widely recognized (such as slavery). Other harms can be identified, and solutions posed, through anthropological approaches that consider social structure, history, language, human biology, and—especially—the lived experience of those most harmed by racialized systems.

FIGURE 14.1

(a) Pioneering civil rights leader Pauli Murray is pictured. **(b)** Murray's now-restored home shows the public cemetery placed immediately uphill, which meant the house was permanently waterlogged. A restoration effort was what kick-started the archaeological investigation of the house and surroundings.

(a)

(b)

people had less power to protest or because other existing disamenities already made the neighborhood undesirable for White families who chose to live elsewhere. Agbe-Davies's excavations showed exactly how much of a disamenity the cemetery placement was for the family. The Maplewood Cemetery drainage system diverted the water and runoff directly onto the Murray property, which saturated and eroded the house foundations, making the entire house unstable. The Murray family well was also unusable, polluted by runoff from decomposing bodies. City archives show that Murray's grandfather tirelessly approached the city for help but was repeatedly ignored. While the story from the written records would have ended there, the archaeological excavations showed how the Murray family attempted to solve the problem. The uncovered brick drains were built to attempt to divert the runoff and create drainage infrastructure to protect their house (**Figure 14.2**). Agbe-Davies's excavations showed how the Murray family responded to one result of structural racism in Durham.

racism Harm and oppression directed at groups or individuals based on societal beliefs of racial hierarchy, such as White superiority.

anti-racism Overturning entrenched structural sources of race-based inequality.

disamenity An environmental hazard or other unwanted or unpleasant environmental feature that reduces quality of life for residents.

minoritize To deny equitable access to power, wealth, or resources within society to a group of people. (In contrast, a minority simply means a group with fewer members than some other group.)

structural racism A system of inequality, often state-sanctioned and created historically, that builds on the belief that people can be classified into distinctive, separate groups on the basis of ancestry or visible body characteristics and that these typologies reflect meaningful biological differences, justifying the belief that members of some groups are superior or inferior to others.

FIGURE 14.2

Excavations at Pauli Murray's childhood home revealed brick features the family built in an attempt to divert the constant runoff away from the house foundations. The brick is in poor shape after 100 years of being waterlogged.

Agbe-Davies's excavations also connect small everyday details to broader themes in history, such as how oppressive and racialized systems operated in the recent past and how people experienced them. Agbe-Davies revealed how structural racism can manifest itself through the placing of more disamenities, such as public cemeteries, factories, or landfills, in the places where minoritized groups live and the resulting environmental degradation of these neighborhoods.

Race is a belief system, not a scientifically valid way to understand human biological variation. In this chapter, we focus on contemporary anthropological research that aims to determine (i) why racialized social systems persist, (ii) what consequences these systems exert on those subjected to them, and (iii) how they can be dismantled to create more equitable and stable societies.

An important note before we move on: Anthropologists are extremely careful to distinguish the terms *race* and *ethnicity*. Race is an imposed social category, as we will explain, in which the features of a group are imagined to be inherited and innate and thus based in biology. It is also a set of historical ideas with the particular capacity to harm, given how tightly welded it is to political and economic power arrangements that have developed and continue to be managed in many societies today. Ethnicity, on the other hand, refers to a social identity that relates to ideas of shared history, language, norms, practices, values, and sometimes ancestry. Ethnicity is one of the many social identities people negotiate in relation to their place in society, alongside other common ones such as gender, age, or occupation. These two terms are often used interchangeably; for example, ethnic groups may be referred to by racialized identity terms such as "Black" or "Asian" because the ethnic categories themselves have become racialized. But, to anthropologists, the distinction is central to understanding what racism is, and how it operates within society.

oppressive system A societal arrangement that permits one group to impose their will on others in burdensome, malicious, or unjust ways.

racialized system A society that is organized to reflect a racial hierarchy; inequality is embedded in the society, and people are rewarded or oppressed on the basis of their place within it.

SCIENCE AND THE ORIGINS OF RACIALIZED SYSTEMS

The fundamental belief in the existence of biological races is rooted in thinking based in typology. This typological thinking attempts to organize highly complex biocultural variation, such as in how people look, into simplified, distinct categories; individual variation within types is not taken into consideration. In this section, we will examine how early anthropologists contributed to the rise of scientific racism and how other anthropologists then refuted these theories.

typology A system imposed to categorize objects together on the basis of specific similarities, emphasizing what is "typical" or "average" for each category.

scientific racism Misinterpretation or use of misleading scientific evidence to justify and support racialized worldviews.

WHAT IS TYPOLOGICAL THINKING?

The use of racial categories to classify humans into types is necessarily highly subjective and arbitrary. Such typological thinking about human variation is based on the idea that human phenotypes can be correctly categorized into discrete types simply on the basis of visible bodily features. This approach was common in early European science.

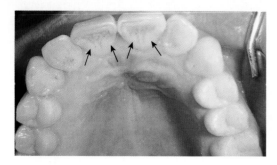

FIGURE 14.3

An example of shovel-shaped incisors is shown. This photo is from a study in Turkey that found 10% of the sample had shovel-shaped incisors.

To understand what makes typological approaches to human biological variation distinct—and wrong—consider the example of human teeth. If you put your tongue against your upper incisors (front teeth), you may feel a different texture than someone else would. This is because for some people the incisors are flat on their back; others have a dip or "shovel" shape formed by ridges on the sides of the tooth. Shovel-shaped incisors are a relatively simple phenotypic trait, because most people (not all) either have the shovel shape or they do not (**Figure 14.3**).

Shovel-shaped incisors are more commonly found in populations on the Asian continent or with ancestry there. According to typological thinking, shovel-shaped incisors then are classified as representing an "Asian" phenotype. By extension, then, any tooth examined that has shovel-shaped incisors becomes classified as being "Asian." And this is exactly what was done when incisor shoveling was used as one assumed skeletal marker of "race."

But such typological thinking, even with the most genetically simple traits, necessarily interprets the evidence of human variation in a very particular and narrow way. As we explored in Chapter 3, humans show complex variation on millions of traits within populations, reflecting the interplay of many different evolutionary forces. Classifying some selected and limited traits (tooth shape, skin color) as "typical" or "normal" requires that we ignore all of this "messy" variation. Moreover, some people with Asian ancestry have flat incisors, and many people from other world regions have the shovel shape (**Figure 14.4**).

FIGURE 14.4

Frequency of shovel-shaped incisors in different world populations, as depicted in this graph, shows that there are no populations where you can clearly define the groups as distinct based on the characteristic shape of the incisors. The data are based on pooling of multiple samples with the vertical line representing the median frequency of shoveling for a population from that geographic region, the blue box indicates the frequency range from the 25th to 75th percentile, and the horizontal lines reflect the total range (highest and lowest frequencies) of samples from each region. The dots represent outliers from studies within each region, further demonstrating how variable the expression of this trait is.

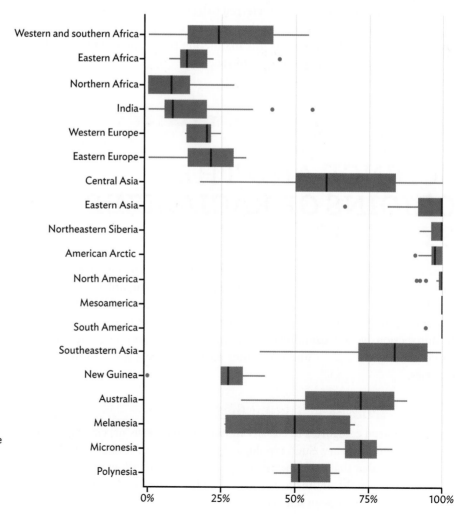

Typological thinking then incorrectly defines someone from Asia with flat incisors as an outlier or abnormality requiring explanation, and it also incorrectly defines people from other parts of the world with shovel-shaped incisors as "having Asian ancestry," completely ignoring the genetics of how these phenotypes develop in an individual.

Essentialized thinking occurs when arbitrary typologies (such as shovel-shaped incisors) are *assumed* to have biologically fixed qualities. For example, an "Asian" person is defined by having shovel-shaped incisors (among other features); a "Caucasian" person is then partially defined by not having them. Essentialized ways of thinking easily slide from physical traits, such as skin color, to wider racist assumptions about how people assigned to given social groupings act, behave, or think.

THE EARLY SCIENCE OF RACE

The concept of biological "race" as it is recognized today originated in the so-called Age of Discovery and the Enlightenment during the 17th and 18th centuries. Europe's wealthy and politically powerful elite became interested in studying the natural world; travelers, missionaries, and merchants brought back knowledge and startling evidence such as unfamiliar rocks, animals, plants, goods, and even people. Museums became one key place where this variety was presented to the European public (**Figure 14.5**). Typological and hierarchical thinking strongly influenced how objects (including the bodies of people who were seen as racialized "others" and even living people treated as objects of display) were displayed and studied. Today we know that typological thinking about human biology is misleading even for characterizing the simplest body traits, such as the shape of our incisors. But at that time, the notion that there were distinct biological types of people aligned well with the beliefs of European elites about their innate superiority in the world.

essentialize To apply the belief of "natural" essential characteristics to culturally defined groups of people (such as on the basis of "race" but also other characteristics such as "sex").

FIGURE 14.5

This is a view of the "Hall of Primitive Medicine" at the Wellcome Historical Medical Museum in London, U.K. The display was based on items collected from around the world by Sir Henry Wellcome, reflecting colonial ideas about "exotic" peoples. The renamed "Medicine Man" gallery was finally shuttered in 2022.

34 QUADRUPEDIA ANTROPOMORPHA.

CLASSIS I.

QUADRUPEDIA

Ordo 1.

ANTROPOMORPHA. *Dentes* primores utrinque quatuor, aut nulli.

1. *HOMO.* *Noſce te ipſum.*

Homo variat: Europæus albus.
Americanus rubeſcens.
Aſiaticus fuſcus.
Africanus niger.

2. *SIMIA.* *Os dentatum.* *Pedes pentadactyli*

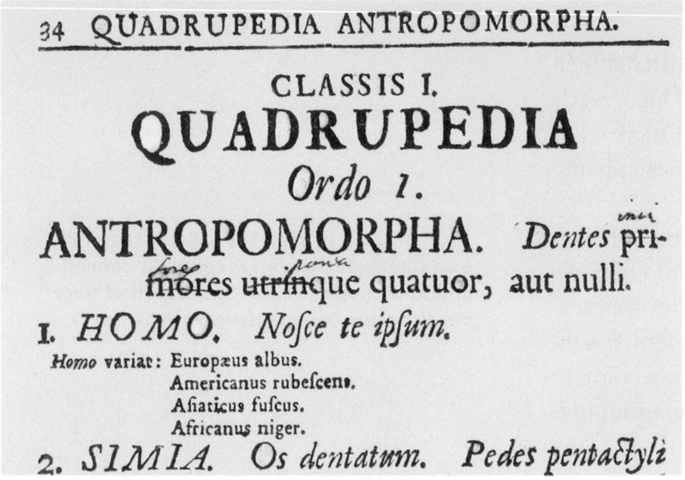

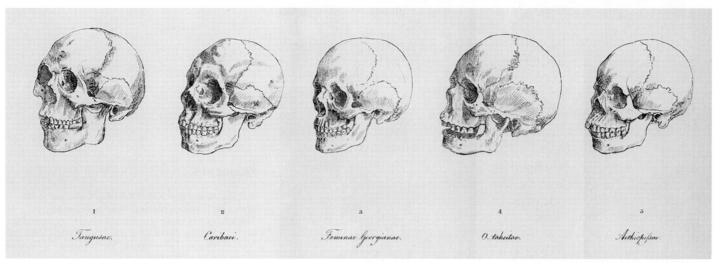

FIGURE 14.6

This section from Linnaeus's *Systema Naturae* was first published in 1735. (1) His typology of "human [*Homo*] variations" is outlined and places people from Europe above those from the Americas and Asia, and then Africa. He also identifies colors associated with his hierarchy. (2) His placement of apes/monkeys (*Simia*) just under humans was far more controversial at the time, because it went against Church teachings.

Hierarchies already dominated much European thinking about how the world worked, and scientific research then (as now) reflected the moral standards of the time. These hierarchies were deeply enmeshed with religious beliefs. The notion of the Great Chain of Being was one dominant idea, a philosophy that humans were given power, by an all-powerful God, to have control over the natural world; this power included the ability to name and label all things. This culminated in matter being organized by European naturalists into a linear and rigid hierarchy with God at the top, humans (meaning Europeans) in the middle, and animals and then trees at the bottom. As European exploration increasingly revealed the variation of humans across the globe, leading scientists such as Carolus Linnaeus (1707–1778)—who devised the taxonomic system of species naming still used today—fully embraced the goal of describing humanity's place in nature and identifying different "types" of humans within that larger model (**Figure 14.6**).

The concept of "race" packaged highly select biological and cultural "evidence" together into neat bins, and these reproduced various hierarchies that always maintained Europeans at the top. In 1753, for example, Linnaeus differentiated four distinct human types based on combinations of skin color and assumed temperament—variously and incorrectly categorizing racial groups as "hearty," "serious," "lazy," or "irascible." These were widely accepted within educated European circles at the time as a serious scientific contribution. Such efforts always relied heavily on the application of rigid geographic classifications based on where people came from.

In an attempt to base the study of race on empirically verifiable observations, German scientist Johann Blumenbach (1752–1840), sometimes considered the first physical anthropologist, developed a taxonomy of five races based on the shape of skulls. Blumenbach praised the beauty of a Georgian skull found in the Caucasus Mountains, from which the term "Caucasian" derives (**Figure 14.7**).

This and other early typological systems used to organize humans were designed by Europe's scientific elites who, in many cases, had no firsthand knowledge of the peoples they were categorizing. Linnaeus himself never left Sweden. His behavioral interpretations of human physical variation relied entirely on the travelogues of returning European explorers and Christian

FIGURE 14.7

This sketch of skulls representing Blumenbach's five races, highlighting their geographic origins, is taken from his 1795 doctoral thesis. These read from left to right, as sourced from Mongolia, the Caribbean, Georgia (a female, which he described as the most "beautiful" skull), Tahiti, and Ethiopia.

missionaries. And scientists couldn't agree on how many races there were, or what they were, because the classifications they were producing were mostly based on their own unscientific and individual impressions and dispositions.

Yet, by the late 1800s, the prevailing view of many scientists and other European elites was not only that races were real, innate, and representative of different kinds of humans, but also that these race categories could be linked to different evolutionary histories. One set of scientific research that supported these inaccurate conclusions was not just the shape but the measuring of skulls, or craniometry. Since skulls hold brains, researchers concluded that skull size and intelligence must be linked (an argument that also had sexist implications, since women tend to have smaller skulls on average). Because racial typologies linked physical differences to cognitive, moral, or behavioral traits, such as criminality and intelligence, this pseudoscience helped justify mistreatment or denial of rights of disfavored groups. If the qualities of so-called races were innate, then social programs and political reforms could be dismissed as a waste of effort. Thus, by promulgating the idea of distinct biological races through these typologies, the European scientific establishment helped provide a rationale for the continued displacement, subjugation, or enslavement of non-Europeans around the globe that was in full force at the time.

Racial typologies were especially embraced by elites in the European colonies most dependent on enslaved labor forces, such as the United States, Brazil, and India. Over time, the notion of races became increasingly embedded in many governmental and other powerful institutions. For example, early-20th-century anti-immigration laws passed in the United States (such as the Chinese Exclusion Act of 1882 or the Immigration Act of 1924) were justified by racist science suggesting that "race mixing" led to declines in intelligence and more crime.

SOCIAL DARWINISM AND EUGENICS

Nineteenth-century Europe witnessed a shift in thinking about race and human variation, which built upon Charles Darwin's groundbreaking theories published in *On the Origin of Species* (1859) and *The Descent of Man* (1871). In particular, Darwin's theories of natural selection inspired some to view inequality as the result of inherent differences between human societies, wherein the most successful groups pass their ability to succeed onto the next generation while less successful groups die off. Herbert Spencer, a contemporary of Darwin, was a key proponent of this viewpoint, which came to be known as "social Darwinism," and it was Spencer who coined the now-famous phrase "survival of the fittest."

This social Darwinism supported the development of eugenics, the study of how to manipulate reproduction within human societies to increase the frequencies of the most desirable traits in future generations. Eugenics had major support in the United States and Europe in the earlier part of the 20th century, including from multiple U.S. presidents and the wider scientific establishment. It was Charles Darwin's son, Leonard, who launched the First International Eugenics Congress in 1912, and a cousin, Francis Galton, was the honorary president of the newly formed Eugenics Education Society in the United Kingdom from 1907 (**Figure 14.8**). Influential economist John Maynard Keynes was also a member. Eugenics policies led to laws against marriage between people assigned to different races, racist immigration laws, and sterilization campaigns in the United States and many other countries, with the goal of "improving" the species. Eugenics was used as a driving ideology in Nazi Germany, where Adolf

pseudoscience Methods, techniques, or beliefs that appear to have scientific validity but are not based on rigorous, empirical hypothesis testing.

eugenics A racist effort to improve the so-called "genetic quality" of human groups by encouraging those socially defined as "the best" to have more children and preventing others deemed "undesirable" from doing so.

FIGURE 14.8

This 1920s British poster promoted eugenic ideas of racial superiority.

Hitler's "Final Solution" enacted large-scale genocide against Jews and other groups with what they defined as socially or politically undesirable traits.

As a political movement, eugenics quickly fell out of favor soon after the war ended, and not only because of public horror around its application to Nazi genocide. Wider scientific rejection of eugenics was spurred by reconsideration of the tenets of Darwin's theory of natural selection, now combined with the principles of genetics through the modern synthesis (see Chapter 3). The concept of "population" came to quickly replace "race" in scientific language. The study of variation replaced the study of categoric averages or types. A static view of a set number of fixed types of people was replaced with a dynamic view of ever-changing and complex webs of human connection with deeply interwoven histories.

PHYSICAL ANTHROPOLOGISTS AND THE SUPPORT OF RACIAL TYPOLOGIES

In the early 20th century, race science was mainstream in anthropology, adding scientific support to racist and eugenic ideas. Influential early physical anthropologists, especially those interested in craniometry (or the measurement of skulls), played a role in the science that established and justified racist worldviews into the mid-20th century. Examples include the work of Aleš Hrdlička (1869–1943), founder of the American Association of Physical Anthropologists (AAPA), which in 2020 was renamed the American Association of Biological Anthropologists to distance the organization from its historical connection with race science. Hrdlička spent much of his career as curator of physical anthropology at what is now the Smithsonian Institution National Museum of Natural History in Washington, DC, United States. He perceived himself as nonracist, but questionable conclusions drawn from his studies of human anatomy reveal his alignment with White supremacy. For example, he insisted that early humans must have evolved in Europe, despite there being no good evidence to support that position at the time.

Harvard professor Earnest Hooton (1887–1954) was another prominent early physical anthropologist who used measurements of skulls to develop detailed racial typologies, most notably those taken from the site of Pecos Pueblo in New Mexico in the southwestern United States. This was considered by many as cutting-edge work at the time for its use of early statistical methods and attempts to describe change through time at a single archaeological site. More controversial was his work in the 1920 and 1930s, applying similar phenotypic measures to thousands of incarcerated men to prove that different body forms (such as low foreheads or short stature) could predict different criminal behaviors. Hooton and other scientists at the time espoused additional theories, since debunked, of criminality being based in biology. Physiognomy and phrenology are two pseudosciences that viewed one's physical appearance as reflecting aspects of one's personality, disposition, or tendency toward specifics types of crime (**Figure 14.9**). Such work has been fully discredited but continues to pervade the public consciousness where the evidence against racist pseudoscience is not systematically taught.

At the same time this discredited work was appearing, credible scientific breakthroughs in understanding evolution had been happening apace. By the 1920s, Darwin's theory of natural selection and the principles of genetic inheritance were gaining acceptance in scientific circles. By the 1950s, the widening field of population genetics was beginning to replace race as the

---

physical anthropology **An outdated term for what is now called biological anthropology, sometimes based in typological approaches to explain human biology.**

White supremacy **A political, economic, and cultural system in which those who are identified as "White" overwhelmingly control power and material resources, conscious and unconscious ideas of White superiority are widespread, racism is daily reenacted, and systematic oppression of non-White people is justified.**

population genetics **The study of genes and gene frequencies within populations, for the purpose of understanding the history of a population and the evolutionary mechanisms that shaped its genetic structure.**

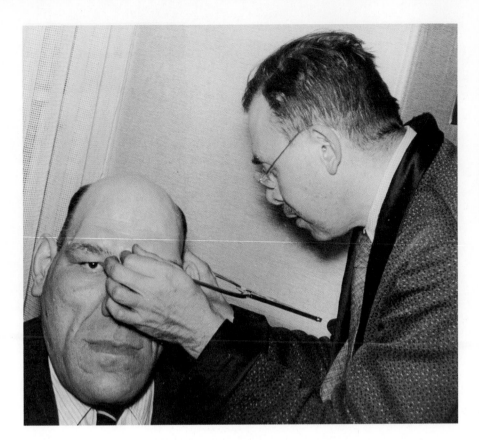

FIGURE 14.9

Earnest Hooton is pictured making head measurements. Hooton's 1926 typology identified four human "types," using racialized terms now discredited, based on skin color, head and nose shape, and hair form. The typology was informed by body measurements collected around the globe by many physical anthropologists trained or working at Harvard University, where Hooton taught for four decades. This work is now uniformly rejected as racist. Two of Hooton's students trained at Harvard, biological anthropologists Sherwood ("Sherry") Washburn (1911–2000) and Gabriel Lasker (1912–2002), went on to advance views of human variation based in population genetics that challenged their advisor's now-discredited typological framework.

scientific paradigm for explaining human variation and its causes (Chapter 3). The study of human variation replaced the study of human types. A static view of a set number of fixed types of people was replaced with a dynamic view of ever-evolving populations that was able to grapple better with the complexities of human difference and continues to help us reinterpret human histories (**Figure 14.10**).

Furthermore, a racial or typological view of human history and variation failed under its own weight of inadequacy to explain the observed patterns of variation anthropologists were observing in living peoples and ancient populations composed of skeletons and fossils. For example, as discussed in Chapter 3, human biological variation is not distributed discretely as a racial model predicts. Furthermore, when different traits are plotted, different groupings of human populations emerge, which suggests little consistency in so-called fixed racial types. However, the biggest challenge to the racial approach to human variation was the increasing recognition that most human variation is found within local populations, meaning it is difficult to look at the entirety of the human genome and see evidence of clear population-based differences, especially at the continental scale.

EARLY ANTHROPOLOGY CHALLENGES SCIENTIFIC RACISM

Not all early anthropologists agreed with the flawed research agenda pursued by physical anthropologists such as Hooton and Hrdlička. There was considerable parallel research by anthropologists that revealed how social institutions (including scientific practices)—not human biology—were responsible for the perpetuation of beliefs in the veracity of race and biological typologies. Over time, these alternative theories of race as a social construct survived rigorous scientific scrutiny, while biological theories did not.

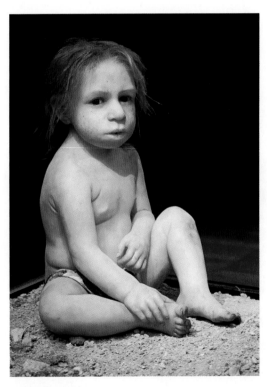

FIGURE 14.10

Analyses of ancient Neanderthal DNA suggest a mutation (such as that of some modern humans descended from populations of northern Europe) associated with a reduction in skin pigmentation. Recent reconstructions of Neanderthals for museums, including this one, are taking this into account.

FIGURE 14.11

(a) Students of W. E. B. Du Bois helped him develop a series of compelling infographics that connected social, economic, and health data to histories of slavery and poverty. This graphic was created for a European audience to explain how long and entrenched enslavement was and how recently emancipation happened. (b) Du Bois is pictured at the 1900 Paris Exposition, where these infographics were showcased.

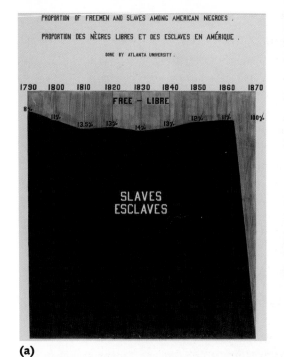

(a)

(b)

W. E. B. Du Bois (1868–1963; pronounced Dew-BOYCE) was one of the earliest to define and advance this effort. An anthropologist–sociologist before such labels existed, he was the first Black American to graduate with a PhD from Harvard. His careful statistical analyses demonstrated how many biological differences otherwise then ascribed to race (such as worse health) were explained by the recency of slavery and lack of access to critical resources such as clean water, adequate nutrition, and education (**Figure 14.11**). "It is not one problem," Du Bois wrote in 1898, "but rather a plexus of social problems, some new, some old, some simple, some complex; and these problems have their one bond of unity in the act that they group themselves above those Africans whom two centuries of slave-trading brought into the land." Du Bois's proposed solution remains current today: moving beyond the typological approaches to human variation popularly applied in both science and medicine.

W. Montague Cobb (1904–1990) was a physical anthropologist trained as a physician at Howard University, and subsequently, he was the first Black American to get a PhD in the then-new field of anthropology (**Figure 14.12**). Described as an activist scholar, Cobb's vision for challenging racist science included curating what remains the largest historical collection of skeletons collected from the remains of Black people. Many human remains came to his collection at Howard University (where he had returned to teach anatomy) because the state had seized the bodies for use as medical cadavers when families couldn't afford burials.

Cobb's work used detailed analysis of both skeletal and living bodies to highlight the central role of material disadvantage in delaying physical growth and producing worse health in Black people in the United States. In an article written in 1936, for example, Cobb used systematic analysis of measurements of track and field athletes to challenge the argument that Black runners (including the incredible Jesse Owens, who dominated the 1936 Olympic Games in Berlin) consistently outperformed other athletes because of innate biological differences. Rather, he showed, their performance was better explained by hard work and training.

FIGURE 14.12

Portrait of William Montague Cobb, who earned an MD in 1929 and was the first Black American to receive a PhD in Anthropology in 1932. He later served as president of the civil rights organization NAACP (National Association for the Advancement of Colored People) from 1976–1982.

In his early career, Cobb often interacted with Franz Boas, arguably the most influential anthropologist of his era. Boas's analysis, published in full form as *Changes in Bodily Form of Descendants of Immigrants* (1911), was a detailed systematic study of over 13,000 immigrants from Europe to New York and their American-born children, based on work commissioned by the U.S. Immigration Commission. By comparing body measurements between the generations, he demonstrated how supposedly fixed and unchanging body features such as height, face shape, and skull shape were in fact *developmentally plastic*. That is, environmental factors such as improved diet had profound impacts on the physical development of head shape and other aspects of phenotype previously described as immutable racial traits. Although some findings from this study are being reassessed, the wide public release of these findings was significant in challenging scientific racism in the decades that followed, and it is one reason that Boas's immigrant research has been considered by many to be an example of early anti-racist anthropology.

Caroline Bond Day (1889–1948) was another early Black American anti-racist anthropologist. She took classes with Earnest Hooton at Harvard; at the time, he was the only physical anthropologist teaching there. Using photographs of phenotypes from Hooton's lab and materials she collected herself, alongside genealogical information from families that included those socially classified as both Black and White, she rejected the idea of innate biological differences explaining individual achievement. Rather, she showed that those who had phenotypes (such as lighter skin color) closer to their White relatives benefited from having greater social and economic privileges.

Another important challenger of scientific and societal racism was Zora Neale Hurston (**Figure 14.13**). She was born in Notasulga, Alabama in the southern United States in 1891, the granddaughter of enslaved people and the daughter of a sharecropper father and schoolteacher mother. She came to the formal study of anthropology relatively late in life, studying as a student of Franz Boas (alongside Margaret Mead and Ruth Benedict at Columbia University in New York) while she pursued a successful career as an author and journalist.

developmental plasticity The capacity of the same genotype to produce distinct phenotypes as a response to the environmental conditions under which development occurs.

FIGURE 14.13

In 1935, Zora Neale Hurston (left) co-led an expedition to the American South and the Bahamas to audio-record and preserve local folk songs. This photo was taken in Eatonville, Florida, where Hurston spent most of her childhood.

Hurston's innovations in ethnographic methods allowed her to present new views of American society and White privilege that challenged harmful entrenched racial stereotypes in the early 20th century. In particular, she used literary skill to align her descriptions of everyday life in Black communities much closer to the way the people she studied actually expressed their experiences of such things as love, music, and work. This approach created a rich and almost poetic scholarship. Her autoethnographic descriptions conveyed more directly what people actually said and how they said it, challenging the contemporary academic writing conventions of the time. She also humanized Black Americans for a wider public audience through her literary classics that exemplify anti-racism, such as *Their Eyes Were Watching God* (1937).

These early anti-racist efforts continue to inspire many anthropologists today. We will further discuss these legacies in Section 14.4.

SECTION 14.2

STRUCTURAL RACISM

In this section, we examine how the social construct of race systematically reinforces inequality in societies by serving as the basis of legal, economic, and social policies and practices. One example studied in detail by anthropologists is health disparities. In the United Kingdom, minoritized groups were four times more likely to die of COVID-19 at the peak of the pandemic. Furthermore, 90% of the doctors who died of COVID-19 were also from minoritized communities. In such cases, it may seem that racial categories explain differences in risk. But anthropological studies have consistently shown how this is best explained by structural racism. Race may be a concept without a biological basis, but experiencing the effects of racism directly affects biology.

health disparity A difference in preventable disease, injury, or violence created through social disadvantage.

RACISM IN THE HOSPITAL: OBSTETRIC CARE

Racism becomes embodied in many different ways, and differential access to, or quality of, medical care is one of the best studied. The United States spends more money per capita on childbirth-related care yet ranks low—alongside lower-income countries such as Afghanistan and Belize—in maternal health measures. In the United States, Black women are three times more likely to die during childbirth than others, and their babies are 50% more likely to be born prematurely and more than twice as likely to die in the first year of life. Though lack of access to healthcare can account for some of these discrepancies, anthropological research is revealing the role of clinical neglect and mistreatment as important factors.

Tennis star Serena Williams has told her own story of giving birth at a top hospital, where she knew her body and that something was wrong after her Cesarean delivery. The nurse dismissed her as confused, accounting for it as postbirth fogginess. This led to a delay in diagnosing blood clots in her lungs, a potentially lethal condition.

Cultural anthropologist Dána-Ain Davis collected and analyzed such birth stories by many professional Black women. All women may encounter mistreatment during obstetric care, but these experiences reveal how persistent racism contributed to patterns of missed diagnoses, neglectful treatment, pain, or coercion to undergo unwanted procedures.

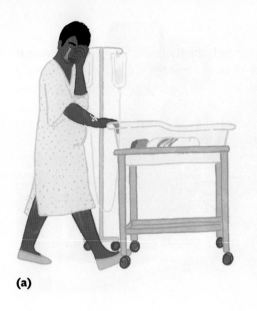

(a)

OBSTETRIC RACISM

DIAGNOSTIC LAPSE

When a clinicians' uninterrogated belief that Blackness is pathological leads them to de-emphasize or exaggerate or ignore a patient's symptoms resulting in an inappropriate or lapsed diagnosis.

NEGLECT, DISMISSIVENESS, OR DISRESPECT

When medical professionals ignore or dismiss a person's expressed need for reproductive help or care and/or treats them with disdain.

INTENTIONALLY CAUSING PAIN

When medical professionals fail to appropriately manage pain, which may be rooted in racialized beliefs about pain immunity and as well as the absence of empathy for Black people's physical suffering, leading to lack of internal motivation to alleviate or reduce Black suffering.

COERCION

When medical professionals perform procedures without consent and/or intimidate patients to make decisions.

CEREMONIES OF DEGRADATION

The ritualistic ways in which patients are humiliated or shamed and includes a sense of being sized up to determine the worthiness of the patient or their support person(s) who may be viewed as a threat. In response, medical staff may deploy security, police, social services or psychiatry to ensure compliance or to remove the "threatening" person.

MEDICAL ABUSE

Can occur when medical professionals engage in experimentation and/or (repetitive) behavior that is motivated not by concern for the patient but serves to validate the clinician's self-worth and upholds their domination over the patient.

RACIAL RECONNAISSANCE

Describes the Herculean effort made by Black women to avoid or mitigate racist encounters including being hypervigilant about procedures and finding providers.

(b)

Davis's research is justice-oriented, seeking to find ways to confront the experiences of medical racism that her work makes clear. Through interviews with doulas and midwives who work outside or at the margins of hospital systems, Davis is also documenting successful efforts to resist and disrupt what she calls obstetric racism through focusing more carefully on listening to women and supporting their sense of control of their own bodies. Davis interprets their stories with the recognition that the ideologies and practices of slavery and racial science both have a long afterlife. For one thing, the medical specialties of obstetrics and gynecology were developed in part through experimentation on enslaved Black women's bodies. Davis also spent seven years interviewing Black women with babies who were admitted to neonatal intensive care units because they were born prematurely or with life-threatening congenital conditions. The interviews were long and often painful, reflecting the interviewees' anxiety and distress in silences, quivering voices, and tears. Women told of the poor treatment of partners or babies too.

Davis has several recommendations, including diversifying medical staff and building knowledge among them about the realities and effects of obstetric racism. To this end, Davis uses what she terms graphic ethnography to explain and share the pains of obstetric racism that Black women experience by witnessing one woman's story through art (**Figure 14.14**).

Davis's research focuses particularly on documenting the experiences of urban professionals. The shared details of their experiences with those collected for other minoritized and lower-income women show these harmful practices are not just related to factors such as poverty; the women she collected stories from were typically well-educated with excellent healthcare insurance. Collated statistics from the United States also show that Black women with the highest levels of educational attainment have worse birth outcomes than do White women with the lowest levels.

FIGURE 14.14

Cultural anthropologist Dána-Ain Davis is committed to the public sharing of insights from her research. Through collaboration with doula and founder of The Educated Birth, Cheyenne Varner, and mother LeConté J. Dil, she **(a)** uses images to help recount moving stories that exemplify experiences of mothers and their babies. She also **(b)** creates readable graphics to outline how racism works within obstetrical practice in U.S. hospitals and suggest changes that will improve outcomes. The intended audience is medical professionals.

obstetric racism **Harmful birth experiences due to racist interactions with physicians, nurses, and other medical professionals.**

FIGURE 14.15

Biological anthropologist Daniel Brown (middle) teaches anthropology students how to test blood pressure. Blood pressure increases when we experience social stresses such as gender or racial discrimination.

RACISM AND EMBODIED STRESS

While influenced by genetics, blood pressure dynamically increases with exposure to social stressors. This is why biological anthropologists use blood pressure as a way to measure the effects of social stress on our bodies (**Figure 14.15**). People in the United States with darker skin have higher rates of hypertension (high blood pressure) than lighter-skinned people living in the same locales. Excessive hypertension is associated with an elevated risk of cardiovascular disease, one of the most notable health disparities in the United States and other higher-income countries. Based on what anthropologists know about human variation, this association then suggests a hypothesis: The social consequences of living with darker skin may lead to heightened stress, and thus elevate blood pressure, which helps explain why people exposed to discrimination experience increased risks for hypertension and other chronic diseases.

Medical anthropologist Lance Gravlee tested this hypothesis with the residents of a middle-sized town, Guayama, in southeastern Puerto Rico. Formerly an important sugar-growing area, the population reflects a diversity of ancestries, including from Spain, Africa, and the mainland United States. Gravlee's team measured people's blood pressure but also used a handheld device to measure the level of reflectance of skin. Darker skin reflects less light, and lighter skin reflects more light. They also asked people to self-identify their ethnicity using local racialized Puerto Rican terms such as *blanco* ("white"), *negro* ("black"), and *trigueño* ("wheat-colored"). It turned out that higher blood pressure was associated with people's classifications of race, such as *negro*, but not with the measurements of skin pigment itself. The hierarchical way Puerto Ricans were classified culturally by color was embodied, with those in lower status categories such as *negro* exhibiting heightened stress effects as seen in their blood pressure. In other words, simply labeling yourself in a lower status category resulted in greater embodied stress markers.

Gravlee expanded this research to Tallahassee, Florida, in the southeastern United States. The work was conducted in partnership with community organizer Miaisha Mitchell, and together they formed the Health Equity Alliance of Tallahassee (HEAT) (**Figure 14.16**). The alliance is a means to guide the research, but it also connects the results back to the community to identify how interventions to reduce racism can improve a range of stress-related health conditions, including high blood pressure, heart disease, and other chronic illnesses.

UNITED STATES

Tallahassee

FLORIDA

North America

Guayama

PUERTO RICO

FIGURE 14.16

The Health Equity Alliance of Tallahassee (HEAT)—a collaboration between community members, community organizer Miaisha Mitchell, and anthropologist Lance Gravlee (second from the left)—is leading efforts to reduce health disparities in historically minoritized neighborhoods in Tallahassee, Florida.

Through collaborations with geneticists, Gravlee's team has also been able to show that people's personal experiences of racism are associated with the shortening of their telomeres, which are small protective structures at the ends of chromosomes. Shortening over time is precipitated by stress and is associated with more rapid biological aging and earlier death. This faster "weathering" of racialized bodies is also worsened by its intersection with the stresses tied to gender, poverty, and other social inequalities.

THE PERSISTENCE OF RACIALIZED SOCIETIES

Racism is what results when racial typologies are maintained within societies, affecting individual treatment, rights, and privileges. The process of *racialization*, the focus of this section, is how that happens. Racialization is the conscious labeling of an individual or a group based on physical (and sometimes aural) characteristics within the context of hierarchical social systems that place some groups as higher in value or more "normal" than others.

Racialization takes many different forms, but all ultimately act toward the same goals of institutionalizing for some advantages within societies and maintaining the racialized status quo. People in racialized societies learn about race categories, and how to place people into them, at very early ages. As with phenotypes such as hair or skin color, language is a social key mechanism for placing people into racialized categories. These lessons are constantly reinforced in a variety of ways: by the state, media, and interpersonal interactions. Racism as an *ideology* maintains power in part because it absorbs and otherwise scavenges and recycles ideas and values from almost every aspect of society, from pop culture to religion to public transportation. Most typically, racialization occurs through a particular kind of racism referred to as White supremacy, as we will explain in this section.

racialize To categorize people into established racist typologies within a given cultural context.

ideology A set of beliefs and practices attached to a group of people that collectively shape a specific worldview (sometimes referred to as a "belief system").

COLORISM AND WHITENESS

Racialization is often (but not always) implemented through systems of colorism. Colorism is a way of understanding access to educational and economic privileges and how these link to life outcomes such as health, prison sentencing, or income. In racialized systems that are based around skin color, the closer one is to "Whiteness," the better one's opportunities and the greater one's advantages are.

In the last half century, this desire for proximity to Whiteness has been targeted more literally through the popularity of skin-whitening products and other lightening beauty practices (such as avoiding the sun and UV exposure). In fact, skin-whitening products are popular today in many places around the globe where light skin is tied to societal advantages. Women more often use lightening products, but men do as well.

Medical anthropologist and physician Gideon Lasco conducted a series of interviews and focus groups with younger men in the western Philippines, comparing those living in a provincial town to those in the bustling regional capital of Quezon City. Lascoe's work explains how many young men in both places expressed anxieties around their masculinity, tied to more women entering the workforce and concerns about getting a good job and being able to support a family. They were highly motivated and tried many different means to lighten their skin, even highly toxic products, for the anticipated professional and social advantages it could offer (**Figure 14.17**).

What is defined as proximity to Whiteness shifts across time and space; it can be many things other than skin color. For example, from the late 1800s through 1945, Japan was aggressively advancing Imperial expansion in China, southeastern Asia, and the Pacific. The very acts of advancing coloniality decreased the perceived distance and difference between Japan and many European empires from a European perspective; that is, if Japan can take over neighboring land and peoples, they must be advanced and "like us," in a mindset that centers coloniality. Additionally, Japan purposefully borrowed concepts from White northern Europe related to everything from the importance of national language to the use of school uniforms and what children should eat. Correspondingly, the importance of proximity to behavioral Whiteness was elevated within Japanese society in this period.

colorism Social advantage based on the proximity of skin color and other features to those defined by others as White.

Whiteness Social identity within a hierarchical structure situated as superior to others, associated with lighter skin and benefiting those defined by it with power, privilege, and wealth.

FIGURE 14.17

Some affordable skin-lightening products used in Asia and elsewhere are highly toxic. Here women stage a mock beauty pageant in the Philippines to warn of the use of popular (if illegal) whitening beauty products that contain mercury.

FIGURE 14.18

Historically, photographic images of people with darker skin were less readily visible or oddly colorized in photographs. This Kodak advertisement from the 1980s promotes improved technologies for photographs of people with darker skin tones.

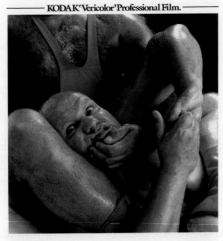

KODAK 'Vericolor' Professional Film.

Holds flesh tones superbly while you wrestle with the composition.

White supremacy can also be reinforced through cultural standards regarding what types of bodies are considered "normal." For example, the entire field of color photography was based on the principle of light skin being the standard; because of this, photography technology has generally advanced in ways that better serve light-skinned people (**Figure 14.18**). Oximeters (which measure oxygen levels in the blood) are a potentially life-saving tool adopted by many people during the COVID-19 pandemic. But the technology is standardized to read oxygen levels most correctly through lighter skin. It accordingly then gives false (overly high) readings for people with darker skin. In these and many other ways, the idea of Whiteness becomes deeply embedded, expected, and normalized within society. But because it is constantly presented as "normal," those categorized as White are often unaware that there is a colorist system that inherently privileges them.

RACIALIZING BY THE STATE: THE CENSUS

The norms and practices of government play a major role in their perpetuation of the belief that racial categories matter and hence in racializing societies. One notable way that governments reinforce racialized systems is through using typological categories, such as in formal census taking (**Figure 14.19**). Nearly two-thirds of nations ask people to identify racialized categories on a census. Census-taking clumps together groups of people with otherwise varied ethnicities, languages, and histories in arbitrary ways. The category "Indigenous" in the

FIGURE 14.19

Census questions on race (sometimes relabeled as "ethnicity" or "population group") from **(a)** South Africa, **(b)** the United States, and **(c)** Brazil, which all incorporate racialized categories in different ways, are compared.

(a)

How would you describe yourself in terms of population group?
1 = Black African
2 = Coloured
3 = Indian or Asian
4 = White
5 = Other

☐ *Write the appropriate code in the box*

(b)

NOTE: Please answer BOTH Question 8 about Hispanic origin and Question 9 about race. For this census, Hispanic origins are not races.

8. Is Person 1 of Hispanic, Latino, or Spanish origin?

☐ **No**, not of Hispanic, Latino, or Spanish origin

☐ Yes, Mexican, Mexican Am., Chicano

☐ Yes, Puerto Rican

☐ Yes, Cuban

☐ Yes, another Hispanic, Latino, or Spanish origin—*Print, for example, Salvadoran, Dominican, Colombian, Guatemalan, Spaniard, Ecuadorian, etc.* ↳

9. What is Person 1's race?
Mark ✗ one or more boxes **AND** print origins.

☐ White—*Print, for example, German, Irish, English, Italian, Lebanese, Egyptian, etc.* ↳

☐ Black or African American—*Print, for example, African American, Jamaican, Haitian, Nigerian, Ethiopian, Somali, etc.* ↳

☐ American Indian or Alaska Native—*Print name of enrolled or principal tribe(s), for example, Navajo Nation, Blackfeet Tribe, Mayan, Aztec, Native Village of Barrow Inupiat Traditional Government, Nome Eskimo Community, etc.* ↳

☐ Chinese ☐ Vietnamese ☐ Native Hawaiian
☐ Filipino ☐ Korean ☐ Samoan
☐ Asian Indian ☐ Japanese ☐ Chamorro
☐ Other Asian— *Print, for example, Pakistani, Cambodian, Hmong, etc.* ↳ ☐ Other Pacific Islander— *Print, for example, Tongan, Fijian, Marshallese, etc.* ↳

☐ Some other race—*Print race or origin.* ↳

(c)

6.06—YOUR COLOR OR RACE IS:

☐ 1—White (If Indigenous land and codes 1 to 4 in this item, go to 6.07) ↳ ☐ 2—Black ☐ 3—Yellow ☐ 4—Brown ☐ 5—Indigenous (Skip to 6.08) ↳

FIGURE 14.20

Legal government identification documents that include racial categories from **(a)** Singapore and **(b)** the United States are pictured.

(a)   (b)

Brazilian census lumps together enormous cultural and language diversity, and in doing so it implies that Indigenous people are fundamentally different from everyone else. While some systems allow people to self-nominate "multiracial" or "mixed-ethnicity" categories, providing these options in itself assumes and shows that racial categories matter.

One of the most complexly racialized census classification systems in the world is the U.S. census, which requires citizens to provide both "ethnic" and "racial" self-identification. Despite this dual identification, the categories presented can be extremely broad; the designations of "European" and "White," for example, each capture an incredible diversity of family histories and phenotypes. In highly racialized countries such as Singapore and the United States, racial categories are even required for the formal legal documents that allow people to participate in society, such as driver's licenses (**Figure 14.20**).

In Brazil, another highly racialized society, there are massive differences in the health, income, and education of people labeled as *branco* ("white," higher status and associated with lighter-skinned phenotypes) versus *negro* ("black," lower status and associated with darker-skinned phenotypes). Yet, the ruling class and government deny that there are racialized divisions within society. This form of "color-blind nationalism" then means there is no requirement to do anything about entrenched racism and the harm it does.

REINFORCING WHITE SUPREMACY THROUGH INSTITUTIONS: POLICING AND POLICE TRAINING

Justice and legal systems also play a major role in maintaining racialized societies.

Cultural anthropologist Laurence Ralph has documented the origins of armed U.S. police forces in his analysis of efforts to limit the freedoms of Black people in New Orleans in the period leading up to the Civil War. The first slave patrol there began in 1764, in an effort to suppress the political alliance between fugitive enslaved people and Indigenous peoples fighting for freedom after the Natchez Massacre. By the early 1800s, New Orleans police were armed with guns in order to limit the immigration of free and enslaved Black people following the Haitian Revolution. Opponents of armed police at the time argued that they were an unjust outgrowth of prior slave patrols. Despite this opposition, race-based policing took on a new form after the Civil War: The Black Codes implemented racist laws that criminalized and imprisoned people for unemployment and homelessness (then called "vagrancy"). Ralph's ethnographic research painstakingly traces how Black people in the United States today connect contemporary anti-Black police violence to the history of the slave patrol in the American South.

A Word on Words for People

Ethnonyms (ethno = nation; nym = name)—the names by which groups of people or ethnic groups are known—change. Ethnonyms vary depending on time and location as well. The ethnonyms our grandparents used have likely fallen out of use. In this textbook, we use the most current ethnonyms as suggested by the American Psychological Association. As such we use Black people (notice the uppercase B) and Latinx people, despite there being ongoing discussions about both of these ethnonyms. We also use White people (notice the uppercase W) as this helps recognize that Whiteness is an ethnic category that is imbued with particular histories and power, not to label a generic category for people of European origin.

Some labels for ethnic groups and people exhibit strong in-group/out-group rules. That is, the label that people within an ethnic group use for one another may be considered a slur if used by people outside the group. To be sure, ethnonyms for African American/Black, Italian, and Irish people in the United States have changed many times over the last century, with the majority of previous ethnonyms now being understood as racial slurs. Consider the changes in ethnonyms for people of Latin-American origins: Hispanic is less frequently used to refer to groups of people (but witness its use on the U.S. census form), and for a while Latino was used, then Latina/o, and now we are frequently seeing and hearing Latinx. This latter term makes space for gender fluidity by using the -x rather than the masculine -o or feminine -a (Chapter 11). Undoubtedly many ethnonyms will continue to change as we recognize the attempt of a label to capture different experiences, histories, and identities.

ethnonym The name by which a group of people or ethnic group is known.

Today, the public outcry over police violence against racialized groups is considerable (**Figure 14.21**). In the United States, improving police-force training on diversity issues has been one common response. Cultural anthropologist Aisha M. Beliso-De Jesús has been studying how police are trained around issues of race. Over a three-year period in California, Florida, and Louisiana, she interviewed police; participated in many everyday policing activities, such as going on ride-alongs and visiting shooting range practice; attended diversity trainings; and spent time alongside cadets.

FIGURE 14.21

Protests against police violence took place in Cleveland, Ohio, in 2020, outside the Justice Center.

FIGURE 14.22

Cadets at a Florida law enforcement academy run in formation as part of their police training.

She found that the training reflected societally held White supremacist beliefs, which then became "molded" into the cadets, including non-White trainees. For example, potentially dangerous suspects in combat training were described in ways that associated and naturalized criminality with non-Whiteness or emphasized that non-White communities were "gang-infested" places to fear, sometimes described as "jungles."

Moreover, cadet training constantly pushed the importance of a shared "blue identity," of police as one homogenous group (**Figure 14.22**). But that "blue identity" fundamentally reflects White (as well as cisgender male) norms and values regarding what a police officer should be. The cover of a cadet fitness log displayed a uniformed White male, exemplifying what an ideal officer should look and be like.

Beliso-De Jesús found that even officer "cultural diversity" trainings reinforce many embedded ideas of White supremacy. For example, while these trainings emphasize avoiding offending people who are not White (or cisgender), many of them encourage officers to actively ignore structural racism. They don't explain the broader racialized system that police are part of, including how mass incarceration is tied to the expansions of for-profit prisons or how court fine systems can push those already on poverty's edge into inescapable debt. Beliso-De Jesús proposes that incorporating these explanations into training could help.

Beliso-De Jesús argues that any effort to confront White supremacy embedded in the United States' policing would ultimately require dismantling the entire current approach to police training. To work with other academics to help build new, globally relevant models for how to rethink the way policing is organized, Beliso-De Jesús has cofounded the Center on Transnational Policing at Princeton University.

Cultural anthropologist Christen Smith studies policing and anti-Black state violence in the Americas, with research that explores the possibilities for **abolition** in Brazil and the United States. Smith's work depicts police violence as an extension of the slavery system, dealing unjust punishment and death to Black families. Smith's ethnography of theatrical performances in Brazil allows her to reveal anti-Black police and state violence (**Figure 14.23**). Smith's

abolition A movement that aims to end oppressive anti-Black institutions (especially prisons and policing) and build alternatives such as community-based justice systems.

FIGURE 14.23

Members of the politically motivated Choque Cultural street theater troupe perform together in Brazil. The actors in white cloth masks represented the police, but this also plays on the fact that masks are often used when committing crimes.

research involved following an Afro-Brazilian street-theater group as they performed in peripheral urban neighborhoods in Bahia, a northeastern state in Brazil. The troupe's signature play, *Pare Para Pensar* (*Stop to Think*), includes reenactment of a police raid that pushes the idea that police violence itself is a performance of racism by racialized individuals. The performance is a way of challenging societal myths that Brazilian racism is benign. Community members can participate by uploading pictures and videos to social media. Smith's research provides an indication of how Black movements throughout the world are using varied means of expression to highlight, call out, and reject the everyday violence that emerges from structurally racist policing.

REINFORCING WHITE SUPREMACY THROUGH INSTITUTIONS: SCHOOLING

Schools serve as vehicles through which racism is taught, enacted, and reinforced. In the United States and Canada, Indigenous children were forced into residential Indian schools and forcibly assimilated into White languages and culture. While these historical examples of educational racism are widely documented and understood, recent anthropological research shows even well-meaning efforts to advance diversity often re-entrench racism.

Savannah Shange is a cultural anthropologist whose book *Progressive Dystopia* focuses on Robeson Justice Academy (a pseudonym) in San Francisco to explain how this happens. Shange applies abolition scholarship, an approach gaining traction in anthropological research on a range of topics around advancing anti-racism, including education and justice reform. Her ethnographic research has shown that even "progressive" institutions—cities or schools that pride themselves on being politically progressive—can nonetheless reinforce White supremacy.

Robeson Justice Academy was created through a vision of a multiracial coalition, designed to advance equality, racial justice, and decolonization through better models for U.S. education. Shange began as a teacher at the school and was able to conduct many years of ethnographic observation in classrooms, assemblies, and teacher meetings; in homes; and during protests—considering the worlds of both teachers (many White) and students (many lower income and Black). Because of the school's efforts to promote progressive values such as racial justice, the academy was especially successful at sending Black students to university. But it also had the highest rate of suspension for Black students in the wider school district. Furthermore, Black students and teachers who challenged policies and curricula were disproportionately marginalized or pushed out.

Shange's study details how the self-defined progressive school paradoxically reproduced the very racist structures it claimed to overturn. The study documents the school's anti-Blackness through the story of sophomore Tarika and other students. Tarika lived in Sunnydale, a nearby low-income housing project with many Black residents. Teachers at Robeson identified Tarika as a troublemaker and a "Sunnydale girl," despite her good academic performance and her commitment to protest and actively engage in justice-seeking. Tarika was ultimately asked to leave Robeson—labeled as too loud, disruptive, disobedient, and defiant. Shange argues that underfunded schools, where old systems are falling apart, are the best places for imagining new anti-racist futures. But she shows that the most seemingly progressive efforts to create change can continue to harm Black youth.

BRAZIL

BAHIA

South America

abolition scholarship A range of theories, concepts, and methods designed to advance racial liberation; it is aligned with decolonizing approaches (see Chapter 2).

FIGURE 14.24

The Asian American Student Association (AASA) at the University of Georgia has a mission to promote cultural and political awareness of Asian and Asian American customs and diversity within the university and the local community.

LEARNING AND READING RACE IN EVERYDAY INTERACTIONS

Racialization also occurs through interpersonal interactions in daily life. A clear example of this is the experience of becoming assigned to new and different racial categories that international students face when moving to the United States. Students from China, for instance, find themselves suddenly being grouped as "Asian" with students from South Korea or Vietnam on the basis of similarities in facial shape and hair type—even though they speak very different languages and come from distinct cultures. Initially this experience can be confusing and hurtful for the student, but often their identity then racializes to conform to their new social category. Studies of Chinese students in the United States, for example, show that on arrival the term "Asian" used to describe them had little or no meaning to them. But within a year of living in the United States, they started to discuss their social identities using terms such as "Asian" or "Asian American" as well as "Chinese," and they began to identify more closely with others sharing the same new identity (**Figure 14.24**).

Ethnographer Viviane Cretton has been doing research in Valais, a French-speaking canton in Switzerland (**Figure 14.25**). Interviewing both lighter-skinned Swiss nationals and new refugees and immigrants to the region, she has found that "Whiteness" and "being Swiss" are perceived as much the same

FIGURE 14.25

A diverse audience watches Swiss cow fighting in Valais, Switzerland.

thing. Having darker skin marks people socially as "immigrants" or "outsiders." This means they face constant reminders that they do not belong, such as questions of "Where do you come from?" Light-skinned Swiss nationals typically claim there is no racism. Importantly, Cretton has shown that darker-skinned Swiss go along with this—pretending such racist interactions aren't happening. This helps them fit in socially, but it also helps to reinforce the social dominance of Whiteness, and therefore it perpetuates the racist interactions even as they are denied to exist. This is one way that White supremacy and other systems of racial superiority become normalized, so that those in power can continue to refuse to see or acknowledge them.

Language—spoken, written, and signed—is often key to the process of sorting people into social categories within racialized societies. When a non-White person speaks standard American English (MWAE, the variant associated with universities and other elite institutions), they are often asked "Where are you really from?" or "How did you learn to speak English so well?" That is, decisions are made on the basis of perceived phenotypes about how people use language. But this also happens in reverse; on hearing someone speak non-MWAE, people will also project an assumed appearance onto them.

As explained in Chapter 7 in detail, interpreting language is never fixed. The way that people decode language reflects their beliefs about the producer of the language and about how meaning should be evaluated. This provides much opportunity to use language as a tool of covert racism. Linguistic anthropologist Jane Hill (1939–2018) used her detailed analysis of "Mock Spanish" by non-Spanish speakers in the United States to show how this works. Used mainly by well-educated White people who may classify their improper use of Spanish as just "having fun," its covert racism is experienced by Spanish speakers as it plays on unflattering stereotypes. Yet at the same time, public spaces in the United States (such as schools or shops) are mostly defined as White, often demanding the use of MWAE varieties by non-English speakers. In these ways, language use in public spaces becomes racialized and racializing (**Figure 14.26**).

By carefully following the cultural standards for actions or language associated with favored racialized identities, people can shift socially toward Whiteness to some degree, even if they are otherwise defined by phenotypes

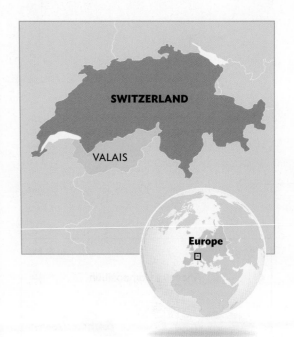

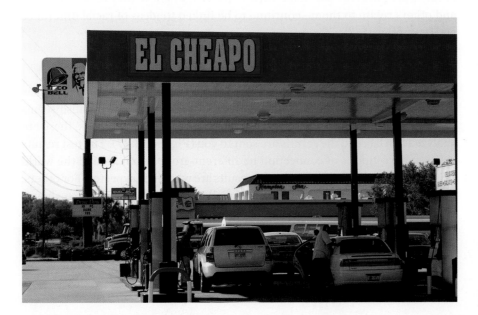

FIGURE 14.26

"El Cheapo" gas is an example of Mock Spanish used in the United States that linguistic anthropologist Jane Hill explained as a form of covert racism based in the purposeful misuse of language.

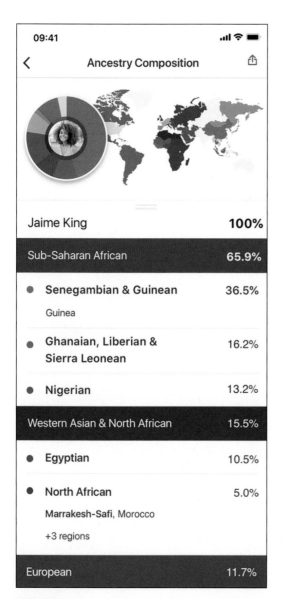

FIGURE 14.27

An example of "ancestry testing" results from 23andMe, one of the larger commercial companies, is illustrated. (© 23andMe, Inc. 2023. All rights reserved and distributed pursuant to a limited license from 23andMe.)

associated with specific other racial typologies within that society. Brazilian society, as noted above, is highly racialized, with clear Black disadvantage across all government and many social institutions. Linguistic anthropologist Jennifer Roth-Gordon has done long-term research in one section of the enormous coastal city of Rio de Janeiro where lower, middle, and higher income families live in particularly close proximity. She has found that people "read" each other—in the ways they move, stand, talk, eat, or dress—to assign degrees of Whiteness and Blackness to them. Those in the middle class, in particular, try hard to exhibit symbolic Whiteness. For example, eating a bologna sandwich can index "lack of civility and refinement," which is then coded by other observers with "Blackness" (or less "Whiteness"). But regardless of whether people are ascribed racial identities by others or purposefully adopt them, the system of White supremacy is still being supported and reproduced because people's core social identities—how they believe they relate to others and others relate to them—continue to be linked to ideas of racial difference and hierarchy.

NEW WAYS TO SELF-RACIALIZE: GENETIC ANCESTRY TESTING

New technologies, such as personal genetic ancestry testing, are opening new ways for people to racialize both themselves and others. The premise seems simple enough. You provide a sample of cells from inside your cheek, these are analyzed in a lab, and the results are sent to you (**Figure 14.27**). The test results give you percentages of connection to different groups from around the world (**Figure 14.28**). For some people, the results are what they expected. For others, there can be surprises, such as finding small percentages of your DNA show a relationship to Ashkenazi Jewish, Cherokee, or eastern African ancestry.

Ancestry testing, as a for-profit business, benefits from consumer's beliefs that such labels extracted from our genetic makeup can and should legitimately construct our social identities. But to Kim TallBear and other Indigenous

FIGURE 14.28

Students at Coretta Scott King Young Women's Leadership Academy in Atlanta, Georgia, United States, review the results of consumer DNA tests, reflecting the percentage of their DNA associated with different world populations.

anthropologists who study the social implications of these new genetic technologies, the idea that someone socially classified as White can declare they are "Native American" by a boxed test—despite having none of the relations or duties necessary for tribal recognition—is yet another way that those who benefit from the arrangements of dominant settler societies in places such as the United States try to harm Indigenous people by devaluing their identities.

ANTHROPOLOGY AND ANTI-RACISM NOW

Much recent anthropological work shows how racism explains many dramatic inequalities within contemporary societies. Inspired by the anti-racist efforts of early anthropologists such as Du Bois, Cobb, Boas, and Neale Hurston, and the clear evidence of the ongoing harms of racialized systems, anti-racist work is increasingly mainstreamed in the discipline.

Social activism aligned with research is one way this is happening. Leith Mullings (1945–2020) was the president of the American Anthropological Association from 2011 to 2013, and she focused her research on structures of inequality and how people resisted them (**Figure 14.29**). She began in Africa, studying lay medicinal and religious practices in Ghana, but eventually turned to community-supporting research in urban U.S. locations, challenging not only discriminatory structures based on race but also others based on gender and inadequate healthcare. She was also one of the founding members of the Black Radical Congress in 1988, an effort based in Chicago that connected scholarly research to activists in grassroots social movements advancing racial justice.

FIGURE 14.29

Cultural anthropologist Leith Mullings was the cofounder of the Black Radical Congress. and president of the American Anthropological Association from 2011 to 2013.

prison abolition A global movement dedicated to eliminating or reducing policing and prisons and replacing this with a system of social services, rehabilitation, and community accountability.

informal justice Activity that is intended to ensure fair treatment but is not regulated or enforced through a formal legal system.

transformative justice A set of practices for dealing with crime that includes transforming oppression, supporting victims of crime, making perpetrators accountable in a way that is sustainable and affirming to communities, and creating norms and values that resist harm.

FIGURE 14.30

Cultural anthropologist Christen Smith (pink T-shirt) works with communities to identify how to create safe societies. Here she sits with other members of the Cite Black Women Collective, who together use podcasts and other means to expand recognition of important scholarly work that is often ignored or sidelined.

Christen Smith, whose research in Brazil we discussed earlier, applies her ethnographic expertise around policing to advance a social movement for prison abolition. One purpose is to support forms of community-based informal justice, a range of dispute resolution mechanisms that may include Indigenous, non-state, customary, familial, nongovernmental, community-based, and norm-based (as opposed to rule-based) approaches, so that families would not need to rely on police for safety and security. The prison abolition movement is creating alternative forms of conflict resolution, beyond trials and courts, based on transformative justice (**Figure 14.30**).

As we explained earlier in the chapter, some (but not all) early physical anthropologists played a central role in promoting the idea of racial typologies, supporting biological justifications for colonialism, slavery, and oppression. Many feel this history creates very particular collective ethical obligations for anthropologists today. Acknowledging that problematic past, in 2020 the membership of the American Association of Physical Anthropologists (AAPA) voted to rename themselves as the American Association of Biological Anthropologists (AABA) and also similarly changed the name of their society's scientific journal. Given the historical connection between this history of physical anthropology and such support of scientific racism, the organization stated that the change recognized responsibilities "to counter the impact of harmful work done by our professional predecessors and to call out scientific racism today."

Training students is another way anthropologists work to advance an anti-racist future. W. Montague Cobb's successes included training diverse biological anthropologists, an important means to address the historical Whiteness of norms and practices in the field. In 1932, he founded the now-named Montague Cobb Research Laboratory at Howard University, where students almost a century later not only continue to learn anatomy but also are inspired by his legacy to bring more diverse perspectives to the study of inequality through skeletal materials and through activism (**Figure 14.31**).

FIGURE 14.31

The W. Montague Cobb Research Laboratory at Howard University, now directed by biological anthropologist Fatimah Jackson, continues to build on the dual inspirations of Cobb's science and activism. Pictured here is biological anthropologist Carter Clinton—who served as assistant curator of the Cobb Research Laboratory when he was a PhD student at Howard University—and a colleague working in a lab to extract ancient DNA.

Michael Blakey, who was previously the Montague Cobb Research Laboratory director, led the community-engaged New York African Burial Ground project discussed in Chapter 13. Such efforts provide a legacy to Cobb's scholarly work by continuing to question the implications of social categories of race through the analysis of skeletal collections.

Such work also helps anthropologists navigate the ethical complexities of working with state and other powerful institutions that continue to organize their activities and mindsets around racial categories. For example, forensic anthropologists have skills that are valuable for law enforcement. They also understand the misuse of racial typologies and collectively agree that races don't exist biologically. In missing persons or murder cases where skeletons need to be identified, there is often insistence by law enforcement that they estimate "race." If apparent age, sex, and "race" can be assigned, then records of missing persons can be searched more efficiently, which goes a long way toward solving a crime and reuniting long-lost bodies with family members.

In navigating such tensions, forensic anthropologists often provide informed guesses at an individual's "race" when asked to do so (**Figure 14.32**). These estimates are based on some key skeletal markers (such as tooth shapes found at high frequencies in those different world regions) that very generally distinguish people of, say, African versus Asian ancestry. However, the ability to discern with some reasonable probability (say 80–90%) whether a skeleton was of European versus African descent does not mean that forensic anthropologists are saying that racial typologies are accurate. But it can nonetheless reinforce that mindset. Such ethical challenges highlight why continued reflection about the connections between anthropology, racial science, and the maintenance of racialized societies will likely remain at the core of the field well into the future.

forensic anthropology A subdiscipline of anthropology focused on the examination of human skeletal remains to assist in the detection of crimes and the identification of victims.

FIGURE 14.32

Debra Prince-Zinni (left) and Jennie Jin (right) are forensic anthropologists who work with the U.S. Department of Defense. Here they secure a case containing the possible remains of U.S. service members lost in the Korean War for transport to their laboratory in Hawaii. Military personnel are often classified in their service records by "race," so forensic identification by anthropologists requires a sophisticated understanding of human variation but also the origins and legacies of socially constructed typologies.

Race and Racialized Societies

A century of anthropological research on human variation shows that biological races don't exist. The myth of races, however, creates and reinforces the realities of harmful, unjust racialized societies.

KEY TERMS
> anti-racism
> disamenity
> minoritize
> oppressive system
> racialized system
> racism
> structural racism

14.1 | Science and the Origins of Racialized Systems

Explain how race is a social construct.

- The typological approach of early physical anthropology supported race science, providing justifications for racism and oppression that linger today.

- Parallel early anthropological research tested alternative theories of race as a social construct. These have survived rigorous scholarly scrutiny, while biological theories have not.

KEY TERMS
> developmental plasticity
> essentialize
> eugenics
> physical anthropology
> population genetics
> pseudoscience
> scientific racism
> typology
> White supremacy

14.2 | Structural Racism

Connect the history of scientific racism to the development and persistence of racialized worldviews.

- Racism persists because it is woven into the wider fabric of the many interconnected, interlocking systems that organize our societies and our place within them, including healthcare, education, immigration, justice, policing, and others.

KEY TERMS
> health disparity
> obstetric racism

14.3 | The Persistence of Racialized Societies

Appraise how racism operates today, including how it creates inequalities and destabilizes societies.

- Racialized systems are most pronounced in societies that have or were colonized, had economies based in slavery, and/or have large or diverse immigrant populations.

KEY TERMS
> abolition
> abolition scholarship
> colorism
> ethnonym
> ideology
> racialize
> Whiteness

14.4 | Anthropology and Anti-Racism Now

Evaluate anthropological approaches for accomplishing anti-racist goals.

- Solutions to racism must change systems, not just the opinions of people within them.

- Anthropologists have ethical responsibilities related to teaching and researching race and racism and working toward the goals of anti-racism.

KEY TERMS
> forensic anthropology
> informal justice
> prison abolition
> transformative justice

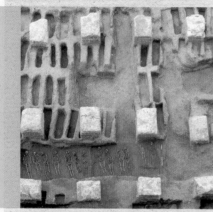

Disease, Health, and Healing

The Museum of London storage rooms are filled from top to bottom with thousands of boxes of human remains. One of the most extensive collections of skeletons was excavated from large medieval burial sites in the center of London, including many remains from East Smithfield cemetery (**Figure 15.1**). Archaeological excavations of the cemetery revealed burials up to five bodies deep. Mass plots were dug there in 1348, in anticipation of an incoming wave of the Black Death pandemic from continental Europe (**Figure 15.2**). The panic around the infectious plague was well-founded; in the following years, half of the population of London would die. The 636 known bodies excavated or still buried at East Smithfield represent just a small sample of all those who succumbed, but they provide important scientific insights into how pandemic disease, society, and human biology interact.

As she pulls boxes from the museum's storage shelves filled with human remains, bioarchaeologist Sharon DeWitte likes to feel some weight (**Figure 15.3**). The more bone material that is available from a deceased individual, the more she can figure out about their health while alive and their cause of death. DeWitte can look in eye sockets for healed lesions that suggest recovery from parasitic infections. Horizontal lines visible on the outer surface of the teeth suggest periods of poor health while the person was growing. Age at death can be estimated by deterioration of the joints and the wear on the teeth. An especially healthy-looking skeleton can suggest a sudden death, such as from an accident, childbirth, or a fast-acting illness like the plague. This quality characterizes many of the skeletons buried in East Smithfield cemetery.

MANY HEALING SYSTEMS

The study of disease, health, and healing by anthropologists engages an array of evidence to understand why we get sick and how to create healthier societies.

LEARNING OBJECTIVES

15.1 Disease and Human History
Identify how disease today relates to human evolution and major social and technological transitions in human history.

15.2 Social Dimensions of Illness
Explain how cultural ideas and social identities shape illness experiences and practices, now and in the past.

15.3 Healing Systems
Characterize biomedicine as a healing system, including as it relates to other healing systems.

15.4 Biomedicine and Power
Identify how disease, illness, and healing systems relate to societal power.

FIGURE 15.1

These burial plots at East Smithfield cemetery were used between 1348 and 1350 as an emergency site for burying bodies of plague victims. Excavations by the Museum of London in the 1980s yielded a large sample of burials, allowing ongoing bioarchaeological study of one of the deadliest pandemics in human history.

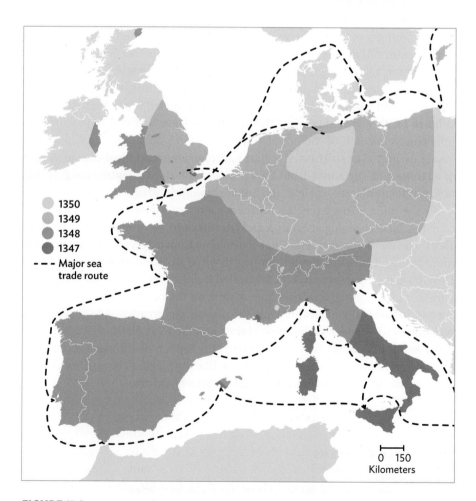

FIGURE 15.2

The "Black Death" plague pandemic spread across Europe and adjacent continents rapidly between 1347 and 1350, killing 30–50% of people. Massive religious, economic, and political changes followed.

Using bioarchaeological techniques to examine skeletons from East Smithfield and other medieval cemeteries in London, DeWitte is contributing to the larger picture of the human history of infectious disease. Newer laboratory techniques can reveal clues from even tiny pieces of bone about what infections an individual's body carried at the time of death. She can identify which of those early Londoners died from the waves of disease caused by *Yersinia pestis*, the bacterium associated with plague cases today, or if other potential infectious agents were involved. Working with geneticists, she can use ancient DNA from small samplings of bones to trace the evolutionary history of different strains of plague, providing clues for understanding and controlling future outbreaks. Her research also shows how existing hunger and extreme economic inequality and histories of malnutrition help explain the incredibly high death rates in London as compared to the experience of other European cities hit by the same plague around the same time.

Human health has long been a concern across many areas of anthropology, and there are many potential applications to improve quality of life today. In this chapter, we focus on two ways that anthropologists are creating new understandings of why we get sick and what helps us become and stay healthy. The first is based on evidence from biological anthropology and archaeology regarding the history of human diseases, including studies like that conducted by DeWitte and her colleagues. This view from human long-term history helps explain why novel diseases emerge, how human biology today reflects past adaptations to them, and how we might treat them. Then we draw on research from medical anthropology (a subfield of cultural anthropology) to understand how humans differently experience, understand, and react to illness within their varied cultural contexts and through varied healing systems, both now and in the past. Finally, we examine how our bodies and our health are embedded in culturally based healing systems, especially *biomedicine*.

FIGURE 15.3

Bioarchaeologist Sharon DeWitte sits in front of the boxes of medieval human remains that provide the basic data from her research into past pandemics.

biomedicine **The use of concepts from biology, biochemistry, and physiology to understand health and disease in the human body; sometimes called "medicine."**

SECTION 15.1

DISEASE AND HUMAN HISTORY

Looking at the long sweep of human history, we can discover how major human cultural and technological changes have not only created illness but also created solutions to it. Human societies, diseases, and human biologies are entwined, adjusting to each other over millennia. With every major transition in human history, humans have had to adapt to the new diseases that these changes brought. And, in turn, many technological and social responses laid additional foundations for the emergence of other diseases (**Table 15.1**).

We have little direct evidence, due to the small number of archaeological skeletons that have been excavated from very early time periods, but the earliest humans were probably affected mainly by physical trauma and parasitic and bacterial infections. Foraging, fishing, hunting, cooking, traveling, and other everyday activities meant risks of debilitating or lethal injuries. Dental disease may also have been painful and disabling, leading to possible sepsis and death. Although early humans were not eating the sugary and processed foods that

TABLE 15.1

Some Diseases That Emerged in Response to Major Changes in Human Societies, Eliciting the Need for Further Human Adaptation

Major Human Behavioral or Societal Changes	Timescale	Relevant Ecological, Social, or Technological Changes	Emerging Diseases	Examples
Big-game collaborative hunting	Since ~1.8 million years ago	Eating more meat	Diseases from parasites in the flesh of other animal species	• Tapeworm
Permanent settlements	Since ~13,000 years ago	Consistent use of common water sources	Diseases from parasites that reproduce in or near fresh water	• Giardiasis • Schistosomiasis
		Heightened contact with human feces	Diseases from parasites carried in human waste	• Roundworm • Hookworm
Domestication of animals	Since ~10,000 years ago	Proximity to livestock	Zoonoses (animal diseases that jump to humans)	• Rabies • Brucellosis • Anthrax
Intensification of agriculture	Since ~10,000 years ago	Land clearance for farming and irrigation systems	Diseases carried by flying insects	• Malaria (mosquito) • Trypanosomiasis/ sleeping sickness (tsetse fly)
Intensification of agriculture and social differentiation	Since ~10,000 years ago	Stored food surpluses such as grain	• Diseases of reliance on single crops or famine • Diseases of tainted food stores • Rodent-borne infectious diseases	• Malnutrition • Pellagra • Botulism • Plague • Rat-bite fever • Lassa fever • Hantavirus
Urbanization	Since ~5,000 years ago	• Increasing population densities • Worse sanitation	Viral and bacterial diseases that require population density for transmission	• Influenza • Measles • Typhoid • Smallpox • Tuberculosis
Long-distance trade and European colonization	Since 1500s	• Transmission of different infectious diseases between continents • Interaction of new diseases	Epidemics of existing diseases	• Epidemic plague • Syphilis
Industrialization	Since 1700s	Air and water pollution	Chronic diseases related to toxin exposure	• Lead poisoning • Cancers • Chronic obstructive pulmonary disease (COPD)

TABLE 15.1

Some Diseases That Emerged in Response to Major Changes in Human Societies, Eliciting the Need for Further Human Adaptation (*continued*)

Major Human Behavioral or Societal Changes	Timescale	Relevant Ecological, Social, or Technological Changes	Emerging Diseases	Examples
Public health systems	Since 1800s	• Emergence of sanitation services • Invention of antibiotics • Mass production of pharmaceuticals	Infectious agents that evolve antibiotic resistance	• Methicillin-resistant *Staphylococcus aureus* (MRSA) infection • Opioid addiction
Globalized food systems	Since 1950s	Highly processed diets	Chronic diseases related to diet	• Diabetes • Cancers • Dental decay
High-speed international travel	Since 1960s	Rapid movement of masses of people across the globe	Pandemics of highly contagious respiratory disease	• Severe acute respiratory syndrome (SARS) • Coronavirus disease 2019 (COVID-19)
Habitat destruction and human-induced climate change	Since 1970s	• Forced migration • Closer contact to wild animals due to habitat destruction • Contamination of soil, water, and air	New, remerging, and resurging infectious diseases	• Human immunodeficiency virus (HIV)/acquired immunodeficiency syndrome (AIDS) • Chikungunya • Ebola • Cholera
Global labor markets and neoliberalism	Since 1980s	Increasingly inequitable distributions of power and resources	Diseases related to stress and unequal access to healthcare	• Depression • Diabetes • Cardiovascular disease • Hypertension

create dental disease now, regular chewing of some tough plant foods can cause rapid wear of the teeth. This can expose the dental pulp to painful and potentially deadly bacterial infections.

The initial transition to eating more meat, from about 1.8 million years ago, also increased human exposures to parasites in the flesh of these animals, such as tapeworms. About 1.2 million years ago, human ancestors began to lose body hair. As hominins moved into cooler climates, adoption of clothing and bedding for warmth would have been advantageous; this then created new welcoming ecosystems for parasitic insects such as bedbugs and body lice—and the diseases they carried.

Handling, cooking, and eating hunted animals also exposed early human communities to zoonotic viral diseases (caused by pathogens transmitted from animals to humans). The clues to this are in the observation that handling and eating "bushmeat" (meat from wildlife species, especially mammals) remains a

Many communities across the globe continue to rely on wild-caught animals to feed or sell to support their families. Here a hunter in southeast Cameroon is shown with game caught in trap lines.

major source of new viral infections (**Figure 15.4**), such as Ebola. Wild chimpanzee meat was probably the original source of the viral strain that became HIV (human immunodeficiency virus, the infectious agent of acquired immunodeficiency syndrome or AIDS). But the risk of infectious disease was limited in the millennia prior to the emergence of crop and animal domestication because communities were small and highly mobile, and population densities were low. When new infectious agents emerged, without new people to infect they died out quickly, rather than being the reservoirs of infection that become epidemics and pandemics today.

From the beginnings of domestication in the Neolithic era, the additional intimacy with animals meant their infections could now be repeatedly transmitted to humans and become *endemic*. Brucellosis is a bacterial infection of goats and cows that does them relatively little harm. But when it is transmitted to humans in raw milk, it causes lifelong pain, disability, and sometimes neurological damage. Domesticated animals also acted as intermediate sources of human-to-human transmitted viral infections, as in the case of bovine (cow) forms of tuberculosis.

Plant domestication brought many benefits, but it also created new disease exposures. Clearing land for crops created ecosystems ideal for the breeding of mosquitos, leading to endemic and deadly mosquito-borne malaria (still a major cause of death globally). Increasing reliance on a very limited number of plants, such as corn, wheat, or rice, also led to harmful nutritional deficiencies. Eating a diet focused on corn alone as a staple, as happened in the southern United States during the Great Depression of the 1930s, can lead to pellagra, a nutritional disease characterized by the "four Ds": dermatitis, diarrhea, dementia, and death. Furthermore, reliance on just a few crop species for food also bought new risks for noninfectious (chronic) disease, such as famine-triggered malnutrition in years of crop failure.

In some cases, the selection and spread of new genetic mutations helped populations to adapt to new diseases (Chapter 3). For example, changes in the shape of blood cells provided protection from malarial parasites in irrigated land, the evolution of new proteins allowed adults to absorb the nutrients from cows' milk, and genetic changes to blood supply increased the oxygen in the body so that humans could survive at high altitudes.

These evolutionary processes continue today. For example, a small number of people have what appears to be genetic resistance to some strains of HIV infection, due to a mutation that inhibits entry of the virus into human cells.

In addition to genetic adaptations, cultural adaptations addressed emerging diseases, such as innovations in food preparation. Cuisines emerged that favored boiled or treated milk, making new reliance on dairy products safer. Much later, new technologies and practices, such as animal vaccines, antibiotics, and pasteurization, helped to control animal-carried diseases.

In Mesoamerica, corn (maize) became a domesticated crop by about 9,000 years ago. By about 3,500 years ago, archaeological evidence appears that indicates cultural practices of treating the kernels by soaking them in an alkaline solution. This soaking greatly improved the nutritional value of corn in a narrow diet of domesticated crops, especially when combined with eating beans.

The rise of the first dense urban settlements, and then industrialization, marked a major shift in the disease history of humans. Sometimes referred to as the first *epidemiological transition*, it marked a new trend toward infectious agents as the primary causes of death (**Figure 15.5**). As communities became more sedentary and more densely populated, the conditions were right for the

endemic Describes a disease maintained over time (usually in a specified geographic area).

epidemiological transition A change through time in the primary diseases and causes of death within a population, linked to a major lifestyle transition.

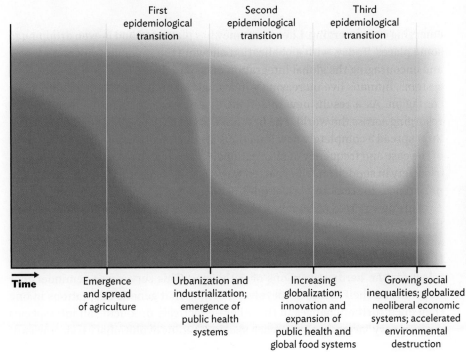

First epidemiological transition

Second epidemiological transition

Third epidemiological transition

Time

Emergence and spread of agriculture

Urbanization and industrialization; emergence of public health systems

Increasing globalization; innovation and expansion of public health and global food systems

Growing social inequalities; globalized neoliberal economic systems; accelerated environmental destruction

FIGURE 15.5

A generalized model of major epidemiological transitions for our species is illustrated, showing how social, environmental, and technological shifts have changed the diseases to which humans must then adapt. These varied causes of disease are not independent, and their co-occurrence can create compounded disease "syndemics" with an amplified capacity to harm. For example, the interaction of COVID-19 infection with widespread existing chronic diseases like diabetes lead to many additional pandemic-related deaths.

Pervailing causes of death and disability

⬤ Physical trauma
⬤ Parasitic and zoonotic diseases
⬤ Highly transmissible infectious diseases
⬤ Non-communicable "chronic" diseases

continuous circulation of contagious human-to-human infectious diseases, meaning they could become endemic. The list of known communicable infectious diseases that emerged in the *first* major transition and remain with us now is long. Among the most notable are smallpox, influenza, cholera, tuberculosis, measles, mumps, dengue fever, yellow fever, and bubonic plague. Waves of such infections—including the Black Death that killed at least one-third of the population of Europe at the time—remained the major human killers until very recently, when public health practices and technologies allowed humans more ways to control their spread.

Increasing societal inequality seems only to accelerate exposure to infectious disease. For example, there was a particularly deadly wave of plague that hit London in the summer of 1665 and again in the spring of 1666, killing as many as 7,000 residents per week. Most of those who died were the city's poorest citizens. Wealthier citizens, including many physicians, had retreated to the relative safety of their country homes. The abandonment of the city by those able to flee also meant city parishes lost the regular relief funds that were particularly needed to assist in the crisis.

The invention of public health systems, and later new science-based technologies such as vaccines and mass-produced pharmaceuticals, led to the *second* major epidemiological transition. Infectious disease was no longer the primary cause of human death. Many states and nations conducted campaigns to promote childhood vaccinations, public sanitation, and food aid (**Figure 15.6**). Life expectancy and quality of life rose dramatically, with many more children surviving childhood and adults living on into old age.

But the same transition was also associated with increasing urbanization and the accompanying sedentary lifestyles, cheaper mass-processed foods, and increasingly high-sugar diets. By the end of the 20th century, this set the stage for the emergence of more chronic (noninfectious) diseases such as cancer, diabetes, and cardiovascular disease, which are now major causes of adult illness and death across the globe.

Currently we are in the midst of a *third* epidemiological transition, where chronic disease remains prominent but harder-to-treat infectious diseases are

(a)

(b)

FIGURE 15.6

People are shown waiting for vaccinations in **(a)** the United States and **(b)** Zimbabwe. Because of the variety of infectious diseases with which humans now coexist, many people in the world rely on similarly organized government medical services, including vaccination programs, as part of their basic efforts to be and stay well.

emerging or reemerging. Life expectancy has plateaued and is even dropping in some places. Today, with globalization allowing the rapid movement of people and encouraging the global integration of economic, dietary, health, and social systems, humans live increasingly in a single, shared ecosystem for infectious contagion. As a result, new infectious diseases are constantly emerging and resurging across the world. The first wave of the COVID-19 pandemic in 2020–2021 spread a completely new infectious agent globally within months because of the ease and frequency of international travel. It also reshaped many aspects of society in sudden and unexpected ways, such as accelerating our capacity and preferences for remote work or online education.

This new period of human-disease history is also marked by new diseases that result from human success in managing previous diseases. Infections with antibiotic-resistant bacteria, such as MRSA, come from the global spread of antibiotic (over)use and the diligent creation of aseptic environments that then select for the hardiest versions of pathogens. This serves as a reminder that humans and their diseases coevolve, meaning that genetic adaptations in one then elicit further changes in the other—effectively producing an interspecies evolutionary "arms race" with each species shaping evolutionary trajectories of the other.

EVOLUTIONARY MEDICINE

The recognition that humans and disease have a lengthy, entwined history that impacts health today is a basic idea behind *evolutionary medicine*, an approach that assesses many medical conditions today as reflecting beneficial past genetic adaptations that nonetheless required some trade-offs. With the eradication of malaria in many parts of the world and better medical treatment options, descendants of past populations that lived in malarial regions deal with the legacies of debilitating sickle-cell anemia (Chapter 3).

Consider the evolution of hominin bipedalism 5–7 million years ago and the increase in brain size that then accompanied an increasing capacity to use tools, outlined in Chapter 5. One trade-off is a level of obstetric (childbirth) pain and complications not faced in other mammals. Now a large human head must pass through a relatively small pelvis. The birth canal can't widen further without compromising our ability to walk upright and have our hands free. Other trade-offs from the evolution of bipedalism are "slipped" disks and a host of back, knee, and foot problems.

Another contribution of evolutionary medicine is different perspectives on "new" diseases, such as the alarming rises in rates of childhood asthma and allergies in highly industrialized nations including Australia and Sweden. Evolutionary medicine's "hygiene hypothesis" provides one possible explanation for the proliferation of such chronic conditions related to dysfunctions in the immune system, and it suggests some possible fixes. Starting at birth, human bodies acquire diverse colonies of microscopic species that live on and in bodies, including in our guts, mouths, and skin (**Figure 15.7**). Many of these microbial species have coevolved with us in ways that support even our most basic physiological processes, such as breaking down food. These are collectively referred to as our *human microbiome*. Anthropological studies comparing average microbiomes across different human groups show that people living in highly industrialized settings tend to have relatively less diverse microbiomes overall. This may result from living in sterilized environments designed to make people safe from germs and the diseases they cause. Chemical treatment of water supplies, food pasteurization, overuse of antibiotics, and widespread availability

evolutionary medicine **The application of evolutionary principles to explain the basis of disease and develop recommendations for improved treatment.**

human microbiome **All the interacting microorganisms—including helpful, harmless, and harmful bacteria, fungi, and viruses—that live in and on our bodies.**

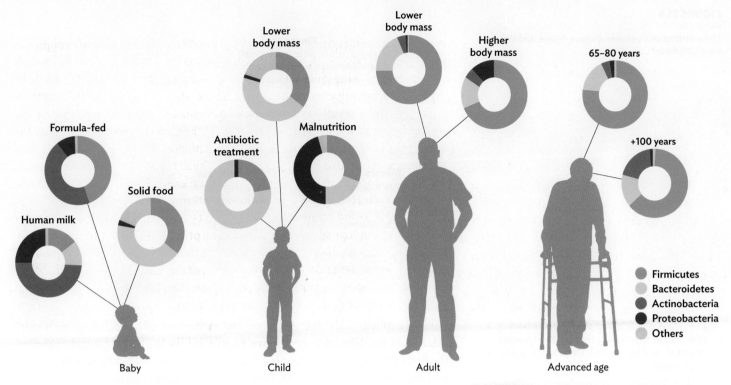

FIGURE 15.7

Genetic estimates of the relative abundance of different types of microbial populations in the human gut microbiome are illustrated with respect to nutritional and body mass differences across the life span.

Legend:
- Firmicutes
- Bacteroidetes
- Actinobacteria
- Proteobacteria
- Others

of antibacterial products all reduce the diversity of microbiomes in and on our bodies. Some other differences, such as lower levels of breastfeeding and less time spent outdoors and around animals, may also contribute to this reduction in the diversity of the species that live so intimately with humans increasingly observed in wealthier, urban populations.

But these changes that reduce the diversity of microbes may not simply protect us from infections. They may also deplete colonies of friendly microbes or parasites that help "educate" the developing human immune system to respond to harmful threats such as viruses and bacteria. Without the early-life exposures to many different, relatively safe microorganisms that have coevolved with humans, the immune system then fails by either overreacting or underreacting. From an evolutionary medicine perspective, it makes sense to encourage new parents to adopt a family dog, use early daycare, and serve more wild-caught or homegrown foods. The goal would be to restore young children's microbiome diversity and safely trigger the immune system so it functions as designed through evolution.

SECTION 15.2

SOCIAL DIMENSIONS OF ILLNESS

For humans, being sick is not just about managing the biological effects of disease. Our physical suffering has social meaning, and our social arrangements help define who suffers and how. How we manifest, experience, and react to signs of illness will vary, depending on the communities to which we belong and our roles within them.

Illness
Subjective suffering, focused on symptoms, signs, and symbols, needing comfort and care

Disease
Impairment of body function usually labeled by experts and identified as requiring treatment

Sickness
Societal recognition of disruption or suffering and expectations for the sick role

disease A physiological change in the body that impairs functioning that can be classified, detected, and targeted for treatment (usually by a specialist).

illness The subjective experience of suffering, anxiety, fear, and pain, eliciting and needing comfort and care.

sickness The social expectations and roles connected to disease and illness, including how the affected individual relates to others.

stigma Being pushed down or out of society by association with unwanted and devalued social identities (such as those tied to specific diseases).

health Well-being due to a relative absence of disease, illness signs, sickness, stigma, and suffering.

This explicit focus on the cultural and social context of health requires clarification of key terminology (**Figure 15.8**). Disease is a physiological change in the body that impairs functioning. Disease is usually labeled by health specialists, such as doctors or healers. Disease can have many causes, including infectious agents (such as viruses or bacteria), injury or wear and tear on the body, exposures to social stress, genetic mutations, or inadequate nutrients. Often greater disease severity results from the interaction of these factors, as when undernutrition worsened the effects of plague infection in London, resulting in sudden and massive numbers of deaths.

Illness refers to the subjective experience of sickness, such as how we experience its symptoms and how it relates to our own suffering. Sickness relates to our ways of dealing with disease or illness in relation to others and wider society, such as how it changes our social roles, obligations, or interactions. Sick people are expected to behave differently than well people, and they are treated differently too. Sometimes they get more care, and sometimes less. Stigma is when the disease characteristics of a person lead to them being socially avoided, mistreated, or rejected. Health, then, can be most simply defined by the absence of disease, illness, sickness, and stigma.

HEALING IN THE HUMAN LINEAGE

Humans have not only gained from genetic and technological adaptations to prevent disease but also developed the capacity to support and aid recovery. Caring for others with pain, trauma, and illness has long been part of our species' behavioral repertoire. Numerous early fossils in the genus *Homo* show evidence of healed injuries. One Neanderthal excavated from the Shanidar Cave site in Iraq from 40,000 years ago survived for many years with a fractured arm that atrophied and a head wound that likely caused partial blindness and deafness. Their survival after the initial wounds could not have happened without ongoing care by others.

Another example of even more intensive intervention to help those suffering is seen in fossil teeth from a hunter-gatherer community in what is now Italy, dating to about 13,000 years ago. The excavated teeth show signs of experimentation with dental work such as drilling and filling (**Figure 15.9**).

We seem to be the only living species that has this evolved capability to respond to disease through complex, coordinated caring behaviors. Caring for others while they are ill became possible due to a number of concurrent evolved human traits including high levels of social cooperation, empathy, the ability to detect and recognize the signs of disease, and the capacity for accumulating knowledge so we can learn from others how best to treat it. One intriguing proposition is that the human loss of most body hair contributed to the long-term success of human species because it helped advertise symptoms such as skin rashes and bloodshot eyes better, leading to better caregiving and so survival.

RECOGNIZING ILLNESS

Significant cultural differences exist in how illness is experienced and diseases are diagnosed, because symptoms are differently understood and interpreted. For example, autism is classed in clinical terms as part of a spectrum of neurological conditions that typically emerge early in childhood, characterized by difficulties in recognizing and acting in accordance with expected forms of social interaction. Children diagnosed with forms of autism may prefer to avoid eye contact, repeat sounds or words, or be more sensitive to sensory input, such as touch or sound.

But here social context matters greatly to what is defined as pathological versus normal. In China, children are often discouraged from making eye contact with adults. So what might be considered elsewhere as early signs of behavioral dysfunction are not treated with such concern. In Ethiopia, greetings are highly ritualized and the form is important. Therefore, the capacity to follow repetitive sequences means the regimented way that children greet adults is not just considered socially appropriate but viewed as a strength. In urban South Korea, meanwhile, diagnoses of autism are so stigmatized that clinicians and parents alike will find any way they can to avoid it, even selecting attachment disorder labels. In all these cases, local cultural norms shape whether caregivers will identify childhood patterns of behavior as a problem requiring intervention. Moreover, the ways children in these contexts experience their illness is very different, and those differences impact how both families and health professionals might best respond—or not—to a perceived pathology in each case.

EXPERIENCING PAIN

Individual illness experience also varies by social position within societies. Pain is one example of a symptom that can be felt and expressed very differently both cross-culturally and also within communities, such as by age and gender. Medical anthropologist Janice Morse conducted a long-term study of childbirth pain among first-time mothers in the island nation of Fiji (**Figure 15.10**). She compared the experiences of Indigenous Fijians, or iTaukei, with Indo-Fijians whose ancestors were transported from India as indentured sugar plantation laborers in the 1800s. Morse spent time watching births, interviewing the attendants and nurses, and talking to mothers and fathers. iTaukei grow up hearing talk about childbirth and attending birth celebrations. As many births take place at home with family nearby, they may even have seen babies born. First-time mothers know what to expect and are excited for their special event.

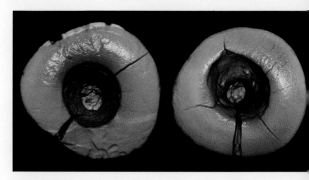

FIGURE 15.9

The computer-generated reconstructions from incomplete archaeological data estimate the form of very early dental work performed in central Italy around 12,900 years ago. The filling material was bitumen, a natural tar used to waterproof containers.

empathy The capacity to relate to the emotional state of others, including their pain and suffering.

diagnosis The process of labeling health conditions by interpreting physiological markers, behavioral patterns, or reported symptoms; implying cause; and suggesting treatments.

symptom An identified marker of illness.

FIGURE 15.10

A new baby is cared for by an Indigenous Fijian (iTaukei) mother and grandmother on Nacula Island in Fiji.

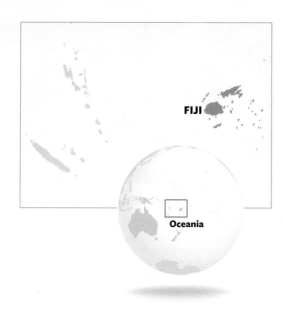

FIJI

Oceania

By contrast, first-time Indo-Fijian mothers are often confused and scared about giving birth. Little has been said to them of sex or the birthing process. While pregnant, women's daily work goes on much the same as before, and often pregnancies are kept quiet. Husbands avoid the birth altogether. Hospital births are particularly frightening, as often women labor without any family support.

Morse found that expression of childbirth pain varied dramatically based on the different social roles and positions of men and women in each group. Indigenous Fijian women rated the pain of childbirth similarly to Indo-Fijian women. Both understood it to be among the most painful events they could experience. But for Indigenous Fijian women, pain was expected and prepared for, and it was seen as part of the valued transition to motherhood. They made much less sound and moved about less during labor. They took pride in enduring the pain. Indigenous Fijian men, helping out with chores and nearby but physically separate, rated the pain of their wives in childbirth as considerably worse than anything they themselves could ever experience, such as a broken leg (**Figure 15.11**). For Indo-Fijian women, on the other hand, the pain was unexpected and frightening. Their subjective experience of the pain was much worse, and they were much more vocal and notably distressed during labor.

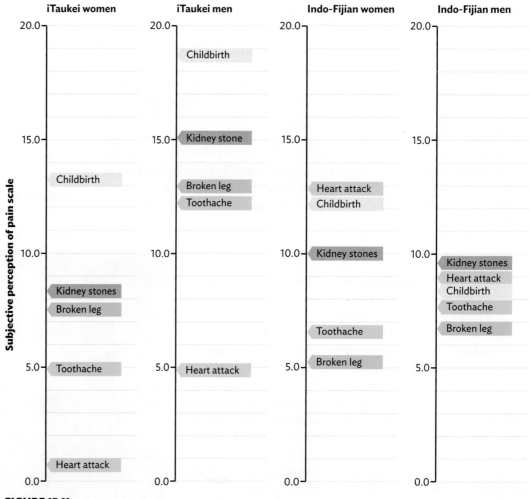

FIGURE 15.11

Scaling and comparison of perceived level of pain in iTaukei and Indo-Fijian women and men, as measured by medical anthropologist Janice Morse, is shown. Her study showed how gender interacts differently with group norms to scale childbirth pain as especially excruciating (iTaukei men) or no different from other sources of pain (Indo-Fijian males).

FIGURE 15.12

Kavadi devotees experience extreme pain and physical stress while carrying heavy burdens, attached through needles or piercings, barefooted over long distances as part of a Tamil Hindu religious ritual.

In some contexts, experiences of pain may even be viewed as a pathway to healing, such as during religious rituals. An example is the *kavadi attam* (burden dance) pilgrimage, such as practiced by Tamil Hindus in many countries (**Figure 15.12**). After piercings with sharp metallic objects such as needles, hooks, and skewers, devotees walk for miles in the hot sun, carrying extremely heavy portable shrines up the steep temple stairs. Psychological anthropologist Dimitris Xygalatas has been testing participants' experiences of pain during this exhausting and painful religious ritual on the small tropical island of Mauritius in the Indian Ocean, and tracking their well-being afterward. Despite extreme stress, no participants reported any long-term negative effects.

Xygalatas also identified that those who had the most illness or felt the most socially isolated opted to bear more pain during the ritual by carrying heavier loads or enduring more body mutilation. Using wearable watches to collect data on aspects of health such as stress levels and sleep patterns along with participants' own reports, he was also able to identify that they then also had the greatest physical and psychological health improvements in the weeks following. This shows how participation in rituals, even extreme and potentially harmful ones, can have positive health effects. The reasons are generally understood but not yet detailed: Anthropological studies are detangling how social support, heightened social status, physiological responses to pain, and our immune systems all interact to explain the positive effects of ritual traumas to body tissue, such as from kavadi attam and similar phenomena like tattooing.

ILLNESS AS COMMUNICATION

Humans use spoken and body language as a means to convey distress to others, as signals of illness and need for care. These rely on metaphors, called *idiom of distress*, that are understandable only in their cultural and social context. For example, people in English-speaking industrialized nations might talk about their "stress" causing stomach ulcers, even though scientifically the

idiom of distress An indirect and culturally specific way of expressing hurt, worry, suffering, conflict, or loss through the language of illness.

cause of ulcers is recognized to be a bacterium (*Helicobacter pylori*). They might say "working so hard is going to give me an ulcer." The reference to ulcers here can be used as a socially acceptable illness metaphor that helps destigmatize communicating feelings of emotional distress.

Idioms of distress provide a culturally meaningful and acceptable way to identify, communicate about, and work to rectify a bad situation. They can—if properly understood—invite and welcome a supportive response from others. Medical anthropologist Lesley Jo Weaver has studied how women in northern India express symptoms of what they call "tension." It can come on rapidly and is characterized by feelings of anger and irritation and by physical symptoms such as stomach pain, insomnia, and high blood pressure. Importantly, these signals of "tension" aren't viewed as something to seek medical treatment for. Rather, the solutions come from getting help from others to fix strained familial relationships or manage the many stresses of fast-paced urban life.

These idioms are always highly localized, reflecting that people learn to express illness in ways that others around them understand. And it can complicate processes of diagnosis that rely on patients reporting their symptoms. In the wake of a massive and dreadful earthquake in Haiti in 2010, a team of medical and psychological anthropologists working in the rural central plateau found that—in the well-intentioned effort to provide aid—medically trained healthcare workers did not understand local ways of communicating distress. This significantly limited their capacity to provide mental health services. Haitians communicated distress using locally understood terms, such as having "loaded head" or "heart that hurts." Clinicians incorrectly interpreted these terms to mean headaches and indigestion and treated these symptoms with pharmaceuticals (**Figure 15.13**), rather than with resources that would have provided social and emotional support. This is why medical anthropologists highlight the importance of understanding how people communicate distress to the effective diagnosis and treatment of pain, mental illness, or any other experienced health conditions.

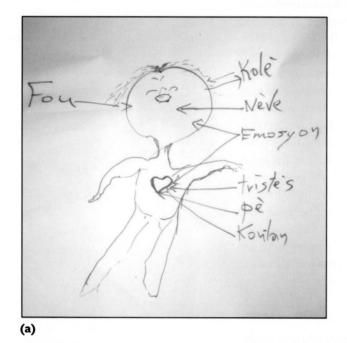

(a)

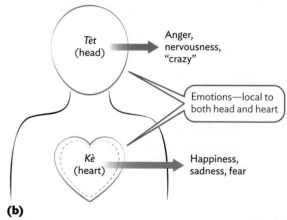

(b)

FIGURE 15.13

Medical and psychological anthropologists in Haiti's central plateau used people's drawings to understand how they experience distress through body symptoms. **(a)** A drawing by Haitian focus group participants indicates the local understanding that emotional distress is situated in the heart and the head. **(b)** The anthropologist's graphic adds clarification and translation. Such studies can improve diagnostic tools for conditions like depression when clinician and patient do not share nuanced cultural understandings of how distress is embodied.

LEARNING STIGMA

When people report or exhibit signs of illness, what ails them is often recognized in alignment with socially recognized labels. For women in northern India, it may be self-identified "tension," while for those in the United States it could be a medical diagnosis with "depression." Diagnosing or otherwise labeling someone as having a condition can have many advantages, in part because it declares one as legitimately "sick." It can trigger support from others, or it can release people from having to meet expected social and productive roles.

But being diagnosed with a disease can also have negative social effects, and these can even make people sicker. This is because disease labels themselves can be very powerful because of their attached moral meanings, pushing people down and out of society. Those diagnosed with the most stigmatized diseases are often denied access to healthcare or other support because they are judged as less worthy or deserving. Leprosy (Hansen's disease), for instance, has often been highly stigmatized. It is caused by a bacterial infection and leads to neurological damage in the cooler parts of the body—the hands, feet, nose, and genitals—leading to secondary infection and disfigurement. But contrary to what many believe, leprosy isn't highly contagious. Still, those diagnosed with the disease often experience a severe drop in social status, up to and including being completely rejected (**Figure 15.14**).

Throughout European history, the physical signs of leprosy, such as skin lesions or other visible disfigurement, were greatly feared, and those affected were cast out from society. But stigmas change through time as ideas about the causes of disease shift. The stigma of leprosy was most intense during periods in which it was explained religiously as a product of sin; as ideas around leprosy changed through time to view the disease more as a trial of suffering from God, much more support was provided by charitable church hospitals to those affected. Similarly, the particularly powerful stigma of a diagnosis of lung cancer

FIGURE 15.14

Leprosy has been an extremely stigmatized disease through much of European history. In this 13th-century French depiction, people labeled with leprosy in a society dominated by Christianity, who were both feared and socially rejected, use rattles to warn others they are "unclean" so they can be avoided, and carry begging bowls so they can eat. Archaeological excavations confirm they were removed further from society by being excluded from burial on consecrated ground, thereby damning them further in the afterlife.

SRI LANKA

Asia

has been recently amplified, reflecting successful public health campaigns that created new social judgment of those who smoke.

Nancy Waxler (1931–2007) explained "learning to be a leper," based on her fieldwork in Sri Lanka with clinic outpatients. In nearby India, people diagnosed with leprosy found their lives in tatters. Doctors would refuse to treat them, families would reject them, and many ended up on the streets as beggars. Yet in Sri Lanka, despite leprosy being highly feared and considered extremely contagious and disfiguring, Waxler found that most of those diagnosed carried on their lives much as before: Schoolteachers were in the classroom and mothers were still at home caring for their children. The case of leprosy in Sri Lanka shows that no disease is innately stigmatized, even a disease that is otherwise feared. Rather, we learn from others who we are expected to care for and who we are socially permitted to dismiss and otherwise reject.

HEALING SYSTEMS

The act of caring for those who are sick is as old as our species, as noted in Section 15.2. But to deal with the particular challenges of coping with disease and restoring health, humans have more recently developed more structured healing systems, or culturally organized ways of caregiving for the ill, that bring the quest for health out of the individual home and into a wider society. All healing systems, including biomedicine, encompass shared symbols and meaning. In this section, we consider some of the challenges and limits of current systems of biomedical practice and training, and we assess the benefits of using or integrating other healing systems.

ethnomedical system The structures, practices, beliefs, and therapeutic techniques that together define a system for healing. Ethnomedical systems can include both lay and specialist knowledge and practices.

Ethnomedical systems are shared, systematic ways of explaining, recognizing, reacting to, accommodating, and treating disease and illness within a society. All healing systems have conventions that participants understand and give meaning to, including different roles and responsibilities for patients and healers, expected causes of illness, and preferred or acceptable modes of treatment.

Healing is not just about removing physical pain, dysfunction, and damage from the body. It is also about restoring our positive connections to others. Some healing systems focus more on the former, and others on the latter. Therefore, medical anthropologists sometimes distinguish between personalistic and naturalistic healing systems. But regardless of the ways illness is explained, every medical system has three basic elements: a theory of what causes illness, a system for diagnosing illness, and a set of techniques deemed to be appropriate for healing.

PERSONALISTIC HEALING SYSTEMS

Personalistic systems see the causes of illness in disrupted relationships between people or with other realms, including the supernatural or spiritual. The causes of illness could be a curse, witchcraft, or retribution for sin. The healing in personalistic systems focuses on fixing relationships between people, deities, or ghosts, righting the proposed wrongs that led to illness in the first place. Shamanic healing is the clearest contemporary example of a personalistic system.

shamanic healing Treatment by a religious practitioner who connects spirit and physical worlds.

FIGURE 15.15

A Buryat healer consults with a patient in her apartment near Ulan-Ude in Siberia.

For the Buryat people, the largest Indigenous group in Siberia (in what is now Russia), visiting a healer was long illegal in the city of Ulan-Ude where the majority of Buryats live. Under seven decades of central Soviet-era control, shamanic healers were oppressed and imprisoned because they challenged the state's stance of forced atheism. But shamanic practices continued quietly, hidden in small pockets in the remote steppes of the expansive countryside. The collapse of Soviet Russia allowed a rapid resurgence in shamanism and a regrowth of the profession.

Buryat healers today practice openly. They describe themselves as compelled by powers outside themselves to serve the desperate and needy in a time of rising capitalism, increasing urban poverty, and reduced state provision of health services. Their work, often done in varied forms of a kitchen, might include libations of vodka or milk, offerings of cooked meat for the spirits, or drumming to dismiss evil thoughts, appease disquieted ancestral spirits, and rebalance the world of patients (**Figure 15.15**). By connecting people to their lost family and performing rituals from the countryside in the Buryat language, the healer links people to lost places and times. And by using the Buryat language in their rituals, they are aiding post-Soviet Indigenous language and cultural revitalization.

Although we can't observe the healing practices themselves, archaeologists have discovered evidence that suggests shamanic traditions in different parts of the world. For example, archaeologists have discovered 61 tattoos on the body of a naturally mummified individual now called "Ötzi," who died 5,300 years ago while journeying across the icy Ötztal Alpine range between what is now Austria and Italy. What makes them particularly interesting is that the tattooed lines and crosses are all located on parts of the body that also show evidence of arthritis, including knee, ankles, wrist, and lower back (**Figure 15.16**). The fact that the markings also cluster around the body points used in contemporary acupuncture treatments suggests the tattooing was a healing practice.

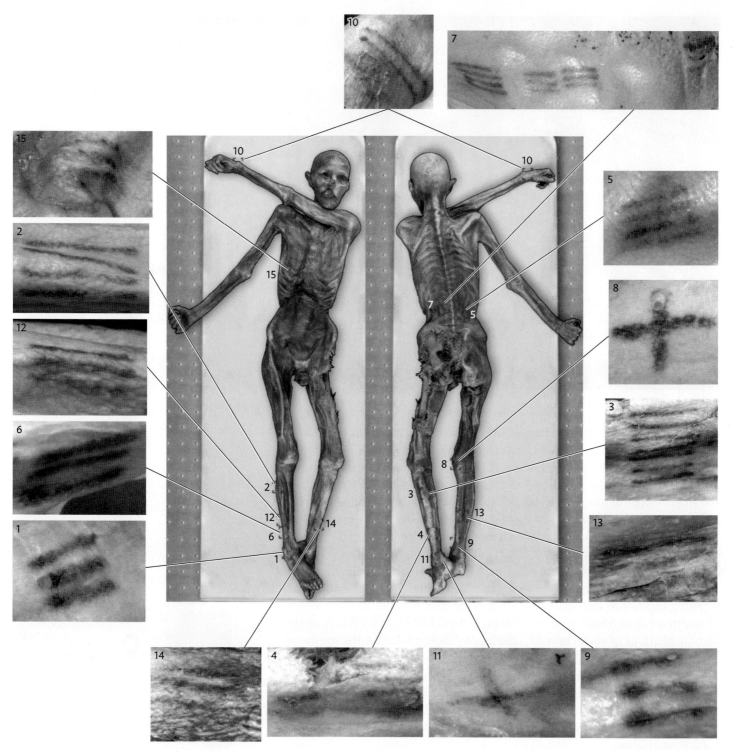

FIGURE 15.16

The body positions of Ötzi's 61 tattoos and some of the designs, made 5,300 years ago, are shown.

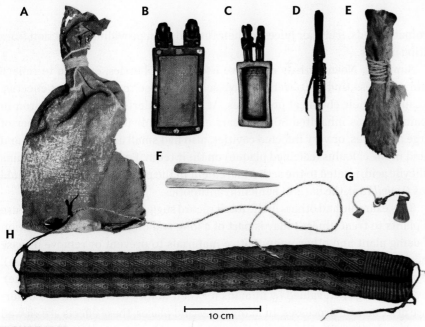

Bolivian Andes

FIGURE 15.17

The 1,000-year-old ritual bundle of a healer found at the Bolivian site of Cueva del Chileno consisted of an outer leather bag (A) that contained carved and decorated wooden snuffing tablets (B, C), a snuffing tube with two human hair braids attached (D), an animal-skin pouch made of three fox snouts snitched together (E), two spatulas made of llama bone (F), pieces of plants attached to wool strings (G), and a multicolored woven headband (H).

Archaeologists have also found evidence of shamanic or personalistic healers in an array of times and places. For example, excavations in the Bolivian Andes in South America revealed the location where a healer was laid to rest in a rock shelter about 1,000 years ago. The individual's remains were missing. But remaining was a leather bag with paraphernalia for crushing and inhaling hallucinogens (**Figure 15.17**). Archaeologist Melanie Miller and her team analyzed the chemical residues inside the bag. They found traces of the *Psychotria viridis* shrub, an ingredient in ayahuasca, and the plant *Anadenanthera*, the source of *vilca*, as well as cocaine from the coca bush. Reality-altering compounds such as those from ayahuasca and vilca are central to many traditional Andean healing rituals, and similar paraphernalia is sometimes carried by traveling healers in Bolivia today.

NATURALISTIC HEALING SYSTEMS

Naturalistic healing systems, of which biomedicine is an example, tend to focus on explaining disease symptoms and illness in proximate terms (such as exposure to an infectious agent). Many Indigenous and other community-based healing systems also incorporate or are fully based on naturalistic notions of the body that favor treatment through chemical or mechanical means, including such practices as bone setting, therapeutic massage, acupuncture, and use of plants. Most humans incorporate these practices into their daily lives without paying much attention, such as stretching before running to prevent injury.

The use of plants to prevent and relieve illness likely pre-dates the emergence of behaviorally modern humans, reflecting an earlier hominin adaptation shared with some other animal species (**Figure 15.18**). Nonhuman primates might swallow nonnutritive leaves, bitter pith, and large seeds in the rainy season to improve their health by removing parasites. Many primates also apply

FIGURE 15.18

Chimpanzees in the wild (shown here in Mahale Mountains National Park, Tanzania) have been repeatedly observed stripping and eating the bitter pith of plants, probably as a curative for parasitic infections.

aromatic seeds, fruits, or juices to their fur and skin, providing protection from biting insects.

Similarly, Neanderthals may have used leaves, berries, or resin to relieve pain or illness, and they seem to have selected those that were most effective because of their chemical properties. At the Neanderthal site of El Sidrón in Spain that was inhabited 50,000 years ago, one individual with a number of large abscesses, or very infected cavities, also had small amounts of poplar and mold in the calculus (calcified plaque) on their teeth. Poplar tree bark contains salicylic acid, related to the active ingredient in the painkiller aspirin. The mold was *Penicillium*, the basis of penicillin antibiotics.

This example and others in the fossil record suggest that pharmaceutical use of plants to treat illness today is part of a long and ongoing hominin tradition of using plant and other nonnutritive materials to prevent or remove disease and assist healing. Psychoactive plants, such as poppies (the source of opium), peyote cactus (the source of mescaline), and coffee beans (a source of caffeine), have also long been valued by humans for their ability to stimulate and otherwise alter mental processes. In many times and places, these effects are viewed as integral parts of legitimate healing systems and health-keeping practices.

Moreover, an array of anthropological research shows how naturalistic healing techniques need not be specialist knowledge. Knowledge about the healing properties of plants is learned from family, friends, and neighbors (**Figure 15.19**). Even for those who rely heavily on biomedicine, minor illnesses are often treated with various trusted home remedies, such as peppermint tea for indigestion or lavender for insomnia.

FIGURE 15.19

Anthropologists study how knowledge of medicinal practices is preserved within communities. Pictured here are Mayan schoolchildren in southern Belize who are working with environmental anthropologist Rebecca Zarger to create medicinal plant trails near their villages, as part of an effort to understand how children learn about plant species and their uses from adults and from each other. The collaboration between anthropologist and participants led to the design of school materials to support long-term preservation of this collective community healing knowledge.

MEDICAL PLURALISM

In our globalizing and urbanizing world, people may have access to several different healing systems. Those visiting a shaman in urban Siberia are often educated and middle-class and have options for biomedical treatment. For people on a quest for health, varied systems of healing are rarely treated as fully distinct and disparate. Rather, people often move between systems, based on what they think the problem is, why it began, what can fix it, what makes them feel comfortable and understood, and what social or economic resources they have available at the time.

In the central Pacific, cultural anthropologist Jessica Hardin has been using ethnographic methods to understand how urban Samoans variously understand and treat Type 2 diabetes (**Figure 15.20**). Her work documents the complexities of how people understand chronic illness in both naturalistic and personalistic terms, and it shows how they seek health practices at the intersection of the two approaches.

Samoans recognize that the naturalistic cause of diabetes is *suka* (sugar), diagnosed by a doctor at a clinic. Yet with widespread adherence to Christianity in the island nation and the central role of the church in daily lives, convening with a church leader and religious prayer are also considered important to recovery (**Figure 15.21**).

Samoa also has a very long and highly trusted tradition of expert healing based on both medicinal plant use and massage. Patients consult village healers to treat many of the symptoms of diabetes, such as skin rashes, numb patches, and failing eyes. Whether they have a diagnosis at the clinic or not, the treatment of the symptoms by a healer is much the same. Ultimately, these patients commonly shift between healing systems as they manage their illness.

The systems themselves are not fully distinct either. Doctors may pray with their patients. Church pastors may visit their parishioners in the hospital or even operate as healers in their own villages, dispensing plant-based medicines. This reality of medical pluralism (or syncretism) means Samoans rarely follow the exact biomedical guidelines for treating their diabetes. But the synergies between the different approaches to healing provides meaningful and socially acceptable ways to grapple with a complex, chronic disease.

FIGURE 15.20

Cultural anthropologist Jessica Hardin (left) conducts an interview in a coffee shop in Apia, Samoa.

medical pluralism **Engagement within and fusing of multiple systems of healing in the quest for health. Also called syncretism.**

FIGURE 15.21

Samoans use prayer as part of healing efforts while waiting for the doctor at a clinic in Apia, Samoa.

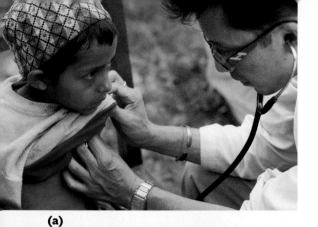

(a)

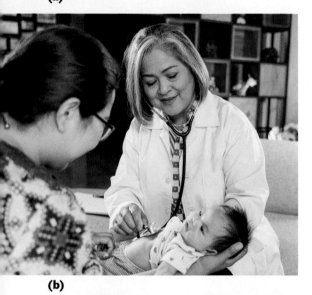

(b)

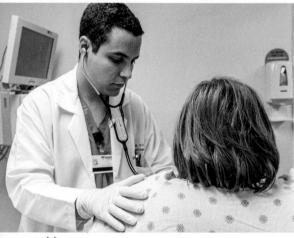

(c)

FIGURE 15.22

The white coat and stethoscope are globally recognized markers of a doctor's status and authority. These pictures were taken in **(a)** Nepal, **(b)** Indonesia, and **(c)** the United States.

social capital **Connections to others that can provide opportunities, information, or material or emotional support.**

BIOMEDICINE AS ETHNOMEDICINE

Biomedicine is a model of naturalistic healing that is purposefully secular and scientifically based. Yet it, too, is often based in cultural meanings and cultural assumptions. Viewed as a wider set of shared practices, biomedicine typically favors aggressive modes of treatment for illness using new practices and technologies, sometimes with the potential of dramatic cures. Whereas more personalistic modes of healing use closeness between patient and healer to build trust, biomedicine often distances the patient from the healer to build the healer's authority.

The doctor's white coat is an important material marker of authority within the biomedical system, one that patients and other staff all understand as indicating a doctor who is clean, competent, caring, and has expert knowledge (**Figure 15.22**). The coat also provides a stark divide within any clinical encounter between healer and patient, reinforcing the differences in both knowledge and power between the two sides of the healing arrangement. It reminds the patient through symbolism that the healer can be trusted to make important decisions about their health.

However, social distancing and status hierarchies can also lead to miscommunication and mistrust between healer and patient in the process of diagnosis and treatment. They can have different ideas regarding their role, and their patients' responsibilities, than their patients themselves do. The further medical staff are from those they treat—in terms of language, culture, socioeconomic status, power status, illness, or life experiences—the wider these gaps of misunderstanding can be.

Consider the global COVID-19 pandemic. The primary scientific approach to reduce the impacts of the disease was population-wide vaccination. Yet many people were hesitant, and mistrust in this specific technology became widespread across communities. Anthropologists were not surprised by this response. Lay ideas of what is healthy or what are appropriate treatments do not always align with those of formal or expert healers within a system. Sometimes they can be at complete odds. Subcultural groups form and act on their own deeply held health belief systems.

In fact, many years prior to the COVID-19 pandemic, clusters of parents in many wealthier countries with excellent preventative services, including Australia, the United Kingdom, and the United States, were hesitant to vaccinate their children against potentially deadly infectious diseases (**Figure 15.23**). Such mistrust of some biomedical technologies and advice played out fully as nations across the globe struggled with universal vaccine uptake as a means to mitigate coronavirus infections in 2021.

Medical anthropologist Elisa Sobo studied parents at a private school in California where vaccine hesitancy had been evident for many years. Her findings suggest that adopting specific health beliefs can act as a form of social capital, facilitating our belonging and acceptance within the communities we want to join and become part of. Social capital is unevenly distributed in society, and it can facilitate access to resources (such as wealth), influence (such as political power), and information (such as safety and health risks). Parents whose children were newly enrolled in the school became increasingly vaccine hesitant over time, even if they had been vaccine acceptors previously. Vaccine refusal seemed to help parents fit in socially with other parents.

This notion of health beliefs as social capital also explains why recent outbreaks of preventable childhood diseases, such as measles, in wealthier sectors of advanced economies tend to pattern within neighborhoods. Sobo suggests that anti-vaccine beliefs spread as people reshape their identity in joining local communities. It's important to note also that vaccine-hesitant parents are struggling to be "good" in their own everyday moral worlds, even if their views are counter to widely accepted medical recommendations.

Anthropologist Heidi Larson, who founded The Vaccine Confidence Project (VCP), advocates for public health strategies that are focused on building trust and conversation, adopting a "We are all in this together" mindset. The solution she proposes is listening and responding to parents' worries rather than labeling their decisions as ignorant or stupid.

To improve biomedical encounters more generally, medical anthropologist and physician Arthur Kleinman developed a strategy based in questions doctors can use to build a conversation—and ultimately the two-way trust necessary to facilitate healing—with the patient. The goal is to close important gaps between how the doctor and patient differently understand their illness by allowing patients to speak with fewer interruptions. Kleinman encourages doctors to make fewer assumptions when interpreting their patients' stories. The questions Kleinman developed include: What do you call this problem? What do you believe causes this problem? How serious is it? How does it affect you? What do you fear most about the condition or the treatment? By asking what resources and support patients have (or don't have) to aid in treatment, physicians may also be able to offer important practical assistance that matters to healing, such as referral to mental health services, information about transport or translation, or mitigation of family tensions.

FIGURE 15.23

Vaccine hesitancy was not created by COVID-19. Medical anthropologists had been documenting and explaining its emergence in wealthier nations for many years prior. After a measles outbreak in Italy in 2017, new laws required additional childhood vaccinations. Public protests followed.

SECTION 15.4

BIOMEDICINE AND POWER

Biomedicine, because of its science-based innovations and global dominance, has an incredible power to reach and heal many people. Yet not everyone gets those benefits because, like all healing systems, biomedicine is embedded within the larger context of government and economies that create power differentials, most especially related to wealth, even when there is universal health care. In this section, we consider how the mechanistic, commodified view of our bodies favored by biomedicine can constantly recreate sickness for many, even though biomedicine is ostensibly focused on healing. We also consider how people in groups with less power and who are subject to the harms of this structural violence create communities of care to help them heal, even as biomedical systems tend to suppress or remove alternatives.

The World Health Organization (WHO) has declared that all people deserve the highest possible standard of health as a basic human right. Yet many people, even within wealthy societies, do not have access to basic and necessary health services. Health inequalities do not just reflect economic inequalities—they drive them. Poor health that is based on poverty and low social status denies people the chance to participate as full productive members of society. This is in part because biomedicine is increasingly a profit-driven enterprise in many places. An examination of these complexities is the focus of this section, with which anthropology helps us grapple.

BIOMEDICALIZATION AND THE COMMODIFICATION OF HEALTH

For most of human history, birth took place much as we described for Indigenous Fijians above: at home attended by families or midwives. It is only in the last century, for example, that pregnancy and childbirth have become biomedical events, overseen by specialist doctors and taking place in hospitals. This is an example of *biomedicalization*, which occurs when conditions are redefined so as to require or presume the need for biomedical interventions.

In wealthier nations, the normal sagging of skin with age has become transformed into a biomedical concern, treated in doctor's offices and hospitals through injections and surgeries. South Korean facial shapes are increasingly reconfigured through surgeries, as the pursuit of beauty has become increasingly medicalized, and invasive cosmetic procedures have been normalized in urban areas of the country (**Figure 15.24**).

In part due to the accelerating medicalization of many aspects of human lives globally, biomedicine is often described by anthropologists as hegemonic, meaning it comes to dominate or control and it makes other options less available or appealing. The increasing role of biomedicine in healing globally means that health is increasingly commodified, based on payments for services and materials, and treated as a commodity that is managed and allocated by market forces. Korean cosmetic surgery is a huge revenue-generating international enterprise that benefits from growing trends in medical tourism, reminding us that biomedicalization and capitalism are closely connected.

Southern India has long had a sophisticated and pluralized system of health self-care based in Ayurveda and Hindu religious practices. This includes a sophisticated set of traditional medicines handmade by local specialists (**Figure 15.25**). Yet the Indian middle and upper classes have a growing preference for commercially produced versions of such medicines, with the appeal generated through the widespread use of advertising by a profit-driven set of

biomedicalization Redefining conditions as benefiting from or needing biomedical treatment.

FIGURE 15.24

Advertisements such as this one for cosmetic surgery are common in Seoul, South Korea, a major global center for using surgical procedures to re-create facial form to adhere to very narrow ideals of beauty.

FIGURE 15.25

An Ayurvedic market sells medicinal plants in the state of Kerala, in southern India.

pharmaceutical Indian companies. This commodification of such items as "male tonics" drives profits from local producers of medicines into the hands of industry.

Although the biomedical industry aims to help people, like other industries within the global capitalist economy, it is concerned with the goal of maximizing profits, and this has led to exploitation. Medical anthropologist Monir Moniruzzaman has been doing long-term ethnographic fieldwork in urban Bangladesh with donors and those who provide their organs for payment (**Figure 15.26**). Through "transplant tourism," those with the financial means (mostly from countries such as Japan, Saudi Arabia, and the United States) work with intermediaries to travel to Bangladesh and other countries to get needed organs unavailable to them at home. Those who give kidneys and other organs described the loss of their organs as a loss of dignity. They were stigmatized, with the mark from their operation signaling their mutilation and desperation as the poorest of the poor (**Figure 15.27**). Long-term medical complications or disability can also result. An organ might yield several thousands of dollars—for

FIGURE 15.26

Medical anthropologist Monir Moniruzzaman (right) interviews an organ donor in the field where he works.

FIGURE 15.27

A resident of a small village in Bangladesh shows the scar from an illegal kidney removal operation. Global trafficking of such organs relies on the economic desperation of those with few other options for supporting themselves and their families.

FIGURE 15.28

Uninsured Appalachian residents wait to receive care at a charitable dental field hospital. Dentistry is a privatized medical specialization in almost every part of the world. Free dental care is rarely available for those who can't afford to pay, and many here spent the night in line hoping for an available slot.

Appalachian region

Rural eastern shore

the poorest of the poor, these represent substantial funds they can't get any other way, allowing them to pay off debts, feed their families, and educate their children. But it is nothing compared to the figures over $200,000 that recipients can pay for the same organ.

Where highly commodified health systems dominate, many people can be excluded because they are unable to afford needed services or products. This lack of access can then precipitate additional forms of harm. Medical anthropologist Sarah Raskin has detailed the experience of living with severe dental decay in rural Appalachia, one of the most economically depressed regions in the United States. For many residents, dental treatment is often financially out of reach (**Figure 15.28**). Over time, this results in both visible decay and terrible pain. But relief from medical clinics or hospitals can be hard to come by. Clinicians "read" severe dental damage as a signal of addiction to methamphetamine, and they refuse requests for prescription drugs that can help with dental pain.

Visibly decayed teeth also make it harder to get the types of jobs that provide dental care, because they categorize a person as undesirable to hire. Raskin's ethnography reveals how dental decay, pain, poverty, stigma, potential addiction, and other illnesses operate to reinforce one another, pushing those with "bad" teeth further down and out from society, including further from adequate medical care or employment that can assist in accessing it.

People who are denied access to, or do not trust, mainstream health services and products may create informal communities of care. Medical anthropologist Thurka Sangaramoorthy began research on the rural eastern shore of Maryland in 2013, observing and interviewing those working in the region's agricultural, poultry, and seafood industries and those making use of free medical clinics (**Figure 15.29**). She found that an overstressed public health infrastructure, lack of money, and undocumented immigrant status meant many workers had precarious access to healthcare. They coped as best they could through networks of improvised care, such as practices of sharing medications between those who have easier access and those who do not.

FIGURE 15.29

Staff at a Maryland migrant clinic conduct mobile tests (for streptococcal infection) in one of the locations where medical anthropologist Thurka Sangaramoorthy did her fieldwork with immigrant workers and those trying to provide them healthcare.

Importantly, her ethnography revealed that many local healthcare professionals were key participants in these informal systems. They explained they were driven to creatively bend (or even break) rules, such as treating patients "off the books," because they believed it was the ethical thing to do when the formal medical system was unable to adequately serve their patients.

BIOPOWER AND BODIES

Health is a central casualty of racism, gender inequality, lack of political power, poverty, and other too-often invisible forms of violence that emerge from inequitable structures—including sometimes public health systems themselves. Biopower is a term coined by French scholar Michel Foucault, whose work has influenced many anthropologists who study health and the human body. Central to the concept of biopower is the question of who is given the authority to make decisions about a person's body. Biopower refers to the capacity of institutions, such as governments or media, to disempower people through regulating bodies. It can be through denying access to health services or banning specific medical procedures. But it is also often achieved through scientific and medical forms of surveillance, such as body measurement or disease tracking.

biopower Institutional power over bodies that is used to control or subjugate.

Anthropologists and medical experts all agree that the black market in organs is dangerous and dreadful, placing donors at risk of extreme exploitation and substandard surgeries. But should international organ selling be banned outright, or should it be better regulated? The answers depend on how you view donor choice in the contexts of extreme poverty: as a form of body autonomy or freedom that gives individuals some power (through money) or as a form of coercion where the rich again have all the advantage.

Government agencies, the media, corporations, and other powerful institutions may all participate in these means of regulating bodies. The so-called "war on obesity" is one example. In 2008, the Japanese government passed the "Metabo Law" that requires companies to monitor their workers' bodies to see if they reach a threshold of body size defined as unhealthy. Media coverage around the dangers of obesity and the social benefits of slimness motivated millions of people to obsessively diet, exercise, and buy products to lose weight.

FIGURE 15.30

Such societal concern around managing, controlling, and removing larger bodies also extends to everyday language practices. Cultural anthropologist Mimi Nichter was studying U.S. teens in Arizona in the 1980s when she identified a phenomenon she termed "fat talk." This same conversational feature has since been observed in many places globally, most especially among young women. Fat talk includes conversational prompts (beginnings) like "Does this make me look fat?" The apparent normality of such a question is a hint of the way even seemingly minor interactions can reflect and feed into wider systems of biopower.

The levers of biopower are also evident in public health practice, where there is institutional oversight over which groups within society are targeted as more deserving of state care and which are not. Medical–linguistic anthropologist Charles Briggs and physician Clara Mantini-Briggs met while they were both working in Venezuela's remote Orinoco Delta region in the wake of a terrible cholera epidemic (**Figure 15.30**). The Warao people who live on the edge of the Orinoco River depend on the river for water, food, and transport. This makes them particularly vulnerable to the spread of cholera, a potentially deadly waterborne infectious disease. Cholera is easily treated if caught early, but if left untreated it can cause death from dehydration within a day. In 1992–1993, some 500 people died from cholera in the Indigenous riverine villages of the Orinoco Delta.

Why so many, for an easily treatable condition? The Briggses' ethnographic study, which included working with public health and other government officials, found that the way they understood cholera risk had become racialized (Chapter 14), deflecting blame from their own institutions and onto those who were ill by labeling them as "unsanitary citizens." This happened easily because the Indigenous Warao were already stigmatized as "dirty" and "disgusting." Such victim-blaming in epidemics of any kind, including cholera, obesity, or COVID-19, can be seen as a form of structural (indirect) violence.

POWER, INEQUALITY, AND BIOMEDICAL TRAINING

A further distinction of biomedicine from other healing systems is that many biomedical practitioners treat patients outside their own communities, and practitioners tend to be considerably more affluent than patients as well. This

can make it difficult for doctors to fully understand the challenges local people face in their daily lives, such as being unable to afford prescribed medications. Outsider doctors might not speak the same language or might use a different dialect. These types of distance in experience between doctor and patient consistently worsen the care given.

This gap is perhaps most evident in the arena of short-term international medical volunteering. Those wanting to enter medical school see the investment of both time and money in such international experience as a valuable résumé builder. Many global health training programs in wealthier nations allow or encourage such placements, providing a means for those with limited practical experience to build their skills through interacting directly with patients served by health systems with fewer resources.

One popular medical "voluntourism" destination is Arusha, Tanzania, with easy access to safari parks and Mount Kilimanjaro. Medical anthropologist Noelle Sullivan spent four summers in Arusha's clinics, observing and talking with local health workers and the paying volunteers placed there (**Figure 15.31**). The volunteers didn't realize that most of their money went to the company arranging the placements, not the hospital or those left on staff trying to manage the mostly untrained volunteers. Sullivan also found that the volunteers, none of whom had any prior practical medical experience, believed themselves to be relative experts, even as compared to the fully trained and highly experienced Tanzanian health workers they were working alongside. They pushed to be allowed to deliver babies, read X-rays, or set broken bones, despite their lack of medical qualification. This was also despite the reality that dispensing the same medical care would have been illegal in their home countries. Accordingly, volunteers constantly strained hospital resources, wasted the local clinicians' time, and exposed patients to additional harms, placing the entire clinic's enterprise at risk while incorrectly believing they were doing good.

One suggested solution to preventing these and other structurally violent and racist abuses within medicine is through teaching "structural competency" as part of medical training in wealthier nations. By learning how to recognize many of the structural barriers to health people face in their everyday lives—whether due to poverty, how people communicate, or social norms about what is appropriate and meaningful treatment—the goal is to improve the effectiveness of the doctor–patient encounter, or at least to encourage biomedical practitioners to ask better questions, listen more, and better understand the answers. But this approach will always be a minor contribution to a much larger and embedded problem in globalized biomedicine: Real improvements in clinical–lay relationships require meaningful intervention not just in the clinic but also in dismantling the institutional structures and barriers, such as racism, gender inequality, poverty, or forced migration, that underpin health inequalities.

The recognition that larger-scale inequalities are not only reflected in ill health but also created by them is one reason the goal of health is so central to advancing human rights globally. The historical scope, weight, resources, authority, and innovation of biomedicine will also be central to this endeavor. Getting it right matters, and this chapter shows the many ways that anthropology is particularly well-placed to identify what the better possibilities might be.

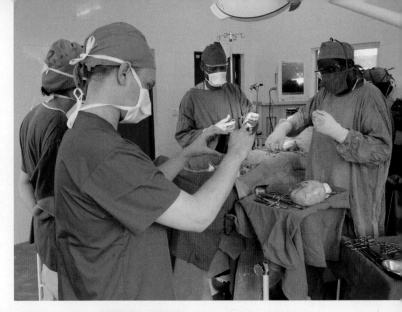

FIGURE 15.31

A short-term foreign medical volunteer takes a photograph during a surgical procedure in Arusha, Tanzania. Medical anthropologists consider both the practical impacts and ethical complexities of such "voluntourism" on local medical systems and quality of care.

15

Disease, Health, and Healing

Anthropologists study human health and disease in many ways, including the evolution of disease, the myriad connections between culture and healing, and how health disparities reflect power. This diversity of evidence provides an array of blueprints for how to reduce individual suffering, prevent and treat diseases, and advance health as a basic human right.

KEY TERM
> biomedicine

15.1 | Disease and Human History

Identify how disease today relates to human evolution and major social and technological transitions in human history.

- Viewed in long-term history, all major human environmental, social, and technological transitions create new disease challenges. New and accelerating diseases can also, in turn, drive rapid social and technological change.

- Humans and their many diseases have coevolved; this recognition provides novel clues on how to treat disease today.

KEY TERMS
> endemic
> epidemiological transition
> evolutionary medicine
> human microbiome

15.2 | Social Dimensions of Illness

Explain how cultural ideas and social identities shape illness experiences and practices, now and in the past.

- Cultural ideas significantly shape how illness is experienced and expressed, what forms of care are given, and how effective treatments will be.

KEY TERMS
> diagnosis
> disease
> empathy
> health
> idiom of distress
> illness
> sickness
> stigma
> symptom

15.3 | Healing Systems

Characterize biomedicine as a healing system, including as it relates to other healing systems.

- Healing is always a social as well as a physical process.

- Biomedicine is a culturally based healing system, like all others, that relies on meaning to be effective.

- People often engage with multiple healing systems.

KEY TERMS
› biomedicine
› ethnomedical system
› medical pluralism
› shamanic healing
› social capital

15.4 | Biomedicine and Power

Identify how disease, illness, and healing systems relate to societal power.

- Biomedicine is a particularly powerful and globally dominant healing system, uniquely positioned to both advance and undermine not only health but also equality, prosperity, and human rights.

KEY TERMS
› biomedicalization
› biopower

16

Anthropology, Environment, and Better Futures

For more than two decades, cultural anthropologist Hilda Lloréns has focused on the lives of Afro-Puerto Rican communities on her home island. Descended from freed slaves and indentured laborers, residents of one off-the-grid rural community live on the mangrove-lined coastal plains once dominated by sugarcane plantations. Residents support themselves via fishing, crab trapping, and foraging for plants and fruit. They make their own electricity from solar panels and windmills. Generations of earned and shared *ecological knowledge* have made it possible for them to thrive.

Lloréns's ethnographic research in such communities—participant observation and interviewing—draws on her own familial ties to Puerto Rico. It allows her to build a detailed picture of people's lives and relationships within broader political and economic processes that connect Puerto Rico, the United States, and beyond. As an Afro-Latinx scholar with Indigenous Taíno roots, Lloréns's work also exemplifies a commitment to decolonial and politically engaged forms of scholarship. She is motivated by research that can support and transform the communities she is studying, one key reason she became an anthropologist.

Her research documents how the ways of life of Afro-Puerto Rican communities are becoming threatened by air, water, and land contamination from oil refineries, pharmaceutical manufacturers, and energy plants that have

LEARNING OBJECTIVES

16.1 The Anthropology of Disaster
Explain how social structures interact with hazards to create disasters.

16.2 Environmental Injustice
Describe the bases of environmental inequalities and the roles anthropologists play in advancing environmental justice.

16.3 Anthropology and Human Ecology
Analyze how anthropology's approaches to studying human–environment interactions emerged and changed.

16.4 Better Ways Forward
Evaluate how anthropologists support the role of Indigenous societies and knowledge in providing pathways for sustainability.

CREATING BETTER FUTURES

An important responsibility of anthropologists is supporting communities that face environmental challenges, such as those in the wake of colonialism, capitalism, and other systems that tend to exaggerate environmental harms. Anthropologists from some of the most affected communities are leading much of this important work.

FIGURE 16.1

This photo, taken by Hilda Lloréns during fieldwork, shows people swimming near the AES coal plant in Guayama, on the southeastern coast of Puerto Rico.

encroached on and polluted the coast (**Figure 16.1**). Puerto Rico is a territory of the United States, a status many contend is the same as being a colony. Denied democratic representation in the U.S. Congress, Puerto Ricans are subject to the decisions of federal policy-makers who are not accountable to them. In Puerto Rico, environmental regulation has been lax and federal disaster aid has been slow and inadequate. Lloréns argues the resulting disproportionate exposure to toxins and disaster risks is a form of environmental racism.

Such challenges are hardly unique to the communities Lloréns studies. Billions of people globally face major environmental hazards such as toxins in their air, food, or water; climate change and unreliable weather; and the threat of disasters and livelihood changes linked to extractive industries, such as large-scale agriculture and commercial fisheries, as well as other profit-seeking industries. Research that can solve, rather than just identify, these pressing environmental challenges is needed now. Anthropologists, including Lloréns, are innovating new ways to do that better.

In this chapter, we begin by examining how anthropologists studying disasters and environmental justice are developing these innovations. We then analyze how approaches to environmental anthropology have evolved over time and how we have now arrived at approaches that recognize the important role played by Indigenous anthropologists.

SECTION 16.1

THE ANTHROPOLOGY OF DISASTER

ecological knowledge Understanding of the environment and its resources derived from interactions with it and other people living in it.

natural hazard A naturally occurring phenomenon, such as a hurricane, earthquake, volcano, or wildfire, that has the potential to harm human societies; it may be fast-moving (like a tornado) or slow-moving (like a drought).

disaster When a natural hazard produces a calamitous impact on human life, health, economics, infrastructure, or society.

Anthropologists don't talk in terms of "natural disasters." Rather, they see hurricanes, floods, and volcanoes as **natural hazards**—events that may or may not damage human societies. For anthropologists, a **disaster** happens when a natural hazard collides with societies that are unprepared, unable to plan, or unwilling to respond because of how they are organized and structured. Disasters result most especially from histories of social, political, and economic inequality. And this is why they cause such massive damage to people's lives, health, income, infrastructure, and cultural heritage. Anthropologists explore how societies, past and present, prepare for and mitigate such disasters.

DISASTER ANTHROPOLOGY IS BORN

Anthony Oliver-Smith is a cultural anthropologist who planned, in 1970, to return to Yungay, Peru, to study how people organized local markets. His earlier work focused on *pishtacos*, monsters of Peruvian folklore who are tall, thin, and White and who attack Indigenous Quechua and Aymara people to suck the fat or life force from their bodies.

Just months before Oliver-Smith was to fly back to the district capital, the "Great Peruvian Earthquake" of 1970—a whopping 7.7 on the Richter scale— struck Yungay. It was a Sunday, and children were gathered in the downtown stadium to see a traveling circus while adults rested after joyous wedding cel- ebrations. The glacier collapse and landslide that followed the earthquake brought about 10 million cubic meters of ice, snow, rocks, mud, and earth (moving 200 miles an hour) down on the town, as well as 150 other towns and 1,500 villages.

It was the worst-ever recorded disaster in the Americas. In all, more than 3 million people were affected, including 50,000 killed and 20,000 presumed dead. In Yungay, the stadium, the circus, and the spectators were buried in the landslide. The entire town was destroyed. All but four of the dozens of palm trees that had originally circled its central plaza were completely buried by the liquified sludge. Survivors took refuge on a cemetery hill. They had to climb over crushed coffins and strewn corpses to get to high land. By the time Oliver-Smith arrived a few months later, the survivors were living in a tent camp on land that they insisted was still Yungay, despite the obliteration of the settlement and all its infrastructure (**Figure 16.2**).

Oliver-Smith decided to stay, do what he could to help, and also learn more about how people managed in the wake of such extreme disaster. He was racked with terror his first night staying with an aid worker, listening to the sharp cracks of the still-collapsing glacier. When he first introduced himself to disaster survivors, one man became inconsolable with grief over the death of his son because Oliver- Smith had the same first name.

Oliver-Smith acknowledged his serious doubts about his mental, physical, and academic ability to conduct the earthquake research. At the time, anthropologists didn't study disas- ters. But he stayed and followed the survivors in Yungay over the next 10 years. The work he ulti- mately produced, including his ethnography *The Martyred City*, revealed the importance of ethnography to understanding the human dimensions of disas- ters. It also signaled the start of the new field of disaster anthropology.

Looking back a decade after the event, Oliver-Smith observed that the earth- quake precipitated or accelerated many large-scale social transitions. Rural-to- urban migration intensified, as people left the Yungay region. The economic value of physical labor increased, with donations and funding from outside the region spurring new construction. Most laborers were Indigenous Quechua people, who gained higher incomes and increased their negotiating power as workers in the postdisaster reconstruction phase. Most of Yungay's upper class were killed or moved to Peru's coast. People were more able to move up in the

FIGURE 16.2

A statue of Christ in the cemetery shown here, and four palm trees in the nearby town plaza, were all that remained of Yungay after the "Great Peruvian Earthquake" of 1970.

disaster anthropology A subfield of anthro- pology that examines the process that precedes, unfolds during, and follows a hazard (often a natural hazard) that creates significant human harms.

social hierarchy of the town. As Oliver-Smith's work shows, the changes that environmental disaster brings can be many and complicated, recasting how societies are organized.

VULNERABILITY AND RESILIENCE

Anthropologists now work alongside geographers, geologists, sociologists, biophysical scientists, and others to predict, study, and respond to disasters. Today, much disaster research is dedicated to predicting who is most vulnerable to disasters (**Figure 16.3**). **Vulnerability** refers to a person's or society's potential to suffer loss or harm—and their ability to anticipate, cope with, and recover from disasters or other environmental challenges.

Early disaster research focused on vulnerability mapping to determine the physical proximity of people and communities to natural hazards. This helps us predict where disasters are most likely to strike human settlements and valuable infrastructure, such as residences or railroads. This kind of vulnerability analysis is still important, but today much vulnerability research is dedicated to understanding how the economic, social, cultural, and political positions of people and communities shape disaster vulnerability.

vulnerability A person's or society's potential to be harmed by or recover from an environmental stressor or disaster. Vulnerability is determined by cultural, economic, political, and other key social structures.

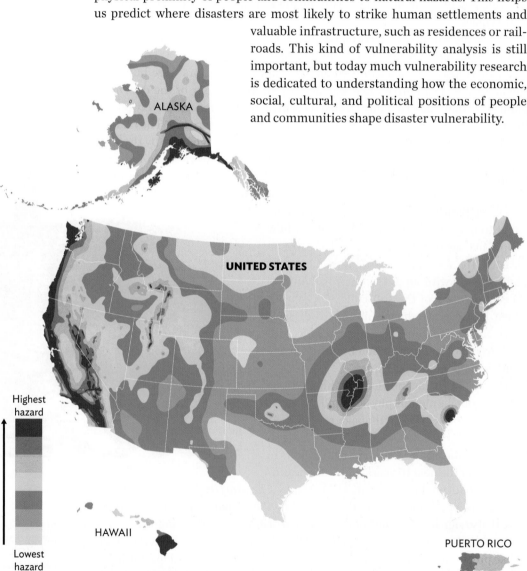

Highest hazard

Lowest hazard

FIGURE 16.3

The U.S. Geological Survey produces national maps showing the physical location of hazards such as earthquakes. An example of a simple national-level hazard map is shown. While such efforts display physical hazards, disasters are created and amplified by social and economic vulnerabilities and map differently as a result.

(a)

(b)

FIGURE 16.4

(a) Over 20,000 people live in proximity to the lava flows and 200,000 live under the ash clouds from the Tungurahua volcano in Ecuador. **(b)** Residents of the village of Manzano work on the village meeting house below Tungurahua.

For example, Tungurahua in Ecuador is an active volcano, and communities have farmed around it for centuries (**Figure 16.4**). Environmental anthropologist A. J. Faas studies different ways to understand personal and societal vulnerability to the volcano's periodic eruptions. Living closer to or further from the volcano is just one limited way of considering who is at greatest risk. Vulnerability is more fully assessed by examining who has the resources to protect against such hazards. When the volcano erupted after a long period of dormancy, both farmers and tourism workers were vulnerable but in different ways. Businesses and local officials dependent on the tourism industry (for example, around the volcanic hot springs) resisted evacuation because they couldn't afford the lost income. Farmers, in contrast, were vulnerable because they lacked transportation and road access to physically evacuate. After the government built new farming settlements several miles farther out from the volcano, the relocated farmers found they couldn't grow enough food to support themselves. Faas describes how some farmers would return to the mountain to farm during the day, even as the ash harmed them, their animals, and their crops.

Risk, Faas argues, is ultimately a culturally constructed idea that is deeply woven into shared understandings of what is valuable and what must be protected. In this case, farmers and tourism workers placed a higher value on their livelihoods than on their health and safety. These values differed from the ones expressed in government policy, and such value conflicts are part of what make risk assessment and disaster prevention so complex and difficult.

The flip side of vulnerability is *resilience*. A concept borrowed from ecology, resilience refers to the capacity of a person or society to cope with, adapt to, or recover from a shock. While resilience is mostly understood to be positive, sometimes resilient systems can stubbornly revert to old, harmful states (e.g., high inequality) even after efforts to reform them. For the communities in Ecuador that Faas was tracking, over time they developed new ways to think about how they related to the volcano. They started working as communities to coexist with the volcano, finding new ways to minimize the hazards. Community

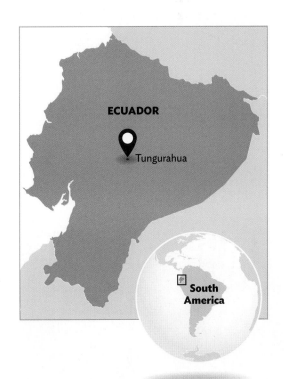

resilience A person's or society's potential to cope, adapt, restore, or recover after a shock or stressor (like a disaster).

FIGURE 16.5

Disaster anthropologist Anaís Roque (second from the left) presents research findings from her work in Puerto Rico as part of her community-based participatory research design.

members are now part of networks of watchers who can identify early warning signs, while others work together to find ways to remove toxic ash from soils so crops can survive.

A team led by Puerto Rican disaster anthropologist Anaís Roque has similarly been studying how social connections created resiliency after the devastation of Hurricane María in Puerto Rico (**Figure 16.5**). Roque interviewed community leaders and community members in two rural towns that were widely recognized for their rapid post-hurricane mobilization. Her goal was to determine what made these communities able to respond more effectively than others.

To deal with the damage of the hurricane, both communities relied not only on the government but also on social capital, the ability to activate networks of people inside and outside the community to help when needed. Right after the hurricane, residents mobilized their relationships to collect tools—ranging from machetes to bulldozers—and clear the streets and ensure access from outside (**Figure 16.6**). Later, they worked with organizations to raise donations for large water purifiers, battery systems for solar panels, and other essentials.

Much anthropological research has shown that cooperation for sharing labor and resources is often galvanized just after disasters. But one key issue with social capital is that people need to have it before the disaster in order to deploy it afterward. People living in poverty or who are otherwise already marginalized tend to have less access to social capital to raise funds, aid, and political help. This makes it harder to respond when faced with recovering from disaster.

ADAPTING TO DISASTERS: ARCHAEOLOGICAL INSIGHTS

Faas's ethnographic work in Ecuador pointed to farming and tourism as two different livelihoods that motivated some small communities to stay close to a dangerous volcano. But if natural hazards such as coastal hurricanes and active volcanoes are so dangerous and harmful, why don't societies avoid them altogether? Many hazard-prone areas offer access to valuable resources, such as fertile land for agriculture or coastal fish, beaches sought by tourists, and other economic opportunities. Archaeological research provides a perspective on how communities over time can develop in ways that help balance the long-term risks and benefits of proximity to natural hazards.

FIGURE 16.6

After Hurricane María in 2017, an important aspect of initial coping in devastated Puerto Rican communities was their ability to draw on existing social connections. Here neighbors are working together to evacuate people using diggers.

FIGURE 16.7

Excavation of a 10th-century Viking farming settlement at Auðkúla, Iceland, is pictured.

Icelandic Volcanoes

In Iceland, there are 30 active volcano systems. The first permanent settlements were built by Vikings from Scandinavia about 1,000 years ago, and volcanic eruptions have occurred regularly for as long as people have been living there. For example, the most fatal volcanic eruption in Iceland's history occurred in 1783 and 1784 when the Laki fissure erupted. Almost a quarter of Iceland's population died, mostly from the poisonous gas and ash emitted from the eruption.

Archaeologists who have studied the long-term human occupation of Iceland have proposed that living with volcanoes has shaped Icelandic society over time in two main ways (**Figure 16.7**). One is the settlement patterns of humans across landscapes. Globally, people are often attracted to the rich and fertile farmland that the ash creates near volcanoes. Yet archaeologists have found that people in Iceland avoided living right next to volcanically active areas. Living in settlements farther away from the volcanos kept Icelanders safer from the risk of volcanic disasters. Archaeologists mapping the farmsteads and settlements in Iceland, and comparing it to geologic evidence of lava flows, have shown that few settlements were destroyed during volcano eruptions.

A second way Icelandic society responded to volcano hazards was through adapting their farming practices. Icelanders began farming grains, such as wheat and other cereals, but—unlike Viking settlements elsewhere—never came to heavily rely on them. Instead, Icelanders focused on raising sheep and cattle. This was also supplemented with fishing in the rivers and ocean, hunting, and gathering eggs and shellfish. Archaeologists argue that Icelandic societies developed this flexible subsistence approach to allow them to change their strategies quickly in the face of natural hazards. For example, if there was an eruption that interfered with their ability to care for their cattle and sheep, they could switch over to fishing instead. Sheep and cows can also be moved from

FIGURE 16.8

A farmer (left) and a rescue worker (right) in Iceland collect sheep during a nearby volcanic eruption in 2011 to move them to safer ground away from toxic ash.

under an ash cloud, whereas crops cannot (**Figure 16.8**). Because Icelanders were not tied to farming crops, they were able to adjust to periodic eruptions.

However, comparing the archaeological history of Viking communities in Iceland with those in Scandinavia that did not face constant volcanic hazards suggests the Icelandic strategy was not without some costs. Until the 1800s, Iceland was a relatively poor country within Europe. If Icelandic society had developed a wider variety of traditional agricultural products, the country may have been wealthier as a result. This case illuminates that organizing societies to manage environmental hazards usually entails significant sustainability trade-offs.

sustainability trade-off A balance of the costs and benefits of different resource management strategies designed to maximize long-term environmental, economic, or societal well-being.

Caribbean Hurricanes

Today, people in the Caribbean often cope initially with incoming coastal hurricanes by evacuating or hunkering down. But people lived in the region for more than 7,000 years before European arrival, and they had developed strategies to deal with such unpredictable and potentially devastating weather events. The islands of Cuba, like much of the Caribbean region, experience frequent hurricanes, resulting in flooding and wind damage. Archaeological evidence shows how people there used varied cultural and social adaptations to manage their ongoing threats. These included (1) living far from coastlines and rivers; (2) building homes with durable hardwood stilts but easily replaced upper materials, such as thatched roofs; and (3) relying on long-distance trade networks to redistribute hurricane risks regionally. On the basis of material remains of life in this Caribbean society before colonization, archaeologists conclude that hurricane risks can be managed via settlement patterns, home construction, and subsistence.

Drought in the Desert

Prolonged drought is a hazard in the arid regions of the world, where water supplies are limited and can make farming to support permanent settlements risky. For example, in the region now known as the southwestern United States, starting around 400 CE, there was a farming society archaeologists describe as the Hohokam archaeological culture. Archaeologists have studied the clay that ceramic vessels were made of, as well as the designs on the pottery found at Hohokam archaeological sites. They have concluded that Hohokam communities, like the Cuban communities discussed above, formed an incredibly dense

(a) **(b)**

FIGURE 16.9

(a) One imagining of Hohokam farming, using canal systems to move water and irrigate land, is depicted. **(b)** The central Arizona canal system can still be seen today, used to move water for irrigation around the same valley.

network of exchange, with frequent travel, migration, and trade, that initially allowed the settlements to thrive.

The southwestern United States is extremely arid, but rivers of water flow into it from the melting snow in the Rocky Mountains. Fed by the Salt and Gila Rivers, hundreds of miles of Hohokam-constructed canals enabled them to use these rivers to farm the desert, growing crops including maize, beans, squash, and cotton (**Figure 16.9a**). The Hohokam canal system grew to become the largest irrigation system in North America; much later, the canals were lined with concrete and are still used to move water all over the city of Phoenix (**Figure 16.9b**). With the success of this massive irrigation system, the Hohokam settlement grew.

Sole reliance on such large-scale irrigation systems to support a large community can solve water supply problems, but it creates other problems. Over time, floods deteriorated the actual canal infrastructure, and salt buildup was a perennial problem. The arrival of more people in the thriving settlement meant more food needed to be grown, and the poor desert soil quality was eventually completely depleted. A major drought began around 1300 CE that included many years of unpredictable rain. Bioarchaeologists have identified increased evidence of disease, undernutrition, and vitamin deficiencies in human remains from this period.

Archaeologists refer to these types of long-term scenarios as *path dependency*. When communities solve environmental challenges in one single way (such as the Hohokam canals), it can make it harder to change and adapt later if the climate changes.

Ultimately, people living at Hohokam archaeological sites responded to their increasing troubles in several ways. Some shifted to methods of farming crops that were less reliant on the massive irrigation system and used more wild desert foods. Others migrated away. By the time the Spanish arrived in what is now Arizona, the inhabitants of Hohokam sites had mostly dispersed to smaller, more far-flung settlements. The former irrigated farming sites were largely abandoned after about 1400 CE. However, it would be incorrect to talk about the Hohokam "collapse" or to say that the Hohokam "disappeared." The O'odham, an Indigenous group whose members live in Arizona today, are connected to them as descendant communities and refer to their O'odham ancestors, many of whom lived during the time period of the Hohokam archaeological culture, as Huhugam.

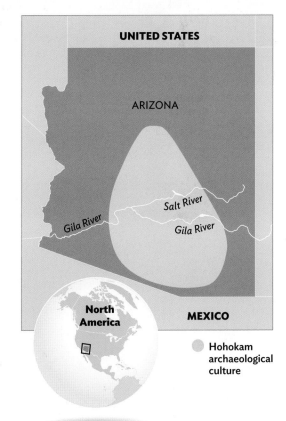

path dependency The tendency to "get stuck" on a trajectory, in which a community becomes overly dependent on certain kinds of technology, settlement patterns, exchange systems, and social organizations, which then creates community-wide vulnerabilities.

DISASTER CAPITALISM: PROFITEERING AND WORLD-BUILDING AFTER ENVIRONMENTAL CRISES

Archaeological studies, such as those of the Hohokam, have taught us that responses to environmental disasters aren't just limited to adapt or collapse. Studies of contemporary societies show how major disruptions can also create opportunities for economic changes. Disaster capitalism, for example, describes the experience in which disasters create opportunities that rapidly shift societies into new forms of privatization, profit-driven decision-making, and market-based management. Such shifts are, most often, to the benefit of those who already possess the most power and wealth. For example, governments can displace marginalized populations from desirable land, or the financial benefits of rebuilding can enrich private corporations.

A massive earthquake hit Haiti in 2010. In the aftermath, the United States proposed a disaster relief and reconstruction package that was contingent on Haiti opening further to U.S. investors and trade. Cultural anthropologist Mark Schuller led a team studying camps for displaced persons in Haiti after the earthquake, identifying how the influx of humanitarian aid impacted those it was intended to help. Almost all decisions were made by foreign workers in nongovernmental organizations (NGOs), who lacked experience in Haiti and understanding of Haitian people. The NGOs competed against each other. The resulting lack of coordination led to major missteps and waste in the efforts to rebuild housing, education, and services (**Figure 16.10**).

One of the worst decisions by the NGOs was their support of evicting displaced people from tent camps. Displaced people were then forced to relocate into the sprawling informal settlements around the capital, where services such as adequate clean water or health care were absent and violence was common. The resulting long-term humanitarian disaster then became the pretext for unpopular economic reforms, such as the privatization of telecommunications, prospecting for mining, and new industrial development—all of which benefited foreign financiers.

Anthropological studies of disaster responses suggest that disaster capitalism tends to have two phases: profiteering and world-ordering. In the shorter,

disaster capitalism Experience in which disaster recovery is used as an opportunity for some to profit by empowering capitalist interests and disempowering marginalized communities.

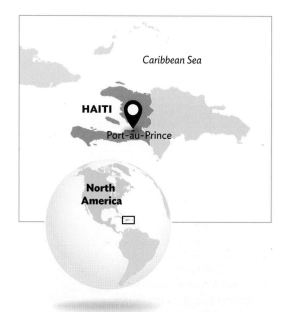

FIGURE 16.10

Informal communities that received people displaced by the earthquake now struggle with additional hazards, such as waterborne illnesses, that have resulted from a large influx of new people moving into already inadequately serviced neighborhoods. Here, a worker from a nongovernmental organization sprays chlorine on water taps in Port-au-Prince, Haiti, in 2010, during efforts to improve water quality in the wake of the earthquake.

earlier profiteering phase, private companies and nongovernmental agencies win governmental contracts to provide disaster relief, making a large profit with little competition or supervision. In the later and longer world-ordering phase, governments fund private companies to build for-profit infrastructure that is designed to permanently replace public services. Disaster capitalism is an important phenomenon to understand, as it is expected to increasingly drive economic shifts as climate change increases the frequency and intensity of natural disasters globally.

SECTION 16.2

ENVIRONMENTAL INJUSTICE

Environmental harms can build slowly and quietly over time, accumulating in such a way that the effects become normalized or taken for granted. The way these effects are felt by different people or groups tends to reflect power structures in how communities are organized. In the United States, for example, Black people are 75% more likely than others to live near hazardous waste facilities. Across a large range of environmental risks—reaching far beyond toxic waste—scholars find that people who are members of minoritized racial/ethnic groups or who live in low-income communities are at much higher risk.

The applied scholarly field of environmental justice was born in the United States in 1987, as part of the broader movement for racial justice. Led by Black civil rights activists, the environmental justice movement has fought for political reforms and public education to address environmental injustices. The public's growing realization that environmental racism is a major driver of health disparities led to protests opposing the location of toxic industries in minoritized communities. At the same time, a field of scholarly research grew to study how and why environmental injustices map onto socioeconomic inequalities. This branch of anthropological research has always been highly action-oriented.

environmental justice Equality for all people and communities in the protections conferred by environmental policies and the vulnerabilities to environmental health risks.

environmental injustice Disproportionate exposure of minoritized racial/ethnic, Indigenous, and low-income communities to higher levels of environmental risk (industrial development, pollution, toxic dumping, etc.) compared to other parts of society.

ENVIRONMENTAL JUSTICE IN THE CITY

Melissa Checker is an environmental anthropologist who is dedicated to using her research as a tool for advancing justice for communities in the United States. Her ethnography *Polluted Promises* traces the origins of environmental justice activism in the predominantly Black Hyde Park neighborhood of Augusta, Georgia, in the southeastern United States. Hyde Park residents live with the legacy of slavery and then sharecropping—an exploitative labor arrangement in which former slaves were often forced into abusive tenant farming. At the time of her study, some 70% of Hyde Park residents were living below the poverty line. Families had worked tirelessly and across generations to liberate themselves from peonage (being bound in service because of debt) and to buy their own land and homes. Most families had grown carefully kept gardens, with bountiful vegetables including okra, greens, and sweet potatoes. Yards contained plum and pecan trees. Beyond providing hearty and healthy foods, these gardens symbolized racial progress, self-sufficiency, and pride for Black families.

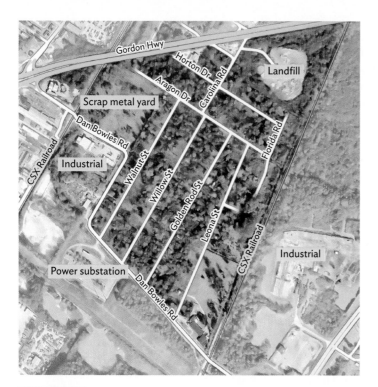

FIGURE 16.11

A scrap metal yard, which contained rusty drums of mercury by the mid-1980s, was located immediately beside the Hyde Park neighborhood, in Augusta, Georgia, until it was closed in 1998. It was one of the many industries that slowly poisoned the Hyde Park neighborhood, reflecting racist planning decisions to locate commercial activities with greatest risk around a community that was 98% minority residents.

However, by the 1990s, children in vibrant, verdant Hyde Park began to suffer from mysterious illnesses. Louvenia, a mother of three, was alarmed when her elementary-aged daughter fainted at school and developed enlarged lymph nodes. Soon her younger son developed unexplained high fevers and weight loss, dropping half his body weight. Ultimately, he was diagnosed and treated for T-cell lymphoma, which the doctor said was caused by toxic chemicals. A few years later, Louvenia's youngest daughter developed asthma, severe allergies, and developmental delays. Louvenia came to believe that her family's illnesses might be connected to the pecans they gathered and ate from their backyard tree. Across Hyde Park, people began to notice something was wrong with the gardens they had once celebrated. Plants withered and rotted on the vine.

Officials from the local university tested the soil and found high levels of chromium and arsenic. Tests also revealed that the groundwater was contaminated. Nearby industrial development was polluting the land, water, and air (**Figure 16.11**). University and public health officials gave conflicting guidance about whether garden harvests were safe to eat, a common experience in communities enduring the legacies of environmental injustices. The Hyde Park and Aragon Park Improvement Committee, founded by residents in the 1960s to advance civil rights, helped advocate. Their initial efforts for city assistance and recognition, like those in so many disadvantaged neighborhoods, were frustrating and fruitless.

Checker joined their fight in the late 1990s as an activist anthropologist. She volunteered with community activists—writing grants, doing cleanups, teaching children, building a website, and getting into local politics (**Figure 16.12**). After many frustrations and failures, Hyde Park activists won a U.S. Environmental Protection Agency Brownfields grant to clean up and redevelop land

FIGURE 16.12

Filmmaker Michelle Hansen and crew work with the residents of Hyde Park to expand and spread knowledge of the long history of environmental racism that Melissa Checker's research helped reveal.

Some Terms Used for Change-Oriented Modes of Anthropology

Applied anthropology is an umbrella term that encompasses a range of approaches anthropologists use, from working with government and business to engaging in activism to address social problems.

Today, the Society for Applied Anthropology (SfAA) is the flagship organization advancing this approach and has heavily supported work like Barbara Rose Johnston's advocacy for legal settlements to be paid to victims of environmental harms (discussed in the next section).

Activist anthropology refers to collaborative research that is conducted between anthropologists and activists engaged in political struggles to improve social conditions.

Ugandan anthropologist Stella Nyanzi, who was sentenced to 18 months in prison, uses a decolonial form of activism called "radical rudeness" to fight for gender and sexual equity in postcolonial contexts.

applied anthropology
The use of anthropological research and expertise in the solution of real-world challenges.

activist anthropology
Collaborative research and action in partnership with communities, usually those with less power or otherwise marginalized, to challenge the political status quo.

Activist anthropologist Stella Nyanzi celebrates with supporters after release from prison; she was jailed for cyberharassment after sharing her "offensive and vulgar" poem on Facebook as a means to critique the president of Uganda.

Radical anthropology describes approaches that identify, critique, and fight exploitation and oppression. Such approaches are often aligned with opposition to social structures that the activists see as oppressive, including racism, colonialism, capitalism, sexism, heterosexism, and binary gender. An important part of radical anthropology is imagining and working toward more just and equitable futures.

Brian Burke's research on bartering markets as an alternative to extractivist capitalism (see Chapter 9) is an example of radical anthropology.

Engaged anthropology refers to approaches that seek to bring about social change through public education, social critique, support, and collaboration with agents of social change.

An example of engaged anthropology is Setha Low's work with the U.S. National Park Service and the City of New York to raise awareness of racialized and gendered disparities in residents' access to public parks.

radical anthropology
Working toward more just and equitable futures by identifying, critiquing, and fighting exploitation through opposing social structures seen as oppressive.

engaged anthropology
Bringing about social change through public education, social critique, support, and collaboration with agents of social change.

with hazardous contaminants. A permit for an unwanted recycling plant, which would be a pollution risk, was revoked, and the mayor promised that no more unwanted industries would be located in Hyde Park. To address the environmental injustices they study, anthropologists including Checker have experimented with a range of remedies, including raising awareness, volunteering with local communities, and joining the fight.

ENVIRONMENTAL JUSTICE IN MICRONESIA

The field of applied anthropology offers a range of ways anthropologists work to solve environmental crises and injustices. Applied anthropologist Barbara Rose Johnston investigated the environmental injustice that resulted from U.S. nuclear detonations at the Pacific Proving Grounds on the Marshall Islands in Micronesia. The U.S. military detonated 43 atomic bombs there between 1946 and 1958 on the tiny, beautiful Marshallese atolls of Enewetok and Bikini, after removing all the Indigenous residents (**Figure 16.13**).

Johnston and her collaborators documented how the communities on nearby unevacuated Rongelap Atoll were exposed to the fallout of nuclear bombs—without their knowledge or consent. When the extent of the fallout became clearer, these communities were evacuated by the U.S. military to their secure base on another Marshallese island, Kwajalein Atoll. There, they became subjects in classified government research on the effects of the radiation exposure.

Decades later, Johnston worked to inform the Marshall Islands Nuclear Claims Tribunal's deliberations on how to compensate the victims, many of whom struggled not only with displacement but also with high rates of thyroid tumors, miscarriages, and other health harms from radiation. Johnston led efforts to develop a consequential damage assessment methodology for establishing compensation for environmental harms suffered by victims of nuclear and industrial disaster. It is designed to center, in legal fights, the

MARSHALL ISLANDS

ENEWETOK   BIKINI

RONGELAP

KWAJALEIN

Oceania

FIGURE 16.13

The residents of Bikini Atoll were removed from their ancestral home in 1946 by the U.S. government prior to test explosions of nuclear bombs.

value that Indigenous people put on local ecologies and livelihoods—such valuation is not constrained by the narrow conceptions of ownership found in Western law.

Johnston has since assisted many other social movements and victims' legal battles related to nuclear fallout, dams, and other environmental harms. An inspiration to the generations of anthropologists who followed in her footsteps, Johnston's model of applied anthropology continues to be influential.

INDIGENOUS ENVIRONMENTAL JUSTICE

The origins of the environmental justice movement are in civil rights activism addressing the legacy of slavery and ongoing racism in the United States. An important insight is that the legacies of *settler colonialism* and ongoing anti-Indigenous violence create similar dynamics of environmental injustice globally. Recent scholarship highlights the forms of ecological violence that are common to settler colonialism. These include the physical displacement of Indigenous peoples, the intentional destruction of systems of relations and caretaking between human and nonhuman ancestors (for example, animals, waters), the importation of nonlocal crops and species to colonized lands, and exploitative and harmful land uses.

The Akwesasne Mohawk Nation straddles the St. Lawrence River on both sides of what is now the U.S.–Canada border, an area of rich wildlife. In the 1950s, St. Lawrence Seaway construction began to spur industrial growth in the state of New York, adjacent to Akwesasne lands and waters (**Figure 16.14**). This included building hydroelectric dams and permitting large industrial corporations, such as car manufacturer General Motors, to operate in direct violation of treaties.

The decisions reflected U.S. government officials' prioritizing of economic development over Indigenous rights and voices, with the process taking advantage of Indigenous groups' lack of political power to fight back at the time. Over the next half century, the government's decisions led to enormous contamination by hazardous chemicals such as polychlorinated biphenyls (PCBs), which are used in aluminum production, upstream from Akwesasne lands and waters.

settler colonialism A system of domination and violence in which people are removed from their land through displacement or genocide; often involves the annihilation of the prior inhabitants' language, culture, livelihoods, and ways of life.

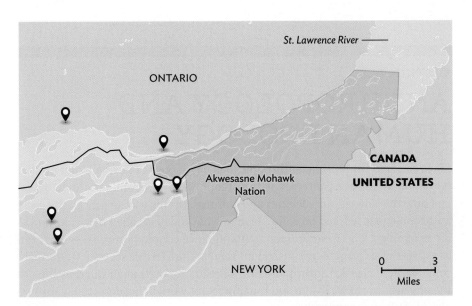

FIGURE 16.14

Locations of the industrial manufacturing plants upstream of Akwesasne Mohawk Nation lands on the U.S.–Canada border are shown.

(a)

(b)

FIGURE 16.15

Mohawk people are shown **(a)** fishing Akwesasne waters for sturgeon and **(b)** cutting wood to smoke it. The waters they have long used to catch traditional foods remain heavily polluted by industrial waste from factories near their lands on the St. Lawrence Seaway, contaminating traditional foods.

ecology The relationship of living organisms to each other and their physical environment.

environmental anthropology A subfield of anthropology that examines the relationship between humans and the world around them.

Adequate cleanup was never done, although three Superfund sites were established by the U.S. Environmental Protection Agency and some of the polluting companies were later fined for illegal use of PCBs. An Akwesasne midwife, who observed high rates of cancer, miscarriages, and birth defects, led her community to launch a major community-based research and environmental justice project to address this. In 1987, the Mohawk Nation formed the Akwesasne Task Force on the Environment (ATFE), as a community-based grassroots activist organization to address this environmental injustice. ATFE built a partnership with professional researchers to understand and fight the harm of exposures to industrial pollutants. As part of the ATFE, biological anthropologists Lawrence Schell and Julia Ravenscroft have been partnering with the task force for many years to identify the long-term impacts of the industrial exposures on Akwesasne. While all those living near the factories have been exposed to PCBs, the Akwesasne had additional risks because the chemical exposure was amplified when eating their traditional foods that are hunted and fished in the area (**Figure 16.15**).

The research partnership has revealed the serious and long-term health effects of those exposures. The very high rates of PCB exposure increase body weight, cholesterol, and triglycerides in Akwesasne adults, all known risk factors for cardiovascular disease. They also inhibit women's reproduction, leading to greater likelihood of infertility. Young Akwesasne men show significantly lower testosterone levels as well. Exposures also appear to be worsening cancer, autoimmune disease, thyroid function, and long-term memory.

One of the key problems is that PCBs persist in the body for a very long time. It may be possible to properly remove the contaminants from the area, but they will continue to harm Akwesasne health. The contaminants and the harm they do to bodies can also be passed on to the next generation through contamination of breast milk.

The Akwesasne Task Force on the Environment continues to work with anthropologists and other researchers to advance human and environmental health and justice among those most impacted by toxic contaminants along the St. Lawrence River. The ATFE is a powerful model for community-based participatory research. It shows the importance of Indigenous leadership and community ecological knowledge to the goals of advancing environmental justice.

SECTION 16.3

ANTHROPOLOGY AND HUMAN ECOLOGY

Since the field's inception, anthropologists have sought to explain and predict how human societies interact within biophysical environments (*ecologies*) and how this shapes our societies and cultures. In this way, nearly all the early anthropologists worked on some form of what today is called *environmental anthropology*. These earlier ideas still influence contemporary research, even as aspects were refuted by subsequent scholarship. In this section, we connect some earlier "classic" anthropological scholarship on human relationships to the physical world we live in and the important work being done today, and we also identify new approaches.

FROM MATERIALISM TO MATERIALITY

Early anthropologists sought to understand how and why cultures change over time. Many of their initial theories were based in conceptions of the physical environment as a driver of cultural variation (**Figure 16.16**). Coining the term cultural ecology, environmental anthropologists tried to understand how the evolution of a "culture core"—that is, cultural features most related to subsistence practices in particular—explained each society's specific configuration of religion, politics, and so on.

Anthropological theorist Marvin Harris took this idea further, arguing the resource base of different ecologies was the ultimate driver of culture. In his controversial 1974 book *Cows, Pigs, Wars, and Witches*, for example, Harris argued that the patriarchy is simply a population control strategy. Women, Harris pointed out, are more biologically valuable than men—they alone can birth and nurse infants, while also being able to do all the jobs men do. If anyone were to predict gender* sex discrimination because of these facts, Harris argued, men would be the victims. However, Harris observed, most societies cross-culturally developed patriarchal structures that highly valued male warriors and warfare. This, he concluded, is a sophisticated cultural strategy to limit overpopulation by undervaluing women and killing off men (**Figure 16.17**).

This approach, called cultural materialism, provided foundational insights for the emerging field of environmental anthropology. But Harris's work was criticized for ignoring historical factors that shaped cultural evolution, such as the role of colonialism in propagating patriarchy. Many

FIGURE 16.16

Cultural anthropologist Julian Steward (1902–1972) is often credited with launching the field of environmental anthropology in the 1940s. Steward used archaeological and ethnographic methods to theorize human–environment relationships through time. Here (right) he is shown in British Columbia, Canada, in 1940 while doing fieldwork, talking with an informant (possibly Nak'azdli Chief Louis-Billy Prince).

cultural ecology The idea that human cultures, including belief systems, are patterned by and arranged around the limits of the physical environments that communities rely on (including other living species).

cultural materialism A theory of culture change that hypothesizes a society's resource base (for example, economics or demography) can explain its cultural characteristics.

SUPERSTRUCTURE

- Art, music, dance, literature, advertising
- Rituals, mythology, religion, ideology, science
- Sports, games, hobbies

STRUCTURE

Domestic economy
- Family structure
- Domestic division of labor
- Socialization, enculturation, education
- Age and sex roles
- Domestic discipline, hierarchy sanctions

Political economy
- Political organization, factions, clubs, associations, corporations
- Division of labor, taxation and tribute
- Class, caste, urban/rural hierarchies
- Discipline, police/military control
- War

INFRASTRUCTURE

Mode of production
- Subsistence technology
- Techno-environmental relationships
- Ecosystems
- Work patterns

Mode of reproduction
- Demography
- Mating patterns
- Fertility and mortality
- Nurturance of infants
- Contraceptives, abortion, technologies, infanticide

FIGURE 16.17

Cultural materialists, led by Marvin Harris and influenced by the ideas of Karl Marx, theorized that infrastructure is the ultimate driver of changes in the superstructure. Put simply, the basic theory was that resources, technologies, and reproduction shape cultures, not the reverse.

environmental determinism A general theory that human societies, cultures, and behaviors are the result of their physical conditions (such as climate and geography).

materiality In anthropology, an approach to studying humans that views their thoughts and behaviors as entangled with physical objects and environments. This work often acknowledges the foundational nature of environment, infrastructure, and politics in shaping human lives.

human behavioral ecology The application of principles from human evolution, such as natural selection, to predict why certain patterns of human cultural behaviors might be favored under different environmental conditions; also called evolutionary ecology or cultural evolution.

anthropologists ultimately concluded his ideas were taken too far, and the backlash against cultural materialism was substantial. Today, most cultural anthropologists are careful to avoid undue emphasis on environmental determinism—the idea that the environment *determines* culture and psychology—in their scholarship.

A newer approach called materiality explores how humans are entangled together in relationships with the material world. Recent scholarship in materiality is seen in studies of infrastructure, focusing especially on inequitable water, electrical, or transportation systems.

HUMAN BEHAVIORAL ECOLOGY

Materialist approaches, along with the parallel developments in studies of human evolution, also informed new anthropological subfields such as human behavioral ecology. Such research, accelerating in the 1980s, examined human behavior through the assumption that cultural patterns may have evolved over time to manage environmental challenges. An example is seen in the work of biological anthropologist Lee Cronk, based on his research among the Mukogodo, a group of East African herders who historically have relied very heavily on their domesticated animals. Cronk identified an unusual demographic pattern: Many more girl children survive than boy children.

The Mukogodo had little prestige among Maa-speaking pastoralists, due to their poverty and ethnic marginalization. For example, Mukogodo men had fewer sheep, goats, and cattle than other groups in this region of Kenya. While there was no evidence at all of infanticide or child abuse, Cronk observed that girl children were breastfed longer, taken to the medical clinic more often when sick, and otherwise cared for more carefully than boys (**Figure 16.18**). Daughters received cattle and other animals as bridewealth when they married, which increased the wealth and health of all their family members. Sons, by contrast, had to give animals away.

Such research is used to suggest that there are special cases in which parents providing preferential care for daughters proves adaptive over time. Hence this behavior persists and spreads, especially when resources (such as livestock) are scarce. In such ways, human behavioral ecologists including Cronk study how evolutionary dynamics—such as natural selection and evolutionary fitness—might explain certain cultural configurations of marriage, reciprocity, and other culturally situated patterns of behavior.

FIGURE 16.18

Detailed anthropological observations have revealed that Mukogodo daughters (as shown here milking a goat) receive better parental treatment, on average, than their brothers. This is associated with better growth in childhood but also with improved prospects for marriage and having children later.

(a)

(b)

(c)

FIGURE 16.19

In 1963, Roy Rappaport photographically documented the complex sequence of events of the *kaiko* or pig festival in one Tsembaga community. **(a)** Here two of Rappaport's informants (cultural guides), Pambo and Rrate, are singeing bristles from a pig that has just been killed. **(b)** Tsembaga men build a ritual fence, through which allies will be fed roasted pork and will watch the community dancing. **(c)** These allies will then breach the ritual fence to join in the festival.

HUMAN ECOLOGIES AS SYSTEMS

New understandings of evolutionary processes in science (such as the modern synthesis discussed in Chapter 3) and ecology led to new research questions. In the 1970s, for example, environmental anthropologists began testing new ideas from ecology about how environments acted as systems.

Roy "Skip" Rappaport's *Pigs for the Ancestors* (1968) drew on his extended doctoral dissertation fieldwork in highland Papua New Guinea earlier that decade. His study examined the role of ritual pig slaughter in highland Tsembaga Maring communities (**Figure 16.19**). Pigs in these communities were central to rituals, social connections, and warfare, and accordingly they were carefully fed, bred, and cared for. Rappaport described how—as the size of the local pig population reached that of the human population—a *kaiko* festival was held. In a special grove, prayers would be made over the pigs in honor of ancestors. The tons of meat and fat from the slaughter that followed were then offered as gifts to allies for joining previous fights against enemy clans. The overall pattern of ritual warfare and feasting was, to Rappaport, evidence that human culture (in this case, pigs and the pig-related rituals) could manage a complicated and delicate balance between limited land, too little food, and too many people. Rappaport's goal was to show how human–environment interactions functioned to maintain a balance locally, through feedback cycles. Criticisms of his work were many: No society is a truly closed system, human religions are too complex to be solely a resource-management tool, and history is crucial to any analysis of contemporary societies. But his broader use of a systems approach to human–environment relations nonetheless remains influential.

A systems approach—in which highly cooperative, creative, social humans are intimately and complexly connected to their environment—can be further extended to encompass longer time frames and help predict what will come next. Significant changes to ecosystems through the evolved human capacity for niche construction began in the Holocene epoch, the geological period in which humans began to domesticate animals and then build and inhabit urban centers (Chapters 8). But the rate and irreversibility of human-influenced environmental change stemming from niche construction have accelerated massively since the 1950s. This is sometimes referred to as the Anthropocene epoch: the time in which human activity has a primary influence on how the whole planet functions.

systems theory The study of how human and nonhuman relationships interact to produce outcomes that are greater than the actions of any one actor, including through feedback loops.

Dispelling Myths and Misconceptions about Humans and the Environment

The urgency of contemporary environmental problems has led to many well-meaning experiments with conservation—as well as some troublesome misconceptions about human/environment relations. Anthropological research, drawing on deep history and cross-cultural evidence, can bring new insights to these efforts. Here are three examples of times anthropologists have been instrumental in dispelling myths and misconceptions about environmentalism.

The "Tragedy of the Commons" Myth

Ecologist Garrett Hardin proposed "the tragedy of the commons" in 1968. This is the incorrect idea that humans cannot collectively self-manage common-pool resources in a sustainable way. Hardin's ideas remain today a popular justification for privatizing commonly managed natural resources, one of the key tenets underlying dispossession in support of capitalist development.

Anthropological myth-busting: Ecological anthropologist Bonnie McCay helped disprove Hardin's proposition using comparative commons research. Working with commercial fisherfolk and other marine experts on commercial tidal oyster harvesting and deeper sea lobster fishing, McCay showed how fishing communities developed their own systems for how to fairly divide up territories and sustainably manage limited marine resources.

Ecological anthropologist Bonnie McCay (right) studies how humans who use marine resources and fishers organize to harvest them, and she is active in developing science-based policies around fisheries and marine conservation.

The "Population Bomb" Myth

Biologist Paul Ehrlich argued in 1968 that a worldwide "population bomb" was about to go off. Overpopulation, it was thought at the time, would drive starvation, mass death, and political collapse. Globally, overpopulation was believed to be the most threatening driver of ecological collapse. This became a popular justification for sterilization, coercive abortions, and birth-control campaigns that disproportionally impacted low-income countries and communities of color.

Anthropological myth-busting: Anthropologists' studies have proven how farmers can manage the need for more food with innovative farming techniques. For example, Robert McC. Netting, in his 1993 book *Smallholders, Householders,* explained how small-scale farming innovations in Africa, Asia, and elsewhere produce more crops, with less energy and ecological degradation, than industrial farms.

The Ecologically "Noble Savage" Myth

The offensively termed "noble savage" concept is attributed to 18th-century philosopher Jean-Jacques Rousseau. It is the simplistic and romanticized idea that all Indigenous peoples previously lived in total harmony with nature. Such mischaracterizations have long been used as the basis of popular justifications to dehumanize, conquer, and exploit Indigenous people.

Anthropological myth-busting: Indigenous people—like all humans—have complex relationships with the environment, as many archaeological studies have shown. Before colonization, some Indigenous societies engaged in unsustainable environmental practices, such as overhunting megafauna or farming in arid regions. And colonization forced many Indigenous peoples into no-win ecologies, rife with environmental injustices. And yet, Indigenous societies have contributed unique and valuable ecological knowledge: identifying life-saving botanical medicines and developing sustainable practices for subsistence farming. And Standing Rock Sioux scholar Vine Deloria Jr. (1933–2005) has documented that very little Indigenous ecological knowledge is in print. We must work harder to make this knowledge available in appropriate ways. Ultimately, stereotypes and slurs are never true. They merely hinder efforts to advance justice and scientific knowledge.

A systems approach recognizes that evolved human biology, social and technological change, and our ecosystems will continue to be inescapably locked together in the future as in the past. So human niche construction is not only creating the conditions under which we will continue to evolve but also concurrently shifting the evolutionary trajectories of many other species across the planet in ways that have dramatic consequences for us too.

For example, as humans continue to remove forests and grow more physical infrastructure, some species become extinct while others thrive. Bats and rats do comparatively well in human-disturbed areas, and they also are hosts of the types of zoonotic viruses that can seed new pandemics (Chapters 15). A systems approach then highlights that preventing future global pandemics can be served by global efforts to protect biodiverse habitats.

SECTION 6.4

BETTER WAYS FORWARD

In the prior sections we encountered many examples of anthropologists who do applied and activist environmental research, united by a goal to help build just and sustainable societies and better human futures. Much of the environmental anthropology research we discussed draws on Indigenous people's knowledge and experiences. In many cases, Indigenous languages and knowledges were interpreted through the interviews and analyses of non-Indigenous anthropologists. This process necessarily removes the ideas and language from their original context and meaning, losing much in translation. Increasingly, Indigenous anthropologists are speaking against these practices, leading the field to realize that the resulting research can be intellectually and ethically problematic.

Here we identify important ways anthropologists are working toward better futures, especially by centering—not just describing—Indigenous worldviews. Led by Indigenous scholars, many anthropologists now believe such research illuminates important, understudied pathways to sustainability.

PRIORITIZING RELATIONALITY

Red River Métis/Otipemisiwak anthropologist Zoe Todd is one of the most impactful theoreticians of Indigenous environmental anthropology today. Her research examines relations between humans and fish in Canada, with a particular focus on how ideas about this relate to Canada's history of settler colonialism.

A pivotal moment came early in her career, when she attended an honorary lecture by a famous scholar who was not from an Indigenous community. The scholar presented to the audience an Inuit concept described as *Sila* (roughly meaning "climate") but never referenced or credited the Indigenous scholars who developed this idea. Furthermore, Todd noted, the climate concept as described in this lecture lacked the richness of Inuit thought—which connected *Sila* to the climate, to the breath of all beings, to an animating life force, and to knowledge and wisdom (**Figure 16.20**). This erasure of foundational Indigenous thinkers from anthropological scholarship, she explains, is why too much environmental anthropology merely represents a watered-down, poor imitation of the powerful Indigenous ideas that anthropologists are meant to be theorizing. Todd's powerful critique helps create new pathways forward for anthropology that will make research more meaningful, impactful, and ethical because it clarifies that anthropological studies are weakened by a lack of true partnership with Indigenous experts.

FIGURE 16.20

Anthropological research in the Canadian Arctic, such as Zoe Todd's research, demonstrates why Indigenous knowledge that treats fish as kin matters—especially as we confront the effects of climate change, as shown here where polar bear tracks traverse melting Arctic ice— because together we share the same ecological fate.

FIGURE 16.21

Pipestone National Monument in Minnesota, in the northern United States, is one historical source of the redstone that is connected to Dakota and Lakota peoples and used for ceremonial pipes. Shown here is pipe carver Billy Bryan.

As importantly, research must be *led* by Indigenous scholars. Todd's approach to studying fish applies relational principles that place fish in a reciprocal, intimate kinship relationship with humans. Anthropologists conducting multispecies ethnography apply field methods such as participant observation to the study of human relations with nonhumans. These studies often use cultural and political economic analysis to understand how humans and nonhuman beings interact. Such research has examined human interactions with dogs, mushrooms, and the microbiome, to name just a few examples. Sisseton-Wahpeton Oyate (Lakota/Dakota) anthropologist Kim TallBear has argued that non-Indigenous perspectives on human connections to other species have been too narrow and limiting because they have focused exclusively on living beings or organisms. Indigenous worldviews look further, to all forces of nature: not only plants and animals but also wind, fire, water, lightning, and so forth.

To illustrate this broader perspective, TallBear explores the example of redstone. Found in prairie quarries of southeastern Minnesota, United States, redstone is used to make ceremonial pipes sacred to Lakota/Dakota people (**Figure 16.21**). A Dakota story tells the history of a flood and how the pooling blood of the people who died colored the stones red. Redstone is now a vibrant and vital part of Lakota/Dakota life, as it plays a central role in connecting people to one another and to the land through prayer and social relations. Drawing a connection to DNA studies of blood and to U.S. Pipestone National Monument, which memorializes the redstone quarries, TallBear explains that non-Indigenous efforts to understand Lakota/Dakota kinship, blood, and redstone have deanimated and deadened these vital ties. This is the cost, she explains, of excluding Indigenous scholars and thinking from efforts to theorize human–environment relations.

Some non-Indigenous anthropologists have accordingly reconsidered the narrower conception of "multispecies" scholarship and begun, instead, to engage in relational approaches to understanding how humans relate to the worlds in which they live.

Diné (Navajo) scholar Melanie K. Yazzie extends theories of relationality to explain how denying the sovereignty of Indigenous nations prevented Diné people from fulfilling human obligations to care for and respect water. In a relational approach, activists defend life. Diné land and water defenders, Yazzie explains, opposed economic development, resource extraction, and colonialism. Diné activists connected this extractivism to a politics of death that brought pollution, racism, and suffering—the opposite of relationality. The commitment to caretaking and defending, she explains, is at the core of

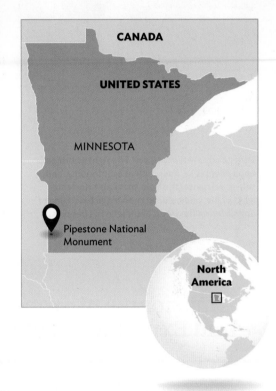

relational approach Based in Indigenous thinking, a central recognition that humans and nonhumans interact in ways that shape each other and their worlds.

extractivism Exploitation of environmental resources at scale to sell globally, with the capitalist goal of making profits.

UNITED STATES

UTAH

Navajo Nation

ARIZONA   NEW MEXICO

MEXICO

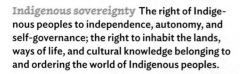

North America

FIGURE 16.22

"Water Is Life" is a call to action that embraces the idea of relationality, such as seen here in Navajo Nation in the southwestern United States.

Indigenous sovereignty The right of Indigenous peoples to independence, autonomy, and self-governance; the right to inhabit the lands, ways of life, and cultural knowledge belonging to and ordering the world of Indigenous peoples.

the activists' refrain "Water Is Life" (**Figure 16.22**). Yazzie and other Indigenous scholars underscore the importance of Indigenous sovereignty—that is, self-governance and self-determination—for reestablishing good relations between humans, water, and the environment more broadly.

As the Indigenous environmental anthropologists whose work is discussed in this section have explained, much is lost when non-Indigenous anthropologists go it alone and reinterpret Indigenous knowledge. Many non-Indigenous anthropologists have come to agree, as is reflected in a 2021 statement from the American Anthropological Association (see box).

American Anthropological Association Apology for Abuse and Exploitation of Indigenous Communities (2021)

"Since its inception, the history of American anthropology has been intertwined with a record of **extractive research** conducted on Indigenous communities. Anthropologists have often assigned themselves the status of 'expert' over the cultural narratives and social histories of the first cultures of the Americas. As 'experts' many anthropologists have neither respected Indigenous knowledge systems and community contributions nor addressed the intended and unintended impacts of anthropological research on those communities. Some anthropologists now acknowledge the harms that have been caused by researchers in the discipline, but it remains the case that anthropology must explicitly address the need to change its ways. . . . The first step for healing starts with a formal and honest acknowledgment and apology of anthropology's exploitation of Indigenous communities, identities, and cultures, and the harms caused by our extractive research. Only then can Indigenous communities begin interrogating the power dynamics and impacts of American anthropology's hegemonic narrative."

extractive research Scholarly investigations that ask questions driven by the interests of the researchers with no community consultation; that remove data and use them to advance discussions outside the community; and that are unconcerned with or disengaged from the needs and well-being of the community.

The emerging consensus is that anthropology needs to redress past and ongoing harms against Indigenous communities. As part of this, anthropologists increasingly recognize that Indigenous scholars are leading new thinking about the environment. This work prioritizes Indigenous self-determination and sovereignty, and it offers new ways to look at the complex challenges of postindustrial capitalism and climate change we face today. These ideas can help us all live more sustainably in the future.

SUSTAINABILITY TRANSITIONS

Relational approaches emphasize an appreciation of deep human intimacy with the world around us and all the other entities that share it with us. But we are rapidly degrading our planetary resources, upending our climates irrevocably, struggling to develop equitable societies, and grappling with zoonotic pandemics. Our societies continue to be defined by entrenched inequalities that make all of these challenges harder and more harmful. But if we step back further and look at the entire human story, there is also reason for optimism. Humans have a remarkable, evolved capacity to manage even extremely complicated challenges via innovation and cooperation. Early in our history we devised new technologies, such as cooking, that expanded what was possible. We found ways—however imperfect—to organize, govern, and find community in increasingly complex societies. And now we have the means to cooperate and make meaning virtually, expanding our communities beyond physical boundaries. We have the capability to use our wisdom, power, and creativity to solve big problems.

Environmental anthropologists, like most environmental scholars, largely believe that our current practices are unsustainable, because (1) they are too extractive and raw materials are running out; (2) they generate too much contamination, trash, and waste; and (3) they contribute to global warming in ways that are expected to destroy existing ecosystems, making parts of the world soon uninhabitable for humans.

The downstream effects on society—from climate migration, to political crises, to death on a massive scale—are projected to be catastrophic. One indicator of the expected impact is that, in the United States, some of the best modeling on climate change is done by the military: Warfare, famine, and political unrest are among the scenarios considered possible. Action to slow, stop, or reverse climate change has been far too little and far too late. Climate-change denialism is one means that both people and organizations can deploy to cope with avoiding recognition of and responsibility for the enormity of the problem. The lack of recognition of materiality—of how the material and human worlds are intimately connected and cocreated—is part of what permits this. As with any disaster, the impacts are expected to continue to fall hardest on the most vulnerable: citizens of island and developing nations, Indigenous and minoritized people, and low-income and socially marginalized groups.

Many environmental anthropologists now argue these conditions must and will bring about a **sustainability transition**. This transition requires new political ecological arrangements that are less extractive, wasteful, and carbon-emitting. In facing down such realities, the most important contribution anthropologists can make is to help plan possible pathways to a better future.

sustainability transition A major or radical transformation in current social–ecological systems to enable long-term environmental, social, and economic well-being.

PLURIVERSE TRANSITIONS

Arturo Escobar, a Colombian American cultural anthropologist proposes three main ways humanity can make sustainability transitions in his book *Pluriversal Politics*. The first way is to focus on improving people's conditions. These

pluriverse transition A vision of the world in which many realities—multiple ways of knowing and being—can coexist, be nurtured, and create positive new ways of living with other humans and nonhumans.

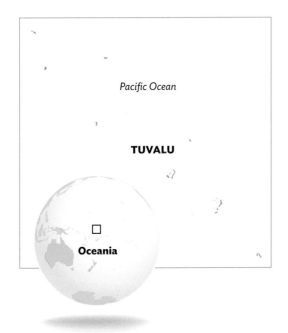

FIGURE 16.23

Here the Minister for Justice, Communication, and Foreign Affairs of Tuvalu, in the central Pacific, appeals to the gathered leaders in Glasgow during the 2021 United Nations Climate Change Conference, standing in the ocean to make a point about the harms of other nations' energy policies on his country's future.

initiatives do not in themselves challenge structural inequalities, but they help create livable futures at an individual level. The second way is to fight for social and environmental justice, human rights, and sustainability. These initiatives will make concrete progress toward a better world. The third approach, and Escobar's main focus, is a *pluriversal* world—one that embraces radical relationality and **pluriverse transitions**. This last option is the one that Escobar really believes is our best hope for the future. But, he argues, it requires us to imagine differently what is real and possible.

To move toward pluriverse transitions, Indigenous leadership in environmental governance and activism is increasingly leading the way. The 2016 #NoDAPL protests of the Dakota Access Pipeline (DAPL) at the Standing Rock Indian Reservation, for example, galvanized a generation of Indigenous and non-Indigenous environmental activists to work together to oppose fossil fuels and water contamination. In 2021, Deb Haaland, member of the Laguna Pueblo, was appointed the first Indigenous U.S. Secretary of the Interior, with power over natural resources, public lands, and wildlife. These events indicate a shift toward Indigenous visions of environmental justice and governance in wider U.S. society. They also help illustrate how an Indigenous approach to sustainability in settler-controlled nations urges us to make profound changes to society.

It is also important to note that many Indigenous-led countries are grappling with consequences of global climate change that greatly threaten their future. People in the small island nations of the central Pacific, including Tuvalu, recognize fully that sea-level rise is happening and that it threatens directly their cultural and economic futures. It is a challenge Tuvaluans cannot fix themselves. Those in the large, industrialized nations that have most contributed to the emissions accelerating climate change have the most power to enact the policy changes needed, yet they are often unwilling to do so. In places such as Tuvalu, it is hard for citizens to understand that groups in other countries believe that climate change is exaggerated or even a hoax (**Figure 16.23**).

Anishinaabe scholar Deborah McGregor, a leading theorist of the relational approach, provides an important example of what pluriverse transitions can look like. Drawing on teachings from grandmothers and other elders, McGregor explains that *zaagidowin* (love) is central to water justice in Anishinaabek society. She argues that water management systems that lacked love—and related values of responsibility, respect, mutuality, reciprocity, and generosity—produced the many water injustices, scarcities, and contaminations we suffer today. The Mother Earth Water Walks were initiated in 2003 to restore loving relationships between the Great Lakes and Anishinaabe people, especially women. Led by Anishinaabe grandmother Josephine Mandamin, the Water Walks were designed to reestablish loving and reciprocal relationships in ways that could restore sustainability for future Anishinaabek generations (**Figure 16.24**). The Water Walks movement ultimately grew and extended into other nations beyond the Anishinaabek. As McGregor explains, past and future generations connect through water because we all interact with the same waters across time and space. These interactions, she explains, also connect us through experiences of water's destruction and its capacity to heal. This is one of the reasons that it is so important to mend human–water relations. McGregor underscores that using love, generosity, responsibility, and mutual respect as the foundation of human–water relations has enabled the Anishinaabek to survive for millennia. On the basis of this evidence, she argues, the Anishinaabek approach is an important one for building a sustainable future.

As this example illustrates, the pluriverse of Indigenous approaches offers different transition strategies from mainstream U.S. environmentalism. A pluriverse approach to sustainable transitions acknowledges and celebrates these differences. Rather than starting with an idea of nature as separate from humanity, Indigenous approaches tend to emphasize reciprocity. This concept of give-and-take between humans and nonhumans highlights the need for relations that are caring and accountable. This includes new ways of engaging with Indigenous communities—prioritizing interactions that are trusting, respectful, and consensual. This approach acknowledges that humans and nonhumans are mutually linked, and one cannot thrive without the other.

A CONCLUDING THOUGHT: MANY WAYS FORWARD

Hilda Lloréns, whose work opened our chapter, advances a vision of sustainability drawn from Black Puerto Rican women's social and environmental justice work. She advocates for external structural changes that will be needed to make any part of our planet habitable for the long term: governmental practices and policies that build equitable societies and redress historical injustice. This is unlikely to happen without extensive and impactful political activism. But her work also underscores the ingenuity and dedication of Taíno and slave-descendant communities in Puerto Rico, in creating livable worlds during the cataclysms of colonization and slavery. She suggests that this same spirit of resistance and renewal can be brought to today's and tomorrow's environmental and climate-induced catastrophes.

However, Lloréns cautions, livelihoods based on Black ecological knowledge cannot continue if the ecosystem itself is destroyed. Defending coastal ecologies also means engaging in activism and, in some cases, refusing unjust governmental programs, such as corrupt disaster aid or polluting industrial development. In place of formal bureaucratic forms of support, many Black Puerto Rican families depend on far-flung kin and **fictive kin** networks. Puerto Ricans' mobility and willingness to migrate to the mainland United States have created a powerful **diaspora** that has generated its own aid in times of need. But Lloréns proposes that this doesn't mean that people should be coerced into constantly harnessing their own resilience. Black Puerto Ricans and other vulnerable communities cannot be expected to forever carry the weight of a system designed to unduly harm them. Rather, pathways toward social and environmental justice must protect ecosystems and rethink life-affirming efforts to create good, sustainable lives for all.

The gravity of environmental challenges facing humanity is clear, from the heart of Puerto Rico to the rest of the globe. Lloréns imagines a better world, based on her careful consideration of the perspectives of one community by one scholar, using one specific set of methods to capture those. Anthropology—as shown in this textbook—works with a massive array of communities, past and present, using many different tools, from different starting positions based on anthropologists' own backgrounds, and accordingly engaging myriad ways to conceptualize what is observed. A diverse anthropology is then able to unite many people and cultures in imagining and devising better ways to address our most pressing human problems. Anthropology is the broadest of all disciplines, uniquely positioned to provide a basic road map for humanity—where we've been, where we can go, and how to get there. We trust in you, our reader, to help take us forward.

FIGURE 16.24

In 2013, Water Walker Sharon Day, Ojibwe (one of the three Anishinaabe nations), carried a ceremonial copper pail of water and Eagle Staff from the headwaters of the Mississippi River to the Gulf of Mexico to raise awareness of pollution in the river.

fictive kin Family relationships that are not based on blood or adoption or marriage. Examples include godparents and found family.

diaspora Refers to people who are living away from their ancestral homeland.

Anthropology, Environment, and Better Futures

This chapter considers the relationship between humans and their environments, with an emphasis on the social structural dynamics that create environmental degradation and how they can be addressed today and in the future.

KEY TERM
> ecological knowledge

16.1 | The Anthropology of Disaster

Explain how social structures interact with hazards to create disasters.

- Human social structures determine the extent to which natural hazards become disasters.

KEY TERMS
> disaster
> disaster anthropology
> disaster capitalism
> natural hazard
> path dependency
> resilience
> sustainability trade-off
> vulnerability

16.2 | Environmental Injustice

Describe the bases of environmental inequalities and the roles anthropologists play in advancing environmental justice.

- Environmental contamination and injustices tend to disproportionately harm minoritized, Indigenous, and low-income people. Anthropologists advance different forms of research to work in solidarity with communities to fight these harms.

KEY TERMS
> activist anthropology
> applied anthropology
> engaged anthropology
> environmental injustice
> environmental justice
> radical anthropology
> settler colonialism

16.3 | Anthropology and Human Ecology

Analyze how anthropology's approaches to studying human–environment interactions emerged and changed.

- Anthropologists have developed and refined many different theories to understand humans as part of the different ecologies we inhabit, including other species.

16.4 | Better Ways Forward

Evaluate how anthropologists support the role of Indigenous societies and knowledge in providing pathways for sustainability.

- Past research with Indigenous communities has been harmful and extractive, but the anthropological community now recognizes that Indigenous knowledge enriches research and suggests new ways to protect our planet.

GLOSSARY

A

abolition A movement that aims to end oppressive anti-Black institutions (especially prisons and policing) and build alternatives such as community-based justice systems. (Ch. 14)

abolition scholarship A range of theories, concepts, and methods designed to advance racial liberation; it is aligned with decolonizing approaches (see Chapter 2). (Ch. 14)

absolute dating A method of determining the age of an artifact or stratum in calendar years. See also *relative dating*. (Ch. 2)

Acheulean A style of tools, dating from around 1.8 million years ago, that includes two-sided handaxes and more functional diversity of tools, created from further working of removed flake edges to shape them. See also *Mousterian* and *Oldowan*. (Ch. 6)

activist anthropology Collaborative research and action in partnership with communities, usually those with less power or otherwise marginalized, to challenge the political status quo. (Ch. 1, 16)

adaptation Any phenotypic variation that improves an organism's fit within a given environment. (Ch. 3)

adaptive radiation A time period during which the number of species increases rapidly, resulting in much greater diversity. (Ch. 4)

advantageous mutation A change in DNA that improves function of the encoded protein. See also *deleterious mutation* and *neutral mutation*. (Ch. 3)

affinal kin Family relationships created through marriage, such as in-laws, or by adoption. See also *consanguineal kin* and *fictive kin*. (Ch. 12)

agency The capacity for individual power, such as acting independently and making free choices. (Ch. 12)

aggression Behavior motivated by a desire to harm another. (Ch. 10)

allele An alternative form of a gene that codes for slightly different proteins that affect the development and expression of a trait (such as blood type or eye color). (Ch. 3)

Allen's rule The tendency for populations living in warmer climates to have slimmer bodies with longer arms and legs than those living in colder climates. (Ch. 3)

alloparents Individuals, who are not the biological parents, that care for offspring. (Ch. 4)

ambilocality A system in which married couples can live near or with either the wife's or the husband's family. (Ch. 12)

amino acid One of 20 compounds that, in different combinations, make up proteins. (Ch. 3)

ancestry A sense of one's biological heritage, often related to a particular group, place, or region. (Ch. 3)

ancient DNA Genetic material (often fragmentary) from humans who lived long ago, extracted from their skeletal or fossil remains. (Ch. 2)

androgyny The quality of being neither specifically feminine nor specifically masculine. (Ch. 11)

angiosperm radiation hypothesis The theory of primate origins based on visual collecting of fruits as the primary adaptation. (Ch. 4)

anthropology The study of what it means to be human, in the broadest possible sense. (Ch. 1)

anti-racism Overturning entrenched structural sources of race-based inequality. (Ch. 14)

applied anthropology The use of anthropological research and expertise in the solution of real-world challenges. (Ch. 1, 16)

arbitrariness The absence of any connection between the sound or form of a word or sign and its referent. (Ch. 7)

arboreal Primarily living in the trees, which could include on the trunks of trees or on the branches. See also *terrestrial*. (Ch. 4)

archaeological context Placement and association of archaeological materials in the archaeological record. (Ch. 2)

archaeological feature A sign of past human activity that loses its form when moved, such as a posthole, hearth, or wall. (Ch. 2)

archaeological record The physical evidence of past human activity, including artifacts, built structures, and animal and plant remains. (Ch. 1)

archaeological survey Systematically mapping a study region and identifying archaeological sites and features, either from the ground or from the air. (Ch. 2)

archaeology The study of material remains as evidence of past human behavior and societies. (Ch. 1)

articulator Any one of several vocal apparatuses used to create and modify sounds. (Ch. 7)

artifact An object that people made or used in the past. (Ch. 1)

ascribed Describes a status that is not earned but rather given, such as inherited wealth. (Ch. 8)

assimilation model A theory of modern human emergence in which modern human anatomy evolved in Africa and spread to other continents by migration of modern humans to other regions, largely replacing but also interbreeding with existing hominins living in Europe and Asia and assimilating their DNA into the modern human gene pool. See also *multiregional model*. (Ch. 6)

assortative mating Nonrandom selection of reproductive partners based on similarity (e.g., speaking the same language or having the same color hair). (Ch. 12)

australopithecine A member of the successful genus of hominins *Australopithecus*, which first evolved around 4.2 million years ago during the Pliocene epoch (5.3–2.6 million years ago) in multiple locations throughout Africa, now extinct. (Ch. 5)

autoethnography Ethnographic research that fully centers on personal experience and reflection as a means to investigate and understand societies. (Ch. 12)

avoidance speech A particular, restricted speech form in some languages that must be used in the presence of, in reference to, or in conversation with certain relatives. (Ch. 12)

B

bacterium (plural, bacteria) A one-celled microorganism, with cell walls but without a nucleus, that can cause disease. (Ch. 13)

balanced reciprocity Giving with the expectation that payback has an equivalent value. (Ch. 9)

band A society of hunter-gatherers in which relationships are generally egalitarian. (Ch. 8)

barter Direct exchange of goods or services, without the use of money. (Ch. 9)

base A building block that pairs in a specific complementary way to form a double-stranded DNA molecule. Cytosine (C) always pairs with guanine (G), and adenine (A) always pairs with thymine (T). (Ch. 3)

Bergmann's rule The tendency for populations living in warmer climates to have more linear, less compact bodies than those living in colder climates. (Ch. 3)

bilophodont molar Describes a back tooth with cusps that form two clear rows, characteristic of cercopithecoids. (Ch. 4)

binary Divided into two oppositional groups. (Ch. 11)

binocular stereoscopic vision The result of two eyes working together to perceive depth and register an object as three-dimensional. (Ch. 4)

binomial nomenclature The "two name" system of naming and defining a species within a genus, for example, *Homo sapiens*. (Ch. 4)

biological anthropology The study of human evolution and biological variation. (Ch. 1)

biological diversity Variability in the biology of a population or species, in all its dimensions. (Ch. 1)

biological species concept A set of organisms that can potentially mate with each other to produce offspring, which can then themselves reproduce. (Ch. 5)

biomedicalization Redefining conditions as benefiting from or needing biomedical treatment. (Ch. 15)

biomedicine The use of concepts from biology, biochemistry, and physiology to understand health and disease in the human body; sometimes called "medicine." (Ch. 15)

biopower Institutional power over bodies that is used to control or subjugate. (Ch. 15)

bipedal Habitually walking on two legs. See also *quadrupedal*. (Ch. 4)

Black Languages English words with Africanized semantic, syntactic, morphological, phonological, and rhetorical patterns originating in the experiences of U.S. slave descendants. (Ch. 7)

body projects Attempts to construct and maintain a desired social identity through attention to the form of the body, especially its surface. (Ch. 9)

bounded rationality The idea that humans make economic choices that are rational given a specific social context, cultural values, and access to information. (Ch. 9)

brachiation Swinging underneath from branch to branch. (Ch. 4)

brideservice Work provided by a prospective or new husband to a bride's family, prior to or early in marriage, cementing his relationship with them. (Ch. 12)

bridewealth Payment to a woman's family to confirm a marriage (also called bride-price) and often to compensate for the loss of a daughter. (Ch. 12)

burial The intentional action of placing the body of a dead individual in a grave or pit. (Ch. 13)

C

canine blunting The wearing of the canines on their tips, dulling the pointed cusp; characteristic of human dentition. (Ch. 5)

capitalism A market-based economy in which private ownership enables some people to profit from others' labor and consumption. (Ch. 9)

catarrhine A monkey or ape of Africa or Asia (and in the past throughout Europe as well). See also *platyrrhine*. (Ch. 4)

cell The smallest basic structural unit of an organism, carrying out specialized functions. (Ch. 3)

cemetery A planned area set aside specifically for the in-ground burial of multiple individuals. (Ch. 13)

cercopithecoid A monkey of Africa or Asia (including langurs, macaques, colobus monkeys, and baboons); the most diverse family of living primates. (Ch. 4)

chattel slavery A form of slavery in which a person is legally transformed into a commodity: The person and all their children become private property and can be owned and sold. (Ch. 9)

chiefdom A hierarchical political unit with kin-based status divisions and composed of several communities with hereditary status. (Ch. 8)

chromosome The structure in the cell nucleus that carries and organizes genes. (Ch. 3)

circulating discourse An idea or belief that moves around communities (large and small) through language. (Ch. 7)

cisgender Having one's internal sense of gender identity align with one's assigned sex at birth. See also *transgender*. (Ch. 11)

citizen A person who has duties and is entitled to rights as a member of a political community. (Ch. 9)

clinal variation A continuous, gradual shift in gene frequencies between one region and the next. (Ch. 3)

clumping The assumption that things are in the same biological category (such as one species) unless there is convincing evidence that they should be divided. See also *splitting*. (Ch. 5)

coalitionary aggression When at least two individuals jointly direct aggression at one or more individuals from the same species. (Ch. 10)

code-switching Moving between two or more language varieties in the same stream of language. (Ch. 7)

codominant Describes alleles that equally influence phenotypic gene expression. See also *dominant* and *recessive*. (Ch. 3)

coevolution A process in which two or more species mutually shape each other's evolutionary trajectories. (Ch. 3)

cognate One of two or more words that have a shared origin. (Ch. 8)

colonialism A system of domination and exploitation, for settlement and other economic benefits, by exerting foreign rule over distant territories and the people in them. (Ch. 2)

coloniality Exploitative and ethnocentric social structures that were established during colonialism and are still in place today. (Ch. 10)

colorism Social advantage based on the proximity of skin color and other features to those defined by others as White. (Ch. 14)

commodification The process by which something that was previously unable to be sold becomes saleable. (Ch. 9)

common-pool resource A natural resource that is finite but difficult to exclude people from using, such as a forest, fishery, grazing pasture, or fresh water. (Ch. 9)

common-pool resource institution A governance arrangement in which a group of people communally owns clearly delineated resources (e.g., land, river water, forest) and collectively makes and enforces rules to protect and distribute these resources. (Ch. 9)

community-based participatory research (CBPR) A collaborative partnering with communities to ensure research is equitable, effective, and properly applied. (Ch. 2)

comparative approach Using data to compare features across societies or species, past or present, with the goal of identifying what is different and what is shared across them. In comparing contemporary human groups, this is sometimes termed cross-cultural research. (Ch. 1)

consanguineal kin Family relationships created through shared blood relationships. See also *affinal kin* and *fictive kin*. (Ch. 12)

constituent An individual piece of language that, in combination with others, makes up the grammar of the language. Subjects and verbs are constituents of every language. (Ch. 7)

consumer A person who buys and uses goods and services. (Ch. 9)

cooperation When members of a group work together for common or mutual benefit. (Ch. 4)

cooperative parenting A system in which children receive care from group members other than their biological parents (such as grandparents or siblings; also called *alloparents*), enhancing the children's well-being and survival. (Ch. 11)

core A piece of stone from which flakes are removed to produce a cutting edge. (Ch. 5)

cosmology A theory of the universe (world) as an ordered whole, including beliefs, knowledge, and interpretations about its origins. (Ch. 8, 9)

craft specialization The assignment of particular productive tasks to subsets of people in a community; these can include tasks that require skill, such as pottery production or weaving. (Ch. 8)

cranial trauma Injury to the head or skull. (Ch. 8)

cranial vault The rounded part of the skull that surrounds the brain. (Ch. 6)

crossing over Exchange of genes between homologous chromosomes during meiosis. (Ch. 3)

cultural anthropology The study of human cultural meanings and variation in social context. (Ch. 1)

cultural capital A set of beliefs and behaviors that can be mobilized to help people enhance their social or economic status. (Ch. 9)

cultural ecology The idea that human cultures, including belief systems, are patterned by and arranged around the limits of the physical environments that communities rely on (including other living species). (Ch. 16)

cultural materialism A theory of cultural change that hypothesizes a society's resource base (for example, economics or demography) can explain its cultural characteristics. (Ch. 16)

cultural relativism The assessment of other cultures in the context of those cultures' own values. (Ch. 1)

cultural theme A recurring symbol (word, image, or action) that defines a social group and reflects their worldview. (Ch. 2)

cultural transmission The process by which cultural elements (behaviors, beliefs, and so on) are shared with and taught to and learned by others. (Ch. 5)

culture Shared meanings, norms, and practices that together shape how people collectively think and act. (Ch. 1)

cumulative culture Traditions (such as tool use) that are built on and modified through time to expand and refine knowledge. (Ch. 5)

cusp A raised point on the crown of a tooth. (Ch. 4)

D

data sovereignty The right of a community to govern how data will be collected from their citizens, stored, protected, and used in research. (Ch. 2)

decanonization Redefining a field's classic texts to include works previously excluded due to the scholar's nationality, race, and/or gender. (Ch. 2)

decedent Term used by forensic anthropologists to refer to a deceased, or dead, individual. (Ch. 13)

decoding In language, the process of producing meaning from someone else's language. See also *encoding*. (Ch. 7)

decolonization The act of challenging and removing enduring power structures created through colonization. (Ch. 10)

decolonizing methodology Designing and conducting research activities that recognize, challenge, and redress the historical and ongoing harms to colonized people, including by researchers. (Ch. 2)

dehumanization The act or process of removing human qualities, traits, or dignity from a person or group of people; this makes the targeted people seem less human and less worthy of human rights. (Ch. 10)

deindustrialization Decline of the manufacturing sector and related social, cultural, and economic changes. (Ch. 9)

deleterious mutation A change in DNA that impairs function of the encoded protein. See also *advantageous mutation and neutral mutation*. (Ch. 3)

Denisovan A now-extinct species of humans that lived primarily in Asia between about 200,000 and 50,000 years ago. (Ch. 6)

derived trait An anatomical feature characteristic of the group in which it occurs that differentiates it from other, closely related groups. See also *primitive trait*. (Ch. 4)

descendant group People with direct and shared personal, spiritual, or ancestral connection to archaeological objects or human remains. (Ch. 1)

developmental adaptation A phenotype, resulting from developmental plasticity, that functions better under local environmental conditions, such as climatic or dietary stress. (Ch. 3)

developmental plasticity The capacity of the same genotype to produce distinct phenotypes as a response to the environmental conditions under which development occurs. (Ch. 3, 14)

diagnosis The process of labeling health conditions by interpreting physiological markers, behavioral patterns, or reported symptoms; implying cause; and suggesting treatments. (Ch. 15)

diarchy A society organized such that women and men generally share power. See also *matriarchy* and *patriarchy*. (Ch. 11)

diaspora Refers to people who are living away from their ancestral homeland. (Ch. 16)

diastema A gap in the tooth row to accommodate large canines when the mouth is closed. (Ch. 5)

disamenity An environmental hazard or other unwanted or unpleasant environmental feature that reduces quality of life for residents. (Ch. 14)

disaster When a natural hazard produces a calamitous impact on human life, health, economics, infrastructure, or society. (Ch. 16)

disaster anthropology A subfield of anthropology that examines the process that precedes, unfolds during, and follows a hazard (often a natural hazard) that creates significant human harms. (Ch. 16)

disaster capitalism Experience in which disaster recovery is used as an opportunity for some to profit by empowering capitalist interests and disempowering marginalized communities. (Ch. 16)

disease A physiological change in the body that impairs functioning that can be classified, detected, and targeted for treatment (usually by a specialist). See also *illness* and *sickness*. (Ch. 15)

diurnal Active during the day. See also *nocturnal*. (Ch. 4)

divergence The emergence of two or more species that shared one common ancestor. (Ch. 5)

DNA Self-replicating material that transmits genetic information in all organisms, including humans. (Ch. 3)

DNA methylation The chemical "locking" of sections of DNA, changing the way a gene codes proteins without changing the DNA itself. (Ch. 3)

DNA replication The process of DNA making copies of itself. (Ch. 3)

domestication The process of adapting plants and animals to be dependent on humans for reproduction and to be used as sources of food, wool and clothing, transport, or milk. (Ch. 8)

dominant Describes an allele that is preferentially expressed in phenotypes. See also *codominant* and *recessive*. (Ch. 3)

dowry Transfer of wealth from a bride's to a groom's family to confirm a marriage (and often to compensate for the cost of supporting their daughter). (Ch. 12)

E

ecofact Material in the archaeological record that was not directly modified by humans, such as plant or animal remains. (Ch. 2)

ecological knowledge Understanding of the environment and its resources derived from interactions with it and other people living in it. (Ch. 16)

ecology The relationship of living organisms to each other and their physical environment. (Ch. 16)

economic Refers to human production, circulation, and consumption of resources. (Ch. 9)

egalitarian A societal model in which access to resources and power is not controlled by some individuals or sectors of society; rather, involvement in decision-making and access to resources is evenly distributed, and social distinctions are based on age, gender, and individual qualities. (Ch. 8, 11)

elite A person with significantly greater power and access to and control of resources than others. (Ch. 8)

embodiment Incorporating and displaying in one's body the material and social worlds in which one lives. (Ch. 3, 11)

empathy The capacity to relate to the emotional state of others, including their pain and suffering. (Ch. 15)

encoding In language, the process of producing speech or signs that reflect what you are thinking about or desiring to express. See also *decoding*. (Ch. 7)

endemic Describes a disease maintained over time (usually in a specified geographic area). (Ch. 15)

endemic warfare Chronic state of low-intensity warfare between groups with little or no death and where the primary aim is not to control or destroy the enemy. (Ch. 10)

engaged anthropology Bringing about social change through public education, social critique, support, and collaboration with agents of social change. (Ch. 16)

endocast A fossilized model of the hollow space inside a skull, often preserving some details of brain anatomy. (Ch. 4, 5, 6)

endogamy A practice that encourages marriage to people inside your own group (also called inmarriage). See also *exogamy*. (Ch. 12)

energy balance The relationship between energy intake (through diet) and energy output (through workload or exercise). (Ch. 3)

environmental anthropology A subfield of anthropology that examines the relationship between humans and world around them. (Ch. 16)

environmental determinism A general theory that human societies, cultures, and behaviors are the result of their physical conditions (such as climate and geography). (Ch. 16)

environmental injustice Disproportionate exposure of minoritized racial/ethnic, Indigenous, and low-income communities to higher levels of environmental risk (industrial development, pollution, toxic dumping, etc.) compared to other parts of society. (Ch. 16)

environmental justice Equality for all people and communities in the protections conferred by environmental policies and the vulnerabilities to environmental health risks. (Ch. 16)

Eocene epoch A division of the geological timescale that lasted from 56 to 33.9 million years ago and is associated with the adaptive radiation of early primates, in particular the adapids and omomyids. (Ch. 4)

epidemiological transition A change through time in the primary diseases and causes of death within a population, linked to a major lifestyle transition. (Ch. 15)

epigenetic Refers to potentially heritable chemical modifications to genes that affect whether genes are switched on or off but do not alter the DNA sequence itself. (Ch. 3)

epigenome The full set of all epigenetic modifications to DNA as seen in a single cell. (Ch. 3)

essentialize To apply the belief of "natural" essential characteristics to culturally defined groups of people (such as on the basis of "race" but also other characteristics such as "sex"). (Ch. 14)

estrus Notable changes in female sexual attractivity (swellings, olfactory, and color changes that attract males), proceptivity (female initiation), and receptivity (willingness to mate) around the time most likely to result in conception. (Ch. 12)

ethics A guiding framework to protect individuals and communities from harm while maximizing the benefits of research. (Ch. 1)

ethnic group People who are identified by shared ancestry or heritage, language, and cultural traditions. (Ch. 8)

ethnoarchaeology. Using participant observation in contemporary groups to understand how archaeological sites could have been created. (Ch. 2)

ethnographic analogy Using evidence from contemporary societies to inform reconstructions of past societies. (Ch. 2)

ethnography A research approach dedicated to describing cultures, based on understanding cultural insiders' own knowledge and worldviews. (Ch. 1)

ethnomedical system The structures, practices, beliefs, and therapeutic techniques that together define a system for healing. Ethnomedical systems can include both lay and specialist knowledge and practices. (Ch. 15)

ethnomusicology The study of music in its social and cultural contexts. (Ch. 7)

ethnonym The name by which a group of people or ethnic group is known. (Ch. 14)

ethnoprimatology The study of human and nonhuman primate interactions in a systemic way, focusing on how they coexist. (Ch. 4)

eugenics A racist effort to improve the so-called "genetic quality" of human groups by encouraging those socially defined as "the best" to have more children and preventing others deemed "undesirable" from doing so. (Ch. 14)

evidentiality A piece of language that indicates how something is known. (Ch. 7)

evolution The scientific theory that explains the appearance of new species as the accumulation of genetic changes across generations. (Ch. 1)

evolutionary medicine The application of evolutionary principles to explain the basis of disease and develop recommendations for improved treatment. (Ch. 15)

excavation Systematic and scientific process of uncovering and recording an archaeological site. (Ch. 2)

exchange system A set of rules and norms that governs how materials, services, symbols, and ideas are transferred between people or groups. (Ch. 9)

exogamy A practice that encourages marriage to people outside your own group (also called outmarriage). See also *endogamy*. (Ch. 12)

extended evolutionary synthesis A revision and expansion of ideas about how evolution works to include mechanisms *beyond* genetic selection, mutation, genetic drift, and gene flow. See also *modern synthesis*. (Ch. 3)

extractive research Scholarly investigations that ask questions driven by the interests of the researchers with no community consultation; that remove data and use them to advance discussions outside the community; and that are unconcerned with or disengaged from the needs and well-being of the community. (Ch. 16)

extractivism Exploitation of environmental resources at scale to sell globally, with the capitalist goal of massive profits. (Ch. 16)

extrapair mating When members of a monogamous species mate outside their bonded pair. (Ch. 12)

F

femininity Along with *masculinity*, the collection of social roles and behaviors that are understood to be expressions of gender within a particular society or community. (Ch. 11)

fictive kin Family relationships that are not based on blood or adoption or marriage. Examples include godparents and found family. See also *affinal kin* and *consanguineal kin*. (Ch. 16)

field notes Detailed notes made during or immediately after participant observation, a primary source of ethnographic evidence. (Ch. 2)

fieldwork The varied processes of collecting new data outside the laboratory, office, or classroom. (Ch. 1)

fission–fusion society A form of primate social group with relatively unstable group membership in which different groups form and dissolve over time depending on circumstances such as food availability. (Ch. 4)

fitness The success of an organism in passing its genes to offspring. (Ch. 3)

flake A piece of stone removed from a core by striking it with a hammerstone. (Ch. 5)

folivore One whose diet is composed mainly of hard-to-digest leaves; examples are mostly monkeys and apes of Africa and Asia. (Ch. 4)

folklore Traditional stories, crafts, rituals, festivals, and so on passed down as local knowledge and practice. (Ch. 5)

food sharing The form of reciprocity most fundamental to the history and survival of our species (and most studied by anthropologists), in which food is given, shared, or exchanged. (Ch. 9)

food sovereignty The right of people to control how food is produced and to exercise this right to produce healthy and culturally valued foods. (Ch. 9)

foramen magnum The hole in the base of the skull that allows the spinal cord to attach to the brain. (Ch. 5)

forensic anthropology A subdiscipline of anthropology focused on the examination of human skeletal remains to assist in the detection of crimes and the identification of victims. (Ch. 13, 14)

formal economy Legally regulated economic activity, estimated to characterize about 40% of the world's employed population. See also *informal economy*. (Ch. 9)

fossil A remainder, trace, petrified form, or impression of a past organism that has been preserved in rock. (Ch. 1)

fossilization The formation of a stone copy of a bone or tooth by slow replacement of inorganic material by other minerals in the environment. (Ch. 4)

founder effect A change in gene frequency that occurs when a larger population divides into smaller separate groups, such as when settling new areas. (Ch. 3)

fraternal polyandrous marriage A system in which a woman marries two or more brothers (who are not her own siblings). (Ch. 12)

frugivore One whose diet is composed mainly of fruits, such as an orangutan. (Ch. 4)

funeral A ceremony honoring a deceased person, usually involving the disposal of their remains. (Ch. 13)

G

gamete A cell that carries genetic material intended for inheritance through reproduction (an ovum or sperm). (Ch. 3)

gender Social, cultural, and/or learned phenomena relating to femininity, masculinity, and gender diversity. (Ch. 11)

gender performance Repetition of socially sanctioned and recognized acts that create and cement gender identities for both self and others. (Ch. 11)

gender script Culturally shared gendered expectations, values, and practices within a society. (Ch. 11)

gender-based violence Serious physical, sexual, verbal, or emotional mistreatment directed at an individual because of gender norms and inequalities. This includes violence in response to perceived violations of the norms associated with assigned sex, gender presentation, or identity. (Ch. 11)

gendered division of labor A system in which gender norms influence the formal or informal work roles assigned to people, such as in household chores or paid employment. (Ch. 11)

gender*sex Whole people and identities; aspects of women, men, and gender/sex-diverse people that involve both gender *and* sex. (Ch. 11)

gene The basic unit of genetic inheritance, identified as a sequence of DNA bases. Some genes provide the instructions to make the proteins needed for human growth, functioning, and reproduction. (Ch. 3)

gene expression The process through which DNA codes for proteins that produce phenotypes. (Ch. 3)

gene flow Movement of genes between populations; it tends to make the populations more genetically similar to one another. (Ch. 3)

generalized Describes species that have not been shaped by evolution to perform one specific function very well but rather have anatomies that can do many things well. (Ch. 4)

generalized dentition Having teeth that can process a diversity of foods, rather than being specialized for processing one type of food. (Ch. 4)

generalized reciprocity Giving without any expectation of direct payback. (Ch. 9)

genetic Related to the basic biological materials of inheritance, which provide instructions for how organisms look and function. (Ch. 1)

genetic ancestry A shared biological history, as defined by genetic similarities. (Ch. 3)

genetic bottlenecking A sharp reduction in population size (from events such as epidemics or natural disasters), resulting in a dramatic change in gene frequencies between one generation and the next. (Ch. 3)

genetic drift Random changes in gene frequencies from one generation to the next. (Ch. 3)

genetic lineage The pattern of mutations in genetic code that connect an ancestor's genome to that of its descendants. (Ch. 6)

genetic mutation A permanent change in the DNA base-pair sequence of one or more genes, sometimes with consequences for how they code for the proteins that control body functions. (Ch. 3)

genocide Sustained and purposeful intent to destroy a group of people, in whole or in part, through killing and other acts of violent removal. (Ch. 10)

genotype The genetic makeup of an organism. See also *phenotype*. (Ch. 3)

globalization The increased economic, social, and political linkages between nations and peoples due to the rapid movement of people and exchange of ideas both within and across national boundaries. (Ch. 10)

governance The formal rules (such as laws) and informal social norms that manage and regulate how people interact within societies. (Ch. 8)

grammar The rules for how words, sentence parts, and sentences are organized to make meanings in a language. (Ch. 7)

grave goods Objects, often valuable, buried with deceased individuals. (Ch. 13)

grief Emotional pain caused by losing someone you care about. (Ch. 13)

grooming claw An anatomical feature of a single claw instead of a nail on one foot digit. (Ch. 4)

growth faltering When the normal growth of children slows or stops because of undernutrition, disease, or mistreatment. (Ch. 11)

gummivore One whose diet is composed mainly of tree sap and gums (usually also with insects); examples are some lemurs and marmosets. (Ch. 4)

H

habituation The process of accustoming animals to be around humans. (Ch. 4)

haft To add a handle or strap to a tool, allowing more precision and force in how it can be used. (Ch. 6)

hammerstone A stone used to strike a core in order to remove flakes. (Ch. 5)

handaxe A multipurpose bifacial stone tool, associated particularly with *Homo erectus*. (Ch. 6)

haplorhine One of a group of "dry-nosed" primates, variously terrestrial and arboreal; this group includes tarsiers, monkeys, apes, and humans. See also *strepsirrhine*. (Ch. 4)

health Well-being due to a relative absence of disease, illness signs, sickness, stigma, and suffering. (Ch. 15)

health disparity A difference in preventable disease, injury, or violence created through social disadvantage. (Ch. 3, 11, 14)

hegemony A process in which dominant groups consolidate consent to govern through shared norms, legitimating discourses, and historical narratives. (Ch. 8)

heteronormativity The assumption that heterosexual orientation and sexual activity are "normal," meaning other sexual configurations are considered abnormal or not considered at all. (Ch. 12)

heterozygous Describes alleles inherited from each parent that have different genetic sequences. See also *homozygous*. (Ch. 3)

hierarchical society A societal model in which people are ranked in grades, orders, or classes, with higher-ranked individuals gaining additional access to resources and power. (Ch. 8)

hierarchy A social arrangement among primates that is based in variations of power, with some individuals having dominance over others. (Ch. 4)

hind-limb dominated location A form of movement in which the body is propelled primarily through the power of the hind limbs. (Ch. 4)

historical trauma Cumulative, multigenerational trauma resulting from extreme physical or psychological violence (including oppression) targeting specific communities, including social decimation and cultural erasures. (Ch. 10)

Holocene epoch A division of the geological timescale that began about 12,000 years ago, after the last major glacial cooling of the planet, and has been associated (until very recently) with a relatively stable climate. (Ch. 8)

hominin A human, extinct human ancestor, or closely related species that is more closely related to modern humans than chimpanzees. (Ch. 1, 5)

hominoid A grouping of primates comprising great apes and lesser apes of Africa and Asia, including gorillas and gibbons, as well as humans. (Ch. 4)

Homo The genus to which humans belong, which first evolved 2.6 million years ago, defined by having a smaller face and teeth and larger brain than other hominins living at the time. (Ch. 5)

Homo sapiens The only remaining species of humans. (Ch. 1)

homologous Having the same purpose or function. For example, homologous chromosomes, inherited from both biological parents, have the same genes that perform the same function in the same places on both halves of the chromosome pair. (Ch. 3)

homozygous Describes alleles inherited from each parent that have the same genetic sequence. See also *heterozygous*. (Ch. 3)

honing chewing A behavior seen in living apes but not in humans, where the combination of a diastema and large canines creates a sharp edge on the canine that helps shred and cut tough plant food. (Ch. 5)

hormone A chemical created in the body that controls and regulates the activities of certain cells or organs. Estrogen (produced in ovaries) and testosterone (produced in testes) are two important hormones that play key roles in reproduction and contribute to differences in secondary sex characteristics that emerge as people mature biologically. (Ch. 11)

household The small group of people who pool basic resources to meet fundamental daily needs (such as sharing meals and shelter); often members are also closely related kin. (Ch. 9)

human behavioral ecology The application of principles from human evolution, such as natural selection, to predict why certain patterns of human cultural behaviors might be favored under different environmental conditions; also called evolutionary ecology or cultural evolution. (Ch. 16)

human–chimp last common ancestor (HC-LCA) The most recent ancestral species before humans diverged into a separate lineage from that of chimpanzees and bonobos. (Ch. 5)

human microbiome All the interacting microorganisms—including helpful, harmless, and harmful bacteria, fungi, and viruses—that live in and on our bodies. (Ch. 15)

humanism An approach focusing on personal experiences, choices, expression, and meanings. (Ch. 1)

hunter-gatherer People who predominantly obtain their food through their knowledge of wild plants and animals, instead of reliance on domesticated plants and animals; sometimes called foragers. (Ch. 2, 8)

hypothesis A proposed explanation for a condition or phenomenon that guides scientific investigation. (Ch. 1)

icon A signifier that resembles the object or concept being signified. See also *index* and *symbol*. (Ch. 7)

ideology A set of beliefs and practices attached to a group of people that collectively shape a specific worldview (sometimes referred to as a "belief system"). (Ch. 14)

idiom of distress An indirect and culturally specific way of expressing hurt, worry, suffering, conflict, or loss through the language of illness. (Ch. 15)

illness The subjective experience of suffering, anxiety, fear, and pain, eliciting and needing comfort and care. See also *disease* and *sickness*. (Ch. 15)

imperialism The efforts of a government to control another country or peoples using military, economic, or political power. (Ch. 10)

incest taboo A cultural rule (usually strictly enforced) that prohibits sexual intimacy between kin defined as too closely related. (Ch. 12)

index A sign that carries social meaning; it provides evidence of something being represented, but it is not physically present in the language used. See also *icon* and *symbol*. (Ch. 7)

indexicality A kind of meaning in language that relies on knowledge of the context in which the language occurred. (Ch. 7)

Indigenous, Aboriginal, and First Nation Terms that refer to original inhabitants of regions and their descendants, who often live with the legacy of being colonized by other groups. (Ch. 1)

Indigenous sovereignty The right of Indigenous peoples to independence, autonomy, and self-governance; the right to inhabit the lands, ways of life, and cultural knowledge belonging to and ordering the world of Indigenous peoples. (Ch. 16)

Indo-European languages A language family that includes the overwhelming majority of Europe, the Iranian plateau, and the northern Indian subcontinent. English is an Indo-European language. (Ch. 8)

industrial capitalism A market-based exchange system using private ownership, wealth accumulation, mechanized production, and new wage-labor arrangements to create profits. (Ch. 9)

informal economy Economic activity that is not legally regulated or protected, estimated to characterize about 60% of the world's employed population (2 billion people). Examples include babysitting, cottage industries, unlicensed street vending, undocumented labor, criminalized sex work, and the black market. See also *formal economy*. (Ch. 9)

informal justice Activity that is intended to ensure fair treatment but is not regulated or enforced through a formal legal system. (Ch. 8, 14)

informed consent Permission granted with adequate knowledge of the possible consequences of participating in research. (Ch. 1)

insectivore One whose diet is composed mainly of insects, such as a tarsier. (Ch. 4)

institution The rules and norms that structure social interactions. (Ch. 8)

interlocutor A person who participates in conversation or interaction with the researcher. (Ch. 2)

introgression The transfer of genetic information (DNA) between diverged populations through limited successive mating, while the gene pools themselves do not merge. (Ch. 6)

isiZulu One of the official languages of South Africa. (Ch. 7)

isolation Physical or social barriers between groups of people that discourage gene flow and encourage genetic drift, meaning groups become less similar over time. (Ch. 3)

isolation event An event that creates a smaller population of animals cut off from others in its species, providing the circumstances for rapid genetic drift and the formation of new species. (Ch. 4)

J

jargon Specialized words used by a group of people or a profession; often the terms are difficult for others to understand. (Ch. 7)

justice A system designed to ensure each person or group gets their fair due. (Ch. 8)

K

key informant A cultural insider whose insights help the anthropologist understand the culture under study. (Ch. 2)

kinship Extremely close social relationships that have a density of expectations and obligations attached to them. (Ch. 8, 12)

knapping Making stone tools by hand. (Ch. 5)

knowledge coproduction A diverse set of research practices that seek to combine scientific integrity with creating knowledge to benefit communities through meaningful collaboration at all stages of a project. (Ch. 1)

knowledge system An organized, systematic, and shared set of related ideas of how something works, based on careful observation, learning, and practice. (Ch. 1)

L

labor Any work, including physical, social, emotional, and intellectual work. (Ch. 9)

lactase persistence (LP) A genetic mutation that continues production of the enzyme lactase into adulthood, allowing digestion of lactose (milk sugar). (Ch. 3)

lactose tolerance or intolerance Ability or inability to digest milk sugar (lactose), related to the presence or absence of the enzyme lactase in the small intestine. (Ch. 3)

lament A type of language and performance used to express grief, usually with weeping and a songlike quality. (Ch. 13)

language A systematic symbol-based signaling system that allows things to get done. (Ch. 1, 7)

language death When a language is no longer used and has no living speakers; also called extinction. (Ch. 10)

language ideology Ideas and beliefs about language and language producers that vary across time, people, and place. (Ch. 7)

language register Different ways of using language according to the audience. (Ch. 12)

language revitalization Process by which a formerly dead or "sleeping" language begins to be used and taught again. (Ch. 10)

language variety A form of a given language that is used regularly by speakers or signers within a society. The variety may be common to a group of age-related users or regional users or some other group within the society. (Ch. 7)

languaging An umbrella term covering all language activities including speaking, hearing, signing, interpreting, reading, writing, and understanding. (Ch. 7)

Latinx A person of Latin American origin or descent. The -x ending indicates all genders. (Ch. 7)

lemur A type of primate found only in Madagascar; mostly nocturnal and tree-dwelling species in which females are often socially dominant. (Ch. 4)

Levant An archaeological term for the general region along the eastern Mediterranean shore where there was early emergence of domestication and complex societies. (Ch. 8)

life history Patterns of growth and reproductive events across the life span. (Ch. 3, 4)

lineage A group of species, both living and extinct, that are all descended from a common ancestor. (Ch. 5, 12)

linguistic anthropology The study of human language variation in its social contexts. (Ch. 1)

linguistic prejudice Having biases or judgments about people based on their language, including the way they speak. (Ch. 7)

linguistic profiling Deciding who someone is with regard to race/ethnicity, age, social class, or national origin based on the way that they speak or sign. (Ch. 7)

linguistic relativity The concept of language as a catalyst for a shift in perspective, such as how people perceive and interact with the worlds around them. (Ch. 7)

local biologies Phenotypic variation resulting from highly localized patterns of physical and social stress and their complex interactions. (Ch. 3)

local knowledge A knowledge system that develops through long-term experience in one place. (Ch. 1)

locomotion How primates typically get around on the ground or in trees, reflected in their anatomy as shaped by evolution. (Ch. 4)

locus The position of a specific gene on a chromosome. (Ch. 3)

longitudinal arch Curvature of the foot from front to back. See also *transverse arch*. (Ch. 5)

M

macroevolution The accumulation of evolutionary changes over long time frames, leading to the emergence of new species. See also *microevolution*. (Ch. 3, 5)

Mainstream White American English (MWAE) Term used in place of "standard English" to make transparent how the assumption of "standard English" represents and legitimizes White, male, upper middle-class, and dominant ways of speaking English. (Ch. 7)

market A place (physical or virtual) where people meet to exchange goods, services, and money. (Ch. 9)

marriage A socially (and often legally) recognized intimate union, creating obligations to each other and other kin. (Ch. 12)

masculinity Along with *femininity*, the collection of social roles and behaviors that are understood to be expressions of gender within a particular society or community. (Ch. 11)

material culture The physical objects humans create, such as pottery or stone tools; once these objects become part of the archaeological record, they are known as artifacts. (Ch. 1)

materiality In anthropology, an approach to studying humans that views their thoughts and behaviors as entangled with physical objects and environments. This work often acknowledges the foundational nature of environment, infrastructure, and politics in shaping human lives. (Ch. 16)

mating system The typical pattern of sexual and reproductive arrangements of a social group or species, such as number of mates acquired. (Ch. 12)

matriarchy A society organized such that women have dominant authority over men. See also *diarchy* and *patriarchy*. (Ch. 11)

matrilineal A societal form in which ancestry, inheritance, and identity are related to women's familial lines. (Ch. 12)

matrilocality A system in which married couples live near or with the wife's family. (Ch. 12)

Maya Indigenous people who inhabit southeastern Mexico, Guatemala, Belize, El Salvador, and Honduras. (Ch. 3)

McGurk effect The perception that results when we hear a sound or a stream of language while viewing an image we associate with a different sound or language. (Ch. 7)

means of production The resources a society uses to produce goods and services. (Ch. 9)

medical pluralism Engagement within and fusing of multiple systems of healing in the quest for health. Also called syncretism. (Ch. 15)

meiosis The process in which a single cell divides twice to create four gametes (sperm or ova) with their own mix of half the genetic information of the original. See also *mitosis*. (Ch. 3)

melanin A pigmented molecule that protects human skin from the harms of ultraviolet radiation. (Ch. 3)

menarche Onset of menstruation during adolescence. (Ch. 3)

merchant capitalism A market-based exchange system using long-distance trade for the acquisition, movement, and sale of raw materials to create profits. (Ch. 9)

Mesolithic period The part of human history during which humans were hunter-gatherers, generally dating to between 20,000 and 10,000 years ago. (Ch. 8)

metaphor theory The idea that metaphors impact how we think about an idea or object. (Ch. 10)

microevolution Any change in gene frequencies in a population between generations and through time. See also *macroevolution*. (Ch. 3)

Middle Pleistocene *Homo* Describes a hominin that anatomically and behaviorally is neither *Homo erectus* nor *Homo sapiens*, who lived in the period between 800,000 and 300,000 years ago. (Ch. 6)

minoritize To deny equitable access to power, wealth, or resources within society to a group of people. (In contrast, a minority simply means a group with fewer members than some other group.) (Ch. 14)

Miocene epoch A division of the geological timescale that lasted from 23 to 5.3 million years ago and is associated with the adaptive radiation of early apes. (Ch. 4, 5)

mitochondrion A plentiful organelle that produces chemical energy for the cell. (Ch. 3)

mitosis Division of a single cell to create two identical cells, crucial to growth and maintenance of the body. See also *meiosis*. (Ch. 3)

mixed economy Economic activity in which multiple sets of rules and norms simultaneously operate to govern how materials, services, symbols, and ideas are transferred between people or groups. (Ch. 9)

mode of production One of the varied ways that a society can organize human labor to produce what they need. Examples include kin-based (domestic) and tributary (ruler/subject) modes. (Ch. 9)

modern synthesis A consolidation of prior research that defined evolution as a change in gene frequencies across generations, potentially leading to new species (through mechanisms such as natural selection). See also *extended evolutionary synthesis*. (Ch. 3)

molecular clock method A method for estimating the possible date of past species' divergence, by comparing their later genetic differences and assuming a known rate of genetic change over time. (Ch. 5)

molecule The smallest unit that has all the properties of a substance. Smaller molecules can combine to form larger molecules: for example, sugars, phosphates, and bases combine to make DNA, and amino acids join together to form proteins. (Ch. 3)

money An object that serves as a medium of exchange and a unit of account in a market economy, such as a coin. (Ch. 9)

monogamy The practice of being with one intimate partner at a time. See also *polyamory*. (Ch. 12)

monolingualism Regular use of only one language. See also *multilingualism*. (Ch. 7)

moral economy A system of economic beliefs and behaviors consisting of (1) shared justice norms that uphold a right to subsistence and survival; (2) economic practices, such as reciprocity, that uphold the justice norms; and (3) social pressure mechanisms such as gossip or protest to enforce justice norms. (Ch. 9)

mortuary practice A rite or activity surrounding death. (Ch. 13)

mosaic When a fossil species contains a mix of primitive traits and derived traits. (Ch. 5)

Mousterian A sophisticated style of tools characterized by a technique of producing and refining sharpened flakes that are particularly suited to hunting. See also *Acheulean* and *Oldowan*. (Ch. 6)

multifactorial Describes a phenotype whose expression is determined by many factors, including the environment in which development happens. (Ch. 3)

multilingualism Regular use of more than one language (characterizes the majority of the world). See also *monolingualism*. (Ch. 7)

multiregional model A theory of modern human emergence in which modern human anatomy is considered to have evolved within each continent slowly through time, where a single species was maintained across time by long-distance gene flow. See also *assimilation model*. (Ch. 6)

multisited ethnography Research that purposefully collapses the distinction between local field sites and the global systems in which they are embedded. (Ch. 12)

N

narrative Using language to create a coherent account of events or experiences. (Ch. 5)

Native American Graves Protection and Repatriation Act (NAGPRA) Legislation passed by the U.S. federal government to protect and return archaeological human remains and culturally significant artifacts to affiliated Native Americans. (Ch. 13)

natural hazard A naturally occurring phenomenon, such as a hurricane, earthquake, volcano, or wildfire, that has the potential to harm human societies; it may be fast-moving (like a tornado) or slow-moving (like a drought). (Ch. 16)

natural selection The theory that a comparatively better match between an individual's phenotype and their environment will favor inheritance of that underlying genotype to the next generation. (Ch. 3)

Neanderthal A now-extinct species of humans that lived primarily in Europe and parts of western Asia between about 430,000 to 35,000 years ago. (Ch. 6)

negative reciprocity Giving where one party benefits more than the other. (Ch. 9)

neoliberalism A system of government that seeks to move service provision from public to market sectors and to move resource ownership and control from the public to the private sphere. (Ch. 9)

Neolithic period The part of human history during which humans domesticated plants and animals, generally beginning about 10,000 years ago. (Ch. 8)

neolocality A system in which married couples move to a new household that is away from both sets of parents. (Ch. 12)

neutral mutation A change in DNA without any change in function. See also *advantageous mutation* and *deleterious mutation*. (Ch. 3)

niche construction The process of an organism altering their adaptive environment, sometimes with consequences for that (and possibly other) species' evolution. (Ch. 3)

nocturnal Active during the night. See also *diurnal*. (Ch. 4)

nonbinary Not identifying as either man or woman. (Ch. 11)

norm A shared set of beliefs of what is ideal, acceptable, or to be avoided. (Ch. 1, 8)

nucleus The information and functional center of a somatic cell. (Ch. 3)

O

obstetric racism Harmful birth experiences due to racist interactions with physicians, nurses, and other medical professionals. (Ch. 14)

occipital torus A thickened shelf of bone near the back of the cranium, characteristic of *Homo erectus* fossils, especially those from Asia. See also *sagittal keel* and *supraorbital torus*. (Ch. 6)

Oldowan A style of very simple hand tools from after 2.6 million years ago, mostly produced by chipping a few flakes off a stone to reveal a single rough working edge. See also *Acheulean* and *Mousterian*. (Ch. 5)

Oligocene epoch A division of the geological timescale that lasted from 33.9 to 23 million years ago and is associated with the adaptive radiation of early haplorhines. (Ch. 4)

omnivore One whose diet is composed of both plant and animal food sources. (Ch. 4)

ontology The study of multiple existing realities. (Ch. 2)

opposable The ability of the thumb or big toe to be placed against the other digits to grasp and hold objects. (Ch. 4, 5)

oppressive system A societal arrangement that permits one group to impose their will on others in burdensome, malicious, or unjust ways. (Ch. 14)

oral tradition Knowledge passed down through generations using stories, song, signs, and other nonwritten means. (Ch. 7)

organelle A structure that has a specialized function within a cell. (Ch. 3)

origin myth A shared, sacred story of where we come from and how and why we are, often including nonhumans (such as gods or animals). (Ch. 7)

P

pair bond A social arrangement of residing and mating with only one other individual at a time. (Ch. 4, 12)

paleoanthropologist An anthropologist who locates, examines, and interprets the early fossil and archaeological evidence for human evolution. (Ch. 5)

Paleocene epoch A division of the geological timescale that lasted from 66 to 56 million years ago and is associated with the adaptive radiation of early mammals closely related to primates. (Ch. 4)

paleoenvironmental reconstruction The scientific determination of ancient environments in which fossil species once lived using methods from zoology, paleontology, and geology. (Ch. 5)

participant observation An ethnographic research method that relies on cultural immersion; the researcher often lives alongside members of the culture under study, conducting careful observation and questioning to facilitate data collection and analysis. (Ch. 1)

paternity certainty The likelihood that a male caring for the offspring of a bonded partner is likely to be caring for his own genetic offspring. (Ch. 12)

path dependency The tendency to "get stuck" on a trajectory, in which a community becomes overly dependent on certain kinds of technology, settlement patterns, exchange systems, and social organizations, which then creates community-wide vulnerabilities. (Ch. 16)

patriarchy A society that is organized such that cisgender men have dominant authority and advantages over women and transgender and nonbinary people. See also *diarchy* and *matriarchy*. (Ch. 11)

patrilineal A societal form in which ancestry, inheritance, and identity are related to men's familial lines. (Ch. 12)

patrilocality A system in which married couples live near or with the husband's family. (Ch. 11, 12)

patron–client relationship An unequal political and economic arrangement in which a person of higher status protects and provides resources to a person of lower status while simultaneously extracting labor or other services from the person of lower status. (Ch. 8)

petroglyph An image carved on rock. (Ch. 7)

phenotype The physical expression of a genetically influenced feature or trait, such as eye color or blood type. See also *genotype*. (Ch. 3)

phonological rule One of a set of conventions, specific to each language, governing how sounds or signs are combined to make a specific language. (Ch. 7)

phylogeny The evolutionary history of a species and its relationship to other taxonomic groupings. (Ch. 4)

physical anthropology An outdated term for what is now called biological anthropology, sometimes based in typological approaches to explain human biology. (Ch. 14)

platyrrhine A monkey of South or Central America (sometimes referred to as a Neotropical primate). See also *catarrhine*. (Ch. 4)

Pleistocene epoch A division of the geological timescale that lasted from 2.6 million until 12,000 years ago and is associated with the beginning use of stone tools and the adaptive radiation of genus *Homo*. (Ch. 5, 6)

plesiadapiform One of an early group of mammals that lived during the Paleocene epoch and were very closely related to the first primate. (Ch. 4)

Pliocene epoch A division of the geological timescale that lasted from 5.3 until 2.6 million years ago and is associated with the evolution of fully bipedal hominins and the genus *Homo*. (Ch. 5)

pluriverse transition A vision of the world in which many realities—multiple ways of knowing and being—can coexist, be nurtured, and create positive new ways of living with other humans and nonhumans. (Ch. 16)

polyamory The practice of being with multiple intimate partners at a time, with the consent of all involved. See also *monogamy*. (Ch. 12)

polyandry A marriage system in which women are permitted or expected to have more than one husband at the same time. See also *polygamy* and *polygyny*. (Ch. 12)

polygamy A marriage system in which a person can have more than one wife or husband at the same time. See also *polyandry* and *polygyny*. (Ch. 12)

polygenic Describes a phenotype whose expression or appearance is determined by multiple genes, each with multiple possible alleles. (Ch. 3)

polygyny A marriage system in which men are permitted or expected to have more than one wife at the same time. See also *polyandry* and *polygamy*. (Ch. 11, 12)

population The set of organisms in the same region that can potentially mate and produce offspring. Human populations are rarely completely isolated from each other. (Ch. 3)

population genetics The study of genes and gene frequencies within populations, for the purpose of understanding the history of a population and the evolutionary mechanisms that shaped its genetic structure. (Ch. 14)

positionality The socioeconomic, political, and cultural positions of the researcher in relation to those of the research participants or communities. (Ch. 2)

postcrania The bones of the skeleton below the cranium. (Ch. 5)

postindustrial capitalism A market-based exchange system that uses knowledge, communications, and services to produce profits. (Ch. 9)

postorbital bar A strut of bone that encircles and protects primate eyes. (Ch. 4)

postprocessual archaeology An archaeological approach focusing on multiple ways of knowing the past. See also *processual archaeology*. (Ch. 2)

power The capacity to do and get what you want, including the ability to access resources and influence the decision-making of others. (Ch. 11)

precision grip The ability to touch the end of the thumb to the end of one or more fingers, allowing the handling of small objects. (Ch. 4)

prefix A string of letters/sounds that go at the start of a root word. (Ch. 8)

prehensile Having the ability to grasp. (Ch. 4)

pressure flaking Applying pressure (using a stick, bone, or antler) to chip away small stone flakes and create more refined shapes and sharper edges. (Ch. 6)

primate One of a group of related mammals that evolved as tree-dwellers with relatively large brains and forward-facing eyes; includes lemurs, monkeys, apes, and humans. (Ch. 1)

primitive trait An anatomical feature inherited from an ancestral species that may have given rise to many descendant species through time. See also *derived trait*. (Ch. 4)

prison abolition A global movement dedicated to eliminating or reducing policing and prisons and replacing this with a system of social services, rehabilitation, and community accountability. (Ch. 14)

private property The bundle of rights that enable an individual or set of individuals to sell, access, manage, withdraw from, and exclude others from land, goods, and other resources. (Ch. 9)

private property regime A governance arrangement in which resources are individually owned, excludable (that is, open only to owners), and often tradable. (Ch. 9)

processual archaeology An archaeological approach that emerged in the 1960s, focusing on scientific study of the processes that created the evidence found at the site being studied. See also *postprocessual archaeology*. (Ch. 2)

proconsulid One of a group of Miocene-epoch African primates that are candidates for early ape ancestors. (Ch. 4)

prognathism The projection of the face forward relative to the braincase, often associated with larger chewing muscles or large snouts in nonprimates. (Ch. 5)

pronoun A word that takes the place of a noun or noun phrase such as a personal name. (Ch. 11)

prosimian A taxonomic classification that recognizes the more primitive appearance of tarsiers and all strepsirrhines but ignores the derived features linking tarsiers to other haplorhines. (Ch. 4)

prosocial behavior Voluntary actions that are intended to help other individuals or groups. (Ch. 8)

protein A large and complex molecule that performs one of many varied and critical functions in the body, such as growth, digestion, blood clotting, or immune response. (Ch. 3)

protein synthesis The process by which cells produce protein molecules, using instructions encoded in DNA. (Ch. 3)

protolanguage A hypothetical undocumented ancestral language. (Ch. 8)

pseudoscience Methods, techniques, or beliefs that appear to have scientific validity but are not based on rigorous, empirical hypothesis testing. (Ch. 14)

Q

quadrupedal Reliant on all four limbs to move about. See also *bipedal*. (Ch. 4)

R

racialize To categorize people into established racist typologies within a given cultural context. (Ch. 7, 14)

racialized system A society that is organized to reflect a racial hierarchy; inequality is embedded in the society, and people are rewarded or oppressed on the basis of their place within it. (Ch. 14)

raciolinguistics The study of how language ideologies produce racial difference and ideologies of racial difference produce linguistic differences. (Ch. 7)

racism Harm and oppression directed at groups or individuals based on societal beliefs of racial hierarchy, such as White superiority. (Ch. 14)

radical anthropology Working toward more just and equitable futures by identifying, critiquing, and fighting exploitation through opposing social structures seen as oppressive. (Ch. 16)

recessive Describes an allele that is expressed phenotypically only in the absence of a dominant gene. See also *codominant* and *dominant*. (Ch. 3)

reciprocity A form of transfer that has specific expectations of give-and-take, is infused with cultural meanings, and depends on the social relationship between people involved. (Ch. 9)

reconciliation A process designed to expose the truth about state repression and violence, establish responsibility for acts of genocide and terror, and enable a society to move forward in peace. (Ch. 10)

recursion Communication that can be made longer and more detailed by adding more language units to it. (Ch. 4)

redistribution A form of economic exchange designed to centralize goods and services and then distribute them out in new patterns. (Ch. 9)

reflexivity Transparent self-reflection on the researcher's own social position, knowledges, and biases and how this shapes the course of research and its conclusions. (Ch. 2)

refusal Acts that reject dominance, such as disobeying unjust laws. (Ch. 10)

register A cluster of language features (such as pronunciation, words, intonation, or other grammatical features) associated with a specific group of people or a specific context. (Ch. 7)

relational approach Based in Indigenous thinking, a central recognition that humans and nonhumans interact in ways that shape each other and their worlds. (Ch. 16)

relative dating A method of determining whether one artifact or stratum is older or younger than another. See also *absolute dating*. (Ch. 2)

religious Describes a set of beliefs and formalized rituals regarding ideology, the supernatural, morals, and values in society. (Ch. 13)

research stakeholder A person with a direct interest or concern in a research project. (Ch. 1)

resilience A person's or society's potential to cope, adapt, restore, or recover after a shock or stressor (like a disaster). See also *vulnerability*. (Ch. 16)

resistance Pushing back against oppression and other forms of structural violence. (Ch. 10)

revolution Challenges to the state with the goal of establishing a new government. (Ch. 10)

rhetoric Persuasive use of written, spoken, and visual language to organize and maintain social groups, construct meanings and identities, and consolidate power. (Ch. 10)

rhinarium A hairless patch of skin connecting the nose to the mouth. (Ch. 4)

ribosome The organelle in which protein synthesis happens. (Ch. 3)

rite of passage A ritual, ceremony, or event marking an important life stage, such as birth, puberty, marriage, or death. (Ch. 13)

ritual Describes a recognized social event that marks a life transition, such as death. (Ch. 6, 13)

romantic love An ideal of courtship and marriage characterized by feelings of desire, emotional intimacy, companionship, and mutual choice. (Ch. 12)

root (word) A word that does not have any affixes such as a prefix or suffix. (Ch. 8)

rule A formal guideline that dictates what can and cannot occur, especially regarding behaviors. (Ch. 8)

rules (of a language) A systematized pattern of use that we learn when we acquire a language, mostly untaught and rarely obvious to speakers or signers. (Ch. 7)

S

sacred Things set apart from society, that are beyond the everyday and treated with care. (Ch. 2)

sagittal crest A prominent ridge of bone projecting upward from the skull that supports extremely strong jaw muscles associated with powerful biting or chewing. (Ch. 4)

sagittal keel A thickened area of bone that runs from the top of the forehead to the back of the cranium, characteristic of *Homo erectus* fossils. See also *occipital torus* and *supraorbital torus*. (Ch. 6)

schema A set of related social norms and rules that establishes how things should be within society. (Ch. 11)

science A systematic approach to creating new knowledge by testing falsifiable predictions about how the world works and came to be. (Ch. 1)

scientific racism Misinterpretation or use of misleading scientific evidence to justify and support racialized worldviews. (Ch. 14)

secular trend A population-wide or group-wide shift in average growth patterns over time. (Ch. 3)

selective pressure An external factor that reduces or enhances the ability of organisms to survive or reproduce in a specific environment. (Ch. 3)

self-governance A system where people regulate their own conduct without intervention from an external authority such as a government. (Ch. 8)

semiotics The study of the way that symbols, including words, make meaning. (Ch. 7)

serial monogamy The practice of engaging in more than one monogamous relationship over one's life span. (Ch. 12)

settler colonialism A system of domination and violence in which people are removed from their land through displacement or genocide; often involves the annihilation of the prior inhabitants' language, culture, livelihoods, and ways of life. (Ch. 10, 16)

sex chromosomes A pair of chromosomes (designated XX, XY, or combinations thereof) that is partially responsible for biological differences in sexual and reproductive anatomy and physiology. Those assigned male at birth are assumed to have XY chromosomes while those assigned female at birth are assumed to have XX chromosomes, though exceptions exist. (Ch. 11)

sex work Labor that employs the body in exchange for money, services, or goods. (Ch. 12)

sexism Ideas and practices suggesting the inferiority of one sex compared to others; usually directed toward women. (Ch. 11)

sexual configuration An approach to describing sexuality that seeks to incorporate as many varied lived experiences as possible, avoiding frameworks that categorize or constrain possibilities. (Ch. 12)

sexual dimorphism The condition when males and females of a species are significantly different in size. (Ch. 4, 11)

sexual orientation The kinds of people, roles, or experiences a person is sexually attracted to or oriented toward. (Ch. 12)

sexual reproduction The process that creates a new organism by combining genetic information from two different individuals. (Ch. 3)

shamanic healing Treatment by a religious practitioner who connects spirit and physical worlds. (Ch. 15)

sickness The social expectations and roles connected to disease and illness, including how the affected individual relates to others. See also *disease* and *illness*. (Ch. 15)

sign(ed) Refers to language produced by using a visual-manual or tactile-manual method. See also *spoken*. (Ch. 7)

singlehood Remaining unmarried or without an intimate partner, including by choice. (Ch. 12)

situated knowledge An understanding that reflects the contexts (including environmental and social) in which meanings are produced and applied. (Ch. 7)

social capital Connections to others that can provide opportunities, information, or material or emotional support. (Ch. 15)

social complexity Describes a society with large numbers of people, large permanent settlements, and many varied social and economic roles. (Ch. 8)

social differentiation The process of creating and reinforcing social hierarchies, aligned with differing roles within society. (Ch. 1)

social identity The self-recognized characteristics that make an individual or social group like or unlike others. (Ch. 1)

social insurance An arrangement in which people can "store" obligations to reciprocate favors or gifts in long-standing relationships and then call on those relationship partners for help during times of scarcity or need. (Ch. 9)

social status A person's standing or importance relative to others in society. (Ch. 8)

social stratification The organization of human groups into different levels (or strata), such as elites and non-elites. (Ch. 8)

socialism A range of redistributive economies with the basic feature of partially or fully communal ownership and control of resources or production. (Ch. 9)

society People in sustained communication, with rules and structures that organize them in relation to one another. (Ch. 1)

solidarity economy An approach to economic development designed to put people over profit, such as fair trade, rotating credit associations, worker cooperatives, and community gardens. (Ch. 9)

somatic cell Any cell in the body other than a gamete. (Ch. 3)

species A group of organisms sufficiently genetically similar to be able to breed with one another. (Ch. 3)

speech act theory A set of ideas arguing that language does not just present information but also performs action. (Ch. 7)

spiritual Describes beliefs relating to unseen realms of existence. (Ch. 13)

splitting The assumption that things are in different biological categories (such as multiple species) unless there is convincing evidence that they should be united. See also *clumping*. (Ch. 5)

spoken Refers to language produced by using an oral method. See also *sign(ed)*. (Ch. 7)

state A large, hierarchical political unit with a centralized government that binds citizens by consensus or coercion and the power to decree and enforce laws. (Ch. 8)

stigma Being pushed down or out of society by association with unwanted and devalued social identities (such as those tied to specific diseases). (Ch. 15)

stone point A shaped piece of rock typically used to create an arrow, spear, or other projectile. (Ch. 6)

stratigraphy The sequence of soil layers (strata) at a location that archaeologists can use to evaluate and date an archaeological site. (Ch. 2)

strepsirrhine One of a group of wet-nosed, mainly arboreal primates with toothcombs; this group includes the lemurs, galagos, and lorises of Africa and Asia. See also *haplorhine*. (Ch. 4)

stress The body's physical reactions to external challenges, both social and environmental. (Ch. 2)

stressor A factor that disrupts normal or healthy physiological processes in an individual's body. (Ch. 3)

strontium isotope analysis An analytical method that compares the abundances of stable isotopes that vary in bedrock and geologic regions; often used by archaeologists to understand how past humans moved around landscapes. (Ch. 9)

structural racism A system of inequality, often state-sanctioned and created historically, that builds on the belief that people can be classified into distinctive, separate groups on the basis of ancestry or visible body characteristics and that these typologies reflect meaningful biological differences, justifying the belief that members of some groups are superior or inferior to others. (Ch. 14)

structural violence When social, economic, and political systems prevent some groups from meeting their basic needs, creating and reinforcing inequities in ways that often benefit other groups with more power. (Ch. 10)

subsistence society A society that produces the basic material necessities for survival, such as food, water, housing, and clothing, but without creating surpluses. (Ch. 9)

suffering Pain, distress, loss, or deprivation that results from the enactment of unequal power structures within society. (Ch. 10)

supraorbital torus A thickened shelf of bone above the eye orbits, characteristic of *Homo erectus* fossils, especially those from Asia. See also *occipital torus* and *sagittal keel*. (Ch. 6)

suspensory Moving through trees by hanging from branches. (Ch. 4)

sustainability trade-off A balance of the costs and benefits of different resource management strategies designed to maximize long-term environmental, economic, or societal well-being. (Ch. 16)

sustainability transition A major or radical transformation in current social–ecological systems to enable long-term environmental, social, and economic well-being. (Ch. 16)

symbol An image, sound, or action that we learn represents (but does not resemble) something else. See also *icon* and *index*. (Ch. 1, 7)

symptom An identified marker of illness. (Ch. 15)

systems theory The study of how human and nonhuman relationships interact to produce outcomes that are greater than the actions of any one actor, including through feedback loops. (Ch. 16)

T

taphonomy Study of the processes that affect human, animal, and plant remains as they decay and become part of the record anthropologists study. (Ch. 13)

taxonomy A scientific system to define and organize species in relation to each other by grouping individuals into like types. (Ch. 4)

terrestrial Primarily living on the ground. See also *arboreal*. (Ch. 4)

threatened Species that are critically endangered, endangered, or vulnerable to extinction due to small or declining numbers and habitat destruction. (Ch. 4)

tool use Manipulation of objects to achieve a goal. (Ch. 4)

toothcomb An anatomical feature of strepsirrhine teeth in which the lower incisors and canine teeth are modified to form a comblike structure. (Ch. 4)

transcription The process of creating a text representing exactly what is said, often with relevant contextual information included. Transcripts are a primary form of evidence used by linguistic anthropologists to record language use. (Ch. 2)

transformative justice A set of practices for dealing with crime that includes transforming oppression, supporting victims of crime, making perpetrators accountable in a way that is sustainable and affirming to communities, and creating norms and values that resist harm. (Ch. 14)

transgender Having one's internal sense of gender identity not align with one's assigned sex at birth. See also *cisgender*. (Ch. 11)

transverse arch Curvature of the foot from side to side. See also *longitudinal arch*. (Ch. 5)

trauma Profound, often ongoing, physical or emotional harms resulting from extremely stressful events or situations. (Ch. 3)

tribal or ethnic warfare Conflict between social groups centered on, or legitimated by, distinctions in their ancestry, traditions, languages, cultures, or ideologies. (Ch. 10)

tribe A small-scale society of agriculturalists where relationships are generally egalitarian. (Ch. 8)

tuberculosis (TB) An infection, caused by the tube-shaped *Mycobacterium tuberculosis* bacterium, that initially affects the lungs. (Ch. 13)

typology A system imposed to categorize objects together on the basis of specific similarities, emphasizing what is "typical" or "average" for each category. (Ch. 14)

U

unbanked Lacking access to formal banking institutions. (Ch. 9)

urban Describes the dense settlement of humans in defined areas. (Ch. 8)

V

valgus knee Location of the knee toward the midline of the body caused by the angulation of the thigh bone. (Ch. 5)

variable In sociolinguistics, a linguistic element that varies based on other linguistic elements but also based on social contexts including class, age, gender/sex, or situation. (Ch. 7)

violence Use of extreme aggression intended to hurt or inflict lethal or nonlethal damage. (Ch. 10)

visual predation hypothesis The theory of primate origins based on visual hunting of insects as the primary adaptation. (Ch. 4)

vocalization Sounds that transfer information to others. (Ch. 4)

vulnerability A person's or society's potential to be harmed by or recover from an environmental stressor or disaster. Vulnerability is determined by cultural, economic, political, and other key social structures. See also *resilience*. (Ch. 16)

W

warfare Organized violence between socially distinct or autonomous groups of people. (Ch. 10)

White supremacy A political, economic, and cultural system in which those who are identified as "White" overwhelmingly control power and material resources, conscious and unconscious ideas of White superiority are widespread, racism is daily reenacted, and systematic oppression of non-White people is justified. (Ch. 14)

Whiteness Social identity within a hierarchical structure situated as superior to others, associated with lighter skin and benefiting those defined by it with power, privilege, and wealth. (Ch. 14)

worker cooperative A business that workers own and self-manage. (Ch. 9)

Y

Y-5 cusp pattern An anatomical feature characteristic of hominoids, whereby the grooves between the cusps on the lower molars (back teeth) form the shape of the letter Y. (Ch. 4)

Z

zoonosis (plural, zoonoses) A disease that can be transferred between animals and humans. (Ch. 13)

zygote The first cell that replicates to create a new sexually reproducing organism, produced through fusion of ovum and sperm. (Ch. 3)

REFERENCES

Abed, E., Schudson, Z., Gunther, O., Beischel, W., & van Anders, S. (2019). Sexual and gender diversity among sexual and gender/sex majorities: Insights via sexual configurations theory. *Archives of Sexual Behavior, 48*(5), 1423–1441. https://doi.org/10.1007/s10508-018-1340-2

Abrahms-Kavunenko, S. (2016). Spiritually enmeshed, socially enmeshed: Shamanism and belonging in Ulaanbaatar. *Social Analysis, 60*(3), 1–16.

Abu-Lughod, L. (2002). Do Muslim women really need saving? Anthropological reflections on cultural relativism and its others. *American Anthropologist, 104*(3), 783–790.

Accomazzo, S. (2012). Anthropology of violence: Historical and current theories, concepts, and debates in physical and socio-cultural anthropology. *Journal of Human Behavior in the Social Environment, 22*(5), 535–552.

Adams, V. (2013). *Markets of sorrow, labors of faith: New Orleans in the wake of Katrina*. Duke University Press.

Addington, L. A., & Rennison, C. M. (2013). Keeping the barbarians outside the gate? Comparing burglary victimization in gated and non-gated communities. *Justice Quarterly, 32*(1), 168–192. https://doi.org/10.1080/07418825.2012.760644

Agbe-Davies, A. (1998). Dealing with "race" in African American archaeology. *Anthropology News, 39*(5), 14. https://doi.org/10.1111/an.1998.39.5.14

Agbe-Davies, A. S. (2004a). The production and consumption of smoking pipes along the tobacco coast. In *Smoking culture: The archaeology of tobacco pipes in eastern North America* (pp. 273–304). University of Tennessee Press.

Agbe-Davies, A. S. (2004b). *Up in smoke: Pipe-making, smoking, and Bacon's Rebellion*. University of Pennsylvania.

Agbe-Davies, A. S. (2010). Concepts of community in the pursuit of an inclusive archaeology. *International Journal of Heritage Studies, 16*(6), 373–389. https://doi.org/10.1080/13527258.2010.510923

Agbe-Davies, A. S. (2016). *Tobacco, pipes, and race in colonial Virginia: Little tubes of mighty power*. Routledge.

Agha, A. (2007). *Language and social relations*. Cambridge University Press.

Ahearn, L. M. (2001). Juggling roles: Daughter, development worker, and anthropologist. In *Invitations to love: Literacy, love letters, and social change in Nepal*. University of Michigan Press.

Ahearn, L. M. (2004). Literacy, power, and agency: Love letters and development in Nepal. *Language & Education: An International Journal, 18*(4), 305–316.

Ahearn, L. M. (2016). *Living language: An introduction to linguistic anthropology*. John Wiley & Sons.

Ahlquist, K. D., Bañuelos, M. M., Funk, A., Lai, J., Rong, S., Villanea, F. A., & Witt, K. E. (2021). Our tangled family tree: New genomic methods offer insight into the legacy of archaic admixture. *Genome Biology and Evolution, 13*(7), Article evab115.

Albury, N. J. (2018). Multilingualism and mobility as collateral results of hegemonic language policy. *Applied Linguistics, 41*(2), 234–259.

Albury, N. J. (2021). Linguistic landscape and metalinguistic talk about societal multilingualism. *International Journal of Bilingual Education and Bilingualism, 24*(2), 207–223.

Aldenderfer, M. (2011). Peopling the Tibetan plateau: Insights from archaeology. *High Altitude Medicine & Biology, 12*, 141–147.

Alexander, G. M., & Hines, M. (2002). Sex differences in response to children's toys in nonhuman primates (*Cercopithecus aethiops sabaeus*). *Evolution and Human Behavior, 23*, 467–479.

Alexander, M. (2012). *The new Jim Crow: Mass incarceration in the age of colorblindness* (with a new foreword by Cornel West). The New Press.

Alim, H. S., Rickford, J. R., & Ball, A. F. (Eds.). (2016). *Raciolinguistics: How language shapes our ideas about race*. Oxford University Press.

Alim, H. S., & Smitherman, G. (2012). *Articulate while Black: Barack Obama, language, and race in the US*. Oxford University Press.

Allen, J. S., & Jobson, R. C. (2016). The decolonizing generation: (Race and) Theory in anthropology since the eighties. *Current Anthropology, 57*(2), 129–148.

Allen, J. S., Park, J., & Watt, S. L. (1994). The chimpanzee tea party: Anthropomorphism, Orientalism, and colonialism. *Visual Anthropology Review, 10*, 45–54. https://doi.org/10.1525/var.1994.10.2.45

Allentoft, M. E., Sikora, M., Sjögren, K.-G., Rasmussen, S., Rasmussen, M., Stenderup, J., Damgaard, P. B.,

Schroeder, H., Ahlström, T., Vinner, L., Malaspinas, A.-S., Margaryan, A., Higham, T., Chivall, D., Lynnerup, N., Harvig, L., Baron, J., Della Casa, P., Dąbrowski, P., . . . Willersley, E. (2015). Population genomics of Bronze Age Eurasia. *Nature, 522*(7555), 167–172.

Alonso Bejarano, C., Juárez, L. L., García, M. A. M., & Goldstein, D. M. (2019). *Decolonizing ethnography: Undocumented immigrants and new directions in social science.* Duke University Press.

Al-Rasheed, M. (2013). *A most masculine state: Gender, politics, and religion in Saudi Arabia.* Cambridge University Press.

Altay, T., Yurdakul, G., & Korteweg, A. (2021). Crossing borders: The intersectional marginalisation of Bulgarian Muslim trans*immigrant sex workers in Berlin. *Journal of Ethnic and Migration Studies, 47*(9), 1922–1939. https://doi.org/10.1080/1369183X.2020.1862646

Álvarez-Sandoval, B. A., Manzanilla, L. R., González-Ruiz, M., Malgosa, A., & Montiel, R. (2015). Genetic evidence supports the multiethnic character of Teopancazco, a neighborhood center of Teotihuacan, Mexico (AD 200–600). *PLOS ONE, 10*(7), Article e0132371.

American Anthropological Association. (2007, August 7). *Eugenics and physical anthropology.* Archived August 10, 2007, at the Wayback Machine. https://web.archive.org/web/20070810204659/http://www.understandingrace.org/history/science/eugenics_physical.html

American Anthropological Association. (2012). *Principles of Professional Responsibility.* https://www.americananthro.org/LearnAndTeach/Content.aspx?ItemNumber=22869&navItemNumber=652

American Anthropological Association. (2022). *AAA Apology to the Indigenous Community.* https://americananthro.org/advocacy-statements/apology-to-the-indigenous-community/

American Association for the Advancement of Science. (2014, August 27). Stone-tipped spears more damaging than sharpened wooden spears. *EurekAlert!* https://www.eurekalert.org/news-releases/652981

Ames, K. M. (1995). Chiefly power and household production on the Northwest Coast. In T. D. Price & G. M. Feinman (Eds.), *Foundations of social inequality* (pp. 155–187). Plenum Press.

Ames, K. M. (2007). The archaeology of rank. In R. A. Bentley, H. D. G. Maschner, & C. Chippindale (Eds.), *Handbook of archaeological theories* (pp. 487–513). AltaMira Press.

Ames, K. M. (2010). Comments on the emergence and persistence of inequality in premodern societies. *Current Anthropology, 51*(1), 95–96.

Ames, M. M. (2007). *Cannibal tours and glass boxes: The anthropology of museums.* UBC Press.

Amrith, M., & Coe, C. M. (2022). Disposable kin: Shifting registers of belonging in global care economies. *American Anthropologist, 124*(2), 307–318.

Anand, N. (2011). Pressure: The politechnics of water supply in Mumbai. *Cultural Anthropology, 26*(4), 542–564.

Anand, N. (2015). Leaky states: Water audits, ignorance, and the politics of infrastructure. *Public Culture, 27*(2), 305–330.

Anderson, B. (1991 [1983]). *Imagined communities: Reflections on the origin and spread of nationalism.* Verso.

Andrews, P., & Kelley, J. (2007). Middle Miocene dispersals of apes. *Folia Primatologica, 78*, 328–343.

Andrikopoulos, A. (2019). Love, money and papers in the affective circuits of cross-border marriages: Beyond the 'sham'/'genuine' dichotomy. *Journal of Ethnic and Migration Studies, 47*(2), 343–360.

Andrikopoulos, A., & Duyvendak, J. W. (2020). Migration, mobility and the dynamics of kinship: New barriers, new assemblages. *Ethnography, 21*(3), 299–318. https://doi.org/10.1177/1466138120939584

Ang, K. (2020, December 14). Leith Mullings, 1945–2020: Anthropologist behind the Sojourner Syndrome. *Social Science Space.* https://www.socialsciencespace.com/2020/12/leith-mullings-1945-2020-a-brilliant-scholar-powerful-inspiration-and-anthropologist-extraordinaire/

Anthony, D. W. (2010). *The horse, the wheel, and language: How bronze-age riders from the Eurasian Steppes shaped the modern world.* Princeton University Press.

Anthony, D. W. & Ringe, D. (2015). The Indo-European homeland from linguistic and archaeological perspectives. *Annual Review of Linguistics, 1*, 199–219.

Antón, S. C. (2012). Early *Homo.* Who, when, and where. *Current Anthropology, 53*, S278–S298.

Antón, S. C., Malhi, R. S., & Fuentes, A. (2018). Race and diversity in US biological anthropology: A decade of AAPA initiatives. *American Journal of Physical Anthropology, 165*, 158–180.

Antrosio, J., & Han, S. (Eds.). (2015, October). The editors' note: Race, racism, and protesting anthropology. *Open Anthropology, 3*(3). https://www.americananthro.org/StayInformed/OAArticleDetail.aspx?ItemNumber=13103

Antrosio, J., & Han, S. (Eds.). (2016, June). The editors' note: Food anthropology. *Open Anthropology, 4*(2), e116–e120. https://www.americananthro.org/StayInformed/OAArticleDetail.aspx?ItemNumber=14852

Apicella, C. L., & Silk, J. B. (2019). The evolution of human cooperation. *Current Biology, 29*(11), R447–R450.

Aranguren, B., Becattini, R., Mariotti Lippi, M., & Revedin, A. (2007). Grinding flour in Upper Palaeolithic Europe (25 000 years bp). *Antiquity, 81*, 845–855.

Arbaci, S. (2019). *Paradoxes of segregation: Housing systems, welfare regimes and ethnic residential change in Southern European cities.* Wiley.

Arbour, L., & Cook, D. (2006). DNA on loan: Issues to consider when carrying out genetic research with aboriginal families and communities. *Community Genetics, 9*, 153–160.

Archambault, J. S. (2016). Taking love seriously in human-plant relations in Mozambique: Toward an anthropology of affective encounters. *Cultural Anthropology, 31*(2), 244–271.

Ardizzone, H. (2006). "Such fine families": Photography and race in the work of Caroline Bond Day. *Visual Studies (Abingdon, England), 21*(2), 106–132.

Are we so different? (n.d.). *Understanding Race.* www.understandingRACE.org

Arizona State University. (2020, June 15). *Belong: What it's like to live in the hyphen with Pardis Mahdavi* [Video]. YouTube. https://www.youtube.com/watch?v=wUNkfNelJgE

Armstrong, C. (2014, December 31). *Dr. Dawnie Steadman—University of Tennessee's FAC Director* [Video]. YouTube. https://www.youtube.com/watch?v=84PHQSpmwJM

Arnauld, M. C., Manzanilla, L. R., & Smith, M. E. (Eds.). (2012). *The neighborhood as a social and spatial unit in Mesoamerican cities.* University of Arizona Press.

Arnold, B. (1990). The past as propaganda: Totalitarian archaeology in Nazi Germany. *Antiquity, 64*(244), 464–478.

Arnold, B., & Wicker, N. L. (2001). *Gender and the archaeology of death.* AltaMira Press.

Ashe, L., Djordjević, I., Weiss, J. E., & Djordjevic, I. (Eds.). (2010). *The exploitations of medieval romance.* Boydell & Brewer Ltd.

Assaf, E., Caricola, I., Gopher, A., Rosell, J., Blasco, R., Bar, O., Zilberman, E., Lemorini, C., Baena, J., Barkal, R., & Cristiani, E. (2020). Shaped stone balls were used for bone marrow extraction at Lower Paleolithic Qesem Cave, Israel. *PLOS ONE, 15*(4), Article e0230972. https://doi.org/10.1371/journal.pone.0230972

Atalay, S. (2006). Introduction: Decolonizing archaeology—Efforts to transform a discipline. *American Indian Quarterly, 30*(3), 269–279.

Atalay, S. (2010a). 'We don't talk about Çatalhöyük, we live it': Building community capacity through archaeological research using a community-based participatory research (CBPR) methodology. *World Archaeology, 42*(3), 418–429.

Atalay, S. (2010b). Indigenous archaeology as decolonizing practice. In M. M. Bruchac, S. M. Hart, & H. M. Wobst (Eds.), *Indigenous archaeologies: A reader on decolonization* (pp. 79–86). Left Coast Press. [Reprint from *American Indian Quarterly, 30*(3), 280–310].

Atalay, S. (2012). *Community-based archaeology: Research with, by and for Indigenous and local communities.* University of California Press.

Athreya, S. (2018). Picking a bone with evolutionary essentialism. *Anthropology News, 59*(5), e55–e60.

Axelsson, E., Ratnakumar, A., Arendt, M., Maqbool, K., Webster, M. T., Perloski, M., Liberg, O., Arnemo, J. M., Hedhammar, Å., & Lindblad-Toh, K. (2013). The genomic signature of dog domestication reveals adaptation to a starch-rich diet. *Nature, 495*(7441), 360–364.

Ayala, F. J. (1995). The myth of Eve: Molecular biology and human origins. *Science, 270*, 1930–1936.

Azcorra, H., Varela-Silva, M. I., Rodriguez, L., Bogin, B., & Dickinson, F. (2013). Nutritional status of Maya children, their mothers, and their grandmothers residing in the City of Merida, Mexico: Revisiting the leg-length hypothesis. *American Journal of Human Biology, 25*(5), 659–665.

Baba, M. (2006). Anthropology and business. In H. J. Birx (Ed.), *Encyclopedia of anthropology* (pp. 83–117). Sage Publications. https://doi.org/10.4135/9781412952453.n35

Baba, M. L. (2012). Anthropology and business: Influence and interests. *Journal of Business Anthropology, 1*(1), 20–71.

Baba, M. L., & Hill, C. E. (2006). What's in the name "applied anthropology"?: An encounter with global practice. *NAPA Bulletin, 25*(1), 176–207.

Bagatell, N. (2010). From cure to community: Transforming notions of autism. *Ethos, 38*(1), 33–55.

Bakdash, T., & Scheper-Hughes, N. (2006). Is it ethical for patients with renal disease to purchase kidneys from the world's poor? *PLOS Medicine, 3*(10), Article e349.

Baker, L. D. (2021). The racist anti-racism of American anthropology. *Transforming Anthropology, 29*(2), 127–142.

Baker-Bell, A. (2020). *Linguistic justice: Black language, literacy, identity and pedagogy.* Routledge.

Ball, C. (2011). Boasian legacies in linguistic anthropology: A centenary review of 2011. *American Anthropologist, 114*(2), 203–216.

Ball, H. L. (2019). Breastfeeding and infant sleep—What medical practitioners need to know. In A. Brown & W. Jones (Eds.), *A guide to supporting breastfeeding for the medical profession.* Routledge.

Bamshad, M. J., Wooding, S., Watkins, W. S., Ostler, C. T., Batzer, M. A., & Jorde, L. B. (2003). Human population genetic structure and inference of group membership. *American Journal of Human Genetics, 72*(3), 578–589.

Barkai, R., Rosell, J., & Gopher, A. (2017). Fire for a reason: Barbecue at Middle Pleistocene Qesem Cave, Israel. *Current Anthropology, 58*(S16), S314–S328. https://doi.org/10.1086/691211

Barker, G. (2009). *The agricultural revolution in prehistory: Why did foragers become farmers?* Oxford University Press.

Baron, J. P. (2018). Making money in Mesoamerica: Currency production and procurement in the classic Maya financial system. *Economic Anthropology, 5*(2), 210–223.

Barrett, R., Kuzawa, C. W., McDade, T., & Armelagos, G. J. (1998). Emerging and re-emerging infectious diseases: The third epidemiologic transition. *Annual Review of Anthropology, 27*(1), 247–271.

Barth, F. (1956). Ecologic relationships of ethnic groups in Swat, North Pakistan. *American Anthropologist, 58*, 1079–1089.

Barth, F. (1969). *Ethnic groups and boundaries: The social organization of culture difference.* Waveland Press.

Barton, L., Newsome, S. D., Chen, F.-H., Wang, H., Guilderson, T. P., & Bettinger, R. L. (2009). Agricultural origins and the isotopic identity of domestication in northern China. *Proceedings of the National Academy of Sciences U.S.A., 106*(14), 5523–5528.

Basso, K. (1996). *Wisdom sits in places: Landscape and language among the Western Apache.* University of New Mexico Press.

Basu, S., Zuo, X., Lou, C., Acharya, R., & Lundgren, R. (2017). Learning to be gendered: Gender socialization in early adolescence among urban poor in Delhi, India, and Shanghai, China. *Journal of Adolescent Health, 61*(4), S24–S29.

Battle-Baptiste, W., & Rusert, B. (Eds.). (2018). *W. E. B. Du Bois's data portraits: Visualizing Black America: The color line at the turn of the twentieth century.* The W. E. B. Du Bois Center at the University of Massachusetts Amherst.

Baugh, J. (2000). Racial identification by speech. *American Speech, 75*(4), 362–364.

Baugh, J. (2018). *Linguistics in pursuit of justice.* Cambridge University Press.

Bauman, R., & Briggs, C. (2003). *Voices of modernity: Language ideologies and the politics of inequality.* Cambridge University Press.

Beall, C. (2007). Two routes to functional adaptation: Tibetan and Andean high-altitude natives. *Proceedings of the National Academy of Sciences U.S.A., 104*(Suppl 1), 8655–8660.

Beall, C. (2014). Adaptation to high altitude: Phenotypes and genotypes. *Annual Review of Anthropology, 43*, 251–272.

Beck, J. (2019, December 17). Why people pretend to talk as their pets. *The Atlantic.* https://www.theatlantic.com/family/archive/2019/12/why-do-people-make-voices-their-pets/603718/

Becker, A. E. (2013). *Body, self, and society: The view from Fiji.* University of Pennsylvania Press.

Becker, A. E. (2018). Sociocultural influences on body image and eating disturbance. In *Eating disorders and obesity: A comprehensive handbook* (pp. 127–133). Guilford Press.

Beckerman, S., Erickson, P. I., Yost, J., Regalado, J., Jaramillo, L., Sparks, C., Iromenga, M., & Long, K. (2009). Life histories, blood revenge, and reproductive success among the Waorani of Ecuador. *Proceedings of the National Academy of Sciences U.S.A., 106*(20), 8134–8139.

Bedford, S., & Spriggs, M. (Eds.). (2019). *Debating Lapita: Distribution, chronology, society and subsistence.* ANU Press.

Begun, D. R. (2007). Fossil record of Miocene hominoids. *Handbook of Paleoanthropology, 2*, 921–977.

Behar, R. (2003). *Translated woman: Crossing the border with Esperanza's story.* Beacon Press.

Beja-Pereira, A., Luikart, G., England, P. R., Bradley, D. G., Jann, O. C., Bertorelle, G., Chamberlain, A. T., Nunes, T., Metodiev, S., Ferrand, N., & Erhardt, G. (2003). Gene-culture coevolution between cattle milk protein genes and human lactase genes. *Nature Genetics, 35*(4), 311–313.

Bejarano, C. A., Juárez, L. L., García, M. A. M., & Goldstein, D. M. (2019). *Decolonizing ethnography: Undocumented immigrants and new directions in social science.* Duke University Press.

Beliso-De Jesús, A. M. (2020). The jungle academy: Molding white supremacy in American police recruits. *American Anthropologist, 122*, 143–156. https://doi.org/10.1111/aman.13357

Beliso-De Jesús, A. M., & Pierre, J. (Eds.). (2020). Special section: Anthropology of white supremacy. *American Anthropologist, 122*(1), 65–75.

Beliso-De Jesús, A. M., & Ralph, L. (2023, Spring). *Policing and militarization today* [Course]. Anthropology@Princeton. https://anthropology.princeton.edu/courses/policing-and-militarization-today

Bellwood, P. (2004). *First farmers: The origins of agricultural societies.* Wiley-Blackwell.

Ben-Dor, M., Sitorli, R., & Barkai, R. (2021). The evolution of the human trophic level during the Pleistocene. *American Journal of Physical Anthropology, 175*(S72), 27–56. https://doi.org/10.1002/ajpa.24247

Benn Torres, J. (2014). Prospecting the past: Genetic perspectives on the extinction and survival of indigenous peoples of the Caribbean. *New Genetics and Society, 33*(1), 21–41.

Benn Torres, J. (2016). A history of you, me, and humanity: Mitochondrial DNA in anthropological research. *AIMS Genetics, 3*(2), 146–156. https://doi.org/10.3934/genet.2016.2.146

Benn Torres, J. (2020). Anthropological perspectives on genomic data, genetic ancestry, and race. *American Journal of Physical Anthropology, 171*, 74–86.

Benn Torres, J., Martucci, V., Aldrich, M. C., Vilar, M. G., MacKinney, T., Gaieski, J. B., Hernandez, R. B., Browne, Z. E., Stevenson, M., Walters, W., Tariq, M., Schurr, T. G., & The Genographic Consortium. (2019). Analysis of biogeographic ancestry reveals complex genetic histories for indigenous communities of St. Vincent and Trinidad. *American Journal of Physical Anthropology, 169*, 482–497. https://doi.org/10.1002/ajpa.23859

Benn Torres, J., & Torres Colón, G. A. (2020). *Genetic ancestry: Our stories, our pasts.* Routledge Press.

Benn Torres, J., Vilar, M., Torres, G., Gaieski, J., Bharath Hernandez, H., Browne, Z., Stevenson, M., Walters, W., Schurr, T. G., & The Genographic Consortium. (2015). Genetic diversity in the Lesser Antilles and its implications for the settlement of the Caribbean Basin. *PLOS ONE, 10*(10), Article e0139192.

Benson, L. V. (2010). Who provided maize to Chaco Canyon after the mid-12th-century drought? *Journal of Archaeological Science, 37*(3), 621–629.

Benson, L., Cordell, L., Vincent, K., Taylor, H., Stein, J., Farmer, G. L., & Futa, K. (2003). Ancient maize from Chacoan great houses: Where was it grown? *Proceedings of the National Academy of Sciences U.S.A., 100*, 13111–13115.

Benson, L. V., & Grimstead, D. N. (2019). Prehistoric Chaco Canyon, New Mexico: Residential population implications of limited agricultural and mammal productivity. *Journal of Archaeological Science, 108*, Article 104971.

Benson, L. V., Grimstead, D. N., Stein, J. R., Roth, D. A., & Plowman, T. I. (2019). Prehistoric Chaco Canyon, New Mexico: Importation of meat and maize. *Journal of Archaeological Science, 111*, Article 105015.

Benson, L. V., Stein, J. R., & Taylor, H. E. (2009). Possible sources of archaeological maize found in Chaco Canyon and Aztec Ruin, New Mexico. *Journal of Archaeological Science, 36*(2), 387–407.

Bentley, G. C. (1987). Ethnicity and practice. *Comparative Studies in Society and History, 29*, 24–55.

Bentley, G. R. (2020). Don't blame the BAME: Ethnic and structural inequalities in susceptibilities to COVID-19. *American Journal of Human Biology, 32*, Article e23478. https://doi.org/10.1002/ajhb.23478

Bentley, G. R., Goldberg, T., & Jasieńska, G. Z. Y. (1993). The fertility of agricultural and non-agricultural traditional societies. *Population Studies, 47*(2), 269–281.

Bentley, R. A., & O'Brien, M. J. (2019). Modeling niche construction in neolithic Europe. In M. Saqalli & M. Vander Linden (Eds.), *Integrating qualitative and social science factors in archaeological modelling* (pp. 91–108). Springer, Cham. https://doi.org/10.1007/978-3-030-12723-7_4

Beresford, M., Wutich, A., Garrick, D., & Drew, G. (2023). Moral economies for water: A framework for analyzing norms of justice, economic behavior, and social enforcement in contexts of water inequality. *WIREs Water*, Article e1627. https://doi.org/10.1002/wat2.1627

Berger, L. R., Hawks, J., de Ruitter, D. J., Churchill, S. E., Schmid, P., Delezene, L. K., Kivell, T. L., Garvin, H. M., Williams, S. A., DeSilva, J. M., Skinner, M. M., Musiba, C. M., Cameron, N., Holliday, T. W., Harcourt-Smith, W., Ackermann, R. R., Bastir, M., Bogin, B., Bolter, D., . . . Zipfel, B. (2015). *Homo naledi*, a species of the genus *Homo* from the Dinaledi Chamber, South Africa. *eLife, 4*, Article e09560.

Bergström, A., Stringer, C., Hajdinjak, M., Scerri, E. M. L., & Skoglund, P. (2021). Origins of modern human ancestry. *Nature, 590*(7845), 229–237. https://doi.org/10.1038/s41586-021-03244-5

Bernard, A. B., & Marshall, A. J. (2020). Assessing the state of knowledge of contemporary climate change and primates. *Evolutionary Anthropology, 29*, 317–331. https://doi.org/10.1002/evan.21874

Besnier, N. (1994). Polynesian gender liminality through time and space. In G. Herdt (Ed.), *Third sex, third gender: Beyond sexual dimorphism in culture and history* (pp. 316–317). Zone Books.

Besnier, N. (2002). Transgenderism, locality, and the Miss Galaxy beauty pageant in Tonga. *American Ethnologist, 29*(3), 534–566.

Betsinger, T. K., & DeWitte, S. N. (2021). Toward a bioarchaeology of urbanization: Demography, health, and behavior in cities in the past. *American Journal of Physical Anthropology, 175*(S72), 79–118.

Bezanson, M., & McNamara, A. (2019). The what and where of primate field research may be failing primate conservation. *Evolutionary Anthropology, 28*, 166–178. https://doi.org/10.1002/evan.21790

Bhana, D. (2013). How to talk about love in Africa: A view from Jennifer Cole. *Agenda, 27*(2), 99–104.

Bhopal, R. (2007). The beautiful skull and Blumenbach's errors: The birth of the scientific concept of race. *BMJ (Clinical Research Edition), 335*(7633), 1308–1309. https://doi.org/10.1136/bmj.39413.463958.80

Binford, L. R. (2014). *Bones: Ancient men and modern myths.* Academic Press.

Biran, A., Schmidt, W. P., Varadharajan, K. S., Rajaraman, D., Kumar, R., Greenland, K., Gopalan, B., Aunger, R., & Curtis, V. (2014). Effect of a behaviour-change intervention on handwashing with soap in India (SuperAmma): A cluster-randomised trial. *The Lancet Global Health, 2*(3), e145–e154.

Bird, D. W., Bird, R. B., Codding, B. F., & Zeanah, D. W. (2019). Variability in the organization and size of hunter-gatherer groups: Foragers do not live in small-scale societies. *Journal of Human Evolution, 131*, 96–108.

Bird, R. B., & Bird, D. W. (2008). Why women hunt: Risk and contemporary foraging in a Western Desert aboriginal community. *Current Anthropology, 49*(4), 655–693.

Bird, R. B., & Codding, B. F. (2015). The sexual division of labor. In R. A. Scott & S. M. Kosslyn (Eds.), *Emerging trends in the social and behavioral sciences.* https://doi.org/10.1002/9781118900772.etrds0300

Biro, D., Humle, T., Koops, K., Sousa, C., Hayashi, M., & Matsuzawa, T. (2010). Chimpanzee mothers at Bossou, Guinea carry the mummified remains of their dead infants. *Current Biology, 20*(8), R351–R352.

Bjork-James, C. (2020a). *The sovereign street: Making revolution in urban Bolivia.* University of Arizona Press.

Bjork-James, C. (2020b). Unarmed militancy: Tactical victories, subjectivity, and legitimacy in Bolivian street protest. *American Anthropologist, 122*(3), 514–527.

Black, S. P. (2012). Laughing to death: Joking as support amid stigma for Zulu-speaking South Africans living with HIV/AIDS. *Journal of Linguistic Anthropology, 22*(1), 87–108.

Black, S. P. (2013). Stigma and ideological constructions of the foreign: Facing HIV/AIDS in South Africa. *Language in Society, 42*(5), 481–502.

Black, S. P. (2016, January 28). To tell or not to tell. *SAPIENS.* https://www.sapiens.org/culture/to-tell-or-not-to-tell/

Black, S. P. (2017). Anthropological ethics and the communicative affordances of audio-video recorders in ethnographic fieldwork: Transduction as theory. *American Anthropologist, 119*, 46–57. https://doi.org/10.1111/aman.12823

Black, S. P. (2019). *Speech and song at the margins of global health: Zulu tradition, HIV stigma, and AIDS activism in South Africa.* Rutgers University Press.

Black, S. P. (2020). Communicability, stigma, and xenophobia during the COVID-19 outbreak: "Common reactions"? *Language, Culture, and Society, 2*(2), 242–251. https://doi.org/10.1075/lcs.00028.bla

Black, S. P., & Falconi, E. A. (2017). Linguistic anthropology and ethnolinguistics. In M. Aronoff & J. Rees-Miller (Eds.), *The handbook of linguistics* (2nd ed., pp. 479–503). John Wiley & Sons, Ltd.

Blakey, M. L. (1987). Skull doctors: Intrinsic social and political bias in the history of American physical anthropology; with special reference to the work of Ales Hrdlicka. *Critique of Anthropology, 7*, 7–35.

Blakey, M. L. (1995). Race, nationalism, and the Afrocentric past. In *Making alternative histories: The practice of archaeology and history in non-Western settings* (pp. 213–228).

Blakey, M. L. (1998). The New York African Burial Ground Project: An examination of enslaved lives, a construction of ancestral ties. *Transforming Archaeology, 7*, 53–58.

Blakey, M. L. (1999). Scientific racism and the biological concept of race. *Literature and Psychology, 45*, 29–43.

Blakey, M. L. (2020). Archaeology under the blinding light of race. *Current Anthropology, 61*(S22), S183–S197.

Blakey, M. L. (2021). Understanding racism in physical (biological) anthropology. *American Journal of Physical Anthropology, 175*(2), 316–325.

Blandy, S., & Lister, D. (2005). Gated communities: (Ne)gating community development? *Housing Studies, 20*(2), 287–301.

Blaser, M., De Costa, R., McGregor, D., & Coleman, W. D. (Eds.). (2011). *Indigenous peoples and autonomy: Insights for a global age.* University of British Columbia Press.

Bleichenbacher, L. (2012). Linguicism in Hollywood movies? Representations of, and audience reactions to multilingualism in mainstream movie dialogues. *Multilingua, 31*(2–3), 76–155.

Block, D. (2018). The political economy of language education research (or the lack thereof): Nancy Fraser and the case of translanguaging. *Critical Inquiry in Language Studies, 15*(4), 237–257.

Blommaert, J. (2010). *The sociolinguistics of globalization.* Cambridge University Press.

Bloomfield, S. F., Rook, G. A., Scott, E. A., Shanahan, F., Stanwell-Smith, R., & Turner, P. (2016). Time to abandon the hygiene hypothesis: New perspectives on allergic disease, the human microbiome, infectious disease prevention and the role of targeted hygiene. *Perspectives in Public Health, 136*(4), 213–224.

Boas, F. (1911). Changes in bodily form of descendants of immigrants (Final Report). Reports of the U.S. Immigration Commission (1907–10). Government Printing Office.

Boas, F. (1912). Changes in the bodily form of descendants of immigrants. *American Anthropologist, 14*(3), 530–562.

Body Worlds. (n.d.). https://bodyworlds.com

Boellstorff, T. (2004). Gay language and Indonesia: Registering belonging. *Journal of Linguistic Anthropology, 14*(2), 248–268.

Boellstorff, T. (2005). *The gay archipelago: Sexuality and the nation in Indonesia.* Princeton University Press.

Boellstorff, T. (2011). But do not identify as gay: A proleptic genealogy of the MSM category. *Cultural Anthropology, 26*(2), 287–312.

Boellstorff, T. (2015). *Coming of age in Second Life: An anthropologist explores the virtually human.* Princeton University Press.

Bogin, B., Varela-Silva, M. I., Rios, L., & Silva M. (2007). Life history trade-offs in human growth: Adaptation or pathology? *American Journal of Human Biology, 19*(5), 631–642.

Bolnick, D. A., Fullwiley, D., Duster, T., Cooper, R. S., Fujimura, J. H., Kahn, J., Kaufman, J. S., Marks, J., Morning, A., Nelson, A., Ossorio, P., Reardon, J., Reverby, S. M., & TallBear, K. (2007). The science and business of genetic ancestry testing. *Science, 318*, 399–400.

Bolnick, D. A., Smith, R. W., & Fuentes, A. (2019). How academic diversity is transforming scientific knowledge in biological anthropology. *American Anthropologist, 121*(2), 464.

Bonilla, Y., & Rosa, J. (2015). #Ferguson: Digital protest, hashtag ethnography, and the racial politics of social media in the United States. *American Ethnologist, 42*(1), 4–17.

Borgstrom, E. (2016). Social death. *QJM: An International Journal of Medicine, 110*(1), 5–7.

Boroditsky, L. (2011a). How languages construct time. In S. Dehaene & E. Brannon (Eds.), *Space, time and number in the brain: Searching for the foundations of mathematical thought* (pp. 333–341). Academic Press.

Boroditsky, L. (2011b, February 1). *How language shapes thought: The languages we speak affect our perceptions of the world.* Scientific American. https://www.scientificamerican.com/article/how-language-shapes-thought/

Boroditsky, L. (2017, November). *How language shapes the way we think* [Video]. TED Conferences. https://www.ted.com/talks/lera_boroditsky_how_language_shapes_the_way_we_think/transcript?language=en

Boroditsky, L., & Gaby, A. (2010). Remembrances of times east: Absolute spatial representations of time in an Australian aboriginal community. *Psychological Science, 21*(11), 1635–1639. https://doi.org/10.1177/0956797610386621

Bos, K. I., Harkins, K. M., Herbig, A., Coscolla, M., Weber, N., Comas, I., Forrest, S. A., Bryant, J. M., Harris, S. R., Schuenemann, V. J., Campbell, T. J., Majander, K., Wilbur, A. K., Guichon, R. A., Steadman, D. L. W., Cook, D. C., Niemann, S., Behr, M. A., Zumarraga, M., . . . Krause, J. (2014). Pre-Columbian mycobacterial genomes reveal seals as a source of New World human tuberculosis. *Nature, 514*, 494–497.

Bos, K. I., Stevens, P., Nieselt, K., Poinar, H. N., DeWitte, S. N., & Krause, J. (2012). *Yersinia pestis*: New evidence for an old infection. *PLOS ONE, 7*(11), Article e49803.

Bossak, B. H., & Welford, M. R. (2016). Spatio-temporal characteristics of the medieval Black Death. In *Spatial analysis in health geography* (pp. 71–84). Routledge.

Bouie, J. (2018, June 5). *The Enlightenment's dark side.* Slate. https://slate.com/news-and-politics/2018/06/taking-the-enlightenment-seriously-requires-talking-about-race.html

Bourdieu, P. (2018). The forms of capital. In M. Granovetter & R. Swedberg (Eds.), *The sociology of economic life* (3rd ed., pp. 78–92). Routledge.

Bourget, S. (2006). *Sex, death, and sacrifice in Moche religion and visual culture.* University of Texas Press.

Bourgois, P. (2001). The power of violence in war and peace: Post–Cold War lessons from El Salvador. *Ethnography, 2*(1), 5–34.

Bourgois, P., & Schonberg, J. (2007). Intimate apartheid: Ethnic dimensions of habitus among homeless heroin injectors. *Ethnography, 8*(1), 7–31.

Bowser, B. J. (2000). From pottery to politics: An ethnoarchaeological study of political factionalism, ethnicity, and domestic pottery style in the Ecuadorian Amazon. *Journal of Archaeological Method and Theory, 7*(3), 219–248.

Boyd, B. (2018). The evolution of stories: From mimesis to language, from fact to fiction. *Wiley Interdisciplinary Reviews: Cognitive Science, 9*(1), Article e1444.

Boyd, R. (2006). The puzzle of human sociality. *Science, 314*(5805), 1555–1556.

Boyd, R. (2018). *A different kind of animal: How culture transformed our species.* Princeton University Press.

Boyd, R., Hardeman, R., Ogunwole, M., Fields, N., Khazanachi, R., Nolen, L., Onuoha, C., Paul, D., & Essien, U. R. (2020, August 25). Racism, police violence, and health. (No. 120) [Podcast episode]. In *Anti-racism in medicine*. Clinical Problem Solvers. https://clinicalproblemsolving.com/2020/08/25/episode-120-antiracism-in-medicine-series-episode-1-racism-police-violence-and-health/

Boyd, R., & Richerson, P. J. (2001). Norms and bounded rationality. In G. Gigerenzer & R. Selten (Eds.), *Bounded rationality: The adaptive toolbox* (pp. 281–296). MIT Press.

Branas, C. C., Dinardo, A. R., Puac Polanco, V. D., Harvey, M. J., Vassy, J. L., & Bream, K. (2013). An exploration of violence, mental health and substance abuse in post-conflict Guatemala. *Health, 5*(5), 825–833.

Branch, G., & Scott, E. C. (2013). Peking, Piltdown, and Paluxy: Creationist legends about paleoanthropology. *Evolution: Education and Outreach, 6*, 27. https://doi.org/10.1186/1936-6434-6-27

Brandes, S. (2000). El día de muertos, el Halloween y la búsqueda de una identidad nacional mexicana. *Alteridades, 10*(20), 7–20.

Brandes, S. (2009). Torophiles and torophobes: The politics of bulls and bullfights in contemporary Spain. *Anthropological Quarterly, 82*(3), 779–794.

Brettell, C. B., & Sargent, C. F. (Eds.). (2012). *Gender in cross-cultural perspective* (6th ed.). Pearson Prentice Hall.

Brewis, A., & Meyer, M. (2005). Demographic evidence that human ovulation is undetectable (at least in pair bonds). *Current Anthropology, 46*(3), 465–471.

Brewis, A., Roba, K. T., Wutich, A., Manning, M., & Yousuf, J. (2021). Household water insecurity and psychological distress in Eastern Ethiopia: Unfairness and water sharing as undertheorized factors. *SSM-Mental Health, 1*, 100008.

Brewis, A., & Wutich, A. (2019). *Lazy, crazy, and disgusting: Stigma and the undoing of global health*. Johns Hopkins University Press.

Brice Heath, S. (1986). What no bedtime story means: Narrative skills at home and school. In B. B. Schieffelin & E. Ochs (Eds.), *Language socialization across cultures* (pp. 97–124). Cambridge University Press.

Briggs, C. L., & Mantini-Briggs, C. (2003). *Stories in the time of cholera: Racial profiling during a medical nightmare*. University of California Press.

Briody, E. K., & Pester, T. M. (2014). The coming of age of anthropological practice and ethics. *Journal of Business Anthropology*, Special Issue 1, 11–37.

Briody, E. K., & Pester, T. M. (2017). Redesigning anthropology's ethical principles to align with anthropological practice. In T. de Waal Malefyt & R. J. Morais (Eds.), *Ethics in the anthropology of business: Explorations in theory, practice, and pedagogy* (pp. 23–44). Routledge.

Briody, E., Pester, T. M., & Trotter, R. (2012). A story's impact on organizational-culture change. *Journal of Organizational Change Management, 25*(1), 67–87.

Brodkin, K., Morgen, S., & Hutchinson, J. (2011). Anthropology as white public space? *American Anthropologist, 113*(4), 545–556.

Brondizio, E. S., Ostrom, E., & Young, O. R. (2009). Connectivity and the governance of multilevel social-ecological systems: The role of social capital. *Annual Review of Environment and Resources, 34*, 253–278.

Brosius, J. P. (2006). Common ground between anthropology and conservation biology. *Conservation Biology, 20*(3), 683–685.

Brosnan, S. F., de Waal, F. B. M., & Proctor, D. (2014). Reciprocity in primates. In S. D. Preston, M. L. Kringelbach, & B. Knutson (Eds.), *The interdisciplinary science of consumption* (pp. 3–31). Boston Review. https://doi.org/10.7551/mitpress/9780262027670.003.0001

Brown, J., & Dye, D. H. (2007). Severed heads and sacred scalplocks: Mississippian iconographic trophies. In R. J. Chacon & D. H. Dye (Eds.), *The taking and displaying of human body parts as trophies by Amerindians* (pp. 278–298). Springer.

Brown, R. A., & Armelagos, G. J. (2001). Apportionment of racial diversity: A review. *Evolutionary Anthropology, 10*, 34–40.

Brownell, S., & Besnier, N. (2013). Gender and sexuality. In J. J. Carrier & D. B. Gewertz (Eds.), *The handbook of sociocultural anthropology* (pp. 239–258). Bloomsbury.

Browning, S. R., Browning, B. L., Zhou, Y., Tucci, S., & Akey, J. M. (2018). Analysis of human sequence data reveals two pulses of archaic Denisovan admixture. *Cell, 173*(1), 53–61. https://doi.org/10.1016/j.cell.2018.02.031

Brumfiel, E. M. (1994). Ethnic groups and political development in ancient Mexico. In E. M. Brumfiel & J. W. Fox (Eds.), *Factional competition and political development in the New World* (pp. 89–102). Cambridge University Press.

Brutsaert, T. (2010). Human adaptation to high altitude. In M. P. Muehlenbein (Ed.), *Human evolutionary biology* (pp. 170–191). Cambridge University Press.

Bruxelles, L., Stratford, D. J., Marie, R., Pickering, T. R., Heaton, J. L., Beaudet, A., Kuman, K., Crompton, R., Carlson, K. J., Jashashvili, T., McClymont, J., Leader, G. M., & Clarke, R. J. (2019). A multiscale stratigraphic investigation of the context of StW 573 'Little Foot' and

Member 2, Sterkfontein Caves, South Africa. *Journal of Human Evolution, 133,* 78–98.

Brynildsrud, O. B., Pepperell, C. S., Suffys, P., Grandjean, L., Monteserin, J., Debech, N., Bohlin, J., Alfsnes, K., Pettersson, J. O. H., Kirkeleite, I., Fandinho, F., Aparecida da Silva, M., Perdigao, J., Portugal, I., Viveiros, M., Clark, T., Caws, M., Dunstan, S., . . . Eldholm, V. (2018). Global expansion of *Mycobacterium tuberculosis* lineage 4 shaped by colonial migration and local adaptation. *Science Advances, 4*(10). https://doi.org/10.1126/sciadv.aat5869

Buikstra, J. E. (1995). Tombs for the living . . . or . . . for the dead: The Osmore ancestors. In T. Dillehay (Ed.), *Tombs for the living: Andean mortuary practices* (pp. 229–279). Dumbarton Oaks.

Buikstra, J. E. (1998). Los cementerios de Chiribaya y Estuquiña. In K. Wise (Ed.), *Moquegua: Los primeros doce mil años* (pp. 91–101). Policrom.

Buikstra, J. E., & Beck, L. A. (Eds.). (2006). *Bioarchaeology: The contextual analysis of human remains.* Academic Press.

Bull, B. (2013). Social movements and the 'Pink Tide' governments in Latin America: Transformation, inclusion and rejection. In *Democratization in the Global South* (pp. 75–99). Palgrave Macmillan.

Burger, J., Link, V., Blöcher, J., Schulz, A., Sell, C., Pochon, Z., Diekmann, Y., Žegarac, A., Hofmanová, Z., Winkelbach, L., Reyna-Blanco, C. S., Bieker, V., Orschiedt, J., Brinker, U., Scheu, A., Leuenberger, C., Bertino, T. S., Bollongino, R., Lidke, G., . . . Wegmann, D. (2020). Low prevalence of lactase persistence in Bronze Age Europe indicates ongoing strong selection over the last 3,000 years. *Current Biology, 30*(21), 4307–4315.

Burke, B. J. (2012). *"Para que cambiemos"/"So we can (ex) change": Economic activism and socio-cultural change in the barter systems of Medellín, Colombia* (Publication No. 3509096) [Doctoral dissertation, The University of Arizona]. ProQuest Dissertations Publishing.

Burke, B. J. (2022). *Social exchange: Barter as economic and cultural activism in Medellín, Colombia.* Rutgers University Press.

Burke, B. J., & Shear, B. (2014). Introduction: Engaged scholarship for non-capitalist political ecologies. *Journal of Political Ecology, 21*(1), 127–144.

Burnet, J. E. (2008). Gender balance and the meanings of women in governance in post-genocide Rwanda. *African Affairs, 107*(428), 361–386.

Burnett, D. (2016). Illuminating the legacy of Zora Neale Hurston: Visionary, architect, and anthropologist of Africana religious subjectivities. *Journal of Africana Religions, 4*(2), 255–266.

Burnett, S., & Irish, J. (Eds.). (2017). *A world view of bioculturally modified teeth.* University Press Scholarship.

BurnSilver, S., Magdanz, J., Stotts, R., Berman, M., & Kofinas, G. (2016). Are mixed economies persistent or transitional? Evidence using social networks from Arctic Alaska. *American Anthropologist, 118*(1), 121–129.

Burton, O. (2015). To protect and serve whiteness. *North American Dialogue, 18*(2), 38–50. https://doi.org/10.1111/nad.12032

Burton, O. (2016). *Attica is: Revolutionary consciousness, counterinsurgency and the deferred abolition of New York State prisons* (Publication No. 10242798) [Doctoral Dissertation, University of North Carolina-Chapel Hill]. ProQuest Dissertations Publishing.

Butler, J. (2002). *Gender trouble.* Routledge.

Caglar, A. (2015). Anthropology of citizenship. In J. D. Wright (Ed.), *International encyclopedia of the social & behavioral sciences* (2nd ed.). Elsevier. https://doi.org/10.1016/B978-0-08-097086-8.12180-4

Caldeira, T. P. (2000). *City of walls: Crime, segregation, and citizenship in São Paulo.* University of California Press.

Callaway, E. (2014). Domestication: The birth of rice. *Nature, 514,* S58–S59.

Callaway, E. (2021). Oldest DNA from a *Homo sapiens* reveals surprisingly recent Neanderthal ancestry. *Nature, 592*(7854), 339.

Cameron, E., Mearns, R., & McGrath, J. T. (2015). Translating climate change: Adaptation, resilience, and climate politics in Nunavut, Canada. *Annals of the Association of American Geographers, 105*(2), 274–283.

Campbell, M. W., & de Waal, F. B. M. (2011). Ingroup-outgroup bias in contagious yawning by chimpanzees supports link to empathy. *PLOS ONE, 6,* 19–22.

Cann, R. L., Stoneking, M., & Wilson, A. C. (1987). Mitochondrial DNA and human evolution. *Nature, 325*(6099), 31–36.

Carayon, D., Adhikari, K., Monsarrat, P., Dumoncel, J., Braga, J., Duployer, B., Delgado, M., Fuentes-Guajardo, M., de Beer, F., Hoffman, J. W., Oettlé, A. C., Donat, R., Pan, L., Ruiz-Linares, A., Tenailleau, C., Vaysse, F., Esclassan, R., & Zanolli, C. A. (2019). Geometric morphometric approach to the study of variation of shovel-shaped incisors. *American Journal of Physical Anthropology, 168,* 229–241. https://doi.org/10.1002/ajpa.23709

Carneiro, R. L. (1970). A theory of the origin of the state. *Science, 169*(3947), 733–738.

Cartmill, M. (1974). Rethinking primate origins. *Science, 184,* 436–443.

Cashdan, E. A. (1985). Coping with risk: Reciprocity among the Basarwa of Northern Botswana. *Man, 20*(3), 454–474.

Caspari, R. (2018). Race, then and now: 1918 revisited. *American Journal of Physical Anthropology, 165*(4), 924–938.

Cepelewicz, J. (2019, August 29). Fossil DNA reveals new twist in Modern Human origins. *Quanta Magazine.* https://www.quantamagazine.org/fossil-dna-reveals-new-twists-in-modern-human-origins-20190829/

CGTN. (2020, October 31). Ancient Denisovan DNA found in Chinese Karst cave. *CTGN.* https://news.cgtn.com/news/2020-10-31/Ancient-Denisovan-DNA-found-in-Chinese-karst-cave—V2yLXz02zK/index.html

Chagnon, N. A., Lynch, R. F., Shenk, M. K., Hames, R., & Flinn, M. V. (2017). Cross-cousin marriage among the Yanomamö shows evidence of parent–offspring conflict and mate competition between brothers. *Proceedings of the National Academy of Sciences U.S.A., 114*(13), E2590–E2607.

Chang, W., Cathcart, C., Hall, D., & Garrett, A. (2015). Ancestry-constrained phylogenetic analysis supports the Indo-European Steppe hypothesis. *Language, 91*(1), 194–244.

Chapman, C. A., Bicca-Marques, J. C., Dunham, A. E., Fan, P., Fashing, P. J., Gogarten, J. F., Guo, S., Huffman, M. A., Kalbitzer, U., Li, B., Ma, C., Matsuda, I., Omeja, P. A., Sarkar, D., Sengupta, R., Serio-Silva, J. C., Tsuji, Y., & Stenseth, N. C. (2020). Primates can be a rallying symbol to promote tropical forest restoration. *Folia Primatologica, 91*, 669–687. https://doi.org10.1159/000505951

Charity Hudley, A. H., Mallinson, C., Bucholtz, M., Flores, N., Holliday, N., Chun, E., & Spears, A. (2018). Linguistics and race: An interdisciplinary approach towards an LSA statement on race. *Proceedings of the Linguistic Society of America, 3*, Article 8.

Checker, M. (2005). *Polluted promises.* New York University Press.

Checker, M. (2007). "But I know it's true": Environmental risk assessment, justice, and anthropology. *Human Organization, 66*(2), 112–124.

Checker, M. (2020). *The sustainability myth: Environmental gentrification and the politics of justice.* New York University Press.

Checker, M., & Fishman, M. (2004). *Local actions: Cultural activism, power, and public life in America.* Columbia University Press.

Checker, M., Vine, D., & Wali, A. (2010). A sea change in anthropology? Public anthropology reviews. *American Anthropologist, 112*(1), 5–6.

Chen, D., Huang, J., Chen, J., You, Z., Wang, H., Wang, X., Yan, X., & Luo, X. (2019). Reappraisal of the Mawangdui Han tomb cadaver thirty years after its unearthing. *Biopreservation and Biobanking, 17*(20), 105–112.

Cheney, D. L., & Seyfarth, R. M. (2018). Flexible usage and social function in primate vocalizations. *Proceedings of the National Academy of Sciences U.S.A., 115*(9), 1974–1979. https://doi.org/10.1073/pnas.1717572115

Christakos, G., Olea, R. A., & Yu, H. L. (2007). Recent results on the spatiotemporal modelling and comparative analysis of Black Death and bubonic plague epidemics. *Public Health, 121*(9), 700–720.

Christensen, A. M., & Passalacqua, N. V. (2018). *A laboratory manual for forensic anthropology.* Academic Press.

Christensen, A. M., Passalacqua, N. V., & Bartelink, E. J. (2014). *Forensic anthropology: Current methods and practice.* Elsevier.

Chua, L., High, C., & Lau, T. (Eds.). (2009). *How do we know? Evidence, ethnography, and the making of anthropological knowledge.* Cambridge Scholars Publishing.

Clancy, K. B., & Davis, J. L. (2019). Soylent is people, and WEIRD is white: Biological anthropology, whiteness, and the limits of the WEIRD. *Annual Review of Anthropology, 48*, 169–186. https://doi.org/10.1146/annurev-anthro-102218-011133

Clancy, K. B., Nelson, R. G., Rutherford, J. N., & Hinde, K. (2014). Survey of academic field experiences (SAFE): Trainees report harassment and assault. *PLOS ONE, 9*(7), Article e102172.

Clarey, T. L. (2017). Disposal of *Homo naledi* in a possible deathtrap or mass mortality scenario. *Journal of Creation, 31*(2), 61–70.

Clark-Decès, I. (2005). *No one cries for the dead: Tamil dirges, rowdy songs, and graveyard petitions.* University of California Press.

Clifford, J., & Marcus, G. E. (Eds.). (1986). *Writing culture: The poetics and politics of ethnography* (a School of American Research advanced seminar). University of California Press.

Cobb, W. M. (1934). The physical constitution of the American Negro. *The Journal of Negro Education, 3*(3), 340–388.

Cobb, W. M. (1936). Race and runners. *Journal of Health and Physical Education, 7*, 1–9.

Coe, S. D., & Coe, M. D. (1996). *The true history of chocolate.* Thames & Hudson.

Cole, J. (2009). Love, money, and economies of intimacy in Tamatave, Madagascar. In J. Cole & L. Thomas (Eds.), *Love in Africa* (pp. 109–134). Chicago Scholarship.

Cole, J. (2010). *Sex and salvation: Imagining the future in Madagascar.* University of Chicago Press.

Cole, J., & Groes, C. (Eds.). (2016). *Affective circuits: African migrations to Europe and the pursuit of social regeneration*. University of Chicago Press.

Colwell, C. (2016). Collaborative archaeologies and descendant communities. *Annual Review of Anthropology, 45*(1), 113–127.

Colwell, C. (2018). The entanglement of Native Americans and colonialist archaeology in the southwestern United States. In B. Effros & G. Lai (Eds.), *Unmasking ideology in imperial and colonial archaeology: Vocabulary, symbols, and legacy* (pp. 151–172). Cotsen Institute of Archaeology Press.

Colwell, C. (2019). Can repatriation heal the wounds of history? *The Public Historian, 41*(1), 90–110.

Colwell, C. (2020). Collaboration is only a tool to decolonize the museum. *TRAJECTORIA, 1*, 1–11.

Colwell, C., & Koyiyumptewa, S. B. (2018). Traditional cultural properties and the Hopi model of cultural preservation. In L. J. Kuwanwisiwma, T. J. Ferguson, & C. Colwell (Eds.), *Footprints of Hopi history: Hopihiniwtiput Kukveni'at* (pp. 16–38). University of Arizona Press.

Commission for Racial Justice, United Church of Christ. (1987). *Toxic wastes and race in the United States*. https://www.nrc.gov/docs/ML1310/ML13109A339.pdf

Conching, A. K. S., & Thayer, Z. (2019). Biological pathways for historical trauma to affect health: A conceptual model focusing on epigenetic modifications. *Social Science & Medicine, 230*, 74–82.

Conkey, M. W., & Spector, J. D. (1984). Archaeology and the study of gender. *Advances in Archaeological Method and Theory, 7*, 1–38.

Conklin, B. (2001). *Consuming grief: Compassionate cannibalism in an Amazonian society*. University of Texas Press.

Constable, N. (2009). The commodification of intimacy: Marriage, sex, and reproductive labor. *Annual Review of Anthropology, 38*, 49–64.

Cooper, D., Delormier, T., & Taualii, M. (2019). 'It's always a part of you': The connection between sacred spaces and Indigenous/Aboriginal health. *International Journal of Human Rights Education, 3*(1). Retrieved from https://repository.usfca.edu/ijhre/vol3/iss1/2

Cooper, J., & Sheets, P. (Eds.). (2012). *Surviving sudden environmental change: Answers from archaeology*. University of Colorado Press.

Coqueugniot, H., Dutour, O., Arensburg, B., Duday, H., Vandermeersch, B., & Tillier, A.-m. (2014). Earliest cranio-encephalic trauma from the Levantine Middle Palaeolithic: 3D reappraisal of the Qafzeh 11 skull, consequences of pediatric brain damage on individual life condition and social care. *PLOS ONE, 9*(7), Article e102822. https://doi.org/10.1371/journal.pone.0102822

Cordain, L., Watkins, B. A., & Mann, N. J. (2001). Fatty acid composition and energy density of foods available to African hominids: Evolution implications for human brain development. *World Review of Nutrition and Dietetics, 90*, 144–161.

Corwin, Z. B., & Clemens, R. F. (2020). Analyzing fieldnotes: A practical guide. In M. R. M. Ward & S. Delamont (Eds.), *Handbook of qualitative research in education* (2nd ed., pp. 409–419). Edward Elgar Publishing.

Costantini, C. (2012, October 1). *Linguists tell New York Times that 'illegal' is neither 'neutral' nor 'accurate'*. ABC News. https://abcnews.go.com/ABC_Univision/linguists-york-times-illegal-neutral-accurate/story?id=17366512#.UHYiAGkzu7M

Coumans, C. (2017). Do no harm? Mining industry responses to the responsibility to respect human rights. *Canadian Journal of Development Studies/Revue canadienne d'études du développement, 38*(2), 272–290.

Coumans, C., & Kirsch, S. (2011). Occupying spaces created by conflict: Anthropologists, development NGOs, responsible investment, and mining. *Current Anthropology, 52*(S3), S29–S43.

Coupland, N. (Ed.). (2003). Sociolinguistics and globalisation [Special issue]. *Journal of Sociolinguistics, 7*(4), 465–623.

Covey, R., & McGraw, W. S. (2014). Monkeys in a West African bushmeat market: Implications for cercopithecid conservation in eastern Liberia. *Tropical Conservation Science, 7*(1), 115–125.

Cowgill, G. L. (1997). State and society at Teotihuacan, Mexico. *Annual Review of Anthropology, 26*, 129–161.

Cowgill, G. L. (2004). Origins and development of urbanism: Archaeological perspectives. *Annual Review of Anthropology, 33*, 525–549.

Cowgill, G. L. (2013). Possible migrations and shifting identities in the Central Mexican epiclassic. *Ancient Mesoamerica, 24*(1), 131–149. https://doi.org/10.1017/S0956536113000060

Cowgill, G. L. (2015). The debated role of migration in the fall of ancient Teotihuacan in Central Mexico. In B. J. Baker & T. Tsuda (Eds.), *Migration and disruptions: Unifying themes in studies of ancient and contemporary migration* (pp. 97–122). University Press of Florida.

Craft, J., Wright, K., Weissler, R., & Queen, R. (2020). Language and discrimination: Generating meaning, perceiving identities, and discriminating outcomes. *Annual Review of Linguistics, 6*, 389–407. https://doi.org/10.1146/annurev-linguistics-011718-011659

Cretton, V. (2018). Performing whiteness: Racism, skin colour, and identity in Western Switzerland. *Ethnic and Racial Studies, 41*(5), 842–859.

Crittenden, A. N., & Marlowe, F. W. (2008). Allomaternal care among the Hadza of Tanzania. *Human Nature, 19*(3), 249–263.

Crittenden, A. N., & Schnorr, S. L. (2017). Current views on hunter-gatherer nutrition and the evolution of the human diet. *American Journal of Physical Anthropology, 162*, 84–109. https://doi.org/10.1002/ajpa.23148

Crombé, P., Aluwé, K., Boudin, M., Snoeck, C., Messiaen, L., & Teetaert, D. (2020). New evidence on the earliest domesticated animals and possible small-scale husbandry in Atlantic NW Europe. *Scientific Reports, 10*(1), Article 20083.

Cronk, L. (1989). Low socioeconomic status and female-biased parental investment: The Mukogodo example. *American Anthropologist, 91*(2), 414–429.

Cronk, L. (1991). Human behavioral ecology. *Annual Review of Anthropology, 20*(1), 25–53.

Cronk, L. (2004). *From Mukogodo to Maasai: Ethnicity and cultural change in Kenya.* Westview Press.

Crowder, L. S. (2000). Chinese funerals in San Francisco Chinatown: American Chinese expressions in mortuary ritual performance. *Journal of American Folklore, 113*(450), 451–463.

Crowther, A., & Faulkner, P. (2021, May 5). A cave site in Kenya's forests reveals the oldest human burial in Africa. *The Conversation.* https://theconversation.com/a-cave-site-in-kenyas-forests-reveals-the-oldest-human-burial-in-africa-160343

Csordas, T. (2004). Evidence of and for what? *Anthropological Theory, 4*(4), 473–480.

Curry, A. (2013). Archaeology: The milk revolution. *Nature, 500*, 20–22. https://doi.org/10.1038/500020a

Daley, J. (2017, April 11). 13,000-year-old fillings were "drilled" with stone and packed with tar. *Smithsonian Magazine.* https://www.smithsonianmag.com/smart-news/researchers-find-filling-made-stone-age-dentist-180962845/

d'Alpoim Guedes, J., Gonzalez, S., & Rivera-Collazo, I. (2021). Resistance and care in the time of COVID-19: Archaeology in 2020. *American Anthropologist, 123*(4), 898–915. https://doi.org/10.1111/aman.13669

Dance, A. (2021, January 21). How to "co-live" with a natural hazard. *SAPIENS.* https://www.sapiens.org/culture/tungurahua/

Danforth, M. E. (1994). Stature change in prehistoric Maya of the southern lowlands. *Latin American Antiquity, 5*(3), 206–211.

D'Aoust, A.-M. (2011). *Love as a border technology: The governmentality of "mail-order brides" and marriage migrants in the United States and Germany* (Publication No. AAI3462193). [Dissertation, University of Pennsylvania]. Penn Libraries, University of Pennsylvania.

D'Aoust, A.-M. (2018). A moral economy of suspicion: Love and marriage migration management practices in the United Kingdom. *Environment and Planning D: Society and Space, 36*(1), 40–59. https://doi.org/10.1177/0263775817716674

Dass, A. (2019, April 12). *Angélica Dass's Humanae project* [Video]. Exploratorium. https://www.exploratorium.edu/video/angelica-dass-humanae-project

Davies, J., & Spencer, D. (2010). *Emotions in the field: The psychology and anthropology of fieldwork experience.* Stanford University Press.

Davis, D.-A. (2019a). *Reproductive injustice: Racism, pregnancy, and premature birth.* New York University Press.

Davis, D.-A. (2019b). Obstetric racism: The racial politics of pregnancy, labor, and birthing. *Medical Anthropology, 38*(7), 560–573.

Davis, D.-A., Varner, C., & Dill, L. J. (2021, August 27). A birth story. *Anthropology News.* https://www.anthropology-news.org/articles/a-birth-story/

Day, C. B. (1932). *A study of some Negro-white families in the United States* [with a foreword and notes on the anthropometric data by Earnest A. Hooton]. Peabody Museum of Harvard University. Reprinted in 1970 by Negro Universities Press.

De Albuquerque, K. (1998). In search of the big bamboo. *Transition,* (77), 48–57.

de la Rocha, M. G. (2001). From the resources of poverty to the poverty of resources? The erosion of a survival model. *Latin American Perspectives, 28*, 72–100. https://doi.org/10.1177%2F009458 2X010/2800405

de la Rocha, M. G. (2007). The construction of the myth of survival. *Development and Change, 38*, 45–66. https://doi.org/10.1111/j.1467-7660.2007.00402.x

de Leeuw, A., Happé, F., & Hoekstra, R. A. (2020). A conceptual framework for understanding the cultural and contextual factors on autism across the globe. *Autism Research, 13*, 1029–1050.

De León, J. (2015). *The land of open graves: Living and dying on the migrant trail.* University of California Press.

de Waal Malefyt, T., & Morais, R. J. (2020). *Advertising and anthropology: Ethnographic practice and cultural perspectives.* Routledge.

Dean, L. G., Vale, G. L., Laland, K. N., Flynn, E., & Kendal, R. L. (2014). Human cumulative culture: A comparative perspective. *Biological Reviews, 89*(2), 284–301.

Deléchat, C., & Medina, L. (2020). *What is the informal economy?* International Monetary Fund Publications. https://www.imf.org/en/Publications/fandd/issues/2020/12/what-is-the-informal-economy-basics

Delgado, A. N. (2018). Science, politics and the production of biological knowledge: New trends and old challenges. *Journal for General Philosophy of Science, 49*(3), 467–473.

Deloria, V., Jr. (1969). *Custer died for your sins: An Indian manifesto.* Macmillan.

Deloria, V., Jr. (1995). *Red earth, white lies: Native Americans and the myth of scientific fact.* Scribner.

Delphy, C. (1993). Rethinking sex and gender. *Women's Studies International Forum, 16*(1), 1–9.

DeLugan, R. M. (2012). *Reimagining national belonging: Post-civil war El Salvador in a global context.* University of Arizona Press.

DeLugan, R. M. (2020). *Remembering violence: How nations grapple with their difficult pasts.* Routledge.

Democracy Now! (2018, October 19). *Dissident Saudi Academic Madawi Al-Rasheed on Khashoggi's disappearance, U.S.-Saudi relations & more* [Video]. YouTube. https://www.youtube.com/watch?v=RetFU-LFL4Y

DeMyers, C., Warpinski, C., & Wutich, A. (2017). Urban water insecurity: A case study of homelessness in Phoenix, Arizona. *Environmental Justice, 10*(3), 72–80.

D'Errico, F., Henshilwood, C., Vanhaeren, M., & van Niekerk, K. (2005). *Nassarius kraussianus* shell beads from Blombos Cave: Evidence for symbolic behaviour in the Middle Stone Age. *Journal of Human Evolution, 48*(1), 3–24.

DeSalle, R., & Tattersall, I. (2018). *Troublesome science. The misuse of genetics and genomics in understanding race.* Columbia University Press.

Deter-Wolf, A., Robitaille, B., Krutak, L., & Galliot, S. (2016). The world's oldest tattoos. *Journal of Archaeological Science: Reports, 5*, 19–24. https://doi.org/10.1016/j.jasrep.2015.11.007

Díaz-Muñoz, S. L. (2011). Paternity and relatedness in a polyandrous nonhuman primate: Testing adaptive hypotheses of male reproductive cooperation. *Animal Behaviour, 82*(3), 563–571.

DiGangi, E. A., & Bethard, J. D. (2021). Uncloaking a lost cause: Decolonizing ancestry estimation in the United States. *American Journal of Physical Anthropology, 175*(2), 422–436.

Dingwall, H. L., Hatala, K. G., Wunderlich, R. E., & Richmond, B. G. (2013). Hominin stature, body mass, and walking speed estimates based on 1.5 million-year-old fossil footprints at Ileret, Kenya. *Journal of Human Evolution, 64*(6), 556–568.

Dirks, P. H. G. M., & Berger, L. R. (2013). Hominin-bearing caves and landscape dynamics in the Cradle of Humankind, South Africa. *Journal of African Earth Sciences, 78*, 109–131. https://doi.org/10.1016/j.jafrearsci.2012.09.012

Dirks, P. H. G. M., Berger, L. R., Hawks, J., Randolph-Quinney, P. S., Blackwell, L. R., & Roberts, E. M. (2016). Deliberate body disposal by hominins in the Dinaledi Chamber, Cradle of Humankind, South Africa. *Journal of Human Evolution, 96*, 145–153.

Dirks, P. H. G. M., Roberts, E. M., Hilbert-Wolf, H., Kramers, J. D., Hawks, J., Dossetto, A., Duval, M., Elliott, M., Evans, M., Grun, R., Hellstrom, J., Herries, A. I. R., Joannes-Boyau, R., Makhubela, T. V., Placzek, C. J., Robbin, J., Spandler, C., Wiersma, J., Woodhead, J., & Berger, L. R. (2017). The age of *Homo naledi* and associated sediments in the Rising Star Cave, South Africa. *eLife, 6*, Article e24231. https://doi.org/10.7554/eLife.24231.001

Dixon, R. M. W. (1990). The origin of 'mother-in-law vocabulary' in two Australian languages. *Anthropological Linguistics, 32*(1/2), 1–56.

Dixon, R. M. W. (2015). *Edible gender, mother-in-law style, and other grammatical wonders: Studies in Dyirbal, Yidiñ, and Warrgamay.* Oxford University Press.

Dixson, A. (2015). Primate sexuality. In A. Bolin and P. Whelehan (Eds.), *The international encyclopedia of human sexuality.* Wiley. https://doi.org/10.1002/9781118896877.wbiehs375

Dobres, M. A., & Robb, J. E. (Eds.). (2000). *Agency in archaeology.* Psychology Press.

Dolgova, O., & Lao, O. (2018). Evolutionary and medical consequences of archaic introgression into modern human genomes. *Genes, 9*(7), 358. https://doi.org/10.3390/genes9070358

Dolhinow, P. (2002). Anthropology and primatology. In A. Fuentes (Ed.), *Primates face to face: The conservation implications of human–nonhuman primate interconnections* (pp. 7–24). Cambridge University Press. https://doi.org/10.1017/CBO9780511542404.004

Dolotovskaya, S., Roos, C., & Heymann, E. (2020). Genetic monogamy and mate choice in a pair-living primate. *Scientific Reports, 10*(1), Article 20328. https://doi.org/10.1038/s41598-020-77132-9

Dolotovskaya, S., Walker, S., & Heymann, E. W. (2020). What makes a pair bond in a Neotropical primate: Female and male contributions. *Royal Society Open Science, 7*(1), Article 191489. https://doi.org/10.1098/rsos.191489

Dominy, M. D. (2018). Reflexivity. In H. Callan (Ed.), *The international encyclopedia of anthropology.* Wiley. https://doi.org/10.1002/9781118924396.wbiea1976

Donnelly, S. (2018, October 10). Kwame Nkrumah (1909–1972)—A term at LSE. *The London School of Economics and Political Science.* https://blogs.lse.ac.uk/lsehistory/2018/10/10/kwame-nkrumah-lse/

Dornan, J. (2002). Agency and archaeology: Past, present, and future directions. *Journal of Archaeological Method and Theory, 9*(4), 303–329.

Douglas, K., & Rasolondrainy, T. (2021). Social memory and niche construction in a hypervariable environment. *American Journal of Human Biology, 33*(4), Article e23557. https://doi.org/10.1002/ajhb.23557

Drennan, R. D., & Peterson, C. E. (2006). Patterned variation in prehistoric chiefdoms. *Proceedings of the National Academy of Sciences U.S.A., 103*(11), 3960–3967.

Du Bois, W. E. B. (1898). The study of the Negro problems. *Annals of the American Academy of Political and Social Science, 11,* 1–23.

DuBois, Z., & Juster, R. P. (2022). Lived experience and allostatic load among transmasculine people living in the United States. *Psychoneuroendocrinology, 143,* Article 105849.

DuBois, Z., & Shattuck-Heidorn, H. (2021). Challenging the binary: Gender/sex and the bio-logics of normalcy. *American Journal of Human Biology, 33,* Article e23623.

Duchêne, A. (2009). Marketing, management and performance: Multilingualism as a commodity in a tourism call center. *Language Policy, 8*(1), 27–50.

Duchêne, A., & Heller, M. (Eds.). (2011). *Language in late capitalism: Pride and profit.* Routledge.

Dugmore, A., & Vésteinsson, O. (2012). Black sun, high flame, and flood: Volcanic hazards in Iceland. In J. Cooper & P. Sheets (Eds.), *Surviving sudden environmental change: Answers from archaeology* (pp. 67–90). University of Colorado Press.

Dunsworth, H., & Eccleston, L. (2015). The evolution of difficult childbirth and helpless hominin infants. *Annual Review of Anthropology, 44*(1), 55–69.

Duranti, A. (2000). An historical perspective on contemporary linguistic anthropology. *Teaching Anthropology: Society for Anthropology in Community Colleges Notes, 7*(2), 20–24.

Duranti, A. (2011). Linguistic anthropology: Language as a non-neutral medium. In R. Mesthrie (Ed.), *The Cambridge Handbook of Sociolinguistics.* Cambridge University Press.

Durington, M. (2009). Suburban fear, media and gated communities in Durban, South Africa. *Home Cultures, 6*(1), 71–88. https://doi.org/10.2752/174063109X380026

Duster, T., Goodman, A., Graves, J. L., Jr., Hammonds, E. M., Hubbard, R., Kaufman, J., Krieger, N., Lancaster, R. N., Leroi, A. M., Lewontin, R. C., Marks, J., Morning, A., Reardon, J., Dunklee, B., Wentworth, K., & Stevens, J. (n.d.). Is race "real"? *Social Science Research Council.* http://raceandgenomics.ssrc.org

Eades, D. (2012). The social consequences of language ideologies in courtroom cross-examination. *Language in Society, 41*(4), 471–497. https://doi.org/10.1017/S0047404512000474

Earle, T. K. (1987). Specialization and the production of wealth: Hawaiian chiefdoms and the Inka Empire. In E. M. Brumfiel & T. K. Earle (Eds.), *Specialization, exchange, and complex societies* (pp. 64–75). Cambridge University Press.

Earle, T. K. (1997). *How chiefs come to power: The political economy in prehistory.* Stanford University Press.

Earle, T. (2011). Redistribution in Aegean palatial societies. Redistribution and the political economy: The evolution of an idea. *American Journal of Archaeology, 115*(2), 237–244.

Eaves, E. R., & Ritenbaugh, C. (2018). Placebo. In H. Callan (Ed.), *The international encyclopedia of anthropology.* Wiley. https://doi.org/10.1002/9781118924396.wbiea2117

Eckert, P. (2008). Variation and the indexical field. *Journal of Sociolinguistics, 12*(4), 453–476.

Edgeworth, M. (2021). Transgressing time: Archaeological evidence in/of the Anthropocene. *Annual Review of Anthropology, 50,* 93–108. https://doi.org/10.1146/annurev-anthro-101819-110118

Edmonds, A. (2010). *Pretty modern: Beauty, sex, and plastic surgery in Brazil.* Duke University Press.

Edmonds, A. (2012, March 24). A right to beauty. *Anthropology Now.* http://anthronow.com/print/alex-edmonds-a-right-to-beauty

Egeland, C. P., Dominguez-Rodriguez, M., Pickering, T. R., Mneter, C. G., & Heaton, J. L. (2018). Hominin skeletal part abundances and claims of deliberate disposal of corpses in the Middle Pleistocene. *Proceedings of the National Academy of Sciences U.S.A., 115*(18), 4601–4606. https://doi.org/10.1073/pnas.1718678115

Eggerman, M., & Panter-Brick, C. (2010). Suffering, hope, and entrapment: Resilience and cultural values in Afghanistan. *Social Science & Medicine, 71*(1), 71–83.

Ehrlich, P. R. (1968). *The population bomb.* Ballantine Books.

Eiberg, H., Troelsen, J., Nielsen, M., Mikkelsen, A., Mengel-From, J., Kjaer, K. W., & Hansen, L. (2008). Blue eye color in humans may be caused by a perfectly associated founder mutation in a regulatory element located within the HERC2 gene inhibiting OCA2 expression. *Human Genetics, 123*(2), 177. https://doi.org/10.1007/s00439-007-0460-x

Ellingson, T. (2001). *The myth of the noble savage.* University of California Press.

Elliston, D. A. (2018). Erotic anthropology: "Ritualized homosexuality" in Melanesia and beyond. In M. Klass & M. Weisgrau (Eds.), *Across the boundaries of belief: Contemporary issues in the anthropology of religion* (pp. 133–158). Routledge.

Ellner, S. (2018). Pink-tide governments: Pragmatic and populist responses to challenges from the right. *Latin American Perspectives, 46*(1), 4–22.

Emery Thompson, M. (2019). How can non-human primates inform evolutionary perspectives on female-biased kinship in humans? *Philosophical Transactions of the Royal Society, B: Biological Sciences, 374*(1780), Article 20180074. https://doi.org/10.1098/rstb.2018.0074

Enard, D., & Petrov, D. A. (2018). Evidence that RNA viruses drove adaptive introgression between Neanderthals and modern humans. *Cell, 175*(2), 360–371. https://doi.org:10.1016/j.cell.2018.08.034

Engel, G. A., Jones-Engel, L., Schillaci, M. A., Suaryana, K. G., Putra, A., Fuentes, A., & Henkel, R. (2002). Human exposure to herpesvirus B–seropositive macaques, Bali, Indonesia. *Emerging Infectious Diseases, 8*(8), 789.

English, N. B., Betancourt, J. L., Dean, J. S., & Quade, J. (2001). Strontium isotopes reveal distant sources of architectural timber in Chaco Canyon, Mexico. *Proceedings of the National Academy of Sciences U.S.A., 98,* 11891–11896.

English-Lueck, J. A. (2017). *Cultures@siliconvalley.* Stanford University Press.

Erlandson, J. M., Zeder, M. A., Boivin, N. L., Crowther, A., Denham, T., Fuller, D. Q., Larson, G., & Petraglia, M. D. (2016). Reply to Ellis et al.: Human niche construction and evolutionary theory. *Proceedings of the National Academy of Sciences U.S.A., 113*(31), 4437–4438. https://doi.org/10.1073/pnas.1609617113

Escobar, A. (2020). *Pluriversal politics: The real and the possible.* Duke University Press.

Estes, A. C. (2011, September 6). It wasn't just Neanderthals: Ancient humans had sex with other hominids. *The Atlantic.* https://www.theatlantic.com/technology/archive/2011/09/it-wasnt-just-neanderthals-ancient-humans-had-sex-other-hominids/338117/

Estrada, A., Garber, P. A., Rylands, A. B., Roos, C., Fernandez-Duque, E., Di Fiore, A., Nekaris, K. A.-I., Nijman, V., Heymann, E. W., Lambert, J. E., Rovero, F., Barelli, C., Setchell, J. M., Gillespie, T. R., Mittermeier, R. A., Arregoitia, L. V., De Guinea, M., Gouveia, S., Dobrovolski, R., . . . Li, B. (2017). Impending extinction crisis of the world's primates: Why primates matter. *Science Advances, 3*(1), Article e1600946.

European Union. (n.d.). *Sham marriages: How the EU is helping mend the heartbreak of human trafficking.* https://wayback.archive-it.org/12090/20210204170202/https://europa.eu/euprotects/our-safety/sham-marriages-how-eu-helping-mend-heartbreak-human-trafficking_en

Excd.lab. (n.d.). *Kinbank: A database for exploring the global diversity of kinship terminologies.* https://excd.org/research-activities/kinbank/

Faas, A. J. (2016). Disaster vulnerability in anthropological perspective. *Annals of Anthropological Practice, 40*(1), 14–27.

Faas, A. J. (2022). *In the shadow of Tungurahua: Disaster politics in highland Ecuador.* Rutgers University Press.

Fabian, T. (2020). The *Cool Runnings* effect: Flexible citizenship, the Global South, and transcultural republics at the Winter Olympic Games. *The International Journal of the History of Sport, 37*(13), 1274–1299.

Falk, D. (1975). Comparative anatomy of the larynx in man and the chimpanzee: Implications for language in Neanderthal. *American Journal of Physical Anthropology, 43*(1), 123–132.

Falls, S. (2017). *White gold: Stories of breast milk sharing.* University of Nebraska Press.

Fan, S., Hansen, M. E., Lo, Y., & Tishkoff, S. A. (2016). Going global by adapting local: A review of recent human adaptation. *Science, 354*(6308), 54–59.

Fanelli, D. (2010). "Positive" results increase down the hierarchy of the sciences. *PLOS ONE, 5*(4), Article e10068.

Fanon, F. (2007). *The wretched of the Earth.* Grove/Atlantic, Inc.

Fanon, F. (2008). *Black skin, white masks.* Grove Press.

Farmer, P. (1996). On suffering and structural violence: A view from below. *Daedalus (Boston), 125*(1), 261–283.

Farmer, P. (1999). *Infections and inequalities: The modern plagues.* University of California Press.

Farmer, P. (2004). *Pathologies of power: Health, human rights, and the new war on the poor.* University of California Press.

Farrell, T. S. C., & Martin, S. (2009). To teach standard English or World Englishes? A balanced approach to instruction. *English Teaching Forum, 47*(2), 2–7.

Fattal, I. (2018, January 4). Why do cartoon villains speak in foreign accents? *The Atlantic.* https://www.theatlantic.com/education/archive/2018/01/why-do-cartoon-villains-speak-in-foreign-accents/549527/

Fausto-Sterling, A. (1993). The five sexes: Why male and female are not enough. *The Sciences, 33*(2), 20–24.

Fausto-Sterling, A., Sung, J., Hale, M., Krishna, G., & Lin, M. (2020). Embodying gender/sex identity during infancy: A theory and preliminary findings. OSF Preprints. https://doi.org/ 10.31219/osf.io/ysrjk

Feinman, G. M. (2013). Crafts, specialists, and markets in Mycenaean Greece. Reenvisioning ancient economies: Beyond typological constructs. *American Journal of Archaeology, 117*(3), 453–459.

Feinman, G. M., & Garraty, C. P. (2010). Preindustrial markets and marketing: Archaeological perspectives. *Annual Review of Anthropology, 39*(1), 167–191. https:// doi.org/10.1146/annurev.anthro.012809.105118

Feldblum, J. T., Manfredi, S., Gilby, I. C., & Pusey, A. E. (2018). The timing and causes of a unique chimpanzee community fission preceding Gombe's "Four-Year War." *American Journal of Physical Anthropology, 166*, 730–744.

Ferguson, J. (1994). *The anti-politics machine: "Development," depoliticization, and bureaucratic power in Lesotho.* University of Minnesota Press.

Fernández, E. (2006). The language of death: Euphemism and conceptual metaphorization in Victorian obituaries. *SKY Journal of Linguistics, 19*, 101–130.

Ferring, R., Oms, O., Agusti, J., Berna, F., Nioradze, M., Shelia, T., Tappen, M., Vekua, A., Zhavania, D., & Lordkipanidze, D. (2011). Earliest human occupations at Dmanisi (Georgian Caucasus) dated to 1.85–1.78 Ma. *Proceedings of the National Academy of Sciences U.S.A., 108*(26), 10432–10436. https://doi.org/10.1073/pnas.1106638108

Fetterman, D. M. (2019). *Ethnography: Step-by-step* (4th ed.). SAGE Publications, Inc.

Fine, C. (2010). *Delusions of gender: The real science behind sex differences.* Icon Books Ltd.

Fischman, J. (2010, September 12). The pressure of race. *The Chronicle of Higher Education.* https://www. chronicle.com/article/To-Battle-a-Plague-an/124337

Flannery, K., & Marcus, J. (2012). *The creation of inequality.* Harvard University Press.

Flewellen, A., Dunnavant, J., Odewale, A., Jones, A., Wolde-Michael, T., Crossland, Z., & Franklin, M. (2021). "The future of archaeology is antiracist": Archaeology in the time of Black Lives Matter. *American Antiquity, 86*(2), 224–243. https://doi.org/10.1017/aaq.2021.18

Flores, N. (2013). The unexamined relationship between neoliberalism and plurilingualism: A cautionary tale. *TESOL Quarterly, 47*(3), 500–520.

Flores, N., & Rosa, J. (2015). Undoing appropriateness: Raciolinguistic ideologies and language diversity in education. *Harvard Educational Review, 85*(2), 149–171.

Foley, W. A. (2012). Anthropological linguistics. In C. A. Chapelle (Ed.), *The encyclopedia of applied linguistics.* Wiley. https://doi.org/10.1002/9781405198431. wbeal0031.pub2

Ford, C. S., & Beach, F. A. (1951). *Patterns of sexual behavior.* Harper and Brothers.

Forte, M. C. (2011). The human terrain system and anthropology: A review of ongoing public debates. *American Anthropologist, 113*, 149–153. https://doi.org/ 10.1111/j.1548-1433.2010.01315

Fortun, K. (2009). *Advocacy after Bhopal.* University of Chicago Press.

Foster, G. M. (1976). Disease etiologies in non-Western medical systems. *American Anthropologist, 78*(4), 773–782.

Foucault, M. (2012). *The birth of the clinic.* Routledge.

Fox, K., Rallapalli, K. L., & Komor, A. C. (2020). Rewriting human history and empowering indigenous communities with genome editing tools. *Genes, 11*(1), Article 88.

Fox, S. H., & Willis, M. S. (2010). Dental restorations for Dinka and Nuer refugees: A confluence of culture and healing. *Transcultural Psychiatry, 47*(3), 452–472.

Frantz, L. A. F., Bradley, D. G., Larson, G., & Orlando, L. (2020). Animal domestication in the era of ancient genomics. *Nature Reviews Genetics, 21*(8), 449–460.

Fraser, H. (2018). Forensic transcription: How confident false beliefs about language and speech threaten the right to a fair trial in Australia. *Australian Journal of Linguistics, 38*(4), 586–606.

Fredlund, J., & Fiaveh, D. Y. (2019). Activist anthropologist sentenced to 18 months in prison. *Anthropology News, 60*(4), e160–e164.

Friedli, A., Gohard-Radenkovic, A., & Ruegg, F. (Eds.). (2017). *Nation-building and identities in post-Soviet societies: New challenges for social sciences.* LIT Verlag.

Friedrich, P. (1989). Language, ideology, and political economy. *American Anthropologist, 91*, 295–312.

Fries-Britt, S., George Mwangi, C. A., & Peralta, A. M. (2014). Learning race in a U.S. context: An emergent framework on the perceptions of race among foreign-born students of color. *Journal of Diversity in Higher Education, 7*(1), 1–13.

Froese, T., Gershenson, C., & Manzanilla, L. R. (2014). Can government be self-organized? A mathematical model of the collective social organization of ancient Teotihuacan, Central Mexico. *PLOS ONE, 9*(10), Article e109966.

Froese, T., & Manzanilla, L. R. (2018). Modeling collective rule at ancient Teotihuacan as a complex adaptive system: Communal ritual makes social hierarchy more effective. *Cognitive Systems Research, 52*, 862–874.

Fruth, B., & Hohmann, G. (2018). Food sharing across borders. *Human Nature, 29*, 91–103. https://doi.org/10.1007/s12110-018-9311-9

Fry, D. P., & Söderberg, P. (2013). Lethal aggression in mobile forager bands and implications for the origins of war. *Science, 341*(6143), 270–273.

Fuentes, A. (1998). Re-evaluating primate monogamy. *American Anthropologist, 100*(4), 890–907.

Fuentes, A. (2012a). Ethnoprimatology and the anthropology of the human–primate interface. *Annual Review of Anthropology, 41*, 101–117.

Fuentes, A. (2012b). *Race, monogamy, and other lies they told you: Busting myths about human nature.* University of California Press.

Fuentes, A. (2018). Niche construction. In W. Trevathan, M. Cartmill, D. Dufour, C. Larsen, D. O'Rourke, K. Rosenberg, & K. Strier (Eds.), *The international encyclopedia of biological anthropology.* Wiley. https://doi.org/10.1002/9781118584538.ieba0342

Fuentes, A. (2019). Identities, experiences, and beliefs: On challenging normativities in biological anthropology. *American Anthropologist, 121*(2), 467–469.

Fuentes, A. (2021a). Searching for the "roots" of masculinity in primates and the human evolutionary past. *Current Anthropology, 62*(S23), S13–S25.

Fuentes, A. (2021b). Biological anthropology's critical engagement with genomics, evolution, race/racism, and ourselves: Opportunities and challenges to making a difference in the academy and the world. *American Journal of Physical Anthropology, 175*(2), 326–338.

Fuhrman, O., & Boroditsky, L. (2010). Cross-cultural differences in mental representations of time: Evidence from an implicit nonlinguistic task. *Cognitive Science, 34*, 1430–1451. https://onlinelibrary.wiley.com/doi/pdf/10.1111/j.1551-6709.2010.01105.x

Fuller, K. C., McCarty, C., Seaborn, C., Gravlee, C. C., & Mulligan, C. J. (2018). *ACE* gene haplotypes and social networks: Using a biocultural framework to investigate blood pressure variation in African Americans. *PLOS ONE, 13*(9), Article e0204127. https://doi.org/10.1371/journal.pone.0204127

Gaby, A. (2012). The Thaayorre think of time like they talk of space. *Frontiers in Psychology, 3*, Article 300. https://doi.org/10.3389/fpsyg.2012.00300

Gaines, A. D., & Davis-Floyd, R. (2004). Biomedicine. In C. R. Ember & M. Ember (Eds.), *Encyclopedia of medical anthropology* (pp. 95–109). Springer. https://doi.org/10.1007/0-387-29905-X_11

Gal, S. (1989). Language and political economy. *Annual Review of Anthropology, 18*, 345–367.

Gal, S. (2019). Making registers in politics: Circulation and ideologies of linguistic authority. *Journal of Sociolinguistics, 23*, 450–466.

Galeano, E. (1997). *Open veins of Latin America: Five centuries of the pillage of a continent.* NYU Press.

Galway-Witham, J., Cole, J., & Stringer, C. (2019). Aspects of human physical and behavioural evolution during the last 1 million years. *Journal of Quaternary Science, 34*, 355–378. https://doi.org/10.1002/jqs.3137

Garcia, A. (2010). *The pastoral clinic: Addiction and dispossession along the Rio Grande.* University of California Press.

Gardner, A. M. (2010). Engulfed: Indian guest workers, Bahraini citizens and the structural violence of the Kafala system. In N. De Genova & N. M. Peutz (Eds.), *The deportation regime: Sovereignty, space, and the freedom of movement.* Duke University Press.

Gargett, R. (1979). Grave shortcomings: The evidence for Neanderthal burial. *Current Anthropology, 30*, 157–190.

Gargett, R. (1999). Middle Palaeolithic burial is not a dead issue: The view from Qafzeh, Saint-Césaire, Kebara, Amud, and Dederiyeh. *Journal of Human Evolution, 37*, 27–90.

Garrison, N. A., Hudson, M., Ballantyne, L. L., Garba, I., Martinez, A., Taualii, M., Arbour, L., Caron, N. R., & Rainie, S. C. (2019). Genomic research through an Indigenous lens: Understanding the expectations. *Annual Review of Genomics and Human Genetics, 20*(1), 495–517.

Garth, H. (2020). *Food in Cuba: The pursuit of a decent meal.* Stanford University Press.

Geber, J. (2015). Victims of Ireland's great famine: The bioarchaeology of mass burials at Kilkenny Union Workhouse. In C. S. Larsen (Ed.), *Bioarchaeological interpretations of the human past: Local, regional, and global perspectives.* University Press of Florida.

Gee, J. (1990). *Social linguistics and literacies: Ideology in discourses* (5th ed.). Routledge.

Geere, J. A. L., Hunter, P. R., & Jagals, P. (2010). Domestic water carrying and its implications for health: A review and mixed methods pilot study in Limpopo Province, South Africa. *Environmental Health, 9*(1), 52.

George, D. R. (2010). Overcoming the social death of dementia through language. *The Lancet, 376*(9741), 586–587.

Gerbault, P., Liebert, A., Itan, Y., Powell, A., Currat, M., Burger, J., Swallow, D. M., & Thomas, M. G. (2011). Evolution of lactase persistence: An example of human niche construction. *Philosophical Transactions of the Royal Society B: Biological Sciences, 366*(1566), 863–877.

Gero, J. M. (1996). Archaeological practice and gendered encounters with field data. In R. P. Wright (Ed.), *Gender and archaeology* (pp. 251–280). University of Pennsylvania Press.

Gibbons, A. (2018). The five refusals of white supremacy. *The American Journal of Economics and Sociology, 77*(3–4), 729–755. https://doi.org/10.1111/ajes.12231

Gibbons, A. (2021, May 10). Neanderthals carb loaded, helping grow their big brains. Science. https://www.science.org/news/2021/05/neanderthals-carb-loaded-helping-grow-their-big-brains

Gifford-Gonzalez, D. P. (2007). On beasts in breasts: Another reading of women, wildness and danger at Catalhoyuk. *Archaeological Dialogues, 14*(1), 91–111.

Gignoux, C. R., Henn, B. M., & Mountain, J. L. (2011). Rapid, global demographic expansions after the origins of agriculture. *Proceedings of the National Academy of Sciences U.S.A., 108*(15), 6044–6049.

Gilby, I. C., Brent, L. J. N., Wroblewski, E. E., Rudicell, R. S., Hahn, B. H., Goodall, J., & Pusey, A. E. (2013). Fitness benefits of coalitionary aggression in male chimpanzees. *Behavioral Ecology and Sociobiology, 67*, 373–381.

Gitschier, J. (2010). All about mitochondrial Eve: An interview with Rebecca Cann. *PLOS Genetics, 6*(5), Article e1000959. https://doi.org/10.1371/journal.pgen.1000959

GLAAD. (n.d.). Transgender people. In *GLAAD Media Reference Guide* (11th ed.). https://www.glaad.org/reference/transgender

Glausiusz, J. (2020). Pulling back layers of history, culture and identity. *Nature, 582*(7811), 306–307.

Glencross, B., & Agarwal, S. C. (2011). An investigation of cortical bone loss and fracture patterns in the neolithic community of Catalhoyuk, Turkey using metacarpal radiogrammetry. *Journal of Archaeological Science, 38*(3), 513–521.

Glick Schiller, N. (2016). Conjectures about conjunctures, decolonization, and the ontological turn [A comment on Allen, J. S., & Johnson, R. C. (2016). The decolonizing generation: (Race and) Theory in anthropology since the eighties]. *Current Anthropology, 57*(2), 140–141.

Gluckman, P., Beedle, A., Buklijas, T., Low, F., & Hanson, M. (2016). *Principles of evolutionary medicine.* Oxford University Press.

Goel, I. (2019, September 26). India's third gender rises again. *SAPIENS.* https://www.sapiens.org/body/hijra-india-third-gender/

Gokcumen, O., & Frachetti, M. (2020). The impact of ancient genome studies in archaeology. *Annual Review of Anthropology, 49*, 277–298. https://doi.org/10.1146/annurev-anthro-010220-074353

Goldstein, D. M. (2004). *The spectacular city.* Duke University Press.

Goldstein, M. C. (1987). When brothers share a wife. *Natural History,* (March 1987), 39–48.

Gonçalves, K., & Kelly-Holmes, H. (Eds.). (2020). *Language, global mobilities, blue-collar workers and blue-collar workplaces.* Routledge.

Gonçalves, K., & Schluter, A. (2017). Please do not leave any notes for the cleaning lady, as many do not speak English fluently: Policy, power, and language brokering in a multilingual workplace. *Language Policy, 16*(3), 242–265.

Gone, J. P., Hartmann, W. E., Pomerville, A., Wendt, D. C., Klem, S. H., & Burrage, R. L. (2019). The impact of historical trauma on health outcomes for Indigenous populations in the USA and Canada: A systematic review. *American Psychologist, 74*(1), 20–35.

González, R. J. (2020). Beyond the Human Terrain System: A brief critical history (and a look ahead). *Contemporary Social Science, 15*(2), 227–240.

González de la Rocha, M. (2020). Of morals and markets: Social exchange and poverty in contemporary urban Mexico. *The Annals of the American Academy of Political and Social Science, 689*(1), 26–45.

Good, M. J. (1995). Cultural studies of biomedicine: An agenda for research. *Social Science & Medicine, 41*(4), 461–473.

Goodall, J. (1986). *The chimpanzees of Gombe: Patterns of behavior.* Belknap Press.

Goodman, A. H. (2016). Disease and dying while black: How racism, not race, gets under the skin. In M. K. Zuckerman & D. L. Martin (Eds.), *New directions in biocultural anthropology* (pp. 67–87). Wiley.

Goodman, A. H., Moses, Y. T., & Jones, J. L. (2012). *Race: Are we so different?* Wiley–Blackwell.

Göttner-Abendroth, H. (2012). *Matriarchal societies: Studies on Indigenous cultures across the globe.* Peter Lang.

Gowland, R. (2018). 'A mass of crooked alphabets': The construction and othering of working class bodies in industrial England. In P. Stone (Ed.), *Bioarchaeological analyses and bodies.* Springer.

Gowland, R. L., & Newman, S. (2017). Children of the revolution: Childhood health inequalities and the life course during industrialization of the 18th and 19th centuries. In P. Beauchesne & S. Agarwal (Eds.), *Childhood in the past* (pp. 294–329). University of Florida Press. https://doi.org/10.5744/florida/9780813056807.003.0010

Gowlett, J. A. J. (2018). Archaeological approaches in anthropology. In H. Callan (Ed.), *The international encyclopedia of anthropology.* Wiley. https://doi.org/10.1002/9781118924396.wbiea2358

Gowlett, J. A. J. (2020). Dating, archaeological. In H. Callan (Ed.), *The international encyclopedia of anthropology*. Wiley. https://doi.org/10.1002/9781118924396.wbiea2335

Gracia, A., Arsuaga, J. L., Martínez, I., Lorenzo, C., Carretero, J. M., Bermúdez de Castro, J. M., & Carbonell, E. (2009). Craniosynostosis in the middle Pleistocene human cranium 14 from the Sima de los Huesos, Atapuerca, Spain. *Proceedings of the National Academy of Sciences U.S.A., 106*, 6573–6578.

Graeber, D. (1995). Dancing with corpses reconsidered: An interpretation of famadihana (in Arivonimamo, Madagascar). *American Ethnologist, 22*(2), 257–277. https://doi.org/10.1525/ae.1995.22.2.02a00030

Graeber, D. (2009). *Direct action: An ethnography.* AK Press.

Graeber, D. (2018). *Bullshit jobs.* Penguin.

Graff, S. R. (2020). Archaeology of cuisine and cooking. *Annual Review of Anthropology, 49*(1), 337–354. https://doi.org/10.1146/annurev-anthro-102317-045734

Graham, F. (2021, June 25). Daily briefing: DNA in Denisova Cave soil records several human species. *Nature.* https://www.nature.com/articles/d41586-021-01771-9

Gravlee, C. C. (2009). How race becomes biology: Embodiment of social inequality. *American Journal of Physical Anthropology, 139*, 47–57.

Gravlee, C. C. (2020, April 15). It's about racism, not race, when coronavirus hits communities of color hard. *Tampa Bay Times.* https://www.tampabay.com/opinion/2020/04/15/its-about-racism-not-race-when-coronavirus-hits-communities-of-color-hard-column/

Gravlee, C. C. (2021, March 27). How whiteness works: JAMA and the refusals of white supremacy. *Somatosphere.* http://somatosphere.net/2021/how-whiteness-works.html/

Gravlee, C. C., Bernard, H. R., & Leonard, W. R. (2003a). Heredity, environment, and cranial form: A re-analysis of Boas's immigrant data. *American Anthropologist, 105*(1), 125–138.

Gravlee, C. C., Bernard, H. R., & Leonard, W. R. (2003b). Boas's changes in bodily form: The immigrant study, cranial plasticity, and Boas's physical anthropology. *American Anthropologist, 105*(2), 326–332.

Gravlee, C. C., & Dressler, W. W. (2005). Skin pigmentation, self-perceived color, and arterial blood pressure in Puerto Rico. *American Journal of Human Biology, 17*(2), 195–206.

Green, L. (1994). Fear as a way of life. *Cultural Anthropology, 9*(2), 227–256.

Green, L. (1999). *Fear as a way of life: Mayan widows in rural Guatemala.* Columbia University Press.

Greene, J., Basilico, M. T., Kim, H., & Farmer, P. (2013). Colonial medicine and its legacies. In P. Farmer, J. Y. Kim, A. Kleinman, & M. Basilico (Eds.), *Reimagining global health: An introduction* (pp. 33–73). University of California Press.

Greer, S. (2010). Heritage and empowerment: Community-based Indigenous cultural heritage in northern Australia. *International Journal of Heritage Studies, 16*(1–2), 45–58.

Grimble, A. F. (1989). *Tungaru traditions: Writings on the atoll culture of the Gilbert Islands.* University of Hawaii Press.

Grinker, R. R. (2007). *Unstrange minds: Remapping the world of autism.* Basic Books.

Grinker, R. R. (2020). Autism, "stigma," disability: A shifting historical terrain. *Current Anthropology, 61*(S21), S55–S67.

Grinker, R. R., & Cho, K. (2013). Border children: Interpreting autism spectrum disorder in South Korea. *Ethos, 41*(1), 46–74.

Gruber, T., & Clay, Z. (2016). A comparison between bonobos and chimpanzees: A review and update. *Evolutionary Anthropology, 25*, 239–252. https://doi.org/10.1002/evan.21501

Grün, R., Pike, A., McDermott, F., Eggins, S., Mortimer, G., Aubert, M., Kinsley, L., Joannes-Boyau, R., Rumsey, M., Denys, C., Brink, J., Clark, T., & Stringer, C. (2020). Dating the skull from Broken Hill, Zambia, and its position in human evolution. *Nature, 580*, 372–375.

Grunspan, D. Z., Nesse, R. M., Barnes, M. E., & Brownell, S. E. (2017). Core principles of evolutionary medicine: A Delphi study. *Evolution, Medicine, and Public Health, 1*, 13–23.

Guedes, C., & Guimarães, S. (2020). Research ethics and Indigenous Peoples: Repercussions of returning Yanomami blood samples. *Developing World Bioethics, 20*(4), 209–215.

Gugliotta, G. (2008, July). The great human migration. *Smithsonian Magazine.* https://www.smithsonianmag.com/history/the-great-human-migration-13561/

Guiterman, C. H., Swetnam, T. W., & Dean, J. S. (2016). Eleventh-century shift in timber procurement areas for the great houses of Chaco Canyon. *Proceedings of the National Academy of Sciences U.S.A., 113*(5), 1186–1190.

Gumbs, A. P. (2020, February 25). Even in the grave, Black people can't rest in Durham. *INDY Week.* https://indyweek.com/news/voices/even-in-the-grave-black-people-cant-rest-in-durham/

Gumperz, J. J., & Levinson, S. C. (Eds.). (1996, May). *Rethinking linguistic relativity* [Papers presented at a conference]. Werner-Gren Symposium 112, Ocho Rios, Jamaica.

Guo, Y., Chang, J., Han, L., Liu, T., Li, G., Garber, P. A., Xiao, N., & Zhou, J. (2020). The genetic status of the critically endangered Hainan gibbon (*Nomascus hainanus*): A species moving toward extinction. *Frontiers in Genetics, 11,* Article 1478. https://doi.org/10.3389/fgene.2020.608633

Gupta, P. (2018, October 16). 'Our vote matters very little': Kim TallBear on Elizabeth Warren's attempt to claim Native American heritage. *Jezebel.* https://theslot.jezebel.com/our-vote-matters-very-little-kim-tallbear-on-elizabeth-1829783321

Gurche, J. (2013). *Shaping humanity: How science, art, and imagination help us understand our origins.* Yale University Press.

Gurven, M., & Hill, K. (2009). Why do men hunt? A reevaluation of "man the hunter" and the sexual division of labor. *Current Anthropology, 50*(1), 51–74.

Gurven, M., & Von Rueden, C. (2006). Hunting, social status and biological fitness. *Social Biology, 53*(1–2), 81–99.

Gusterson, H. (2006). Where are we going? Engaging dilemmas in practicing anthropology. *Anthropology News, 47*(5), 26.

Haak, W., Brandt, G., de Jong, H. N., Meyer, C., Ganslmeier, R., Heyd, V., Hawkesworth, C., Pike, A. W. G., Meller, H., & Alt, K. W. (2008). Ancient DNA, strontium isotopes, and osteological analyses shed light on social and kinship organization of the Later Stone Age. *Proceedings of the National Academy of Sciences U.S.A., 105*(47), 18226–18231. https://doi.org/10.1073/pnas.0807592105

Haak, W., Lazaridis, I., Patterson, N., Rohland, N., Mallick, S., Llamas, B., Brandt, G., Nordenfelt, S., Harney, E., Stewardson, K., Fu, Q., Mittnik, A., Bánffy, E., Economou, C., Francken, M., Friederich, S., Garrido Pena, R., Hallgren, F., Khartanovich, V., . . . Reich, D. (2015). Massive migration from the Steppe was a source for Indo-European languages in Europe. *Nature, 522,* 207–211.

Haas, R., Watson, J., Buonasera, T., Southon, J., Chen, J. C., Noe, S., Smith, K., Llave, C. V., Eerkens, J., & Parker, G. (2020). Female hunters of the early Americas. *Science Advances, 6*(45), Article eabd0310.

Haber, A. (2016). Decolonizing archaeological thought in South America. *Annual Review of Anthropology, 45*(1), 469–485.

Hagelberg, E., Hofreiter, M., & Keyser, C. (2015). Introduction: Ancient DNA: The first three decades. *Philosophical Transactions of the Royal Society, B: Biological Sciences, 370*(1660), Article 20130371. https://doi.org/10.1098/rstb.2013.0371

Hahn, H. P. (2018). Material culture. In H. Callan (Ed.), *The international encyclopedia of anthropology.* Wiley. https://doi.org/10.1002/9781118924396.wbiea1789

Haile-Selassie, Y., Latimer, B. M., Alene, M., Deino, A. L., Gibert, L., Melillo, S. M., Saylor, B. Z., Scott, G. R., & Lovejoy, C. O. (2010). An early *Australopithecus afarensis* postcranium from Woranso-Mille, Ethiopia. *Proceedings of the National Academy of Sciences U.S.A., 107*(27), 12121–12126. https://doi.org/10.1073/pnas.1004527107

Hajdinjak, M., Mafessoni, F., Skov, L., Vernot, B., Hubner, A., Fu, Q., Essel, E., Nagel, S., Nickel, B., Richter, J., Moldovan, O. T., Constantin, S., Endarova, E., Zahariev, N., Spassov, R. Welker, F., Smith, G. M., Sinet-Mathiot, V., Paskulin, L., . . . Paabo, S. (2021). Initial Upper Paleolithic humans in Europe had recent Neanderthal ancestry. *Nature, 592,* 253–257.

Hale, C. R. (2006). Activist research v. cultural critique: Indigenous land rights and the contradictions of politically engaged anthropology. *Cultural Anthropology, 21*(1), 96–120.

Hames, R. (2007). The ecologically noble savage debate. *Annual Review of Anthropology, 36,* 177–190.

Hamilton, M. J., Milne, B. T., Walker, R. S., Burger, O., & Brown, J. H. (2007). The complex structure of hunter-gatherer social networks. *Proceedings of the Royal Society, B: Biological Sciences, 274,* 2195–2203.

Hammarström, H., Forkel, R., Haspelmath, M., & Bank, S. (Eds.). (2022). Glottolog 4.7: An initiative of the Max Planck Institute for Evolutionary Anthropology. https://doi.org/10.5281/zenodo.7398962 (Available online at https://glottolog.org)

Hannaford, D. (2014). *Married to the mobile: Migration, gender, class, and kinship in contemporary Senegal* [Doctoral dissertation, Emory University]. Emory Theses and Dissertations.

Hannaford, D. (2015). Technologies of the spouse: Intimate surveillance in Senegalese transnational marriages. *Global Networks (Oxford), 15*(1), 43–59. https://doi.org/10.1111/glob.12045

Hannaford, D. (2017). *Marriage without borders: Transnational spouses in neoliberal Senegal.* University of Pennsylvania Press.

Hannaford, D., & Foley, E. E. (2015). Negotiating love and marriage in contemporary Senegal: A good man is hard to find. *African Studies Review, 58*(2), 205–225.

Haraway, D. (2003). *The companion species manifesto: Dogs, people, and significant otherness.* Prickly Paradigm Press.

Harcourt-Smith, W., Throckmorton, Z., Congdon, K. A., Zipfel, B., Deane, A. S., Drapeau, M., Churchill, S. E., Berger, L. R., & DeSilva, J. M. (2015). The foot of *Homo naledi*. *Nature Communications, 6*(1), 1–8.

Hardin, G. (1968). The tragedy of the commons: The population problem has no technical solution; it requires a fundamental extension in morality. *Science, 162*(3859), 1243–1248.

Hardin, J. (2016). Claiming *pule*, manifesting *mana*: Ordinary ethics and Pentecostal self-making in Samoa. In M. Tomlinson & T. P. K. Tengan (Eds.), *New Mana: Transformations of a classic concept in Pacific languages and cultures* (pp. 257–284). ANU Press.

Hardy, K., Buckley, S., Collins, M. J., Estalrrich, A., Brothwell, D., Copeland, L., García-Tabernero, A., García-Vargas , S., de la Rasilla, M., Lalueza-Fox, C., Huguet, R., Bastir, M., Santamaría, D., Madella, M., Wilson, J., Fernández Cortés, A., & Rosas, A. (2012). Neanderthal medics? Evidence for food, cooking, and medicinal plants entrapped in dental calculus. *Naturwissenschaften, 99*(8), 617–626.

Hardy, K., Buckley, S., & Copeland, L. (2018). Pleistocene dental calculus: Recovering information on Paleolithic food items, medicines, paleoenvironment and microbes. *Evolutionary Anthropology: Issues, News, and Reviews, 27*(5), 234–246.

Harkin, M. E. (2010). Uncommon ground: Holism and the future of anthropology. *Reviews in Anthropology, 39*(1), 25–45.

Härkönen, H. (2019). Money, love, and fragile reciprocity in contemporary Havana, Cuba. *The Journal of Latin American and Caribbean Anthropology, 24*(2), 370–387.

Harmand, S., Lewis, J. E., Feibel, C. S., Lepre, C. J., Prat, S., Lenoble, A., Boës, X., Quinn, R. L., Brenet, M., Arroyo, A., Taylor, N., Clément, S., Daver, G., Brugal, J. P., Leakey, L., Mortlock, R. A., Wright, J., Lokorodi, S., Kirwa, C., . . . Roche, H. (2015). 3.3-million-year-old stone tools from Lomekwi 3, West Turkana, Kenya. *Nature, 521*, 310–315.

Harris, M. (1968). *The rise of anthropological theory: A history of theories of culture.* AltaMira Press.

Harris, M. (1974). *Cows, pigs, wars & witches: The riddles of culture.* Vintage.

Harris, R. (1981). *The language myth.* London.

Harrison, F. V. (2011). *Decolonizing anthropology: Moving further toward an anthropology for liberation.* American Anthropological Association.

Hart, K. (1985). The informal economy. *Cambridge Anthropology, 10*(2), 54–58.

Harvey, D. (2005). *The new imperialism.* Oxford University Press.

Hatala, K. G., Dingwall, H. L., Wunderlich, R. E., & Richmond, B. G. (2013). The relationship between plantar pressure and footprint shape. *Journal of Human Evolution, 65*(1), 21–28. https://doi.org/10.1016/j.jhevol.2013.03.009

Hatala, K. G., Roach, N. T., Ostrofsky, K. R., Wunderlich, R. E., Dingwall, H. L., Villamore, B. A., Green, D. J., Harris, J. W. K., Braun, D. R., & Richmond, B. G. (2016). Footprints reveal direct evidence of group behavior and locomotion in *Homo erectus. Scientific Reports, 6,* Article 28766. https:/doi.org/10.1038/srep28766

Hatala, K. G., Wunderlich, R. E., Dingwall, H. L., & Richmond, B. G. (2015). Interpreting locomotor biomechanics from the morphology of human footprints. *Journal of Human Evolution, 90,* 38–48.

Hauser-Schäublin, B. (2005). Temple and king: Resource management, rituals, and redistribution in early Bali. *Journal of the Royal Anthropological Institute, 11*(4), 747–771.

Haviland, J. (1993). Anchoring, iconicity, and orientation in Guugu Yimidhirr pointing gestures. *Journal of Linguistic Anthropology, 3*(1), 3–45.

Haviland, J. (1998). Guugu Yimithirr cardinal directions. *Ethos, 26*(1), 25–47.

Hawks, J., Elliott, M., Schmid, P., Churchill, S. E., de Ruiter, D. J., Roberts, E. M., Hilbert-Wolfe, H., Garvin, H. M., Williams, S. A., Delenze, L. K., Feuerrigiel, E. M., Randolph-Quinney, P., Kivell, T. L., Laird, M. F., Tawane, G., DeSilva, J. M., Bailey, S. E., Brophy, J. K., Meyer, M. R., . . . Berger, L. R. (2017). New fossil remains of *Homo naledi* from the Lesedi Chamber, South Africa. *elife, 6,* Article e24232.

Hedenstierna-Jonson, C., Kjellström, A., Zachrisson, T., Krzewińska, M., Sobrado, V., Price, N., Günther, T., Jakobsson, M., Götherström, A., & Storå, J. (2017). A female Viking warrior confirmed by genomics. *American Journal of Physical Anthropology, 164*(4), 853–860. https://doi.org/10.1002/ajpa.23308

Hegmon, M. (2016). Archaeology of the human experience: An introduction. *Archaeological Papers of the American Anthropological Association, 27*(1), 7–21.

Heider, K. G. (1996). *Grand Valley Dani: Peaceful warriors.* Wadsworth Publishing.

Heller, M. (2011). *Paths to post-nationalism: A critical ethnography of language and identity.* Oxford University Press.

Henderson, J. S., Joyce, R. A., Hall, G. R., Hurst, W. J., & McGovern, P. E. (2007). Chemical and archaeological evidence for the earliest cacao beverages. *Proceedings of the National Academy of Sciences U.S.A., 104*(48), 18937–18940.

Hendricks, R., & Boroditsky, L. (2015). Constructing mental time without visual experience. *Trends in Cognitive Sciences, 19*(8), 429–430. https://doi.org/10.1016/j.tics.2015.06.011

Hendry, A., Gotanda, K., & Svensson, E. (2017). Human influences on evolution, and the ecological and societal consequences. *Philosophical Transactions of the Royal Society, B: Biological Sciences, 372,* Article 20160028.

Henrich, J. (2020). *The WEIRDest people in the world: How the West became psychologically peculiar and particularly prosperous.* Farrar, Straus and Giroux.

Henrich, J., Albers, W., Boyd, R., Gigerenzer, G., McCabe, K. A., Ockenfels, A., & Young, H. P. (2001). What is the role of culture in bounded rationality? In G. Gigerenzer & R. Selten (Eds.), *Bounded rationality: The adaptive toolbox* (pp. 343–359). MIT Press.

Henrich, J., Boyd, R., Bowles, S., Camerer, C., & Fehr, E. (2001). Cooperation, reciprocity and punishment in fifteen small-scale societies. *Santa Fe Institute.* https://www.santafe.edu/research/results/working-papers/cooperation-reciprocity-and-punishment-in-fifteen-

Henrich, J., Boyd, R., & Richerson, P. J. (2012). The puzzle of monogamous marriage. *Philosophical Transactions of the Royal Society of London, B: Biological Sciences, 367*(1589), 657–669. https://doi.org/10.1098/rstb.2011.0290

Henrich, J., Heine, S. J., & Norenzayan, A. (2010). Most people are not WEIRD. *Nature, 466*(7302), 29. https://doi.org/10.1038/466029a

Henton, E., Meier-Augenstein, W., & Kemp, H. (2009). The use of oxygen isotopes in sheep molars to investigate past herding practices at the Neolithic settlement of Çatalhöyük, Central Anatolia. *Archaeometry, 52*(3), 429–449.

Herdt, G. (2010). Anthropological foundations of sexuality, health and rights. In P. Aggleton & R. Parker (Eds.), *Routledge handbook of sexuality, health and rights.* Routledge.

Hestermann, M., Ziegler, T., Van Schaik, C. P., Launhardt, K., Winkler, P., & Hodges, J. K. (2001). Loss of oestrus, concealed ovulation and paternity confusion in free-ranging Hanuman langurs. *Proceedings of the Royal Society of London, B: Biological Sciences, 268*(1484), 2445–2451.

Hewlett, B. S. (1993). *Intimate fathers: The nature and context of Aka Pygmy paternal infant care.* University of Michigan Press.

High, C. (2010). Warriors, hunters, and Bruce Lee: Gendered agency and the transformation of Amazonian masculinity. *American Ethnologist, 37*(4), 753–770.

High, C. (2020). "Our land is not for sale!" Contesting oil and translating environmental politics in Amazonian Ecuador. *The Journal of Latin American and Caribbean Anthropology, 25*(2), 301–323.

Hill, J. H. (1998). Language, race, and white public space. *American Anthropologist, 100*(3), 680–689. https://doi.org/10.1525/aa.1998.100.3.680

Hill, J. H. (2008). *The everyday language of white racism.* Wiley Blackwell.

Hill, J. H., & Mannheim, B. (1992). Language and world view. *Annual Review of Anthropology, 21,* 381–406.

Hill, K., Barton, M., & Hurtado, A. M. (2009). The emergence of human uniqueness: Characters underlying behavioral modernity. *Evolutionary Anthropology: Issues, News, and Reviews, 18*(5), 187–200.

Hirsch, J. S., & Wardlow, H. (Eds.). (2006). *Modern loves: The anthropology of romantic courtship and companionate marriage.* University of Michigan Press.

Hirsch, J. S., Wardlow, H., & Smith, D. J. (2009). *The secret: Love, marriage, and HIV.* Vanderbilt University Press.

History on the Net. (n.d.). *The September 11 attacks: Pop culture reaction.* https://www.historyonthenet.com/authentichistory/2001-2008/1-911/3-reaction/1-cartoons/index.html

Hlusko, L. J., Carlson, J. P., Chaplin, G., Elias, S. A., Hoffecker, J. F., Huffman, M., Jablonski, N. G., Monson, T. A., O'Rourke, D. H., Pilloud, M. A., & Scott, G. R. (2018). Environmental selection during the last ice age on the mother-to-infant transmission of vitamin D and fatty acids through breast milk. *Proceedings of the National Academy of Sciences U.S.A., 115*(19), E4426–E4432.

Ho, K. (2009). *Liquidated: An ethnography of Wall Street.* Duke University Press.

Hodder, I. (1997). 'Always momentary, fluid and flexible': Towards a reflexive excavation methodology. *Antiquity, 71*(273), 691–700. https://doi.org/10.1017/S0003598X00085410

Hodder, I. (2005). Women and men at Catalhoyuk. *Scientific American Special Editions, 15*(1S), 34–41. https://doi.org/10.1038/scientificamerican0105-34sp

Hodder, I. (2006). *The leopard's tale: Revealing the mysteries of Çatalhöyük.* Thames and Hudson.

Hodder, I. (Ed.). (2014). *Religion at work in a Neolithic society: Vital matters.* Cambridge University Press.

Hodder, I. (2018). Post-processual archaeology. In C. Smith (Ed.), *Encyclopedia of global archaeology.* Springer. https://doi.org/10.1007/978-1-4419-0465-2_269

Hodder, I. (Ed.). (2019). *Religion, history, and place in the origin of settled life.* University Press of Colorado.

Hodder, I., & Hutson, S. (2003). *Reading the past: Current approaches to interpretation in archaeology.* Cambridge University Press.

Hodder, I., Karlsson, H., & Olsen, B. (2008). 40 years of theoretical engagement: A conversation with Ian Hodder. *Norwegian Archaeological Review, 41*(1), 26–42.

Hodges, A. (2011). *The "war on terror" narrative: Discourse and intertextuality in the construction and contestation of sociopolitical reality.* Oxford University Press.

Hoefinger, H. (2013). *Sex, love and money in Cambodia: Professional girlfriends and transactional relationships.* Routledge. https://doi.org/10.4324/9780203550786

Hoffman, B. W. (1999). Agayadan Village: Household archaeology on Unimak Island, Alaska. *Journal of Field Archaeology, 26*(2), 147–161.

Hofmann, B. (2002). On the triad disease, illness, and sickness. *Journal of Medicine and Philosophy, 27,* 651–673.

Hoke, M. K. (2018, January 10). Baby fat is about more than cuteness. *SAPIENS.* https://www.sapiens.org/biology/baby-fat-is-about-more-than-cuteness/

Holborow, M. (2018). Language, commodification and labour: The relevance of Marx. *Language Sciences, 70,* 58–67.

Holbraad, M. (2012). *Truth in motion: The recursive anthropology of Cuban divination.* University of Chicago Press.

Holbraad, M., & Pedersen, M. (2017). *The ontological turn: An anthropological exposition.* Cambridge University Press.

Holloway, R. L., Hurst, S. D., Garvin, H. G., Schoenemann, P. T., Vanti, W. B., Berger, L. R., & Hawks, J. (2018). Endocast morphology of *Homo naledi* from the Dinaledi Chamber, South Africa. *Proceedings of the National Academy of Sciences U.S.A., 115*(22), 5738–5743.

Holmes, D. R., & Marcus., G. E. (2008). Collaboration today and the re-imagination of the classic scene of fieldwork encounter. *Collaborative Anthropologies, 1*(1), 81–101.

Holmes, S. M. (2006). An ethnographic study of the social context of migrant health in the United States. *PLOS Medicine, 3*(10), Article e448.

Holmes, S. M. (2007). "Oaxacans like to work bent over": The naturalization of social suffering among berry farm workers. *International Migration, 45*(3), 39–68.

Holmes, S. M. (2013). *Fresh fruit, broken bodies.* University of California Press.

Hommon, R. J. (2013). *The ancient Hawaiian state: Origins of a political society.* Oxford University Press.

hooks, b. (2014). *Ain't I a woman: Black women and feminism* (2nd ed.). Routledge.

Hooton, E. A. (1926). Progress in the study of race mixtures with special reference to work carried on at Harvard University. *Proceedings of the American Philosophical Society, 65*(4), 312–325. http://www.jstor.org/stable/984239

Hooton, E. A. (1939). *The American criminal: An anthropological study.* Harvard University Press.

Horton, S., & Barker, J. C. (2010). Stigmatized biologies: Examining the cumulative effects of oral health disparities for Mexican American farmworker children. *Medical Anthropology Quarterly, 24*(2), 199–219.

Hoskins, J. (1988). Matriarchy and diarchy: Indonesian variations on the domestication of the savage woman. In D. Gewertz (Ed.), *Myths of matriarchy reconsidered* (pp. 34–56). University of Sydney.

Houldcroft, C. J., & Underdown, S. J. (2016). Neanderthal genomics suggests a Pleistocene time frame for the first epidemiologic transition. *American Journal of Physical Anthropology, 160,* 379–388.

Hrdy, S. B. (2011). *Mothers and others.* Harvard University Press.

Hubisz, M. J., Williams, A. L., & Siepel, A. (2020). Mapping gene flow between ancient hominins through demography-aware inference of the ancestral recombination graph. *PLOS Genetics, 16*(8), Article e1008895. https://doi.org/10.1371/journal.pgen.1008895

Hublin, J. (2009). The prehistory of compassion. *Proceedings of the National Academy of Sciences U.S.A., 106*(16), 6429–6430.

Huerta-Sanchez, E., Jin, X., Bianba, A., Bianba, Z., Peter, B. M., Vickenbosch, N., Liang, Y., Yi, X., He, M., Somel, M., Ni, P., Wang, B., Ou, X., Luosang, H., Luosang, J., Xi, Z., Cuo, P., Li, K., Gao, G., . . . Nielsen, R. (2014). Altitude adaptation in Tibetans caused by introgression of Denisovan-like DNA. *Nature, 512,* 194–197.

Huffman, M. A., & Pebsworth, P. A. (2018). Medicinal plant use by nonhuman primates. In W. Trevathan, M. Cartmill, D. Dufour, C. Larsen, D. O'Rourke, K. Rosenberg, & K. Strier (Eds.), *The international encyclopedia of biological anthropology.* Wiley. https://doi.org/10.1002/9781118584538.ieba0315

Humphrey, C. (1999). Shamans in the city. *Anthropology Today, 15*(3), 3–10.

Hunter, E., Smith, M., & Tanner, K. (2011). Gender differences affecting vocal health of women in vocally demanding careers. *Logopedics Phoniatrics Vocology, 36*(3), 128–136.

Hunter, M. (2010). *Love in the time of AIDS: Inequality, gender, and rights in South Africa.* Indiana University Press.

Hutchings, R. M. (2021). Whistlin' Dixie? Comments on the Association for Washington Archaeology's Statement on Racism, Anti-Racism, Diversity, and Inclusion. *Journal of Northwest Anthropology, 55*(1), 189–201.

Hutchinson, P., & Moerman, D. E. (2018). The meaning response, "placebo," and method. *Perspectives in Biology and Medicine, 61*(3), 361–378.

Iantaffi, A., Barker, M.-J., van Anders, S., & Scheele, J. (n.d.). *Mapping your sexuality: From sexual orientation to sexual configurations theory.* https://www.queensu.ca/psychology/van-anders-lab/SCTzine.pdf

Idrus, M. M., Ismail, H., Saad, N. S. M., Abdullah, H., Puteh-Behak, F., Darmi, R., Baharun, H., Ali, S. M., & Haliza Harun, H. (2021). Generating alternatives to dominant ideology of English language position in Malaysia: A colonial vision or postcolonial revision? *Globalizations, 19*(5), 711–724. https://doi.org/10.1080/14747731.2021.1934961

Ifekwunigwe, J. O., Wagner, J. K., Yu, J. H., Harrell, T. M., Bamshad, M. J., & Royal, C. D. (2017). A qualitative analysis of how anthropologists interpret the race construct. *American Anthropologist, 119*(3), 422–434.

Ingold, T. (2018). *Anthropology: Why it matters.* John Wiley & Sons.

Inhorn, M. C., & Smith-Hefner, N. J. (Eds.). (2020). *Waithood: Gender, education, and global delays in marriage and childbearing.* Berghahn Books.

Inoue, Y., Sinun, W., Yosida, S., & Okanoya, K. (2017). Combinatory rules and chunk structure in male Mueller's gibbon songs. *Interaction Studies, 18*(1), 1–25. https://doi.org/10.1075/is.18.1.01ino

Inoue-Nakamura, N., & Matsuzawa, T. (1997). Development of stone tool use by wild chimpanzees (*Pan troglodytes*). *Journal of Comparative Psychology, 111*(2), 159–173.

interACT. (n.d.). What is intersex? *interACT: Advocates for Intersex Youth.* https://interactadvocates.org

International Labor Organisation. (2018). *Women and men in the informal economy: A statistical picture* (3rd ed.). International Labour Office. https://www.ilo.org/global/publications/books/WCMS_626831/lang—en/index.htm

Iowa State University. (2009, December 17). *Chimps' spear from discovery by ISU's Pruetz to be in Smithsonian exhibit.* https://www.news.iastate.edu/news/2009/dec/Smithsonian

Irvine, J. T. (1989). When talk isn't cheap: Language and political economy. *American Ethnologist, 16,* 248–267.

Isaac, G., Bojorquez, A., & Nichols, C. (2012). Dying to be represented: Museums and Día de los Muertos collaborations. *Collaborative Anthropologies, 5*(1), 28–63.

Itan, Y., Jones, B. L., Ingram, C. J., Swallow, D. M., & Thomas, M. G. (2010). A worldwide correlation of lactase persistence phenotype and genotypes. *BMC Evolutionary Biology, 10*(1), Article 36. https://doi.org/10.1186/1471-2148-10-36

Jablonski, N. G. (2004). The evolution of human skin and skin color. *Annual Review of Anthropology, 33,* 585–623.

Jablonski, N. G. (2012). *Living color: The biological and social meaning of skin color.* University of California Press.

Jablonski, N. G. (2018). Skin color. In W. Trevathan, M. Cartmill, D. Dufour, C. Larsen, D. O'Rourke, K. Rosenberg, & K. Strier (Eds.), *The international encyclopedia of biological anthropology.* Wiley. https://doi.org/10.1002/9781118584538.ieba0456

Jablonski, N. G., & Chaplin, G. (2000). The evolution of human skin coloration. *Journal of Human Evolution, 39*(1), 57–106.

Jablonski, N. G., & Chaplin, G. (2010). Human skin pigmentation as an adaptation to UV radiation. *Proceedings of the National Academy of Sciences U.S.A., 107*(Suppl 2), 8962–8968.

Jackson, F. L. C. (2018). Cobb, William Montague. In W. Trevathan, M. Cartmill, D. Dufour, C. Larsen, D. O'Rourke, K. Rosenberg, & K. Strier (Eds.), *The international encyclopedia of biological anthropology.* Wiley. https://doi.org/10.1002/9781118584538.ieba0574

Jaeggi, A. V., De Groot, E., Stevens, J. M. G., & Van Schaik, C. P. (2013). Mechanisms of reciprocity in primates: Testing for short-term contingency of grooming and food sharing in bonobos and chimpanzees. *Evolution and Human Behavior, 34*(2), 69–77. https://doi.org/10.1016/j.evolhumbehav.2012.09.005

Jaeggi, A. V., & Gurven, M. (2013). Reciprocity explains food sharing in humans and other primates independent of kin selection and tolerated scrounging: A phylogenetic meta-analysis. *Proceedings of the Royal Society, B: Biological Sciences, 280*(1768), Article 20131615. https://doi.org/10.1098/rspb.2013.1615

Jaeggi, A. V., Trumble, B. C., Kaplan, H. S., & Gurven, M. (2015). Salivary oxytocin increases concurrently with testosterone and time away from home among returning Tsimané hunters. *Biology Letters, 11*(3), Article 20150058.

Jagger, G. (2008). *Judith Butler: Sexual politics, social change and the power of the performative.* Routledge.

Jain, S. L. (2013). *Malignant: How cancer becomes us.* University of California Press.

Jakubiak, C. (2020). "English Is Out There—You Have to Get with the Program": Linguistic instrumentalism, global citizenship education, and English-language voluntourism. *Anthropology & Education Quarterly, 51*(2), 212–232.

Jankowiak, W. R., & Fischer, E. F. (1992). A cross-cultural perspective on romantic love. *Ethnology, 31*(2), 149–155.

Janson, C. H. (2000). Primate socio-ecology: The end of a golden age. *Evolutionary Anthropology, 9,* 73–86.

JHU Online Program in the History of Medicine. (2020, April 23). *Addressing resistance to social distancing with compassion, not judgment* [Video]. YouTube. https://www.youtube.com/watch?v=cjWWRAdPiA0

Jiao, T. (2001). Gender studies in Chinese Neolithic archaeology. In B. Arnold & N. Wicker (Eds.), *Gender and the archaeology of death* (pp. 51–64). AltaMira Press.

Jing, Y., & Flad, R. K. (2002). Pig domestication in ancient China. *Antiquity, 76*(293), 724–732.

Johansson, S. (2015). Language abilities in Neanderthals. *Annual Review of Linguistics, 1,* 311–332. https://doi.org/10.1146/annurev-linguist-030514-124945

Johnson, K. M. (2020). Exploring family, ethnic, and regional identities among Tiwanaku-affiliated communities in Moquegua, Peru. In K. J. Knudson & C. M. Stojanowski (Eds.), *Bioarchaeology and identity revisited* (pp. 20–55). University Press of Florida.

Johnson, P. L., & Wood, J. W. (1991). Gainj. In T. E. Hays (Ed.), *Encyclopedia of world cultures, Volume 2: Oceania.* G. K. Hall & Company.

Johnston, B. R. (1994). *Who pays the price: The sociocultural context of environmental crisis.* Island Press.

Johnston, B. R. (2020). Comments on anthropology as activism. In A. J. Willow & K. A. Yotenbleng (Eds.), *Anthropology and activism* (pp. 143–145). Routledge.

Jolly, A. (1966). *Lemur behavior: A Madagascar field study.* University of Chicago Press.

Jolly, M. (2018). Dowry. In H. Callan (Ed.), *The international encyclopedia of anthropology.* Wiley. https://doi.org/10.1002/9781118924396.wbiea2374

Jones, D., & Hill, K. (1993). Criteria of facial attractiveness in five populations. *Human Nature, 4*(3), 271–296.

Jones, S. (1997). *The archaeology of ethnicity.* Routledge.

Jones-Engel, L., Engel, G. A., Schillaci, M. A., Rompis, A., Putra, A., Suaryana, K. G., Fuentes, A., Beer, B., Hicks, S., White, R., Wilson, B., & Allan, J. S. (2005). Primate-to-human retroviral transmission in Asia. *Emerging Infectious Diseases, 11*(7), 1028–1035.

Jordan, B. (1992). *Birth in four cultures: A cross cultural investigation of childbirth in Yucatan, Holland, Sweden, and the United States.* Waveland Press.

Jordan, F. M., Gray, R. D., Greenhill, S. J., & Mace, R. (2009). Matrilocal residence is ancestral in Austronesian societies. *Proceedings of the Royal Society, B: Biological Sciences, 276*(1664), 1957–1964. https://doi.org/10.1098/rspb.2009.0088

Joyce, R. A. (2011, March 5). Sex work and archaeology. *Ancient Bodies, Ancient Lives.* https://ancientbodies.wordpress.com/2011/03/05/sex-work-and-archaeology/

Julian, C. G., & Moore, L. G. (2019). Human genetic adaptation to high altitude: Evidence from the Andes. *Genes, 10*(2), Article 150. https://doi.org/10.3390/genes10020150

Jungk, M., Chichester, O., & Fletcher, C. (2018, September 14). In search of justice: Pathways to remedy at the Porgera Gold Mine. Business for Social Responsibility. https://www.bsr.org/en/our-insights/report-view/porgera-gold-mine-barrick-pathways-to-remedy.

Kaba, M. (2021). *We do this 'til we free us: Abolitionist organizing and transformative justice.* Haymarket Books.

Kacki, S., Trinkaus, E., Schotsman, E. M. J., Courtard, P., Dori, I., Dutailly, B., Guyomarc'h, P., Mora, P., Sparacello, V. S., & Villotte, S. (2020). Complex mortuary dynamics in the Upper Paleolithic of the decorated Grotte de Cussac, France. *Proceedings of the National Academy of Sciences U.S.A., 117*(26), 14851–14856. https://doi.org/10.1073/pnas.2005242117

Kahlenger, S. M., & Wrangham, R. W. (2010). Sex differences in chimpanzees' use of sticks as play objects resemble those of children. *Current Biology, 20,* R1067–R1068.

Kampourakis, K., & Peterson, E. L. (2023). The racist origins, racialist connotations, and purity assumptions of the concept of "admixture" in human evolutionary genetics. *Genetics, 223*(3), Article iyad002. https://doi.org/10.1093/genetics/iyad002

Kang, O., Rubin, D., & Lindemann, S. (2015). Mitigating U.S. undergraduates' attitudes toward international teaching assistants. *TESOL Quarterly, 49,* 681–706. https://doi.org/10.1002/tesq.192

Kaplan, H., Hill, K., Hawkes, K., & Hurtado, A. (1984). Food sharing among Ache hunter-gatherers of Eastern Paraguay. *Current Anthropology, 25*(1), 113–115. https://doi.org/10.1086/203089

Kauanui, J. K. (2008). *Hawaiian blood: Colonialism and the politics of sovereignty and indigeneity.* Duke University Press.

Kawano, S. (2004). Scattering ashes of the family dead: Memorial activity among the bereaved in contemporary Japan. *Ethnology, 43*(3), 233–248.

Kay, G. L., Sergeant, M. J., Zhou, Z., Chan, J., Millard, A., Quick, J., Szikossy, I., Pap, I., Spigelman, M., Loman, N. J., Achtman, M., Donoghue, H. D., & Pallen, M. J. (2015). Eighteenth-century genomes show that mixed infections were common at time of peak tuberculosis in Europe. *Nature Communications, 6*, Article 6717.

Kay, R. F. (1975). The functional adaptations of primate molar teeth. *American Journal of Physical Anthropology, 43*, 195–215.

Kean, W. F., Tocchio, S., Kean, M., & Rainsford, K. D. (2013). The musculoskeletal abnormalities of the Similaun Iceman ("ÖTZI"): Clues to chronic pain and possible treatments. *Inflammopharmacology, 21*(1), 11–20.

Kelly-Holmes, H. (2000). *Bier, Parfum, Kaas*: Language fetish in European advertising. *Cultural Studies, 3*(1), 67–82.

Kemeny, R. (2019, March 31). Fat, not meat, may have led to bigger hominin brains. *Scientific American*. https://www.scientificamerican.com/article/fat-not-meat-may-have-led-to-bigger-hominin-brains/

Kendal, J., Tehrani, J. J., & Odling-Smee, J. (2011). Human niche construction in interdisciplinary focus. *Philosophical Transactions of the Royal Society of London, B: Biological Sciences, 366*(1566), 785–792. https://doi.org/10.1098/rstb.2010.0306

Kennett, D. J., Plog, S., George, R., Culleton, B., Watson, A., Skoglund, P., Rohland, N., Mallick, S., Stewardson, K., Kistler, L., LeBlanc, S., Whiteley, P., Reich, D., & Perry, G. (2017). Archaeogenomic evidence reveals prehistoric matrilineal dynasty. *Nature Communications, 8*, Article 14115.

Kennett, D. J., Prufer, K. M., Culleton, B. J., George, R. J., Robinson, M., Trask, W. R., Buckley, G. M., Moes, E., Kate, E. J., Harper, T. K., O'Donnell, L., Ray, E. E., Hill, E. C., Alsgaard, A., Merriman, C., Meredith, C., Edgar, H. J. H., Awe, J. J., & Gutierrez, S. M. (2020). Early isotopic evidence for maize as a staple grain in the Americas. *Science Advances, 6*(23), Article eaba3245.

Kenney, A. D., Dowdle, J., Bozzacco, L., McMichael, T. M., St. Gelais, C., Panfil, A., Sun, Y., Schlesinger, L. S., Anderson, M. Z., Green, P. L., López, C. B., Rosenberg, B. R., Wu, L., & Yount, J. S. (2017). Human genetic determinants of viral diseases. *Annual Review of Genetics, 51*, 241–263.

Kenoyer, J. M. (1997). Trade and technology of the Indus Valley: New insights from Harappa, Pakistan. *World Archaeology, 29*(2), 262–280.

Kenoyer, J. M. (2010). Measuring the Harappan world: Insights into the Indus order and cosmology. In I. Morley & C. Renfrew (Eds.), *The archaeology of measurement: Comprehending heaven, earth and time in ancient societies* (pp. 106–121). Cambridge University Press.

Kenoyer, J. M., Price, T. D., & Burton, J. H. (2013). A new approach to tracking connections between the Indus Valley and Mesopotamia: Initial results of strontium isotope analyses from Harappa and Ur. *Journal of Archaeological Science, 40*(5), 2286–2297.

Kertzer, D., & Arel, D. (Eds.). (2002). Census and identity: The politics of race, ethnicity and language in national censuses. Cambridge University Press. https://doi.org/10.1017/CBO9780511606045

Kessler, S. E., Bonnell, T. R., Setchell, J. M., & Chapman, C. A. (2018). Social structure facilitated the evolution of care-giving as a strategy for disease control in the human lineage. *Scientific Reports, 8*, Article 13997.

Kessler, S. J. (1990). The medical construction of gender: Case management of intersexed infants. *Signs, 16*(1), 3–26.

Ketz, K. A., Abel, E. J., & Schmidt, A. J. (2005). Public image and private reality: An analysis of differentiation in a nineteenth-century St. Paul bordello. *Historical Archaeology, 39*(1), 74–88.

Keys, H. M., Kaiser, B. N., Kohrt, B. A., Khoury, N. M., & Brewster, A. R. T. (2012). Idioms of distress, ethnopsychology, and the clinical encounter in Haiti's Central Plateau. *Social Science & Medicine, 75*(3), 555–564.

Khalid, A., & Quiñonez, C. (2015). Straight, white teeth as a social prerogative. *Sociology of Health & Illness, 37*(5), 782–796.

Kiesling, S. F. (2004). Dude. *American Speech, 79*(3), 281–305.

Kim, J. Y., Millen, J. V., Irwin, A., & Gershman, J. (2000). *Dying for growth: Global inequalities and the health of the poor*. Common Courage Press.

Kim, P. S., Coxworth, J. E., & Hawkes, K. (2012). Increased longevity evolves from grandmothering. *Proceedings of the Royal Society, B: Biological Sciences, 279*(1749), 4880–4884.

Kimmerle, E. H. (2014). Forensic anthropology in long-term investigations: 100 cold years. *Annals of Anthropological Practice, 38*(1), 7–21.

Kimmerle, E., & Edwards, J. (2022). *We carry their bones: The search for justice at the Dozier School for Boys*. CELA.

King, T. E., Fortes, G. G., Balaresque, P., Thomas, M. G., Balding, D., Delser, P. M., Neumann, R., Parson, W., Knapp, M., Walsh, S., Tonasso, L., Holt, J., Kayser, M., Appleby, J., Forster, P., Ekserdjian, D., Hofreiter, M., & Schürer, K. (2014). Identification of the remains of King Richard III. *Nature Communications, 5*(5631), Article 5631. https://doi.org/10.1038/ncomms6631

King Richard III Visitor Centre. (n.d.). https://kriii.com/

Kintigh, K. W., Altschul, J. H., Beaudry, M. C., Drennan, R. D., Kinzig, A. P., Kohler, T. A., Limp, W. F., Maschner, H. D., Michener, W. K., Pauketat, T. R., Peregrine, P., Sabloff, J. A., Wilkinson, T. J., Wright, H. T., & Zeder, M. A. (2014). Grand challenges for archaeology. *Proceedings of the National Academy of Sciences U.S.A., 111*(3), 879–880. https://doi.org/10.1073/pnas.1324000111

Kirch, P. V. (1997). *The Lapita peoples: Ancestors of the oceanic world.* Blackwell.

Kirch, P. V. (2010). *How chiefs became kings: Divine kingship and the rise of archaic states in ancient Hawai'i.* University of California Press.

Kirch, P. V., & Sahlins, M. (1994). *Anahulu: The anthropology of history in the kingdom of Hawaii. Volume 2: The archaeology of history.* University of Chicago Press.

Kissel, M., & Fuentes, A. (2018). 'Behavioral modernity' as a process, not an event, in the human niche. *Time and Mind, 11*(2), 163–183.

Kissel, M., & Kim, N. C. (2019). The emergence of human warfare: Current perspectives. *American Journal of Physical Anthropology, 168,* 141–163.

Kiyamu, M., Bigham, A., Parra, E., León-Velarde, F., Rivera-Chira, M., & Brutsaert, T. D. (2012). Developmental and genetic components explain enhanced pulmonary volumes of female Peruvian Quechua. *American Journal of Physical Anthropology, 148*(4), 534–542.

Kleinman, A., & Benson, P. (2006). Anthropology in the clinic: The problem of cultural competency and how to fix it. *PLOS Medicine, 3*(10), Article e294.

Knauft, B. M. (2003). What ever happened to ritualized homosexuality? Modern sexual subjects in Melanesia and elsewhere. *Annual Review of Sex Research, 14*(1), 137–159.

Knudson, K. J., Williams, S. R., Osborne, R., Forgey, K., & Williams, P. R. (2009). The geographic origins of Nasca trophy heads in the Kroeber collection using strontium, oxygen, and carbon isotope data. *Journal of Anthropological Archaeology, 28*(2), 244–257.

Kohler, T. A., & Smith, M. E. (Eds.). (2018). *Ten thousand years of inequality: The archaeology of wealth differences.* University of Arizona Press.

Kohler, T. A., Smith, M. E., Bogaard, A., Feinman, G. M., Peterson, C. E., Betzenhauser, A., Pailes, M., Stone, E. C., Prentiss, A. M., Dennehy, T. J., Ellyson, L. J., Nicholas, L. M., Faulseit, R. K., Styring, A., Whitlam, J., Fochesato, M., Foor, T. A., & Bowles, S. (2017). Greater post-Neolithic wealth disparities in Eurasia than in North America and Mesoamerica. *Nature, 551,* 619–622.

Kohn, E. (2015). Anthropology of ontologies. *Annual Review of Anthropology, 44,* 311–327.

Kohrt, B. A., Worthman, C. M., Adhikari, R. P., Luitel, N. P., Arevalo, J. M., Ma, J., McCreath, H., Seeman, T. E., Crimmins, E. M., & Cole, S. W. (2016). Psychological resilience and the gene regulatory impact of posttraumatic stress in Nepali child soldiers. *Proceedings of the National Academy of Sciences U.S.A., 113*(29), 8156–8161. https://doi.org/10.1073/pnas.1601301113

Kolopenuk, J. (2020). Provoking bad biocitizenship. *Hastings Center Report, 50,* S23–S29.

Kolstø, P., & Høivik, S. (2018). *Political construction sites: Nation-building in Russia and the post-Soviet states.* Routledge.

Koops, K., Furuichi, T., Hashimoto, C., & van Schaik, C. O. (2015). Sex differences in object manipulation in wild immature chimpanzees (*Pan troglodytes schweinfurthii*) and bonobos (*Pan paniscus*): Preparation for tool use? *PLOS ONE, 10*(10), Article e0139909.

Kothari, A., Salleh, A., Escobar, A., Demaria, F., & Acosta, A. (2019). *Pluriverse. A post-development dictionary.* Tulika Books.

Kottak, C. P. (1999). The new ecological anthropology. *American Anthropologist, 101*(1), 23–35.

Kozaitis, K. A. (2018). Ethnocentrism. In H. Callan (Ed.), *International encyclopedia of anthropology.* Wiley–Blackwell.

Krieger, N. (2003). Genders, sexes, and health: What are the connections—and why does it matter? *International Journal of Epidemiology, 32,* 652–657.

Kubota, R. (2016). The multi/plural turn, postcolonial theory, and neoliberal multiculturalism: Complicities and implications for applied linguistics. *Applied Linguistics, 37*(4), 474–494.

Kuhn, S. L., & Stiner, M. C. (2019). Hearth and home in the Middle Pleistocene. *Journal of Anthropological Research, 75*(3), 305–327. https://doi.org/10.1086/704145

Kuipers, J. (2013). Evidence and authority in ethnographic and linguistic perspective. *Annual Review of Anthropology, 42,* 399–413. https://doi.org/10.1146/annurev-anthro-081309-145615

Kutlu, E. (2020a). Now you see me, now you mishear me: Raciolinguistic accounts of speech perception in different English varieties. *Journal of Multilingual and Multicultural Development.* [Published online October 22, 2020.] https://doi.org/10.1080/01434632.2020.1835929

Kutlu, E. (2020b). Where do negative stereotypes come from? The case of Indian English in the USA. *Proceedings of the Linguistic Society of America, 5*(1), 74–82.

Kutlu, E., Tiv, M., Wulff, S., & Titone, D. (2022). The impact of race on speech perception and accentedness judgments in racially diverse and non-diverse groups. *Applied Linguistics, 43*(5), 867–890. https://doi.org/10.1093/applin/amab072

Kuwayama, T. (2003), "Natives" as dialogic partners: Some thoughts on native anthropology. *Anthropology Today, 19*, 8–13.

Kuzawa, C. (2018). Developmental plasticity. In W. Trevathan, M. Cartmill, D. Dufour, C. Larsen, D. O'Rourke, K. Rosenberg, & K. Strier (Eds.), *The international encyclopedia of biological anthropology* (pp. 71–73). Wiley. https://doi.org/10.1002/9781118584538.ieba0133

Kuzawa, C. W., & Gravlee, C. C. (2016). Beyond genetic race: Biocultural insights into the causes of racial health disparities. In M. K. Zuckerman & D. L. Martin (Eds.), *New directions in biocultural anthropology* (pp. 89–102). Wiley. https://doi.org/10.1002/9781118962954.ch5

La Fundación de Antropología Forense de Guatemala (FAFG). (n.d.). https://fafg.org/home/

Laderman, C., & Roseman, M. (Eds.). (1996). *The performance of healing.* Routledge.

Lai, V. T., & Boroditsky, L. (2013). The immediate and chronic influence of spatio-temporal metaphors on the mental representations of time in English, Mandarin, and Mandarin-English speakers. *Frontiers in Psychology, 4*, Article 142. https://doi.org/10.3389/fpsyg.2013.00142

Laing, M. (2013). *A linguistic atlas of early Middle English, 1150–1325*, version 3.2. The University of Edinburgh. http://www.lel.ed.ac.uk/ihd/laeme2/laeme2.html

Lake, R. W. (1993). Rethinking NIMBY. *Journal of the American Planning Association, 59*(1), 87–93.

Laland, K. N., & O'Brien, M. J. (2010). Niche construction theory and archaeology. *Journal of Archaeological Method and Theory, 17*(4), 303–322.

Laland, K. N., Odling-Smee, F. J., & Feldman, M. W. (2001). Cultural niche construction and human evolution. *Journal of Evolutionary Biology, 14*, 22–33.

Laluk, N. C. (2021). Changing how archaeology is done in Native American contexts: An *Ndee* (Apache) case study. *Journal of Social Archaeology, 21*(1), 53–73.

Lamb, S. (2000). *White saris and sweet mangoes: Aging, gender and body in North India.* University of California Press.

Lamb, S. (2001). Being a widow and other life stories: The interplay between lives and words. *Anthropology and Humanism, 26*(1), 16–34.

Lamb, S. (2018). Being single in India: Gendered identities, class mobilities, and personhoods in flux. *ETHOS, 46*(1), 49–69.

Lambert, H. (2009). Evidentiary truths? The evidence of anthropology through the anthropology of medical evidence. *Anthropology Today, 25*(1), 16–20.

Lambert, P. M. (2009). Health versus fitness: Competing themes in the origins and spread of agriculture? *Current Anthropology, 50*(5), 603–608.

Landau, M. (1984). Human evolution as narrative: Have hero myths and folktales influenced our interpretations of the evolutionary past? *American Scientist, 72*(3), 262–268.

Landsman, G. (2008). *Reconstructing motherhood and disability in the age of perfect babies.* Routledge.

Langley, M. (2018, August 19). How "bling" makes us human. *The Conversation.* https://theconversation.com/how-bling-makes-us-human-101094

Lappan, S. (2008). Male care of infants in a siamang (*Symphalangus syndactylus*) population including socially monogamous and polyandrous groups. *Behavioral Ecology and Sociobiology, 62*(8), 1307–1317.

Lappan, S., Malaivijitnond, S., Radhakrishna, S., Riley, E. P., & Ruppert, N. (2020). The human–primate interface in the New Normal: Challenges and opportunities for primatologists in the COVID-19 era and beyond. *American Journal of Primatology, 82*(8), Article e23176.

Larsen, C. S. (Ed.). (2001). *Bioarchaeology of Spanish Florida: The impact of colonialism.* University Press of Florida.

Larsen, C. S. (2015). *Bioarchaeology: Interpreting behavior from the human skeleton* (2nd ed.). Cambridge University Press.

Larsen, C. S., Griffin, M. C., Hutchinson, D. L., Noble, V. E., Norr, L., Pastor, R. F., Ruff, C. B, Russell, K. E., Schoeninger, M. J., Schultz, M., Simpson, S. W., & Teaford, M. F. (2001). Frontiers of contact: Bioarchaeology of Spanish Florida. *Journal of World Prehistory, 15*(1), 69–123.

Larsen, C. S., Hillson, S. W., Boz, B., Pilloud, M. A., Sadvari, J. W., Agarwal, S. C., Glencross, B., Beauchesne, P., Pearson, J., Ruff, C. B., Garofalo, E. M., Hager, L. D., Haddow, S. D., & Knüsel, C. J. (2015). Bioarchaeology of Neolithic Çatalhöyük: Lives and lifestyles of an early farming society in transition. *Journal of World Prehistory, 28*, 27–68.

Larsen, C. S., Knüsel, C. J., Haddow, S. D., Pilloud, M. A., Milella, M., Sadvari, J. W., Pearson, J., Ruff, C. B., Garofalo, E. M., Bocaege, E., Betz, B. J., Dori, I., & Glencross, B. (2019). Bioarchaeology of Neolithic Catalhöyük reveals fundamental transitions in health, mobility, and lifestyle in early farmers. *Proceedings of the National Academy of Sciences U.S.A., 116*(26), 12615–12623.

Larson, H. J., Cooper, L. Z., Eskola, J., Katz, S. L., & Ratzan, S. (2011). Addressing the vaccine confidence gap. *The Lancet, 378*(9790), 526–535.

Lasco, G. (2019, June 6). The dark side of skin whitening. *SAPIENS.* https://www.sapiens.org/biology/skin-whitening/

Lasco, G., & Hardon, A. P. (2020). Keeping up with the times: Skin-lightening practices among young men in the Philippines. *Culture, Health & Sexuality, 22*(7), 838–853.

Lassek, W. D., & Gaulin, S. J. (2009). Costs and benefits of fat-free muscle mass in men: Relationship to mating success, dietary requirements, and native immunity. *Evolution and Human Behavior, 30*(5), 322–328.

Lassiter, L. E. (2005). Collaborative ethnography and public anthropology. *Current Anthropology, 46*(1), 83–106.

Law, R. (2006). Moving mountains: The trade and transport of rocks and minerals within the Greater Indus Valley Region. In E. C. Robertson, J. D. Seibert, D. C. Fernandez, & M. U. Zender (Eds.), *Space and spatial analysis in archaeology* (pp. 301–313). University of Calgary Press.

Lawson, D. W., James, S., Ngadaya, E., Ngowi, B., Mfinanga, S. G., & Mulder, M. B. (2015). No evidence that polygynous marriage is a harmful cultural practice in northern Tanzania. *Proceedings of the National Academy of Sciences U.S.A., 112*(45), 13827–13832.

Leap, W., & Boellstorff, T. (Eds.). (2004). *Speaking in queer tongues: Globalization and gay language.* University of Illinois Press.

Lee, D. D. (1938). Conceptual implications of an Indian language. *Philosophy of Science, 5,* 89–102.

Lee, N. K., & Scott, J. N. (2019). Introduction: New directions in African diaspora archaeology. *Transforming Anthropology, 27*(2), 85–90. https://doi.org/10.1111/traa.12164

Lee, R. (1979). *The Dobe !Kung.* CBS College Publishing.

Lee, S.-H., & Hudock, A. (2021). Human evolution in Asia: Taking stock and looking forward. *Annual Review of Anthropology, 50,* 145–166. https://doi.org/10.1146/annurev-anthro-101819-110230

Lehrner, A., & Yehuda, R. (2018). Cultural trauma and epigenetic inheritance. *Development and Psychopathology, 30,* 1–15. https://doi.org/10.1017/S0954579418001153

Leonard, W. R., Snodgrass, J. J., & Robertson, M. L. (2010). *Evolutionary perspectives on fat ingestion and metabolism in humans.* CRC Press/Taylor & Francis.

Leonard, W. Y. (2021). Toward an anti-racist linguistic anthropology: An Indigenous response to white supremacy. *Journal of Linguistic Anthropology, 31*(2), 218–237.

Lepore, J. (2020, July 20). The invention of the police. *The New Yorker.* https://www.newyorker.com/magazine/2020/07/20/the-invention-of-the-police

Lessard-Phillips, L., & Nagai, N. (2021). Empirical perspectives on citizenship and migration: The challenge of capturing complexity. In M. Giugni & M. Grasso (Eds.), *Handbook of citizenship and migration* (pp. 37–51). Edward Elgar Publishing.

Levine, N. E. (1987a). Differential child care in three Tibetan communities: Beyond son preference. *Population and Development Review, 13*(2), 281–304.

Levine, N. E. (1987b). Fathers and sons: Kinship value and validation in Tibetan polyandry. *Man, 22*(2), 267–286.

Levine, N. E. (1988). *The dynamics of polyandry: Kinship, domesticity, and population on the Tibetan border.* University of Chicago Press.

Levine, N. E. (2008). Alternative kinship, marriage, and reproduction. *Annual Review of Anthropology, 37,* 375–389.

Levine, N. E., & Silk, J. B. (1997). Why polyandry fails: Sources of instability in polyandrous marriages. *Current Anthropology, 38*(3), 375–399.

Lewis, M. E., & Gowland, R. (2007). Brief and precarious lives: Infant mortality in contrasting sites from medieval and post-medieval England (AD 850–1859). *American Journal of Physical Anthropology, 134*(1), 117–129.

Lewis, R. J. (2018). Female power in primates and the phenomenon of female dominance. *Annual Review of Anthropology, 47*(1), 533–551. https://doi.org/10.1146/annurev-anthro-102317-045958

Lewontin, R. C. (1972). The apportionment of human diversity. In T. Dobzhansky, M. K. Hecht, & W. C. Steere (Eds.), *Evolutionary Biology* (pp. 381–398). Springer. https://doi.org/10.1007/978-1-4684-9063-3_14

Li, B., Li, M., Li, J., Fan, P., Ni, Q., Lu, J., Zhou, X., Long, Y., Jiang, Z., Zhang, P., Huang, Z., Huang, C., Jiang, X., Pan, R., Gouveia, S., Dobrovolski, R., Grueter, C. C., Oxnard, C., Groves, C., . . . Garber, P. A. (2018). The primate extinction crisis in China: Immediate challenges and a way forward. *Biodiversity and Conservation, 27*(13), 3301–3327.

Li, D. (2004). Echoes of violence: Considerations on radio and genocide in Rwanda. *Journal of Genocide Research, 6*(1), 9–27.

Li, D. (2019). *The universal enemy: Jihad, empire, and the challenge of solidarity.* Stanford University Press.

Lieberman, D. (2020). *Exercised: Why something we never evolved to do is healthy and rewarding.* Pantheon Books.

Lieberman, D. E., Mahaffey, M., Quimare, S. C., Holowka, N. B., Wallace, I. J., & Baggish, A. L. (2020). Running in Tarahumara (Rarámuri) culture: Persistence hunting, footracing, dancing, work, and the fallacy of the athletic savage. *Current Anthropology, 61*(3), 356–379. https://doi.org/10.1086/708810

Liebmann, M., & Murphy, M. S. (Eds.). (2010). *Enduring conquests: Rethinking the archaeology of resistance to Spanish colonialism in the Americas.* School for Advanced Research Press.

Liese, K. L., Davis-Floyd, R., Stewart, K., & Cheyney, M. (2021). Obstetric iatrogenesis in the United States: The spectrum of unintentional harm, disrespect, violence, and abuse. *Anthropology & Medicine, 28*(2), 188–204.

Lindo, E., Nolen, L., Paul, D., Ogunwole, M., Fields, N., Onuoha, C., Williams, J., Essien, U. R., & Khazanchi, R. (2020, November 17). Dismantling race-based medicine, part 1: Historical & ethical perspectives (No. 141) [Podcast episode]. In *Anti-racism in medicine.* Clinical Problem Solvers. https://clinicalproblemsolving.com/2020/11/17/episode-141-antiracism-in-medicine-series-episode-1-dismantling-race-based-medicine-part-1-historical-and-ethical-perspectives-with-edwin-lindo/

Lippi, R. (2012). Teaching children how to discriminate: What we learn from the big bad wolf. Excerpted from *English with an accent: Language, ideology and discrimination in the United States* (2nd ed.). Routledge. https://rosinalippi.com/weblog/shorter-works-essays/teaching-children-how-to-discriminate-what-we-learn-from-the-big-bad-wolf/

Lippi-Green, R. (2011). *English with an accent: Language, ideology, and discrimination in the United States* (2nd ed.). Routledge.

Little, M. A. (2018). Adaptation. In W. Trevathan, M. Cartmill, D. Dufour, C. Larsen, D. O'Rourke, K. Rosenberg, & K. Strier (Eds.), *The international encyclopedia of biological anthropology.* Wiley. https://doi.org/10.1002/9781118584538.ieba0005

Liu, L., Bestel, S., Shi, J., Song, Y., & Chen, X. (2013). Paleolithic human exploitation of plant foods during the last glacial maximum in North China. *Proceedings of the National Academy of Sciences U.S.A., 110*(14), 5380–5385.

Liu, W., Athreya, S., Xing, S., & Wu, X. (2022). Hominin evolution and diversity: A comparison of earlier-Middle and later-Middle Pleistocene hominin fossil variation in China. *Philosophical Transactions of the Royal Society B, 377*(1847), Article 20210040.

Live Science Staff. (2011, September 8). Image gallery: Our closest human ancestor. *Live Science.* https://www.livescience.com/15953-image-gallery-closest-human-ancestor.html

Livingstone, F. (1962). On the non-existence of human races. *Current Anthropology, 3*(3), 279–281.

Lloréns, H. (2018a). Ruin nation: In Puerto Rico, Hurricane Maria laid bare the results of a long-term crisis created by dispossession, migration, and economic predation. *NACLA Report on the Americas, 50*(2), 154–159.

Lloréns, H. (2018b). Imaging disaster: Puerto Rico through the eye of Hurricane María. *Transforming Anthropology, 26*(2), 136–156.

Lloréns, H. (2019). US media depictions of climate migrants. In Y. Bonilla & M. LeBrón (Eds.), *Aftershocks of disaster: Puerto Rico before and after the storm.* Haymarket Books.

Lloréns, H. (2021). *Making livable worlds: Afro-Puerto Rican women building environmental justice.* University of Washington Press.

Lock, M. M. (2002). *Twice dead: Organ transplants and the reinvention of death.* University of California Press.

Lock, M. (2013). The epigenome and nature/nurture reunification: A challenge for anthropology. *Medical Anthropology, 32*(4), 291–308.

Lock, M. (2015). Comprehending the body in the era of the epigenome. *Current Anthropology, 56*(2), 151–177.

Lomawaima, K. T., Brayboy, B. M. J., & McCarty, T. L. (Eds.). (2018). Editors' introduction to the special issue: Native American boarding school stories. *Journal of American Indian Education, 57*(1), 1–10.

Lomnitz, L. A. (1988). Informal exchange networks in formal systems: A theoretical model. *American Anthropologist, 90*(1), 42–55. https://doi.org/10.1525/aa.1988.90.1.02a00030

Lomnitz, L. A. (2014). *Networks and marginality: Life in a Mexican shantytown.* Academic Press.

Long, B. (2021, June 23). DNA from sediment reveals epic history of Denisova Cave. *Phys Org.* https://phys.org/news/2021-06-dna-sediment-reveals-epic-history.html

Longman, D. P., Wells, J. C. K., & Stock, J. T. (2020). Human athletic paleobiology; using sport as a model to investigate human evolutionary adaptation. *American Journal of Biological Anthropology, 171*(S70), 42–59. https://doi.org/10.1002/ajpa.23992

Lonsdorf, E. V. (2017). Sex differences in nonhuman primate behavioral development. *Journal of Neuroscience Research, 95,* 213–221.

Lordkipanidze, D., Vekua, A., Ferring, R., Rightmire, G. P., Agusti, J., Kiladze, G., Mouskhelishvili, A., Nioradze, M., Ponce de León, M. S., Tappen, M., & Zollikofer, C. (2005). The earliest toothless hominin skull. *Nature, 434*(7034), 717.

Love, N. (2017). On languaging and languages. *Language Sciences, 61*, 113–147.

Low, S. M. (2001). The edge and the center: Gated communities and the discourse of urban fear. *American Anthropologist, 103*, 45–58. https://doi.org/10.1525/aa.2001.103.1.45

Low, S. (2004). *Behind the gates: Life, security, and the pursuit of happiness in fortress America.* Routledge.

Low, S. (2010). A nation of gated communities. In H. Gusterson & C. Besteman (Eds.), *The insecure American: How we got here and what we should do about it* (pp. 27–44). University of California Press.

Low, S. (2017). Security at home: How private securitization practices increase state and capitalist control. *Anthropological Theory, 17*(3), 365–381.

Low, S., Taplin, D., & Scheld, S. (2009). *Rethinking urban parks: Public space and cultural diversity.* University of Texas Press.

Lozada Cerna, M. C., & Buikstra, J. E. (2002). *El Señorío de Chiribaya en la costa sur del Perú.* Instituto de Estudios Peruanos.

Lubick, N. (2020, August 6). What milk-sharing communities reveal. *SAPIENS.* https://www.sapiens.org/culture/milk-sharing/

Lucy, J. A. (1992). *Language diversity and thought: A reformulation of the linguistic relativity hypothesis.* Cambridge University Press. https://doi.org/10.1017/CBO9780511620843

Lucy, J. A. (1997). Linguistic relativity. *Annual Review of Anthropology, 26*, 291–312. https://doi.org/10.1146/annurev.anthro.26.1.291

Lucy, S. (2005). Ethnic and cultural identities. In M. Díaz-Andreu, S. Lucy, S. Babic, & D. N. Edwards (Eds.). *The archaeology of identity: Approaches to gender, age, status, ethnicity, and religion* (pp. 86–109). Routledge.

Lugli, F., Di Rocco, G., Vazzana, A., Genovese, F., Pinetti, D., Cilli, E., Carile, M. C., Silvestrini, S., Gabanini, G., Arrighi, S., Buti, L., Bortolini, E., Cipriani, A., Figus, C., Marciani, G., Oxilia, G., Romandini, M., Sorrentino, R., Sola, M., & Benazzi, S. (2019). Enamel peptides reveal the sex of the Late Antique 'Lovers of Modena.' *Scientific Reports, 9*(1), Article 13130.

Lulewicz, J. (2019). The social networks and structural variation of Mississippian sociopolitics in the southeastern United States. *Proceedings of the National Academy of Sciences U.S.A., 116*(14), 6707–6712.

Lupack, S. (2011). Redistribution in Aegean palatial societies. A view from outside the palace: The sanctuary and the *Damos* in Mycenaean economy and society. *American Journal of Archaeology, 115*(2), 207–217.

Lynn, C. D., Howells, M., Herdrich, D., Ioane, J., Hudson, D., & Fitiao, S. A. T. U. (2020). The evolutionary adaptation of body art: Tattooing as costly honest signaling of enhanced immune response in American Samoa. *American Journal of Human Biology, 32*(4), Article e23347.

Lyon, S. (2020). Economics. In N. Brown, T. McIlwraith, & L. T. de González (Eds.), *Perspectives: An open introduction to cultural anthropology.* American Anthropological Association. http://perspectives.americananthro.org

Ma, Y., Fuller, B. T., Sun, W., Hu, S., Chen, L., Hu, Y., & Richards, M. P. (2016). Tracing the locality of prisoners and workers at the mausoleum of Qin Shi Huang: First Emperor of China (259–210 BC). *Scientific Reports, 6*(1), Article 26731.

MacDonald, K., Scherjon, F., van Veen, E., Vaesen, K., & Roebroeks, W. (2021). Middle Pleistocene fire use: The first signal of widespread cultural diffusion in human evolution. *Proceedings of the National Academy of Sciences U.S.A., 118*(31), Article e2101108118. https://doi.org/10.1073/pnas.2101108118

Macfarlane, A. (2009, March 26). Interview of James Scott [Video]. http://www.alanmacfarlane.com/ancestors/scott.htm

Macgregor, S., Bellis, C., Lea, R. A., Cox, H., Dyer, T., Blangero, J., Visscher, P. M., & Griffiths, L. R. (2010). Legacy of mutiny on the *Bounty*: Founder effect and admixture on Norfolk Island. *European Journal of Human Genetics, 18*, 67–72. https://doi.org/10.1038/ejhg.2009.111

Mackey, D. A., Sherwin, J. C., Kearns, L. S., Ma, Y., Kelly, J., Chu, B. S., Macmillan, R., Barbour, J. M., Wilkinson, C. H., Matovinovic, E., Cox, H. C., Bellis, C., Lea, R. A., Quinlan, S., Griffiths, L. R., & Hewitt, A, W. (2011). The Norfolk Island Eye Study (NIES): Rationale, methodology and distribution of ocular biometry (biometry of the Bounty). *Twin Research and Human Genetics, 14*(1), 42–52.

Mageo, J. M. (1992). Male transvestism and cultural change in Samoa. *American Ethnologist, 19*(3), 443–459.

Magilton, J., Lee, F., & Boylston, A. (Eds.). (2008). *Lepers outside the gate: Excavations at the cemetery of the hospital of St. James and St. Mary Magdalene, Chichester, 1986–87 and 1993.* Council for British Archaeology.

Mahbub, A. (2008). *Social dynamics of CLTS: Inclusion of children, women and vulnerable.* Institute of Development Studies (IDS) Conference on Community-Led Total Sanitation (CLTS), December 16–18, 2008, Brighton, U.K.

Mahdavi, P. (2009). *Passionate uprisings: Iran's sexual revolution.* Stanford University Press.

Malinowski, B. (1929). *The sexual life of savages in northwestern Melanesia.* Routledge.

Maloney, T., Dilkes-Hall, I. E., & Davis, J. (2017). Indigenous led archaeological excavation at Moonggaroonggoo, Gooniyandi country, Western Australia, reveals late Holocene occupation. *Australian Archaeology, 83*(3), 178–184.

Manzanilla, L. R. (2009). Corporate life in apartment and barrio compounds at Teotihuacan, Central Mexico: Craft specialization, hierarchy, and ethnicity. In L. R. Manzanilla & C. Chapdelaine (Eds.), *Domestic life in prehispanic capitals: A study of specialization, hierarchy, and ethnicity* (pp. 21–42). University of Michigan Museum of Anthropology.

Manzanilla, L. R. (2012). Neighborhoods and elite "houses" at Teotihuacan, Central Mexico. In M. C. Arnauld, L. R. Manzanilla, & M. E. Smith (Eds.), *The neighborhood as a social and spatial unit in Mesoamerican cities* (pp. 55–73). University of Arizona Press.

Manzanilla, L. R. (2015). Cooperation and tensions in multiethnic corporate societies using Teotihuacan, Central Mexico, as a case study. *Proceedings of the National Academy of Sciences U.S.A., 112*(30), 9210–9215.

Manzanilla, L. R. (2017). *Multiethnicity and migration at Teopancazco: Investigations of a Teotihuacan neighborhood center.* University Press of Florida.

Marchi, R. M. (2006). El Dia de los Muertos in the USA: Cultural ritual as political communication. In *Spontaneous shrines and the public memorialization of death* (pp. 261–283). Palgrave Macmillan.

Marchi, R. M. (2009). *Day of the Dead in the USA: The migration and transformation of a cultural phenomenon.* Rutgers University Press.

Marciniak, S., Bergey, C. M., Silva, A. M., Hałuszko, A., Furmanek, M., Veselka, B., Velemínský, P., Vercellotti, G., Wahl, J., Zariṇa, G., Longhi, C., Kolář, J., Garrido-Pena, R., Flores-Fernández, R., Herrero-Corral, A. M., Simalcsik, A., Müller, W., Sheridan, A., Miliauskienė, Ž., . . . Perry, G. H. (2022). An integrative skeletal and paleogenomic analysis of stature variation suggests relatively reduced health for early European farmers. *Proceedings of the National Academy of Sciences U.S.A., 119*(15), Article e2106743119.

Marks, J. (2017). *Is science racist?* John Wiley & Sons.

Marler, P. (1999). How much does a human environment humanize a chimp? *American Anthropologist, 101*(2), 432–436. https://doi.org/10.1525/aa.1999.101.2.432

Marlowe, F. (2002). Why the Hadza are still hunter-gatherers. In S. Kent (Ed.), *Ethnicity, hunter-gatherers, and the 'other'* (pp. 247–281). Smithsonian Institution Press.

Marshall, L. (1959). Marriage among !Kung bushmen. *Africa: Journal of the International African Institute, 29*(4), 335–365.

Marshall, L. (1976). *The !Kung of the Naye Naye.* Harvard University Press.

Marshall, M. (1979). *Weekend warriors: Alcohol in a Micronesian culture.* McGraw-Hill Humanities Social.

Martin, D. L., & Harrod, R. P. (2015). Bioarchaeological contributions to the study of violence. *American Journal of Physical Anthropology, 156,* 116–145.

Martin, E. (2001). *The woman in the body: A cultural analysis of reproduction.* Beacon Press.

Martin, L. (1986). "Eskimo words for snow": A case study in the genesis and decay of an anthropological example. *American Anthropologist, 88*(2), 418–423.

Martin, R. D. (1990). *Primate origins and evolution.* Princeton University Press.

Martinez, D. (2014). Indigenous archaeologies. In C. Smith (Ed.), *Encyclopedia of global archaeology* (pp. 3772–3776). Springer. https://doi.org/10.1007/978-1-4419-0465-2_1

Martinon-Torres, M., d'Errico, F., Santos, E., Gallo, A. A., Amano, N., Archer, W., Armitage, S. J., Arsuaga, J. L., de Castro, J. M. B., Blinkhorn, J., Crowther, A., Douka, K., Dubernet, S., Faulkner, P., Fernandez-Colon, P., Kourampas, N., Garcia, J. G., Larreina, D., Le Bourdonnec, X., . . . Petraglia, M. D. (2021). Earliest known human burial in Africa. *Nature, 593,* 95–100. https://doi.org/10.1038/s41586-021-03457-8

Marx, K. (1867). *Capital: A critique of political economy.* Verlag von Otto Meisner.

Masao, F. T., Ichumbaki, E. B., Cherin, M., Barili, A., Boschian, G., Iurino, D. A., Menconero, S., Moggi-Cecchi, J., & Manzi, G. (2016). New footprints from Laetoli (Tanzania) provide evidence for marked body size variation in early hominins. *eLife, 5,* Article e19568.

Masterson, E. E., Fitzpatrick, A. L., Enquobahrie, D. A., Mancl, L. A., Conde, E., & Hujoel, P. P. (2017). Malnutrition-related early childhood exposures and enamel defects in the permanent dentition: A longitudinal study from the Bolivian Amazon. *American Journal of Physical Anthropology, 164,* 416–423.

Matthews, A. S. (2020). Anthropology and the Anthropocene: Criticisms, experiments, and collaborations. *Annual Review of Anthropology, 59*, 67–82. https://doi.org/10.1146/annurev-anthro-102218-011317

Mattingly, C. (2010). *The paradox of hope: Journeys through a clinical borderland.* University of California Press.

Mattison, S. M., Shenk, M. K., Thompson, M. E., Borgerhoff Mulder, M., & Fortunato, L. (2019). The evolution of female-biased kinship in humans and other mammals. *Philosophical Transactions of the Royal Society, B, 374*(1780), Article 20190007.

Mattison, S. M., Smith, E. A., Shenk, M. K., & Cochrane, E. E. (2016). The evolution of inequality. *Evolutionary Anthropology, 25*, 184–199.

Mauss, M. (2002). *The gift: The form and reason for exchange in archaic societies.* Routledge Classics. (Original work published 1925)

Maxwell, S. J. (2018). *The quality of the early hominin fossil record: Implications for evolutionary analysis.* [Doctoral dissertation, University College London—Birkbeck]. https://core.ac.uk/download/pdf/161939043.pdf

McCabe, S. C. J. (2017). Aegyptopithecus. In A. Fuentes (Ed.), *The international encyclopedia of primatology.* https://doi.org/10.1002/9781119179313.wbprim0398

McCay, B. J., & Acheson, J. M. (Eds.). (1987). *The question of the commons: The culture and ecology of communal resources.* University of Arizona Press.

McCoy, R. C., Wakefield, J., & Akey, J. M. (2017). Impacts of Neanderthal-introgressed sequences on landscape of the human gene expression. *Cell, 168*(5), 916–927. https://doi.org/10.1016/j.cell.2017.01.038

McCulloch, G. (2020). *Because internet: Understanding the new rules of language.* Riverhead Books.

McDowell, E. (2019, September 1). Trowel blazers: Dr. Pauli Murray. North Carolina Office of State Archaeology. https://archaeology.ncdcr.gov/blog/2019-09-01/trowel-blazers-pauli-murray

McGregor, D. (2015). Indigenous women, water justice and zaagidowin (love). *Canadian Woman Studies, 30*(2–3), 71. https://link.gale.com/apps/doc/A438562132/AONE?u=maine_oweb&sid=googleScholar&xid=261091bf

McGregor, W. (1989). Gooniyandi mother-in-law 'language': Dialect, register, and/or code? In U. Ammon (Ed.), *Status and function of languages and language varieties* (pp. 630–657). De Gruyter Press.

McKenna, J. J., Ball, H. L., & Gettler, L. T. (2007). Mother–infant cosleeping, breastfeeding and sudden infant death syndrome: What biological anthropology has discovered about normal infant sleep and pediatric sleep medicine. *American Journal of Physical Anthropology, 134*(S45), 133–161.

McNamara, T. (2019). *Language and subjectivity.* Cambridge University Press.

Mead, M. (1963). *Sex and temperament in three primitive societies.* William Morrow. (Original work published 1935)

Melian-Zamora, R. E., & Behar, R. (2020). Translations of the self: Moving between objects, memories, and words: A dialogue with Ruth Behar. *American Anthropologist, 122*(3), 568–580.

Meloni, M. (2015). Epigenetics for the social sciences: Justice, embodiment, and inheritance in the postgenomic age. *New Genetics and Society, 34*(2), 125–151. https://doi.org/10.1080/14636778.2015.1034850

Meloni, M. (2016). *Political biology: Science and social values in human heredity from eugenics to epigenetics.* Springer.

Mendez, F. L., Poznik, G. D., Castellano, S., & Bustamante, C. D. (2016). The divergence of Neanderthal and modern human Y chromosomes. *American Journal of Human Genetics, 98*(4), 728–734. https://doi.org/10.1016/j.ajhg.2016.02.023

Meredith, S. L. (2012). *The development of adult sex-typed social behavior in Lemur catta.* [Doctoral dissertation, Arizona State University]. CORE. https://core.ac.uk/download/pdf/79563846.pdf

Meredith, S. (2015a). Anchoring the clade: Primate-wide comparative analysis supports relationship between juvenile interest in infants and adult patterns of infant care. *Folia Primatologica, 86*(1–2), 117–123.

Meredith, S. L. (2015b). Comparative perspectives on human gender development and evolution. *American Journal of Physical Anthropology, 156*, 72–97. https://doi.org/10.1002/ajpa.22660

Meredith, S. L. (2018). Sex-typed social development in *Lemur catta. Folia Primatologica, 89*(3–4), 224–239.

Meredith, S. L., & Schmitt, C. A. (2019). The outliers are in: Queer perspectives on investigating variation in biological anthropology. *American Anthropologist, 121*(2), 487–489.

Metraux, R., & Segel, S. (1980). Margaret Mead: Anthropologist of our time (photo essay). *Studies in Visual Communication, 6*(1), 4–14.

Metzl, J. M., & Hansen, H. (2014). Structural competency: Theorizing a new medical engagement with stigma and inequality. *Social Science & Medicine, 103*(3), 126–133.

Meyer, M., Arsuaga, J.-L., de Filippo, C., Nagel, S., Aximu-Petri, A., Nickel, B., Martínez, I., Gracia, A., Bermúdez de Castro, J. M., Carbonell, E. Viola, B., Kelso, J.,

Prüfer, K., & Pääbo, S. (2016). Nuclear DNA sequences from the Middle Pleistocene Sima de los Huesos hominins. *Nature, 531*, 504–507.

Meyer, M., Gibson, E., & Costello, J. (2005). City of angels, city of sin: Archaeology in the Los Angeles red-light district ca. 1900. *Historical Archaeology, 39*, 107–125.

Miao, P. (2003). Deserted streets in a jammed town: The gated community in Chinese cities and its solution. *Journal of Urban Design, 8*(1), 45–66.

Mignolo, W. D. (2007). Delinking: The rhetoric of modernity, the logic of coloniality and the grammar of de-coloniality. *Cultural Studies, 21*(2–3), 449–514.

Mignolo, W. D. (2018). Foreword: On pluriversality and multipolarity. In B. Reiter (Ed.), *Constructing the pluriverse* (pp. ix–xvi). Duke University Press.

Mikaere, A. (1994). Maori women: Caught in the contradictions of a colonised reality. *Waikato Law Review, 2*, 125.

Millar, K. M. (2020). Garbage as racialization. *Anthropology and Humanism, 45*(1), 4–24.

Miller, M. J., Albarracin-Jordan, J., Moore, C., & Capriles, J. M. (2019). Chemical evidence for the use of multiple psychotropic plants in a 1,000-year-old ritual bundle from South America. *Proceedings of the National Academy of Sciences U.S.A., 116*(23), 11207–11212.

Mine, J. G., Slocombe, K. E., Willems, E. P., Gilby, I. C., Yu, M., Thompson, M. E., Muller, M. N., Wrangham, R. W., Townsend, S. W., & Machanda, Z. P. (2022). Vocal signals facilitate cooperative hunting in wild chimpanzees. *Science Advances, 8*(30), Article abo5553.

Mitani, J. C. (1985). Sexual selection and adult male orangutan long calls. *Animal Behaviour, 33*(1), 272–283.

Mitchell, A. (2020, June 19). Interview with Kelly Wright, Sociolinguist. *Medium.* https://vincennes.medium.com/interview-with-kelly-wright-sociolinguist-8878ddd857ae

Mitchell, M., Guilfoyle, D. R., Reynolds, R.D., & Morgan, C. (2013). Towards sustainable community heritage management and the role of archaeology: A case study from Western Australia. *Heritage & Society, 6*(1), 24–45.

Modan, G., & Brill, S. B. (2014). Engaging death: Narrative and constructed dialogue in advance care planning discussions. *Communication & Medicine, 11*(2), 153–165.

Mohai, P., Pellow, D., & Roberts, J. T. (2009). Environmental justice. *Annual Review of Environment and Resources, 34*, 405–430.

Molnar, S. (2002). *Human variation: Races, types, and ethnic groups* (5th ed.). Prentice Hall.

Moniruzzaman, M. (2016). Spare parts for sale: Violence, exploitation, suffering. In P. J. Brown & S. Closser (Eds.), *Understanding and applying medical anthropology* (3rd ed., pp. 277–285). Routledge.

Moniruzzaman, M. (2019). "The heavier selves": Embodied and subjective suffering of organ sellers in Bangladesh. *Ethos, 47*(2), 233–253.

Montoya, T. (2017). Yellow water: Rupture and return one year after the Gold King Mine spill. *Anthropology Now, 9*(3), 91–115.

Moore, R. (2015). Meaning and ostension in great ape gestural communication. *Animal Communication, 19*(1), 223–231.

Morais, R. J., & de Waal Malefyt, T. (2014). Ethics in business anthropology: Crossing boundaries. *Journal of Business Anthropology* (Special issue 1), 1–10.

Moran, E. F. (2000). *Human adaptability: An introduction to ecological anthropology.* Westview Press.

Moret, J., Andrikopoulos, A., & Dahinden, J. (2021). Contesting categories: Cross-border marriages from the perspectives of the state, spouses and researchers. *Journal of Ethnic and Migration Studies, 47*(2), 325–342.

Morgan, T. J. H., Uomini, N. T., Rendell, L. E., Choiunard-Thuly, L., Street, S. E., Lewis, H. M., Cross, C. P., Evans, C., Kearney, R., de la Torre, I., Whitten, A., & Laland, K. N. (2015). Experimental evidence for the co-evolution of hominin tool-making teaching and language. *Nature Communications, 6*, Article 6029. https://doi.org/10.1038/ncomms7029

Moriarty, E. (2020). Sign to me, not the children: Ideologies of language contamination at a deaf tourist site in Bali. *Language and Communication, 74*, 195–203.

Morning, A. (2012). Multiraciality and census classification in global perspective. In R. Edwards, S. Ali, C. Caballero, & M. Song (Eds.), *International perspectives on racial and ethnic mixedness and mixing* (pp. 10–22). Routledge.

Morning, A. (2015). Ethnic classification in global perspective: A cross-national survey of the 2000 census round. In *Social statistics and ethnic diversity* (pp. 17–37). Springer.

Morse, J. M. (1989). Cultural responses to parturition: Childbirth in Fiji. *Medical Anthropology, 12*, 35–44.

Moser, S. (2007). On disciplinary culture: Archaeology as fieldwork and its gendered associations. *Journal of Archaeological Method and Theory, 14*(3), 235–263.

Moses, Y. T. (2018). Determinism, biological. In H. Callan (Ed.), *The international encyclopedia of anthropology.* Wiley. https://doi.org/10.1002/9781118924396.wbiea2295

Mourant, A. E., Kopec, A. C., & Domaniewska-Sobczak, K. (1976). *The distribution of human blood groups and other polymorphisms.* Oxford University Press.

Mulder, M. B. (1990). Kipsigis women's preferences for wealthy men: Evidence for female choice in mammals? *Behavioral Ecology and Sociobiology, 27,* 255–264.

Mulligan, C. J. (2016). Early environments, stress, and the epigenetics of human health. *Annual Review of Anthropology, 45,* 233–249.

Mullings, L., Benn Torres, J., Fuentes, A., Gravlee, C. C., Roberts, D., & Thayer, Z. (2021). The biology of racism. *American Anthropologist, 123*(3), 671–680.

Nakassis, D., Parkinson, W. A., & Galaty, M. L. (2011). Redistribution in Aegean palatial societies. Redistributive economies from a theoretical and cross-cultural perspective. *American Journal of Archaeology, 115*(2), 177–184.

Nanda, S. (1999). *Neither man nor woman: The hijras of India.* Cengage Learning.

Nanda, S. (2018). *Love and marriage: Cultural diversity in a changing world.* Waveland Press.

Narang, S. (2018, May 25). Navajo women struggle to preserve traditions as climate change intensifies. *The World.* https://theworld.org/stories/2018-05-25/navajo-women-struggle-preserve-traditions-climate-change-intensifies

Nascimento, G., & Windle, J. (2021). The unmarked whiteness of Brazilian linguistics: From Black-as-theme to Black-as-life. *Journal of Linguistic Anthropology, 31,* 283–286. https://doi.org/10.1111/jola.12321

Nasser El-Dine, S. (2018). Love, materiality, and masculinity in Jordan: "Doing" romance with limited resources. *Men and Masculinities, 21*(3), 423–442.

National Academies. (n.d.). *Evolution resources at the National Academies.* https://www.nationalacademies.org/evolution/science-and-religion#sl-three-columns-c73fd162-02a3-4d3c-b354-b526b19029c9

National Academies of Sciences, Engineering, and Medicine. (2022). *Measuring sex, gender identity, and sexual orientation.* The National Academies Press. https://doi.org/10.17226/26424

National Geographic. (2019). Hadza. *National Geographic.* https://www.nationalgeographic.org/encyclopedia/hadza/

Nations, M., Corlis, J., Feitosa, J. I., Caprara, A., Farfan-Santos, E., Hadad, S. C., Hinton, D. E., Mayblin, M., de Souza Minayo, M. C., Pinto, S., & Rebhun, L. A. (2015). Cumbered cries: Contextual constraints on maternal grief in northeast Brazil. *Current Anthropology, 56*(5), 613–637.

Nazarea, V., Rhoades, R., Bontoyan, E., & Flora, G. (1998). Defining indicators which make sense to local people: Intra-cultural variation in perceptions of natural resources. *Human Organization, 57*(2), 159–171.

NC Department of Natural and Cultural Resources. (2019, June 20). *Archaeology at the Pauli Murray family home: The state of research 2019* [Video]. YouTube. https://www.youtube.com/watch?v=jSr407TOayo

NCD Risk Factor Collaboration. (2016). A century of trends in adult human height. *eLife, 5,* Article e13410.

Nelson, R. G. (2016). Residential context, institutional alloparental care, and child growth in Jamaica. *American Journal of Human Biology, 28*(4), 493–502.

Nelson, R. G. (2018). Stress and growth. In W. Trevathan, M. Cartmill, D. Dufour, C. Larsen, D. O'Rourke, K. Rosenberg, & K. Strier (Eds.), *The international encyclopedia of biological anthropology.* Wiley. https://doi.org/10.1002/9781118584538.ieba0380

Nelson, R. G. (2021). The sex in your violence: Patriarchy and power in anthropological world building and everyday life. *Current Anthropology, 62*(S23), S92–S102.

Nesse, R. M., & Williams, G. C. (2012). *Why we get sick: The new science of Darwinian medicine.* Vintage.

Netting, R. McC. (1993). *Smallholders, householders: Farm families and the ecology of intensive, sustainable agriculture.* Stanford University Press.

Nicholas, G. P. (2008a). Melding science and community values: Indigenous archaeology programs and the negotiation of cultural difference. In S. W. Silliman (Ed.), *Collaboration at the trowel's edge: Teaching and learning in Indigenous archaeology* (pp. 228–249). University of Arizona Press.

Nicholas, G. (2008b). Native peoples and archaeology. In D. M. Pearsall (Ed.), *Encyclopedia of archaeology* (pp. 1660–1669). Academic Press. https://doi.org/10.1016/B978-012373962-9.00203-X

Nicholas, G. (2018, February 14). It's taken thousands of years, but Western science is finally catching up to Traditional Knowledge. *The Conversation.* https://theconversation.com/its-taken-thousands-of-years-but-western-science-is-finally-catching-up-to-traditional-knowledge-90291

Nicholas, G. P., & Andrews, T. D. (1997). Indigenous archaeology in the postmodern world. In G. P. Nicholas & T. D. Andrews (Eds.), *At a crossroads: Archaeology and First Peoples in Canada* (pp. 1–18). Simon Fraser University Press.

Nicholas, G. P., & Hollowell, J. (2007). Ethical challenges to a postcolonial archaeology: The legacy of scientific colonialism. In Y. Hamilakis & P. Duke (Eds.), *Archaeology and capitalism: From ethics to politics* (pp. 59–82). Left Coast Press.

Nichter, M. (1989). Pharmaceuticals, health commodification, and social relations: Ramifications for primary health care. In *Anthropology and international health* (pp. 233–277). Springer.

Nichter, M. (2008). *Global health: Why cultural perceptions, social representations, and biopolitics matter.* University of Arizona Press.

Nichter, M. (2009). *Fat talk.* Harvard University Press.

Nichter, M. (2010). Idioms of distress revisited. *Culture, Medicine, and Psychiatry, 34*(2), 401–416.

Nichter, M. (2021). Idioms of distress. In H. Callan (Ed.), *The international encyclopedia of anthropology.* Wiley. https://doi.org/10.1002/9781118924396.wbiea2018

Nielsen, M. W., Alegria, S., Börjeson, L., Etzkowitz, H., Falk-Krzesinski, H. J., Joshi, A., Leahey, E., Smith-Doerr, L., Woolley, A. W., & Schiebinger, L. (2017). Opinion: Gender diversity leads to better science. *Proceedings of the National Academy of Sciences U.S.A. 114*(8), 1740–1742.

Nielsen, R., Akey, J. M., Jakobsson, M., Pritchard, J. K., Tishkoff, S., & Willerslev, E. (2017). Tracing the peopling of the world through genomics. *Nature, 541*(7637), 302–310. https://doi.org/10.1038/nature21347

Nkrumah, K. (1967). African socialism revisited. In *Africa: National and social revolution.* Peace and Socialism Publishers. https://www.marxists.org/subject/africa/nkrumah/1967/african-socialism-revisited.htm

Nkrumah, K., Arrigoni, R., & Napolitano, G. (1963) *Africa must unite.* Heinemann.

Nnaemeka, O. (2005). African women, colonial discourses, and imperialist interventions: Female circumcision as impetus. In O. Nnaemeka (Ed.), *Female circumcision and the politics of knowledge: African women in imperialist discourses* (pp. 27–46). Praeger.

Nordling, L. (2020, July 17). Who gets to study whom? *SAPIENS.* https://www.sapiens.org/culture/anthropology-colonial-history/

North-Hager, E. (2012, September 24). One of the gang. *USCDornsife.* https://dornsife.usc.edu/news/stories/1245/one-of-the-gang/

Novak, S. A. (2009). Beneath the facade: A skeletal model of domestic violence. In R. Gowland & C. J. Knüsel (Eds.), *Social archaeology of funeral remains* (pp. 238–252). Oxbow Books.

Oakland Rodman, A. (1992). Textiles and ethnicity: Tiwanaku in San Pedro de Atacama, North Chile. *Latin American Antiquity, 3*(4), 316–340.

Ochs, E. (2008). Talking to children in Western Samoa. *Language in Society, 11*(1), 77–104. http://www.sscnet.ucla.edu/anthro/faculty/ochs/articles/ochs1982a.pdf

Ochs, E. (2017). Lecture by E. Ochs, November 17, 2017. *Berkeley Language Center, University of California,* *Berkeley.* http://blc.berkeley.edu/2017/08/09/lecture-by-e-ochs-november-17-2017/

Ochs, E., & Schieffelin, B. B. (1984). Language acquisition and socialization: Three developmental stories and their implications. In R. Shweder & R. Levine (Eds.), *Culture theory: Essays on mind, self and emotion* (pp. 276–320). Cambridge University Press. http://www.sscnet.ucla.edu/anthro/faculty/ochs/articles/Language_acquisition_and_socialization.pdf

O'Connell, J. (2011). Remembering Lew Binford. *Mitteilungen der Gesellschaft für Urgeschichte, 20,* 79–89.

Ode, K. (2016, July 22). Pipestone National Monument offers a glimpse into the past, as it still is practiced today. *StarTribune.* https://www.startribune.com/pipestone-national-monument-offers-a-glimpse-into-the-past-as-it-still-is-practiced-today/387695401/

Okiror, S. (2020, February 21). Stella Nyanzi marks release from jail in Uganda with Yoweri Museveni warning. *The Guardian.* https://www.theguardian.com/global-development/2020/feb/21/stella-nyanzi-marks-release-from-jail-in-uganda-with-yoweri-museveni-warning

Okura, K. (2021). There are no Asians in China: The racialization of Chinese international students in the United States. *Identities: Global Studies in Culture and Power, 28*(2), 147–165. https://doi.org/10.1080/1070289X.2019.1663053

Oliver-Smith, A. (1986). *The martyred city: Death and rebirth in the Andes.* University of New Mexico Press.

Oliver-Smith, A., & Hoffman, S. M. (Eds.). (1999). *The angry earth: Disaster in anthropological perspective.* Routledge.

Omi, M., & Winant, H. (2014). *Racial formation in the United States* (3rd ed.). Routledge.

Ong, A. (1999). *Flexible citizenship: The cultural logics of transnationality.* Duke University Press.

Ong, A., Dominguez, V. R., Friedman, J., Schiller, N. G., Stolcke, V., Wu, D. Y., & Ying, H. (1996). Cultural citizenship as subject-making: Immigrants negotiate racial and cultural boundaries in the United States [and comments and reply]. *Current Anthropology, 37*(5), 737–762.

Organ, C., Nunn, C. L., Machanda, Z., & Wrangham, R. W. (2011). Phylogenetic rate shifts in feeding time during the evolution of *Homo. Proceedings of the National Academy of Sciences U.S.A., 108*(35), 14555–14559. https://doi.org/10.1073/pnas.1107806108

Orlove, B. S. (1980). Ecological anthropology. *Annual Review of Anthropology, 9*(1), 235–273.

Orr, T. J., Burns, M., Hawkes, K., Holekamp, K. E., Hook, K. A., Josefson, C. C., Kimmitt, A., Lewis, A. K., Lipshutz,

S., Lynch, K., Sirot, L., Stadtmauer, D., Staub, N., Wolfner, M., & Hayssen, V. (2020). It takes two to tango: Including a female perspective in reproductive biology. *Integrative and Comparative Biology, 60*(3), 796–813.

Ortiz, A. (1969). *The Tewa world: Space, time, being, and becoming in a Pueblo society.* University of Chicago Press.

Ostrom, E. (1990). *Governing the commons: The evolution of institutions for collective action.* Cambridge University Press.

Ottman, N., Smidt, H., de Vos, W. M., & Belzer, C. (2012). The function of our microbiota: Who is out there and what do they do? *Frontiers in Cellular and Infection Microbiology, 2,* 104.

Oxilia, G., Fiorillo, F., Boschin, F., Boaretto, E., Apicella, S. A., Matteucci, C., Panetta, D., Pistocchi, R., Guerrini, F., Margherita, C., Andretta, M., Sorrentino, R., Boschian, G., Arrighi, S., Dori, I., Mancuso, G., Crezzini, J., Riga, A., Serrangeli, M. C., . . . Benazzi, S. (2017). The dawn of dentistry in the late upper Paleolithic: An early case of pathological intervention at Riparo Fredian. *American Journal of Physical Anthropology, 163,* 446–461.

Pabst, M. A., Letofsky-Papst, I., Bock, E., Moser, M., Dorfer, L., Egarter-Vigl, E., & Hofer, F. (2009). The tattoos of the Tyrolean Iceman: A light microscopical, ultrastructural and element analytical study. *Journal of Archaeological Science, 36*(10), 2335–2341.

Paciulli, L. M., & Emer, L. K. (2018). Sociosexual behavior (nonhuman primates). In W. Trevathan, M. Cartmill, D. Dufour, C. Larsen, D. O'Rourke, K. Rosenberg, & K. Strier (Eds.), *The international encyclopedia of biological anthropology.* https://doi.org/10.1002/9781118584538.ieba0459

Padilla, M. B. (2007). *Caribbean pleasure industry: Tourism, sexuality, and AIDS in the Dominican Republic.* University of Chicago Press.

Palmer, D. A., Tse, M. M., & Colwell, C. (2019). Guanyin's limbo: Icons as demi-persons and dividuating objects. *American Anthropologist, 121*(4), 897–910.

Palmquist, A. (2015, January 5). Who is milk sharing online? *Anthrolactology.* https://anthrolactology.com/2015/01/05/who-is-milk-sharing-online/

Palmquist, A. E. L., & Doehler, K. (2014). Contextualizing online human milk sharing: Structural factors and lactation disparity among middle income women in the U.S. *Social Science & Medicine, 122,* 140–147.

Panofsky, A., Dasgupta, K., & Iturriaga, N. (2021). How white nationalists mobilize genetics: From genetic ancestry and human biodiversity to counterscience and metapolitics. *American Journal of Physical Anthropology, 175*(2), 387–398.

Pareja, M. N., McKinney, T., Mayhew, J. A., Setchell, J. M., Nash, S. D., & Heaton, R. (2020). A new identification of the monkeys depicted in a Bronze Age wall painting from Akrotiri, Thera. *Primates, 61,* 159–168.

Park, J. (2000). "The worst hassle is you can't play rugby": Haemophilia and masculinity in New Zealand. *Current Anthropology, 41*(3), 444–453.

Park, J., Scott, K., York, D., & Carnahan, M. (2019). *Haemophilia in Aotearoa New Zealand: More than a bleeding nuisance.* Routledge.

Parker, G. (2014). Mothers at large: Responsibilizing the pregnant self for the "obesity epidemic." *Fat Studies, 3*(2), 101–118.

Parker, G., & Pausé, C. (2018). Pregnant with possibility: Negotiating fat maternal subjectivity in the "war on obesity." *Fat Studies, 7*(2), 124–134. https://doi.org/10.1080/21604851.2017.1372990

Parker, R. (1991). *Bodies, pleasures and passions.* Beacon Press.

Parker, R. (2007). Sexuality, health, and human rights. *American Journal of Public Health, 96,* 972–973.

Parker, R. (2009). Sexuality, culture and society: Shifting paradigms in sexuality research. *Culture, Health & Sexuality, 11*(3), 251–266.

Parker Pearson, M. (2000). *The archaeology of death and burial.* Texas A&M University Press.

Parkinson, W. A., Nakassis, D., & Galaty, M. L. (2013). Crafts, specialists, and markets in Mycenaean Greece. *American Journal of Archaeology, 117*(3), 413–422.

Parsons Dick, H. (2011). Making immigrants illegal in small-town USA. *Journal of Linguistic Anthropology, 21*(S1), E35–E55.

Pascoe, C. J. (2007). *Dude, you're a fag: Masculinity and sexuality in high school.* University of California Press.

Pascoe, C. J. (n.d.). Selected media. *C. J. Pascoe.* https://www.cjpascoe.org/media

Patterson, O. (2018). *Slavery and social death: A comparative study* (with a new preface). Harvard University Press.

Pauli, J. (2019). *The decline of marriage in Namibia: Kinship and social class in a rural community.* Transcript Verlag. https://doi.org/10.14361/9783839443033

Pauli, J., & Dawids, F. (2017). The struggle for marriage: Elite and non-elite weddings in rural Namibia. *Anthropology Southern Africa, 40*(1), 15–28.

Pauli Murray Center for History and Social Justice. (n.d.). https://www.paulimurraycenter.com/

Pawłowska, K. (2015). The smells of Neolothic Çatalhöyük, Turkey: Time and space of human activity. *Journal of Anthropological Archaeology, 36,* 1–11.

Pawłowski, B. (2015). Ovulation, concealed. In P. Whelehan & A. Bolin (Eds.), *The international encyclopedia of human sexuality*. Wiley. https://doi.org/10.1002/9781118896877.wbiehs325

Paz, A. I. (2019). Communicating citizenship. *Annual Review of Anthropology, 48*(1), 77–93.

Peacock, J. L. (2001). *The anthropological lens: Harsh light, soft focus*. Cambridge University Press.

Pearson, G. (2018). Gender and globalization. In H. Callan (Ed.), *The international encyclopedia of anthropology*. https://doi.org/10.1002/9781118924396.wbiea2303

Peccerelli, F. (2014, November). *A forensic anthropologist who brings closure for the "disappeared"* [Video]. TEDYouth 2014. https://www.ted.com/talks/fredy_peccerelli_a_forensic_anthropologist_who_brings_closure_for_the_disappeared?language=en#t-103399

Pels, P. (2021). Classification revisited: On time, methodology and position in decolonizing anthropology. *Anthropological Theory, 22*(1), 78–101. https://doi.org/10.1177/14634996211011749

Pennisi, E. (2021, June 23). Ancient Siberian cave hosted Neanderthals, Denisovans, and modern humans – possibly at the same time. *Science*. https://www.science.org/news/2021/06/ancient-siberian-cave-hosted-neanderthals-denisovans-and-modern-humans-possibly-same

Peregrine, P., Moses, Y. T., Goodman, A., Lamphere, L., & Peacock, J. L. (2012). What is science in anthropology? *American Anthropologist, 114*, 593–597.

Perez, S. I., Tejedor, M. F., Novo, N. M., & Aristide, L. (2013). Divergence times and the evolutionary radiation of New World monkeys (Platyrrhini, Primates): An analysis of fossil and molecular data. *PLOS ONE, 8*(6), Article e68029.

Pérez Rodríguez, V., de León, R. H. P., & Tuñón, A. M. (2017). Skeletal health and the abandonment of a late-terminal formative urban center in the Mixteca Alta: A bioarchaeological analysis of human remains from Cerro Jazmín. *Journal of Archaeological Science: Reports, 13*, 729–736.

Pérez Rodríguez, V., Kellner, C. M., & Ponce de León, R. H. (2020). Urban to the bone: Isotopic and faunal dietary data from Formative-period Cerro Jazmín, Mixteca Alta, Oaxaca, México. *Journal of Archaeological Science, 121*, Article 105177.

Pérez Rodríguez, V., & Tuñón, A. M. (2020). Political strategies and the urban spaces that reflect them in Formative-period Cerro Jazmín, Oaxaca. *Ancient Mesoamerica, 31*(3), 386–397.

Perry, G. H. (2014). Parasites and human evolution. *Evolutionary Anthropology, 23*(6), 218–228.

Petersdorf, M., & Higham, J. P. (2017). Mating systems. In M. Bezanson, K. C. MacKinnon, E. Riley, C. J. Campbell, K. Nekaris, A. Estrada, A. F. Di Fiore, S. Ross, L. E. Jones-Engel, B. Thierry, R. W. Sussman, C. Sanz, J. Loudon, S. Elton, & A. Fuentes (Eds.), *The international encyclopedia of primatology*. Wiley. https://doi.org/10.1002/9781119179313.wbprim0212

Petersdorf, M. & Higham, J. P. (2018). Mating systems (primates). In W. Trevathan, M. Cartmill, D. Dufour, C. Larsen, D. O'Rourke, K. Rosenberg, & K. Strier (Eds.), *The international encyclopedia of biological anthropology*. Wiley. https://doi.org/10.1002/9781118584538.ieba0308

Petryna, A., & Follis, K. (2015). Risks of citizenship and fault lines of survival. *Annual Review of Anthropology, 44*, 401–417.

Pickering, R., Herries, A. I. R., Woodhead, J. D., Hellstrom, J. C., Green, H. E., Paul, B., Ritzman, T., Strait, D. S., Schoville, B. J., & Hancox, P. J. (2019). U–Pb-dated flowstones restrict South African early hominin record to dry climate phases. *Nature, 565*, 226–229.

Piel, F., Patil, A., Howes, R., Nyangiri, O. A., Gething, P. W., Williams, T. N., Weatherall, D. J., & Hay, S. I. (2010). Global distribution of the sickle cell gene and geographical confirmation of the malaria hypothesis. *Nature Communications, 1*, Article 104. https://doi.org/10.1038/ncomms1104

Pilbeam, D. R., & Lieberman, D. E. (2017). Reconstructing the last common ancestor of chimpanzees and humans, In M. N. Muller, R. W. Wrangham, & D. R. Pilbeam (Eds.), *Chimpanzees and human evolution* (pp. 22–141). Harvard University Press.

Pitluck, A. Z., Mattioli, F., & Souleles, D. (2018). Finance beyond function: Three causal explanations for financialization. *AnthroSources, 5*(2), 157–171. https://doi.org/10.1002/sea2.12114

Plafker, G., Ericksen, G. E., & Concha, J. F. (1971). Geological aspects of the May 31, 1970, Perú earthquake. *Bulletin of the Seismological Society of America, 61*(3), 543–578.

Plummer, T. W., Ditchfield, P. W., Bishop, L. C., Kingston, J. D., Ferraro, J. V., Braun, D. R., Hertel, F., & Potts, R. (2009). Oldest evidence of toolmaking hominins in a grassland-dominated ecosystem. *PLOS ONE, 4*(9), Article e7199. https://doi.org/10.1371/journal.pone.0007199

Pobiner, B. (2016). Meat-eating among the earliest humans. *American Scientist, 104*(2), 110. https://doi.org/10.1511/2016.119.110

Pocock, R. I. (1918). On the external characters of the lemurs and of *Tarsius*. *Proceedings of the Zoological Society of London, 1918*, 19–53.

Podesva, R. (2007). Phonation type as a stylistic variable: The use of falsetto in constructing a persona. *Journal of Sociolinguistics, 11*(4), 478–504.

Polese, A., Morris, J., Pawłusz, E., & Seliverstova, O. (Eds.). (2017). *Identity and nation building in everyday post-socialist life*. Routledge.

Ponce de Leon, M. S., Bienvenu, T., Marom, A., Engel, S., Tafforeau, P., Warren, J. L. A., Lordkipanidze, D., Kurniawan, I., Murti, D. B., Suriyanto, R. A., Koesbardiati, T., & Zollikofer, C. F. (2021).The primitive brain of early *Homo*. *Science, 372*(6538), 165–171. https://doi.org/10.1126/science.aaz0032

Pontzer, H., & Wood, B. M. (2021). Effects of evolution, ecology, and economy on human diet: Insights from hunter-gatherers and other small-scale societies. *Annual Review of Nutrition, 41*, 363–385. https://doi.org/10.1146/annurev-nutr-111120-105520

Porr, M., & Matthews, J. (Eds.). (2019). *Interrogating human origins: Decolonisation and the deep human past*. Routledge.

Poplett, E. (2019, February 28). *Uncovering histories*. Carolina Center for Public Service. https://ccps.unc.edu/uncovering-histories/

Power, S. (2001). Bystanders to genocide: Why the United States let the Rwandan genocide happen. *Atlantic Monthly, 288*(2), 89.

Price, N., Hedenstierna-Jonson, C., Zachrisson, T., Kjellström, A., Storå, J., Krzewińska, M., Günther, T., Sobrado, V., Jakobsson, M., & Götherström, A. (2019). Viking warrior women? Reassessing Birka chamber grave Bj.581. *Antiquity, 93*, 181–198.

Price, T. D. (1995). Social inequality at the origins of agriculture. In T. D. Price & G. M. Feinman (Eds.), *Foundations of social inequality* (pp. 129–151). Springer.

Price, T. D., & Gebauer, A. B. (Eds.). (1995). *Last hunters, first farmers: New perspectives on the prehistoric transition to agriculture*. School of American Research Press.

Proffitt, T., Luncz, L., Falótico, T., Ottoni, E. B., de la Torre, I., & Haslam, M. (2016). Wild monkeys flake stone tools. *Nature, 539*, 85–88.

Pruetz, J., Bertolani, P., Boyer Ontl, K., Lindshield, S., Shelley, M., & Wessling, E. G. (2015). New evidence on the tool-assisted hunting exhibited by chimpanzees (*Pan troglodytes verus*) in a savannah habitat at Fongoli, Sénégal. *Royal Society Open Science, 2*(4), Article 140507.

Pruetz, J. D., & Herzog, N. (2017). Chimpanzees at Fongoli, Senegal navigate a burned landscape. *Current Anthropology, 58*(S16), S337–S350.

Prüfer, K., Racimo, F., Patterson, N., Jay, F., Sankararaman, S., Sawyer, S., Heinze, A., Renaud, G., Sudmant, P. H., de Filippo, C., Li, H., Mallick, S., Dannemann, M., Fu, Q., Kircher, M., Kuhlwilm, M., Lachmann, M., Meyer, M., Ongyerth, M., . . . Pääbo, S. (2014). The complete genome sequence of a Neanderthal from the Altai Mountains. *Nature, 505*(7481), 43–49. https://doi.org/10.1038/nature12886

Pullum, G. (1989). The great Eskimo vocabulary hoax. *Natural Language & Linguistic Theory, 7*(2), 275–281.

Quer, J., & Steinbach, M. (2019). Handling sign language data: The impact of modality. *Frontiers in Psychology, 10*, Article 483. https://doi.org/10.3389/fpsyg.2019.00483

Quijada, J. B., Graber, K. E., & Stephen, E. (2015). Finding "their own": Revitalizing Buryat culture through shamanic practices in Ulan-Ude. *Problems of Post-Communism, 62*(5), 258–272. https://doi.org/10.1080/10758216.2015.1057040

Quijano, A. (2000). Coloniality of power and Eurocentrism in Latin America. *International Sociology, 15*(2), 215–232.

Quijano, A. (2007). Coloniality and modernity/rationality. *Cultural Studies, 21*(2–3), 168–178.

Quillen, E. E., Norton, H. L., Parra, E. J., Lona-Durazo, F., Ang, K. C., Illiescu, F. M., Pearson, L. N., Shriver, M. D., Lasisi, T., Gokcumen, O., Starr, I., Lin, Y. L., Martin, A. R., & Jablonski, N. G. (2019). Shades of complexity: New perspectives on the evolution and genetic architecture of human skin. *American Journal of Physical Anthropology, 168*(67), 4–26.

Quinlan, M. B. (2011). Ethnomedicine. In M. Singer & P. I. Erickson (Eds.), *A companion to medical anthropology* (pp. 379–403). Wiley. https://doi.org/10.1002/9781444395303.ch19

Rabinow, P. (2007). *Reflections on fieldwork in Morocco* (with a new preface by the author). University of California Press.

Raffield, B., Price, N., & Collard, M. (2017). Polygyny, concubinage, and the social lives of women in Viking-age Scandinavia. *Viking and Medieval Scandinavia, 13*, 165–209.

Raharijaona, V., & Kus, S. (2001). Matters of life and death: Mortuary rituals as part of a larger whole among the Betsileo of Madagascar. In M. S. Chesson (Ed.), *Social memory, identity and death: Anthropological perspectives on mortuary rituals* (pp. 56–69). Archaeological Papers of the American Anthropological Association.

Rahman, T. (2009). Language ideology, identity and the commodification of language in the call centers of Pakistan. *Language in Society, 38*, 233–258.

Rahmstorf, L. (2018). Of middens and markets: The phenomenology of the market place in the Bronze Age and beyond. In H. P. Hahn & G. Schmitz (Eds.), *Market as place and space of economic exchange: Archaeological and anthropological perspectives* (pp. 20–40). Oxbow Books.

Ralph, L. (2014). *Renegade dreams: Living through injury in gangland Chicago.* University of Chicago Press.

Ralph, L. (2015). Becoming aggrieved: An alternative framework of care in black Chicago. *RSF: The Russell Sage Foundation Journal of the Social Sciences, 1*(2), 31–41.

Ralph, L. (2019). The logic of the slave patrol: The fantasy of black predatory violence and the use of force by the police. *Palgrave Communications, 5,* Article 130. https://doi.org/10.1057/s41599-019-0333-7

Rana, J. (2020). Anthropology and the riddle of white supremacy. *American Anthropologist, 122*(1), 99–111.

Ranere, A. J., Piperno, D. R., Holst, I., Dickau, R., & Iriarte, J. (2009). The cultural and chronological context of early Holocene maize and squash domestication in the Central Balsas River Valley, Mexico. *Proceedings of the National Academy of Sciences U.S.A., 106*(13), 5014–5018.

Rankin-Hill, L. M., & Blakey, M. L. (1994). W. Montague Cobb (1904–1990): Physical anthropologist, anatomist, and activist. *American Anthropologist, 96*(1), 74–96.

Rappaport, R. (1968). *Pigs for the ancestors: Ritual in the ecology of a New Guinea people.* Yale University Press.

Raskin, S. E. (2015). *Decayed, missing, and filled: Subjectivity and the dental safety net in Central Appalachia* (Publication No. 3725587) [Doctoral dissertation, University of Arizona]. ProQuest Dissertations Publishing.

Ravenscroft, J., Schell, L. M., & Akwesasne Task Force on the Environment. (2018). Patterns of PCB exposure among Akwesasne adolescents: The role of dietary and inhalation pathways. *Environment International, 121,* 963–972.

Ray, I. (2007). Women, water, and development. *Annual Review of Environment and Resources, 32,* 421–449.

Raymond, H. (2007). The ecologically noble savage debate. *Annual Review of Anthropology, 36,* 177–190.

Reardon, J., & TallBear, K. (2012). "Your DNA is our history": Genomics, anthropology, and the construction of whiteness as property. *Current Anthropology, 53*(S5), S233–S245.

Reddy, W. (2012). *The making of romantic love: Longing and sexuality in Europe, South Asia, and Japan, 900–1200 CE.* University of Chicago Press.

Redfern, R. C. (2017). Identifying and interpreting domestic violence in archaeological human remains: A critical review of the evidence. *International Journal of Osteoarchaeology, 27*(1), 13–34. https://doi.org/10.1002/oa.2461

Redford, K. H. (1991). The ecologically noble savage. *Cultural Survival Quarterly, 15*(1), 46–48.

Reese, A. M. (2019). *Black food geographies: Race, self-reliance, and food access in Washington, DC.* UNC Press Books.

Reichard, U. H. (2018). Monogamy in primates. In W. Trevathan, M. Cartmill, D. Dufour, C. Larsen, D. O'Rourke, K. Rosenberg, & K. Strier (Eds.), *The international encyclopedia of biological anthropology.* Wiley. https://doi.org/10.1002/9781118584538.ieba0326

Rej, P. H., HEAT Steering Committee, Gravlee, C. C., & Mulligan, C. J. (2020). Shortened telomere length is associated with unfair treatment attributed to race in African Americans living in Tallahassee, Florida. *American Journal of Human Biology, 32*(3), Article e23375.

Relton, C. L., Hartwig, F. P., & Davey Smith, G. (2015). From stem cells to the law courts: DNA methylation, the forensic epigenome and the possibility of a biosocial archive. *International Journal of Epidemiology, 44*(4), 1083–1093. https://doi.org/10.1093/ije/dyv198

Restrepo, E., & Escobar, A. (2005). 'Other anthropologies and anthropology otherwise': Steps to a world anthropologies framework. *Critique of Anthropology, 25*(2), 99–129.

Reyes, A. (2017). Inventing postcolonial elites: Race, language, mix, excess. *Journal of Linguistic Anthropology, 27*(2), 210–231.

Reyes-Foster, B. M., Carter, S. K., & Hinojosa, M. S. (2015). Milk sharing in practice: A descriptive analysis of peer breastmilk sharing. *Breastfeeding Medicine, 10*(5), 263–269.

Reyes-García, V. (2001). *Indigenous people, ethnobotanical knowledge, and market economy: A case study of the Tsimané Amerindians in lowland Bolivia* (UMI No. 3039808) [Doctoral dissertation, University of Florida]. ProQuest Dissertations Publishing.

Reyes-García, V. (2019). Mothering in the field: Participant observation and cultural transmission. In B. Hewlett (Ed.), *The secret life of anthropologists.* Springer.

Reyes-García, V., Broesch, J., & TAPS Bolivian Study Team. (2013). The transmission of ethnobotanical knowledge and skills among Tsimané in the Bolivian Amazon. In R. Ellen, S. J. Lycett, & S. E. Johns (Eds.), *Understanding cultural transmission in anthropology: A critical synthesis* (pp. 191–212). Berghahn.

Reyes-García, V., Luz, A. C., Gueze, M., Paneque-Gálvez, J., Macía, M. J., Orta-Martínez, M., Pino, J., & TAPS Bolivian Study Team. (2013). Secular trends on traditional ecological knowledge: An analysis of different domains of knowledge among Tsimané men. *Learning and Individual Differences, 27,* 206–212.

Reyes-García, V., & Sunderlin, W. D. (2011). Why do field research? In A. Angelsen, H. O. Larsen, J. F. Lund, C. Smith-Hall, & S. Wunder (Eds.), *Measuring livelihoods and environmental dependence: Methods for research and fieldwork* (pp. 17–32). Earthscan.

Richards, M. P., Pearson, J. A., Molleson, T. I., Russell, N., & Martine, L. (2003). Stable isotope evidence of diet at Neolithic Catalhoyuk, Turkey. *Journal of Archaeological Science, 30*(1), 67–76.

Rick, T. C., & Sandweiss, D. H. (2020). Archaeology, climate, and global change in the Age of Humans. *Proceedings of the National Academy of Sciences U.S.A., 117*(15), 8250–8253. https://doi.org/10.1073/pnas.2003612117

Rickford, J. R., & Rickford, A. E. (1976). Cut-eye and suck-teeth: African words and gestures in New World guise. *The Journal of American Folklore, 89*(353), 294–309.

Riley, E. P. (2007a). Flexibility in diet and activity patterns of *Macaca tonkeana* in response to anthropogenic habitat alteration. *International Journal of Primatology, 28*(1), 107–133.

Riley, E. P. (2007b). The human–macaque interface: Conservation implications of current and future overlap and conflict in Lore Lindu National Park, Sulawesi, Indonesia. *American Anthropologist, 109*(3), 473–484.

Riley, E. (2013). Contemporary primatology in anthropology: Beyond the epistemological abyss. *American Anthropologist, 115*(3), 411–422. https://doi.org/10.1111/aman.12025

Rippon, G. (2019). *The gendered brain: The new neuroscience that shatters the myth of the female brain.* Random House.

Ritchie, H., & Roser, M. (2018, September). Urbanization. *Our World in Data.* https://ourworldindata.org/urbanization

Rival, L., & McKey, D. (2008). Domestication and diversity in manioc (*Manihot esculenta* Crantz ssp. *esculenta,* Euphorbiaceae). *Current Anthropology, 49*(6), 1109–1117.

Rivers-Moore, M. (2011). Imagining others: Sex, race, and power in transnational sex tourism. *ACME: An International Journal for Critical Geographies, 10*(3), 392–411.

Rivers-Moore, M. (2012a). Almighty gringos: Masculinity and value in sex tourism. *Sexualities, 15*(7), 850–870.

Rivers-Moore, M. (2012b). Becoming middle class? Consumption, respectability, and place in sex tourism. In *Consumer culture in Latin America* (pp. 207–219). Palgrave Macmillan.

Rivers-Moore, M. (2014). Waiting for the state: Sex work and the neoliberal governance of sexuality. *Social Politics, 21*(3), 403–429.

Rivers-Moore, M. (2016). *Gringo Gulch: Sex, tourism, and social mobility in Costa Rica.* University of Chicago Press.

Robben, A. C. G. M. (Ed.). (2004). *Death, mourning, and burial: A cross-cultural reader* (2nd ed.). Blackwell.

Roberts, C., & Buikstra, J. E. (2003). *The bioarchaeology of tuberculosis: A global view on a reemerging disease.* University Press of Florida.

Robinson, S. (2011). *Split intransitivity in Rotokas, a Papuan language of Bougainville* [Doctoral dissertation, Radboud University Nijmegen]. https://pure.mpg.de/rest/items/item_795664_8/component/file_795665/content

Robson, A. J., & Kaplan, H. S. (2006). The economics of hunter-gatherer societies and the evolution of human characteristics. *Canadian Journal of Economics/Revue canadienne d'économique, 39*(2), 375–398. https://doi.org/10.1111/j.0008-4085.2006.00351.x

Rodney, N. C., & Mulligan, C. J. (2014). A biocultural study of the effects of maternal stress on mother and newborn health in the Democratic Republic of Congo. *American Journal of Physical Anthropology, 155*(2), 200–209.

Rodrigues, M. A. (2017). Female spider monkeys (*Ateles geoffroyi*) cope with anthropogenic disturbance through fission–fusion dynamics. *International Journal of Primatology, 38,* 838–855.

Rodríguez, D., Hermida, A., & Huesca, J. (2012). El altar de muertos: Origen y significado en México. *Revista de Divulgación Científica y Tecnológica de la Universidad Veracruzana, 25*(1). https://docplayer.es/10826625-El-altar-de-muertos-origen-y-significado-en-mexico.html

Rogers, J., & Gibbs, R. (2014). Comparative primate genomics: Emerging patterns of genome content and dynamics. *Nature Reviews Genetics, 15,* 347–359. https://doi.org/10.1038/nrg3707

Rojas, R. (2017). The ebbing "pink tide": An autopsy of left-wing regimes in Latin America. *New Labor Forum, 26*(2), 70–82. https://doi.org/10.1177%2F1095796017700136

Rooker, K., & Gavrilets, S. (2020). On the evolution of sexual receptivity in female primates. *Scientific Reports, 10,* Article 11945. https://doi.org/10.1038/s41598-020-68338-y

Roque, A., Pijawka, D., & Wutich, A. (2020). The role of social capital in resiliency: Disaster recovery in Puerto Rico. *Risk, Hazards & Crisis in Public Policy, 11*(2), 204–235.

Rosa, J. (2016). Standardization, racialization, language-lessness: Raciolinguistic ideologies across communicative contexts. *Journal of Linguistic Anthropology, 26*(2), 162–183.

Rosa, J. (2019). *Looking like a language, sounding like a race: Raciolinguistic ideologies and the learning of Latinidad.* Oxford University Press.

Rosa, J., & Bonilla, Y. (2017). Deprovincializing Trump, decolonizing diversity, and unsettling anthropology. *American Ethnologist, 44*(2), 201–208.

Rosa, J., & Díaz, V. (2020). Raciontologies: Rethinking anthropological accounts of institutional racism and enactments of white supremacy in the United States. *American Anthropologist, 122*(1), 120–132.

Rosa, J., & Flores, N. (2017). Unsettling race and language: Toward a raciolinguistic perspective. *Language in Society, 46*(5), 621–647.

Rosen, L. (1989). *The anthropology of justice: Law as culture in Islamic society.* Cambridge University Press.

Ross, C. T., Borgerhoff Mulder, M., Oh, S-Y., Bowles, S., Beheim, B., Bunce, J., Caudell, M., Clark, G., Colleran, H., Cortez, C., Draper, P., Greaves, R., Gurven, M., Headland, T., Headland, J., Hill, K., Hewlett, B., Kaplan, H., Koster, J., . . . Ziker, J. (2018). Greater wealth inequality, less polygyny: Rethinking the polygyny threshold model. *Journal of the Royal Society, Interface, 15*(144), Article 20180035.

Roth, W. D., Yaylaci, S., Jaffe, K., & Richardson, L. (2020). Do genetic ancestry tests increase racial essentialism? Findings from a randomized controlled trial. *PLOS ONE, 15*(1), Article e0227399. https://doi.org/10.1371/journal.pone.0227399

Roth, W. E. (1897). *Ethnological studies among the north-west-central Queensland Aborigines.* Edmund Gregory.

Roth-Gordon, J. (2016). *Race and the Brazilian body.* University of California Press.

Rowe, M. (2011). *Bonds of the dead: Temples, burial, and the transformation of contemporary Japanese Buddhism.* University of Chicago Press.

Rubin, D. (1992). Nonlanguage factors affecting undergraduates' judgments of nonnative English-speaking teaching assistants. *Research in Higher Education, 33*(4), 511–531.

Rubin, D. L. (1998). Help! My professor (or doctor or boss) doesn't talk English. In J. Martin, T. Nakayama, & L. Flores (Eds.), *Readings in cultural contexts* (pp. 149–160). Mayfield Press.

Ruff, C. B., Holt, B., Niskanen, M., Sladek, V., Berner, M., Garofalo, E., Garvin, H. M., Hora, M., Junno, J.,

Schuplerova, E., Vilkama, R., & Whittey, E. (2015). Gradual decline in mobility with the adoption of food production in Europe. *Proceedings of the National Academy of Sciences U.S.A., 112*, 7147–7152.

Running Bear, U., Thayer, Z. M., Croy, C. D., Kaufman, C. E., Manson, S. M., & the AI-SUPERPFP Team. (2019). The impact of individual and parental American Indian boarding school attendance on chronic physical health of Northern Plains Tribes. *Family & Community Health, 42*(1), 1–7.

Rushohora, N. A. (2015). An archaeological identity of the Majimaji: Toward an historical archaeology of resistance to German colonization in southern Tanzania. *Archaeologies: Journal of the World Archaeological Congress, 11*, 246–271.

Rutherford, A. (2021). Race, eugenics, and the canceling of great scientists. *American Journal of Physical Anthropology, 175*(2), 448–452.

Ruvolo, M., Disotell, T. R., Allard, M. W., Brown, W. M., & Honeycutt, R. L. (1991). Resolution of the African hominoid trichotomy by use of a mitochondrial gene sequence. *Proceedings of the National Academy of Sciences U.S.A., 88*(4), 1570–1574. https://doi.org/10.1073/pnas.88.4.1570

Rwanda Social Security Board. (2019). Maternity leave. *Rwanda Social Security Board.* http://www.rssb.rw/content/maternity-leave

Rylko-Bauer, B. (2015). An SfAA oral history interview with Barbara Rose Johnston: The intersections of environment, health, and human rights. *Society for Applied Anthropology, November 2017 Newsletter.* https://www.appliedanthro.org/application/files/7615/6157/1347/Barbara_Rose_Johnston.pdf

Sahlins, M. (2017). *Stone age economics.* Routledge Classics. (Original work published 1972)

Salah, N. M., & Ayad, H. M. (2018). Why people choose gated communities: A case study of Alexandria metropolitan area. *Alexandria Engineering Journal, 57*(4), 2743–2753.

Saleh, F. (2020). Transgender as a humanitarian category: The case of Syrian queer and gender-variant refugees in Turkey. *TSQ, Transgender Studies Quarterly, 7*(1), 37–55.

Salhi, B. (2016). Beyond the doctor's white coat: Science, ritual, and healing in American biomedicine. In P. J. Brown & S. Closser (Eds.), *Understanding and applying medical anthropology* (3rd ed., pp. 204–212). Routledge.

Samanta, T. (2020). Living solo at midlife: Can the pandemic de-stigmatize living alone in India? *Journal of Aging Studies, 56*, Article 100907.

Sampathkumar, Y. (2020, May 13). Searching for the sources of water scarcity. *SAPIENS*. https://www.sapiens.org/culture/water-scarcity/

Samson, D. R. (2021). The human sleep paradox: The unexpected sleeping habits of *Homo sapiens*. *Annual Review of Anthropology, 50*, 259–274. https://doi.org/10.1146/annurev-anthro-010220-075523

Samson, D. R., & Nunn, C. L. (2015). Sleep intensity and the evolution of human cognition. *Evolutionary Anthropology: Issues, News, and Reviews, 24*(6), 225–237.

San Roque, L. (2019). Evidentiality. *Annual Review of Anthropology, 48*, 353–370. https://doi.org/10.1146/annurev-anthro-102218-011243

Sanchez-Mazas, A., Černý, V., Di, D., Buhler, S., Podgorná, E., Chevallier, E., Brunet, L., Weber, S., Kervaire, B., Testi, M., Andreani, M., Tiercy, J.-M., Villard, J., & Nunes, J. M. (2017). The HLA-B landscape of Africa: Signatures of pathogen-driven selection and molecular identification of candidate alleles to malaria protection. *Molecular Ecology, 26*(22), 6238–6252.

Sangaramoorthy, T. (2014). *Treating AIDS: Politics of difference, paradox of prevention*. Rutgers University Press.

Sangaramoorthy, T. (2018). "Putting Band-Aids on things that need stitches": Immigration and the landscape of care in rural America. *American Anthropologist, 120*, 487–499. https://doi.org/10.1111/aman.13054

Sanjek, R. (Ed.). (2019). *Fieldnotes: The makings of anthropology*. Cornell University Press.

Sauther, M. L., Sussman, R. W., & Gould, L. (1999). The socioecology of the ringtailed lemur: Thirty-five years of research. *Evolutionary Anthropology: Issues, News, and Reviews, 8*, 120–132.

Savage-Rumbaugh, E. S., McDonald, K., Sevcik, R. A., Hopkins, W. D., & Rupert, E. (1986). Spontaneous symbol acquisition and communicative use by pygmy chimpanzees (*Pan paniscus*). *Journal of Experimental Psychology, 115*, 211–235.

Sawyer, S., Renaud, G., Viola, B., Hublin, J., Gansauge, M., Shunkov, M. V., Derevianko, A. P., Prüfer, K., Kelso, J., & Pääbo, S. (2015). Nuclear and mitochondrial DNA sequences from two Denisovan individuals. *Proceedings of the National Academy of Sciences U.S.A., 112*(51), 15696–15700. https://doi.org/10.1073/pnas.1519905112

Sayers, K., Raghanti, M. A., & Lovejoy, C. O. (2012). Human evolution and the chimpanzee referential doctrine. *Annual Review of Anthropology, 41*, 119–138.

Scarupa, H. J. (1988). W. Montague Cobb: His long, storied, battle-scarred life. *New Directions, 15*(2), Article 2. http://dh.howard.edu/newdirections/vol15/iss2/2

Schaffnit, S. B., Urassa, M., & Lawson, D. (2019). "Child marriage" in context: Exploring local attitudes towards early marriage in rural Tanzania. *Sexual and Reproductive Health Matters, 27*(1), 93–105. https://doi.org/10.1080/09688080.2019.1571304

Schaffnit, S. B., Wamoyi, J., Urassa, M., Dardoumpa, M., & Lawson, D. W. (2020). When marriage is the best available option: Perceptions of opportunity and risk in female adolescence in Tanzania. *Global Public Health, 16*(12), 1820–1833. https://doi.org/10.1080/17441692.2020.1837911

Schaller, M. (2015). The behavioral immune system. In D. M. Buss (Ed.), *The handbook of evolutionary psychology*. Wiley. https://doi.org/10.1002/9781119125563.evpsych107

Scheffler, C., & Hermanussen, M. (2018). Growth in childhood and adolescence. In W. Trevathan, M. Cartmill, D. Dufour, C. Larsen, D. O'Rourke, K. Rosenberg, & K. Strier (Eds.), *The international encyclopedia of biological anthropology*. Wiley. https://doi.org/10.1002/9781118584538.ieba0537

Schell, L. M. (2020). Modern water: A biocultural approach to water pollution at the Akwesasne Mohawk Nation. *American Journal of Human Biology, 32*(1), Article e23348.

Schell, L. M., Gallo, M. V., Denham, M., Ravenscroft, J., DeCaprio, A. P., & Carpenter, D. O. (2008). Relationship of thyroid hormone levels to levels of polychlorinated biphenyls, lead, *p,p'*-DDE, and other toxicants in Akwesasne Mohawk youth. *Environmental Health Perspectives, 116*(6), 806–813.

Schell, L. M., Gallo, M. V., Ravenscroft, J., & DeCaprio, A. P. (2009). Persistent organic pollutants and anti-thyroid peroxidase levels in Akwesasne Mohawk young adults. *Environmental Research, 109*(1), 86–92.

Schell, L. M., Ravenscroft, J., Cole, M., Jacobs, A., Newman, J., & Akwesasne Task Force on the Environment. (2005). Health disparities and toxicant exposure of Akwesasne Mohawk young adults: A partnership approach to research. *Environmental Health Perspectives, 113*(12), 1826–1832.

Schell, L. M., & Tarbell, A. M. (1998). A partnership study of PCBs and the health of Mohawk youth: Lessons from our past and guidelines for our future. *Environmental Health Perspectives, 106*(Suppl 3), 833–840.

Scheper-Hughes, N. (1992). *Death without weeping: The violence of everyday life in Brazil*. University of California Press.

Scheper-Hughes, N. (1995). The primacy of the ethical: Propositions for a militant anthropology. *Current Anthropology, 36*(3), 409–440.

Scherer, A. K. (2018). Head shaping and tooth modification among the classic Maya of the Uscamacinta River Kingdoms. In V. Tiesler & M. C. Lozada (Eds.), *Social skins of the head: Body beliefs and ritual in ancient Mesoamerica and the Andes* (pp. 59–80). University of New Mexico Press.

Schieffelin, B., Woolard, K., & Kroskrity, P. (Eds.). (1998). *Language ideologies: Practice and theory.* Oxford University Press.

Schlegel, A., & Eloul, R. (1988). Marriage transactions: Labor, property, status. *American Anthropologist, 90,* 291–309. https://doi.org/10.1525/aa.1988.90.2.02a00030

Schmidt, J. (2016). Being 'like a woman': Fa'afāfine and Samoan masculinity. *The Asia Pacific Journal of Anthropology, 17*(3–4), 287–304. https://doi.org/10.1080/14442213.2016.1182208

Schmitt, D. P. (2015). Fundamentals of human mating strategies. In D. M. Buss (Ed.), *The handbook of evolutionary psychology.* Wiley. https://doi.org/10.1002/9781119125563.evpsych111

Schnegg, M. (2015). Epistemology: The nature and validation of knowledge. In H. R. Bernard & C. C. Gravlee (Eds.), *Handbook of methods in cultural anthropology* (2nd ed., pp. 21–53). Rowman & Littlefield.

Schneider, T. D., & Hayes, K. (2020). Epistemic colonialism: Is it possible to decolonize archaeology? *American Indian Quarterly, 44*(2), 127–148.

Schoenemann, P. T., Budinger, T. F., Sarich, V. M., & Wang, W. S.-Y. (2000). Brain size does not predict general cognitive ability within families. *Proceedings of the National Academy of Sciences U.S.A., 97*(9), 4932–4937. https://doi.org/10.1073/pnas.97.9.4932

Schon, R. (2011). Redistribution in Aegean palatial societies. By appointment to his majesty the *Wanax*: Value-added goods and redistribution in Mycenaean palatial economies. *American Journal of Archaeology, 115*(2), 219–227.

Schoville, B. (2021, March 31). Ancient southern Kalahari was more important to human evolution than previously thought. *The Conversation.* https://theconversation.com/ancient-southern-kalahari-was-more-important-to-human-evolution-than-previously-thought-155047

Schoville, B. J., Brown, K. S., Harris, J. A., & Wilkins J. (2016). New experiments and a model-driven approach for interpreting Middle Stone Age lithic point function using the edge damage distribution method. *PLOS ONE, 11*(10), Article e0164088. https://doi.org/10.1371/journal.pone.0164088

Schoville, B. J., Wilkins, J., Ritzman, T., Oestmo, S., & Brown, K. S. (2017). The performance of heat-treated silcrete backed pieces in actualistic and controlled complex projectile experiments. *Journal of Archaeological Science, 14,* 302–317.

Schuller, M. (2012). *Killing with kindness: Haiti, international aid, and NGOs.* Rutgers University Press.

Schwartz, T. (2019, May 2). Haiti anthropology brief: Cultural materialist cake of culture. *Schwartz Research Group.* https://timothyschwartzhaiti.com/cake-of-culture/

Schweitzer, T. (1997). Embeddedness of ethnographic cases: A social networks perspective. *Current Anthropology, 38*(5), 739–760. https://doi.org/10.1086/204665

Science Magazine. (2021, June 22). *Snippet: Ancient Siberian cave hosted Neanderthals, Denisovans, and modern humans* [Video]. YouTube. https://www.youtube.com/watch?v=I954Aqf9T5A

Scott, A., Power, R. C., Altmann-Wendling, V., Artzy, M., Martin, M. A. S., Eisenmann, S., Hagan, R., Salazar-García, D. C., Salmon, Y., Yegorov, D., Milevski, I., Finkelstein, I., Stockhammer, P. W., & Warinner, C. (2021). Exotic foods reveal contact between South Asia and the Near East during the second millennium BCE. *Proceedings of the National Academy of Sciences U.S.A., 188*(2), Article e2014956117.

Scott, J. C. (1976). *The moral economy of the peasant: Rebellion and subsistence in Southeast Asia.* Yale University Press.

Scott, J. C. (1985). *Weapons of the weak: Everyday forms of peasant resistance.* Yale University Press.

Scott, J. C. (1990). *Domination and the arts of resistance: Hidden transcripts.* Yale University Press.

Scott, K. A., & Davis, D. (2021). Obstetric racism: Naming and identifying a way out of Black women's adverse medical experiences. *American Anthropologist, 123*(3), 681–684.

Scott, M. W. (2013). The anthropology of ontology (religious science?). *Journal of the Royal Anthropological Institute, 19*(4), 859–872.

Segata, N. (2015). Gut microbiome: Westernization and the disappearance of intestinal diversity. *Current Biology, 25*(14), R611–R614.

Semaw, S., Rogers, M. J., Quade, J., Renne, P. R., Butler, R. F., Dominguez-Rodrigo, M., Stout, D., Hart, W. S., Pickering, T., & Simpson, S. W. (2003). 2.6-Million-year-old stone tools and associated bones from OGS-6 and OGS-7, Gona, Afar, Ethiopia. *Journal of Human Evolution, 45*(2), 169–177.

Serano, J. (2007). *Whipping girl: A transsexual woman on sexism and the scapegoating of femininity*. Seal Press.

Setchell, J. M., Fairet, E., Shutt, K., Waters, S., & Bell, S. (2017). Biosocial conservation: Integrating biological and ethnographic methods to study human–primate interactions. *International Journal of Primatology, 38*, 401–426. https://doi.org/10.1007/s10764-016-9938-5

Shahack-Gross, R., Berna, F., Karkanas, P., Lemorini, C., Gopher, A., & Barkai, R. (2013). Evidence for the repeated use of a central hearth at Middle Pleistocene (300 ky ago) Qesem Cave, Israel. *Journal of Archaeological Science, 44*, 12–21. https://doi.org/10.1016/j.jas.2013.11.015

Shanee, N., Mendoza, A. P., & Shanee, S. (2015). Diagnostic overview of the illegal trade in primates and law enforcement in Peru. *American Journal of Primatology, 79*(11), Article e22516. https://doi.org/10.1002/ajp.22516

Shange, S. (2017a). *Progressive dystopia*. Duke University Press.

Shange, S. (2017b). *Progressive dystopia: Multiracial coalition and the carceral state* (Publication No. 2579) [Doctoral Dissertation, University of Pennsylvania]. https://repository.upenn.edu/edissertations/2579.

Shange, S. (2022). Abolition in the clutch: Shifting through the gears with anthropology. *Feminist Anthropology, 3*(2), 187–197.

Sharp, G. C., Lawlor, D. A., & Richardson, S. S. (2018). It's the mother! How assumptions about the causal primacy of maternal effects influence research on the developmental origins of health and disease. *Social Science & Medicine, 213*, 20–27.

Sharp, G. C., Schellhas, L., Richardson, S. S., & Lawlor, D. A. (2019). Time to cut the cord: Recognizing and addressing the imbalance of DOHaD research towards the study of maternal pregnancy exposures. *Journal of Developmental Origins of Health and Disease, 10*(5), 509–512.

Shaw, C. N., & Stock, J. T. (2013). Extreme mobility in the Late Pleistocene? Comparing limb biomechanics among fossil *Homo*, varsity athletes and Holocene foragers. *Journal of Human Evolution, 64*(4), 242–249.

Sheff, E. (2005). Polyamorous women, sexual subjectivity and power. *Journal of Contemporary Ethnography, 34*(3), 251–283.

Shell-Duncan, B., Naik, R., & Feldman-Jacobs, C. (2016). *A state-of-the-art synthesis on female genital mutilation/cutting: What do we know now?* Population Council.

Shenk, M. K., & Mattison, S. M. (2011). The rebirth of kinship. *Human Nature, 22*(1), 1–15.

Sherwin, J., Kearns, L. S., Hewitt, A. W., Ma, Y., Kelly, J., Griffiths, L. R., & Mackey, D. A. (2011). Prevalence of chronic ocular diseases in a genetic isolate: The Norfolk Island Eye Study (NIES). *Ophthalmic Epidemiology, 18*(2), 61–71.

Shipman, P., Bosler, W., Davis, K., Behrensmeyer, A. K., Dunbar, R. I. M., Groves, C. P., Thackeray, F., Harris Van Couvering, J. A., & Stucky, R. K. (1981). Butchering of giant geladas at an Acheulian site [and comments and reply]. *Current Anthropology, 22*(3), 257–268.

Shurkin, J. (2014). Animals that self-medicate. *Proceedings of the National Academy of Sciences U.S.A., 111*(49), 17339–17341.

Shutt, K., Heistermann, M., Kasim, A., Todd, A., Kalousova, B., Profosouva, I., Petrzelkova, K., Fuh, T., Dicky, J.-F., Bopalanzognako, J.-B., & Setchell, J. M. (2014). Effects of habituation, research and ecotourism on faecal glucocorticoid metabolites in wild western lowland gorillas: Implications for conservation management. *Biological Conservation, 172*, 72–79.

Sicoli, M. A., & Holton, G. (2014). Linguistic phylogenies support back-migration from Beringia to Asia. *PLOS ONE, 9*(3), Article e91722. https://doi.org/10.1371/journal.pone.0091722

Sievert, L. L., & Kiely, D. (2018). Menopause. In W. Trevathan, M. Cartmill, D. Dufour, C. Larsen, D. O'Rourke, K. Rosenberg, & K. Strier (Eds.), *The international encyclopedia of biological anthropology*. Wiley. https://doi.org/10.1002/9781118584538.ieba0317

Silcock, J. L. (2018). Aboriginal translocations: The intentional propagation and dispersal of plants in Aboriginal Australia. *Journal of Ethnobiology, 38*, 390–405.

Silk, J. B., Altmann, J., & Alberts, S. C. (2006). Social relationships among adult female baboons (*Papio cynocephalus*) I. Variation in strength of social bonds. *Behavioral Ecology and Sociobiology, 61*, 183–195.

Silk, J. B., Cheney, D., & Seyfarth, R. (2013). A practical guide to the study of social relationships. *Evolutionary Anthropology: Issues, News, and Reviews, 22*(5), 213–225.

Silk, J. B., & House, B. R. (2011). Evolutionary foundations of human prosocial sentiments. *Proceedings of the National Academy of Sciences U.S.A., 108*(Suppl 2), 10910–10917.

Sillén-Tullberg, B., & Moller, A. P. (1993). The relationship between concealed ovulation and mating systems in anthropoid primates: A phylogenetic analysis. *The American Naturalist, 141*(1), 1–25.

Silverstein, M. (1979). Language structure and linguistic ideology. In P. Clyne, W. F. Hanks, & C. L. Hofbauer

(Eds.), *The elements: A parasession on linguistic units and levels.* Chicago Linguistic Society.

Silverstein, M. (2017). Standards, styles, and signs of the social self. *Journal of the Anthropological Society of Oxford Online, 9*(1), 134–164.

Simmen, B., Pasquet, P., Masi, S., Koppert, G. J. A., Wells, J. C. K., & Hladik, C. M. (2017). Primate energy input and the evolutionary transition to energy-dense diets in humans. *Proceedings of the Royal Society, B: Biological Sciences, 284*(1856), Article 20170577.

Simons, E. (1995). Egyptian Oligocene primates: A review. *American Journal of Physical Anthropology, 38*(S21), 199–238.

Simpson, A. (2007). On ethnographic refusal: Indigeneity, 'voice' and colonial citizenship. *Junctures: The Journal for Thematic Dialogue,* No. 9. https://junctures.org/index.php/junctures/article/view/66/60

Simpson, A. (2014). *Mohawk interruptus: Political life across the borders of settler states.* Duke University Press.

Sion, L. (2006). "Too Sweet and Innocent for War"?: Dutch peacekeepers and the use of violence. *Armed Forces & Society, 32*(3), 454–474. https://doi.org/10.1177/0095327X05281453

Sion, L. (2007). Reinterpreting combat masculinity: Dutch peacekeeping in Bosnia and Kosovo. *Sociologie, 3*(1), 95–110.

Slater, P. A., Hedman, K. M., & Emerson, T. E. (2014). Immigrants at the Mississippian polity of Cahokia: Strontium isotope evidence for population movement. *Journal of Archaeological Science, 44,* 117–127.

Slicox, M. T. (2014). Primate origins and the plesiadapiforms. *Nature Education Knowledge, 5*(3), 1.

Slon, V., Hoppe, C., Weiss, C. L., Mafessoni, F., de la Rasilla, M., Lalueza-Fox, C., Rosas, A., Soressi, M., Knul, M. V., Miller, R., Stewart, J. R., Derevianko, A. R., Jacobs, Z., Li, B., Roberts, R. G., Shunkov, M. V., De Lumley, H., Perrenound, C., Gusic, I., . . . Meyer, M. (2017). Neanderthal and Denisovan DNA from Pleistocene sediments. *Science, 356*(6338), 605–608. https://doi.org/10.1126/science.aam9695

Small, M. F. (1993). *Female choices: Sexual behavior of female primates.* Cornell University Press.

Smedley, A., & Smedley, B. D. (2005). Race as biology is fiction, racism as a social problem is real: Anthropological and historical perspectives on the social construction of race. *American Psychologist, 60*(1), 16–26. https://doi.org/10.1037/0003-066X.60.1.16

Smith, B. D. (1995). Seed plant domestication in eastern North America. In T. D. Price & A. B. Gebauer (Eds.), *Last hunters, first farmers: New perspectives on the prehistoric transition to agriculture* (pp. 193–214). School of American Research Press.

Smith, B. D. (2001). Low-level food production. *Journal of Anthropological Research, 9,* 1–43.

Smith, B. D. (2006). Eastern North America as an independent center of plant domestication. *Proceedings of the National Academy of Sciences U.S.A., 103*(33), 12223–12228.

Smith, B. D. (2008). Winnowing the archaeological evidence for domesticated sunflower in pre-Columbian Mesoamerica. *Proceedings of the National Academy of Sciences U.S.A., 105*(30), Article E45.

Smith, B. D. (2014). Failure of optimal foraging theory to appeal to researchers working on the origins of agriculture worldwide. *Proceedings of the National Academy of Sciences U.S.A., 111,* Article E2829.

Smith, C. A. (2015). Blackness, citizenship, and the transnational vertigo of violence in the Americas. *American Anthropologist, 117*(2), 384–392.

Smith, C. A. (2016). *Afro-paradise: Blackness, violence, and performance in Brazil.* University of Illinois Press.

Smith, C. A. (2021a). Counting frequency: Un/gendering anti-Black police terror. *Social Text, 39*(2), 25–49.

Smith, C. A. (2021b). Impossible privacy: Black women and police terror. *The Black Scholar, 51*(1), 20–29.

Smith, D., Schlaepfer, P., Major, K., Dyble, M., Page, A. E., Thompson, J., Chaudhary, N., Salali, G. D., Mace, R., Astete, L., Ngales, M., Vinicius, L., & & Migliano, A. B. (2017). Cooperation and the evolution of hunter-gatherer storytelling. *Nature Communications, 8*(1), Article 1853.

Smith, L. T. (1999). *Decolonizing methodologies: Research and Indigenous Peoples.* Zed Books.

Smith, M. E. (2004). The archaeology of ancient state economies. *Annual Review of Anthropology, 33*(1), 73–102.

Smith, M. E. (2010). The archaeological study of neighborhoods and districts in ancient cities. *Journal of Anthropological Archaeology, 29*(2), 137–154.

Smith, M. E. (2017). The Teotihuacan anomaly: The historical trajectory of urban design in ancient Central Mexico. *Open Archaeology, 3*(1), 175–193.

Smith, M. E., Chatterjee, A., Huster, A. C., Stewart, S., & Forest, M. (2019). Apartment compounds, households, and population in the ancient city of Teotihuacan, Mexico. *Ancient Mesoamerica, 30*(3), 399–418.

Smith, M. E., & Novic, J. (2012). Neighborhoods and districts in ancient Mesoamerica. In M. C. Arnauld, L. R. Manzanilla, & M. E. Smith (Eds.), *The neighborhood* as a social and spatial unit in Mesoamerican cities (pp. 1–26). University of Arizona Press.

Smith, R. W., & Archer, S. M. (2019). Bisexual science. *American Anthropologist, 121*(2), 491–492.

Smith, R. W., & Bolnick, D. A. (2019). Situating science: Doing biological anthropology as a view from somewhere. *American Anthropologist, 121*(2), 465–467.

Snowdon, C. (2018). Cognitive components of vocal communication: A case study. *Animals, 8*(7), Article 126. https://doi.org/10.3390/ani8070126

Sobo, E. J. (2015). Social cultivation of vaccine refusal and delay among Waldorf (Steiner) school parents. *Medical Anthropology Quarterly, 29*, 381–399. https://doi.org/10.1111/maq.12214

Sobo, E. J. (2020). *Dynamics of human biocultural diversity: A unified approach.* Routledge.

Soffer, O. (2004). Recovering perishable technologies through use wear on tools: Preliminary evidence for Upper Paleolithic weaving and net making. *Current Anthropology, 45*, 407–413.

Solecki, R. S. (1975). Shanidar IV, a Neanderthal flower burial in northern Iraq. *Science, 190*(4217), 880–881. https://doi.org/10.1126/science.190.4217.880

Sontag, S. (2001). *Illness as metaphor and AIDS and its metaphors.* Macmillan.

Spears, A. (2009). Writing truth to power: Racism as statecraft. In A. Waterston & M. D. Vesperi (Eds.), *Anthropology off the shelf: Anthropologists on writing.* Wiley–Blackwell. https://doi.org/10.1002/9781444308822.ch9

Spears, A. (2020). Racism, colorism, and language within their macro contexts. In H. S. Alim, A. Reyes, & P. Kroskrity (Eds.), *The Oxford handbook of language and race* (pp. 47–67). Oxford University Press.

Spears, A. (2021). White supremacy and antiblackness: Theory and lived experience. *Journal of Linguistic Anthropology, 31*(2), 157–179.

Speed, S. (2019). The persistence of white supremacy: Indigenous women migrants and the structures of settler capitalism. *American Anthropologist, 122*(1), 76–85.

Spektor, B. (2020, April 3). World's oldest human DNA found in 800,000-year-old tooth of a cannibal. *Live Science.* https://www.livescience.com/oldest-human-ancestor-dna-homo-antecessor.html

Speller, C. F., Kemp, B. M., Wyatt, S. D., Monroe, C., Lipe, W. D., Arndt, U. M., & Yang, D. Y. (2010). Ancient mitochondrial DNA analysis reveals complexity of indigenous North American turkey domestication. *Proceedings of the National Academy of Sciences*

U.S.A., 107*(7), 2807–2812. https://doi.org/10.1073/pnas.0909724107

Spikins, P., Needham, A., Wright, B., Dytham, C., Gatta, M., & Hitchens, G. (2019). Living to fight another day: The ecological and evolutionary significance of Neanderthal healthcare. *Quaternary Science Reviews, 217*, 98–118.

Sponheimer, M., Alemseged, Z., Cerling, T. E., Grine, F., E., Kimbel, W. H., Leakey, M. G., Lee-Thorp, J. A., Manthi, R. K., Reed, K. E., Wood, B. A., & Wynn, J. G. (2013). Isotopic evidence of early hominin diets. *Proceedings of the National Academy of Sciences U.S.A., 110*(26), 10513–10518. https://doi.org/10.1073/pnas.1222579110

Spradley, J. P. (1980). Doing participant observation. In J. P. Spradley, *Participant observation* (pp. 53–62). Waveland Press, Inc.

Springer, K., Stellman, J., & Jordan-Young, R. (2012). Beyond a catalogue of differences: A theoretical frame and good practice guidelines for researching sex/gender in human health. *Social Science & Medicine, 74*, 1817–1824.

Spronk, R. (2012). *Ambiguous pleasures: Sexuality and middle class self-perceptions in Nairobi.* Berghahn Books.

Squires, S., & Byrne, B. (Eds.). (2002). *Creating breakthrough ideas: The collaboration of anthropologists and designers in the product development industry.* Bergin & Bargey.

Squires, S., & Mack, A. (2012). Renewing our practice: Preparing the next generation of practitioners. *Ethnographic Praxis in Industry Conference (EPIC) Proceedings, 2012*(1), 296–310.

Stanford, C. B. (2012). Chimpanzees and the behavior of *Ardipithecus ramidus. Annual Review of Anthropology, 41*(1), 139–149.

Stansbury, J., Mathewson-Chapman, M., & Grant, K. (2003). Gender schema and prostate cancer: Veterans' cultural model of masculinity. *Medical Anthropology, 22*(2), 175–204.

Starkweather, K., & Hames, R. (2012). A survey of non-classical polyandry. *Human Nature, 23*(2), 149–150. https://doi.org/10.1007/s12110-012-9144-x

Steadman, D. W. (1998). The population shuffle in the Central Illinois Valley: A diachronic model of Mississippian biocultural interactions. *World Archaeology, 30*, 306–326.

Steinberg, M. K., Height, C., Mosher, R., & Bampton, M. (2006). Mapping massacres: GIS and state terror in Guatemala. *Geoforum, 37*(1), 62–68.

Steward, J. H. (1955). *Theory of culture change: The methodology of multilinear evolution.* University of Illinois Press.

Stewart (Strathern), P. J., & Strathern, A. J. (2020, February 20). Gossip—A thing humans do. *Anthropology News.* https://www.anthropology-news.org/articles/gossip-a-thing-humans-do/

Stiner, M. C., Barkai, R., & Gopher, A. (2009). Cooperative hunting and meat sharing 400–200 kya at Qesem Cave, Israel. *Proceedings of the National Academy of Sciences U.S.A., 106*(32), 13207–13212. https://doi.org/10.1073/pnas.0900564106

Stiner, M. C., Gopher, A., & Barkai, R. (2011). Hearth-side socioeconomics, hunting and paleoecology during the Late Lower Paleolithic at Qesem Cave, Israel. *Journal of Human Evolution, 60*(2), 213–233.

Stinson, S., Bogin, B., Huss-Ashmore, R., & O'Rourke, D. (2000). *Human biology: An evolutionary and biocultural perspective.* Wiley.

Stojanowski, C. M. (2004). Population history of native groups in pre- and postcontact Spanish Florida: Aggregation, gene flow, and genetic drift on the southeastern U.S. Atlantic coast. *American Journal of Physical Anthropology, 123*(4), 316–332.

Stojanowski, C. M. (2005a). Spanish colonial effects on Native American mating structure and genetic variability in northern and central Florida: Evidence from Apalachee and Western Timucua. *American Journal of Physical Anthropology, 128*(2), 273–286.

Stojanowski, C. M. (2005b). The bioarchaeology of identity in Spanish colonial Florida: Social and evolutionary transformation before, during, and after demographic collapse. *American Anthropologist, 107*(3), 417–431.

Stojanowski, C. M. (2009). Bridging histories: The bioarchaeology of identity in postcontact Florida. In K. J. Knudson & C. M. Stojanowski (Eds.), *Bioarchaeology and identity in the Americas* (pp. 59–81). University Press of Florida.

Stojanowski, C. M., Carver, C. L., & Miller, K. A. (2014). Incisor avulsion, social identity and Saharan population history: New data from the Early Holocene southern Sahara. *Journal of Anthropological Archaeology, 35,* 79–91.

Stone, A. C., & Ozga, A. T. (2019). Ancient DNA in the study of ancient disease. In *Ortner's identification of pathological conditions in human skeletal remains* (pp. 183–210). Academic Press.

Stout, D., Toth, N., Schick, K., & Chaminade, T. (2008). Neural correlates of Early Stone Age toolmaking: Technology, language and cognition in human evolution.

Philosophical Transactions of the Royal Society, B: Biological Sciences, 363(1499), 1939–1949. https://doi.org/10.1098/rstb.2008.0001

Strang, V. (2005). Knowing me, knowing you: Aboriginal and European concepts of nature as self and other. *Worldviews: Global Religions, Culture, and Ecology, 9*(1), 25–56.

Strang, V. (2006). A happy coincidence? Symbiosis and synthesis in anthropological and Indigenous knowledges. *Current Anthropology, 47*(6), 981–1008.

Strassmann, B. I. (2013). Concealed ovulation in humans: Further evidence. In K. Summers & B. Crespi (Eds.), *Human social evolution: The foundational works of Richard D. Alexander* (pp. 139–151). Oxford University Press.

Strathern, M. (1988). *Gender of the gift: Problems with women and problems with society in Melanesia.* University of California Press.

SturtzSreetharan, C., Agostini, G., Wutich, A., Mitchell, C., Rines, O., Romanello, B., & Brewis, A. (2019). "I need to lose some weight": Masculinity and body image as negotiated through fat talk. *Psychology of Men & Masculinities, 21*(1), 148–161. https://doi.org/10.1037/men0000219

SturtzSreetharan, C., & Brewis, A. (2019). Rice, men, and other everyday anxieties: Navigating obesogenic urban food environments in Osaka, Japan. In I. Vojnovic, A. Pearson, G. Asiki, G. DeVerteuil, & A. Allen (Eds.), *Handbook of global urban health* (pp. 662–681). Routledge.

SturtzSreetharan, C., Brewis, A., Hardin, J., Trainer, S., & Wutich, A. (2021). *Fat in four cultures: A global ethnography of weight.* University of Toronto Press.

Suchak, M., & de Waal, F. B. M. (2012). Monkeys benefit from reciprocity without the cognitive burden. *Proceedings of the National Academy of Sciences U.S.A., 109*(38), 15191–15196. https://doi.org/10.1073/pnas.1213173109

Sugiyama, N., & Somerville, A. D. (2017). Feeding Teotihuacan: Integrating approaches to studying food and foodways of the ancient metropolis. *Archaeological and Anthropological Sciences, 9,* 1–10.

Sullivan, N. (2018). International clinical volunteering in Tanzania: A postcolonial analysis of a Global Health business. *Global Public Health, 13*(3), 310–324. https://doi.org/10.1080/17441692.2017.1346695

Sunderland, P. L., & Denny, R. M. (2016). *Doing anthropology in consumer research.* Routledge.

Sussman, R. W. (1991). Primate origins and the evolution of angiosperms. *American Journal of Primatology, 23,* 209–223.

Swan, K. (2018, May 31). Researcher proposes study on how residential school trauma may have affected genes. *CBC News.* https://www.cbc.ca/news/indigenous/residential-school-trauma-epigenetics-1.4681966

TallBear, K. (2011, November 18). Why interspecies thinking needs Indigenous standpoints. *Cultural Anthropology.* https://culanth.org/fieldsights/why-interspecies-thinking-needs-indigenous-standpoints

TallBear, K. (2013). *Native American DNA: Tribal belonging and the false promise of genetic science.* University of Minnesota Press.

TallBear, K. (2019). Feminist, queer, and Indigenous thinking as an antidote to masculinist objectivity and binary thinking in biological anthropology. *American Anthropologist, 121*(2), 494–496.

TallBear, K. (2019, January 17). Elizabeth Warren's claim to Cherokee ancestry is a form of violence. *High Country News.* https://www.hcn.org/issues/51.2/tribal-affairs-elizabeth-warrens-claim-to-cherokee-ancestry-is-a-form-of-violence

TallBear, K. (n.d.). About the blogger. *The Critical Polyamorist.* http://www.criticalpolyamorist.com/about.html

TallBear, K., Bear, T., Lindquist, K., & Mounsef, D. (n.d.). *Tipi confessions: Sexy storytelling, performances, and anonymous audience confessions.* https://tipiconfessions.com/

TallBear, K., & Willey, A. (2019). Critical relationality: Queer, Indigenous, and multispecies belonging beyond settler sex & nature. *Imaginations: Journal of Cross-Cultural Image Studies, 10*(1), 5–15.

Tanner, S. (2018). Growth, environmental influences on. In W. Trevathan, M. Cartmill, D. Dufour, C. Larsen, D. O'Rourke, K. Rosenberg, & K. Strier (Eds.), *The international encyclopedia of biological anthropology.* Wiley. https://doi.org/10.1002/9781118584538.ieba0158

Teaford, M. F., & Ungar, P. S. (2000). Diet and the evolution of the earliest human ancestors. *Proceedings of the National Academy of Sciences U.S.A., 97,* 13506–13511.

Teaiwa, K. M. (2004). Multi-sited methodologies: "Homework" in Australia, Fiji, and Kiribati. In L. Hume & J. Mulcock (Eds.), *Anthropologists in the field: Case studies in participant observation* (pp. 216–234). Columbia University Press.

Teaiwa, K. M. (2014). *Consuming Ocean Island: Stories of people and phosphate from Banaba.* Indiana University Press.

Tedlock, B. (1991). From participant observation to the observation of participation: The emergence of narrative ethnography. *Journal of Anthropological Research, 47*(1), 69–94.

TEDx Emory. (2019, June 28). *John Baugh: The Significance of Linguistic Profiling* [Video]. YouTube. https://youtu.be/GjFtIg-nLAA

TEDx Talks. (2014, February 27). *It's not all sex and violence: Agustin Fuentes at TEDxUND* [Video]. YouTube. https://www.youtube.com/watch?v=66IeDfeGbzA

Templeton, A. R. (2002). Out of Africa again. *Nature, 416*(6876), 45–51.

Templeton, A. R. (2013). Biological races in humans. *Studies in History and Philosophy of Science Part C: Studies in History and Philosophy of Biological and Biomedical Sciences, 44*(3), 262–271.

Thayer, Z. (2018). Developmental adaptation. In W. Trevathan, M. Cartmill, D. Dufour, C. Larsen, D. O'Rourke, K. Rosenberg, & K. Strier (Eds.), *The international encyclopedia of biological anthropology.* Wiley. https://doi.org/10.1002/9781118584538.ieba0132

Thayer, Z., Bécares, L., & Carr, P. A. (2019). Maternal experiences of ethnic discrimination and subsequent birth outcomes in Aotearoa New Zealand. *BMC Public Health, 19*(1), Article 1271.

Thayer, Z. M., & Kuzawa, C. W. (2015). Ethnic discrimination predicts poor self-rated health and cortisol in pregnancy: Insights from New Zealand. *Social Science & Medicine, 128,* 36–42.

Thayer, Z. M., & Non, A. L. (2015). Anthropology meets epigenetics: Current and future directions. *American Anthropologist, 117,* 722–735. https://doi.org/10.1111/aman.12351

The Asthma Files. (n.d.). Platform for Experimental, Collaborative Ethnography. https://theasthmafiles.org/

The British Museum. (n.d.). *The museum of the world.* https://britishmuseum.withgoogle.com/

The Economist. (2020, June 13). Language is a telling clue to unacknowledged racial attitudes. *The Economist.* https://www.economist.com/books-and-arts/2020/06/12/language-is-a-telling-clue-to-unacknowledged-racial-attitudes

The Educational Linguist. (2016, August 21). When is it appropriate for a white person to use Spanish with Latinxs? *The Educational Linguist.* https://educationallinguist.wordpress.com/page/4/

The Maya Project. (n.d.). *The Maya Project: A blend of art and academic research portraying the biosocial realities of the Maya in Mesoamerica.* http://mayaproject.org.uk/

The siratany initiative. (2016, July). *Bezà Mahafaly, Madagascar.* https://campuspress.yale.edu/bezamahafaly/the-siratany-initiative/

Thibault, P. J. (2017). The reflexivity of human languaging and Nigel Love's two orders of language. *Language Sciences, 61,* 74–85.

Thibodeau, P. H., & Boroditsky, L. (2013). Natural language metaphors covertly influence reasoning.

PLOS ONE, 8(1), Article e52961. https://doi.org/10.1371/journal.pone.0052961

Thomas, D. A. (2011). *Exceptional violence: Embodied citizenship in transnational Jamaica.* Duke University Press.

Thompson, J. J., Ritenbaugh, C., & Nichter, M. (2009). Reconsidering the placebo response from a broad anthropological perspective. *Culture, Medicine, and Psychiatry, 33*(1), 112–152.

Thoradeniya, T., & Jayasinghe, S. (2021). COVID-19 and future pandemics: A global systems approach and relevance to SDGs. *Globalization and Health, 17,* Article 59. https://doi.org/10.1186/s12992-021-00711-6

Thornton, R. (2016). Who owns our past? The repatriation of Native American human remains and cultural objects. In S. Lobo, S. Talbot, & T. L. Morris (Eds.), *Native American voices: A reader* (pp. 311–322). Routledge.

Throop, C. J., & Duranti, A. (2015). Attention, ritual glitches, and attentional pull: The president and the queen. *Phenomenology and the Cognitive Sciences, 14,* 1055–1082. http://www.sscnet.ucla.edu/anthro/faculty/duranti/reprints/DurantiThroop2015-Obamaand-thequeen.pdf

Tiippana, K. (2014). What is the McGurk effect? *Frontiers in Psychology, 5,* Article 725. https://doi.org/10.3389/fpsyg.2014.00725

Tishkoff, S. A., Reed, F. A., Ranciaro, A., Voight, B. F., Babbitt, C. C., Silverman, J. S., Powell, K., Mortensen, H. M., Hirbo, J. B., Osman, M., Ibrahim, M., Omar, S. A., Lema, G., Nyambo, T. B., Ghori, J., Bumpstead, S., Pritchard, J. K., Wray, G. A., & Deloukas, P. (2007). Convergent adaptation of human lactase persistence in Africa and Europe. *Nature Genetics, 39*(1), 31–40. https://doi.org/10.1038/ng1946

Todd, Z. (2016). An Indigenous feminist's take on the ontological turn: 'Ontology' is just another word for colonialism. *Journal of Historical Sociology, 29*(1), 4–22.

Toepel, U., Knebel, J.-F., Hudry, J., le Coutre, J., & Murray, M. M. (2009). The brain tracks the energetic value in food images. *NeuroImage, 44*(3), 967–974. https://doi.org/10.1016/j.neuroimage.2008.10.005

Tolbert, E. (1990). Women cry with words: Symbolization of affect in the Karelian lament. *Yearbook for Traditional Music, 22,* 80–105.

Tomori, C., Palmquist, A. E., & Dowling, S. (2016). Contested moral landscapes: Negotiating breastfeeding stigma in breastmilk sharing, nighttime breastfeeding, and long-term breastfeeding in the U.S. and the U.K. *Social Science & Medicine, 168,* 178–185.

Torres-Rouff, C. (2002). Cranial vault modification and ethnicity in Middle Horizon San Pedro de Atacama, Chile. *Current Anthropology, 43*(1), 163–171.

Torres-Rouff, C. (2008). The influence of Tiwanaku on life in the Chilean Atacama: Mortuary and bodily perspectives. *American Anthropologist, 110*(3), 325–337.

Torres-Rouff, C. (2009). The bodily expression of ethnic identity: Head shaping in the Chilean Atacama. In K. J. Knudson & C. M. Stojanowski (Eds.), *Bioarchaeology and identity in the Americas* (pp. 212–277). University Press of Florida.

Torres-Rouff, C., & Knudson, K. J. (2017). Integrating identities: An innovative bioarchaeological and biogeochemical approach to analyzing the multiplicity of identities in the mortuary record. *Current Anthropology, 58*(3), 381–409.

Tortorici, Z., Whitehead, N. L., & Sigal, P. (2020). *Ethnopornography: Sexuality, colonialism, and anthropological/archival knowledge.* Duke University Press.

Toth, N., Schick, K., & Semaw, S. (2006). A comparative study of the stone tool-making skills of *Pan, Australopithecus,* and *Homo sapiens.* In N. Toth & K. Schick (Eds.), *The Oldowan: Case studies into the earliest Stone Age* (pp. 155–222). Stone Age Institute. https://www.stoneageinstitute.org/pdfs/oldowan-ch6-toth-etal.pdf

Toups, M. A., Kitchen, A., Light, J. E., & Reed, D. L. (2011). Origin of clothing lice indicates early clothing use by anatomically modern humans in Africa. *Molecular Biology and Evolution, 28*(1), 29–32.

Townsley, G. (2009, October 26). The evolution of motherhood [interview with Sarah Hrdy]. *NOVA.* https://www.pbs.org/wgbh/nova/article/evolution-motherhood/

Tran, A. L. (2018). The anxiety of romantic love in Ho Chi Minh City, Vietnam. *Journal of the Royal Anthropological Institute, 24*(3), 512–531.

Tran, C. N. H., & Schroeder, L. (2021). Common evolutionary patterns in the human nasal region across a worldwide sample. *American Journal of Physical Anthropology, 176*(3), 422–433. https://doi.org/10.1002/ajpa.24378

Trevathan, W. R. (1995). Evolutionary medicine: An overview. *Anthropology Today, 11*(2), 2–5.

Trevathan, W. (2018). Life history (human). In W. Trevathan, M. Cartmill, D. Dufour, C. Larsen, D. O'Rourke, K. Rosenberg, & K. Strier (Eds.), *The international encyclopedia of biological anthropology.* Wiley. https://doi.org/10.1002/9781118584538.ieba0296

Trinkaus, E. (1983). *The Shanidar Neandertals.* Academic.

Trinkaus, E. (2018). One hundred years of paleoanthropology: An American perspective. *American Journal of Physical Anthropology, 165*(4), 638–651.

Trnka, S. (2007). Languages of labor: Negotiating the "real" and the relational in Indo-Fijian women's expressions of physical pain. *Medical Anthropology Quarterly, 21*(4), 388–408.

Trumble, B. C., & Finch, C. E. (2019). The exposome in human evolution: From dust to diesel. *The Quarterly Review of Biology, 94*, 333–394.

Trumble, B. C., Smith, E. A., O'Connor, K. A., Kaplan, H. S., & Gurven, M. D. (2014). Successful hunting increases testosterone and cortisol in a subsistence population. *Proceedings of the Royal Society, B: Biological Sciences, 281*(1776), Article 20132876.

Tsosie, K. (2018, October 17). Elizabeth Warren's DNA is not her identity. *The Atlantic.* https://www.theatlantic.com/ideas/archive/2018/10/what-make-elizabeth-warrens-dna-test/573205/

Tsosie, K. S. (2021). Ancient-DNA researchers write their own rules. *Nature, 600*(7887), 37.

Tsosie, K., & Anderson, M. (2018, October 22). Two Native Americans geneticists interpret Elizabeth Warren's DNA test. *The Conversation.* https://theconversation.com/two-native-american-geneticists-interpret-elizabeth-warrens-dna-test-105274

Tuck, E., & Yang, K. W. (2012). Decolonization is not a metaphor. *Decolonization: Indigeneity, Education & Society, 1*(1), 1–40.

Tumilowicz, A., Habicht, J. P., Pelto, G., & Pelletier, D. L. (2015). Gender perceptions predict sex differences in growth patterns of indigenous Guatemalan infants and young children. *The American Journal of Clinical Nutrition, 102*(5), 1249–1258.

Tung, J., & Gilad, Y. (2013). Social environmental effects on gene regulation. *Cellular and Molecular Life Sciences, 70*, 4323–4339. https://doi.org/10.1007/s00018-013-1357-6

Tung, T. A. (2012a). *Violence, ritual, and the Wari Empire: A social bioarchaeology of Wari imperialism in the ancient Andes.* University Press of Florida.

Tung, T. A. (2012b). Violence against women: Differential treatment of local and foreign females in the heartland of the Wari Empire. In D. L. Martin, R. P. Harrod, & V. R. Perez (Eds.), *The bioarchaeology of violence* (pp. 180–200). University Press of Florida.

Tung, T. A. (2021). Making and marking maleness and valorizing violence: A bioarchaeological analysis of embodiment in the Andean past. *Current Anthropology, 62*(S23), S125–S144.

Tung, T. A., & Knudson, K. J. (2011). Identifying locals, migrants, and captives in the Wari heartland: A bioarchaeological and biogeochemical study of human remains from Conchopata, Peru. *Journal of Anthropological Archaeology, 30*(3), 247–261.

Turner, B. L., & Thompson, A. L. (2013). Beyond the Paleolithic prescription: Incorporating diversity and flexibility in the study of human diet evolution. *Nutrition Reviews, 71*(8), 501–510. https://doi:10.1111/nure.12039

Turner, T. R., Bernstein, R. M., Taylor, A. B., Asangba, A., Bekelman, T., Cramer, J. D., Elton, S., Harvati, K., Williams-Hatala, E. M., Kauffman, L., Middleton, E., Richtsmeier, J., Szathmáry, E., Torres-Rouff, C., Thayer, Z., Villaseñor, A., & Vogel, E. (2018). Participation, representation, and shared experiences of women scholars in biological anthropology. *American Journal of Physical Anthropology, 165*, 126–157.

Turp, A. B., Guler, I., Bozkurt, N., Uysal, A., Yilmaz, B., Demir, M., & Karabacak, O. (2018). Infertility and surrogacy first mentioned on a 4000-year-old Assyrian clay tablet of marriage contract in Turkey. *Gynecological Endocrinology, 34*(1), 25–27.

Twiss, K. C., Bogaard, A., Charles, M., Henecke, J., Russell, N., Martin, L., & Jones, G. (2009). Plants and animals together: Interpreting organic remains from building 52 at Catalhoyuk. *Current Anthropology, 50*(6), 885–895.

UC Berkeley. (2015, January 13). *Watch how Stone-Agers made butchering tools* [Video]. YouTube. https://www.youtube.com/watch?v=fmOGTKt0HYs.

UNC. (2018, May 5). Block party for archaeology [Event]. *UNC Department of Anthropology Public Archaeology class and the Pauli Murray Project.* https://agbedavies.web.unc.edu/wp-content/uploads/sites/7160/2018/04/PM-Event-Flyer_FINAL.pdf

Undocumented Migration Project. (n.d.). https://www.undocumentedmigrationproject.org/installation

Unicode. (n.d.). Full emoji list, v15.0. *Unicode.* https://unicode.org/emoji/charts/full-emoji-list.html

University of Wollongong. (2020, June 16). French cave reveals secrets of life and death from the ancient past. *Phys Org.* https://phys.org/news/2020-06-french-cave-reveals-secrets-life.html

Uperesa, F. (2010). A different weight: Tension and promise in Indigenous anthropology. *Pacific Studies, 33*(2), 280.

Upton, D. (2017, September 13). Confederate monuments and civic values in the wake of Charlottesville. *Society of Architectural Historians (SAH) Blog.* https://www.sah.org/publications-and-research/sah-blog/sah-blog/2017/09/13/confederate-monuments-and-civic-values-in-the-wake-of-charlottesville#commentsWidget,

Urciuoli, B. (2008). Skills and selves in the new workplace. *American Ethnologist, 35*(2), 211–228.

USC. (2012, August 15). *Embedded with the MS-13* [Video]. YouTube. https://www.youtube.com/watch?v=JugCQAZUrCA

Val, A. (2016). Deliberate body disposal by hominins in the Dinaledi Chamber, Cradle of Humankind, South Africa. *Journal of Human Evolution, 96*, 145–148.

Valeggia, C. R., & Núñez-de la Mora, A. (2015). Human reproductive ecology. In M. P. Muehlenbein (Ed.), *Basics in human evolution* (pp. 295–308). Academic Press. https://doi.org/10.1016/B978-0-12-802652-6.00021-9

Valentine, D. (2007). *Imagining transgender: Ethnography of a category.* Duke University Press.

Valenzuela, P. (2000). Major categories in Shipibo ethnobiological taxonomy. *Anthropological Linguistics, 42*(1), 1–36.

van Anders, S. M. (2015). Beyond sexual orientation: Integrating gender/sex and diverse sexualities via sexual configurations theory. *Archives of Sexual Behavior, 44*, 1177–1213. https://doi.org/10.1007/s10508-015-0490-8

van Anders, S. M., Schudson, Z. C., Abed, E. C., Beischel, W. J., Dibble, E. R., Gunther, O. D., Kutchko, V. J., & Silver, E. R. (2017). Biological sex, gender, and public policy. *Policy Insights from the Behavioral and Brain Sciences, 4*(2), 194–201. https://doi.org/10.1177/2372732217720700

Van Arsdale, A. P. (2019). Population demography, ancestry, and the biological concept of race. *Annual Review of Anthropology, 48*, 227–241.

Van der Geest, S., & Finkler, K. (2004). Hospital ethnography: Introduction. *Social Science & Medicine, 59*(10), 1995–2001.

Van Willigen, J. (1984). Truth and effectiveness: An essay on the relationships between information, policy and action in applied anthropology. *Human Organization, 43*(3), 277–282.

Van Wolputte, S. (2016). Sex in troubled times: Moral panic, polyamory and freedom in north-west Namibia. *Anthropology Southern Africa, 39*(1), 31–45.

Vance, C. S. (1991). Anthropology rediscovers sexuality: A theoretical comment. *Social Science & Medicine, 33*(8), 875–884.

Vasey, P. L., & Jiskoot, H. (2010). The biogeography and evolution of female homosexual behavior in Japanese macaques. *Archives of Sexual Behavior, 39*, 1439–1441.

Vásquez-Léon, M. (2017). Smallholder cooperativism as a development strategy in Latin America. In T. J. Finan, B. J. Burke, & M. Vásquez-Léon (Eds.), *Cooperatives, grassroots development, and social change: Experiences from rural Latin America.* University of Arizona Press.

Vayda, A. P., & McCay, B. J. (1975). New directions in ecology and ecological anthropology. *Annual Review of Anthropology, 4*(1), 293–306.

Velasco, M. C. (2018). Ethnogenesis and social difference in the Andean Late Intermediate Period (AD 1100–1450): A bioarchaeological study of cranial modification in the Colca Valley, Peru. *Current Anthropology, 59*(1), 98–106.

Vélez-Ibáñez, C. G. (2004). Regions of refuge in the United States: Issues, problems, and concerns for the future of the Mexican-origin populations in the United States. *Human Organization, 63*(1), 1–20. https://doi.org/10.17730/humo.63.1.ru1h227tgeyh8dm3

Verdu, P. (2020). Sociocultural behavior and human genetic diversity. In H. Callan (Ed.), *The international encyclopedia of anthropology.* Wiley. https://doi.org/10.1002/9781118924396.wbiea1891

Vernot, B., & Akey, J. M. (2014). Resurrecting surviving Neanderthal lineages from modern human genomes. *Science, 343*(6174), 1017–1021. https://doi.org/10.1126/science.1245938

Villarosa, L. (2020, July 28). Pollution is killing Black Americans. This community fought back. *The New York Times Magazine.* https://www.nytimes.com/2020/07/28/magazine/pollution-philadelphia-black-americans.html

Villmoare, B., Hatala, K. G., & Jungers, W. (2019). Sexual dimorphism in *Homo erectus* inferred from 1.5 Ma footprints near Ileret, Kenya. *Scientific Reports, 9*, Article 7687. https://doi.org/10.1038/s41598-019-44060-2

Villmoare, B., Kimbel, W. H., Seyoum, C., Campisano, C. J., DiMaggio, E. N., Rowan, J., Braun, D. R., Arrowsmith, J. R., & Reed, K. E. (2015). Early *Homo* at 2.8 Ma from Ledi-Geraru, Afar, Ethiopia. *Science, 347*(6228), 1352–1355.

Viveros, A. (2021, August 13). U.S. chimp sanctuary is poised to give its primates a COVID-19 vaccine—will others follow its lead? *Science Insider.* https://www.science.org/content/article/us-chimp-sanctuary-poised-give-its-primates-covid-19-vaccine-will-others-follow-its

Voss, B. L. (2000). Feminisms, queer theories, and the archaeological study of past sexualities. *World Archaeology, 32*(2), 180–192.

Voss, B. L. (2008). Sexuality studies in archaeology. *Annual Review of Anthropology, 37*(1), 317–336.

Voss, B. L. (2020). History, the family, and household archaeology. In M. Boyd, J. C. Erwin, & M. Hendrickson (Eds.), *The entangled past: Integrating history and archaeology* (pp. 292–301). University of Calgary Press.

Wade, L. (2019, November 7). Caribbean excavation offers intimate look at the lives of enslaved Africans. *Science*. https://www.sciencemag.org/news/2019/11/caribbean-excavation-offers-intimate-look-lives-enslaved-africans

Wade, L. (2020, May 14). From Black Death to fatal flu, past pandemics show why people on the margins suffer most. *Science*. https://www.sciencemag.org/news/2020/05/black-death-fatal-flu-past-pandemics-show-why-people-margins-suffer-most

Wagner, J. K., Colwell, C., Claw, K. G., Stone, A. C., Bolnick, D. A., Hawks, J., Brothers, K. B., & Garrison, N. A. (2020). Fostering responsible research on ancient DNA. *The American Journal of Human Genetics, 107*(2), 183–195.

Wagner, J. K., Yu, J. H., Ifekwunigwe, J. O., Harrell, T. M., Bamshad, M. J., & Royal, C. D. (2017). Anthropologists' views on race, ancestry, and genetics. *American Journal of Physical Anthropology, 162*(2), 318–327.

Wales, N. (2012). Modeling Neanderthal clothing using ethnographic analogues. *Journal of Human Evolution, 63*(6), 781–795. https://doi.org/10.1016/j.jhevol.2012.08.006

Walker, P. L. (2001). A bioarchaeological perspective on the history of violence. *Annual Review of Anthropology, 30*, 573–596.

Walker, P. L., & Cook, D. C. (1998). Brief communication: Gender and sex: Vive la difference. *American Journal of Physical Anthropology, 106*(2), 255–259.

Walter, B. S., & DeWitte, S. N. (2017). Urban and rural mortality and survival in medieval England. *Annals of Human Biology, 44*(4), 338–348.

Ward, T. W. (2013). *Gangsters without borders: An ethnography of a Salvadoran street gang.* Oxford University Press.

Wardlow, H. (2004). Anger, economy, and female agency: Problematizing "prostitution" and "sex work" among the Huli of Papua New Guinea. *Signs, 29*(4), 1017–1040.

Warin, M., Kowal, E., & Meloni, M. (2020). Indigenous knowledge in a postgenomic landscape: The politics of epigenetic hope and reparation in Australia. *Science, Technology, & Human Values, 45*(1), 87–111.

Warren, M. (2019, June 26). Move over, DNA: Ancient proteins are starting to reveal humanity's history. *Nature.* https://www.nature.com/articles/d41586-019-01986-x

Washington, H. A. (2006). *Medical apartheid: The dark history of medical experimentation on Black Americans from colonial times to the present.* Doubleday.

Watanabe, K., Urasopon, N., & Malaivijitnond, S. (2007). Long-tailed macaques use human hair as dental floss. *American Journal of Primatology, 69*(8), 940–944. https://doi.org/10.1002/ajp.20403

Watkins, R. J. (2007). Knowledge from the margins: W. Montague Cobb's pioneering research in biocultural anthropology. *American Anthropologist, 109*, 186–196.

Watkins, R. J. (2012). Biohistorical narratives of racial difference in the American Negro: Notes toward a nuanced history of American physical anthropology. *Current Anthropology, 53*(S5), S196–S209.

Watkins, R., & Muller, J. (2015). Repositioning the Cobb human archive: The merger of a skeletal collection and its texts. *American Journal of Human Biology, 27*(1), 41–50. https://doi.org/10.1002/ajhb.22650

Waxler, N. E. (1981). Learning to be a leper: A case study in the social construction of illness. In E. Mishler (Ed.), *Social contexts of health, illness, and patient care* (pp. 169–174). Cambridge University Press.

Weaver, J. (2010, January 12). Monkeys go out on a limb to show gratitude. *Nature.* https://doi.org/10.1038/news.2010.9

Weaver, L. J. (2017). Tension among women in North India: An idiom of distress and a cultural syndrome. *Culture, Medicine, and Psychiatry, 41*(1), 35–55.

Weinstein, K. J. (2005). Body proportions in ancient Andeans from high and low altitudes. *American Journal of Physical Anthropology, 128*(3), 569–585.

Weinstein, K. J. (2007). Thoracic skeletal morphology and high-altitude hypoxia in Andean prehistory. *American Journal of Physical Anthropology, 134*(1), 36–49.

Weinstein, K. J. (2017). Morphological signatures of high-altitude adaptations in the Andean archaeological record: Distinguishing developmental plasticity and natural selection. *Quaternary International, 461*(15), 14–24.

Weismantel, M. (2004). Moche sex pots: Reproduction and temporality in ancient South America. *American Anthropologist, 106*(3), 495–505.

Weismantel, M. (2021). *Playing with things: Engaging with the Moche sex pots.* University of Texas Press.

Weissbrod, L., Marshall, F. B., Valla, F. R., Khalaily, H., Bar-Oz, G., Auffray, J.-C., Vigne, J.-D., & Cucchi, T. (2017). Origins of house mice in ecological niches created by settled hunter-gatherers in the Levant 15,000 y ago. *Proceedings of the National Academy of Sciences U.S.A., 114*(16), 4099–4104.

Weitz, S., Ricci, L. A., Davoren, J., Vullo, C., Salado, M., & Peccerelli, F. (2009). DNA profiling of skeletal samples from the disappeared in Latin America. *Forensic Science International: Genetics Supplement Series, 2*(1), 245–247.

Wendland, C. L. (2012). Moral maps and medical imaginaries: Clinical tourism at Malawi's College of Medicine. *American Anthropologist, 114*(1), 108–122.

Wesley, L. (2008). When is an 'extinct language' not extinct? Miami, a formerly sleeping language. In K. King, N. Schilling-Estes, J. J. Lou, L. Fogle, & B. Soukup (Eds.), *Sustaining linguistic diversity: Endangered and minority language and language varieties* (pp. 23–37). Georgetown University Press.

Westbrook, L., & Saperstein, A. (2015). New categories are not enough: Rethinking the measurement of sex and gender in social surveys. *Gender & Society, 29*(4), 534–560.

Westin, J. L. (2017). Habituation to tourists: Protective or harmful? In K. M. Dore, E. P. Riley, & A. Fuentes (Eds.), *Ethnoprimatology: A practical guide to research at the human–nonhuman primate interface* (pp. 15–28). Cambridge University Press.

Weston, K. (1991). *Families we choose: Lesbians, gays, kinship.* Columbia.

Weyrich, L., Duchene, S., Soubrier, J., Arriola, L., Llamas, B., Breen, J., Morris, A. G., Alt, K. W., Caramelli, D., Dresely, V., Farrell, M., Farrer, A. G., Francken, M., Gully, N., Haak, W., Hardy, K., Harvati, K., Held, P., Holmes, E. C., . . . Cooper, A. (2017). Neanderthal behaviour, diet, and disease inferred from ancient DNA in dental calculus. *Nature, 544*, 357–361.

White, C. D., Spence, M. W., Longstaffe, F. J., & Law, K. R. (2004). Demography and ethnic continuity in the Tlailotlacan enclave of Teotihuacan: The evidence from stable oxygen isotopes. *Journal of Anthropological Archaeology, 123*(4), 385–403.

White, T. D., Asfaw, B., Beyene, Y., Haile-Selassie, Y., Lovejoy, C. O., Suwa, G., & WoldeGabriel, G. (2009). *Ardipithecus ramidus* and the paleobiology of early hominids. *Science, 326*(5949), 64–86.

White Hughto, J., Reisner, S., & Pachankis, J. (2015). Transgender stigma and health: A critical review of stigma determinants, mechanisms, and interventions. *Social Science & Medicine, 147*, 222–231.

Whiten, A. (2000). Primate culture and social learning. *Cognitive Science, 24*, 477–508.

Whyte, K. (2018). Settler colonialism, ecology, and environmental injustice. *Environment and Society, 9*(1), 125–144.

Wiessner, P. (1982). Risk, reciprocity and social influences on !Kung San economics. In E. Leacock & R. Lee (Eds.), *Politics and history in band societies* (pp. 61–84). Cambridge University Press.

Wiessner, P. W. (2014). Embers of society: Firelight talk among the Ju/'hoansi bushmen. *Proceedings of the National Academy of Sciences U.S.A., 111*(39), 14027–14035.

Wilce, J. (2008). *Crying shame: Metaculture, modernity, and the exaggerated death of lament.* Wiley.

Wilce, J., & Fenigsen, J. (2015). Mourning and honor: Register in Karelian lament. In A. Agha & Frog (Eds.), *Registers of communication* (pp. 187–209). Finnish Literature Society.

Wiley, A. S. (2004). "Drink milk for fitness": The cultural politics of human biological variation and milk consumption in the United States. *American Anthropologist, 106*(3), 506–517.

Wiley, A. S. (2011). Milk for "growth": Global and local meanings of milk consumption in China, India, and the United States. *Food and Foodways, 19*(1–2), 11–33.

Wilkins, J. (2020a). Is it time to retire NASTIES in Southern Africa? Moving beyond the culture-historical framework for Middle Stone Age Lithic assemblage variability. *Lithic Technology, 45*(4), 295–307. https://doi.org/10.1080/01977261.2020.1802848

Wilkins, J. (2020b). Learner-driven innovation in the stone tool technology of early *Homo sapiens. Evolutionary Human Sciences, 2*, 1–15.

Wilkins, J., Pickering, R., Schoville, B., Meyer, M., Collins, B., & Maape, S. (2021, March 31). Investigating human origins in the Kalahari. *Social Sciences.* https://socialsciences.nature.com/posts/investigating-the-origins-of-homo-sapiens-in-the-kalahari

Wilkins, J., Schoville, B. J., & Brown, K. S. (2014). An experimental investigation of the functional hypothesis and evolutionary advantage of stone-tipped spears. *PLOS ONE, 9*(8), Article e104514. https://doi.org/10.1371/journal.pone.0104514

Wilkins, J., Schoville, B. J., Brown, K. S., & Chazan, M. (2012). Evidence for early hafted hunting technology. *Science, 338*(6109), 942–946. https://doi.org/10.1126/science.1227608

Wilkins, J., Schoville, B. J., Pickering, R., Gliganic, L., Collins, B., Brown, K. S., von der Meden, J., Khumalo, W., Meyer, M. C., Maape, S., Blackwood, A. F., & Hatton, A. (2021). Innovative *Homo sapiens* behaviours 105,000 years ago in a wetter Kalahari. *Nature, 592*, 248–252.

Willey, A. (2016). *Undoing monogamy: The politics of science and the possibilities of biology.* Duke University Press.

Williams, H. (1995). There are no free gifts! Social support and the need for reciprocity. *Human*

Organization, 54(4), 401–409. https://doi.org/10.17730/humo.54.4.w233493122q420v7

Williams, S. R. (2018). Ancient DNA. In W. Trevathan (Ed.), *The international encyclopedia of biological anthropology*. Wiley. https://doi.org/10.1002/9781118584538.ieba0022

Willis, A., & Oxenham, M. F. (2013). The Neolithic demographic transition and oral health: The Southeast Asian experience. *American Journal of Physical Anthropology, 152*, 197–208.

Willis, M. S., Harris, L. E., & Hergenrader, P. J. (2008). On traditional dental extraction: Case reports from Dinka and Nuer en route to restoration. *British Dental Journal, 204*(3), 121–124.

Wilson, A. (2019). Queer anthropology. In *The open encyclopedia of anthropology*. http://doi.org/10.29164/19queer

Wilson, M. L., Boesch, C., Fruth, B., Furuichi, T., Gilby, I. C., Hashimoto, C., Hobaiter, C., Hohmann, G., Itoh, N., Koops, K., Lloyd, J., Matsuzawa, T., Mitani, J. C., Mjungu, D. C., Morgan, D., Muller, M. N., Mundry, R., Nakamura, M., Pruetz, J., . . . Wrangham, R. W. (2014). Lethal aggression in *Pan* is better explained by adaptive strategies than human impacts. *Nature, 513*, 414–417.

Winking, J. W. (2005). *Fathering among the Tsimane of Bolivia: A test of the proposed goals of paternal care* (Publication No. 3201660) [Doctoral dissertation, University of New Mexico]. ProQuest Dissertations Publishing.

Winking, J., Eastwick, P. W., Smith, L. K., & Koster, J. (2018). Applicability of the Investment Model Scale in a natural-fertility population. *Personal Relationships, 25*(4), 497–516. https://doi.org/10.1111/pere.12257

Winterhalder, B., & Kennett, D. J. (2009). Four neglected concepts with a role to play in explaining the origins of agriculture. *Current Anthropology, 50*(5), 645–648.

Wittfogel, K. (1955). Developmental aspects of hydraulic societies. In *Irrigation civilizations: A comparative study* (pp. 43–57). Social Science Monographs, Department of Cultural Affairs, Pan American Union.

Wolf, E. R. (1982). *Europe and the people without history*. University of California Press.

Wolfe, S. H., & Handwerker, W. P. (2010). Where bad teeth come from: A study in how cultures exert causal force. *Human Organization, 69*(4), 398–406.

Wong, K. (2014, August 27). Archaeologists assess killing power of Stone Age weapons. *Scientific American*. https://blogs.scientificamerican.com/observations/archaeologists-assess-killing-power-of-stone-age-weapons/

Wood, B., & Strait, D. (2004). Patterns of resource use in early *Homo* and *Paranthropus*. *Journal of Human Evolution, 46*(2), 119–162.

Wood, J. W. (2017). *Dynamics of human reproduction: Biology, biometry, demography*. Routledge.

Woolard, K., & Schieffelin, B. (1994). Language ideology. *Annual Review of Anthropology, 23*, 55–82.

Woolf, G. (2020). *The life and death of ancient cities: A natural history*. Oxford University Press.

Worthman, C. M. (2019). Shared and local pathways in suffering and resilience: Keeping the body in mind. *Transcultural Psychiatry, 56*(4), 775–785.

Worthman, C. M., & Melby, M. K. (2002). Toward a comparative developmental ecology of human sleep. In M. A. Carskadon (Ed.), *Adolescent sleep patterns: Biological, social, and psychological influences* (pp. 69–117). Cambridge University Press.

Wright, K. E. (2017). *The reflection and reification of racialized language in popular media*. [Master's thesis, University of Kentucky]. https://uknowledge.uky.edu/cgi/viewcontent.cgi?article=1018&context=ltt_etds

Wright, K. I. (2014). Domestication and inequality? Households, corporate groups and food processing tools at Neolithic Çatalhöyük. *Journal of Anthropological Archaeology, 33*, 1–33.

Wright, L. E., & White, C. D. (1996). Human biology in the classic Maya collapse: Evidence from paleopathology and paleodiet. *Journal of World Prehistory, 10*(2), 147–198.

Wright, R. P. (Ed.). (1996). *Gender and archaeology*. University of Pennsylvania Press.

Wutich, A. (2009). Intrahousehold disparities in women and men's experiences of water insecurity and emotional distress in urban Bolivia. *Medical Anthropology Quarterly, 23*(4), 436–454.

Wutich, A. (2011). The moral economy of water reexamined: Reciprocity, water insecurity, and urban survival in Cochabamba, Bolivia. *Journal of Anthropological Research, 67*(1), 5–26.

Wutich, A., Beresford, M., & Carvajal, C. (2016). Can informal water vendors deliver on the promise of a human right to water? Results from Cochabamba, Bolivia. *World Development, 79*, 14–24.

Wutich, A., Beresford, M., Montoya, T., Radonic, L., & Workman, C. (2021). Water security and scarcity. In M. Aldenderfer (Ed.), *Oxford research encyclopedia of anthropology*. Oxford University Press. https://doi.org/10.1093/acrefore/9780190854584.013.475

Xiang, H., Gao, J., Yu, B., Zhou, H., Cai, D., Zhang, Y., Chen, X., Wang, X., Hofreiter, M., & Zhao, X. (2014). Early

Holocene chicken domestication in northern China. *Proceedings of the National Academy of Sciences U.S.A., 111*(49), 17564–17569.

Xygalatas, D., Khan, S., Lang, M., Kundt, R., Kundtová-Klocová, E., Krátký, J., & Shaver, J. (2019). Effects of extreme ritual practices on psychophysiological well-being. *Current Anthropology, 60*(5), 699–707.

Yakushko, O., & Rajan, I. (2017). Global love for sale: Divergence and convergence of human trafficking with "mail order brides" and international arranged marriage phenomena. *Women & Therapy, 40*(1–2), 190–206.

Yang, F., & Hu, A. (2012). Mapping Chinese folk religion in mainland China and Taiwan. *Journal for the Scientific Study of Religion, 51*(3), 505–521.

Yang, L. (2016). At the bottom of the heap: Socioeconomic circumstances and health practices and beliefs among garbage pickers in peri-urban China. *Critical Asian Studies, 48*(1), 123–131.

Yates-Doerr, E. (2011). Bodily betrayal: Love and anger in the time of epigenetics. In F. E. Mascia-Lees (Ed.), *A companion to the anthropology of the body and embodiment* (pp. 292–306). Wiley–Blackwell.

Yatsuka, H. (2015). Reconsidering the "indigenous peoples" in the African context from the perspective of current livelihood and its historical changes: The case of the Sandawe and the Hadza in Tanzania. *Center for African Area Studies, 36*(1), 27–48. https://doi.org/10.14989/197193

Yatsunenko, T., Rey, F. E., Manary, M. J., Trehan, I., Dominguez-Bello, M. G., Contreras, M., Magris, M., Hidalgo, G., Baldassano, R. N., Anokhin, A. P., Heath, A. C., Warner, B., Reeder, J., Kuczynski, J., Caporaso, J. G., Lozupone, C. A., Lauber, C., Clemente, J. C., Knights, D., . . . Gordon, J. I. (2012). Human gut microbiome viewed across age and geography. *Nature, 486*, 222–227. https://doi.org/10.1038/nature11053

Yazzie, M. K. (2018). Decolonizing development in Diné Bikeyah: Resource extraction, anti-capitalism, and relational futures. *Environment and Society, 9*(1), 25–39.

Yeoman, B. (2018, August 30). The hidden resilience of "food desert" neighborhoods. *SAPIENS.* https://www.sapiens.org/culture/food-deserts-washington-dc/

Yoder, P. S., & Wang, S. (2013). *Female genital cutting: The interpretation of recent DHS data.* DHS Comparative Reports No. 33, ICF International. https://dhsprogram.com/pubs/pdf/cr33/cr33.pdf

Yong, E. (2015, September 10). 6 tiny cavers, 15 odd skeletons, and 1 amazing new species of ancient human: The inside story behind a spectacular new hominin find. *The Atlantic.* https://www.theatlantic.com/science/archive/2015/09/homo-naledi-rising-star-cave-hominin/404362/

Yong, E., Essien, U. R., Nolen, L., Khazanchi, R., Ogunwole, M., Fields, N., Onuoha, C., Williams, J., & Paul, D. (2020, December 3). Structural inequalities and the pandemic's winter surge (No. 141) [Podcast episode]. In *Anti-racism in medicine.* Clinical Problem Solvers. https://clinicalproblemsolving.com/2020/12/02/episode-145-antiracism-in-medicine-series-episode-3-structural-inequities-and-the-pandemics-winter-surge/

Yuasa, I. P. (2010). Creaky voice: A new feminine voice quality for young urban-oriented upwardly mobile American women? *American Speech, 85*(3), 315–337.

Zall, C. (2016, October 14). How the Miami Tribe got its language back. *The World.* https://theworld.org/stories/2016-10-14/how-miami-tribe-got-its-language-back

Zarger, R., & Stepp, J. (2004). Persistence of botanical knowledge among Tzeltal Maya children. *Current Anthropology, 45*(3), 413–418.

Zeberg, H., & Paabo, S. (2020). The major genetic factor for severe COVID-19 is inherited from Neanderthals. *Nature, 587*, 610–612.

Zeder, M. A. (2006). Central questions in the domestication of plants and animals. *Evolutionary Anthropology: Issues, News, and Reviews, 15*(3), 105–117.

Zeder, M. A. (2008). Domestication and early agriculture in the Mediterranean Basin: Origins, diffusion, and impact. *Proceedings of the National Academy of Sciences U.S.A., 105*(33), 11597–11604.

Zeder, M. A. (2015). Core questions in domestication research. *Proceedings of the National Academy of Sciences U.S.A., 112*(11), 3191–3198.

Zeder, M. A, & Hesse, B. (2000). The initial domestication of goats (*Capra hircus*) in the Zagros Mountains 10,000 years ago. *Science, 287*(5461), 2254–2257.

Zeder, M. A., & Smith, B. D. (2009). A conversation on agricultural origins: Talking past each other in a crowded room. *Current Anthropology, 50*(5), 681–691.

Zefferman, M. R., & Mathew, S. (2015). An evolutionary theory of large-scale human warfare: Group-structured cultural selection. *Evolutionary Anthropology: Issues, News, and Reviews, 24*(2), 50–61.

Zefferman, M. R., & Mathew, S. (2020). An evolutionary theory of moral injury with insight from Turkana warriors. *Evolution and Human Behavior, 41*(5), 341–353.

Zefferman, M. R., & Mathew, S. (2021). Combat stress in a small-scale society suggests divergent evolutionary roots for posttraumatic stress disorder symptoms.

Proceedings of the National Academy of Sciences U.S.A., 118(15), Article e2020430118.

Zhang, H., Wang, C., Turvey, S. T., Sun, Z., Tan, Z., Yang, Q., Long, W., Wu, X., & Yang, D. (2020). Thermal infrared imaging from drones can detect individuals and nocturnal behavior of the world's rarest primate. *Global Ecology and Conservation, 23*, Article e01101.

Zhang, X. L., Ha, B. B., Wang, S. J., Chen, Z. J., Ge, J. Y., Long, H., He, W., Da, W., Nian, X. M., Yi, M. J., Zhou, X. Y., Zhang, P. Q., Jin, Y. S., Bar-Yosef, O., Olsen, J. W., & Gao, X. (2018). The earliest human occupation of the high-altitude Tibetan Plateau 40 thousand to 30 thousand years ago. *Science, 362*, 1049–1051.

Zhao, L. X., & Zhang, L. Z. (2013). New fossil evidence and diet analysis of *Gigantopithecus blacki* and its distribution and extinction in South China. *Quaternary International, 286*, 69–74.

Zhu, H. (2020). Countering COVID-19-related anti-Chinese racism with translanguaged swearing on social media. *Multilingua, 39*(5), 607–616.

Zhu, L. (2012). *National holidays and minority festivals in Canadian nation-building* (Publication No. uk.bl. ethos.557557) [Ph.D. thesis, University of Sheffield]. White Rose eTheses Online.

Zhu, Z., Dennell, R., Huang, W., Wu, Y., Qiu, S., Yang, S., Rao, Z., Hou, Y., Xie, J., Han, J., & Ouyang, T. (2018). Hominin occupation of the Chinese Loess Plateau since about 2.1 million years ago. *Nature, 559*, 608–612.

Zilhão, J., Angelucci, D. E., Badal-García, E., d'Errico, F., Daniel, F., Dayet, L., Douka, K., Higham, T. F. G., Martínez-Sánchez, M., Montes-Bernárdez, R., Murcia-Mascarós, S., Pérez-Sirvent, C., Roldán-García, C., Vanhaeren, M., Villaverde, V., Wood, R., & Zapata, J. (2010). Symbolic use of marine shells and mineral pigments by Iberian Neanderthals. *Proceedings of the National Academy of Sciences U.S.A., 107*, 1023–1028. https://doi.org/10.1073/pnas.0914088107

Zimman, L. (2013). Hegemonic masculinity and the variability of gay-sounding speech: The perceived sexuality of transgender men. *Journal of Language & Sexuality, 2*(1), 1–39.

Zuckerman, M., Harper, K., Barrett, R., & Armelagos, G. (2014). The evolution of disease: Anthropological perspectives on epidemiologic transitions. *Global Health Action, 7*(1), Article 23303.

Zulaika, J. (1995). The anthropologist as terrorist. In C. Nordstrom & A. C. G. M. Robben (Eds.), *Fieldwork under fire: Contemporary studies of violence and survival* (pp. 206–222). University of California Press.

CREDITS

Table of Contents

Photos: TOC 1: Robert Mora / Alamy Stock Photo; **TOC 2:** Anamaria Mejia/Shutterstock; **TOC 3:** Science History Images / Alamy Stock Photo; **TOC 4:** Avalon.red / Alamy Stock Photo; **TOC 5:** Bone Clones, Inc. / Science Source; **TOC 6:** Richard 'Bert' Roberts, University of Wollongong; **TOC 7,** top: NK Sanford / Alamy Stock Photo; **TOC 7,** bottom: KVASVECTOR/Shutterstock; **TOC 8,** top: blickwinkel / Alamy Stock Photo; **TOC 8,** bottom: Tuca Vieira; **TOC 9:** ML Harris / Alamy Stock Photo; **TOC 10,** top: Danita Delimont / Alamy Stock Photo; **TOC 10,** bottom: Tim Graham / Alamy Stock Photo; **TOC 11:** akg-images / Werner Forman; **TOC 12:** John Henshall / Alamy Stock Photo; **TOC 13:** DEA / G. DAGLI ORTI/ De Agostini via Getty Images; **TOC 14:** Mark Kanning / Alamy Stock Photo; **TOC 15,** top: MOLA/Getty Images; **TOC 15,** bottom: Hemis / Alamy Stock Photo; **TOC 16,** top: USGS/Science Source; **TOC 16,** bottom: MARK RALSTON/AFP via Getty Images

Chapter 1

Photos: Chapter-opening photos, clockwise from top: **1.COa:** Matt Hahnewald Photography / Alamy Stock Photo; **1.COb:** REUTERS/Charles Platiau/Alamy Stock Photo; **1.COc:** PRISMA ARCHIVO / Alamy Stock Photo; **1.COd:** Robert Mora / Alamy Stock Photo; **1.02:** Sheela Athreya; **1.03:** Li Liu, Stanford University; **1.04a:** Henk Meijer / Alamy Stock Photo; **1.04b:** Robert Fried / Alamy Stock Photo; **1.04c:** Michele Oenbrink / Alamy Stock Photo; **1.05:** Sandra Mu/Getty Images; **1.06:** Elisa Nino-Sears; **1.07a:** ERIC LAFFORGUE / Alamy Stock Photo; **1.07b:** imageBROKER / Alamy Stock Photo; **1.07c:** RooM the Agency / Alamy Stock Photo; **1.08:** Apata, M, Arriaza, B, Llop, E, Moraga, M. Human adaptation to arsenic in Andean populations of the Atacama Desert. Am J Phys Anthropol. 2017; 163: 192– 199. https://doi.org/10.1002/ajpa.23193; **1.09:** PRISMA ARCHIVO / Alamy Stock Photo; **1.10:** Tony Rinaldo Photography; **1.11:** blickwinkel / Alamy Stock Photo; **1.12:** Prostock-studio / Alamy Stock Photo; **1.13:** Lisa Matisoo-Smith; **1.14:** Amy Smotherman Burgess – USA TODAY NETWORK; **1.15:** Lysandra Marquez/Cronkite News; **1.16:** REUTERS / Alamy Stock Photo; **1.17:** Marco Hill; **1.18:** AP Photo; **1.2 review:** Elisa Nino-Sears

Chapter 2

Photos: Chapter-opening photos, clockwise from top: **2.COa:** Benjamin Reed; **2.COb:** Ayana Omilade Flewellen; **2.COc:** Anamaria Mejia/Shutterstock; **2.COd:** Alexandra Brewis; **2.01:** Workers digging for phosphate, Banaba, Kiribati. Arundel, Lilian Mary Izod, 1883: Alexander Turnbull Library, Wellington, New Zealand; **2.02:** Katerina Teaiwa; **2.03a:** Wellcome Library, London; **2.03b:** Yale Archives; **2.04b:** Susanne Kuehling, University of Regina; **2.05:** Roy Rappaport Papers, Special Collections & Archives, UC San Diego; **2.06:** Tom Bukowski; **2.07:** James Broesch; **2.09a:** Ruth Behar; **2.09b:** Rolando Estévez; **2.10:** Library of Congress; **2.12:** Cécile Evers-Traore; **2.13a-b:** Nick Enfield; **2.14:** Erin Moriarty Harrelson; **2.15:** Image created by Juan C

Fernandez-Diaz from airborne lidar data collected by NCALM for the Pacunam Lidar Initiative (PLI) and first published by LiDAR Magazine Vol. 9 No. 2 Airborne Lidar for Archaeology in Central and South America; **2.16:** Ayana Omilade Flewellen; **2.17:** Chris Searles, Diving With a Purpose; **2.19a:** University of Auckland, Department of Anthropology, Anthropology Photographic Archive; **2.20:** Howard Crosby Butler Archive, Department of Art and Archaeology, Princeton University; **2.21:** Clive Gamble; **2.22:** Scott Donald Haddow; **2.23a-b:** Verónica Pérez Rodríguez; **2.24:** Benjamin Reed; **2.25:** Carolyn Freiwald; **2.26a-b:** Dr. Michelle A. Rodrigues; **2.27:** Alyssa Crittenden; **2.28:** Courtesy of University of Adelaide Library, Rare Books and Manuscripts; **2.29:** Lisa Maree Williams/Getty Images; **2.30:** Jim Wilson/The New York Times/ Redux; **2.31:** NAGPRA Comics; **2.32:** Iain Bond Photography; **2.33:** Daniel J.Sauve

Other: Fig. 2.8: Reprinted from *Learning and Individual Differences* 27, Victoria Reyes- García, Ana C. Luz, Maximilien Gueze, et al., "Secular Trends on Traditional Ecological Knowledge: An Analysis of Changes in Different Domains of Knowledge among Tsimane' Men," pp. 206-212, Copyright 2023, with permission from Elsevier. **Fig. 2.11:** Sicoli, Mark A., and Gary Holton. 2014. "Linguistic Phylogenies Support Back-Migration from Beringia to Asia." *PLoS ONE* 9(3): e91722. https://doi.org/10.1371/journal. pone.0091722. © 2014 Sicoli and Holton. This is an open-access article distributed under the terms of the Creative Commons Attribution License, which permits unrestricted use, distribution, and reproduction in any medium, provided the original author and source are credited. https://creativecommons.org/licenses/by/4.0/. **Fig. 2.18:** Crow Canyon Archaeological Center. n.d. "Archaeological Dating." https://www.crowcanyon.org/education/learn-about-archaeology/archaeological-dating/. Adapted with permission from Crow Canyon Archaeological Center. **Fig. 2.19b:** Adapted from Irwin, Geoff. 2017. "Pacific Migrations – Into Remote Oceania: Lapita People." *Te Ara – The Encyclopedia of New Zealand*. Last revised February 8, 2017. http://www.TeAra.govt.nz/en/map/1767/ sites-of-lapita-pottery. Reused with permission.

Chapter 3

Photos: Chapter-opening photos, clockwise from top: **3.COa:** David Bagnall / Alamy Stock Photo; **3.COb:** Maria A. Nieves Colón; **3.COc:** Science History Images / Alamy Stock Photo; **3.COd:** imageBROKER / Alamy Stock Photo; **3.COe:** paul prescott / Alamy Stock Photo; **3.01:** Paul H. Stob; **3.02:** John de la Bastide/Shutterstock; **3.06:** Wellcome Images / Science Source; **3.10a:** Science History Images / Alamy Stock Photo; **3.10b:** Michelle Gilders / Alamy Stock Photo; **3.10c:** Ralph Lee Hopkins / Alamy Stock Photo; **3.10d:** Nature Picture Library / Alamy Stock Photo; **3.11b:** Douglas Peebles Photography / Alamy Stock Photo; **3.12:** Maciej Dakowicz / Alamy Stock Photo; **3.14:** Maria A. Nieves Colón; **3.15:** paul prescott / Alamy Stock Photo; **3.16a:** imageBROKER / Alamy Stock Photo; **3.16b:** kielcscn / Alamy Stock Photo; **3.19:** Ashley Cooper pics /

Chamber, South Africa." *eLife* 4. https://doi.org/10.7554/eLife.09561. © 2015, Dirks et al. http://creativecommons.org/licenses/by/4.0/. **Fig. 5.5:** Adapted from National Natural History Museum. "Human Evolution Interactive Timeline." With permission of Smithsonian Human Origins Program. **Fig. 5.17:** Based on illustration by David Brill. Courtesy of David Brill.

Chapter 6
Photos: Chapter-opening photos, clockwise from top: **6.COa:** S. Entressangle / E. Daynes / Science Source; **6.COb:** Suzanne Long / Alamy Stock Photo; **6.COc:** Jayne Wilkins; **6.COd:** Album /Alamy Stock Photo; **6.COe:** JEFF PACHOUD/AFP via Getty Images; **6.COf:** Fine Art Images/Heritage Images/Getty Images; **6.COg:** Richard 'Bert' Roberts, University of Wollongong; **6.01a-b:** Jayne Wilkins; **6.02a-b:** Wilkins J, Schoville BJ, Brown KS (2014) An Experimental Investigation of the Functional Hypothesis and Evolutionary Advantage of Stone-Tipped Spears. PLoS ONE 9(8): e104514. https://doi.org/10.1371/journal.pone.0104514; **6.03-1:** Courtesy of and © National Museum of Tanzania & Eric Delson (photo by C. Tarka); **6.03-1a:** FOSSIL CREDIT: National Museums of Kenya. Photo Credit: David Brill; **6.03-2:** REUTERS / Alamy Stock Photo; **6.03-3:** Milford Wolpoff; **6.03-4:** ARTIFACT CREDIT: American Museum of Natural History PHOTO CREDIT: © 1996 David L. Brill; **6.03-5:** Bone Clones, Inc. / Science Source; **6.04a:** Vasil Gabunia/Shutterstock; **6.04b:** Elisabeth Daynes / Science Source; **6.04c:** Drawn by Ofer Bar-Yosef; **6.05:** National Museum of Kenya; photo by A. Walker; **6.06a-b:** Kevin Hatala; **6.08:** P. Thomas Schoenemann, Thomas F. Budinger, Vincent M. Sarich, and William S.-Y. Wang. (2000). Brain size does not predict general cognitive ability within families, 97 (9) 4932-4937 https://doi.org/10.1073/pnas.97.9.4932, Copyright (2000) National Academy of Sciences, U.S.A.; **6.09:** M. Ponce de León and Ch. Zollikofer/University of Zurich; **6.10a:** Michael J. Rogers, Southern Connecticut State University; **6.10b-c:** Michael J. Rogers, Southern Connecticut State University; **6.11:** Nick Walton; **6.13:** Handout/Reuters; **6.14:** Ferraro JV, Plummer TW, Pobiner BL, Oliver JS, Bishop LC, Braun DR, et al. (2013) Earliest Archaeological Evidence of Persistent Hominin Carnivory. PLoS ONE 8(4): e62174. https://doi.org/10.1371/journal.pone.0062174; **6.15a-b:** Barkai, Ran, et al. "Fire for a Reason: Barbecue at Middle Pleistocene Qesem Cave, Israel." Current Anthropology, vol. 58, no. S16, Aug. 2017, Figure3 https://doi.org/10.1086/691211; **6.16 left:** JINI Xinhua/eyevine/Redux; **6.16 right:** JACK GUEZ/AFP via Getty Images; **6.19:** clockwise from top: **6.19a:** Dr. Jeffrey H. Schwartz; **6.19b:** State Museum of National History Stuttgart; **6.19c:** Milford Wolpoff; **6.19d:** Danita Delimont / Alamy Stock Photo; **6.19e:** Courtesy of and © of Eric Delson; **6.19f:** Courtesy of and © of Eric Delson; **6.19g:** John Reader / Science Source; **6.19h:** FOSSIL CREDIT: Musee De l'Homme Photo Credit: David Brill; **6.19i:** Sabena Jane Blackbird / Alamy Stock Photo; **6.21a:** Shannon McPherron/MPI EVA Leipzig/UPI /Alamy Stock Photo; **6.21b:** Callaway, E. Oldest Homo sapiens fossil claim rewrites our species' history. Nature (2017). https://doi.org/10.1038/nature.2017.22114; **6.22a:** The Natural History Museum / Alamy Stock Photo; **6.22b:** The Natural History Museum / Alamy Stock Photo; **6.22c:** H. Rougier, et al. Peştera cu Oase 2 and the cranial morphology of early modern Europeans. Copyright (2007) National Academy of Sciences, U.S.A. https://doi.org/10.1073/pnas.0610538104; **6.22d:** FOSSIL CREDIT: Peabody Museum Harvard University PHOTO CREDIT: ©1985 David L. Brill; **6.22e:** Fabrice Demeter; **6.22f:** ©2001 David L. Brill, humanoriginsphotos.com; **6.22g:** Milford Wolpoff; **6.22h:** The Natural History Museum / Alamy Stock Photo; **6.26:** David Wall / Alamy Stock Photo; **6.27a:** Fine Art Images/Heritage Images/Getty Images; **6.27b:** Album /Alamy Stock Photo; **6.27c:** JEFF PACHOUD/AFP via Getty Images; **6.28:** V. Feruglio/ PCR Cussac/French Ministry of Culture; **6.29:** Natural History Archive / Alamy Stock Photo; **6.30:** Giovanni Caselli; **6.31a:** Mellars P. et al. Genetic and archaeological perspectives on the initial modern human colonization of southern Asia. fig 4. PNAS v110 no. 26 10699-10704 2013; **6.31b:** Bouzouggar A. et al. 2007. 82 000-year-old shell beads from North Africa and implications for the origins of modern human behavior. Fig. 3. PNAS 104:9964-9969; **6.32a-c:** James Steele Margaret Clegg and Sandra Martelli. Comparative Morphology of the Hominin and African Ape Hyoid Bone a Possible Marker of the Evolution of Speech. Human Biology 2013 85 (5) 639-672 https://doi.org/10.3378/027.085.0501; **6.34c:** S. Entressangle / E. Daynes / Science Source; **6.35:** ARTIFACT CREDIT: courtesy Denise de Sonneville-Bordes. Photo Credit: David Brill; **6.36:** Chen, F., Welker, F., Shen, CC. et al. A late Middle Pleistocene Denisovan mandible from the Tibetan Plateau. Nature 569, 409–412 (2019). https://doi.org/10.1038/s41586-019-1139-x. Copyright ©2019 Karger Publishers, Basel, Switzerland.; **6.37a:** Nastya Smirnova RF/Shutterstock; **6.37b:** Used with permission of Springer Nature BV, from Nature, Douka, et. al, Age estimates for hominin fossils and the onset of the Upper Palaeolithic at Denisova Cave. Volume 565 (2019); permission conveyed through Copyright Clearance Center, Inc.; **6.37c:** Richard 'Bert' Roberts, University of Wollongong; **6.38a:** Suzanne Long / Alamy Stock Photo; **6.38b:** Mauricio Anton / Science Source; **6.39b:** Tim Wiencis/Splash News/Newscom; **6.39c:** Javier Trueba/MSF/Science Source; **6.1 review:** Kevin Hatala

Other: **Fig. 6.7a:** From *Evolution of African Mammals*, edited by Vincent J. Maglio and H. B. S. Cooke, Cambridge, Mass.: Harvard University Press, Copyright © 1978 by the President and Fellows of Harvard College. Used by permission. All rights reserved. **Fig. 6.17:** Adapted from National Natural History Museum. "Human Characteristics: Brains." With permission of Smithsonian Human Origins Program. **Fig. 6.18:** Top used with permission of University of Chicago Press – Journals, from Aiello, Leslie C., and Peter Wheeler. 1995. "The Expensive-Tissue Hypothesis: The Brain and the Digestive System in Human and Primate Evolution." *Current Anthropology* 36(2): 199-221; permission conveyed through Copyright Clearance Center, Inc. Bottom adapted from Grube, Natalia, Hector H. Garcia, and George H. Perry. 2021. "Human Diet Evolution: Meat, Fire, and Tapeworms." *Frontiers for Young Minds* 9: 555342. Copyright © 2021 Grube, Garcia and Perry. This is an open-access article distributed under the terms of the Creative Commons Attribution License (CC BY). https://creativecommons.org/licenses/by/4.0/. **Fig. 6.20:** Adapted from Debets, G. F. 1955. "Paleoanthropological Finds at Kostenki." *Sovetskaya Arkheologiya* 1: 43-54. With permission from *Russian Archaeology*. **Fig. 6.37d:** From Slon, Viviane, Charlotte Hopfe, Clemens L. Weiss, et al. 2017. "Neandertal and Denisovan DNA from Pleistocene Sediments." *Science* 356(6338): 605-608. Reprinted with permission from AAAS. **Fig. 6.41:** Adapted from Dolgova, Olga, and Oscar Lao. 2018. "Evolutionary and Medical Consequences of Archaic Introgression into Modern Human Genomes." *Genes* 9(7): 358. https://doi.org/10.3390/genes9070358. © 2018 by the authors. Licensee MDPI, Basel, Switzerland. This article is an open access article distributed under the terms and conditions of the Creative Commons Attribution (CC BY) license (http://creativecommons.org/licenses/by/4.0/). **Fig. 6.42:** Adapted from Ahlquist, K. D., Mayra M. Bañuelos, Alyssa Funk, et al. 2021. "Our Tangled Family Tree: New Genomic Methods Offer Insight into the Legacy of Archaic

Chapter 7

Photos: Chapter-opening photos, clockwise from top: **7.COa:** ADI WEDA/EPA-EFE/Shutterstock; **7.COb:** Guy Corbishley / Alamy Stock Photo; **7.COc:** KVASVECTOR/Shutterstock; **7.COd:** AP Photo/Diane Bondareff; **7.COe:** NK Sanford / Alamy Stock Photo; **7.01:** AP Photo/Diane Bondareff; **7.03:** ZUMA Press, Inc. / Alamy Stock Photo; **7.05:** Rotokas Ecotourism; **7.07:** Getty Images/iStockphoto; **7.09:** NK Sanford / Alamy Stock Photo; **7.10:** Richard Maschmeyer / Alamy Stock Photo; **7.11:** Richard Levine / Alamy Stock Photo; **7.12a:** Rachel Kolokoff Hopper / Alamy Stock Photo; **7.12b:** James Davis Photography / Alamy Stock Photo; **7.14:** ADI WEDA/EPA-EFE/Shutterstock; **7.15:** REUTERS / Alamy Stock Photo; **7.16a:** Richard Levine / Alamy Stock Photo; **7.16b:** Guy Corbishley / Alamy Stock Photo; **7.17:** Lera Boroditsky; **7.18:** AP Photo/Record Searchlight, Andreas Fuhrmann; **7.20:** Darryl W. Moran Photography; **7.21:** Maximum Film / Alamy Stock Photo; **7.22:** Johnny Nunez/WireImage/Getty Images; **7.01 review:** Getty Images/iStockphoto; **7.04 review:** Guy Corbishley / Alamy Stock Photo

Other: Fig. 7.2: From Black, Steven P. 2013. "Stigma and Ideological Constructions of the Foreign: Facing HIV/AIDS in South Africa." *Language in Society* 42(5): 481-502. Copyright © Cambridge University Press 2013. Reproduced with permission of the Licensor through PLSclear. **Fig. 7.13:** Adapted from Hammarström, Harald, Robert Forkel, Martin Haspelmath, and Sebastian Bank (eds.). 2011. *Glottolog 4.7.* Glottolog 4.7 edited by Hammarström, Harald & Forkel, Robert & Haspelmath, Martin & Bank, Sebastian is licensed under a Creative Commons Attribution 4.0 International License. https://creativecommons.org/licenses/by/4.0/.

Chapter 8

Photos: Chapter-opening photos, clockwise from top: **8.COa:** blickwinkel / Alamy Stock Photo; **8.COb:** Linda R. Manzanilla; **8.COc:** Tuca Vieira; **8.COd:** Michael Rooney / Alamy Stock Photo; **8.COe:** The Print Collector / Alamy Stock Photo; **8.01:** Michael Rooney / Alamy Stock Photo; **8.02:** Linda R. Manzanilla; **8.03:** Emmanuel LATTES / Alamy Stock Photo; **8.04:** PA Images / Alamy Stock Photo; **8.05:** BIOSPHOTO / Alamy Stock Photo; **8.06:** Monika Hrdinova / Dembinsky Photo Associates / Alamy Stock Photo; **8.07:** The Print Collector / Alamy Stock Photo; **8.10:** Michel Arnault / Alamy Stock Photo; **8.11:** Nicolle Rager Fuller, National Science Foundation; **8.12:** Eddie Gerald / Alamy Stock Photo; **8.13:** Thomas O'Neill/NurPhoto via Getty Images; **8.14:** blickwinkel / Alamy Stock Photo; **8.15:** Ekin Yalgin / Alamy Stock Photo; **8.18:** robertharding / Alamy Stock Photo; **8.19:** Brian Overcast / Alamy Stock Photo; **8.20:** Ben Trumble; **8.21:** © British Library Board. All Rights Reserved / Bridgeman Images; **8.22:** Dylan Garcia Photography / Alamy Stock Photo; **8.24:** Christian Kober 1 / Alamy Stock Photo; **8.25:** AsiaDreamPhoto / Alamy Stock Photo; **8.26:** Tuca Vieira; **8.1 review:** Dylan Garcia Photography / Alamy Stock Photo

Other: Fig. 8.8: Drazen Tomic, *The Human Past*, 4th Edition, by Chris Scarre, published by Thames & Hudson. Reused by permission of Thames & Hudson. **Fig. 8.16:** Used by permission, © SIL

International. *Ethnologue: Languages of the World.* Twenty-sixth edition. Dallas, Texas: SIL International. 2023. Online version: http://www.ethnologue.com. Further redistribution prohibited without permission.

Chapter 9

Photos: Chapter-opening photos, clockwise from top: **9.COa:** Norman Price / Alamy Stock Photo; **9.COb:** Richard Levine / Alamy Stock Photo; **9.COc:** The Print Collector / Alamy Stock Photo; **9.COd:** ML Harris / Alamy Stock Photo; **9.COe:** The British Museum / Trustees of the British Museum; **9.01:** Ashanté M. Reese; **9.02:** Fruth, B., Hohmann, G. Food Sharing across Borders. Hum Nat 29, 91–103 (2018). https://doi.org/10.1007/s12110-018-9311-9; **9.03a:** Hemis / Alamy Stock Photo; **9.03b:** Richard Ellis / Alamy Stock Photo; **9.03c:** Mike Goldwater / Alamy Stock Photo; **9.05:** Baz Ratner/Reuters/Alamy Sotck Photo; **9.06:** E. Assaf et al, Shaped stone balls were used for bone marrow extraction at Lower Paleolithic Qesem Cave, Israel, https://doi.org/10.1371/journal.pone.0230972; **9.08:** Oramstock / Alamy Stock Photo; **9.09:** Avalon.red/Alamy Stock Photo; **9.11:** ML Harris / Alamy Stock Photo; **9.13b:** The British Museum / Trustees of the British Museum; **9.14:** Danita Delimont / Alamy Stock Photo; **9.15:** Lewis Hine/National Archives; **9.16:** Bettmann Archive/Getty Images; **9.17:** Peter Marshall/Alamy Stock Photo; **9.18:** AAMIR QURESHI/AFP via Getty Images; **9.20:** lucky-photographer / Alamy Stock Photo; **9.21:** WENN Rights Ltd / Alamy Stock Photo; **9.22:** Eitan Simanor / Alamy Stock Photo; **9.26:** The Print Collector / Alamy Stock Photo; **9.27:** Janzig/USA/Alamy Stock Photo; **9.28:** Jean Williamson / Alamy Stock Photo; **9.29:** American Museum of Natural History; **9.30:** Kent Raney / Alamy Stock Photo; **9.31:** Illinois State Museum; **9.32:** World History Archive / Alamy Stock Photo; **9.33:** Roberto Machado Noa/Getty Images; **9.34a:** Norman Price / Alamy Stock Photo; **9.34b:** Richard Levine / Alamy Stock Photo; **9.35:** David Mercado/Reuters/Alamy Stock Photo; **9.37:** GUILLERMO LEGARIA/AFP via Getty Images; **9.38:** Courtesy of Andres Gonzalez Aguilera; **9.1 review:** ML Harris / Alamy Stock Photo; **9.3 review:** The Print Collector / Alamy Stock Photo; **9.4 review:** Norman Price / Alamy Stock Photo

Other: Fig. 9.4: Adapted from Yellen, J. E. 1979. "Cultural Patterning in Faunal Remains: Evidence from the !Kung Bushmen." In *Experimental Archaeology*, edited by D. Ingersoll, J. E. Yellen, and W. Macdonald. With permission from John E. Yellen. **Fig. 9.7:** From Sahlins, Marshall. 1972. *Stone Age Economics.* London: Routledge. Copyright © 1972 by Marshall Sahlins. Reproduced by permission of Taylor and Francis Group, LLC, a division of Informa plc. **Fig. 9.10:** Used with permission of University of Chicago Press – Journals, from Schweizer, Thomas. 1997. "Embeddedness of Ethnographic Cases: A Social Networks Perspective." *Current Anthropology* 38(5): 739-760; permission conveyed through Copyright Clearance Center, Inc. **Fig. 9.25:** Adapted from Nakassis, Dimitri, William A. Parkinson, and Michael L. Galaty. 2011. "Redistribution in Aegean Palatial Societies. Redistributive Economies from a Theoretical and Cross-Cultural Perspective." *American Journal of Archaeology* 115(2): 177-184. Courtesy Archaeological Institute of America and the American Journal of Archaeology.

Chapter 10

Photos: Chapter-opening photos, clockwise from top: **10.COa:** Danita Delimont / Alamy Stock Photo; **10.COb:** Danita Delimont / Alamy Stock Photo; **10.COc:** agefotostock / Alamy Stock Photo; **10.COd:** Tim Graham / Alamy Stock Photo; **10.01:** Fundación de Antropología Forense de Guatemala (FAFG); **10.02:** Danita

Delimont / Alamy Stock Photo; **10.03a:** agefotostock / Alamy Stock Photo; **10.05:** Simon Kachenge; **10.06:** Everett Collection; **10.07a:** Paolo Bona / Alamy Stock Photo; **10.07b:** imageBROKER / Alamy Stock Photo; **10.08:** Kent Raney / Alamy Stock Photo; **10.09:** dpa picture alliance / Alamy Stock Photo; **10.10:** Cam Cardow, Courtesy of Cagle Cartoons **10.11:** Jens Meierhenrich; **10.12:** Tim Graham / Alamy Stock Photo; **10.13:** Danita Delimont / Alamy Stock Photo; **10.14:** Larsen, C.S., Griffin, M.C., Hutchinson, D.L. et al. Frontiers of Contact: Bioarchaeology of Spanish Florida. Journal of World Prehistory 15, 69–123 (2001). https://doi.org/10.1023/A:1011180303211; **10.15:** Public Domain; **10.16:** Zaneta Thayer; **10.17:** Rebecca E. Rollins / PIH; **10.18:** © 2006 Seth M. Holmes; **10.19:** Gareth Dewar / Alamy Stock Photo; **10.20:** Prisma by Dukas Presseagentur GmbH / Alamy Stock Photo; **10.21:** Rushohora, N.A. Facts and Fictions of the Majimaji War Graves in Southern Tanzania. Afr Archaeol Rev 36, 145–159 (2019). https://doi.org/10.1007/s10437-019-09324-2; **10.22:** Christopher Pillitz/In Pictures via Getty Images Images; **10.23:** Carwil Bjork-James; **10.4 review:** Tim Graham / Alamy Stock Photo

Other: p. 286, left: Reprinted from *Geoforum* 37(1), Michael K. Steinberg, Carrie Height, Rosemary Mosher, et al. "Mapping Massacres: GIS and State Terror in Guatemala," pp. 62-68, Copyright 2006, with permission from Elsevier. **Fig. 10.3b:** Used with permission of John Wiley & Sons, from Kissel, Marc, and Nam C. Kim. 2019. "The Emergence of Human Warfare: Current Perspectives." *American Journal of Physical Anthropology* 168 Suppl 67: 141-163; permission conveyed through Copyright Clearance Center, Inc. **Fig. 10.4:** Adapted from Wendorf, Fred. 1968. *The Prehistory of Nubia*, Volume 2. Southern Methodist University Press. With permission from the Fred Wendorf Estate. **Fig. 10.14a:** Courtesy of American Museum of Natural History. **Fig. 10.14b:** Adapted from Larsen, Clark Spencer, Mark C. Griffin, Dale L. Hutchinson, et al. 2001. "Frontiers of Contact: Bioarchaeology of Spanish Florida." *Journal of World Prehistory* 15(1): 69-123. https://doi.org/10.1023/A:1011180303211. With permission from Mark C. Griffin and Northern Illinois University.

Chapter 11

Photos: Chapter-opening photos, clockwise from top: **11.COa:** akg-images / Werner Forman; **11.COb:** AB Forces News Collection / Alamy Stock Photo; **11.COc:** Uno surgery erwin/Shutterstock; **11.COd:** Science History Images / Alamy Stock Photo;**11.COe:** Ben Trumble; **11.01:** Tetra Images / Alamy Stock Photo; **11.02:** AB Forces News Collection / Alamy Stock Photo; **11.04:** Roy LANGSTAFF / Alamy Stock Photo; **11.05:** Alexandra Brewis; **11.06:** ZUMA Press, Inc. / Alamy Stock Photo; **11.07:** Janine Wiedel Photolibrary / Alamy Stock Photo; **11.09:** Image Professionals GmbH / Alamy Stock Photo; **11.10:** Tuul and Bruno Morandi / Alamy Stock Photo; **11.12:** Science History Images / Alamy Stock Photo; **11.14:** Barry Hewlett; **11.15:** Images of Africa Photobank / Alamy Stock Photo; **11.16:** Ben Trumble; **11.17:** Rebecca Bliege Bird;**11.18:** Randy Haas; **11.19:** akg-images / Werner Forman; **11.20:** Uno surgery erwin/Shutterstock; **11.21:** anthony asael / Alamy Stock Photo; **11.23:** Alexandra Brewis; **11.24:** Christina Torres; **11.26:** Courtesy of Madawi Al-Rasheed; **11.27:** Michele Burgess / Alamy Stock Photo; **11.4 review:** Alexandra Brewis

Other: Fig. 11.3: Adapted from Ainsworth, Claire. 2015. "Sex Redefined." *Nature* 518: 288-291. https://doi.org/10.1038/518288a. Reproduced with permission from Springer Nature. **Fig. 11.18:** Reprinted with permission from AAAS. Haas, Randall, James Watson, Tammy Buonasera, et al. 2020. "Female Hunters of the Early Americas." *Science Advances* 6(45). © The Authors, some rights reserved; exclusive licensee AAAS. This work is distributed under a CC BY-NC 4.0 License (http://creativecommons.org/licenses/by-nc/4.0/). **Fig. 11.22:** Reprinted from *The American Journal of Clinical Nutrition* 102(5), Alison Tumilowicz, Jean-Pierre Habicht, Gretel Pelto, et al. "Gender Perceptions Predict Sex Differences in Growth Patterns of Indigenous Guatemalan Infants and Young Children," pp. 1249-1258, Copyright 2015, with permission from American Society for Nutrition. **Fig. 11.25:** Adapted from Taylor, Jerome, 2020. "Global Gender Gap Report 2020." Last modified February 20, 2020. https://commons.wikimedia.org/wiki/File:Global_Gender_Gap_Report_2020.png. The copyright holder of this file allows anyone to use it for any purpose, provided that the copyright holder is properly attributed. Redistribution, derivative work, commercial use, and all other use is permitted.

Chapter 12

Photos: Chapter-opening photos, clockwise from top: **12.COa:** John Henshall / Alamy Stock Photo; **12.COb:** IanDagnall Computing / Alamy Stock Photo; **12.COc:** Paul Rushton / Alamy Stock Photo;**12.COd:** imagebroker / Alamy Stock Photo; **12.01:** Dinah Hannaford; **12.02:** Brisbane, Aus.: Edmund Gregory, Government Printer, 1897; **12.03:** Jules Scheele; **12.04a:** IanDagnall Computing / Alamy Stock Photo; **12.04b:** Mark Green / Alamy Stock Photo; **12.04c:** Album / Alamy Stock Photo; **12.05:** Riza Azhari / Sijori Images/ZUMAPRESS/Newscom; **12.06:** Jani-Markus Häsä / Alamy Stock Photo; **12.07:** uskarp / Alamy Stock Photo; **12.08:** Jun Kamata; **12.09:** INTERFOTO / Alamy Stock Photo; **12.12a:** Charlotte Thege / Alamy Stock Photo; **12.12b:** John Henshall / Alamy Stock Photo; **12.13:** AP Photo/Laurent Rebours; Table **12.3a:** imagebroker / Alamy Stock Photo; Table **12.3b:** Malcolm Schuyl / Alamy Stock Photo; Table **12.3c:** Steve Bloom Images / Alamy Stock Photo; Table **12.3d:** Paul Maguire / Alamy Stock Photo; **12.14:** Avalon.red / Alamy Stock Photo; **12.16:** Punit Paranjpe/Reuters/Redux; **12.19:** Beate Apfelbeck; **12.21:** LEO RAMIREZ/AFP/Getty Images; **12.22:** Paul Rushton / Alamy Stock Photo; **12.23:** Steve Allen Travel Photography / Alamy Stock Photo; **12.24:** Laura M. Ahearn Annual Review of Anthropology 2001 30:1, 109-137; **12.25:** xPACIFICA/Redux; **12.26:** Julia Pauli; **12.27:** imageBROKER / Alamy Stock Photo; **12.28:** peter dench / Alamy Stock Photo; **12.29:** David Bokuchava / Alamy Stock Photo; **12.4 review:** Julia Pauli

Other: Fig. 12.11: Adapted from Schacht, Ryan, and Karen L. Kramer. 2019. "Are We Monogamous? A Review of the Evolution of Pair-Bonding in Humans and Its Contemporary Variation Cross-Culturally." *Frontiers in Ecology and Evolution* 7. https://doi.org/10.3389/fevo.2019.00230. © 2019 Schacht and Kramer. This is an open-access article distributed under the terms of the Creative Commons Attribution License (CC BY). https://creativecommons.org/licenses/by/4.0/. **Fig. 12.14:** From Ember, C. R. et al., *Anthropology*, 13th Ed., © 2010. Reprinted by permission of Pearson Education, Inc. **Fig. 12.17:** Used with permission of The Royal Society, from Jordan, Fiona M., Russell D. Gray, Simon J. Greenhill, and Ruth Mace. 2009. "Matrilocal Residence Is Ancestral in Austronesian Societies." *Proceedings of the Royal Society of London. Series B: Biological Sciences* 276(1664): 1957-1964; permission conveyed through Copyright Clearance Center, Inc. **Fig. 12.18:** Adapted from Haak, Wolfgang, Guido Brandt, Hylke N. de Jong, et al. 2008. "Ancient DNA, Strontium Isotopes, and Osteological Analyses Shed Light on Social and Kinship Organization of the Later Stone Age." *PNAS* 105(47): 18226-18231. Copyright 2008 National Academy of Sciences, U.S.A. With permission from National Academy of Sciences, U.S.A. **Table 12.1:** From Schudson, Z. S., E. R. Dibble, and S. M. van Anders. 2023. "Sexual

Configurations Theory Interview Workbook." https://www.queensu.ca/psychology/van-anders-lab/sctworkbook.pdf. Adapted with permission from the authors.

Chapter 16

Photos: Chapter-opening photos, clockwise from top: **16.COa:** Cavan Images / Alamy Stock Photo; **16.COb:** Art Wager/Getty Images; **16.COc:** Ingolfur Juliusson/Reuters/Redux; **16.COd:** Nativestock.com/Marilyn Angel Wynn / Alamy Stock Photo **16.01:** Hilda Lloréns; **16.02:** USGS/Science Source; **16.04a:** KalypsoWorldPhotography / Alamy Stock Photo; **16.04b:** A.J. Faas;**16.05:** Anais Roque; **16.06:** Yuisa Rios/FEMA/AB Forces News Collection / Alamy Stock Photo;**16.07:** Margrét Hallmunds-dóttir; **16.08:** Ingolfur Juliusson /Reuters/Redux; **16.09a:** Nativestock.com/Marilyn Angel Wynn / Alamy Stock Photo; **16.09b:** Art Wager/Getty Images; **16.10:** Kena Betancur/Reuters/ Redux; **16.12:** Michelle Hansen; 16 A: Luke Dray/Getty Images; **16.13:** Svintage Archive / Alamy Stock Photo; 16.15a-b: Cavan Images / Alamy Stock Photo; **16.16:** Shim Harno / Alamy Stock Photo; **16.18:** Lee Cronk; 16.19a-c: Roy Rappaport Papers, Special Collections & Archives, UC San Diego; 16 B: Bonnie McCay; **16.20:** MB Photography/Getty Images; **16.21:** David Joles/Star Tribune via Getty Images; **16.22:** MARK RALSTON/AFP via Getty Images; **16.23:** EyePress/Newscom; **16.24:** ZUMA Press Inc / Alamy Stock Photo; **16.4 review:** David Joles/Star Tribune via Getty Images **Other:** **Fig. 16.17:** Adapted from Schwartz, Timothy. 2019. "Haiti Anthropology Brief: Cultural Materialist Cake of Culture." Schwartz Research Group. Last modified May 2, 2019. https:// timothyschwartzhaiti.com/cake-of-culture/. Reused with permission of the author. **American Anthropological Association Apology for Abuse and Exploitation of Indigenous Communities:** From American Anthropological Association. "AAA Apology to the Indigenous Community." November 17, 2021. https://www. americananthro.org/StayInformed/NewsDetail.aspx?ItemNumber=528239. Reproduced by permission of the American Anthropological Association. Not for sale or further reproduction.

INDEX

Note: A page number in *italics* refers to a figure, and a page number followed by *t* indicates a table.

A

abolition
    of anti-Black institutions, *420*, 420–21
    prison abolition movement, 426
abolition scholarship, 421
Aboriginal communities (Australia), 6
absolute dating methods, 36, 37*t*
Abu-Lughod, Lila, 340
Acheulean tools, 157*t*, 164, *164*
activist anthropology, 14, *15*, 475
acupuncture, 447, 449
adapids, *108*, 109
adaptations, 61
    to climate, *66*, 66–67
    to disease, *68*, 68–69, *69*, 436, 438
    to ultraviolet radiation, *67*, 67–68, *68*
adaptive radiation
    defined, 97
    of haplorhines, 96
    of *Homo* in Pleistocene, 125
    of platyrrhines, 98
adornment, *182*, 182–83
    of Neanderthals, 186
advantageous mutations, 60
Aegyptopithecus, *108*, 110, *111*
affinal kin, 354–56, 355*t*
Africa
    emergence of anatomically modern humans in, 64
    genetic diversity in, 64, 177, *177*
    migration of humans from, 64, 65–66
African Burial Ground, 396–97, *397*, 427
Afro-Puerto Rican communities, 463–64, *464*
afterlife, beliefs about, 381
Agbe-Davies, Anna, 401–3
agency
    private sexual activity and, 353
    of sex workers, 373
aggression, 286
    coalitionary, 287–88, 290, 292, 293
    See also violence
agricultural cooperatives, 278–79, *279*
agriculture
    development projects and, 306
    diseases emerging with, 434*t*, *437*
    emergence of states and, 235
    feudalism and, 238, *238*, 239

industrial farming, 266
    with large draft animals, 237
    large-scale in early cities, 236
    migrant labor in, 304, *304*
    in small egalitarian groups, 236
    small-scale innovations in, 482
    spread of languages and, 234, *234*
    transition to, 227, 230–33, *233*, 235, 236–37
    tribes and chiefdoms based on, 236
Ahearn, Laura, 369, *369*
Aka, equitable division of labor, 328, *329*
Akwesasne Mohawk Nation, *477*, 477–78, *478*
Alaska, Agayadan Village in, 360
Alim, Samy, 200
allele frequencies. *See* microevolution
alleles, 55, 57–58
Allen's rule, 67
alloparents, 92, 332
Al-Rasheed, Madawi, 340, *340*
Amazonian region
    Indigenous communities in, *26*, 26–27
    Waorani peaceful protest, 296, *296*
ambilocality, 364, *364*
American Anthropological Association (AAA)
    apology for extractive research, 486
    ethical principles of, 16, 17*t*
American Sign Language (ASL), 199, 208–9
amino acids, 54
anatomically modern humans, 173–78, 173*t*, *174*
    emergence as a species, 64
    key fossil finds, *175*, 175–76
    See also Homo sapiens
ancestry, 51–52, *52*
ancient DNA, 41, *65*, 65–66, 103
    medieval plague and, 433
The Ancient One, 396
androgyny, 322
angiosperm–primate radiation hypothesis, 109
Anthropocene epoch, 481
anthropology
    defined, 3
    diversity within, 46–47, *47*, 489
    subfields of, *4*, 4–10
anti-racism, 401, 402, 411, 412, 425–27
apes, 95, 98
    geographic distribution, 99, *99*
    Miocene evolution of, *108*, 125

threatened with extinction, 113
    See also specific apes
Appalachia
    [aks] used in, 201, *201*
    dental care unaffordable in, 456, *456*
applied anthropology, 14–15, 475
arbitrariness of symbols, 203
arboreal adaptations
    in hominins, 122, 136, 137, 138, 141
    lacking in *Homo erectus*, 160
arboreal primates, 89–90
archaeological context, 35
archaeological features, 33, *33*
archaeological record, 5
    site preservation and, 35
archaeological survey, 33, *33*
archaeology
    dating methods in, 36, 37*t*, 105, 128
    defined, 5
    gender differences in practice of, 324, *324*
    Indigenous and descendant rights in, 45, *45*, 46, *46*
    Indigenous researchers in, 47, *47*
    material culture and, 7
    methodological specialties in, 38
    postprocessual, *39*, 39–40
    practice of, 33–40
    processual, 38–39, *39*, 40
    sexualities depicted in, 349–51, *350*
    teeth in, 8–9, *9*, 103
archaic *Homo sapiens*, 165–66
"Ardi," 137, *137*, 151
Ardipithecus
    Australopithecus descended from, 138, *138*
    habitat of, 137, *137*
Ardipithecus kadabba, *124*, 136
Ardipithecus ramidus, *124*, 136–37, *137*, 151
art, *179*, 179–80, *180*
    Upper Paleolithic, 226, *226*
Arthur G. Dozier School, lost boys, 14–15, *15*, 44, 311
articulators, 198–99, *199*
artifacts, 5
    controlled by foreign interests, 151, *151*
    controlling use and preservation of, 45
    as social constructions, 39
ascribed status, 238, 239
Asfaw, Berhane, *151*
[ask]/[aks], *201*, 201–2
assigned sex, 316, 317, 320*t*
    limitations of, 318–19, *318–19*

assimilation, forced, 300, 301, 421
assimilation model, 173
assortative mating, 366, 367
Atalay, Sonya, *46*
Athreya, Sheela, 4, *5*
atlatl, 180, *180*, 332
audiovisual recordings, 32, *32*
Austin, J. L., 204–5
Australia. *See* Indigenous Australians
australopithecines, *124*, *138*, 138–41
    ancestral to genus *Homo*, 125, 144
    defined, 122
    evolved from bipedal apes, 125
    Homo naledi and, 122, 123
    radiation of, *138*, 139–41
Australopithecus afarensis, *140*, 140–41, 144, *330*
Australopithecus africanus, 141, *141*, 144, 330
Australopithecus anamensis, 139–40
Australopithecus deyiremeda, 140
Australopithecus garhi, 140, 144, 146
Australopithecus platyops, 140
Australopithecus sediba, 141, *141*, 157
autism, 441
autoethnography, 354, 355, 412
avoidance speech, 355–56, *355t*
Ayurveda, 454, *455*
Aztec market system, 259–60, *260*

B
baboons, 88, 92, 98, *98*
    confronting predators, 225, *225*
bacteria, 394
Bahasa gay, 352
Bahrain, migrant workers in, 305, *305*
Baker-Bell, April, 202
balanced reciprocity, 254, *254*
Baldwin, Daryl, 309–10
Ball, Helen, 12
Banaba (Ocean Island), 21–22, *22*, 43, *43*
band, 236
barefoot running, 135
Barnett, Kristen, 47
barter
    markets based on, 258–59, 278, *278*
    in recession of late 2000s, 254
base camps, *252*, 252–53
bases in DNA, 54, *54*
    mutations and, 58, *59*
    similarity of all humans and, 66
Baugh, John, 217, *217*
BCE (before the common era), 36
Beach, Frank, 347
Becker, Anne, 265
Begay, David, *47*
Behar, Ruth, 28–29, *29*, 44
Bejarano, Carolina Alonso, 307–8
Beliso-De Jesús, Aisha M., 419–20

Bellecourt, Vernon, *16*
Benedict, Ruth, 411
Benn Torres, Jada, 51–52, *52*, 65
Berger, Lee, 121, 123, *123*
Bergmann's rule, 66–67
Beringia, 234
big toes
    nonopposable in bipeds, 133
    opposable, *88*, 90, 91, 137
bilophodont molars, 98, *98*
binary gender schemas, 316–17, *320t*, 321
Binford, Lewis, 38–39, *39*
binocular stereoscopic vision, 90, 91
binomial nomenclature, 93
bioarchaeology, 8
biological anthropology, 4, *5*
    culture and, 6–7
    practice of, 40–43
    teeth in, 9, *9*
biological diversity, 4
biological samples, and community values, 45–46, *46*
biological species, 128
    early humans and, 190
biomedicalization, 454
biomedicine, 433, 449
    building trust between patient and healer, 453
    commodification of, 454–57, *455*, *456*
    distancing patient from healer, 452, *452*, 458–59
    informal access to, 456–57, *457*
    power differentials and, 453
    See also vaccination
biopower, 457–58
bipedalism
    anatomical markers of, 131–33, *132*
    in australopithecines, 138, 140, *140*
    benefits and costs, 133, *134*, 134–35, 438
    of earliest hominins, 131–35, *134*
    of *Homo erectus*, 160–61, *161*
    in Miocene apes, 125
bipedal primates, 89
    human distinctiveness, 103
BISINDO (Indonesian Sign Language), 208–10, *209*
Bjork-James, Carwil, 311, *311*
Black, Steven, 195–96
Black Codes, 418
Black Death, 14th-century, 431, *432*, 433, 437
Black Englishes
    [aks] in, 201–2
    code-switching and, 217
    of Disney villains, 217
Black Languages, 202, 217
black market, in Cuba, 273

Black people, as ethnonym, 419
Black people in U.S.
    health disparities of, 410
    near hazardous waste facilities, 473
Black Radical Congress, 425, *425*
Black women, obstetric racism and, 412–13, *413*
blades, 180, 181
Blakey, Michael, 396, 426–27
Bliege Bird, Rebecca, 332
blood pressure, 414, *414*
blood types, 57–58, 65, *65*
blue eyes, 58–59
Blumenbach, Johann, 406, *406*
Boas, Franz, 16, 44, 411
BODIES exhibit, 385
body
    commodification of, 264–66, *265*
    moving and holding as gender marker, 323, *323*
bodybuilding competitions, *265*
body image in women, 265
    "fat" and, 211, *211*, 458
body projects, 265, *265*
body shape, and climate, *66*, 66–67
body size
    diet of primate and, 106
    of extinct primates, 105
    global human increase in, 265
body weight, secular trend in, 75
Body Worlds exhibit, 385, *385*
Boellstorff, Tom, 25–26, *26*
Bolivia
    exploitation of natural gas, 311
    personalistic healers in, 449, *449*
    privatization of water, 311
    water insecurity, 275, *275*
    Zona Sur self-governance, 243–44
bonobos, 95, 99, *101*, 101–2, 111
    cognitive abilities, 107, *107*
    estrus in, 362, *362*
    food sharing in, *251*
    Kanzi creating signs, 198
    relation to humans, 129
    sexual behavior, 362
Boroditsky, Lera, 212–13, *213*
bottlenecking, genetic, 62, *63*, 65–66
bounded rationality, 266–67
Bourdieu, Pierre, 264–65
brachiation, 89, 100
brain death, 391
brain development, and meat, 103
brain regions, 162–63
brain size
    of australopithecines, 139
    climate fluctuations and, 170, *170*
    dietary transitions and, 170, *171*
    of hominins increasing 2.8 mya, 131
    of *Homo erectus*, *162*, 162–63, *163*

of Middle Pleistocene *Homo*, 166, 170, *170*, *171*
of modern humans, 162, *163*
of primates, *88*, 91, 107–8
Brazil
anti-Black police violence in, 420–21
ascribing racial identities in, 424
fortified enclaves in São Paulo, 245, *245*
racialized census in, *417*, 418
brideservice, *362*, 363
bridewealth, *362*, 362–63, 370, 480
Briggs, Charles, 458
Briody, Elizabeth, 15
Brown, Daniel, *414*
Bryan, Billy, *485*
Bryant, Elmore, *15*
Buddhist family altar, 387–88, *388*
built structures, early production of, 181, *181*
burial rituals, 180, 186
first apparently intentional, 378–80
first for anatomically modern humans, *380*, 380–81
green burials, 385
Neanderthals and, *379*, 379–80
social stratification and, 237
in United States, 385
See also mortuary practices
Burke, Brian, 278, 475
Bush, George W., 296
bushbabies, 96, 102
butchering
cannibalism and, 288
food sharing and, *252*, 252–53, *253*
by Middle Pleistocene *Homo*, 165, 167–68, *168*
by Neanderthals, 185
by Pliocene hominins, 144, 146, *146*
techniques of, 39, *39*
See also hunting
Butler, Howard Crosby, *38*
Butler, Judith, 316

C

cacao beans
in Aztec society, 260
at Chaco Canyon, 270, *270*
Cahokia, *270*, 270–71, *271*, 295
Caldeira, Teresa, 245, *245*
call center, international, *263*, 263–64
Cambodia, "hostess bars" in, 373, *373*
canine blunting, 134, *134*
canine teeth
of apes vs. humans, 134, *134*, 136, 137
of australopithecines, 139, *139*
sexual dimorphism and, 106
cannibalism
in early *Homo* species, 288, *289*
of Wari' dead, 382, *382*

canon, 44
canonical self-interest model, 266
capitalism
biomedicalization and, 454–55
cultural capital in, 264–66, *265*
defined, 260
disasters creating opportunities for, 472–73
gifts and exchanges of labor in, 274
globalized, 263–64, 271
industrial, 261, *261*, 262
neoliberal, 262, 272, 276
postindustrial, 264, 487
sustainability and, 487
transitions to, 260–62, *261*
See also privatization
Caribbean people
genetic ancestry of, 51–52, *52*, 65
managing hurricane risks, 470
See also Cuba
Carneiro, Robert, 235, 290
cassava, 13
Çatalhöyük, 39, *39*, 44, *232*, 232–33, *233*, 235
catarrhines, *95*, 97, *97*, 98
Aegyptopithecus as ancestor of, 110
cave dwelling, and food sharing, 252–53, *253*
cave etchings, 180, *180*
cave paintings, 179, *179*
CE (common era), 36
cells, 53, *53*
cemeteries, 381, 383, 385
census, *417*, 417–18
centralized government
in complex societies, 239, 242
of first cities, 236
of Teotihuacan, 221, 222
cercopithecoids, *95*, 98
Chaco Canyon, 268–70, *269*, *270*
charitable donations, 254–55, *255*
chattel slavery, 261. *See also* slavery
Checker, Melissa, 473–74, *474*, 476
cheek-pouch monkeys, 98, *99*
chiefdoms, 236
Hawaiian, 239–40, *240*
childbirth
biomedicalization of, 454
bipedalism and, 438
pain of, *441*, 441–42, *442*
racism in experience of, 412–13, *413*
childcare
by Aka men, 328, *329*
of Hadza in Tanzania, 42, *42*
in Papua New Guinea, 327
weak reciprocity and, 276
women's responsibility for, 329
child development
developmental plasticity, 72–73
growth, 75–77, 337

growth faltering, 336–37
trauma, 77, 79
child labor, in agricultural societies, 231
child soldiers, 79, *79*
chimpanzees, 88, 89, *95*, 101–3
anthropomorphizing of, *87*
coalitionary aggression in, 287–88, 293
cognitive abilities, 107–8
evolutionary origin of, 111
genetics of humans and, 101, *101*, 129
geographic distribution, *99*
grief apparently displayed by, 378
healing plants used by, *449*
HIV acquired from meat of, 436
learned behaviors in, 148, *148*
life history, *92*
male violence in, 298
threatened by human encroachment, 112–13
chin, 161, 167, 174
China
marriage corners in, 368, *368*
QingMing Festival, 388, *389*
socialism with markets in, 275
Chinese American funerals, 382–83, *383*
Chinese dynasties, 240, *241*
cholera in Orinoco Delta, 458, *458*
choppers, 107, 146, 155, 168
chromosomes, 54–55, *55*
circulating discourses, 211
cisgender people, 317, 320*t*
cities
emergence of, *235*, 235–36
fortified enclaves in, 245, *245*
inequalities in, *244*, 244–45, *245*
reliance on massive systems, 224
social stratification in, 236–37, *237*, 242
Teotihuacan, 221–23, *222*, *223*, 230, 244, 245
warfare in archaeological record, 290
citizens, 262, 263
Civil Rights Movement, 401
environmental justice and, 477
clavicle, 90
Claw, Katrina, 47, *47*
climate, and body shape, *66*, 66–67
climate change
impacting the most vulnerable, 487
increasing natural disasters, 473
Indigenous knowledge and, 487
Pacific island nations and, 488, *488*
as threat to primates, 113
unsustainable practices and, 487
climate changes in past
Middle Pleistocene *Homo* and, 171, *172*
spread of modern humans and, 177
transition to agriculture and, 227
See also cooling climate
climate fluctuations, and hominin brain

size, 170, *170*
clinal variation, 65, *65*
clothing
    as gender marker, 322, *322*
    invented by *Homo sapiens*, 181
    Neanderthals and, 185
    parasitic insects and, 435
clumping, 128–29
coalitionary aggression, 287
    in chimpanzees, 287–88, 293
    warfare as, 290, 292, 293
    See also group violence
Cobb, W. Montague, *410*, 410–11, 426–27
code-switching, 217
codominant alleles, 57–58
coevolution, 71–72, *73*
    of humans and diseases, 438
    of humans and microbiome, 438–39
cognate, 234
cognitive ability
    behavioral modernity and, 178
    brain of *Homo erectus* and, 162–63
    brain size of primates and, 107–8
    of *Homo* species, 125
    See also brain size
collarbone, 90
Colombia, bartering markets in, 278, *278*
colonialism
    capitalism and, 261
    complex societies and, 300
    current global system and, 302
    decolonizing methodologies and, 44
    defined, 22
    diseases in European rise of, 434t
    European patriarchy and, 334
    as form of imperialism, 300
    genocide in North America and,
        294–95
    health disparities and, 79, *301*, 301–4
    impacts on Banaban people, 21–22, *22*,
        43, *43*
    Indigenous societies and, 483
    international development as, 306
    racial typologies and, 407
    rights of descendant groups and, 45
    sexualizing "native" peoples, 347, *347*
    See also imperialism; settler colonialism
coloniality, 303–4
    anthropologists' research practices and,
        307–8
    Whiteness in Japan and, 416
colorism, *416*, 416–17, *417*
color photography, 417, *417*
color vision, 90, 97
commodification
    of basic rights in neoliberalism, 304
    of the body, 264–66, *265*
    in capitalist systems, 260
    cultural capital and, 264–66, *265*

defined, 260
    of health, 454–57, *455*, *456*
    of physical and emotional intimacies, 373
    of social lives in neoliberalism, 276
common-pool resource, 261
common-pool resource institution, 261
community-based participatory research
    (CBPR), 44
community food stores, 249–50
community gardens, 250, *250*, 273, 279
comparative approaches, 11–12
    to primate evolution, 105–8
compassionate cannibalism of Wari', 382,
    382
complex societies. *See* social complexity
Conklin, Beth, 382, *382*
consanguineal kin, 354–55
constituents of language, 200
consumer goods, commodification of,
    264–65, *265*
consumerism, 306
consumers, 262, 263
cooking, 168–69, *169*
    brain size and, 170, *171*
    Homo floresiensis and, 188
    by Neanderthals, 185
    See also fire
cooling climate, 125, *126*, 133, 142
    fire and, 169
    Homo erectus adapted to, 158
    hunting of herbivores and, 165
    Middle Pleistocene *Homo* and, 167
    small island *Homo* species and, 188
    warming in Holocene, 227
cooperation
    along gender lines, 252
    in caring for sickness, 441
    in chimpanzees, 102–3
    food sharing and, 251–52
    human culture and, 149
    in hunter-gatherer societies, 226, *226*
    kinship and, 223–24
cooperative parenting, 332
coproduced knowledge, 13, 29, 44
cores, 145, *145*, 146
corn. *See* maize (corn)
co-sleeping, 12, *12*
cosmetic surgery
    in Brazil, 334–35
    in Korea, 454, *454*
    as medical pursuit of beauty, 454
    in Saudi Arabia, 340
cosmology, 223
    of Cahokia, 271
cousin marriage, 357, 367, *367*
COVID-19 pandemic
    animal–human transmission, 115
    color-based oximeters in, 417
    foreign language terms about, 200

globalization of infectious disease and,
        438
    globally emerging strains of, 395
    migrant workers' risk of, 305
    minoritized groups dying from, 412
    Neanderthal ancestry and, 190
    vaccination hesitancy in, 452
    victim-blaming in, 458
    women staying home during, 329
craft specialization
    in Çatalhöyük, 233
    in complex societies, 239
    food surpluses and, 236
cranial anatomy
    of *Homo erectus*, 161, *162*, 166
    of *Homo floresiensis*, 189
    of *Homo sapiens*, 166, 173–74, *174*
    of Middle Pleistocene *Homo*, 166,
        166–67, 172, *172*
    of Neanderthals, *185*
cranial capacity, and cognitive abilities,
    107–8
cranial trauma, in Çatalhöyük, 233
cranial vault, 161
craniometry, 407, 408. *See also* skulls
creaky voice, 323
cremation
    Hindu practices, *381*, 381–82
    in United States, 385
Cretaceous period, *105*, 109
Cretton, Viviane, 422–23
criminality, discredited theories of,
    408
Crittenden, Alyssa, 42, *42*
Cronk, Lee, 480
cross-cousin marriage, 357, 367, *367*
cross-cultural studies, 11–12
crossing over, 56, *56*
cross-species comparisons, 11–12
Cruz-Torres, Maria, 14, *14*
cryptocurrency, 264
Cuba
    hurricane risks in, 470
    redistributive economy, 272–73, *273*
    religious and spiritual healing in, 28
cultural anthropology, 6–7, *7*
    practice of, 23–29
    teeth as seen in, 8, *8*
cultural capital, 264–66, *265*
cultural ecology, 479
cultural learning, 148–49
cultural materialism, *479*, 479–80
cultural relativism, 11, 23
cultural themes, 25
cultural transmission, *148*, 148–49
culture, 6, *6*
    of colonized people, 301
    microevolution and, 69–72
cumulative culture, 149

cusps, 98, *98*

D

dairying traditions, 71, *71*, *72*
Dakota Access Pipeline, 488
Dani in New Guinea
    endemic warfare, *292*, 292–93
    grief, 386–87, *387*
Dart, Raymond, 149, 151
Darwin, Charles, 60, 149, 407, 408
Darwin, Leonard, 407
Darwin's finches, *60*, 60–61
data sovereignty, 46, *46*, 47
dating methods, 36, 37t, 105, 128
Davis, Dána-Ain, 412–13, *413*
Dawn Ape, 110
Day, Caroline Bond, 411
Day, Sharon, *489*
Dead Birds (film), 292, *292*
dead bodies, study of, 392–96
    ethical and legal issues, 396–97
dead incorporated into life, 387–91
    Buddhist family altar, 387–88, *388*
    Día de los Muertos, *389*, 389–90
    Malagasy in Madagascar and, 390, *390*
    QingMing Festival, 388, *389*
    trophy heads, 390–91, *391*
death
    animals' responses to, 378, *379*
    determining the moment of, 391
    full comprehension emerging, 378–80
    "home death" movement, 385
    medical aid in, 391–92
    of migrants crossing Mexico–U.S.
        border, 377–78, *378*, 397, *397*
    See also burial rituals; mortuary
        practices
decanonization, 44
decedent, 393
decoding language, 203–4, 215–17
decolonization, 307–8, 309
    activist anthropology and, 475
    defined, 307
    justice systems and, 243
decolonizing methodologies, 44
dehumanization, 296, *296*
deindustrialization, 261
De León, Jason, 377–78, *378*, 397
deleterious mutations, 60
Deloria, Ella, 16
Deloria, Vine, Jr., 16, *16*, 483
DeLugan, Robin Maria, 242
democratic governance, 242
    urban self-governance, 245
dendrochronology, 37t
Denisovans, 186, *186*, *187*, 188
    mating with *Homo sapiens*, 188, *189*,
        189–90, *190*, *191*
Densmore, Frances, *30*

dental calculus
    phytoliths in, 259
    poplar and mold in, 450
dental care
    13,000 years ago, 440, *441*
    unaffordable in Appalachia, 456, *456*
dental decay
    in agricultural societies, 232
    in Çatalhöyük, 233
    in commodified health systems, 456
dental disease, in early humans, 433, 435
dentition, 8
    of apes vs. humans, 134, *134*, *139*
    of australopithecines, 138–39, *139*
    generalized, 90, *91*
    for omnivorous human diets, 11
    See also teeth
derived traits
    defined, 88
    of haplorhines, 96
    of primates, 88, *88*
descendant communities, 6
    biological samples and, 45–46
    excavated materials and, 45, *45*, 46, *46*
    as research stakeholders, 13
desert taphonomy, 377
development, as form of colonialism, 306
developmental adaptations, 73, *73*
developmental plasticity, 72–77, 411
development projects, 305–7
DeWitte, Sharon, 431, 433, *433*
Día de los Muertos (Day of the Dead), *389*,
    389–90
diagnosis, 441
    communication and, 444, *444*
diarchy, 336
diaspora
    defined, 489
    Puerto Rican, 489
diastema, 134, *134*, *139*
diets
    of australopithecines, 139
    brain size and, 170, *171*
    of hominins vs. apes, 131, 133–34, *134*
    human dentition and, 11
    of Middle Pleistocene *Homo*, 167
    of paranthropines, 142
    primate teeth and, 90, 106
    Spanish missions in Americas and, 301
    See also meat eating
Dill, LeConté J., *413*
dimples, 57, *57*, 62
Dinknesh ("Lucy"), 140, *140*, 141, 151
disamenities, in minoritized communities,
    402–3
disaster
    archaeology of, 468–71
    defined, 464
    resilience in, 467–68, *468*

vulnerability to, *466*, 466–67, *467*
disaster anthropology, 465–66
disaster capitalism, 472–73
disease, 440, *440*
    adaptations to, 68, 68–69, *69*
    changes in human societies and, 433,
        434t–35t, 435–38
    colonialism in Americas and, 300, 310
    evolution of caring behavior for, 440–41,
        441
    stigmatized, *445*, 445–46
Disney animation, language varieties in,
    216–17, *217*
diurnal primates, 88
divergence from common ancestor, 130
diverse human phenotypes. *See*
    adaptations
diversity within anthropology, 46–47, *47*, 489
Dmanisi, *159*, 159–60
DNA
    chimp similarity to humans, 129
    of Denisovans, 186, *187*, 188
    epigenetic changes to, *77*, 77–79, *78*, 302
    identifying genocide victims, 285
    interbreeding of *Homo* species and,
        188–90, *189*
    mitochondrial, 53, 176, *187*, 189, 231
    molecular clock method, 130
    mutations in, 58–60, *59*
    Native American remains, 396
    of Neanderthals, 184, 185, 186, *187*, 188
    in nucleus, 53
    past marriage practices and, 364–65, *365*
    protein synthesis and, 54–55
    samples shared without consent, 46, *46*
    from skeletal or fossil remains, 41, *65*,
        65–66, 103, 433
    structure of, 54, *54*
    of tuberculosis strains, 394–95
DNA methylation, *78*, 78–79
DNA replication, 55, *56*, 58, *59*
domestication, *228*, 228–30
    diseases associated with, 434t, 436
    of large draft animals, 237
    of maize, *229*, 229–30
    starting in Holocene, 227
domestic mode of production, 262
dominant alleles, 57, *57*
dowry, *362*, 363
Dozier School, lost boys, 14–15, *15*, 44, 311
"drag queen," 325
dress. *See* clothing
drought, 470–71
Du Bois, W. E. B., 410, *410*
DuBois, Zachary, 324–25
Duke Lemur Center, 117, *117*
Dunnavant, Justin, *34*
Duranti, Alessandro, 202

E

early hominins, 136–44
   at Miocene–Pliocene boundary, 136–38, *138*
   Pliocene–Pleistocene radiation, *126, 138,* 139–44
   woodland/grassland habitats, 137, *137*
   See also australopithecines
East African Rift System, 127, *127*
Eaves, Lindsay, 121
ecofacts, 34
ecological knowledge, 463, 464
ecology, 478
economic behavior, 250, 251
economic system, revolt against, 272
ecotourism, *114,* 114–16, *115,* 117
Ecuador, living with volcano, *467,* 467–68
Edmonds, Alexander, 334–35
egalitarian social structures, 226, *226*
   in bands and tribes, 236
   Çatalhöyük and, 233
   defined, 328
   of small agriculturalist groups, 236
Ehrlich, Paul, 482
electron spin resonance (ESR), 37*t*
elephants, mourning, 378, *379*
elites
   in agricultural societies, 237, *237*
   capitalism and, 261–62
   control of resources by, 238
   defined, 222
   in early European science, 405–7
   in governance, 242
   in neoliberal economy, 262
   spectacular tombs of, 383–84, *384, 385*
   of Teotihuacan, 222
Elliott, Marina, 121, *122*
El Salvador, recreating national identity, 242, *243*
embodiment
   communication of distress and, 444, *444*
   defined, 336
   of gender inequality, *336,* 336–38, *337*
   of stress in phenotypes, 77
   of stress of racism, *414,* 414–15
emojis, 203, *203,* 210
empathy, 441
empire. *See* imperialism
encoding language, 203
endemic diseases, 436, 437
endemic warfare, 290–93, *291, 292*
endocasts, 108, 163
   of australopithecines, 139
   of *Homo erectus,* 163, *163*
endogamy, 366–67
energy balance, 75
   reproduction and, *75,* 75–76

Enfield, Nick, 32, *32*
engaged anthropology, 475
English
   compulsory in federal boarding schools, 310
   as Indo-European language, 235
   pronouns in, 323
   upward mobility in Pakistan and, 263, *263*
entrepreneurs, and rotating credit associations, 277
environment
   developmental plasticity and, 411
   myths about humans and, 482–83
environmental anthropology, 478–79, *479*
   Indigenous knowledge and, 483–84, 486
   systems approach in, 481, 483
   unsustainable practices and, 487
environmental degradation, in minoritized communities, 403
environmental determinism, 480
environmental hazards, 464
environmental injustices, 473
   industrial pollution in the city, 473–74, *474,* 476
   industrial pollution of Indigenous lands and waters, *477,* 477–78, *478*
   Marshall Islands nuclear fallout, *476,* 476–77
environmental justice, 473, 488, 489
environmental racism, 464, 473, *474*
Eocene epoch, *108,* 109
epidemiological transitions, 436–38, *437*
epigenetic change, *77,* 77–79, *78*
   institutional violence and, 302
epigenome, 78
epochs, *105, 108*
eras, *105*
eroticism, 348, *348*
Escobar, Arturo, 487–88
essentialized thinking, 405
estrus, 362, *362*
ethics of anthropology, 13, 16–17
   basic principles of AAA, 16, 17*t*
   causes of violence and, 311
   extractive archaeology and, *38*
   of international development projects, 307
   in studies of human remains, 396–97
ethnic groups
   defined, 222
   in Teotihuacan, 222
ethnicity, as social identity, 403
ethnoarchaeology, 38–39
ethnographic analogies, 42–43
ethnography, 6, 23–29
   in linguistic anthropology, 31
   multispecies, 485
ethnomedical systems, 446

ethnomusicology, 195
ethnonyms, 419
ethnoprimatology, 114–17
eugenics, *407,* 407–8
euthanasia, 391–92
Evers, Cecile, *31*
evidentiality, 213–14
evolution, 4
   extended synthesis, 69
   gradualism vs. punctuated equilibrium, 129
   human niche construction and, 483
   modern synthesis, 61, 408
   See also microevolution
evolutionary anthropology. *See* biological anthropology
evolutionary medicine, 438–39
excavation, 34, *34*
   extractive practices in, *38*
   gender differences in practice of, 324, *324*
   pedestals in, 324, *324*
exchange systems
   defined, 251
   Polanyi's three forms of, 257–58, *258*
   reciprocity underlying, 250
   See also reciprocity
exogamy, 366–67
extended evolutionary synthesis, 69
extractive practices, 487
extractive research, 486
extractivism
   in colonies, 271
   by companies, 306
   defined, 485
   opposite of relationality, 485
eyes
   forward-facing, 109
   of primates, 90, *90*
   See also vision

F

fa`afafine, 325, *325*
Faas, A. J., 467–68
facial reconstructions, 149–50, *150*
fair trade cooperatives, 279, *279*
"fake news," 214
Farmer, Paul, *303,* 303–4
farming populations
   reproductive hormones in, 75–76
   See also agriculture
"fat"
   meaning of, 211, *211*
   See also obesity
fat talk, 458
Fausto-Sterling, Anne, 319
Fayum Depression, 110, *110, 111*
feces
   reproductive hormones in, 86
   stress hormones in, 114

female genital cutting/mutilation, 335
femininity
    defined, 316
    enacted in high school, 315–16, *316*
feudal agricultural societies, 238, *238,* 239
Feuerriegel, Elen, 121
fictive kin, 489
field notes, 25, *25*
field schools, 21, *41*
fieldwork, 10–11, *11*
    online, 25–26, *26*
Fiji
    childbirth pain in, *441,* 441–42, *442*
    earliest colonization of, 36, *36*
    forcible resettlement in, 21, *22,* 43
    women's body ideals, 265
financial crisis of 2007–2009
    banking culture and, 264
    barter networks in, 254
fire, 168–69, *169*
    at home bases, 252–53
    Homo floresiensis and, 188
    Neanderthals' use of, 185
    See also cooking
First Nations, 6
fishing communities, 482
fishing tools, 180
fission–fusion society, 101
fitness, 61
flakes, 145, *145,* 146
Flewellen, Ayana, *34*
Flores, Nelson, 216, *216*
folivores, 106
folklore, 149
food
    archaeological record of trade in, 259
    global capitalism and, 264–66
    Indigenous systems of, 273–74
food banks, 267
food self-reliance, 250, 279
food sharing
    community gardens and, 279
    early evidence of, *252,* 252–53, *253*
    explanations for, 251–52
    global capitalism and, 265
    human social life and, 251, *251*
    by nonhuman primates, 251, *251*
food sovereignty, 273
food surpluses, and social stratification, 236
foot bones
    of *A. afarensis,* 141
    bipedalism and, *132,* 133, 135
footprints
    barefoot biomechanics and, 135
    Ileret near Lake Turkana, 160–61, *161,* 165
    at Laetoli, *140,* 140–41

foragers. *See* hunter-gatherers
foramen magnum, 132, *132*
Ford, Clennan, 347
forensic anthropology, 14, *14*
    decomposition studies in, 393, 396
    Guatemalan massacres and, 285–86, *286,* 311
    issues with estimating race, 427, *427*
    of migrants dying on Mexico–U.S. border, 377–78, *378,* 397, *397*
    solving crimes, 393
fossilization, 103, *104*
fossils
    in biological anthropology, 4
    dating of, 105, 128
    of early hominins, 126–28, *127*
    of hominin skeletons, 41
    removed by foreign interests, 151, *151*
fossil teeth, 9, *9,* 103
Foucault, Michel, 457
founder effect, 62, *63*
Fox, Keolu, 47
FOXP2, 183, 186
fraternal polyandrous marriage, 358, *358,* 366
frugivores, 106
funerals, 378, 385, 386. *See also* mortuary practices

G

Gainj, late menarche in, 75
Gal, Susan, 210
galagos, 93–94, *94,* 96
Galápagos finches, *60,* 60–61
Galton, Francis, 407
gametes, 53, 55–56, *56*
Ganges River, *381,* 381–82
Gardner, Andrew, 305
Garth, Hanna, 273
"gay"
    communities defined by label of, 352
    fa'afafine seen as, 325
    transgender women defining themselves as, 351
gay men
    creaky voice and, 323
    sex work, 372
    with wives and children, 351
Geber, Jonny, 392–93
Gee, James, 204
gender
    childbirth pain and, 442, *442*
    defined, 316, 320*t*
    distinction between sex and, 317
gender-based violence, 338
gendered division of labor, 326–29, *328, 329*
    consistent across many societies, 328
    food sharing and, 252

    likely emerging in hominins, 330–331
    more equitable among Aka, 328, *329*
    in the new millennium, 328–29
    in past societies, 328, *328*
    women's social status and, 336
gender expression, 321*t*
    in Japanese society, 322, *323*
gender identity, 321*t*
    social media and, 341
gender inequality
    embodiment of, *336,* 336–38, *337*
    national rankings of, *339,* 339–40
gender norms, 321*t*
gender performance, 316, 324
gender reveals, 318, *318*
gender roles, 11, 321*t. See also* gendered division of labor
gender schemas, 320*t,* 321
gender scripts, 316, 321–22
gender*sex, 319, 320*t*
    in flux, 340–41
    pronouns and, 323
    sexual configurations and, 348–49, 348*t,* 349
gender terms, 320*t*–21*t*
gene expression, 77
gene flow, 62, *64,* 64–65
    in *Homo erectus,* 160
    isolation and, 66, *66*
    modern human emergence and, 172–73
generalized dentition, 90, *91*
generalized reciprocity, 253–54, *254*
generalized species, 89
General Motors, ethnography in, 15
genes, 55
genetic ancestry, 52, *52*
    commercial tests of, *424,* 424–25, *425*
genetic bottlenecking, 62, *63,* 65–66
    in spreading of modern humans, 177
genetic code, 54
genetic diversity, 64–66, *65*
    distance from Africa and, 177, *177*
genetic drift, 61–64, *63*
    isolation and, 66, *66,* 99
    in Middle Pleistocene *Homo,* 171
genetic lineage, 176, *176,* 177
genetic markers, 4
genetic mutations, 58–60, *59*
genetics, 53–58
genocide
    defined, 285
    in Guatemala, 285–86, *286*
    against Indigenous North Americans, 294–95
    by Nazi Germany, 294, 407–8
    Rwandan, 297, *297,* 336
    in settler colonialism, 300
    threat to group identity and, 297
genotype, 52

geological timescale, 105, *105*
  fossil evidence and, *108*, 108–9
Gero, Joan, 324, *324*
gestation times, in primates, 92–93
Ghanaian independence, *271*, 271–72
gibbons, 88, 89, *95*, 99, 100, *100*
  extrapair mating in, 361
  geographic distribution, *99*
  pair bonds in, 88, 92, 100, 361
  postorbital closure in, *90*
  rare Hainan gibbon, 113
gift giving, 253–55, *255*
  in reciprocal exchange systems, 256, *256*
Gigantopithecus, *108*, 110, *111*
gig economy, 276
glaciers, 227. *See also* cooling climate
globalization
  of capitalist economy, 261, 263–64
  development projects and, 306
  extractivism in, 271, 306
  infectious diseases and, *437*, 437–38
  of political and economic system, 302
  of sex work, 371–72
  structural violence and, *304*, 304–5,
    305
Global North, 302–3
Global South, 302–3
Goldstein, Daniel, 243–44
Gona, Ethiopia, stone tools, 146–47, *147*,
    164
González, Mercedes, 276
Goodall, Jane, 287, *287*
gorillas, 88, 89, 92, *95*, 100, *101*
  geographic distribution, *99*
  plastinated exhibit, 385, *385*
  sagittal crest, 106, *107*
  tool use, 102
  wildlife tourists and, 114, *114*
gossip, 205, *205*
  discouraging violence, 295
  as resistance, 308
  small-group alliances and, 294
governance, 240
  of states, 242, *243*
  unequal power and wealth in, 245
gradualism, 129
Graeber, David, 262, *262*
grammar, 197, 198, 200
Gran Dolina, Spain, 288, *289*
grave goods
  of anatomically modern humans,
    380–81
  defined, 380
  of enslaved woman buried in America,
    396
  lacking with Neanderthals, 380
Gravettian societies, 226, *226*
Gravlee, Lance, 414–15

great apes, *95*, 99
  communication by, *197*, 197–98
  relationships to humans, *101*, 101–2
  See also specific apes
Great Chain of Being, 406
Great Recession, 264
  stress on men, 335
Green, Linda, 286
grief, 386
  animals' apparent display of, 378
grieving rituals
  of Dani women, 386–87, *387*
  Karelian laments, 386
  of poor women in northeastern Brazil,
    387
Grimble, Arthur, 43, *43*
grooming claw, 96, 97
group identity, 293–96, *294*
  promoting organized aggression, 297
group violence
  archaeological rationales for, 294–95
  cultures socialized against, 295–96
  rhetoric in motivation for, 296–98, *297*
  See also coalitionary aggression;
    warfare
Guatemala
  feeding of Mayan boys and girls, *336*,
    336–37, *337*
  forensic analysis of massacres, 285–86,
    286, 311
  trend in women's height, *74*, 74–75
"guest workers" in Bahrain, 305, *305*
gummivores, 106
Gurche, John, 150
Gurtov, Alia, 121

H

Haaland, Deb, 488
habituation, of primates to humans, 114, *114*
Hadza communities in Tanzania, *42*,
    42–43
hafts, 155, *156*
Haile-Selassie, Yohannes, 151, *151*
Haiti
  communication of distress in, 444, *444*
  earthquake of 2010, 472
  HIV/AIDS in, 303, *303*
  impact of coloniality, 303–4
  Vodou (VooDoo) in, 383
hammerstone, 145, *145*
handaxe, 164
Hannaford, Dinah, 345–46, *346*
Hansen, Michelle, *474*
haplorhines, 93, *94–95*, 96–103
  Oligocene fossils and, 110
Hardin, Garrett, 482
Hardin, Jessica, 451, *451*
Harris, Marvin, 479, *479*

Havasupai, sovereignty and blood samples,
    46, *46*
Hawaiian chiefdoms, 239–40, *240*
HC-LCA. *See* human–chimp last common
    ancestor (HC-LCA)
head size and form
  climate and, 67
  See also skulls
healing systems, 446
  ethnomedical, 446
  naturalistic, 449–50, *450*
  personalistic, 446–49, *447*, *449*
  religious and spiritual in Cuba, 28
  three basic elements of, 446
  See also biomedicine
health
  commodification of, 454–57, *455*, *456*
  defined, 440
  transition to agriculture and, 232, 233
health disparities, 79
  of Black people in U.S., 410
  environmental racism and, 473
  between genders, *336*, 336–38, *337*, *338*
  historical trauma and, 79
  racism and, 412–15, *413*
Health Equity Alliance of Tallahassee
    (HEAT), 414–15, *415*
health inequalities, 459
  global, 302
Hedenstierna-Jonson, Charlotte, 333
hegemony, 242
  of American anthropology, 486
  of biomedicine, 454
  formalized justice systems and, 243
height
  secular trend in, *74*, 74–75
  social stress and, 76–77
Henrich, Joe, 266–67, *267*
Hernández, Esperanza, 28–29, *29*, 44
hernandez, féi, 325
heteronormativity, 351–53, *352*
heterozygous genotype, 57
Hewlett, Barry, 328
hierarchical societies
  complexity of, 239
  defined, 222
  of first cities, 236
  governance of, 242
  racialization in, 415
  social differentiation in, 9
  of Teotihuacan, 221
hierarchy
  defined, 86
  early European scientists and, 405–6,
    406
  of Puerto Rico's racialized terms, 414
high altitude, 72–73, *73*, 78
hijra, 326, *326*

Hill, Jane, 423
Hinduism
    cremation in, *381*, 381–82
    health self-care and, 454
    kavadi attam ritual, 443, *443*
Hispanic people, 419
historical trauma, 302
Hitler, Adolf, 407
HIV/AIDS. *See* human immunodeficiency
    virus (HIV)
Ho, Karen, 264, *264*
Hodges, Adam, 296
Hoefinger, Heidi, 373
Hohokam communities, 470–72, *471*
Holbraad, Martin, 28
Holmes, Seth, 304, *304*
Holocene epoch, 227, 481
hominin habitats
    fragmented forests, 125, 167
    of Middle Pleistocene *Homo*, 167
    open grasslands, 158
    woodland/grassland, 137, *137*, 139
hominins
    arboreal adaptations in, 122, 136, 137,
        138, 141
    becoming early humans, 157
    challenges of scarce data, 125–29
    dating of, 128
    defined, 3, 121
    divergence from chimps, *129*, 129–31, *131*
    earliest, *136*, 136–38, *137*, *138*
    ethnographic analogies and, 42–43
    fossil evidence, 41, 126–28, *127*
    gender likely emerging in, 330–31
    identifying species, 128–29
    at Miocene–Pliocene boundary, *136*,
        136–38, *137*, *138*
    Pliocene–Pleistocene radiation, *126*, *138*,
        139–44
    relational perspective on, 125
    See also australopithecines
hominoids, *95*, 98, 99–103. *See also specific*
    apes
Homo
    defining characteristics, 125
    diverse interbreeding species, 188–91,
        189, *191*
    early species, 125, *126*, 142–44, *143*, *144*
    fossils with healed injuries, 440
    speech capability, 183
Homo economicus, 266
Homo erectus, 157–65
    alongside Middle Pleistocene *Homo*, 172
    archaeological sites, *158*
    brain size, *162*, 162–63, *163*
    cranial appearance, 161, *162*, *166*
    Dmanisi site, *159*, 159–60
    expansion beyond Africa, 157–59, *158*

footprints, *160*, 160–61
    important fossil finds, *158*
    interbreeding with early humans, 190
    Neanderthals evolved from, 184
    regions not reached by, 176–77
    remaining questions about, 165
    small species descended from, 188
    stature of, *160*, *160*
    tool traditions, *164*, 164–65
Homo ergaster, 159
Homo floresiensis, 188, *188*, *189*
Homo habilis, 142–44, 146, 155, 157, 164
Homo heidelbergensis, 151
homologous chromosomes, 55, *55*
Homo luzonensis, 188
Homo naledi, 123, *123*, 188
Homo rudolfensis, 144, 157
Homo sapiens, 3, 173–83
    anatomically modern, 64, 173–78, 173*t*,
        174, *175*
    assimilation model of emergence, 173
    behaviorally modern, 173*t*, 178–83
    challenges of 21st century, 191
    changing ecosystems, 178, *178*
    cranial features, *166*, 173–74, *174*
    definitive fossil sites, *175*, 175–76
    Denisovan ancestry in, 188, *189*, 189–90,
        190, 191
    genetic diversity in, 64–66, *65*, *177*
    genetics of emergence and spread, *176*,
        176–77, *177*
    interbreeding with other species,
        188–91, *189*, *190*, *191*
    as last surviving humans, 191
    likely direct ancestors, 171, 176
    major waves of migration, 176–78, *177*
    Middle Pleistocene *Homo* and, 165–66,
        166, 171, 173, 174
    multiregional model of, 172–73
    Neanderthal ancestry in, 188–89, *189*,
        190, 191
    related to apes, *95*, 99, *101*, 101–2
    transitional fossil sites, 174, *174*
homozygous genotype, 57
honing chewing, 134, *134*
Hooton, Earnest, 408, 409, *409*, 411
hormones, 318, 319
household, 250, 251, *251*
    marriage systems and, 360
houses, and social stratification, 237
howler monkeys, 92
Hrdlička, Aleš, 408, 409
human behavioral ecology, 480, *480*
human–chimp last common ancestor
    (HC-LCA), *129*, 129–30, *131*
    first hominins evolved from, 136–38,
        138
    tool use by, 135

human immunodeficiency virus (HIV)
    activist choir and, 195–97, *196*
    apes as source of, 115, 436
    genetic resistance to, 436
    in Haiti, 303, *303*
    in South Africa, 195–97
humanism, 12–13
    in archaeology, 38
humanness, 173, 173*t*
human–primate interactions, 114–17
humans. *See Homo sapiens*
human variation
    evolutionary view of, 407, 408–9
    mostly in local populations, 409
    See also genetic diversity; phenotypes
hunter-gatherers
    Aka division of labor, 328, *329*
    between Asia and Alaska, 234
    bands of, 236
    climate warming and, 227
    contemporary mixed economies, 275
    cooperation among, 226, *226*
    cultivating wild plants, 228
    decreased world population of, 227, *227*
    defined, 226
    ethnographic analogies and, 42–43
    hunting by women, 332
    invading cities or states, 240, *241*
    in large chiefdoms, 236
    of Pacific Northwest, 236
    rich archaeological record of, 226, *226*
    social stratification among, 236, 237, *237*
    strengthened by communication, 294
    transition to agriculture, 5, 230–31, *231*
    violent events among, 295–96
hunting
    of "bushmeat" today, 435–36, *436*
    by chimpanzees, *102*, 102–3
    diseases associated with, 434*t*
    by *Homo erectus*, 165
    of marine mammals with tuberculosis,
        394
    meat eating and, 157
    by men versus women, 331, *332*, 332–33,
        333
    by Middle Pleistocene *Homo*, 165, 167, *167*
    of primates by humans, 113
    social status from prowess in, 237, *237*
    tools of *Homo sapiens*, 180, *180*
    See also butchering
hunting and butchering techniques, 39, *39*
Hurley, Elizabeth, *363*
hurricanes, Caribbean, 470
    Maria in Puerto Rico, 468, *468*
Hurston, Zora Neale, *411*, 411–12
hygiene hypothesis, 438
hyoid bone, 183, *183*, 198
hypotheses, 4

I

Icelandic volcanoes, *469*, 469–70, *470*
icons, 203–4
ideology, 415. *See also* language ideologies
idioms of distress, 443–44, *444*
illness, 440
    as communication, 443–44, *444*
    cultural differences in, 441
    medicinal plants for prevention and relief of, *449*, 449–50, *450*
immigrant rights, 307–8
immigrants
    Boas's studies of phenotypes of, 411
    English language use and, 7, 14
    Hungarian politics and, 210
    informal healthcare for, 456–57, *457*
    skin color as social marker of, 422–23
    unauthorized, 14, 277, 307–8, 372, 377, 456
    to U.S. during Irish potato famine, 392
    See also migrant workers
immigration
    arming of police and, 418
    neoliberalism and, 304
    racist laws affecting, 407
imperialism, 299–302. *See also* colonialism
incest taboo, 347
incisors
    diets of primates and, 106
    shovel-shaped, *404*, 404–5
index, 203, *203*
indexicality, 202
Indian Englishes, 215
Indigenous ancestry, 51–52, *52*, 424–25
Indigenous anthropologists, 47, *47*, 483–87
Indigenous archaeologists, 47, *47*
Indigenous Australians
    forced removals of children, 79
    hunting by Martu women, 332, *332*
    Kow Swamp cemetery, 381
    language register of, 355–56, *355t*
Indigenous communities
    coproduced knowledge and, 44
    extractive research and, 486
    food sovereignty in, 273–74
    local knowledge of, 13
    new ways of engaging with, 489
    rights over excavated materials, 6, 45, *45*, 46, *46*
Indigenous knowledge, 483–84, 486. *See also* local knowledge
Indigenous languages
    North American, *30*, 30–31, *31*
    in shamanic healing, 447
    tracing origins through, 30–31, *31*
Indigenous-led countries, 488

Indigenous North Americans
    colonists' acceptable sexualities and, 354
    crossing from Siberia, 234
    European settler colonialism and, 300–302, 309–10
    extractive research and, 486
    fugitive slaves allied with, 418
    genocide against, 294–95
    government boarding schools, 301–2, *302*, 310, 421
    language revitalization, 309–10, *310*
    mounds built by, 294–95, *295*
    new diseases introduced to, 300, 310
    Spanish missions and, 300–301, *301*
Indigenous people
    defined, 6
    "noble savage" myth and, 482–83
    relationships with environment, 483
Indigenous scholars, 484–87
Indigenous sovereignty, 485–86, 487
individualism
    capitalist values and, 306
    neoliberalism and, 370
Indo-European languages, *234*, 234–35
Indonesia, gay sexualities in, 352, *352*
Indonesian Sign Language (BISINDO), 208–10, *209*
industrial capitalism, 261, *261*, 262
industrialization
    diseases and, *434t*, 436–37, *437*, 438
    microbiome and, 438
industrial pollution
    in the city, 473–74, *474*, 476
    in Indigenous communities, *477*, 477–78, *478*
inequality
    cultural values and, 272
    disasters and, 464
    gender and, 317
    ill health and, 459
    infectious disease and, 437, *437*
    redistribution as driver of, 267
    reinforced by racism, 412
    social Darwinism and, 407
    in socialist Cuba, 272–73
    in Teotihuacan, 222
    in urban societies, 242
    worsened by neoliberalism, 262
    See also gender inequality; health disparities; social stratification
informal economy, 277–78
informal justice, 243–44, 245, 426
informed consent, 16, 395–96
infrastructure, *479*, 480
inmarriage, 366–67
insectivores, 106
institutions, 242
insular dwarfism, 188

intelligence
    racist science and, 407
    See also cognitive ability
interlocutors, 28
international call center, *263*, 263–64
international development projects, 305–7
intersex, 318, 319, *321t*, 326, 341
introgression, *189*, 190
Iran, young people in, 353, *353*
Ireland, Great Famine in, 392–93, *393*
irrigation, 221, 228, 230, 231
    in complex societies, 235, 239
    drought in southwestern U.S. and, 470–71, *471*
IsiZulu, 196
isolation, 66, *66*
isolation event
    apes and, 111
    monkeys and, 98–99

J

Jackson, Fatimah, *426*
Jacobs, Zenobia, *187*
Japan
    body size regulation in, 457
    Buddhist family altar, 387–88, *388*
    gender expressions in, 322, *323*
    "host clubs" catering to women in, 372
    organ transplants unacceptable in, 391
    proximity to Whiteness and, 416
    unmarried women in, 371
Japanese verb forms, 206–7, *206t*
jargon, 196
Jebel Irhoud Cave, Morocco, 174, *174*
Jebel Sahaba, violent deaths, 290, *290*
jewelry, 182–83
    as grave goods, 380
Jin, Jennie, *427*
Johanson, Donald, 140, 151
Johnston, Barbara Rose, 475, 476–77
Joseph, Acephie, 303–4
Ju/'hoansi (!Kung), *252*, *255*, 255–56, *256*, 276
    strengthening community, 294, *294*
justice systems, 243
    informal, 243–44, 245, 426

K

Kabwe ("Broken Hill") cranium, *151*
kafala system, 305
kaiko pig festival, 481, *481*
Kanjera South, Kenya, 168, *168*
Kanzi the bonobo, 198
Kardashian, Kim, *265*
Karelian laments, 386
Kathu Pan, 155–57, *156*
Kennewick Man, 396
Kenyanthropus platyops, 140
key informants, 25

Keynes, John Maynard, 407
Kimeu, Kamoya, 151, *151, 160*
Kimmerle, Erin, 14–15, *15,* 44
kinship, 223–24, *224*
    defined, 355
    in domestic mode of production, 262
    language and, 355–56, 355*t*
    marriage and, 354–56, *356,* 362
    status in chiefdoms and, 236
Kleinman, Arthur, 453
knapping, 145
knowledge coproduction, 13, 29, 44
knowledge systems, 13. *See also* local
    knowledge
knuckle-walking, 89, 101, 136
Knudson, Kelly, 390–91
Kohrt, Brandon, 79, *79*
Koko the gorilla, 197, *197*
Korisettar, *5*
Kula exchange system, 23–24, *24*
!Kung. *See* Ju/'hoansi
Kutlu, Ethan, 215–16

L

labor
    capitalism and, 261, *261,* 262
    defined, 252
    in lower-income countries, 304, 306
    mechanization of, 264
    See also gendered division of labor
labrets (lip plugs), 338, *338*
lactase persistence (LP), *70,* 70–72, *72*
lactose tolerance or intolerance, *70,* 70–71
Laetoli footprints, *140,* 140–41, *330*
Lake Mungo, Australia, 45, *45*
Laluk, Nicholas, 47
laments, 386
Landau, Misia, 149–50
language
    7,000 currently used, 198
    adopting words from other languages,
        200
    anatomical capability of, 183, *183,* 198
    of caregiver to child, 208, *208*
    commodification of, 263–64
    defined, 7, 197
    between doctor and patient, 459
    "fat talk" in, 458
    as gender marker, 322–23, *323*
    grammatical number in, 212
    of *hijra,* 326
    human distinctiveness and, 103
    as identity marker, 206–7
    idioms of distress in, 443–44
    immigrants and, 7, 14, 210, *210*
    kin relations and, 355–56, 355*t*
    mixed French and Arabic in Marseille,
        31
    Neanderthals and, 186

pronouns in, 323, 341
in racialized societies, 415, 423, *423*
recording of, 31–33
recursive, 103
sexual identities and, 352
as social action, 202, 204–5, *210,* 210–11,
    211
social organization and, *207,* 207–10
social status and, 202, 206–7, 206*t,* 208,
    208
spatial organization in, 212–13, *213*
spreading in Mesolithic and Neolithic,
    234–35
as system of signs, 202–4, *203*
See also linguistic anthropology;
    speech
language death, 301
language families, 234, *234*
language ideologies, 197, 207
    signers in Indonesia and, 208–10, *209*
    stigmatized groups and, 210, *210*
language register, 355–56, 355*t*
    social status and, 206–7
language revitalization, 309–10, *310*
language varieties, 198, 200–202
    of English in Pakistan, 263–64
    in multilingual societies, 215–16
    prejudice against, 216–17, *217*
    speaker's appearance and, *215,* 215–16
languaging, 210
Lapita, 36, *36*
Larsen, Clark Spencer, 233
Larson, Heidi, 453
Lasco, Gideon, 416
Latinx, 216, *216,* 419
Lau, Timm, 29
laws, 243
Leakey, Jonathan, 142
Leakey, Louis, 142, *143,* 146, 151
Leakey, Mary, 140, 142, 146, 151
learned behaviors, 148
lemurs, 87, 93–94, *94,* 96
    conservation efforts, *116,* 116–17, *117*
    hunted for food, 113
    life history, *92*
    postorbital bar in, *90*
    pygmy mouse, 88
    ring-tailed, 85–87, *86,* 89, *96,* 113, 116,
        117, *117*
    toothcomb of, *96*
leprosy, *445,* 445–46
"lesbian," 352
Lesotho, cattle farming in, 306–7, *307*
lesser apes, *95,* 99, 100, *100. See also*
    gibbons
Levant, 230–31, *231*
Levine, Nancy, 358
Levi-Strauss, Claude, 44
LGBTQIA+ communities, 339, 341

Li, Bo, *187*
Li, Darryl, 297–98
Lieberman, Daniel, 135
life history
    in humans, 76, *76,* 92
    in primates, *92,* 92–93
lineage, 357
linguistic anthropology, 7, *7*
    practice of, 30–33
    tooth-associated sounds and, 8, 10
    See also language
linguistic prejudice, 216–17, *217*
linguistic profiling, 217
linguistic relativity, 212–14, *213*
Linnaeus, Carolus, 406, *406*
Lippi-Green, Rosina, 216–17
Lloréns, Hilda, 463–64, *464,* 489
local biologies, 74
local knowledge, 13
    of Tsimané people, 26–27, *27*
locomotion
    of extinct primates, 106
    of primates, 89–90
locus on a chromosome, 58
Lomnitz, Larissa, 256–57, *257*
longitudinal arch, 133
López Juárez, Lucia, 308
lorises, 93–94, *94, 96, 96*
love, romantic, 368–70, *369, 370*
"Lovers of Modena," 350
Low, Setha, 475
Lucy, John, 212
"Lucy," 140, *140,* 141, 151
Lui, Li, 5, *5*

M

macaques, 92
    cheek pouches, 98, *99*
    interactions with humans, *115,* 115–16,
        116, 148
    life history, *92*
    tool use by, 148, *149*
MacDonald, John, 215
macroevolution, 61, 128
Madagascar
    endangered primate species in, 113
    famadihana rituals in, 390, *390*
    lemurs in, 85, *86, 96,* 116, 117
Mainstream White American English
    (MWAE). *See* MWAE
maize (corn)
    in Chaco Canyon, 269
    domestication of, *229,* 229–30, 436
    nutritional improvement of, 436
    pellagra from reliance on, 436
    Spanish missions and, 301
    in Teotihuacan, 221, 230
Majimaji war, 309, *309*
malaria, *68,* 68–69, *69,* 436, 438

Malinowski, Bronislaw, 16, *23*, 23–24, 28, 44, 347
Mandamin, Josephine, 488
Mantini-Briggs, Clara, 458
Manzanilla, Linda, 221–23, *222*
Māori
    as first settlers of New Zealand, 178, *178*
    gender-based roles of, 334, *334*
Maricela from Ecuador, 377
markets, 258, *258*
    in Cuban food system, 273, *273*
    defined, 258
    early trade routes and, 258–59, *259*
    money and, 259–60
    neoliberalism and, 262
    as special case of reciprocity, 258
    See also capitalism
marmosets
    as gummivores, 106
    pygmy, *94*, 114, *114*
marriage
    age trending upward, 370
    alternatives to, 370–71
    arranged, 366, 367, 369, 370
    defined, 346, 354
    economic arrangements of, *362*, 362–63, 370
    expensive rituals in Namibia, 370, *370*
    family members' influence on, 362
    kinship and, 354–56, *356*
    as legally codified institution, 354, *354*
    living arrangements in, *364*, 364–65, *365*
    matchmaking, 368, *368*
    norms for selecting a spouse, 366–68
    political alliances and, 356, *356*
    romantic love and, 368–70, *369*, *370*
    same-sex, 370
    transnational, 345–46, *346*, 364
    of women at young ages, 365–66
marriage corners in China, 368, *368*
marriage systems, 356–60, *357*, *358*
Marshall Islands, nuclear testing harms and legacy, *476*, 476–77
Marx, Karl, 262, *479*
masculinity
    clients of sex work and, 372
    defined, 316
    enacted in high school, 315–16, *316*
    military service and, *298*, 298–99
    NATO peacekeepers and, 298–99
    skeletal trauma and, 338
    skin-lightening products and, 416
mass incarceration, 420
masturbation, 350, *350*
"matched guise" experiments, 215, 216
matchmaking, 368, *368*
material culture, 7
    stone tools, 147

materiality, 480, 487
Mathew, Sarah, *291*, 291–92, 293
mating systems
    human, 360, 362
    in nonhuman primates, 360–62, *361t*
Matisoo-Smith, Lisa, 13, *13*
matriarchy, 335
matrilineal societies, 365
matrilocality, 364, *364*
Maude, Henry, 43, *43*
Mauss, Marcel, 254
Maya people, 74
    feeding of boys and girls, *336*, 336–37, *337*
    height of women, *74*, 74–75
    Yucatec speakers, 212
McCay, Bonnie, 482, *482*
McGregor, Deborah, 488–89
McGurk, Harry, 215
McGurk effect, 215
Mead, Margaret, 16, *327*, 327–28, 347, 411
meaning, 202–4
    changes in, 210
    circulating discourses and, 211
means of production, 262
meat eating
    brains of human ancestors and, 103, *171*
    cooking and, 168, *169*
    exposure to diseases from, 435–36
    by hominins, 131, 133
    by *Homo erectus*, 165, *165*
    by *Homo* species, 125
    hunting and, 157
    by Middle Pleistocene *Homo*, 167–68, *168*, *169*
    by Neanderthals, 185
    primates hunted for, 113
    scavenging and, 165, *165*
    See also butchering; hunting
medical anthropology, 8
medical pluralism, 451, *451*
medical volunteering, short-term international, 459, *459*
medicine. *See* biomedicine
meiosis, 55–56, *56*
melanin, 68, *68*
menarche, onset of, 75, *75*
merchant capitalism, 261
Meredith, Stephanie, 85–87, *86*, 116
Mesolithic period, 231
    spread of language in, 234–35
metaphor theory, 296, *296*
Mexico
    deaths while crossing U.S. border, 377–78, *378*, 397, *397*
    Día de los Muertos, *389*, 389–90
Mexico City, reciprocal exchange in, 256–57, *257*

microbiome, human, 438–39, *439*
microevolution, 51, 52
    human culture and, 69–72
    human diversity and, 64–66
    mechanisms of, 58–64
microliths, 180
Middle Pleistocene *Homo*, 165–73
    anatomical variation in, 167
    brain size, 166, 170, *170*, 171
    butchering by, 165, 167–68, *168*
    cranial anatomy, *166*, 166–67
    cranial variation, 172, *172*
    defined, 165
    dietary flexibility, 167
    fire used by, 168–69, *169*
    Homo sapiens and, 165–66, *166*, 171, 173, 174
    hunting by, 165, 167, *167*
    interpersonal violence in, 288, *289*
    Neanderthals evolved from, 184
    regional distinctiveness in, 171–73, *172*
    tool-making by, 167, *167*
    varied habitats, 167
migrants crossing Mexico–U.S. border, 377–78, *378*, 397, *397*
migrant workers, *304*, 304–5, *305*
    development creating pool of, 307
    sex workers and, 371
    unauthorized, 14, 307–8, 377
    See also immigrants
Mijangos García, Mirian, 308
Miller, Melanie, 449
Minangkabau, power sharing in, 335, *335*
minoritized communities, 401–2
    toxic industries in, 473, *474*
Miocene epoch, *108*, 110–11, 125
missing link, 129
Mississippian culture, 270–71, *271*
Mitchell, Miaisha, 414
mitochondria, 53, *53*
mitochondrial DNA, 53, 176, *187*, 189
    agricultural societies and, 231
mitosis, 55, *55*
Mitterrand, François, *359*
Miura, Ryosuke, *323*
mixed economies, *274*, 274–75
    defined, 273
    food sovereignty and, 273
    informal elements of, 278
    moral economies and, 275–76
Moche ceramic vessels, 350, *350*
Mock Spanish, 423, *423*
modern synthesis, 61, 408
modes of production, *258*, 262
molars, 90, *91*
    bilophodont, 98, *98*
    diet and, 106
    of *Homo erectus*, 161
    of humans vs. apes, 134

of leaf-eating monkeys, 98
    Y-5 cusp pattern, 99, *99*, 110
molecular clock method, 130
molecules, 54
money, 259–60
Moniruzzaman, Monir, 455, *455*
monkeys
    adaptive radiation of, 111
    classification of, *94–95*
    tool use by, 147, 148, *149*
    See also macaques
Monks Mound, Cahokia, *270, 271*
monogamy
    conditions conducive to, 359
    defined, 355
    documented in societies, *357*
    with informal polygyny, 358–59
    males and females similar in size, 9, *9*
    most common form of marriage, 358, 360
    in nonhuman primates, 360–62, 361t
    serial, 359
    settler colonialism and, 354
monolingualism, 210
moral economies, *275*, 275–76
Morales, Evo, 311
Moriarty, Erin, 33, *33*, 208–9
Morocco, justice systems in, 243
morphological rules, 198, 199
Morris, Hannah, 121
Morse, Janice, 441–42, *442*
mortuary practices, 381–83
    beliefs about afterlife and, 381
    cemeteries, 381, 383, 385
    defined, 381
    Haitian Vodou (Voodoo), 383
    Hindu cremation, *381*, 381–82
    in San Francisco Chinatown, 382–83, *383*
    social status and, 383–85
    in United States, 385
    Wari' cannibalism, 382, *382*
    See also burial rituals
mosaic of traits, 136, 137
mother-in-law language, 355–56, 355t
Mountain Chief, *30*
Mousterian tools, 185, *185*
Mukogodo, preference for daughters, 480, *480*
Mulligan, Connie, 78–79
Mullings, Leith, 425, *425*
multifactorial phenotypes, 58
multilingualism, 210
    comprehension and, 215–16
multiregional model of human evolution, 172–73
multisited ethnography, 345
multispecies ethnography, 485
Murray, Pauli, 401–2, *402*
Muslim women, 340, *341*
mutations, 58–60, *59*

mutual aid networks, 245
MWAE (Mainstream White American English)
    code-switching and, 217
    defined, 200
    of Disney heroes, 217
    evidentiality in, 213
    grammatical number in, 212
    non-White speaker of, 215, 216, 423
    speaking to babies and, 208
Mycenaean Greece, 268, *268*
Mycobacterium tuberculosis, *394*, 394–95, *395*
myths
    about humans and environment, 482–83
    origin myths, 204
    as resistance, 308

N

nails on fingertips, *88*, 90
    of plesiadapiforms, 109
Nakayama, Satsuki, 322
Nanda, Serena, 326
Nariokotome Boy, 160, *160*
narrative
    in paleoanthropology, 125, 149–50, *150*, 151
    rationalizing group violence, 294–95
nationally important artifacts, 151, *151*
Native American Graves Protection and Repatriation Act (NAGPRA), 396
Native Americans. *See* Indigenous North Americans
Natufians, 230–31, *231*
natural hazards
    adapting to proximity of, 468–71
    defined, 464
naturalistic healing systems, 449–50, *450*
natural selection, 59, 60–61, 66
    cultural behavior patterns and, 480
    human variation and, 407, 408–9
Nayar, Arun, *363*
Nazi Germany, 294, 407–8
Neanderthals, 184–86
    anatomy of, 185, *185*
    behaviorally modern, 185–86
    caring for injuries, 440
    in Denisova Cave, 186, *187*, 188
    evolution of, 184
    gender likely emerging in, 330
    healing plants used by, 450
    introgression and other hominins, 188–89, *189, 190, 191*
    limitations of, 186
    range of, 184, *184*
    skin reflectance (pigmentation) and, *409*
    tool style, *185*, 185–86

negative reciprocity, 254, *254*
Nelson, Robin, *76*, 76–77
neoliberalism, 262, 272
    cheap labor for global agribusinesses and, 304
    eroding reciprocity, 276
    eroding social connections, 276
    individualism and, 370
    structural violence and, 304
Neolithic period, 231
    spread of language in, 234–35
    See also Çatalhöyük
neolocality, 364, 369
Neotropical monkeys, 98. *See also* platyrrhines
Nepomnaschy, Pablo, 42
netnography, 25–26, *26*
Netting, Robert McC., 482
neutral mutations, 59
new archaeology. *See* processual archaeology
New Zealand
    British patriarchy introduced to, 334
    historical trauma in, 302, *302*
    last settled land mass, 178, *178*
    See also Māori
Nez, Jason, *180*
niche construction
    around dairying, 70–72, *72*
    changing ecosystems, 178, 481, 483
Nichter, Mimi, 458
Nieves-Colón, Maria, *65*
Nkrumah, Kwame, *271*, 271–72
"noble savage" myth, 482–83
nocturnal primates, 88
nonbinary identities, 317, 320t, *325*, 325–26, *326*, 341, 353
non-fungible tokens (NFTs), 264
nongovernmental organizations (NGOs), in disasters, *472*, 472–73
norms
    culture defined by, 6
    defined, 240
    gossip and, 205
    institutions and, 242
    justice systems and, 243
nuclear family, 369
nucleus, 53, *53*
nurturance, 348, *348*
Nyanzi, Stella, *475*

O

obesity
    state regulation of, 457
    stigma, 458
    See also "fat"
obsidian hydration, 37t
obstetric racism, 412–13, *413*
occipital torus, 161, *162*

Occupy movement, 262
Ochs, Elinor, 208
O'Gorman, Kieran, *187*
Oldowan tools, *145*, 146–47, *147*, 157t
    of *Homo erectus*, 164, *164*
    Homo floresiensis and, 188
    at Kathu Pan, 155
Olduvai Gorge, 142, *143*, 145, 146
Oligocene epoch, *108*, 110, *111*
Oliver-Smith, Anthony, 465–66
omnivores, 90
omomyids, *108*, 109
online fieldwork, 25–26, *26*
ontology, 28
opposable thumbs and big toes, *88*, 90, 91
oppressive systems, 403
oral sex, 350, *350*
oral traditions, 204
orangutans, 88, *95*, *100*, 100–101, *101*
    geographic distribution, *99*
organelles, 53, *53*
organ transplants, 391, 396
    global trafficking in, *455*, 455–56, 457
origin myths, 204
Orrorin tugenensis, *124*, 136, *138*
Ötzi, 447, *448*
Ouranopithecus macedoniensis, 130, *131*
outmarriage, 366–67
Owens, Jesse, 410
oxygen isotopes, 391

P
Padilla, Mark, 372
pain
    of childbirth, *441*, 441–42, *442*
    of kavadi attam pilgrimage, 443, *443*
pair bond, 88, 92, 106
    defined, 355
    evolutionary benefits of, 360
    in gibbons, 88, 92, 100
    marriage as, 354
    See also monogamy
Pakistan, call centers in, *263*, 263–64
paleoanthropologists, 121, *123*
paleoanthropology
    diversity in, 151, *151*
    fossil evidence in, 126–28, *127*
    as a narrative, 125, 149–50, *150*, 151
Paleocene epoch, *108*, 109
Papua New Guinea
    gendered division of labor in, 327, *327*
    pig festival in, 481, *481*
parallel cousin marriage, 367
Paranthropus, *138*, 141–42, *142*
Paranthropus aethiopicus, *124*, *138*, 142, *142*
Paranthropus boisei, *124*, *138*, 142, *142*
Paranthropus robustus, *124*, *138*, 142, *142*,
    157, 330

participant observation, 6
    different modes of, 25–26, *25t*
    by linguistic anthropologists, 31
Pascoe, C. J., 315–16
paternity certainty, 360
path dependency, 471
patriarchy, 333–36, 340
    Harris on, 479
patrilineal societies, 365–66
patrilocality, 334, *364*, 364–65
    DNA evidence of, 364–65, *365*
    marriage of young women and, 366
patron–client relationship, 238, *238*
Pauli, Julia, 370, *370*
Peccerelli, Fredy, 285, *286*, 311
Peixotto, Becca, 121, *122*
Pérez Rodríguez, Verónica, 40, *40*
periods, *105*, *108*
personal experiences
    of ethnographer, 29
    of excavator, 39
personalistic healing systems, 446–49,
    447, *448*, *449*
Peru
    earthquake of 1970, *465*, 465–66
    trophy heads in Nasca Valley, 390–91,
    391
    Wari empire, 300, *300*
petroglyphs, 204, *204*
pet trade, illegal, 113–14, *114*
phenotypes, 52, 56–58
    racial typologies and, 403–5, *404*
    regional variations in, 66–69
    See also human variation
phonological rules, 198, 199
phrenology, 408
phylogeny, 93
physical anthropology
    racial typologies in, 408–9, *409*, 426
    See also biological anthropology
physiognomy, 408
phytoliths, 259
Pitcairn Island, 62, *63*
plague
    in London of 1665–66, 437
    See also Black Death, 14th-century
plants
    domestication of, *228*, 228–30, *229*
    healing uses of, *449*, 449–50, *450*, 451
    psychoactive, 450
platyrrhines, *94–95*, *97*, 97–98, *98*
Pleistocene epoch, 125, 155
    evolutionary synergies in, 170, *171*
    Homo erectus adapted to, 158
plesiadapiforms, *108*, 109, *109*
Pliocene epoch, 125
Pliocene–Pleistocene hominin radiation,
    126, *138*, 139–44

pluriverse transitions, 487–89
Pobiner, Briana, 165, *165*
Polanyi, Karl, 257–58, *258*
police training, White supremacy in, 420,
    420
police violence, 418–21
    protests against, *419*, *420*, 420–21
pollution. *See* industrial pollution
polyamory, 354, 355
    Herero in Namibia and, 357, *358*
polyandry, *357*, 357–58, *358*, 366
    in nonhuman primates, 361t
polygamy, 357
polygenic phenotypes, 58
polygynandry, in nonhuman primates,
    361t
polygyny, 327, 357, *358*
    concentrated resources and, 359
    informal with legal monogamy, *358*,
    358–59, *359*
    in majority of societies, 357, *357*
    in nonhuman primates, 360, 361t
    of Senegalese men, 345–46
    in Viking-age Scandinavia, 360
    wealth required for, 359
population bomb myth, 482
population genetics, 408–9
population growth, and agriculture, 231,
    235
populations, defined, 52
positionality
    in archaeology, 39
    in cultural anthropology, 29
postcrania, 137
postindustrial capitalism, 264
postorbital bar, 90, *90*
postorbital closure, *90*, 96
postprocessual archaeology, *39*, 39–40
post-traumatic stress disorder (PTSD), *79*
    endemic warfare and, 292
potassium–argon (K–Ar) dating, 37t
potatoes, 232, *232*
    Great Famine in Ireland and, 392–93, *393*
poverty
    black market in organs and, *455*,
    455–56, 457
    coloniality and, 303
    court fine systems and, 420
    cultural values and, 272
    eroding social connections, 276
    sex work and, 371, 372
    worsened by development projects, 306
power
    biopower, 457–58
    defined, 335
    of descendants of colonizers, 45
    in ethnographic relationships, 29
    gender norms and, 85

hegemony and, 242
in hierarchy, 86
to impose monolingualism, 210
in language, 31
modes of production and, 262
in postindustrial capitalism, 264
resource inequalities and, 238
shared by genders in Minangkabau, 335, *335*
structural violence and, 299
pragmatic rules, 198, 199
prayer, in healing efforts, 451, *451*
precision grip, 90, 91
tool-making and, 144
predators, group protection from, 225, *225*
prefix, 234
prehensile hands and thumbs, *88*, 90
prehensile tails, 98, *98*, 99
pressure flaking, 167
primary sex characteristics, 318, 320*t*
primate evolution
comparison to living species, 105–8
fossil evidence, *108*, 108–11
fossilization and, 103–5, *104*
geological timescale and, 105, *105*, *108*, 108–9
primates
anatomy of, *88*, 89–90, *90*
behavior of, 91–93
biological anthropology and, 4
captive breeding of, 117, *117*
comparisons of different species, 11–12, 41–42
conservation of, 42, *42*, 114–17
derived traits of, 88, *88*
diseases of humans and, 115–16
ethics of working with, 16
food sharing by, 251, *251*
gender roles and, 329–30
geographical distribution, 87, *87*
living in groups, 224–25, *225*
napping and sleeping in groups, 12, *12*
number of living species, 87
plants used for healing by, 449, *449*
social arrangements, 91, 91–92
species diversity in world regions, *112*
taxonomy of, 93–103, *94–95*
teeth of, 9, *9*, 90, *91*
threatened, *112*, 112–14
trade in, *113*, 113–14, *114*
primitive traits, 94, 108
Prince-Zinni, Debra, *427*
prison abolition, 426
private property, 260–61, 264
private property regime, 261
privatization
disasters as opportunity for, 472
of government services, 262

of land held as commons, 306–7
tragedy of the commons and, 482
of water in Bolivia, 311
processual archaeology, 38–39, *39*, 40
proconsulids, *108*, 110
production
means of, 262
modes of, *258*, 262
prognathism
in australopithecines, 138
less in *Homo erectus*, 161
in Middle Pleistocene *Homo*, 167
pronouns, and gender*sex, 323, 341
prosimians, 97
prosocial behavior, 225
proteins, 53, 54
protein synthesis, 54–55
protolanguage, 234
Pruetz, Jill, 102, *102*
pseudoscience, 407, 408
public health systems, 437, *437*, 457
victim-blaming by, 458
Puerto Rico
environmental hazards in, 463–64, *464*
Hurricane Maria in, 468, *468*
livable worlds created in, 463, 489
racialized terms in, 414
punctuated equilibrium, 129
Punnett squares, 57, *57*
pygmy marmosets, *94*, 114, *114*

Q

Qesem Cave, Israel, 169, *169*, 253, *253*
QingMing Festival, 388, *389*
Qin Shi Huang, tomb of, 384, *384*, *385*
quadrupedal leaping, 89
quadrupedal primates, 89
quantitative research methods, 26–27, *27*, 41
queer communities, 339, 341, *352*

R

race
early science of, *405*, 405–7, *406*
forensic anthropology and, 427, *427*
reconsideration of science of, 408
as social construct, 403, 409, 412
racialization, 216, 415
children's entertainment and, 216–17, *217*
racialized systems, 403
census taking in, *417*, 417–18
colorism in, *416*, 416–17, *417*
everyday interactions in, 422–24
language in, 415, 423, *423*
legal government documents in, 418, *418*
police violence in, 418–21, *419*, *420*
trying to exhibit Whiteness in, 423–24
See also White supremacy

raciolinguistics, 216, *216*
racism
in biomedicine, 459
defined, 402
of early anthropologists, 347, 408–9, *409*
embodied stress of, *414*, 414–15
environmental, 464, 473, *474*
language as covert tool of, 423
language uses and, 217
in legal history of U.S., 418
obstetric, 412–13, *413*
pseudosciences based on, 408
reinforced in schools, 421
resistance against, 401
scientific, 403, 411
of sex tourists, 373
structural, 402–3, 412
radical anthropology, 475
radiocarbon dating, 36, 37*t*
radiopotassium dating, 37*t*
Rahman, Tariq, 263
Ralph, Laurence, 11, *11*, 418
Ramaphosa, Cyril, *123*
Rappaport, Roy, *25*, 481, *481*
Rarámuri runners, 135, *135*
Raskin, Sarah, 456
rationality model, 266
Ravenscroft, Julia, 478
recessive alleles, 57, *57*
reciprocal exchange systems, 255–57, *256*
neoliberal economy and, 276
reciprocity
defined, 251
eroded by poverty, 276
fundamental to human exchange, 250
Indigenous approach and, 489
markets and, 258
in Polanyi's analysis, 258, *258*
reliance on weak forms of, 276
as social insurance, 255–57
three forms of, 253–54, *254*
See also food sharing
reconciliation, 311
recursion, 103
red blood cells
malaria and, 68–69, *69*
sickle-shaped, 69, *69*
Redford, Robert, *327*
redistribution, *258*, 267–74
archaeological record of, 268–71
defined, 267
in postcolonial world, 271–72
in systems today, 272–74
redstone, 485, *485*
Reed, Kaye, 144, 151
Reese, Ashanté, 249–50, *250*
reflexivity, 28–29

refugees
forced into sex work, 372
nonbinary, seeking political asylum, 353
resettlement of, 9–10
refusal, 310
register in language, 355–56, 355t
social status and, 206–7
relational approaches, 125, 485–86, 486, 487, 488
relative dating, 36, 128
religion, and power in Saudi Arabia, 340
religious beliefs, 381
religious communities
justice systems in, 243
marriage in, 367
religious conversion, and imperialism, 300, 301
religious rituals
kavadi attam pilgrimage, 443, 443
in U.S. funerals, 385
See also mortuary practices
reproduction
energy balance and, 75, 75–76
sexual, 53
reproductive hormones, in feces, 86
research materials, community control of, 45, 45–46, 46
research stakeholders, 13
resilience, 467–68, 468
resistance, 308–10, 309, 310
to oppression of sexuality, 353, 353–54, 354
revolution, 311, 311
Reyes-García, Victoria, 26–27, 27
rhetoric
defined, 296
willingness to fight and, 296–98, 297, 299
rhinarium, 93–94, 95
ribosomes, 53, 53
rice, 229, 229, 230
Riley, Erin, 115–16, 116
ring-tailed lemur, 85–87, 86, 89
conservation efforts, 116, 117, 117
endangered status, 113
toothcomb of, 96
See also lemurs
Rising Star cave system, 121–23, 122, 123, 127, 127, 128, 149
risk, culturally constructed, 467
rite of passage, 386
rituals
in burial of the dead, 180, 186
in Çatalhöyük, 233
after combat-induced trauma, 292
Dani warfare as, 292
defined, 180, 378
first intentional burials, 378–80
grieving rituals, 386–87, 387

of Hawaiian chiefdoms, 239–40, 240
kaiko pig festival, 481, 481
kavadi attam pilgrimage, 443, 443
mortuary rituals, 380–83
spaces in houses for, 237
in Teotihuacan, 223, 223
in U.S. funerals, 385
Rivera, Diego, 260
Rivers-Moore, Megan, 372
Rodrigues, Michelle, 42, 42
Rogers, Michael, 164
Romani (Roma), 210
romantic love, 368–70, 369, 370
root (word), 234
Roque, Anais, 468, 468
Rosa, Jonathan, 7, 7, 14
rotating credit associations, 276–78, 277
Roth, Walter, 346–47, 347
Roth-Gordon, Jennifer, 424
Rotokas speakers, 200, 200
Rousseau, Jean-Jacques, 482
rules of a language, 200
rules of a society, 240
rules of urban enclave, 245
Rushohora, Nancy, 309
Rwandan genocide
radio broadcasts and, 297, 297
women's upward mobility following, 336

S

sacred meanings, 45
of biological samples, 45–46
sagittal crest, 106, 107
in Paranthropus, 142
sagittal keel, 161, 162
Sahelanthropus tchadensis, 124, 136, 136
Sahlins, Marshall, 253–54, 254, 262
Saleh, Fadi, 352–53
Samoa
healing systems used in, 451, 451
third gender in, 325, 325
Sangaramoorthy, Thurka, 456–57, 457
SARS-CoV-2, 115
Saudi Arabia, women in, 340
scams, 254, 305
Schaffnit, Susan, 366
Schell, Lawrence, 478
schemas, 316
schools
language of immigrant youth in, 7
reinforcing White supremacy, 421
Schoville, Benjamin, 155–57, 156
Schuller, Mark, 472
Schweitzer, Thomas, 256
science, 12–13
ethnographic research as, 26–27, 27
scientific racism, 403, 411
Scott, James, 308–9
secondary sexual characteristics, 318, 320t

Second Life (online platform), 25–26, 26
secular trends, 74, 74–76
selective pressure, 66, 67
self-governance, 243–45
self-interest model, 266
Semai people of Malay Peninsula, 295
Semaw, Sileshi, 164
semiotics, 198, 202
Senegal, transnational marriages, 345–46, 346, 364
serial monogamy, 359
settler colonialism, 300
defined, 477
ecological violence in, 477, 477–78, 478
of Europeans in the Americas, 300–302, 309–10
humans and fish in Canada and, 484, 485
romantic love and, 369
sex assignment. See assigned sex
sex between men, in archaeological record, 349–50
sex chromosomes, 318–19, 318–19
sexism, 335
of British in New Zealand, 334
sex spectrum, 318–19, 320t
sex terms, 320t–21t
sex tourism, 371–73
female, 372, 372
sex trafficking, 372
sexual configuration theory, 347–49, 348t, 349
sexual dimorphism, 100, 101, 321t
in australopithecines, 138
in early hominins, 330, 330
of extinct primates, 106, 110
mating systems and, 360
in modern humans, 330
survival advantage for hominins, 331
sexual identities, 11, 348t
communities defined by labels, 352
sexualities in archaeological record, 349–51, 350
sexual orientation, 346, 347–48, 348t
archaeological record and, 349–50
sexual reproduction, 53
sexual status, 348t
challenging oppression, 353
sex work, 371–73
brothel excavations in U.S., 351
difficulty of defining exploitation, 372–73
as exploitable labor, 371–72
Seyoum, Chalachew, 144
shamanic healing, 446–47, 447, 449, 451
Shange, Savannah, 421
shared knowledge, 44
sharing relationships. See reciprocity
shelter, early production of, 181, 181

shovel-shaped incisors, *404*, 404–5
siamangs, 99, *99*, 100
sickle-cell alleles, 69, *69*, 438
sickness, 440
sign(ed) languages, 33, *33*, 197
  currently used, 198
  articulators of, 199
  rules of, 199
  taught to great apes, *197*, 197–98
  by world region, 208, *209*
signs, language as system of, 202–4, *203*
Simpson, Audra, 310
singlehood, 371
Sion, Liora, 298–99
sitting postures, and gender*sex, 323, *323*
situated knowledge, 204, 216
Sivapithecus, *108*, 110
skeletal remains
  African Burial Ground project, 410, *426*, 426–27
  in archaeology of tuberculosis, 394, 395
  from Black Death pandemic, 431, 433, *433*
  forensic anthropology and, 393
  from Irish potato famine, 392–93
  See also fossils
skin reflectance (color), *67*, 67–68, *68*
  Neanderthal mutation and, *409*
  social and economic privilege and, 411
skin-whitening products, 416, *416*
skulls
  Boas's work on environment and, 411
  in early racial science, 406, *406*, 407, 408, *409*
slavery
  African Burial Ground and, 396
  expansion in 1600s, 261
  medical experimentation and, 413
  police violence as extension of, 418, 420
  Puerto Rican descendants from, 463, 489
  racial typologies and, 407, 410
  in settler colonialism, 300
  sex trafficking as, 372
  as structural violence, 299
sleep
  co-sleeping, 12, *12*
  napping and in groups, 11–12, *12*
smartphones
  romantic love and, 370
  transfers of cash, 346
smell, sense of
  low primate reliance on, 90
  in strepsirrhines, 93
Smith, Christen, 420–21, 426, *426*
Sobo, Elisa, 452–53
social anthropology. *See* cultural anthropology

social capital
  disaster recovery and, 468
  health beliefs as, 452–53
social complexity
  defined, 223
  inequality and, 237–39, *238*
  patriarchy and, 334
  reasons for, 237–39
  state governance in, 242, *243*
social Darwinism, 407
social democracies, 274–75
social differentiation, 9
  diseases emerging with, 434*t*
social identities, 9–10
  ethnicity as, 403
  of international students in U.S., 422
  personal adornment and, 183
  of racial difference and hierarchy, 424
social insurance
  defined, 255
  eroded by neoliberalism, 276
  reciprocity and, 255–57, 276
socialism
  contemporary forms of, 268
  in Cuba, 272–73
  defined, 268
  markets integrated with, 268, 275
  in postcolonial world, 271–72
social media
  body projects and, 265–66
  connecting single people, 371
  gender identities and, 341
  violence against minorities and, 298
  willingness to fight and, 296
social status
  brothel excavations in U.S. and, 351
  capitalism and, 262, 264–65, *265*
  in chiefdoms, 236
  cosmetic surgery in Brazil and, 334–35
  Dani warfare and, 292
  defined, 236
  gifts and, 254, 255
  Japanese verb forms and, 206–7, 206*t*
  language varieties and, 202
  marriage and, 370
  mortuary practices and, 383–85
  registers of language and, 206–7
  Samoan, 208, *208*
  women's lack of power and, 336
social stratification
  in Cahokia, 271
  in Çatalhöyük, 233
  defined, 236
  in early cities, 236–37, *237*
  of *hijra*, 326
  in hunter-gatherers, 236, 237, *237*
  reasons for, 237–39
  transition to agriculture and, 236–37
  See also inequality; social status

social stressors
  children's growth and, 76–77
  DNA methylation and, 78
  embodied racism and, 414–15
society, defined, 6
solidarity economies, 279
solitary primates, 92, 224
  orangutans, 100–101
somatic cells, 53, 55
Spanish-English
  Mexican-style, 217
  racialization and, 216, *216*
Spanish missions in North America, 300–301, *301*
spears
  hafted stone points, 155–57, *156*
  of Middle Pleistocene *Homo*, 167, *167*
  of Neanderthals, 185
species, 61
  blurred concept for humans, 190
speech
  anatomical capability of, 183, *183*
  gay men's voices, 323
  gender*sex and, 323
  Neanderthals and, 186
  See also language
speech act theory, 205
Spencer, Herbert, 407
spiritual beliefs, about afterlife, 381
splitting, 128–29
spoken language, 197
stable isotope analysis, 40
stakeholders, 13
standard English, 200, 201. *See also* MWAE (Mainstream White American English)
states
  defined, 222
  emergence of, 235
  governance of, 242, *243*
  inequality in, 242
  of Teotihuacan, 221
Steadman, Dawnie Wolfe, 14, *14*
Steward, Julian, *479*
stigma, 440
stigmatized diseases, *445*, 445–46
Stone, Anne, 394
stone points, 155–57, *156*
stone tools
  beginning 2.6 mya, 131
  at Gona, Ethiopia, 146–47, *147*, *164*
  of *Homo erectus*, 159, *159*
  of Neanderthals, *185*, 185–86
  specialized by *Homo sapiens*, 180
  types of, 157*t*
  See also tool-making
storytelling
  hunter-gatherer bonding and, 294, *294*
  as resistance, 308

stratigraphy, 34, *35*
strepsirrhines, 93–94, *94, 95,* 96
stress, 42, *42*
   communications about, 443–44, *444*
   embodied, *414,* 414–15
   overcrowding in Çatalhöyük and, 233
   from water scarcity, 338
stressors, 67
   children's growth and, 76–77
   DNA methylation and, 78–79
   environmental, 66–67, *77,* 77–79
   primate habituation to humans and, 114
strontium isotope analysis, 269, 365, 391
structural racism, 402–3
   health disparities and, 412
   police training and, 420
structural violence, 299–308
   contemporary suffering and, 302–5,
      303, 304, 305
   defined, 299
   in European colonialism/imperialism,
      300–302, *301, 302*
   fighting back against, 308–11
   globalization and, 304
   health as casualty of, 457, 458, 459
   migrant workers and, *304,* 304–5, *305*
   neoliberalism and, 304
   root sources of, 299–302
SturtzSreetharan, Cindi, 322, *323*
subsistence societies, 275
Sudanese refugees, 9–10
suffering
   coloniality and, 303
   settler colonialism and, 300–301
   structural violence and, 299, 302–5,
      303, 304, 305
Sullivan, Noelle, 459
supraorbital torus, 161, *162*
survey
   archaeological, 33, *33*
   for fossils, 41, *41*
"survival of the fittest," 407
suspensory primates, 89
sustainability trade-offs, 470
sustainability transitions, 487–89
symbols, 6, *6*
   arbitrariness of, 203
   as cultural themes, 25
   defined, 203
symptoms, 441
syntax rules, 198, 199, 200
Syrian refugees, nonbinary, 353
systems theory, 481, 483

T

Taj Mahal, *369*
TallBear, Kim, 354, *354,* 424–25, 485

tandas, 276–78, *277*
Tanzania
   Hadza communities in, *42,* 42–43
   marriages of young women in, 366, *366*
   medical volunteering in, 459, *459*
   polygynous marriages in, 359
   resistance to German rule, 309, *309*
taphonomy, 377, 378, 393
Tapsell, Paul, 6, *7*
tarsiers, *94,* 97, *97*
tattoos
   as healing practice, 447, *448*
   as ritual trauma, 443
taxation, redistribution through, 267, 268
taxonomy, 93
Teaiwa, Katerina, 21–22, *22,* 43–44
technologies
   agricultural, 234
   of hunter-gatherers, 226
   industrial capitalism and, 261, *261*
   postindustrial capitalism and, 264
   spread of languages and, 234–35
teeth
   African practice of ablation, 9–10
   diet and, 90, 106
   fossilized, 8–9, *9,* 103
   four subfields and, 3, *8,* 8–10, *9*
   hominins' gendered damage to, 330
   of *Homo erectus,* 161
   of *Homo sapiens,* 174, *174*
   of Middle Pleistocene *Homo,* 166, *166*
   premolars in haplorhines, 97
   See also canine teeth; dental decay;
      dentition; incisors; molars
telomeres, shortening of, 415
Teotihuacan, 221–23, *223*
   low levels of inequality, 222, 244
   maize in, 221, 230
   monumental buildings, 221, *222, 223*
   neighborhood enclaves, 222, 245
terrestrial primates, 89, 106
terrorist attack of 9/11, 296, *296*
Tertiary period, *108,* 109
Thayer, Zaneta, 302, *302*
thermoluminescence (TL), 37*t*
third gender, 320*t*
thumbs, opposable, *88,* 90, 91
Tibetan socialization, 29
timescale, geological, 105, *105*
   fossil evidence and, *108,* 108–11
Todd, Zoe, *484,* 484–85
tool-making
   by *Homo erectus, 164,* 164–65
   by *Homo* species, 125
   by Middle Pleistocene *Homo,* 167, *167*
   by Neanderthals, *185,* 185–86
   by Pliocene hominins, 144–47, *145*

specialized by *Homo sapiens,* 180, *180*
   See also stone tools
tool use
   by chimpanzees, 148, *148*
   defined, 107
   by great apes, 102, *102,* 107, *107,* 135, 147
   by *Homo erectus,* 164–65
   by *Homo* species, 125
   by monkeys, 147, 148, *149*
toothcomb, 96, *96*
tooth suck, 8
Torres, Christina, 338
Torres Colón, Gabriel, *52*
trade
   of Chaco Canyon people, 268–70
   development of, 181–82
   diseases emerging with, 434*t*
   in market economies, 259, *259*
   of Mississippian culture, 270–71, *271*
   spread of languages and, 234–35
tragedy of the commons, 482
transcription, 32, *32*
transformative justice, 426
transgender men, transition experience,
   324–25
transgender people, 317, 320*t*
   changing medical practices, 341
   communities defined by label of, 352
   normalized in entertainment, 341
transgender women
   among *hijra,* 326
   defining themselves as "gay," 351
   forced into sex work, 372
transverse arch, 133
trauma
   colonialism as source of, 301, 302
   epigenetic effects of, 78–79, *79,* 302
   forensic anthropology and, 393
   historical, 302
   in male skeletons, 338
   violent, 289–90, 292, 338
   from women's household tasks, *337,*
      337–38
tribal or ethnic warfare, 289–90, *290*
tribes, 236
tributary mode of production, 262
Triqui migrant farmworkers, 304, *304*
Trobriand Islands, *23,* 23–24, *24*
trophy heads, Nasca Valley in Peru,
   390–91, *391*
Tsimané people
   gendered division of labor, 331, *331*
   local knowledge of, 26–27, *27*
tuberculosis (TB), *394,* 394–95, *395*
Turkana in Kenya, endemic warfare, *291,*
   291–92, 293
Tuvalu, and climate change, 488, *488*

Tuyuc Velásquez, Rosalina, *286*
Twin Towers terrorist attack, 296, *296*
typological thinking, 403–7
    replaced by human variation, 408–9, 410

U

ultraviolet radiation, *67*, 67–68, *68*
unauthorized immigrants
    decolonizing study of, 307–8
    forced into sex work, 372
    informal healthcare among, 456
    rotating credit associations and, 277
unbanked persons, 277
underwater archaeology, 34, *34*
Undocumented Migration Project, 397, *397*
urban areas, defined, 222
urbanization
    diseases emerging with, 434*t*, 436–37,
      437
    origins of, *235*, 235–36
Urban Revolution, 236
Uruk, 235, *235*

V

vaccination, 437, *437*
vaccination hesitancy, 452–53, *453*
Valentine, David, 351
valgus knee, 133
van Anders, Sari, 319, 348–49, *349*
variable linguistic element, 201
Varner, Cheyenne, *413*
Vásquez-León, Marcela, 278
veiling of Muslim women, 340, *341*
Vélez-Ibáñez, Carlos, 276–77
Victoria, Queen of England, 356, *356*
vigilante lynchings, 244
Vikings
    female warrior, 332–33, *333*
    polygyny among, 360
    settlements near volcanoes, *469*, 469–70
violence, 286
    cultures socialized against, 295–96
    in early *Homo* species, 288, *289*
    gender-based, 338
    in Middle Pleistocene *Homo*, 288, *289*
    mostly male, 298–99
    symbolic, 308
    See also aggression; genocide; group
      violence; structural violence; warfare
viral diseases
    domesticated animals and, 436
    from hunting and eating animals,
      435–36, *436*

vision
    binocular stereoscopic, 90, 91
    color, 90, 97
    primates' reliance on, *88*, 90
visual predation hypothesis, 109
vitamin D, 68
vocal apparatus, 198, *199*
vocal fry, 323
vocalizations, of nonhuman primates, 85,
    103, 107, 197
Vodou (Voodoo), Haitian, 383
volcanoes
    Icelandic, *469*, 469–70, *470*
    Tungurahua in Ecuador, *467*, 467–68
vulnerability mapping, 466, *466*
vulnerability to disaster, 466–67, *467*

W

Wall Street bankers, 264
Waorani in Ecuador, peaceful protest by,
    296, *296*
warfare, 286, 287–93
    child soldiers in, 79, *79*
    climate change and, 487
    competition for resources and, 290, 292
    endemic, 290–93, *291*, *292*
    group identities and, 293–96, *294*
    for ideological reasons, 286, 288
    masculine identities and, *298*, 298–99
    maternal trauma and, 78–79
    in the past, 288–90
    for psychological reasons, 288
    tribal or ethnic, 289–90, *290*
    violent trauma in, 338
    Wari empire and, 300
    willingness for, 293–99
    See also group violence
Wari empire, Peru, 300, *300*
Wari' in Brazil, funeral rituals, 382, *382*
water
    commodified in capitalism, 260
    Indigenous relations to, 485–86, *486*,
      488–89
    international development projects and,
      306
    moral economy near Cochabamba and,
      275, *275*
    privatization in Bolivia, 311
    women's trauma related to, *337*, 337–38
Water Walks, 488–89, *489*
Waxler, Nancy, 446
Weaver, Lesley Jo, 444
Weismantel, Mary, 350

Whiteness, 416, 419, 423–24
White privilege, 412
White supremacy
    defined, 408
    in early physical anthropology in police
      training, 420, *420*
    racialized societies and, 415–17
    reinforced by schools, 421
    skin color in Switzerland and, 422–23
    on social media, 298
Wiessner, Polly, 255, *256*, 294
Wilkins, Jayne, 155–57, *156*
Williams, Holly Ann, 254–55
Williams, Serena, 412
Willis, Mary, 9–10, 14
Wilson, Chris, 47
Wintu language, 214, *214*
Wittgenstein, Ludwig, 204
Wolf, Eric, 13, 262, *262*
wooden spears, of Middle Pleistocene
    Homo, 167, *167*
worker cooperatives, 278–79, *279*
writing, 236
Wutich, Amber, 275

X

Xi'an, tomb of Qin Shi Huang, 384, *384*,
    385
Xygalatas, Dimitris, 443

Y

Y-5 cusp pattern, 99, *99*, 110
Yanomamö people, 367, *367*
Yazzie, Melanie K., 485–86
Yucatec Maya speakers, 212

Z

Zarger, Rebecca, *450*
Zhao, Hao, *5*
Zimman, Lal, 323
Zona Sur, self-governance, 243–44
zoonoses, 393–95, *394*, *395*
    human niche construction and, 483
    from hunting and eating animals,
      435–36, *436*
zygote, 53, 54, 55